ANCIENT INDIAN TRADITION AND MYTHOLOGY

Translated by
BOARD OF SCHOLARS

Edited by
PROF. G.P. BHATT

VOLUME 37

ANCIENT INDIAN TRADITION AND MYTHOLOGY

Mahāpurāṇas *Translated into English*

Gen. Ed. DR. G.C. TRIPATHI

Founder Eds. LATE J.L. SHASTRI and LATE G.P. BHATT

PUBLISHED VOLUMES

Vols. 1-4	ŚIVA PURĀṆA *Tr.* J.L. Shastri
Vol. 5-6	LIṄGA PURĀṆA *Tr.* J.L. Shastri
Vol. 7-11	BHĀGAVATA PURĀṆA *Tr.* G.V. Tagare
Vol. 12-14	GARUḌA PURĀṆA *Tr.* J.L. Shastri
Vol. 15-19	NĀRADA PURĀṆA *Tr.* G.V. Tagare
Vol. 20-21	KŪRMA PURĀṆA *Tr.* G.V. Tagare
Vol. 22-26	BRAHMAṆḌA PURĀṆA *Tr.* G.V. Tagare
Vol. 27-30	AGNI PURĀṆA *Tr.* N. Gangadharan
Vol. 31-32	VARĀHA PURĀṆA *Tr.* S. Venkitasubramonia Iyer
Vol. 33-36	BRAHMA PURĀṆA *Tr.* J.L. Shastri
Vol. 37-38	VĀYU PURĀṆA *Tr.* G.V. Tagare
Vol. 39-48	PADMA PURĀṆA *Tr.* N.A. Deshpande
Vol. 49-71	SKANDA PURĀṆA *Ed.* G.P. Bhatt, *Tr. & Annot.* Shridhar Balooni & Pratosh Panda
Vol. 72-73	VĀMANA PURĀṆA *Tr. & Annot.* R.S. Shiva Ganesha Murthy
Vol. 74-76	GAṆEŚA PURĀṆA *Tr. & Annot.* Greg Bailey
Vol. 77-80	BRAHMAVAIVARTA PURĀṆA *Tr. & Annot.* G.P. Bhatt
Vol. 81-82	ŚRĪ VIṢṆU PURĀṆA *Tr. & Annot.* T.K. Narsimhan
Vol. 86	MĀRKAṆḌEYA PURĀṆA *Tr. & Annot.* I.S. Madugula

PURĀṆA*S* UNDER PREPARATION

Harivamśa Purāṇa • Bhaviṣya Purāṇa • Matsya Purāṇa

Devī Bhāgavata Purāṇa • Kālikā Purāṇa • Viṣṇudharmottara Purāṇa

THE VĀYU-PURĀṆA

Translated and Annotated by
DR. G.V. TAGARE

PART I

MOTILAL BANARSIDASS
PUBLISHING HOUSE • DELHI
Email: mlbd@mlbd.in • Website: www.mlbd.in
@mlbdofficial

3rd Reprint: Delhi, 2023
First Edition: Delhi, 1987

UNESCO COLLECTION OF REPRESENTATIVE WORKS—*Indian Series*
This book has been accepted in the Indian Translation Series of the UNESCO Collection of Representative Works, jointly sponsored by the United Nations Educational, Scientific and Cultural Organization (UNESCO) and the Government of India

ISBN: 978-93-5676-230-5 (Hardcover)
ISBN: 978-93-5676-231-2 (Paperback)

Printed & Published by
Rajendra P Jain *for*
Motilal Banarsidass Publishing House
A-44, Naraina Industrial Area, Phase I,
New Delhi–110 028 (INDIA)
Email: naraina@mlbd.in Website: www.mlbd.in
Tel.: (+91-11)4751 1592
Showroom:
4637/20, F-2, Hari Sadan, First Floor, Ansari Road, Daryaganj
Delhi–110 002 (Opp. Fire Station) ***Tel.*** : (+91-11)4559 7999

PUBLISHER'S NOTE

The purest gems lie hidden in the bottom of the ocean or in the depth of rocks. One has to dive into the ocean or delve into the rocks to find them out. Similarly, truth lies concealed in the language which with the passage of time has become obsolete. Man has to learn that language before he discovers that truth.

But he has neither the means nor the leisure to embark on that course. We have, therefore, planned to help him acquire knowledge by an easier course. We have started the series of Ancient Indian Tradition and Mythology in English Translation. Our goal is to universalize knowledge through the most popular international medium of expression. The publication of the Purāṇas in English Translation is a step towards that goal.

PREFACE

This thirty-seventh volume in the series on *Ancient Indian Tradition and Mythology* constitutes the first part (Pūrvārdha) of the *Vāyu Purāṇa* of which the second part (Uttarārdha) also is in press and will follow shortly as the thirty-eighth volume. This part contains the English translation of Chapters 1-61 comprising the first two Pādas or Sections out of the total four Pādas into which the Purāṇa is divided, viz. *Prakriyā*, *Upodghāta*, *Anuṣaṅga* and *Upasaṁhāra* Pādas.

The project of this series was envisaged in 1970 by the late Lala Sundar Lal Jain of Messrs. Motilal Banarsidass. Thirty-seven volumes of the series, including the present one, have so far been published and others are in progress. Complete sets of ten major Purāṇas, viz. *Agni*, *Bhāgavata*, *Brahma*, *Brahmāṇḍa*, *Garuḍa*, *Kūrma*, *Liṅga*, *Nārada*, *Śiva* and *Varāha* have already been made available in English to the lovers of ancient Indian wisdom and it is hoped that this eleventh one, Vāyu Purāṇa, will also be complete much before the end of the year.

The Vāyu or Vāyavīya Purāṇa gets its name from the Wind-god who is said to be its promulgator, and it is a Śaiva Purāṇa in the sense that it has been composed for the propagation of devotion to and worship of god Śiva. It discusses the well known five topics of the Purāṇas, viz. creation, dissolution and re-creation, genealogy of gods, sages etc., periods called Manvantaras, and description of royal dynasties. In the present part cosmogony is discussed in great detail and a good deal of geographical material is found. The translation is preceded by a long scholarly *Introduction* highlighting the salient features of the Purāṇa.

It is our pleasant duty to put on record our sincere thanks to Dr. R. N. Dandekar and the UNESCO authorities for their kind encouragement and valuable help which render this work more useful than it would otherwise have been. We are extremely grateful to Dr. G. V. Tagare for translating the text and contributing the *Introduction*. We are also thankful to all those who have been helpful in our project. *—Editor*

CONTENTS

ABBREVIATIONS

Common and self-evident abbreviations such as Ch(s)—Chapter(s), p—page, pp—pages, V—Verse, VV—Verses, Ftn—footnote, Hist. Ind. Philo.—History of Indian Philosophy are not included in this list.

ABORI	*Annals of the Bhandarkar Oriental Research Institute*, Poona
AGP	S. M. Ali's *The Geography of Purāṇas*, PPH, New Delhi, 1973
AIHT	*Ancient Indian Historical Tradition*, F. E. Pargiter, Motilal Banarsidass (MLBD), Delhi
AITM	*Ancient Indian Tradition and Mythology* Series, MLBD, Delhi
AP	*Agni Purāṇa*, Guru Mandal Edition (GM), Calcutta, 1957
Arch.S.Rep.	Archaeological Survey Report
AV	*Atharva Veda*, Svādhyāya Mandal, Aundh
Bd. P.	*Brahmāṇḍa Purāṇa*, MLBD, Delhi 1973
BG	*Bhagavadgītā*
Bh. P.	*Bhāgavata Purāṇa*, Bhagavat Vidyapeeth, Ahmedabad
Br.	*Brāhmaṇa* (preceded by name such as Śatapatha)
BS. P.	*Bhaviṣya Purāṇa*, Vishnu Shastri Bapat, Wai
BV. P.	*Brahma Vaivarta Purāṇa*, GM, 1955-57
CC	*Caturvarga Cintāmaṇi* by Hemādri
CVS	*Caraṇa Vyūha Sūtra* by Śaunaka, Com. by Mahidāsa
DB	*Devī Bhāgavata*, GM, 1960-61
De or GDAMI	*The Geographical Dictionary of Ancient and Mediaeval India*, N. L. De, Oriental Reprint, Delhi, 1971
Dh. S.	*Dharma Sūtra* (preceded by the author's name such as Gautama)
ERE	*Encyclopaedia of Religion and Ethics* by Hastings
GP	*Garuḍa Purāṇa*, ed. R. S. Bhattacharya, Chowkhamba, Varanasi, 1964

GS	*Gṛhya Sūtra* (preceded by the name of the author such as Āpastamba)
HD	*History of Dharma Śāstra*, P. V. Kane, G. O. S.
IA	*The Indian Antiquary*
IHQ	*The Indian Historical Quarterly*
JP	*Purāṇa* (Journal of the Kashiraj Trust), Varanasi
KA	*Kauṭilya Arthaśāstra*
KP	*Kūrma Purāṇa*, Veṅkaṭeśvara Press Edn., Bombay; also Kashiraj Trust Edn., Varanasi, 1971
LP	*Liṅga Purāṇa*, GM, 1960; also MLBD, Delhi, 1981
Manu.	*Manusmṛti*
Mbh.	*Mahābhārata*, Gītā Press, Gorakhpur, VS 2014
MkP	*Mārkaṇḍeya Purāṇa*
MN	*Mahābhārata Nāmānukramaṇī*, Gītā Press, Gorakhpur, VS 2016
MtP	*Matsya Purāṇa*, GM, 1954
MW	Monier Williams' *Sanskrit-English Dictionary*, MLBD, Delhi, 1976
NP	*Nāradīya* or *Nārada Purāṇa*, Veṅkaṭeśvara Press, Bombay
PCK	*Bhāratavarṣīya Prācīna Caritrakośa*, Siddheshwar Shastri, Poona, 1968
Pd.P.	*Padma Purāṇa*, GM, 1957-59
PE	*Purāṇic Encyclopaedia*, V. Mani, English version, MLBD, Delhi, 1975
PR or PRHRC	*Puranic Records on Hindu Rites and Customs*, R. C. Hazra, Calcutta, 1948
ṚV	*Ṛg-Veda*, Svādhyāya Mandal, Aundh
Śat.Br.	*Śatapatha Brāhmaṇa*
SC or SMC	*Smṛti Candrikā* by Devanna Bhaṭṭa
SEP	*Studies in Epics and Purāṇas*, A.D. Pusalkar, Bharatiya Vidya Bhavan (BVB), Bombay

INTRODUCTION

1. THE TITLE *VĀYU PURĀṆA*

This close-cousin of the Bd. P. (*Brahmāṇḍa Purāṇa*) is one of the oldest and authoritative Purāṇas. *Nibandhakāras* (writers on Dharma-Śāstra) like Aparārka, Ballālasena, Devaṇa Bhaṭṭa profusely quote it on *Śrāddha*, *Dāna*, *Tirtha*, *Āśrama* etc., designating their source as '*Vāyavīya*'. They use this term to imply this Purāṇa and *not* the '*Vāyavīya*' *Saṁhitā* in *Śiva Purāṇa*. It is called 'Vāyu' or 'Vāyavīya' as Vāyu narrated it[1] to elucidate Dharmas and the glory of Rudra and it pertains to Śveta Kalpa. The Vā. P. (*Vāyu Purāṇa*) states that it consists of 12000 verses and is divided into four pādas[2].

The traditional division is into four parts (*pādas*) of unequal length, as can be seen below[3]:

I. *Pūrvārdha*

1. *Prakriyā Pāda* (Chs. 1-6)
2. *Upodghāta Pāda* (Chs. 7-64)

II. *Uttarārdha* (Chs. 1-3 of Upodghāta Pāda) and

3. *Anuṣaṅga Pāda* (Chs. 4-37)
4. *Upasaṁhāra Pāda* (Chs. 38-42 and includes Gayā Māhātmya 43-50).

A (Ānandāśrama edt. of the Vā. P.) follows the older tradition and does not divide the text into *Pūrvārdha* and *Uttarārdha* and gives the following break-up into four *Pādas*:

1. *Prakriyā* (Chs. 1-6),
2. *Upodghāta* (Chs. 7-64),

---

1. Mt.P. 53.18, NP. I. 95, Devi Bhāgavata I.3.7, Vā. P. II.41.44-45.
2. *evam dvādaśa-sāhasraṁ purāṇam kavayo viduḥ //*
yathā vedaś catuṣpādaḥ....
catuṣpādaṁm surāṇāṁ tu brahmaṇā vihitaṁ purā //
—Vā. P. I. 32.63b-64.
3. According to Venkateshwar Press edition.

3. *Anuṣaṅga* (Chs. 65-99),
4. *Upasaṁhāra* (Chs. 100-112)

In this break-up, the problem of spilling over three chapters of *Upodghāta Pāda* (Chs. 62, 63, 64 in A) into *Uttarārdha* (as Chs. 1-3) does not arise.

Even our text (Venkateshwar Press Edition) states that the original *Saṁhitā* was divided into four *Pādas* (I.61.5). Later on it specifically confirms it and states that Vāyu-god is its narrator.

"The Wind-god himself......has narrated this popular Purāṇa consisting of four *Pādas*, viz. *Prakriyā* the first section where the story is taken up (the other *Pādas* or Sections being), *Anuṣaṅga*, *Upodghāta* and *Upasaṁhāra*.[1] —II.41.44-45.

The division of the Purāṇa into *Pūrvārdha* and *Uttarārdha* is of a later date.

The original Vā. P. ended with Ch. 41 of *Uttarārdha* (Ch. 103 in A). The sages who listened to Sūta's narration of the Vā. P. expressed their satisfaction at the narration of the Vā. P. They gratefully honoured the Sūta. The end of the narration of the Purāṇa and the conclusion of the sacrificial session (*Satra*) at Naimiṣāraṇya synchronised. The sacrificers had their valedictory (*Avabhṛtha*) bath and they went to heaven (II.41.42).

The last redactor of this Purāṇa exhorts his listeners to worship deities, perform sacrifices and go to heaven at the end of the life (II.41.43).

The same chapter traces the genealogy of teachers who transmitted the text of the Vā. P. from god Brahmā to Sūta and Śāṁsapāyana (II.41.58-66). After stating the 'fruit' of listening to this Purāṇa (*Phala-śruti*) and laying down prohibition of the transmission of the Purāṇa to undeserving persons,

---

1. *prakriyā prathame pāde kathā-vastu-parigrahaḥ /*
anuṣaṅga upodghāta upasaṁhāra eva ca //
evam etac catuṣpādam purāṇaṁ loka-sammatam /
uvāca bhagavān sākṣād vāyur loka-hite rataḥ //

—Vā. P. II.41.44-45

the author concludes the Purāṇa with salutations[1] to the Lord Maheśvara (II.41.73).

As shown in the notes to II.42, that chapter is a later accretion as it comes after *Phala-Śruti*, accepts *Adhyāsavāda* (vv.30-31) of Śaṅkara (c. 650-725 A.D.), quotes from the *Spanda-kārikā* of Vasugupta (c. 825 A.D.) and advocates Kashmiri Trika-Śaivism (v.33), brings in Rādhā-Kṛṣṇa cult (vv.44-45) and Vyāsa's dejection after completing (so called) eighteen Purāṇas[2] which is an echo of Bh. P. I.4.26-31 and subsequent chapters (I. 5 & 6). One wonders why the Agni P., Viṣṇu P. and Liṅga- P. which are uniformly found in the standard lists of Purāṇas are deleted here and one '*Ādi Purāṇa*' is added to the list.

About the number of verses, no criticism is necessary as these Purāṇa-writers depend on hearsay or traditional information in this matter and did not count the verses. It may how-

---

1. taṁ deva-devaṁ jananaṁ janānāṁ....
varaṁ varāṇāṁ varadaṁ maheśvaram,
Brahmāṇam ādim prayato namasye //

—Vā. P. II.41.73

2. Though the traditional number eighteen of Mahāpurāṇas is mentioned in the text, actually only sixteen Purāṇas are enumerated as follows : (Total number of verses in each is given within brackets after the name of the Purāṇa.)

1. Matsya (14000),
2. Bhaviṣya (14500),
3. Mārkaṇḍeya (9000),
4. Brahma-vaivarta (18000),
5. Brahmāṇḍa (12100),
6. Bhāgavata (18000),
7. Brahma (10000),
8. Vāmana (10000),
9. Ādi-Purāṇa (?) (10600),
10. Vāyu (23000),
11. Nāradiya (23000),
12. Garuḍa (19000),
13. Padma (55000)
14. Kūrma (17000),
15. Varāha (24000),
16. Skanda (81900).

—Vā.P.II.42.3-11.

ever be argued that these numbers of verses actually existed then in the MSS of Purāṇas available to those Purāṇa redactors. Gayā-māhātmya (II, Chs. 43-50) is obviously an interpolation. The motive of this interpolation may be synthesising Śaivism and Vaiṣṇavism. The Vā. P. mainly advocates Śaivism and to counter-balance it, *Gayā-māhātmya* which emphasizes Vaiṣṇavism appears to have been added here. This *māhātmya* has a nominal, tenuous connection with the Vāyu P.—only the first verse of the Māhātmya is attributed to Vāyu. The real interlocutors are Nārada and Sanatkumāra.

Moreover a considerable number of verses are common to this *Gayā Māhātmya* and those in the Mbh., Vana, Chs. 84-95; NP, Uttarabhāga, Chs. 44-47; GP, Chs. 82-86; AP, 114-116; KP, II.35. It shows that there must have been an independent work called the *Gayā Māhātmya* from which these Purāṇas borrowed these verses.

2. THE EXTENT

The following total numbers of verses are attributed to the Vā. P. by Anukramaṇī-writers of Purāṇas :

(1)	Devī Bhāgavata I.3.7	24600
(2)	Mt. P. 53.18	24000
(3)	NP I.95.2	
(4)	AP 272. 4-5	14000
(5)	Vā. P. I. 32.63	12000

Actually however, there are 10991 verses[1]

These differences may be due to the difference in the time of the last redaction of these Purāṇas and/or the availability of different Purāṇic texts to these Anukramaṇī-writers. It may also be due to the actual difference in the contents of the Vā.P. before these writers.

We do not know the contents of the Vā. P. mentioned in the Mbh. Vana 191.16 but NP I.95 gives the detailed contents of the Vā. P. According to it, the first part of the Vā. P. contained the story of killing of Gayāsura and the glory of different

1. Ā. Poona and GM Calcutta editions of the Vā.P. I used these editions while writing on the Bd. P.

months and the second part has Revā-Māhātmya—details not found in to-day's editions of the Vā. P. Eggeling's *Catalogue* shows that the Lakṣmī-Saṁhitā once formed a part of the Vā. P. (MS No. 3599). It, however, appears that although these parts of Vā. P. became separate as independent works in due course, they have preserved the name of the Vā. P. as their original source in the colophons as follows :

(1) *Vāyu-purāṇāntargata-Revā-Māhātmyam* /

(2) *iti Śrī-Vāyu-Pūraṇe Lakṣmi-Saṁhitāyām ānanda-kānana-māhātmye......*

3. POSITION IN THE MAHĀPURĀṆAS

The Problem :

Mt. P. (53.18), NP (I.95), DB (I.3.7) and AP (274.4-5) regard Vā. P. as a Mahā-Purāṇa implying its fourth place in the list of Mahāpurāṇas. But Bh. P. (XII. 7.23 ff.), LP (I.36. 61ff), Brahma-Vaivarta (III.133.14ff), Mārkaṇḍeya (137.8ff) and VP (III.6.21ff) do not mention Vā. P. in their list of Mahāpurāṇas, but substitute Śiva Purāṇa instead of Vā. P. KP I.1.13-15 includes both Vā. P. and Śiva P. in its list of nineteen Mahāpurāṇas[1].

The problem is which of the two has a better claim to be the fourth Mahāpurāṇa, as majority is not the criterion in such matters[2].

The consensus of these Purāṇas (or rather Anukramaṇī-writers) about the fourth Mahāpurāṇa is that :

(I) It consists of two parts and 24000 verses, and

(II) Is declared by Vāyu (Wind-god) with reference to Śveta-Kalpa. NP which gives 4th place to Vā. P. in the list of Mahāpurāṇas states its contents also. It includes the five characteristics (*pañca-lakṣaṇa*)

1. The text need not be strained and interpreted "and the eighteenth Vāyaviya called also Brahmāṇḍa" in order to stick to the traditional number eignteen. Purāṇa-writers are not very particular in such matters. For example, our text (Vā. P. II. 42.2-11) records that Vyāsa wrote 18 Purāṇas but the list actually contains only sixteen Purāṇas.

2. M. Winternitz, *Calcutta Review*, December 1924, p. 330.

of Purāṇas, the story of Gayāsura in the first part, *Māsa-Māhātmya* especially that of the month of Māgha, *Dāna-dharmas*, *Rāja-dharmas*, *Vratas* (religious observances) etc. The second part (*Uttara-bhāga*) describes Revā Māhātmya and Śiva Māhātmya.

Let us consider whether Śiva Purāṇa satisfies these conditions :

1. Out of the seven Saṁhitās of Śiva Purāṇa, only one Saṁhitā—*Vāyaviya Saṁhitā*—is declared by Vāyu. Hence the whole of Śiva Purāṇa cannot claim to be declared by Vāyu, and thus claim fourth place in the heirarchy of Mahāpurāṇas.

2. *Vāyaviya Saṁhitā* which claims to have been narrated by Vāyu with reference to Śveta Kalpa[1] (as in the case of Vā. P.) cannot claim to be the 4th Mahāpurāṇa for the following reasons :

(A) *Vāyaviya Saṁhitā* does not satisfy the *Pañca-lakṣaṇa criterion* of a Mahāpurāṇa while Vā. P. does (vide '*Va. P. as a Mahāpurāṇa*').

(B) *Vāyaviya Saṁhitā* consists of 4000 verses only. Vā. P. is nearer the mark to deserve the traditional epithet *dvādaśa-sāhasri saṁhitā* (a text with 12000 verses).

(C) *Vāyaviya Saṁhitā* does not contain the Gayāsura episode in the Pūrvārdha or the Revā Māhātmya in the Uttarārdha.

An extra-textual and hence extraneous argument to support the claim of *Vāyaviya Saṁhitā* is advanced as follows :

Śrīdhara in his Com. on Bh. P. I.1.4 quotes the following verse giving the etymology of the word *Naimiṣa* :

---

1. *śaivaṁ tatra purāṇam vai*
caturarthaṁ sapta-saṁhitam /
—*Vāyavīya Saṁhitā*
I.1.58

vakṣyāmi paramam puṇyaṁ veda-
sammitam /
śveta-kalpa-prasaṅgena vāyunā
kathitam purā
—*Vāyavīya Saṁhitā*
I.1.22-23.

tathā ca vāyaviye :
etan manoramaṁ cakraṁ
mayā sṛṣṭam visṛjyate |
yatrāsya śiryate nemiḥ
sa deśas tapasaḥ śubhaḥ ||

Our text (Vā. P. I. 2.7) has the following verse to explain the etymology of *Naimiṣa.*

bhramato dharmacakrasya yatra
nemir aśiryata |
karmaṇā tena vikhyātaṁ
naimiṣam munipūjitam ||

It is true that Śrīdhara's quotation is found in *Vāyaviya Saṁhitā* (I.2.88). But in olden times, people depended more on memory and did not care to give actual references to MS—*Pustakasthā vidyā*—every now and then. Śrīdhara, being a human being, mixing up of references of similar versesis highly probable. It is equally probable that the MS of Vā. P. before Śrīdhara had a verse with different readings.

I, however, do not understand how a verse incidentally giving the etymology of 'Naimiṣa' is going to refute the strong textual evidence against the position of *Vāyaviya Saṁhitā.*

The presumption that at the time of Śrīdhara (1300-1400 A.D.) Śiva Purāṇa completely eclipsed *Vāyu Purāṇa* and that people regarded *Vāyaviya Saṁhitā* as *Vāyu Purāṇa* need not be seriously considered. For *Nibandhakāras* and commentators on *Smṛtis* from the time of Aparārka quote from *Vāyu Purāṇa* in preference to *Śiva Purāṇa* and these '*Vāyaviya*' quotations are traceable to *Vāyu Purāṇa* only and not to *Vāyaviya Saṁhitā.* And a number of these *Nibandhakāras* are from the region of Śrīdhara Svāmin.[1]

The testimony of these Nibandha-writers disproves the above presumption. Nor should Śrīdhara be accused of confusing *Vāyv Purāṇa* and *Vāyaviya Saṁhitā* when the whole galaxy of writers on Dharma Śāstra and commentators on

1. For the verses quoted from *Vāyu Purāṇa* or *Vāyavīya* by the Nibandhakāras, see Appendix to R.C. Hazra's article 'The Vāyu Purāṇa', IHQ XIV, 2, pp. 337-339. The list of these Dharma Śāstra writers includes Aparārka, Ballālasena, Kullūka Bhaṭṭa, Devaṇa Bhaṭṭa and others.

Smṛtis are definite about the distinction between the two Purāṇas.

The enormous amount of Tāntric Śaiva ritual in Śiva Purāṇa and quotations from a late writer like Vasugupta (circa 825 A.D.) show there had been a lot of late accretion to Śiva Purāṇa. Vāyu like Brahmāṇḍa touches the beginning of the Gupta dynasty (500 A.D.). It will thus be seen that the evidence about the fourth position in the list of Mahāpurāṇas tilts in favour of Vāyu Purāṇa.

4. TRANSMISSION OF THE TEXT

Vā.P. II.41.58-66 gives the following line of transmission of this text:

God Brahmā → Mātariśvan (Wind-god) → Uśanas → Bṛhaspati → Savitṛ → Mṛtyu (god of Death) → Indra → Vasiṣṭha→Sārasvata→Tridhāman→ Śāradvata → Triviṣṭapa → Antarikṣa→Trayyāruṇa→Dhanañjaya→Kṛtañjaya →Tṛṇañjaya →Bharadvāja→Gautama→Niryyantara→Vājaśravas → Soma→ Śuṣma→Tṛṇabindu→Dakṣa→Śakti→Parāśara (while in womb) →Jātukarṇa→Dvaipāyana (Vyāsa)→Sūta (Romaharṣaṇa).

There are two surprising yet similar transmissions. (1) Śakti was the son of Vasiṣṭha. But Śakti did not receive this Purāṇa directly from his father Vasiṣṭha. Fifteen generations of teachers or contemporary teachers had to intervene for its transmission when the father (Vasiṣṭha) could have directly transmitted it to his son (Śakti). Similarly Parāśara did not teach the Purāṇa to Dvaipāyana (Vyāsa) but to Jātukarṇa who taught it to Vyāsa. The birth story of Vyāsa explains why Parāśara was not available to Vyāsa. But the need of fifteen teachers intervening between Vasiṣṭha and his legitimate son Śakti is inexplicable.

This very list of transmission of Bd. P. is given in Bd. P. III. iv. 4. 58-66.

5. VĀYU AS A MAHĀPURĀṆA

The division of this ancient Purāṇa was originally into four sections (*Pādas*), viz. *Prakriyā*, *Anuṣaṅga*, *Upodghāta* and *Upasaṁhāra* (I.i.4.12-14). But due to the popularity of *Pañca-lakṣaṇa* theory at the time of the last redaction the verse[1] enumerating the five characteristics (*lakṣaṇas*) of the Purāṇa, viz.

(1) *Sarga* (Creation of the Universe),
(2) *Pratisarga* (Dissolution and recreation of the Universe),
(3) *Vaṁśa* (Genealogies of gods, the Patriarchs, the Sun, the Moon etc.),
(4) *Manvantaras* (Aeons presided over by Manus),
(5) *Vaṁśānucarita* (Accounts of dynasties of different ruling families),

precedes (I.i.4.10) the older classification

I. *Sarga—Creation of the Universe*

We find the following theories of creation in this Purāṇa:

(i) THE VEDĀNTIC-SĀṄKHYA THEORY

The creation starts with the principle called *Mahat* and ends with *Viśeṣa* i.e. the differentiation amongst the five elements on the grossest plane of matter.[2] But the source of the Universe is the eternal Brahman, beginningless and endless, unborn, incomprehensible. It was in the beginning and it pervaded the entire Universe which was enveloped in darkness (was unmanifest), the Guṇas being in the state of equilibrium. Brahman is also called Ātman.

At the beginning of creation Kṣetrajña (the Supreme Deity) presided over *Pradhāna*, agitated the guṇas and the principle *Mahat* was evolved. When the Sattva-guṇa became dominant in *Mahat*, the psychic subtle body was evolved and was presided over by *Kṣetrajña*. The Purāṇa gives popular etymologies of the synonyms of Brahman, Kṣetrajña etc.—a sort of *samanvaya* of different current terms and theories. When *Mahat* is impelled (by God's will), it creates this great Universe—*Saṅkalpa* (thought-power) and *Adhyavasāya* (determination) are his two tendencies (*vṛtti-dvayam*) (I.i.4.16ff).

---

1. This verse is found in AP I.14, Bd. P. I.i.37b-38, BS.P.I.2.4.5, GP I 215.14, KP I.i.12 to mention a few Purāṇas. Amara Siṁha (5th cent. A.D.) records it in his *Kośa* I.6.5. Curiously enough the Purāṇa texts handed down to us hardly conform to this definition (*The Hist. and Culture of Indian People* Vol. III, p. 292).

2. V.S. Agrawala, *Mt.P.—A Study*, pp. 41-43; also vv. 61-62 below.

This Sāṅkhya-Vedānta synthesis in the theory of creation is found in other Purāṇas also, e.g. AP 17.2-26, Bd. P. I.i.3.6ff, KP I.2.3ff.

(ii) THE PURĀṆIC THEORY

Kṣetrajña called Brahmā awoke in the Cosmic Egg. He is the first embodied being. He is the creator of all *Bhūtas* (elements or beings). This four-headed *Hiraṇyagarbha* is the *Kṣetrajña* both at the time of creation and destruction of the Universe.

This Cosmic Egg contains seven worlds, the earth along with its seven continents, oceans—everything including the Sun, the Moon, Stars, both Loka and A-Loka. From outside, the Cosmic Egg is enveloped with seven sheaths[1]—the first four consisting of four elements, viz. water, fire, wind and ether—*ākāśa*, each sheath being ten times bigger than the former and three more sheaths consisting of *Bhūtādi*, *Mahat* and the Unmanifest *Pradhāna*.

This *Avyakta* (Unmanifest) it called *Kṣetra* and Brahmā is called *Kṣetrajña*. This *Prākṛta-sarga* is presided over by Brahmā. The creation took place without pre-planning (*abuddhipūrvaka*) like a flash of lightening (I.i.4.68-78).

(iii) THE SĀṄKHYA THEORY

The Vedānta, Sāṅkhya and Purāṇic theories are mixed up here. A clear analysis shows that *Prākṛta Sarga* is creation from *Prakṛti*. The Theistic Sāṅkhya position is more explicitly stated in the next chapter (I.i.5) as follows :—

Before the creation of the Universe there was *laya* (equilibrium) of all Guṇas. In the Unmanifest—*Avyatka*—all Guṇas lay potentially like ghee in milk. The great Lord, by His Yogic power created disequilibrium of the guṇas and the trinity of gods, Brahmā (from *rajas*), Fire or Rudra (from *Tamas*) and Viṣṇu (from *Sattva*) are created. It is the Lord who divides Himself into three for these functions.

1. See I.1.1. 44-45.

(iv) THE NINE CREATIONS OF BRAHMĀ

A more popular Purāṇic theory is explained in the next chaptet (I.i.6) :

At the beginning there was one vast ocean—(*Ekārṇava* also called *mahārṇava* or *yugānta-toya* 'water at the end of Yuga' in other Purāṇas). This primeval *Ekārṇava* expresses the unmanifest cause of the Universe (called *Kāraṇa Brahman* by Nīlakaṇṭha in *Harivaṁśa P.* 3.9.1-4). Brahmā named Nārāyaṇa with a thousand (innumerable) heads slept there for a thousand Yugas. At the end of the night, Brahmā assuming the form of the wind moved over the ocean for reconnaissance and discovered the earth as lying within the water. He assumed the form of a boar to lift it—a belief as old as *Tait. Br.* I.2.1-3. The beautiful description of the boar in Yajña terminology found herein is given in other Purāṇas also (e.g. Bm. P. 213.33-42, Bh. P. III. 13.34-39)and even Śaṅkara adopted it in *Viṣṇu-sahasra-nāma* 110.[1] After uplifting the earth, He re-arranged the mountains, oceans as before, as at the beginning of every Kalpa (I.i.6.27-32). When Brahmā consciously (*buddhi-pūrvaka*) began to meditate, *Avidyā* with its five 'knots', viz. *Tamas* (ignorance), *Moha* (delusion), *Mahāmoha* (great delusion) and others unfolded itself and immobile (*mukhya* or *sthāvara*) creation took place. Being dissatisfied with it, Brahmā began to meditate and created the lower creatures and animal-world called *tiryaksrotas* as it functioned 'obliquely' and was Tāmasika and ignorant. Not being satisfied, he created the third Sāttvika or divine creation of gods (called here *ūrdhvasrotas*) (vv. 33-48).

Later, Brahmā created the 'down-currented' (*arvāksrotas*) reation of human beings, Gandharvas, of Rajas and Tamas yet capable of achieving knowledge(vv. 49-52). The fifth creation is called *Anugraha Sarga* (the favoured creation). It is of four types through *Viparyaya* (contrariety?), *Śakti* (power), *Tuṣṭi* (satisfaction) and *Siddhi* (achievement). These creatures have the knowledge of the past and the present (v. 53). The sixth (repeated as the eighth creation) creation is *Bhūtādi* (of elements and Tanmātras?). The Purāṇa gives three more creations, viz.

1. Vide Fns. on p. 45 *infra.*

(7) the creation of *Mahat*, (8) the creation of Tanmātras also called Bhūtasarga (as 6 above) and (9) the *Vaikārika Sarga* (evolutes of Prakṛti) perceptible by senses.

In summary, the author calls the last three as *Prākṛta* (Primary) and the first set (*Mukhya* to *Anugraha*) as *Vaikṛta* (Secondary). The Purāṇa mentions the creation of mental sons (*Kaumāra* creations) eg. of Sanaka, Sanandana who however refused to participate in creation (vv.65-66). The Ṛgvedic idea of creation of Varṇas from the parts of Brahmā's body is also repeated (v.71).

Thus the theories of creation (Chs. 3-6) show the influence of Theistic Sāṅkhya, Vedānta and Purāṇic lore.

II. *Pratisarga or Pratyāhāra (Dissolution and Recreation)*

The theories are scattered over I.ii.7 and II.iv.40-41, They may be summarised as follows :

Dissolution is of four types :

(1) *Nitya*—usual,
(2) *Naimittika*—periodical,
(3) *Prākṛtika*—of Prakṛti, the primordial and
(4) *Ātyantika*—Final or absolute

(cf. KP II.45.1-10; VP I.7.41-43, VI.3.2 ff.)

Out of these (1) *Nitya Pralaya* is the daily disappearance of the world in darkness while *Ātyantika Pralaya* takes place in the case of individuals who obtain spiritual knowledge (I.ii.7.38, II.iv.40.41-45). (2) *Naimittika Pralaya* takes place at the end of the Kalpa (i.e. one thousand sets of four Yugas), when god Brahmā absorbs the creation within himself by creating drought, Saṁvartaka fires and heavy downpour creating one vast sheet of water. He becomes one with a thousand heads, feet, eyes. He sleeps in the *Ekārṇava* (Cosmic waters) for a period of the same duration as the day and re-creates the Universe *de novo* (I.ii.7.40-65) (3) *Prākṛtika Pralaya* takes place at the end of god Brahmā's life. When the time of this dissolution (*Pratyāhāra*) arrives, evolutes of Prakṛti from *Viśeṣas* to *Mahat* are destroyed. Thus the earth gets burnt up, water swallows up the special quality viz. smell, of the earth and is absorbed in it. Thus each element is absorbed by the higher one till *Ākāśa* is 'swallowed up' by *Bhūtādi*. Thus each higher evolute of *Prakṛti* 'swallows up' the lower one till *Mahat* dissolves itself into the equilibrium of guṇas and the dissolution of Prakṛti is complete and only Ātman remains. This process is recurrent (II.iv.40). [Cf. AP 368.1-2; VP I.7.41-43, VI.3.2.ff.; KP II. 45.1-10]

IV. *Manvantaras*[1]

The Vā.P. regards Time as the unconquerable Mahādeva himself.[2] The four faces of Kāla are the four Yugas.[3] He creates all and annihilates all and is subject to none[4]. Its calculation from Nimeṣa to Mahāyuga is given in I.ii.50. 168-182 and also in I.ii.57.7 ff.

(i) *Kalpa* : Vā.P. claims to deal with Kalpa, Manvantaras and Yugas. Though a belief in the periodic creation and destruction of the world is found in AV (X.8.39,40), the theory of Kalpa is not found even in old Upaniṣads. The Buddhists and Jaina Āgamas use the term *Kappa* (Kalpa) in the sense of a long period of time, possibly related to cosmic life, but never in the sense of a period of 1000 Yugas, 14 Manvantaras or 432 million human years[5]

(ii) *Manvantara* : A Manvantara is a period presided over by a Manu as its lord. In every Kalpa, there are fourteen Manus[6] after whom the Manvantara is named. The names are as follows :

---

1. III *Vaṁśa* and V *Vaṁśānucarita* are combined in the next section.
2. I.ii.32.13b.
3. For a beautiful reification of Time with the characteristics of each Yuga vide I.ii.32.13-20.
4. I.ii. 32.29-32. Cf. KP II. 3-16.
5. Vide Vā.P. I.ii.61.136-142 for the duration of Manvantaras and a Kalpa.
6. I ii. 26.30-47; curiously enough 14 vowels (*Svaras*) are traced to 14 Manus.

(1) Svāyambhuva, (2) Svārociṣa, (3) Auttama, (4) Tāmasa, (5) Raivata or Cāriṣṇava, (6) Cākṣuṣa, (7) Vaivasvata, (8) Meru-Sāvarṇi (9) Dakṣa-Sāvarṇi (10) Brahma-Sāvarṇi, (11) Dharma-Sāvarṇi, (12) Ṛtu (Rudra)-Sāvarṇi, (13) Raucya, (14) Bhautya—the Kalpa, Brahmā's day, ends with this Manvantara.

Every Manu has his separate list of sons, gods, seven sages, Indra and an incarnation of Viṣṇu also.[1] They exercise the same powers as mentioned in the Purāṇas. Vā. P. names 33 Kalpas (I.ii.21.26-72 and Ch. 22) while Mt. 290 enumerates 30 names and Bd.P. II.31-119 states that the number of Kalpas is exactly thirtyfive. The destruction of the Universe at the end of a Kalpa and receration at the beginning of a new one on the same lines as in previous Kalpa is described in the above section.

(iii) *Yuga* : The Manvantaras are based on the concept of Yugas. A Yuga originally was a period of five years[2] called (1) Saṁvatsara, (2) Parivatsara, (3) Iḍ or Iḍāvatsara, (4) Anuvatsara and (5) Vatsara. We find the same duration of Yuga in Mbh.[3], Kauṭilya[4] and Vedāṅga Jyotiṣa.[5] Later on the period of four Yugas came to be extended to 12000 years in all[6], a period endorsed by Manu (1.71) and Mbh. (Vana. 188-27).

But now here it is hinted that these are 'divine' years and not human.

Later on these were converted into 'divine years' corresponding to 4320000 human years[7]. The day of god Brahmā consists of 1000 caturyugas in which 14 Manus rule. This means a manvantara $= \frac{1000 \text{ Caturyugas}}{14}$ or $71\frac{6}{14}$ Caturyugas or 306720000 human years.

1. For details vide II. 38 in Upasaṁhāra Pada.
2. Probably 'Yuga' in RV. III.26.3, implies this—Kane-HD.
3. *Sabhā* 11.37-38.
4. Pañca-saṁvatsaram yugam—*Arthaśāstra* II.20. P. 109.
5. Pañca-saṁvatsara-mayam yugādhyakṣam prajāpatim—V.1.
6. Vide Fn 1 p. 396 infra.
7. Vide Vā. P. I.ii Chs. 21,22,57,58. This new concept is adopted by Purāṇas such as KP I. Chs. 51,53, NP I-41, VP I.3 and even in the Mbh. *Vana* Chs. 149, 188.

Curiously enough this Yuga-theory is strictly limited to Bhāratavarṣa as has been thrice asserted by this Purāṇa.[1]

CHARACTERISTICS OF THE YUGAS

Kṛta Yuga : It was a period of social equality. All people were ever young, equal in beauty and longevity with malice towards none. They were houseless nomads resorting to mountains or seashores. The climate was pleasant. The institution of *Varṇāśrama-dharma* or Sacraments did not as yet evolve. The vegetable world and animal kingdom did not exist.[2] Meditation was valued most then. Events happened unplanned (*abuddhi-pūrvakam*).

Tretā Yuga :

The advent of Tretā Yuga was marked by rainfall and luxuriant vegetation. Trees supplied food, clothing and ornaments to people. Giving up their nomadic habits, people began to settle down by river-banks and mountain ridges or hills. They evolved units of measurements and began to construct houses, establish villages and townships. Women came to have monthly menstruation.

In course of time people became greedy and began to over-exploit the trees. The earth, therefore 'swallowed up" the trees and she had to be 'milked' (i.e. Agriculture had to be developed to meet the need of food).

The Purāṇas believe in the eternity of Mantras. The Mantras which disappeared at the end of the last Kalpa, manifested themselves to sages who by their penance qualified themselves to be the recipients of those Mantras. The Veda which was one became "four-feeted" (*Catuṣpāda*). Practice of sacrifices, *dāna* (religious gifts), penance and truthfulness was the Dharma in Tretā Yuga. *Saptarṣis* (the set of seven prominent sages) laid down *Śrauta* and *Smārta Dharma*. The institution of Kingship, Law and order (*Daṇḍa-nīti*) was established (Vā.P.I.ii.8.75 ff., I.ii.57.81-94).

1. *Catvāri Bhārate Varṣe yugāni munayo viduḥ*—Vā.P.I.ii.24.1, I.ii.57, I.ii.46.137.

2. I.8.46-63.

Dvāpara Age :

Dharma became 'two-legged' in Dvāpara and there was increasing deterioration of social, moral and religious conditions. Composition of rival scriptures as against the traditionally respected ones, diversions and variations in the text of Śrutis, ancillaries of Vedas and Smṛtis, intermixture of holy rites cause break-down in the systems and rules of Varṇas and Āśramas. Greed, slaughter, diseases and social and religious confusion greatly increase.[1]

To re-arrange the floating Mantras into four Vedic Saṁhitās, one sage functions as Vyāsa in each Dvāpara. The list of such Vyāsas is given in VP III.3, Bh.P.I.4.14-25, KP I.52, Bd.P.I.ii.35.116-126 with some variations in the names and even in number (e.g. 32 Vyāsas in Bd.P., 25 in KP) but the total of 28 Vyāsas is asserted.

In our text the following is the list of Vyāsas[2]: (1) God Brahmā (?), (2) Satya, (3) Bhārgava, (4) Aṅgiras (5) Savitṛ, (6) Mṛtyu, (7) Śatakratu (Indra), (8) Vasiṣṭha, (9) Sārasvata, (10) Tridhāman, (11) Trivṛt, (12) Śata-tejas, (13) Dharma (Nārāyaṇa), (14) Surakṣaṇa, (15) Āruṇi, (16) Sañjaya, (17) (Deva) Kṛtañjaya, (18) Ṛtañjaya, (19) Bharadvāja, (20) Vācaḥśravas, (21) Vācaspati, (22) Śuklāyana, (23) Tṛṇabindu, (24) Ṛkṣa, (25) Śakti, (26) Parāśara, (27) Jātūkarṇya, (28) Dvaipāyana.

Kali Yuga :

In a predictive tone, our text records the following characteristics and happenings in Kali Age:

Prevalence of violence, falsehood, deception, slaughter of ascetics, negligence of Vedic Studies and Yajñas, total crumbling down of the Varṇa and Āśrama system, Śūdra Kings obeyed by Brāhmaṇas, elimination of Kṣattriyas and Vaiśyas, Śūdras behaving as Brāhmaṇas and *vice versa*, Śūdra ascetics (with shaven heads and ochre-coloured clothes) performing sacred rites, prevalence of heretics like Bauddhas, Jainas,

1. I.ii.56.22-28.
2. I.ii.23.105-214.

Kāpālikas, men and women characterless, kings becoming robbers and robbers kings, maximum life span one hundred years etc. (I.ii.58.32-70).

It is a terribly gloomy picture. But similar conditions in Kali Age are recorded in other Purāṇas e.g. Mbh. *Vana.* 188.190, *Śānti* 69.80-97, Bd.P.I.ii.29.5-21, Bh.P.XII. 1-2, VP VI.1. As pointed out by R.C. Hazra that was the actual condition of the Hindu Society, after Aśoka and before 200 A.D.[1].

Pramati, an incarnation of Viṣṇu, will restore order with a strong hand and enter the confluence of Gaṅgā and Yamunā.[2] To redeem the fallen, Lord Śiva takes an incarnation in each Kaliyuga as follows[3] : (1) Śveta, (2) Sutāra, (3) Damana (Madana in KP), (4) Suhotra, (5) Kaṅga (Kaṅkaṇa in KP), (6) Lokākṣi, (7) Jaigiṣavya, (8) (not mentioned) (Dadhivāha in KP), (9) Ṛṣabha, (10)(not mentioned) (Bhṛgu in KP), (11) (not mentioned) (Ugra in KP), (12) Atri (13) Vāli, (14) Gautama, (15) Vedaśiras, (16) Gokarṇa, (17) Guhā (-Vāsa (?) as in KP), (18) Śikhaṇḍin, (19) Jaṭāmāli, (20) Aṭṭa (-hāsin), (21) Dāruka, (22) Lāṅgalin, (23) Śveta (Mahāyāma in KP), (24) Śūlin, (25) Muṇḍīśvara, (26) Sahiṣṇu, (27) Somaśarman, (28) Nakulin (occupied a Yogic body at Kāyārohaṇa in Gujarat).

Śiva has taken these incarnations to redeem people and hearten them against the fear of Kali.[4]

A happy feature of Kali Yuga is that Dharma practised gives its fruit that very day while it takes a year in Tretā and one month in Dvāpara[5].

III & V. *Vaṁśa and Vaṁśānucarita*

Our Purāṇa describes the race of gods like Agni (I. ii.Ch. 29), Varuṇa (II.iv.22), Gods (I.ii.32), Svāyambhuva Manu

---

1. *Puranic Records on Hindu Rites and Customs*, II. Ch. 1.
2. Vā.P.I.ii. 58.85-88.
3. The list is based on I.ii.23.105-214.
4. *tasmāt kaliyugaṁ prāpya lokānāṃ hita-kāraṇāt |*
   tasmād bhayaṁ na kāryam kalim prāpya mahaujasaḥ ||
   —I.ii.26.2-3.
5. I.ii.58.72.

(I.ii.33), Vaivasvata Manu (II. iii. Chs. 23, 24, 26, 27), the Moon-god (II. iii. Chs. 29, 30), dynasties of kings like Ikṣvāku (II. ii. 26), Nimi (II. iii. 27), Yadu (II. iii. 32 ff) Pṛthu and of sages like Kaśyapa (II. iii. Chs. 6, 7, 8), Atri (II. iii. 9. 67-78) Vasiṣṭha II. iii.9.80-92).

Vā.P. gives the following dynasties of the Kali Age : (i) Pauravas—from Parīkṣit to Kṣemaka (Vā. P. II. iii. 37.245-275) ; (ii)Aikṣvākus—from Bṛhadratha to Sumitra (op. cit. vv. 276-288) ; (iii) Bārhadrathas (op. cit. vv. 289-303), (iv) Pradyotas (op. cit. vv. 304-308a), (v) Śiśunāgas (op. cit. vv. 308b-313), (vi) Nandas (vv. 320-324), (vii) Mauryas (vv. 324-330), (viii) Śuṅgas (vv. 331-336), (ix) Kāṇvas (vv. 337-341), (x) Āndhras (vv. 341b-352).

Out of these (iii) to (x) (Bārhadrathas to Āndhras) have been discussed under "*Historical Tradition in Vā. P.*". It is difficult to fix up the time-frame or chronology of these dynasties. Earlier scholars disbelieved the Purāṇic chronology. The works of F. E. Pargiter (*Ancient Indian Historical Tradition*), S.N. Pradhan (*Chronology of Ancient India*), H. C. Roychaudhary (*Political History of Ancient India*), A.D. Pusalkar (*Vedic Age*), M. K. Acharya (*Dates of Ancient Indian History*), D. R. Mankad (*Puranic Chronology*) have modified this disbelief. In my Introduction to the Bd. P. I accepted tentatively 3102 B.C. as the beginning of Ancient Indian chronology as proposed by A.D. Pusalkar in the *Vedic Age*. My further studies lead me to believe that the date proposed by Megasthenes, the Greek ambassodor in the court of Candragupta, is more reliable than 3102 B.C. proposed by A.D. Pusalkar. The point however needs more debate (vide my long footnote under "*Historical Tradition in the Va. P.*"-

Thus our Purāṇa meets all the five characteristics expected of a Mahāpurāṇa.

6. RELIGIOUS SECTS IN VĀ. P.

Vā. P. believes in the Supreme God—Maheśvara, corresponding to the Upaniṣadic Para-Brahman. The trinity of gods entrusted with the functions of creation, maintenance and absorption (not destruction) of the Universe, viz. Brahmā,

Viṣṇu and Rudra is at a lower level. Vā. P. is traditionally regarded as a Śaiva Purāṇa and its main emphasis is on the glory of Śiva. But as the section of Viṣṇu—Gayā-Māhātmya (and reference to the oneness of Śiva and Viṣṇu at so many places in Vā. P.) shows, like Bd. P., Vā. P. also tries to integrate the society by synthesizing the -isms associated with these gods.

To respect the susceptibilities of traditionalists I do not use here speculative terms like 'Dravidian' Śiva, 'Pre-Vedic', 'Pre-Āryan' etc. but will simply make factual statements.[1]

---

1. The following is the stance of the traditionalists :

(i) *The so-called Āryan invasion of India* : There is no evidence or basis for this myth in the Vedas or in the Purāṇas.

(ii) *The so-called Dravidian Indus civilization and its destruction by invading Āryans.*

The Ṛgveda has no vocable like 'Draviḍa' or 'Nāga' to indicate a people (vide : *Ṛgveda Saṁhitā* Vol. V., Indices, Edt. S. N. Sonatakke and C. G. Kashikar, Vaidika Samsodhana Mandala, Pune, 1951), though it mentions the different peoples who participated in the Dāśarājña war. Had the Vedic speakers fought with Draviḍas or Nāgas, they would have certainly recorded the names of their enemies as they did in the case of the ten participating kings and peoples in the Dāśarājña war.

(iii) Further research in the Indus civilization shows that it disappeared through natural calamities like floods etc.—a fact refuting the theory of the destruction of that civilization by invaders.

(iv) There is no fool-proof evidence to claim the Indus civilization as 'Dravidian' or 'Non-Āryan'. The seals in the Indus-Script as deciphered by Dr. S. R. Rao disclose Vedism. The claim of Russian scholars about the Dravidianism of the seals is countered by the researches of Dr. S.R. Rao. I however, regard this as an open question.

(v) There is a strong ethnological evidence to show that the so-called Aryans were inhabitants of India even before the time of 'The Indus Civilization'.

(vi) Purāṇic India is not contained in the pre-partition political map of India drawn by European cartographers. It is true that they based the map on the political realities of British India in the 19th cent. Purāṇic India extended much to the north and to the west of that map. See the notes on the place-names in the Vā.P.

The above note is based on *Vedic Age* (BVB), pp. 220-221; B.N. Dutta, *Man in India* 1936-37; Kedarnath Śastri, *New Light on the Indus Civilization*; D. K. Chakrabarti, *Indian Studies—Past and Present*, Vol. IX, pp. 343, 358, 1968; B. K. Thaper; *The Aryan : A Reappraisal of the problem*

ŚAIVISM

As stated above, Maheśvara is the Supreme Deity in Vā. P. The author presents obeisance to Him both in the *Maṅgalācaraṇa*[1] and in the concluding verse of the original Purāṇa.[2] Śiva, a deity on a lower plane, was born of Brahmā as 'Nīla-Lohita'[3] (which is obviously a name indicating the colours of the fire). As he cried for personal epithets, god Brahmā gave him the following names :

Rudra, Bhava, Śiva (Śarva in Bd.P.), Paśupati (*Paśūnām patiḥ* in the text), Īśa (Īśāna in Bd. P.), Bhīma, Ugra and Mahādeva[4].

Most of these names are those of Agni according to the *Vāj.S.*[5], *Atharva Veda*[6], and *Śatapatha Br.*[7] Out of the names, Rudra, Bhīma and Ugra indicate the terrific or destructive aspect of Rudra, while the remaining ones show his auspicious nature. But both these aspects are found in Maheśvara (in the Liṅga-form) who is identical with Para Brahman, *Om*, and the Supreme Region.[8]. Whenever Maheśvara is eulogised, He is regarded as the Supreme Lord[9].

Vā. P. gives the details of bodies etc. assigned to the names of Nīlalohita[10].

(UNESCO symposium at Dushambe, Tadzhik Republic, U.S.S.R. 1977 on "The genesis and interaction of nomadic and sedentary societies); K.C. Varma in ABORI LXIV (1983) pp. 335-337, to mention a few.

1. Vā. P. I.i.1.1.
2. Op. cit. II. iv. 42.73.
3. Op. cit. I.ii.27.4.
4. Ibid vv. 6-16.
5. V. 8 (Aundh Edt. p. 14).
6. AV. XI.2.1.
7. I.7.3-8.
8. Vā. P. I.ii. 55.32. The whole *Stotra* (vv. 30-50) shows the supreme nature of Maheśvara.
9. For example Śukra's eulogy of Nīla-Lohita (Vā.P.II.35.162-203). Many of his epithets are drawn from Vedic Literature.
10. Vā.P. I.ii.27.49-58.

Sr.No.	*Names*	*Body*	*Wife*	*Son*
1.	Rudra	Sun	Survarcalā	Śanaiścara (Saturn)
2.	Bhava	Waters	Uṣā	Uśanas (Venus).
3.	Śarva	Earth	Vikeśī	Aṅgāraka (Mars)
4.	Īśāna	Wind	Śivā	Manojava
5.	Paśupati	Fire	Svāhā	Skanda
6.	Bhīma	Ether (Ākāśa)	Diks (Quarters)	Svarga (Heaven)
7.	Ugra	Sacrificer (Initiated Brāhmaṇa).	Dīkṣā	Santāna
8.	Mahādeva	Moon	Rohiṇī	Budha (Mercury)

The assignment of bodies, wife etc. is a Purāṇic development.

MYTHOLOGICAL LEGENDS

The chief and most quoted feat ascribed to Rudra in Purāṇas is the destruction of Dakṣa's sacrifice (e.g. Bh. P. IV.5, LP. I.99 and 100, NP II.66.5-16, Śiva II.1.1-36). The legend is recorded in *Śatapatha* and *Kauṣītaki Brāhmaṇas* but the reason of destruction is Dakṣa's moral turpitude (illict relation with his daughter). There is no Vedic evidence to show that Śiva married Dakṣa's daughter.[1]

Mbh.[2] (*Śānti.* 283.26-33) attributes the destruction of the sacrifice to denial of his due share to Rudra. But in the next chapter, sage Dadhīci condemns Dakṣa for not inviting Śiva and cursed that the sacrifice would not be completed.[3] There is no reference to Satī's self-immolation at the insult of her husband by Dakṣa as in Bd. P. I. ii.13.45ff. and in our text I.ii.30.52-55). As compared with other Purāṇas the

1. Rudra-Śiva, pp. 78-80.
2. Mbh. Śānti. 283-26-33.
3. Op. cit. 284.12-21.

version of Satī's self-immolation and destruction of Dakṣa's sacrifice is probably of an ancient date[1].

Another extraordinary miracle attributed to Śiva is drinking of the Halāhala poison which emerged while churning the ocean for Amṛta. Śiva drank it at the request of Brahmā and saved the world, but he himself became blue-throated.[2] Śiva's blue-throatedness is recorded in the Vāj. S.[3] and Tait. S[4]., but it is not attributed to drinking of any poison. Mbh.[5] attributes it to the strangling of Śiva's throat by Viṣṇu in a fight.

The poison-drinking theory seems to be a post-Mbh. development.

LIṄGA-WORSHIP

The symbolic appearance of Śiva was the manifestation of a column of fire, the root and end of which could not be reached by gods Viṣṇu and Brahmā.[6] It is described in similar terms in other Purāṇas.[7] Rudra and Agni are identified since the Vedic times.[8] When Brahmā and Viṣṇu praised this fire-manifestation of the Liṅga, they used the terms attributed to the Supreme Diety who creates, permeates, protects and destroys the world. It is called Para-Brahman, the highest goal etc.[9]

In general we do not find Liṅga-worship in Vā. P. and I agree with D.R. Patil that it antedates the age of the Guptas in this respect :[10]

---

1. H. H. Wilson, Viṣṇu Purāṇa (Translation), pp. 61ff. and note 1.
2. Vā.P.I.ii. 94.90-25; Bd. P.I.ii.23.86-91.
3. XVI.7.51.2-4
4. IV.5.1-9.
5. Śānti 342.114-115.
6. Vā. P.I.ii.55.19-27.
7. For ex. Bd.P. I.ii.26.18-28; KP I.26.66-99.
8. RV II.1.6, AV VII.8.3, Śatapatha III.1.3 also I.7.3.8.
9. Vā. P.I.ii. 55.30-50.
10. *Vā.P.—Cultural History*, p. 186.

Even in the incident of the falling of Śiva's phallus in Dāruvana in Bd. P. I.ii.27, Śiva came there to teach Pāśupata Yoga to the sages and his queer behaviour is called '*dvāra*' in Pāśupata Yoga. There too the Liṅga is without Yoni and Liṅga-worship is not prescribed—see my Intro. to the Bd.P. Xlvi.

SKANDA

Vā. P.[1] gives the legend of the birth of Skanda. It grants him the parentage of Śiva and Umā, though originally according to Mbh.[2], he is the son of Agni and Svāhā who, to please the polygamous nature of Agni, assumed the forms of six wives of Saptarṣis except that of Arundhatī whose power of chastity was beyond the ability of Svāhā's impersonation. The Vā. P. legend is a later version in which Agni's parentage is retained by impregnating him with Śiva's semen. The rest of the story, Agni's interference in the sexual intercourse of Śiva and Umā etc., is practically the same as in Bd. P.[3] Skanda's status in the Gṛhya Sūtra period (in *Pāraskara Gr.S.*) is not much elevated. Even in Mbh.[4], his mothers appear to be evil spirits and his army consisted mainly of goblins and evil spirits (*Pramathas* and *Vināyakas*) in addition to Devas.

Skanda's status became more elevated in the post-Mbh. period. A cult of Skanda-worshippers was in vogue at the time of Patañjali (1st cent. A.D.).

Kushan seals from the 1st to 3rd cent. A.D. represent Skanda or Kārtikeya holding a javelin and a cock. His installation as the leader of the Deva army by gods Brahmā and Śiva(?) by seating him on a peacock is represented on a seal of the 5th cent. A.D. at Mathura. The names of the rulers of the Gupta dynasty, e.g. Skanda Gupta, Kumāra Gupta, confirm his exalted status.

The status given to Skanda in Vā. P. shows its pre-Gupta version probably reflecting the beliefs in *Pāraskara Gr.S.*

GAṆEŚA

'Gaṇeśa' means 'the lord or commander of gaṇas of Śiva'. He is not necessarily auspicious like the elephant-headed son of

1. II.iii.11.20-50.
2. *Vana* Chs. 224 & 225.
3. II.iii.10.22.51.
4. *Vana*. 226.22.

Umā and Śiva. Gaṇeśa in Vā. P. is a demon (Rākṣasa) called Kṣemaka or Nikumbha who was commisioned by Śiva to get the prosperous city of Vārāṇasī ruled by Divodāsa, vacated for his residence with Umā. After his marriage with Umā, Śiva stayed with his father-in-law but Umā's mother expressed to Umā her exasperation with the unconventional behaviour of Śiva and his followers. Umā felt insulted and urged Śiva to find out residence elsewhere. Śiva selected Vārāṇasī and instructed Nikumbha to use very soft means, as Divodāsa was a very powerful king (II.30.37).

Kṣemaka went into the dream of a barber named Maṅkaṇa and asked him to instal his image at the outskirt of the city (*nagaryante*) with the permission of the king. This Gaṇeśa (Nikumbha) went on giving munificent gifts according to the wishes of all his worshippers.

King Divodāsa was issueless, but after some hesitation, he directed his senior queen Suyaśā to worship this Gaṇeśa and pray to him to grant a son. In spite of repeated services for a long time, Nikumbha purposely did not grant the boon. The king lost his patience: "The god is munificent to my subject but is ungrateful enough to grant me nothing in spite of our rich services. This is no god but a goblin (*bhūtam*). I shall now destory his shrine (vv. 47-50).

When the king destroyed Nikumbha's shrine in desperation, Nikumbha, posing wounded innocence, approached the king and cursed him that as he destroyed Nikumbha's shrine without any reason, his capital city would be deserted (vv. 51-53).

And the great god lived happily with Umā there :

Divodāsa founded a new city on the river Gomatī. At the end of the period of the curse, king Mahābāhu killed demon Kṣemaka and rehabilitated the beautiful city of Vārāṇasī (v. 69).

The curse motif of the desertion of Vārāṇasī is used in Harivaṁśa, Brahma P. and Bd. P. Pargiter records it as a phase in the conflict between Haihayas and kings of Vārāṇasī (AIHT, p. 263).

Gaṇeśa in Vā. P. is 'a jungle genius' as Getty calls it (*Gaṇeśa*, Intro., p. XX).

VAIṢṆAVISM

In the early Viṣṇuism, Viṣṇu (√*viṣ* 'to pervade') represented pervasion—omnipresence of universal character—a protector promoting continuance (vegetation, fecundation and fertilization) of the world and ensuring well-being (*Śrī*), victory, welfare (*bhūti*) and morality[1]—a view supported in our text (I.i.5.26, 33-35): "He is threefold according to Guṇas, fourfold according to Vyūhas (His manifestations such as Vāsudeva, Saṅkarṣaṇa). He is the protector and hence OM. He divides himself into three and carries out the functions of creation, protection and destruction. At the time of destruction he absorbs the Universe and goes to sleep on his ocean-bed (cf. I.ii.24.9ff). At the time of creation he is Brahmā-Nārāyaṇa[2] (I.ii.6.2-6). For lifting up the earth from the bottom of the ocean, Brahmā (Nārāyaṇa) assumed the form of a boar (I. i. 6.10 ff.)".

Owing to the curse of Bhṛgu for killing his wife and for restoration of Dharma and sacrificial order, Viṣṇu underwent the following ten (?) incarnations[3]. Out of these, three were among gods and seven among men as follows:—

Incarnation No.	Period	Name of the incarnation	Name of his preceptor and other details
1.	Cākṣuṣa Manvantara	Nārāyaṇa (Son of Dharma)	Promulgated the institution of sacrifice (*Yajña*).
2.	Vaivasvata Manvantara	Narasiṁha[4]	For killing Hiraṇyakaśipu. (His birth within the sea

1. J. Gonda—*Aspects of Early Viṣṇuism*, pp. 172-175.
2. *Nārāyaṇa means 'one who lies on waters'*
   āpo nārā vai tanava ityapāṁ nāma śuśrumaḥ /
   apsu śete ca yat tasmāt tena Nārāyaṇaḥ smṛtaḥ // —I.ii.6.5.
3. Vā. P. II.36.68-111.
4. V. 72a if emended as '*tu Vainyasya*' as in Bd. P. 2.3.73.72 for the obscure '*tadānyasya*' it means 'Pṛthu' was Viṣṇu's incarnation with god Brahmā as his preceptor (*Purohita*).

			implies a reference to the boar-incarnation).*
3.	7th Tretā Yuga (of the present Manvantara)	Vāmana	Begged in a Baṭu-form three paces of land from Bali but assumed Cosmic Form and covered the Universe in two paces and thus drove Bali to Pātāla for non-fulfilment of the promise.

The following seven (?) incarnations are among human beings.

4.	10th Tretā Yuga	Dattātreya	Son of Atri. Preceptor—Mārkaṇḍeya
5.	15th Tretā Yuga	Māndhātā	A Supreme Ruler (*Cakravartin*). His preceptor—Viśvāmitra.
6.	19th Tretā Yuga	Paraśurāma	Son of Jamadagni. His preceptor—Viśvāmitra.
7.	24th Tretā Yuga	Rāma	Son of Daśaratha; preceptor—Vasiṣṭha; mission—slaying Rāvaṇa.
8.	28th Dvāpara	Vedavyāsa	Son of Parāśara. Preceptor—Jātukarṇa.
9.	-do-	Kṛṣṇa	Son of Vasudeva. Preceptor—Sāndīpani. Mission—to kill Asuras and restore Dharma.

Future incarnation(s)

10.		Kalki—Viṣṇuyaśas	of Parāśara Gotra. Preceptor—Yājñavalkya To massacre the wicked.
10A.	In the 25th Kalpa at the end of Kali Age	Pramati	He was formerly Viṣṇu by name. Pramati was of Candramas Gotra.

*Our text has skipped over two incarnations viz. Pṛthu and Varāha which preceded Narasiṁha. The text if emended as per Bd. P. will more explicitly refer to these two incarnations.

Now-a-days the standard list of the ten incarnations of Viṣṇu does not include King Pṛthu, Māndhātā, Dattātreya, Vyāsa and Pramati. The non-inclusion of Varāha incarnation in spite of its detailed description elsewhere[1] is inexplicable as the germ of this incarnation is traceable to *Tait. Br.* and is elaborately described by other Purāṇas[2] like Bh. P., Mt. P. etc.

Although Śiva and Viṣṇu are treated separately here, Vā. P. insists upon their unity. "It is one God whose oneness and separateness and speciality are described here" declares our Text.[3] As stated above the trinity of Brahmā, Viṣṇu and Śiva represents three Guṇas (of Sāṅkhyas) to explain the creation, maintenance and destruction of the Universe.

RELIGIOUS SECTS IN VĀ.P.

Sun-worship

Although there is no reference to the Sun-worshipping Brahmins in Vā. P. as in the Bhaviṣya Purāṇa, there are some positive indications of the prevalence of Sun-worship, though on a smaller scale. Thus, after re-canting the Yajurveda at the order of his preceptor Vaiśaṁpāyana, Yājñavalkya meditated upon the Sun-god. The recanted Mantras went up to the Sun-god who gave them to Yājñavalkya. Yājñavalkya alias Brahma-rāti assumed the form of a horse and received the Yajurveda (I.ii.61.18-22). Hence it came to be known as Vājasaneyī Saṁhitā. This story appears in Mbh. *Śānti* 318.1-12 but in Mbh. Yājñavalkya was not ordered by Vaiśaṁpāyana to recant Yajurveda and it is the Sun-god and not Yājñavalkya, who assumed the form of a horse at the time of the transmission of the Veda. Mbh. *Śanti* above states that at the behest of the Sun-god, Yājñavalkya opened his mouth and goddess Sarasvatī entered in it (*Op.cit.* 318.7).

---

1. I.ii.6.9-25.
2. Vide Foot-note 1 on p. 44 *infra.*
3. *ata ūrdhvaṁ Brahmaṇaśca Viṣṇoścaiva Bhavasya ca |*
ekatvaṁ ca pṛthaktvaṁ ca viśeṣatvaṃ ca kīrtyate ||
Vā. P.I.1.120

The generosity of the Sun-god in gifting away his Syamantaka jewel to his friend and devotee Śakrajit is mentioned in II.iii.34.20-28. The mythical "astronomy" in Vā.P. gives a poetic description of the Sun's chariot and his attendants, sages, Yātudhānas, Serpents etc. At the Sun-god's residential forest in Kiṁśuka Vana, Siddhas pay homage to him (I.ii. 38.27-32) ; the Wind-god established the image of the Sun-god (Vāḍāditya) in his capital.

An Obscure Cult

Śiva's bull, the son of the divine cow Surabhi, explained the Cult of the Bull (*Go-dharma*) to Dīrghatamas when he caught him by both of his horns (II.iii.37.48-57). Says the bull, "We do not distinguish between what should or should not be eaten or drunk or with whom we cohabit. No sin is committed by us".

Buddha ridiculed the go-dharma by remarking that such persons would be bulls in the next birth. In Va.P. however Dīrghatamas was exonerated for his rape and his eyesight was restored to him by Surabhi.

Non-Vedic Religions

There are direct references to the Buddhists, Jainas and Kāpālikas as the dominant faiths in Kaliyuga.[1]

It is doubtful whether the term Nirvāṇa in the prediction of the impossibility of its attainment in Kali Yuga (I.ii.32.20) can be restricted to Buddhism as the vocable is found in BG VI.15. By the reference to Nirvāṇa in the same line along with *Kṣaṇikavāda* as in

Buddhāvasthā...avyakte saṁpraliyante, te sarve kṣaṇadarśinaḥ/

—II.iii.39.82-85.

---

1. *Śukla-dantā....muṇḍāḥ kāṣāyavāsasaḥ /*
śūdrā dharmaṁ cariṣyanti....

—Vā.P.I.58.59.

Kaṣāyiṇaś ca nirgranthās
tathā kāpālinaśca ha //

—Ibid. 58. 64.

Along with these, apostate Brahmins who 'sold' the Vedas and sacred places are included (58. 65).

one may be tempted to regard this as a reference to Buddhism but the context is that of Brahmanism. '*Buddha*' is an epithet of Śiva[1], but when *buddha* is called the "Shadow of Hari" (II.iii.42.82) it may imply Śākyamuni.

There is so much similarity in rules of discipline of a Brahmanical *Yati* and Bauddha and Jaina *Bhikṣus* (recluses), that it is difficult to determine their particular sect. God Svayaṁbhū is said to have promulgated this "*Śaucācāra-dharma*" to Brahmanical forest-hermits.[2] Even Ahiṁsā[3] is strictly to be observed by all Yatis.

Jaina terms such as *Autpattikas*, *Nārakas* in classifying Jivas (II.iii,39.189-90) and the mention of Mt. Veyardha (AMg. Veyaḍḍha in I.ii.15.36-37) are found in this Purāṇa but there is very little philosophical exposition of non-Vedic sects.

7. (i) VĀ.P. AND DHARMA-ŚĀSTRA

Quotations from Pūraṇas pertaining to Dharma-Śāstra in the *Āpastamba Gr.S.* (I.6.19.13; II.9.23.3-6; II.9.24.6) show that material on Dharma Śāstra came to be included in the Purāṇas since the 5th century B.C. Mediaeval writers on Dharma Śāstra quoted Purāṇas as an authority like Smṛtis.[4] Vā.P. as an authority on Dharma Śāstra is quoted by Aparārka (Com. on. *Yāj. Smṛ*), Ballālasena (in *Adbhuta-Sāgara* and *Dāna-Sāgara*), Kullūka Bhaṭṭa (Com. on *Manu-Smṛ*), Madanapāla (in *Madana Pārijāta*), Śūlapāṇi (in *Prāyaścitta Viveka*), Vācaspati Miśra (in *Tirtha-cintāmaṇi*)—to mention a few prominent authors of the mediaeval period. They use the title of their source as 'Vāyavīya' implying our text—Vāyu Purāṇa and *not* Vāyavīya Saṁhitā of Śiva Purāṇa.

As the titles of the above works indicate, the following topics from Vā.P. have been quoted by the mediaeval authors : (1) *Śrāddha*, (2) *Dāna* (religious gifts), (3) *Tirtha* (sacred places

1. *namaḥ śuddhāya buddhāya* / I.ii.30.45

2. Vide the rules in the whole of the chapter I.ii.16

3. '*Bhikṣūṇām ahiṁsā paramārthitā* / I.ii.16.18.

4. See my Introductions to the KP p. XIV, NP p. 52, Bd.P. pp. VIII-IX.

like Gayā), (4) Duties of persons belonging to different Varṇas and Āśramas, (5) *Yoga*, (6) *Mokṣa*.

Out of these, Śrāddha Kalpa (II.iii. Chs. 10-21) is profusely quoted. The details of actual performance of Śrāddha such as metal pots to be used in Śrāddha, the procedure of offering Piṇḍas, *Agnau-karaṇa*, rites of purification, appropriate and inappropriate acts in Śrāddha are the same as those in Bd.P. But its distinguishing feature not found in Manu and Yājñavalkya is the special importance of Yogins in Śrāddha (vide Vā.P. II.iii.10.50 ff. especially vv. 66 & 67) where a meal to a Yogin is stated as surpassing in merit the offering of meal (food) to a thousand of Brāhmaṇas. Also vide II.iii.17.92-93 where the omnipresence, omnipotence and omniscience of Yogins is extolled. The influence of Pāñcarātra system in the post-Manu-Yājñavalkya period may be the reason. But the Brahmanical Yogī is adorable and not non-Vedic recluses, those who have shaven their heads (muṇḍas), ascetics with matted hair (*Jaṭila*) and the wearers of Kaṣāya garments (*Kaṣāya*). The nudes (*nagnādayaḥ*) i.e. those who are not covered by Vedic religion or not showing allegiance to Vedas should not be allowed to have a look at the food prepared for Śrāddha (*ibid.* Ch. 16.24). The list includes the followers of Sāṅkhyas, Śaivas like Kāruṣa.[1] The belief that the sight of non-Vedic persons pollutes the Śrāddha food is found in Gautama Dh.S. 15-25-28, Manu III.239-42, KP II.22. 34-35, VP III.16. 12-14—to mention a few.

It is rather self-contradictory to enumerate the qualities of Brahmins to be invited to Śrāddha (*Op. cit* Ch.17) and state that it is not necessary to do so.

The importance of Śrāddha is so great that the Tīrtha-Section is subordinated to it informing us of ancient Indian geographical places[2] where Śrāddha performance will be more

---

1. *Vide op. cit*: Ch. 17.66-83.

2. Op. cit. ch. 15. It is not clear why places like Orissa, Telangana or regions north of the Indus were declared unfit for performance of Śrāddha (Ch. 16.22-23). Were they the strongholds of non-Vedic sects ? The words '*pranaṣṭāśrama-dharmāśca* (Lands from which the rules of Āśramas etc. have disappeared i.e. are not observed, lends support to this conjecture.

beneficial. The same is the case about *Tithis* and *Nakṣatras* regarding the fruit of the performance of Śrāddha on those tithis[1] and Nakṣatras. The latter chapter (on Śrāddha under different Nakṣatras) is incorporated from Mbh. *Anuśāsana* 89 and the topic is dealt with in Viṣṇu Dh. S. 78.8-15, Yaj. Smṛ. I.265-268, MK.P.30.8-16, KP.II.23.9-15, Bd. P.2.3-18 but there are some disagreements about the benefit promised.

The Vedic counting of Nakṣatras beginning from Kṛttikā (and not from Aśvinī as we find it to-day) shows that this chapter (or rather its source Mbh. *Anuśāsana* 89) was written some time before 500 A.D.

The topic of *Dāna* (religious gifts) is subservient to *Śrāddha*.

Ch. 21 deals with the period of satisfaction derived by Pitṛs by eating (through Brāhmaṇas) flesh of various animals. *Āpastamba Dh. S.* (600 B.C.) makes flesh-serving at Śrāddhas obligatory and enumerates the animals the flesh of which gratifies Pitṛs for a specified period[2]. For example: *Saṁvatsaram gavayena tṛptiḥ* 'The gratification (of Pitṛs) lasts for a period of one year by (eating through the invited Brāhmaṇas) the flesh of a gavaya, a cow-like animal'. (For details vide *Āpastaṁba Dh. S.* II.7.16-25; II.7.173). Refusal to accept non-vegetarian food at a Śrāddha results in detention in hell (*Viṣṇu-dharmottara* I.140. 49.-50; also Manu V. 35; KP.II.17.40).

Non-vegetarianism in religious and ritualistic acts in ancient India is undeniable despite the story of Uparicara Vasu's fall to Pātāla for advising animal slaughter in sacrifices.

In Southern India, strict vegetarianism is observed at Śrāddhas though neither *Mitākṣarā* nor *Kalpataru* have prohibited flesh-diet at Śrāddha.

The classification of Pitṛs into seven in II.iii.11. 1 ff (Cf. Pd.P. Sṛṣṭi 2.2-4) is a later development.

---

1. *Op. cit.* Ch. 19 and 20.

2. It is not our text only which prescribes flesh-eating and the specific flesh gratifying to the Pitṛs for a particular period. We find the same in Manu III. 267-272, Yāj. Smṛ. I.258-260, Mbh. *Anuśāsana* Ch. 88, *Kātyāyāna Śrāddha-Sūtra* (Kāṇḍikā 7-8), KP. II. 20.40-42, Mt. P. 17-31-35, Bd. P. 2.3.19.

7. (ii) VĀ.P. AND YOGA

The system of psychical and moral discipline called Yoga can be claimed as the special contribution of India to the world. We have traces of it in RV[1]. but it was fully developed at the time of Kaṭha Up.[2] Bd.P offers little about the path of Yoga.[3] But the treatment of Yoga in Vā.P. is comprehensive (I.ii.Chs. 11 to 15)[4]. Thus we are told the four objectives of Breath-control (Prāṇāyāma), viz. *Śānti*, *Praśānti*, *Dipti* and *Prasāda* (explained in 11.4-9); the details of stages, viz. postures (*āsanas*), *prāṇāyāma*, *Pratyāhāra*, *Dhāraṇā* and the resulting *Siddhi* (11.12-30); the places to be avoided for the practice of Yoga (11.31-34); the dangers or physical disability resulting from mistaken practice of *Prāṇāyāma* (11.35-37) and the remedies of them (11.38.58). The signs of progress of a student of Yoga described in 11. 60-61, viz. strength, health, indifference to sensual objects, lustrous complexion, auspicious smell etc. are echoes[5] of Śvet. Up. II.11.

The next chapter (ch. 12) deals with *Upasargas* (troubles, obstacles) that obstruct the path of Yoga and advises how to overcome them. Ch. 13 details the usual eight supreme powers (*aiśvarya-guṇa*) accruing from the practice of Yoga. The list is common to other treatises on Yoga but their classification into *Sāvadya*, *Niravadya* and *Sūkṣma* is peculiar. *Sāvadya* comprises five elements, *Niravadya* five elements and sense-organs, *Sūkṣma* adds to these mind, ego and intellect (13.5-8).

---

1. For example

(i) *Yuñjate mana uta yuñjate dhiyā/* RV.V.81.1 found also in Tait.S. I.2.13.1, Vaj. S. 11.4, Śvet Upa II.4. (ii) RV.I.18.7 repeated in Tait. S.IV.1.1.1, Vaj. S. XI.1, Svet. Up. II.1.

2. Note the wording of Kaṭha VI.8 : *Mṛtyu-proktaṁ Naciketo 'tha labdhvā vidyāmetām yoga-vidhim ca kṛtsnam etc.*

3. Vide Intro. to Bd. P. 1 XIV.

4. Only Chs. and Verses mentioned.

5. *Sattvaṁ tathārogyam alolupatvam varṇa-prabhā susvara-saumyatā ca /*
gandhaḥ śubho mūtrapūrīṣam alpam yoga-
pravṛttiḥ prathamā śarīre //

Vā. P. 11.60.

Compare :
laghutvam ārogyam alolupatvaṁ varṇa-
prasādaḥ svara-sauṣṭhavaṁ ca /
gandhaḥ śubho mūtra-purīṣam alpam
yoga-pravṛttim prathamām vadanti //

—Sv. Up. II.13

The next chapter mainly deals with the transmigration of the soul and states the primitive ideas about embryology. The tortures in hell (commonly described in other Purāṇas) have one relieving feature. The principle of redemption is accepted in Hinduism and not eternal punishment as in Semitic religions.

Ch. 15 describes the procedure of the daily practice of Pāśupata Yoga.

These five chapters—a *purāṇic* compendium on Yoga resembles Pātañjala Yoga to a great extent but it is called Pāśupata Yoga or Yoga of Maheśvara as it consists of five 'Dharmas' proclaimed by Maheśvara, viz. (1) Prāṇāyāma, (2) Dhyāna, (3) Pratyāhāra, (4) Dhāraṇa, and (5) Smaraṇa. It will be seen that here the stage of 'Samādhi' in Patañjali is substituted by 'Smaraṇa'.

7. (iii) ANCIENT LORES IN VĀ. P.

In Vā. P. I.ii.61.62-73 we find information about Vedic Saṁhitās. As I have said in my notes on 'The Schools of Vedas' (*Op. cit.* vv. 1-60), our text differs from the information in the CVS (Śaunaka's *Caraṇa-Vyūha-Sūtra*). About the number of Mantras in the Vedas. our Purāṇa-writer appears to have depended on traditional or rather hearsay report and given approximate round figures without verifying (i.e. counting the Mantras in) the original Saṁhitās as can be seen from the following comparative table :

Name of the Veda	*Total No. of Mantras as per Vā. P.*	*Total No. of Mantras in the Svādhyāya Maṇḍala (Satavalekar) edition, Aundh*
1. Ṛgveda	8635	10,552 (the same in CVS)
2. Sāmaveda	8014 (CVS endorses this)	1810 (But only 75 Sāman Mantras)
3. Ādhvaryava (Black Yajurveda)	12000	12330

4.	Vâjasaneyī Saṁhitā (White Yajurveda)	1900 (8880 when Śukriya Sāmans and Khila Mantras are added)	3988
5.	Atharva Veda	6026	5977

2. As I stated above, Vā. P. differs from CVS about its statements regarding the names of sages, their lineage, the branches of the Vedas.

Purāṇa-writers believe in the eternal nature of Mantras. They (Mantras) become unmanifest at the end of a Kalpa and manifest themselves at the beginning of a new Kalpa (*Op. Cit.* v. 75).

3. Traditionally the number of Lores was fourteen (4 Vedas + 6 Vedāṅgas + Mīmāṁsā, Nyāya, Dharma Śāstra, Purāṇa). It became 18 after the additions of four subsidiary Vedas. CVS, p. 47 gives the following relation between the Veda and its subsidiary Veda:

Veda	*Upa-Veda*
1. Ṛgveda	Āyur Veda (the Science of Medicine).
2. Yajur Veda	Dhanur Veda (Military Science).
3. Sāma Veda	Gāndharva Veda (Musicology).
4. Atharva Veda	Artha-Śāstra (Politics, Economics & Administration).

THE SCIENCE OF MUSIC[1]

The *Svara-maṇḍala* is comprised of seven *Svaras* (notes), three *Grāmas* (basic scales), twentyone *Mūrcchanās* (the modes

1. The note is based on the translation and annotations of Vā. P. II. iii.24.36-66 and Ch. 25. Though similar sections in other Purāṇas like Bd.P, NP. and some later works like *Saṅgīta-Ratnākara* which preserve the Purāṇic tradition are used, the text is still obscure. The ancient Sāma-gāna tradition is still current in Kerala, Tamilnadu, Gujarat but that of music in Purāṇas is unfortunately not preserved anywhere. Hence some guesswork is attempted.

of gradual ascent and descent of the seven notes of the Basic Scales) and fourtynine *Tānas*.

The seven notes (*Svaras*) are *Ṣadja* (*Sa*), *Ṛṣabha* (*Ri*), *Gāndhāra* (*Ga*), *Madhyama* (*Ma*), *Pañcama* (*Pa*), *Dhaivata* (*Dha*), *Niṣāda* (*Ni*).

Our text mentions that there are three *Grāmas* (basic scales of the above group of seven notes), viz. (i) *Ṣaḍja Grāma*, (ii) *Madhyama Grāma* and (iii) *Gāndhāra Grāma* translated here as the *Sa-scale*, the *Ma-scale* and the *Ga-scale*. They are so-called as they have respectively *Sa*, *Ma* and *Ga* as the starting note. Thus (i) the *Sa-scale* would have *Sa*, *Ri*, *Ga*, *Ma*, *Pa*, *Dha*, *Ni* as the order of notes (*Svaras*); (ii) the *Ma-scale* would have *Ma*, *Pa*, *Dha*, *Ni*, *Sa*, *Ri*, *Ga*; and (iii) the *Ga-scale* would have *Ga*, *Ma*, *Pa*, *Dha*, *Ni*, *Sa*, *Ri* as the order of notes.

The *Ga-scale* "went to heaven" i.e. fell into disuse for reasons explained in Part II, p. 662, Fn. 2. infra.

The number of *Śrutis* (microtones) in the *Saptaka* as fixed by Bharata is 22. The *Śruti*-intervals were distributed in the notes as follows :—

Sa scale : 4 *Sa*, 3 *Ri*, 2 *Ga*, 4 *Ma*, 4 *Pa*, 3 *Dha*, 2 *Ni* = 22
Ma scale: 4 *Ma*, 3 *Pa*, 4 *Dha*, 2 *Ni*, 4 *Sa*, 3 Ri, 2 Ga = 22

Mūrcchanā (√*Mūrcch*—'to increase', 'to pervade') was the gradual ascent and descent of the seven notes of the basic scale. As *Mūrcchanās* started from each note of the scale, there were seven *Mūrcchanās* of each scale. Thus the *Mūrcchanās* of the three *Grāmas* numbered twentyone. *Mūrcchanās* served as the basis of different types of songs and brought in the notes of the low (*Mandra*) and high (Tāra) registers (*Sthāna*)[1]. A *Tāna*[2] is like a *Mūrcchanā* in which one or two specific notes are dropped.

When one specific *Svara* (Note) is dropped, it is called *Ṣāḍava Tāna* (a *Tāna* consisting of six notes). When two specific notes are dropped, it is called *Auḍuva Tāna*. According to

1. For detailed discussion of *Mūrcchanās* vide Part II, p. 662, Fn. 3. infra, where terms like *Antara Ga*, *Kākali Ni*, *Sādhāraṇīkṛta Mūrcchanā* are explained.

2. The Purāṇic concept of *Tāna* is different from that of the present times. For details about *Tāna*, see Part II, p. 663, Fn. 1 infra.

Purāṇas, there were twenty *Tānas* of *Madhyama Grāma*, fourteen of *Ṣaḍja Grāma* and fifteen of *Gāndhāra Grāma*. Thus the number of *Tānas* of three Grāmas is given as fortynine.

The Purāṇa mentions two authorities, viz. *Bhimasena* and *Nārada* on Music. The names of *Mūrcchanās* with their presiding deities (Part II, 24.50-62) are for the present mere names till some explanatory text is discovered. Two old terms, viz. *Antara Gāndhāra* and *Kākali Niṣāda* are now known as *Śuddha Gāndhāra* and *Tivra Niṣāda*.

The text on this topic is corrupt and hence obscure.

ALAṄKĀRAS IN MUSIC[1]

Alaṅkāras[2] (embellishments of music) are to be explained along with their *Varṇas* (movement of notes such as 'steady', 'ascending' etc.) as their specific basis and also along with their associated configuration (*Saṁsthāna*), always in regard to dramatic performance[3] etc. The *Varṇas* are (1) *Sthāyin*, (*Sa, Sa, Sa*), (2) *Ārohin* (*Sa, Ri, Ga* etc.), (3) *Avarohin* (*Ni, Dha, Pa* etc.), (4) *Sañcārin* (*Sa, Ri, Sa, Ri, Ga* etc.). *Alaṅkāras* are said to be thirty in number but their explanation is scrappy and unintelligible.

Due to employment of *Varṇa* and *Sthāna* having the measures of *Kāla* and *Mātrā* are configuration, proportion, modifications and characteristics :

varṇa-sthāna-prayogena kāla-mātrā
pramāṇataḥ//
saṁsthānañ ca pramāṇañ ca vikāro
lakṣaṇam tathā/
caturvidham idam jñeyam alaṅkāra-
prayojanam//

---

1. Ref. to Part II, p. 663, Fn. 1 infra for further details.

2. Based on Vā. P. II.25 and *Saṅgīta Ratnākara* I.VI (Section on *Alaṅkāras*). *Saṅgīta Ratnākara* though much late in date than Vā. P. is used, as it preserves Purāṇic material on music. Vā. P. II, Ch. 25 however is full of corrupt readings and many verses (as stated in the translation) are obscure.

3. *Vide* Bharata's *Nāṭyaśāstra* Vol. IV, pp. 79-92 (Baroda Fdt).

The author emphasizes the use of the right Alaṅkāra at the place (Part II, 25.23-25). He gives the local varieties of music proper such as Mandraka, Aparāntika (cf. Ibid 25.33-37).

In spite of its scrappiness and obscurity, Vā.P. seems to follow Bd. P. in the matter about *Tāla* and says that there are two even measures—*Caturasra* (four beats and eight Mātrās) and *Tryasra* (four beats and six Mātrās).

Lastly he mentions three *Vṛttis*, *Citrā*, V*ṛtti* and *Dakṣiṇā*. The explanation in the text being scrappy and obscure, I may quote the explanation from my *Introduction to Bd.P.* (p. lxiii):

(i) In *Cittrā*, the music of stringed instruments was prominent and the song was subservient.

(ii) In *Dakṣiṇā*, the song was prominent and instrumentation subservient and

(iii) in V*ṛtti*, both have equal status.[1]

8. RELIGION AND PHILOSOPHY IN VĀ.P.

In the section on Religious Sects, we have seen the different Vedic and non-Vedic sects current at the time of Vā. P. Now we shall consider a few schools of philosophy mentioned therein :

(i) VEDĀNTA

In the *Maṅgalācaraṇa* (benedictory verses) at the beginning of the Purāṇa, the author identifies the Great God (Mahādeva) Śiva with Upaniṣadic Brahman and applies these epithets to Him. He is the eternal Lord, immutable, imperishable, great soul, Lord, protector of the world (I.i.1.1). The epithets of Brahman are applied to God Śiva in I.ii.24.90-164, II.iii.35. 162-202 (which are strongly influenced by Rudrādhyāya, *Tait. S.* IV.v and vii, *Vāj. S.* Chs. 16 & 18). In II.iii.42.28-43, Brahman is stated to be the greatest, beginningless and endless, omnipresent, one without multiplicity, the source of and the final resolvers of crores of Brahmāṇḍas, the underlying

1. Bharata's *Nāṭya-Śāstra* Vol. IV. pp. 100-101. *Saṅgīta-Ratnākara* V 10-16, VI. 165-167.

reality of the superimposed Universe, an embodiment of existence (*Sat*), knowledge (*cit*) and bliss (*ānanda*)[1].

(ii) SĀṄKHYA

It is the theistic Sāṅkhya. Though Kapila, Āsuri and Pañcaśikha are at best agnostics (if not atheists), they are claimed to be the 'sons' (disciples) of an Avatāra of Śiva. The Sāṅkhya in Vā. P. is strongly influenced by Vedānta as can be seen from the relevant section on 'Vā. P. as a Māhapurāṇa'—*Sarga* i.e. evolution of the Universe. The involution or absorption (Pralaya) of the Universe is described in details as follows: The higher element 'swallows' the special characteristic of the lower element which then automatically becomes a part and parcel of the higher element (e.g. water 'swallows up' the 'smell' (*Gandha*) characteristic of earth etc.). Thus when Ākāśa 'swallows' all the lower Mahābhūtas, it gets merged in the *Cosmic Ego* (*Bhūtādi*) until there is complete balance of all Guṇas (*Guṇa-sāmya*) and Brahma remains in the end (II. iv. 40.2-36).

(iii) YOGA

See the special note in section 7 (ii).

There are references to the external characteristics of Jainas and Buddhists and other non-Vedic (*nagna*—non-covered by the Veda) sects, but their special philosophies are not elucidated.

A few more points:

Ahiṁsā—The Purāṇa supports *Ahiṁsā* by interpreting '*Aja*' as 'a non-germinating seed' and not 'a goat' in performing a sacrifice[2] and by making the pious king Upari-cara (Heaven moving) Vasu fall down in Pātāla for supporting Indra's violence-prone interpretation of '*Aja*'[3] (the story is corroborated in Mbh. Śānti 337.24-27). But the problem arises why this same Purāṇa which denounces *Hiṁsā* so strongly should prescribe

---

1. I regard this chapter (II.iii.42) as a later accretion as the *adhyāsavāda* of Śaṅkara and a quotation from Vasugupta's *Spanda-kārikā* are found in it.
2. I.ii.57.92-110 also Bd. P. I.2.30.11-32.
3. Op. cit. vv. 103-111.

so many varieties of non-vegatarian dishes to Pitṛs in Śrâddha (II.iii.21.3-10).

FREE-WILL AND DESTINY :

The Purāṇa emphasizes the inexorable Law of Karman (I.ii.9.52-56). Destiny is Karma in previous births. Destiny and Karma are inseparable from each other. Neither one is superior to the other i.e. both factors are necessary for achieving the fruit. (Cf. Bd.P. I.ii.8.61-62, Mbh. *Śānti* 238.4-5 which are quoted verbatim in the above Purāṇas.)

9. HISTORICAL TRADITION IN VĀ. P.

Due to the historic role played by Magadha in establishing itself as the paramount power in ancient India—an achievement unanimously attested by Brahmanical, Buddhist and Jaina sources—we find Purāṇas presenting the history of eight successive Magadhan dynasties mentioning the name and the years of reign of each king.

The dynasties so described by Purāṇas like Vā. P., Bd. P., Mt. P. are as follows :

(1) Bârhadratha, (2) Pradyata, (3) Śiśunāga, (4) Nanda, (5) Maurya, (6) Śuṅga, (7) Kāṇva, and (8) Āndhra.

The first king of the first dynasty is Jarâsandha, the powerful monarch who was killed by the mighty Pāṇḍava Bhīma. In the following list of kings, the number of the years each king ruled, is mentioned within brackets after the name of the king.

(1) THE BĀRHADRATHA DYNASTY
(Vā. P. II.37.289-303)

Jarâsandha⟶Sahadeva (killed in the Bhārata war)→ Somādhi (Somāpi in Bd.P.) (58 years)→Śrutaśravas (64)→ Ayutāyu (26)→Nirāmitra (100)→Sukṛtta (56)→Bṛhatkarman (23)→Senajit (the contemporary ruler of Vā.P. and Bd.P.).

FUTURE RULERS :

Śrutañjaya (40) → Mahābala (Ripuñjaya in Bd. P.) (35)→Śuci (58)→Kṣema (28)→Bhuvata (Suvrata in Bd. P.)

(64)→Dharmanetra[1] (58)→Suvrata (Suśarman in Bd. P.) (38) →Dṛḍhasena (58)→Sumati (33)→Sucala[2] (22)→Sunetra (40) →Satyajit (83) →Vīrajit (Viśvajit in Bd. P.) (35) →Ariñjaya (50).

These thirtytwo future kings will rule for 1000 years.

As a matter of fact, the actual number of kings is different even in the case of Bārhadratha. The author seems to have recorded the names of important kings only.

atītā vartamānāśca bhaviṣyāśca
tathā punaḥ !
prādhānyataḥ pravakṣyāmi.........

According to Vā. P., Munika (Śunaka in Bd. P. and Pulaka in Mt. P.) will kill his master Ariñjaya and instal his son Pradyota on the throne of Magadha in the teeth of all Kṣattriyas. He was of Vītihotra class and was a powerful unscrupulous king.

(2) THE PRADYOTA DYNASTY
(II. 37.304-308A)

Pradyota (23) →Pālaka (24) →Viśākhayūpa (50) →Ajaka (31) →Vartivardhana (Nandi-vardhana in Bd. P. (20).

Vā. P. states that this dynasty will rule for 138 years. Actually there is a discrepancy of ten years which can be rectified by accepting the emendation from the Bd. P. which limits the reign of Ajaka to 21 years.

Both Vā. P. and Bd. P. were misinformed about Pradyota who was really a ruler of Malwa at Ujjayinī. Bhāsa has immortalised the romantic elopement of Pradyota's daughter Vāsavadattā with king Udayana of Kauśāmbī in *Pratijñā-Yaugandharāyaṇa*. In *Mṛcchakaṭika* Śūdraka records the political revolution after which Pālaka became the king at Ujjayinī. According to Pāli records, Bimbisāra, the king of Magadha, was a contemporary of Udayana and Pradyota. There is no reliable evidence

1. 297b and 298a taken together mean : He was crowned at the age of five and ruled for 58 years.

2. Not mentioned in Bd. P. but "Sumati (33)" is named instead.

to presume a Pradyota dynasty in Magadha immediately after Bārhadrathas.[1]

(3) THE ŚIŚUNĀGA DYNASTY
(II. 37.308b-313)

Śiśunāka (Śiśunāga in Bd. P.) of Vārāṇasī will vanquish Pradyotas and shift his capital to Girivraja (Rājagṛha in Buddhist records; modern Rajgir, Bihar).

The following will be the kings in this dynasty :

Śiśunāka (Onāga) (40) →Śakavarṇa (Kākavarṇa in Bd. P) (63) → Kṣemavarmā (20) → Ajātaśatru (25) → Kṣatraujas (40) →Vivisāra[2] (Bimbisāra) (28) →Darśaka (25) (He was a contemporary of Udayana as recorded in Bhāsa's *Svapnavāsavadatta*) →Udāyin (33) (He was the founder of Kusumapura or Pāṭalīputra, (Mod. Patna) → Nandivardhana (42) →Mahānandī (43).

(4) THE NANDA DYNASTY
(II. 37.320-323)

The credit of building a vast empire in north India goes to this dynasty. Its founder Mahāpadma (Ugrasena according to Buddhist and Greek sources) will be the son of Mahānandī (of Śiśunāga dynasty) from a Śūdra woman. Vā. P. predicts : "Henceforth all kings will be of Śūdra origin (*Śūdra-yonayaḥ*) and Mahāpadma will be the sole emperor with the earth under one umbrella.[3] Mahāpadma will rule for 28 years (*aṣṭaviṁśati*[4]). His eight sons will rule after him for 12 years. The dynasty will rule for 100 years.

---

1. *The Vedic Age*, p. 328.

2. According to Bd. P. Vidhisāra (Bimbisāra) was succeeded by Ajātaśatru—a fact supported by other records (*vide The Age of Imperial Unity*, pp. 22-28). Vā. P. is obviously wrong in making Ajātaśatru the grandfather of Vivisāra.

3. *tataḥ prabhṛti rājāno bhaviṣyāḥ*
śūdra-yonayaḥ /
ekarāṭ sa Mahāpadma ekacchatro
bhaviṣyati //

—*Op. cit.* v. 321.

4. It should be 88 years as in the Bd. P. for only 12 years are allotted to his sons and the total duration of the dynasty is 100 years.

(5) THE MAURYA DYNASTY
(II. 37.324-330)

Kauṭilya, a Brahmin, will exterminate all Nandas and instal Candragupta Maurya as the King. The following will be the rulers of this dynasty :

Candragupta (24) →Bhadrasāra or Bindusāra (25) →Aśoka (26 but 36 in Bd. P.) →Kuṇāla (8)→Bandhupālita (8)→Indrapālita (10) →Devavarmā (7) →Śatadhara (Śatadhanu in Bd. P.) (8) →Bṛhadaśva (7).

This dynasty of nine kings will rule for 137 years[1]. Mt. P., VP. and Bh. P. give ten as the total of kings in this dynasty.

(6) THE ŚUṄGA DYNASTY
(II. 37.331-336)

Puṣpamitra (Puṣyamitra in Bd. P. and other Purāṇas), the commander-in-Chief of the last Maurya king (mentioned as Bṛhadratha in v. 331, though named as Bṛhadaśva in v. 329) will uepose his master and establish his dynasty. The rulers of this dynasty are as follows :

Puṣpa (Puṣya) mitra (60 but 36 as per other Purāṇas) →Agnimitra[2] (7) →Vasumitra (10) →Dhruka (Bhadra in Bd. P.) (2) → Pulindaka (3) → Ghoṣasuta (3) → Vikramitra (Vajramitra in Bd. P.) (7) →Bhāgavata (32) → Kṣemabhūmi (Devabhūmi in Bd. P.) (10).

Thus 10 kings of Śuṅga dynasty will rule for 112 years. Actually, however the period in Vā.P. comes to 134 years.

(7) THE KĀṆVA DYNASTY
(II. 37.337-341)

V. 337 of the Vā. P. is defective. If emended as per Bd.P. 2.3.74, it means, the last king Devabhūmi being dissolute from his childhood, will be overthrown by his Kāṇvāyana minister Vasudeva.

---

1. Some versions of Vā. P. add the following Kings after Bandhupālita : Daśona (7)→Daśaratha (8) → Samprati (9)→Śāliśuka (13). This, however, disturbs the traditional period of the Maurya dynasty.

2. The hero of Kālidāsa's play *Mālavikāgnimitra*. Bd. P. adds Sujyeṣṭha (7) after Agnimitra but Vā. P. ignores it.

The following will be the kings of Kāṇva dynasty: Vasudeva (9) ⟶Bhūtimitra (24) ⟶Nārāyaṇa (12) ⟶Suśarmā (10).

These Brāhmaṇa kings of Kaṇṭha (Kāṇva) Gotra will rule for 45 years[1].

(8) THE ĀNDHRA DYNASTY
(II. 37.341b to 352)

Overpowering Suśarman and his forces, Sindhuka (Simuka) the Āndhra, will found his dynasty. Vā., Bd., Bh., and V. Purāṇas agree that there will be 30 kings in that dynasty, the actual number of kings listed is different in each of the above Purāṇas. Only Mt. P. gives a list of 30 kings.

Vā. P. gives the following list of Āndhra kings:

Sindhuka (Simuka) (23)→Bhāta i.e. Kṛṣṇa[2] (18)→Śātakarṇi (56)→Āpādabaddha[3] (10+24+6=40 ?)→Nemi Kṛṣṇa (25)→Hāla[4] (1)→(Pattallaka[5]) (5 years as per Bd.P. which reads:

---

1. *Op. cit.* v. 341a. The period of 45 years does not tally with the total number of the regnal years of these kings. Bd. P. gives 5 years as the period of Vasudeva's rule and 4 years as that of Suśarmā.

2. Bd. P. V. 343b reads:

aṣṭau bhātaśca varṣāṇi tasmād
daśa bhaviṣyati |

If this obscure line is emended as per Bd. P. 2.3.74.162a:

kṛṣṇo bhrātāsya varṣāṇi
so 'smād daśa bhaviṣyati

it would mean, "(Simuka's) brother Kṛṣṇa will rule for ten years". This conforms to the statements in other Purāṇas.

3. Bd. P. gives the following Kings instead of Āpādabaddha: Apolava (12)→Paṭumān (24)→Aniṣṭakarmā (25).

4. According to text adopted in Pargiter's *Dynasties of Kali Age*, p. 41, Hāla ruled for 5 years.

5. Vā. P.v. 347a reads:

Pañca saptaka rājāno bhaviṣyantt mahābalāḥ |

'Five or seven powerful kings' are anonymous in Vā. P. but Bd. P. quoted above is supported in history (*The Age of Imperial Unity*, p. 706).

Pañca pattallako nāma bhaviṣyati mahābalaḥ).

(After Pattallaka → Putrikaṣeṇa (Purikasena in Bd. P.) (21)→Sātakarṇi (1)→Śivasvāmin (28)→Gautamīputra (21)→ Yajñaśrī Śātakarṇi (19)→Vijaya (6)→Daṇḍaśrī Śātakarṇi (3) →Pulova (Pulomâvi in Bd.P.) (7)

Vā.P. states that 30 Āndhra kings will rule over the earth for 456 years[1] but actually it lists only 14 kings and the total number of years they ruled comes to 269.

A comparison of this list with that in the Mt. P. Ch. 273 shows that both Vā.P. and Bd.P. were inadequately informed as they could list only 14 and 13 kings and account for a period of 269 and 262 years respectively, though both agree in stating that the Āndhras ruled for 456 years.

The other local dynasties mentioned in Vā. P. with the total number of the years of their dynastic period are as follows :

Total No. of kings in the Dynasty	*Total No. of years of the dynastic rule*
7 Āndhras (Āndhrabhṛtyas?)	300
10 Ābhīras	—
7 Gardabhins	—
10 Śakas	380
8 Yavanas	80
14 Tuṣā (-khā-) ras	500
13 Maruṇḍas (Mlecchas)	350
18 Mauṇas	300 (? Bd.P)

Afterwards 11 Mlecchas will rule for 300 years. Then the Śūdra tribe Kolikila (Kilakila in Bd.P.) will rule for the same period. Vindhyaśakti (circa 300 A.D.) will take over from Kolikila and rule for 96 years.

This Vindhyaśakti, the founder of the Vākāṭaka dynasty was a Brahmin of Viṣṇuvṛddha Gotra, and 96 years is probably the span of his life. Vindhyaśakti's son Pravīra (Pravarasena I)

1. Op. cit. v. 352 reads :
samāḥ śatāni catvāri pañca ṣaḍ vai tathaiva ca /

Literally translated : (The rule of Āndhras will be) four hundred, five and six". This will mean 411 years. But here 'five' stands in ten's place and as such must be interpreted as "fifty". Thus Vā.P. regard 456 years as the period of the Āndhra dynasty.

performed Vājapeya sacrifice[1]—a sort of a public declaration of the end of Mleccha rule.

(9) THE NĀGA DYNASTY OF VIDIŚĀ

This dynasty is mentioned only in Vā. P. and Bd. P. The following is the line of kings :
Sadācandra alias Candrāṁśa (Xandrames, a contemporary of Alexander according to Greek writers) ⟶ Nakhavān ⟶ Dhanadharma⟶Viṁśaja⟶ Bhūtinanda.

A number of minor dynasties are mentioned after this but Viśvaphaṇi of King Nala's race is specially mentioned as a powerful ruler who conquered Magadha. He was a very pious ruler who caste his body in the Gaṅgā.

(10) THE GUPTA DYNASTY

Verse 377 (II.37) mentions the establishment of the Gupta rule. They "will enjoy the territories near the Gaṅgā, such as Prayāga, Sāketa (Ayodhyā) and Magadha."

Before closing this section, I would like to invite the attention of readers to an important statement of Megasthenes, the Greek representative of the Bactrian Kingdom at the court of Pāṭaliputra in 302 B.C. We definitely know that Alexander the Great invaded India in 326 B.C.[2] and that the credit of starting the Gupta era on December 20, 318 A. D. or February 26, 320 A.D. is given to Candra Gupta I of the Gupta dynasty.[3]

The proposed theory of contemporaneity of Megasthenes with Candra Gupta I of the Gupta dynasty[4] needs more debate and if proved with more convincing data, will revolutionize ancient India chronology.

1. *The Age of Imperial Unity*, pp. 219-220.
2. *The Age of Imperial Unity*, p. 47.
3. *The Classical Age*, p. 4.
4. Vide : K.D. Sethna—"Megasthenes and the Indian Chronology as based on the Purāṇas" in *Purana* VIII.1 pp. 9-37 and in the same journal VIII.2. pp. 276-294. Sethna concludes that Candragupta I of the Gupta dynasty was crowned in 325 or 324 BC. He follows up his theory and shows that Xandrames of Greek writers is Candrāṁśa of Nāga dynasty (*Purana* IX.I. pp. 121-139). Also vide, R. D. Karamarkar—"The First Greek conqueror of India" ABORI XXXI-i-iv pp. 238-249.

RECONSIDERATION OF ANCIENT INDIAN CHRONOLOGY

The statement of Megasthenes in *Indika* as quoted by Pliny (VI. XXI.4.5), Solinus (52.5) and Arrian (*Indica* I. IX), that there had been 153 kings intervening between the first king Dionysus and Alexander the Great and the period of their reigns is 6451 years and 3 months tallies with the above Purāṇic list. As Megasthenes was accredited to the court of Sandrocottus (Candra-Gupta) at Pali-bothra (Pāṭalīputra), his informants must have supplied the list of Magadhan kings. According to Vā.P. (II.I 131 ff) Pṛthu, the son of Vena was annointed by gods as the *first king* (ādirāja). Purāṇas tell us that he levelled the whole earth, clearing it of ups and downs, encouraged agriculture, cattle-breeding, commerce and building cities and villages. The list of kings between Pṛthu and Candragupta I (of the Gupta dynasty and NOT Candragupta Maurya) is of 153 kings. (154 if Bharadvāja, the adopted son of Bharata is included, though he got his son Vitatha crowned and did not rule himself).

The period of 6451 years also tallies with the period from Pṛthu as given in the Purāṇas. But this statement make Alexander the great a contemporary of Candragupta I of the Gupta dynasty.

10. THE DATE OF VĀ.P.

Vā.P. is one of the oldest and most authoritative Purāṇas. It is mentioned in Mbh. *Vana*. 191.16, but we do not know what Text was before them then. Nor can we say anything about the nature of the text when it came to be narrated by Sūta, in the reign of King Adhisīma Kṛṣṇa, the fourth descendant of Parīkṣit.[1]

---

1. Bd. P.II.iii. 74.227 states that 1050 years intervened between the birth of Parīkṣit (the Bhārata War) and the coronation of Mahāpadma Nanda (382 B.C.). Thus if Parīkṣit was born in 1432 B.C. according to the Bd. P., the reign of Adhisīma Kṛṣṇa, his fourth descendant, may be taken one century later (30x4=120 years) in 1300 B.C. The statement of Megasthenes discussed elsewhere and our traditional belief about the beginning of the Kali Age in 3102 B.C. (fixing 3138 B.C. as the birth-date of Parīkṣit) if found correct, will upset our present chronological frame.

As Vā.P. is quoted as an authority by mediaeval writers on Dharma Śāstra like Aparārka (c. 1125 A.D.) or Kullūka Bhaṭṭa (c. 1150 A.D.?), Vā.P. must be assigned to a period not later than 1000 A.D.[1]

But we have earlier references and quotations from Vā.P. Śaṅkara in his Com. on the *Brahma Sūtra* (Br. Sū.) quotes verses from the present day text of the Vā.P. For example:

(1) In his Com. on *Br.Sū.* I.3.30:

samāna-nāma-rūpatvāc......
......darśanāt smṛteśca/, he quotes Vā.P.I.ii.8.32-33
teṣām ye yāni karmāṇi prāk sṛṣṭyām pratipedire...... (upto)
tad bhāvitaḥ prapadyante।

(II) In the Com. on the same Sūtra, he further quotes Vā.P. I.ii.9.58.59:

ṛṣiṇāṁ nāmadheyāni...... (upto)
tathā bhāvā yugādiṣu/

(III) In his Com. on Br.Sū.II.I.I:

smṛtyanavakāśā.....doṣa-prasaṅgāt

he quotes Vā.P. I.i.185

ataśca saṅkṣepam imaṁ śṛṇudhvam.....
saṁhāra-kāle ca tadatti bhūyaḥ//

The quotations are enough to show that Śaṅkara regarded Vā.P. as an authority like Smṛtis worth-quoting while explaining Br.Sū. It means that to reach that authoritative position, Vā.P must have existed at least about one century or so before Śaṅkara.

Now the date of Śaṅkara as presumed at present (viz. 8th cent. A.D.) needs correction in view of recent researches. Śaṅkara calls Gauḍapāda as 'his teacher's teacher' *guror guruḥ* (*Upadeśa-sāhasrī* II. 18.2). Gauḍapāda's *Māṇḍūkyakārikās* are

1. Anukramaṇis (Table of Contents) generally given in the 1st chapter of a Purāṇa, were composed later in the 11th cent. A.D. and some attempt is made later to make the Purāṇa text conform to the *Anukramaṇī* (A.D. Pusalkar—*Siudies in Epics and Purāṇas*, p. 70). This has made the problem of fixing the date more complicated.

taken as *Pūrva-pakṣa* in Bhavya's *Madhyamakahṛdaya*[1] Ch. 8. Bhavya (A.D. 490-570) was a Buddhist philosopher of Madhyamaka school and a founder of its branch Svātantrika[2]. To select Gauḍapāda's *Māṇḍūkya-kārikās* for refutation implies a respectable status of Gauḍapāda and his Kārikās. To attain this position as the opponent of Buddhism worth-challenging, by a prominent Buddhist philosopher implies Gauḍapāda's seniority in time to Bhavya, at least by 25 to 50 years. If this conjecture is reasonable, Gauḍapāda must be located somewhere in the later half of the 5th century (A.D. 450+) and automatically Śaṅkara, the disciple's disciple of Gauḍapāda cannot be removed from him by more than 50 or 60 years (25 or 30 years per generation × 2). When Śaṅkara is thus located in the early part of the 6th cent. A.D. Vā. P., to attain an authoritative position to be quotable in Com. on Br. Sū. may be posted in the 5th cent. A.D.

Bāṇa (6th cent. A.D.) mentions Vā.P. in *Harṣacarita* (III. 4th para) as follows :

pustaka-vācakaḥ sudṛṣṭiḥ...... gitvā,
pavamānoktaṁ purāṇam papāṭha|

In *Kādaṁbari* (Pūrvabhāga para 37) :—

Purāṇe Vāyu-pralapitam ('In Purāṇa that is narrated by Vāyu i.e. Va.P'.). As Bāṇa's date—early in the 6th cent. A.D.—is accepted by scholars, Vā.P. may be assigned at least a century earlier to command the respect of scholars like Bāṇa.

It is enough to quote some prominent authors and philosophers—Brahmanical and Buddhist—to show that Vā.P. is reasonably located in the 5th cent. A.D. Vā.P. narrates the future kings upto Gupta period which agrees with the above finding.[3]

Though this is the usual way of determining the date of an old work, Purāṇas, being a literature of growth, have archaic,

---

1. The Sanskrit version of the Tibetan original was published by Prof. V.V. Gokhale. It is reprinted in Hajime Nakamura's *History of Early Vedanta Philosophy* Vol. I pp. 184-185 (Motilal Banarsidas, Delhi 1983).

2. *Op. cit.* p. 206.

3. If we accept Megasthenes' view as explained by K.D. Sethna in *Purāṇa* VIII.i. pp. 9-37 and op. cit. ii. pp. 276-294 Candragupta I of the Gupta dynasty and Megasthenes (302 B.C.) will become contemporaries.

ancient and comparatively modern materials in one and the same chapter and one has to analyse the chapter and fix the dates of those parts.

Dr. D.R. Patil has analysed and tried to fix up the date(s) of the different materials so determined.[1]

The classification is as follows :

(1) *Remains of archaic period*: Kṣattriya-Brāhmaṇa struggle, Kṛsattriya Brāhmaṇas, *Godharma*, *Niyoga* (levirate), cow as means of exchange etc.

(2) *Remains of the ancient periods* :

Old theories regarding kingship, references to Vārtā, Daṇḍanīti etc. as in old portions of Mbh., Kauṭalīya *Arthaśāstra*, popular institutions like *Sabhā*, *Saṁsad*, *Paura Jānapada*, older units of measurement of distance, non-vegetarianism is Śrāddha.

(3) *Some (comparatively) modern features*:

Yuga-system of chronology, ten Avatāras of Viṣṇu (with variations), twenty-eight incarnations of Śiva including Lakulīśa, emphasis on Śaiva religion..

But these elements are so mixed up that one will have to assign different periods to portions forming but one and the same chapter.

11. GAYĀ MĀHĀTMYA (G.M.)

This '*Sthala Purāṇa*' of about 560 verses glorifies the sacredness of the precincts of modern Gayā. It is appended to the Vā. P. after the concluding (*Phala-Śruti*) verses of the Vā. and has a totally different pair of interlocutors. It is found in different works such as Mbh. Vana Chs. 84-95, Garuḍa Chs. 82-86, AP Chs. 114-116, KPII.35, NPII.Chs. 44-47—all having practically similar contents and common verses. This shows that the G.M. must have been an independent work adopted and adapted by various Purāṇa-writers.

The place got its name from a pious Asura[3] King Gaya. He is different from the Vedic seer Gaya (of RV.X.63 and

1. Dr. D. R. patil—*Cultural History from the Vāyu Purāṇa*, pp. 14-15.

2. Based on : (i) The text of G. M. and notes (ii) Nārāyaṇa Bhaṭṭa's *Tristhalī Setu* (TSS), (iii) L. P. Vidyarthi's *The Sacred Complex of Hindu Gaya* (SCHG), (iv) P. V. Kane's *History of Dharma Śāstra* Vol. IV.

3. '*Asura*' is a respectable vocable of Indo-Iranian antiquity (cf. *Ahura* in the Avesta) and means 'spiritual' or 'divine' in the Vedic SK. and the

64) whose father was Plati[1], while our Gaya, according to *Uttarādhyana Sūtra* was the son of Samudravijaya, King of Rajagṛha (mod. Rajgir in Bihar). Buddha visited Gayāsīsa (Gayāśīrṣa) and Kāśyapa's hermitage at Gayā (*Mahāvagga* I. 21.1, also Aśvaghoṣa's *Buddhacarita* XII.87-88, XVII.8). The mention of king Gaya and the sacred place Gayā in Pāli and AMg. canons and in Brahmanical Purāṇas shows that Gaya must have been a historical person in hoary antiquities and the hermitage or the home-town of king Gaya probably became known as Gayā.

The story of Gaya is variously interpreted—as the defeat of Buddhism by Brahmanism[2] or the amalgamations of Brahmanism with the more ancient popular demonolatry[3] or an invention to impress the sanctity of the range of Gayā hills[4]. If this legend be an invention of the Brahmanical Purāṇa-writer, he must have been more sympathetic and respectful to the Asura King Gaya than to his own gods. After reviewing the materials of the sacred geography of Gayā, L.P. Vidyarthi finds the inclusion of the elements of folk tradition in this great traditional and "essentially Sanskritic" holy centre.[5] The story of the great penance of Gaya and the appeal to the generosity of the noble-hearted king by crafty Devas and their subsequent cruel treatment meted out to him is interestingly told in the Purāṇa.[6] Various legends etc. about sacred places (temples, tanks, rivers etc.) at Gayā have been discussed in details in the notes.

---

ancient god Varuṇa is called 'Asura' in the Vedas. '*Sura*' is a later development from '*Asura*' as '*sita*' from '*asita*' (MW, 121.) Asuras was a cousin tribe of Suras and had intermarriages between them. Lord Kṛṣṇa was an Asura from his mother's side (S.K. Chatterji—*Selected Writings*).

1. See *Prācīna Caritra Kośa* by Siddheshwar Shastri Chitrava, p. 308, under '*Gaya Plāta*'. 'Plati' is the name of the father of the Vedic seer Gaya.
2. Rajendra Lal Mitra—*Bodha Gayā*, pp. 14-18.
3. O'Malley—*JASB* LXXII.iii 7,1904.
4. B.M. Barua—*Gayā and Buddha Gayā*, p. 1934.
5. L. P. Vidyarthi—*The Sacred Complex in Hindu Gayā*, p. 29,1978.
6. Vā. P. II. Ch. 44.

The following is a brief outline of the traditional performance of pilgrimage at Gayā which lasts for seven days :

1st day	Entrance into Gayā; bath in the river Phalgu; performance of Śrāddha and Tarpaṇa; visit to Preta Śilā; bath, Śrāddha etc. at Rāma Tīrtha; offering Bali to Yama and Dharma and the two dogs Śyāma and Śabala.
2nd day	Visit Pretaparvata; bath, Śrāddha etc. at Brahma Kuṇḍa; offer *piṇḍas* to Pitṛs invoking gods to witness one's repayment of the debt of the Pitṛs.
3rd day (1st day of Pañcā Tīrthī rites).	*Pañca-Tīrthī* rites (including those at Dakṣiṇa and Uttara Mānasas, Kanakhala); visit to Phalgu; bath, Śrāddha etc.
4th day (2nd day of Pañca-Rites)	Visit to Dharmāraṇya; bath etc. at Mātaṅgavāpī and Brahma Tīrtha; visit Mahābodhi tree; and performance of Śrāddha there.
5th day (3rd of Pañca-Rites)	Bath etc. at Brahmasaras; Śrāddha between Brahmakūpa and Brahmayūpa; circumambulation of Brahmayūpa; watering mango trees at Gopracara; offering Bali to Yama and Dharma and the two dogs of Yama.
6th day (4th of the Pañca-Rites)	Bath at Phalgu; Śrāddhas at various footprints (*Padas*) on Gayā Śiras (which extends from Krauñcapada to Phalgu Tīrtha); Śrāddha and offering Piṇḍas on Viṣṇu Pada is most important. Also Piṇḍa-offerings on Rudra, Brahmā and other 14 Pādas.
7th Day (5th day of Pañca Rites)	Bath, Śrāddha etc. at Gadālola; Śrāddha at Akṣayavaṭa; honour the Gayāvala Brahmin. Bow and worship to the Akṣayavaṭa and to Prapitāmaha.

The special feature of Gayā Yātrā is that there is no tonsure; the Gayawal alone and not other Brāhmaṇas are to be honoured; and that anyone may offer a Piṇḍa to anybody by uttering his name and gotra and can offer a piṇḍa to oneself*.

Gayā is thus the most sacred centre to pay the debt of our ancestors and to redeem them from their plights and secure for them the highest abode.

*For details see Va. P. II. Chs. 45-50. There are of course a few divergences in other Purāṇas about the details of the Yātrā but TSS follows Vā. P.

VĀYU PURĀṆA

PART I

SECTION 1 : PRAKRIYĀ PĀDA

CHAPTER ONE

(*Summary of Contents*)

Obeisance to Śrī Gaṇeśa

One should read or recite any *Purāṇa* or *Itihāsa* text[1] after having paid obeisance to Nārāyaṇa[2] and Nara,[3] the most excellent of men, as well as to goddess Sarasvatī.

---

1. This verse, originally used at the beginning of the Mbh. is adopted by Purāṇa-writers as well, for example, Bh. P. I. 2. 4; and the word '*Jaya*' therein is interpreted by the commentators Vīra Rāghava and Śukadeva as another name of the Bh. P. Thus the word '*Jaya*' became a generic term used both for Itihāsa (Mbh.) and Purāṇa texts (Bh. P., Va. P.). Hence '*Jaya*' is interpreted as 'any Purāṇa or Itihāsa' here. Bhaviṣya Purāṇa states :

Tathaiva viṣṇudharmāśca śivadharmāśca śāśvatāḥ/
Jayeti nāma teṣām ca pravadanti manīṣiṇaḥ//

Compare KP I. 53. 33; II. 46.

2. *Nārāyaṇa* : The god who lay on cosmic waters of the deluge before creation. This aspect of this deity is recorded in the etymology of his name in Manu 1. 10, Mbh. Śānti 328. 25 :

Āpo nārā iti proktā, āpo vai narasūnavaḥ/
Tā yadasyāyanaṁ pūrvaṁ tena nārāyaṇa smṛtaḥ//

In early Viṣṇuism, Viṣṇu and Nārāyaṇa were not identical; the amalgamation of Viṣṇu of Vedic Brāhmaṇism and Nārāyaṇa of the Pañcarātras was a later development (vide J. Gonda, *Aspects of Early Viṣṇuism*; also G. V. Tagare, *Bhāgavata Purāṇa* (AITM), Part I, Introduction, pp. xlii-xlv).

3. *Nara* : An incarnation of Viṣṇu : born of Dharma and Mūrti, daughter of Dakṣa; a constant associate of Nārāyaṇa while performing penance at Badarikāśrama. The Mahābhārata heroes Kṛṣṇa and Arjuna are regarded as incarnations of Nārāyaṇa and Nara.

Victory to Vyāsa,[1] the son of Parāśara and the gladdener of the heart of Satyavatī—Vyāsa from whose lotus-like mouth flowed forth the nectar of words, which the whole universe imbibes.

1. I seek refuge in Lord Īśāna (Śiva), the eternal, steady, immutable, great god of noble soul, the lord of the entire universe.

2-6. Desirous of knowing (more about) *Purāṇas*, legends, (etc.) I seek refuge in Lord Brahmā, the creator of the worlds, (who is) omniscient, unvanquished, the noble lord of (everything) past, present and future; God Brahmā, the lord of the universe in whom are inherent the four divine excellences, viz. unparalleled knowledge, detachment, supremacy and virtue (*dharma*); (Lord Brahmā) who for ever visualizes all beings (irrespective of their being) manifest or unmanifest, which re-enter the Lord (Brahmā) for cessation of activities (at the time of the dissolution of the universe); (God Brahmā) the creator of the world, the knower of the reality of the world, the knower of the principles, who, resorting to Yoga, created all living beings mobile and immobile; the unborn lord, the creator of everything, the lord in the form of consciousness and the cosmic witness of the world.

7-9. After bowing with devoted and pious mind to Brahmā, Vāyu and Indra, to the noble-souled Vasiṣṭha, the most excellent of the sages, and to his (Vasiṣṭha's) great-grandson, Vyāsa, Kṛṣṇa Dvaipāyana, who had attained pre-eminent fame as a sage of great purity, and to sage Jātukarṇa,[2] I shall

1. *Vyāsa* : Vyāsa means "an arranger". In every Dvāpara Yuga, the work of arranging the floating Vedic Mantras into *Saṁhitās*—compilation—is done by a person. And he is called Vyāsa. The compilation of the Mbh. and eighteen Purāṇas is assigned to him. The present Vyāsa is the son of Satyavatī, the incarnation of Vāsavī, the daughter of Pitṛs. His father was sage Parāśara, the grandson of sage Vasiṣṭha. He was dark in complexion and was concealed in an islet in a river by Satyavatī (Mbh. Ādi. 63. 68). Hence he came to be known as 'Kṛṣṇa Dvaipāyana'.

2. *Jātukarṇa*; (also Jātukarṇya) : A sage noted for self-control; a member of Yudhiṣṭhira's court (Mbh. Sabhā. 4.14). One wonders why Parāśara did not teach the Purāṇas (for example this and Bd. P.) directly to his son Vyāsa but did so through Jātukarṇa.

(now) narrate this *Purāṇa* related by Brahmā, which is on a par with the Vedas and which is embellished by sacred treatises consisting of sections on *Dharma* (virtue), *Artha* (wealth) and *Nyāya* (justice or right conduct).

10-12. While Asīmakṛṣṇa,[1] the valiant king of unequalled splendour and the most excellent among sovereigns was ruling over the Earth righteously, the sages of well-disciplined souls performed a sacrifice of long duration in the holy land of Kurukṣetra[2] on the sacred bank of the river Dṛṣadvatī.[3] The sages were devoted to truth and holy rites. They were straightforward. Their sins had been quelled. They were quiescent, had full mental control and had conquered the sense-organs. They were within the precincts of the Naimiṣa[4] forest and had been initiated in accordance with the sacred scriptures.

---

1. *Asīmarkṛṣṇa* : or *Adhisīmakṛṣṇa* :

The great-grandson of Janamejaya III who was the great-grandson of the Mahābhārata hero Arjuna. He was a contemporary of Divākara, king of Ayodhyā and king Senajit of Magadha. All these kings belonged to the 6th or 7th generation of their forebears who participated in the Bhārata war. It was during the reign of Asīmakṛṣṇa that the great *Sattra* of 12 years took place at Kurukṣetra on the bank of the Dṛṣadvatī. The date assigned to this king, viz. B. C. 850 by Pargiter is now discarded.

2. *Kurukṣetra* : The famous battlefield where the war between Kauravas and Pāṇḍavas was fought. The different battles in that war were fought at and around Thaneswar in Haryana. Thus Abhimanyu was killed at Amin, 5 miles south of Thaneswar; Bhiṣma died at Nagdu, 11 miles to the south-west of Thaneswar. Historic battles were fought here from Vedic times to A. D. 1761, the date of the third battle of Panipat, ancient Paṇiprastha—a village claimed by Yudhiṣṭhira from Duryodhana (De, 110).

3. *Dṛṣadvatī* : The Chitang—a tributary of the Ghaggar between the Yamuna and Sutlej—M. Ali, p. 115. De has accepted this identification as correct (p. 58.) instead of with the Ghaggar.

4. *The Naimiṣa forest* : The description here shows that this forest must be located in Kurukṣetra (Kane, *H. D.* IV, 783). It is possible that there were two Naimiṣa forests, the original one on the bank of the Gomati round Nimsār, 45 miles from Lucknow and one in Kurukṣetra as Vā. P. is positive about the performance of the *Sattra* on the Dṛṣadvatī. Was it that sages resident of Naimiṣa forest on the Gomati in U. P. migrated to Kurukṣetra and the sages being Naimiṣeyas (inhabitants of Naimiṣāraṇya), the area of this *Sattra* came to be called Naimiṣāraṇya in Kurukṣetra?

13-16. The highly intelligent Sūta[1] who was the most excellent among the reciters of *Purāṇas* came there to see the sages.

He became well-known to the world as Lomaharṣaṇa[2] (the Thriller who made hair stand on their ends) as he thrilled the members of his audience with delight by his excellent (absorbing) narration.

He was the most intelligent disciple of the sage Vedavyāsa, the store-house of penance, Vedic learning and good conduct.

The association of the sages of Naimiṣāraṇya and their performance of a *Sattra* is as old as Vedic times. According to Kane (ibid) "*Naimiṣyā vai sattram āsata*" occurs in Kāṭhaka Saṁhitā X. 6 (I could not trace it). But if the references given by him to the Saṁhitā and Brāhmaṇas be correct and if the direction of the spread of Aryandom from the West to the East be presumed the Vedic references might be to the Naimiṣāraṇya in the Kurukṣetra area.

1. *Sūta* :

As stated below in vv. 26-33, Sūta is the offspring of a Brāhmaṇa woman from a Kṣatriya male, a view endorsed by Manu X. 11, Yājñavalkya I.93. He was not eligible for Vedic lore but was to recite *Itihāsa* and *Purāṇa*. Gautama regards Sūta as a *Pratiloma* (*Dharma Sūtra* 15-16). Kauṭilya agrees with this status of a Sūta but distinguishes this Sūta, the narrator of Purāṇas probably as a sage different from ordinary Sūtas (*Paurāṇikas tvanyaḥ sūto māgadhaśca brahmakṣattrād viśeṣataḥ—Artha Śāstra* III. 7, p. 165).

There is another derivation of *Sūta* from √*Su*—'to extract (Soma juice)'. In the sacrifice of King Pṛthu, Sūta appeared for the first time while extracting Soma on the prescribed day (*Sutyāha*) but the libations of Soma intended for Bṛhaspati got mixed with that for Indra and were offered to Indra. Hence he became of a mixed class (vv. 28-30). KP. I. 1. 6 regards Romaharṣaṇa as an incarnation of Viṣṇu born on *Sutyāha* with the mission of recounting Purāṇa-Saṁhitā. Romaharṣaṇa, however, does not claim here to be Viṣṇu's incarnation. The birth of Sūta on the *Sutyāha* is recorded in Bd. P. II. 36. 158-73, Pd. P. II. 27. 65-87, Sk. P. Prabhāsa 1. 8.

2. *Ro* (*Lo*) *ma-harṣaṇa*:

This appears to be the special designation of this Sūta as he thrilled the audience with delight and made their hair stand on their end. Hence Brāhmaṇa performers of sacrifices offered him a higher place while he narrated a Purāṇa. This post of honour above the Brāhmaṇas cost him his life as the hot-headed Balarāma killed him when during his visit to Naimiṣāraṇya, he found Romaharṣaṇa occupying a higher seat in the assembly of Brāhmaṇas (Bh. P. X. 78. 28). Our Purāṇa pays high tribute to his scholarship (vv. 13-16, 21-24).

He was well-known in the three worlds. The entire Purāṇic lore was well established in him. His scholarship had become extensive through his study of the Mahābhārata. Stories conducive to (four *Puruṣārthas*, viz.) *Dharma* (virtue), *Artha* (wealth), *Kāma* (desire) and *Mokṣa* (liberation) were firmly rooted in him. Wise sayings and sage discourses came forth from him as medicinal herbs from the (mother) earth.

17. He (the Sūta) who was an adept in decorum, approached the highly intelligent and prominent sages as per proper procedure. After coming near, he paid them obeisance with folded palms.

That brilliant scholar pleased those sages by prostrating himself before them (to show respect).

18. The lustrous sages who were performing sessional sacrifices were delighted; so also were the members of the sacrificial assembly. They duly greeted him with gentle words and honoured him.

19. On seeing that highly reliable scholar Lomaharṣaṇa, there arose in them the desire to hear the Purāṇa.

20. The chief householder (the sponsor) of that sacrificial session who was an expert in all (sacred) lores, understood their desire from their gestures. Consequently, he urged the Sūta (as follows):

21. "O Sūta! For learning *Itihāsa* and *Purāṇas*, the venerable and highly intelligent sage Vyāsa, the greatest among the knowers of Brahman (or Vedas), has been properly served and propitiated by you. And you have (as if) milked from his intellectual store, legends based on ancient tradition.

22. The prominent sages are anxious to hear the Purāṇa. Therefore it behoves you to narrate those legends to them.

23. All the noble persons, the knowers of Brahman (or Veda) who have assembled here, belong to different clans (*gotras*). May they hear about their respective clan-genealogies through the *Purāṇas*.

24. Please expound (the Purāṇa) to these sages, who, along with their sons, have assembled here for this sacrifice of

a long duration. Indeed, you have been (strongly) remembered by us while we were being consecrated for this sacrifice."

25. Urged thus for (narrating) the *Purāṇa* by the sages who were interested in (had some knowledge of) the Purāṇas and were devoted to truth and holy rites, the Sūta agreed to the proposal (and said).

Sūta said :

26-27. It is the incumbent duty of the Sūta, ordained by saintly men of yore to preserve the genealogies of gods, sages and the most glorious kings and the traditions of great men as recorded in (earlier) *Itihāsas* and *Purāṇas* by those well-versed in the Vedic lore (or expounders of Brahman).

28-29. But nowhere is the eligibility of the Sūta for the Vedic lore (such as recitation of the Veda etc.) seen (prescribed). While the sacrifice of the noble-souled (king) Pṛthu, the son of Vena, was being performed, Sūta appeared for the first time extracting Soma (on the prescribed *Sutyā* day) for offering unto the fire, but he became of a mixed caste as the oblation intended for Bṛhaspati was got mixed up with the one intended for Indra and was offered to god Indra. Therefrom was born the Sūta due to this grievous mistake and expiatory rites had to be performed (in that sacrifice) as atonement for the error.

30. As he was born (as a *pratiloma* child) from a Kṣatriya (male), a lower caste man, of a Brāhmaṇa woman, on account of his similarities of the inherent qualities of the former (i.e. Kṣatriya), he is proclaimed as having similar duties (like those of a Kṣatriya).

31. Thus the Sūta who was born of a Brāhmaṇa receptacle from a Kṣatriya source, has (some) qualities with the former (caste) and so has some identity of duties with them.

32. His middling duty (way of maintenance) is the pursuit depending on Kṣatriya profession such as maintaining chariots, elephants and horses. Practice of medicine was his inferior duty.

33. Since I have been commanded by expounders of Brahman like you, to follow my duty, how can I decline to narrate to you in details the *Purāṇa* so highly worshipped by sages.

34. Vāsavī[1] was born as the mental daughter of the Pitṛs (manes). Being cursed by her father, she was born in the species (womb) of a fish.[2]

35. Vyāsa, the great yogin and the foremost among the knowers of the Vedas, was born of her, just as fire is born of the *araṇi* stick.

36. I make obeisance to Vyāsa, the venerable sage, protagonist of Bhṛgu's lore, the ancient Puruṣa, the great lord Viṣṇu in the guise of a human being.

37. Even as he was born, the entire Vedic lore in all its compendiums appeared before him, but he formally attained it from Jātukarṇa, as it was his duty to study it from a preceptor.

38. He churned the ocean of the Vedas with the churning-rod of his intellect and produced the Moon in the form of the Mahābhārata.

39. Just as a tree proliferates into many branches after reaching fertile soil and in congenial season, the tree in the form of the Veda spread out in different branches after reaching him (Vyāsa).

40. I have listened to this Purāṇa from that omniscient expounder of Brahman, who is conversant with the Vedas, who is honoured by all and is of blazing brilliance.

41. I shall now relate in detail the Purāṇa narrated by Vāyu formerly[3], when he was urged by the noble sages of Naimiṣa.

---

1. *Vāsavī* :

Mbh. Ādi. (63. 51-73) endorses this legend but there she is said to be born of Uparicara Vasu and Adrikā, a celestial damsel cursed to be a female fish and was then in her fish-form. The Mbh. records that twins were found in the belly of the defunct Apsarā-fish. The king of the place adopted the boy who became known as a pious king called Matsya and the girl with the foul smell was handed over to Dāśa-rāja. She became a sweet-smelling lady through the favour of sage Parāśara when she responded to his overtures (*Ibid. Ādi*. 63. 70-85).

2. Satyavati, the mother of Vyāsa, was born in the womb of a fish. (*vide Mbh. Ādi*. 63. 50-69).

3. It means that the present Purāṇa which is being narrated by the Sūta at Kurukṣetra was formerly recited by Vāyu to the sages of Naimiṣa forest (mod. Nimsār in U. P.)

42. The ultimate cause is the four-armed, four-faced, supreme Maheśvara, the unmanifest, the inconceivable, the inscrutable and the self-born god.

43. It is certain that he created the unmanifest cause and whatever is permanent, in the form of existent and non-existent, beginning with *Mahat* (the great principle, the cosmic intellect) and ending with *Viśeṣa*.[1]

44-45. The incomparable golden cosmic egg was born from it. The cosmic egg was enveloped by the waters; the waters by the fire; the fire by the wind; the wind by the ether; the ether by the cosmic Ego; that Ego by the cosmic intellect (*Mahat*) and that intellect by the Unmanifest (*avyakta*).[2]

46-47. Hence in this Purāṇa, the origins of all the gods and sages are narrated. The origin of rivers and mountains is explained; all the Manvantaras and Kalpas are described; legends about Brāhmaṇas and Kṣatriyas and the birth of Brāhmaṇas are retold.

48. Then the creatorship of Brahmā and the creation of the subjects (beings) are explained as also the various states of Brahmā, born of the Unmanifest.

49. The number of years of the Kalpas, the establishment of the worlds, the slumber of Viṣṇu and the uplift of the Earth (are described).

50. The mode of planning cities etc. in accordance with castes and stages of life; the cutting of trees planted in dwelling places and those naturally grown (in the forest) (are discussed).[3]

---

1. The phrase '*mahadādi viśeṣānta*' is popular with Purāṇa-writers in describing the evolution of the universe. It means the group with *Mahat* at one end and *Viśeṣa* at the other. The term *Viśeṣa* means *Bhūtas* (gross elements, *Tanmātras*, sense-organs), the *Tāmasī Sṛṣṭi*. It is so called as it indicates the differentiation between gross elements where five senses cognise five sense-objects (*viṣayas*) and *Bhūtas* in a specialised (individual) manner.

2. These are the seven 'Sheaths' of this cosmic Egg. They mention these later (*infra* 4. 75-77). The number seven has a special significance in Purāṇas, e.g. 7 Lokas, 7 Seas, 7 Dvīpas (continents), 7 Mountains etc. (*infra* 4. 72).

3. A. reads *Siddhīnām*: "of the *Siddhis* providing homes under trees (?)"

51. A detailed description of the paths and their measurements and the allocation of places in the heaven to the mortals of this world (is given).

52. Description of (different species of) trees, medicinal trees, plants and creepers (is given). How mortals attain the status of trees, Hellish beings, and insects is also explained.

53. The two paths of the deities and the sages are mentioned. The creation and destruction of food etc., and of bodies is also mentioned.

54. In the beginning, out of sacred literature, the Purāṇa was remembered by Brahmā.[1] Then the Vedas came forth out of his mouths.

55. The ancillaries of the Vedas, the Dharmaśāstras (codes of the law like *Smṛtis*), holy rites, religious observances and restraints, origin of animals and human beings are explained.

56. Similarly are explained the total components of Kalpas; the nine types of unintentional creation by Brahmā are described.

57. Then the three creations without the cosmic intellect; how the worlds came into being and Dharma (virtue) etc. originated from the limbs of Brahmā's body.

58. The twelve species of beings that are born again and again in a Kalpa; the duration of Kalpas and the period of transition from one Kalpa to another.

59. The origin of *Adharma* from Brahmā on being enveloped by Tamas; the birth of Śatarūpā,[2] thereafter (is described).

60. The birth of Priyavrata, Uttānapāda, Prasūti and Ākūti —the sinless ones in whom the subjects are established.

61. The birth of twins to Ākūti by Ruci, the Prajāpati, and the birth of daughters of Dakṣa through Prasūti.

---

1. This self-glorificatory claim for precedence over the Vedas is chronologically justifiable as some compilation called Purāṇa did exist before the Atharva Veda (AV. XI. 7. 24, XV. 6. 11).

2. Śatarūpā: The spouse of Svāyambhuva Manu. The pious lady, a performer of penance was accepted in marriage by Manu. They had two sons—Priyavrata and Uttānapāda and two daughters Prasūti and Ākūti. Prasūti married the Patriarch Dakṣa and Ākuti, Ruci, the Prajāpati (VP. I. 7. 17-18). Probably Manu and Śatarūpā represent the original darents.

62. The procreation by great-souled Dharma from Dakṣa's daughters like Śraddhā, of a race characterised by Sattvaguṇa giving rise to happiness.

63. As well as the race of *Adharma* (unrighteousness) from Hiṁsā (violence) characterised by Tamoguṇa and inauspiciousness. Then is glorified the progeny of Maheśvara from Satī.

64. The receptacle of Yoga recounted again to the twice-born ones (who were) desirous of liberation that type of Yoga (which was) mentioned to blemishless (god) Brahmā.

65. The incarnation and the supreme glory of Rudra, the legends relating to the three Vedas and the great dialogue are then mentioned.

66. Eulogies of Lord Śiva by Brahmā and Nārāyaṇa at which that God was pleased, has been described.

67. The manifestation of Lord Rudra from Brahmā's body and the origin of the name Rudra because he, the Lord, had cried, (has been glorified).

68. How that God obtained the eight names such as Rudra and others from Brahmā and how the three worlds constituting the mobile and immobile beings are pervaded by them.

69. The creation of progeny by Bhṛgu and other sages as well as the glorification of the lineage of Vasiṣṭha, the Brāhmaṇa sage, (is described) here.

70. The progeny of Agni through Svāhā[1] and that of the Pitṛs[2] of two classes through Svadhā, thereafter (are mentioned).

71-72. In the context of the line of Pitṛs, the cursing of Dakṣa, and intelligent (sages like) Bhṛgu and others for the sake of Satī and the counter-curse of Rudra by Dakṣa of wonderful

1. The three fires in every ancient Aryan home, viz. Gārhapatya or Pavamāna, Dakṣiṇāgni or Pāvaka and Āhavanīya or Śuci are regarded as the progeny of Agni from Svāhā (*vide infra* Ch. 29, Agnivaṁśa).

2. The two types of Pitṛs mentioned here (*infra* Ch. 30. 6-7 etc.) are *Agniṣvāttas* and *Barhiṣadas*. The *Śatapatha Brāhmaṇa* and *Tait. Brāhmaṇa* I. 6. 9. 5 mention one more class viz. *Somavantaḥ*. Those who performed a Soma sacrifice are *Somavantaḥ*; those who offered cooked oblations (like *caru* or Puroḍāśa) and secured the next world are *Barhiṣadas* and those who did neither and are consumed by fire after death are *Agniṣvātta*.

activities and the ultimate termination of the enmity between them has been narrated in details here.

73[1]. Their individual appointments in different continents and lands and the description of creation by Svāyambhuva Manu.

74. The creation of Nābhi and the noble-souled Rajas; the enumeration of continents, oceans and mountains.

75. The description of different Varṣas (sub-continents), rivers and their tributaries and the numerous divisions of the seven main continents.

76. The extent of the zones of the continent of Jambū Dvīpa and the ocean; their extent in Yojanas along with their mountains (are mentioned).

77. The mountains in the sub-continents, mountain (ranges) dividing (this) sub-continent, viz. Himavān, Hemakūṭa, Niṣadha, Meru, Nīla, Śveta and Sṛṅgavān.[2]

78. Their internal dimensions, heights, lengths and extents (measured) in Yojanas, and the residents are described.

79. The sub-continents such as Bhārata; the rivers and mountains therein, as inhabited by the stable and moving beings.

---

1. Ref. to Bd. P. I. 65. 66 shows that a line is missing here: The line means : "Herein the details of the sons of Priyavrata are described such as : Their appointments etc."

2. These are the mountain-systems of India as understood by the Purāṇa-writers. They are identified as follows :—

(1) Himavān : The great Himalayan range
(2) Hemakūṭa : Ladakh-Kailash, the trans-Himalayan chain
(3) Niṣadha : Hindu Kush-Kunlun chain
(4) Meru : The Pamirs
(5) Nīla : Zarafshan-Trans-Alai-Tien-Shan chain
(6) Śveta : Nura Tau-Turkistan-Atbashi chain
(7) Śṛṅgavān : Kara Tau-Kirghiz-Ketman chain

Soviet archaeologists and Indologists now testify to the existence of Vedic Aryans from the lower reaches of the Dnieper, Crimea, the northern Black Sea area, through the Soviet republics of Central Asia. *Vide* for example O. N. Trubachev's 'Linguistic periphery of the ancient Slavs', 'Indo-Aryans in Northern Black Sea Area'; B. A. Rybakov's 'The Paganism of the Ancient Slavs and others'. But due to the colonial legacy of mental slavery, many of us still disbelieve the geographical evidence in the Purāṇas.

80. The continents Jambū etc. encricled by the seven oceans, the watery land (?) and the Lokāloka are described.

81. These worlds and the earth with its seven continents as enveloped by the cosmic egg; the worlds Bhū etc., and their natural surroundings are described.

82. Everything is described in brief along with its diameter and circumference even to the smallest fraction of the whole measure.

83. The magnitudes of the sun, the moon and the earth in Yojanas with their present presiding deities. So also the holy assemblies of Mahendra and others on the northern peak of Mānasa.

84. Thereafter, the movement of heaven like the circular movement of the fire-brand, is mentioned. The characteristics of Nāgavīthi and Ajavīthi[1] are also described.

85. Then is stated the Yojanas of the two extremities, the two borders and the zones of Lokāloka. The extent of twilight, day and the equinoxes is mentioned.

86-87. Then the guardians of the world who are stationed in the four quarters are described. The southern and the northern paths of the manes and the deities, the paths of householders and the ascetics as based on the qualities of Rajas and Sattva are described. The region of Viṣṇu where Dharma etc. are established is glorified.

88. The course of movements of the sun, moon, planets and luminaries due to the (controlling) power of Dhruva, the pole-star, and the auspicious and inauspicious effects (of their movement) on the people.

89. The chariot of the sun prepared by Brahmā himself for some special purpose is mentioned. Seated on this chariot, the Sun-god moves in the firmament.

90. That chariot is occupied by the gods, the different suns, sages, divine musicians, celestial damsels, Yakṣas, serpents and Rākṣasas.

---

1. *Vīthis* are the courses of the sun in the sky. Thus *Ajavīthi* is one of the three divisions of the Southern path in the sky in which the sun, the moon and the planets move comprehending the *Nakṣattras* (costellations) Mūla, Pūrvāṣāḍhā and Uttarāṣāḍhā.

91. So also the chariot of the moon which is constituted of the essence of waters is described. The increase and decrease of the moon, caused by the sun, are also mentioned.

92. The movement of the chariots of the sun and others (starting) from the pole-star is described in details, as also the tortoise-shaped arrangement of the heavenly bodies with the pole-star stationed at the tail (end) (is narrated).

93. The stars in the form of constellations are mentioned along with the planets wherein are situated the residences of the gods who have performed meritorious acts.

94-106. The exudation of rain, chilliness and heat from the thousand rays of the sun and the division of rays by their names, functions and purpose; the magnitude of the planets and their courses depending on the sun; the manner how the throat of Śiva became blue on account of poison;[1] how the trident-bearing lord swallowed poison when implored by Brahmā; the eulogy of the supreme lord Śiva by Viṣṇu who is eulogised by the gods; the holy sin-dispelling narrative of the origin of the *Liṅga*.[2] Wonderful transformation of Pradhāna through the cosmic form; the narrative of the greatness of Purūravas, son of Ilā; the propitiation of the two classes of manes by means of nectar; the Parvans (auspicious occasions based on the position of the moon) as also their junctures; the propitiation by means of Śrāddha of the two classes of manes, viz. those who have gone to the heaven and those who have fallen down to the nether regions; the duration and the number of Yugas.[3] The introduction of agriculture and such occupations as means of livelihood in Tretā Yuga due to their decrease in comparison with Kṛta Yuga; the enumeration of the castes and stages of life and the narration of

1. This refers to Śiva's swallowing the *Halāhala* poison which came up while gods and demons were churning the sea for obtaining *Amṛta*. For saving the world from its deadly effect, god Brahmā requested Siva to drink it up (*vide infra* Ch. 54).

2. This refers to Śiva's manifestation in the *liṅg* form as a column of fire the dimension of which could not be comprehended by gods Viṣṇu and Brahmā both of whom were contending for personal superiority. For details : *vide infra* Ch. 55.

3. *Vide infra* Ch. 58; compare Bd. P. Ch. I. 2. 31.

their activities. The establishment of the castes and stages of life by virtuous means; the introduction of the institution of sacrifice; the dialogue between the sages with Vasu and Vasu's descent (to the nether worlds);[1] the inexpressibility of (answers to) questions except by Svāyaṁbhuva Manu. The merits of penance, the periods of Yugas in their entirety, the brief narration of the events in Dvāpara and Kali Yugas; the magnitudes of the girth, height and longevity of gods, animals and human beings in the different Yugas according to the efficacy and power of the Yugas; the characteristics of the good and their advent; the narration of the Vedic and non-Vedic Mantras; the extent of the branches (of the Vedas); the appellation of Vedavyāsa and others; the dissolution of Manvantaras and their re-creation after dissolution—all these are mentioned in detail.

107. Since the account of (creation etc.) of the deities, sages, Manus and the Pitṛs cannot be given in detail, hence they are mentioned briefly.

108. The number of years of the present Manvantara is mentioned in terms of human years. The same applies to all Manvantaras.

109-110. The description of the past and future Manvantaras is given on the basis of the present Manvantara. So also the characteristics and the time duration of the transition from period of the past and future Manvantaras are given with reference to the Svāyaṁbhuva Manvantara. The scheme of three Manvantaras and the knowledge of time are also recounted.

111-112. The account of Devas and Prajāpatis in the Manvantaras, Dakṣa's grandsons, the sons of his favourite daughters and those that were procreated by Brahmā and others as well

---

1. This Vasu was an ancient pious king of Pūru dynasty. Due to his piety, he moved through the sky without touching the earth. There was dispute between sages and gods about the interpretation of '*Aja*' in the Vedic injunction '*Ajena Yaṣṭavyam*'. Gods interpreted it as 'a goat', while the sages held that it meant 'seeds incapable of germination'. When Uparicara Vasu whom both the parties accepted as the judge, decided in favour of gods, even though it involved injury to life, sages cursed him and he fell down from his exalted position into the nether world (*Mbh. Śanti Ch.* 337).

as by the intelligent Dakṣa. The Manus, viz. Sāvarṇi and others, residing on the Meru; the description of the lineage of Dhruva, the son of Uttānapāda[1].

113. The milking of the Earth (as started) by Pṛthu,[2] son of Vena; the specification of vessels and their content of milk; the description of races[3] as well as how formerly this earth was milked by Brahmā and others.

114. The birth of Dakṣa, the intelligent Prajāpati in Māriṣā from the ten Pracetas through a part of the moon.

115. The sovereignty of Mahendras over the beings of the past, present and future, the creation of Manus and others and the various anecdotes of their lives.

116. The creative activity of Vaivasvata Manu is recounted in details. So also is narrated the birth of Bhṛgu and others from the semen of god Brahmā at the time of the great sacrifice when the Lord assumed Varuṇa's form.

117. After the narration of the auspicious creation (Procreative activity) of Cākṣuṣa Manu that of Dakṣa by means of meditation is narrated.

118. Nārada, son of Brahmā, destroyed the mighty sons of Dakṣa after speaking pleasing words to them. He thus invited (Dakṣa's) curse.

119. Then Dakṣa procreated in Vīriṇī his renowned daughters. The procreation (procreative) activity sanctioned by religion (law) of the intelligent Kāśyapa is then narrated.

120. Thereafter, the unity, diversity and specialities of Brahmā, Viṣṇu and Śiva are narrated.

---

1. The reading *Auttānapāda* as in Bd. P. I. 1. 104 is more appropriate.

2. The legend of King Pṛthu milking the earth is a Purāṇic version of the Vedic conception of milking of the *Virāj* cow. The *Virāj Sūkta* (AV VIII. 10) is probably the basis of the legend. This Pṛthu, the son of the tyrant Vena, is a Vedic king. AV VIII. 10. 24 records that Pṛthu milked the *Virāj* cow with the earth as a milking pail and Vaivasvata Manu as the calf. Here (*infra.* II. 1. 174) Cākṣuṣa Manu is made the calf as in Bd. P. I. 2. 36. 202.

3. *Vaṁśānām* 'of the races' is inappropriate. Later on there is a specific mention of who was 'the calf' at the time of each milking of the earth. '*Vatsānāṁ*' the reading in Bd. P. I. 1. 196 is more appropriate.

121. How gods were cursed from being all-powerful by the self-born Brahmā (is narrated). The attainment of Marut-hood by the Maruts born of Diti from divine elements is then narrated.

122. The classification of Maruts into seven groups of seven each, their attainment of god-hood, the order of the Pitṛs and fixation of their abodes in Vāyu are narrated.

123. The creation of Daityas, Dānavas, Gandharvas, serpents, Rākṣasas, goblins, ghosts, animals, birds, creepers and the celestial damsels is then narrated in great detail.

124. The birth of the elephant Airāvata from the ocean, the birth of Garuḍa and his coronation (are also narrated).

125-126. Detailed narration (is then made) of the descendants of Bhṛgu, Aṅgiras, Kaśyapa, Pulastya, the noble Atri and the sage Parāśara. The progeny of Devas and the sages is described thereafter.

127. The three Virgins in whom all the worlds are founded are then glorified. Then the grandsons of the Pitṛs are mentioned and the birth of Devas is described.

128. A detailed description of the Lord and that of the five souls and the progeny of Ilā and then that of Āditya (the Sun-god) is given.

129. The legend of Vikukṣi,[1] the slaying of Dhundhu, and the line of rulers from Ikṣvāku to Bṛhadbala are briefly related.

130. The progeny from Nimi to Jahnugaṇa and even that of king Yayāti is described.

131. The description of the dynasties of Yadu, Haihaya and later that of Kroṣṭṛ is given.

---

1. Vikukṣi was king Ikṣvāku's son. One day Ikṣvāku decided to conduct a great sacrifice (*Mahāpralaya Śrāddha*) to his manes and sent his son Vikukṣi to forest to bring flesh of hunted animals. On his way home, Vikukṣi became hungry and ate a rabbit. When the flesh for sacrifice was to be sprinkled with sacred water, Vasiṣṭha declared that it was 'a remnant' and not acceptable for sacrifice. The Prince confessed but was expelled by Ikṣvāku. As Vikukṣi ate a rabbit, he became known as *Śaśāda*. After his father's death, Vikukṣi returned to rule over Ayodhyā.

132. The glory of Jyāmagha,[1] the creation of subjects of the noble souls Devāvṛdha, Arka and Vṛṣṭi are described.

133. The divine accusation of Viṣṇu, the attainment of a precious jewel from the Sun-god (are described).

134. The creation of the progeny of noble-souled Yudhājit as well as that of the glorious royal sage Devamīḍhuṣa are narrated.

135-136. Again the birth and doings of the great-souled (Viṣṇu), the wickedness of Kaṁsa, the birth in seclusion of Viṣṇu the Prajāpati as the son of Vasudeva and Devakī and later the procreation by Viṣṇu (Kṛṣṇa).

137. In the feud between Devas and Asuras, when, while protecting Indra, a woman (Bhṛgu's wife, Śukra's mother) was slain by Viṣṇu, He incurred the curse of Bhṛgu. Bhṛgu however brought back to life the divine lady, Śukra's mother.

138. There were wars between Devas and Asuras for twelve myriads of years entailing great loss of life. (The exploits of) Narasiṁha and others are extolled.

139. Propitiation of god Śiva was achieved through performance of penance by wise Śukra. Being intensly desirous of getting a boon, he eulogised Śiva. Thereafter are described the activities of gods and demons.

140. While the noble-souled Śukra was engaged with Jayantī, the intelligent Bṛhaspati, assuming the form of Śukra deluded the Asuras. So the mighty brilliant Śukra cursed them (all).

141. Next, the birth and glory of Lord Viṣṇu are described. Turvasu was the grandson of Śukra, born of his daughter Devayānī, from Yadu. Kings Anu, Druhyu and Pūru were the sons of Yayāti.

---

1. The word 'glory' refers to the fortunate end of a henpecked exiled king, son of Rukma-Kavaca. He was issueless. Once in a fight, he got a girl and brought her home. Jyāmagha's queen Śaibyā asked him who she was. The henpecked husband replied, 'Your daughter-in-law'. 'Where is the Son ?' retorted Śaibyā. Jyāmagha performed penance, got a son and the girl then became their daughter-in-law. Vide infra, II. 33.30-35.

142. Noble and excellent kings of this family endowed with brilliance and wealth and possessing eternal fame are described.

143-144a. The close adherence to Dharma by the Brāhmaṇa sage Kauśika is narrated, and also how Surabhi (the divine cow) dispelled the curse of Bṛhaspati.

144b. The praise of the family of Jahnu as also the prowess of Śantanu are also narrated.

145. A brief description of the seven Manus of the future and a description of the destruction (of the universe) at the end of Kaliyuga of the last (Bhauma) Manvantara (are given).

146. The significance of the terms *Para* and *Parārdha* (is explined) and the ascertainment of the extent of the universe in terms of Yojanas (is done).

147. Three types of dissolutions of all living beings, viz. *Naimittika* (periodical), *Prākṛtika* (of prakṛti—primordial nature) and *Ātyantika* (ultimate) are then described.

148-149. Then, there is the description of the drought caused by the sun, of the terrible fire Saṁvartaka, of the cloud, of the single vast ocean, of the wind, of the noble soul's (Brahmā's) night and of the calculation of periods, especially the period of Brahmā. Then the description of the seven worlds beginning with the earth (Bhū) and of hells beginning with Raurava is given.

150. The excellent abode of Śiva lies above the region of Brahmā where all living beings attain merger at the time of annihilation (of the universe).

151-152. Then the end of all living beings, the total annihilation after the death (lit. destruction) of Brahmā, the eight kinds and the eight forms of the vital breath, the upward and downward course (of the deceased) due to their resorting to virtuous and evil deeds in life.

153. Repeated destruction of the Mahābhūtas (the primary elements), the non-eternality of (even) god Brahmā after enumeration of miseries (are described).

154-155. The evil nature of pleasures and the ascertainment of their result, difficulties of attaining liberation, perception of defects through detachment, establishment of the being in

Brahman after casting away the manifest and the unmanifest and its realisation through the knowledge of diversity are all described in details.

156. The supreme bliss of Brahman is stated to be free from threefold distress, formless and unsullied. He who has realized it, has no fear from anywhere.

157. A further creation by another Brahmā is then narrated as before and so also the race of sages and the destruction of all sins.

158. Thus have been described the contents of this Purāṇa. Therein are also described the changes, and dissolutions of the universe, as also the tendencies of the living beings and the fruits of abstention from worldly acts.

159. The birth of Vasiṣṭha and his son Śakti, the slaying of Śakti by (Kalmāṣapāda), son of Sudās at the instigation of the sage Viśvāmitra (are described).

160. The birth of Parāśara (from Adṛśyantī) and how the sage Vyāsa was born of the daughter of Pitṛs from that holy sage.

161. The birth of Śuka; how the intelligent Parāśara and his son (Vyāsa) incurred the wrath of Viśvāmitra.

162. And how the sacrificial fire was kindled by Vasiṣṭha, how that sacrifice was shrewdly spoiled by divine means by lord Skanda, seeking the welfare of the sage Viśvāmitra, and for the sake of progeny.

163. How the holy sage Vyāsa, by the power of his intelligence, divided the single Veda into four ones and how, further, these were redacted into several branches by his disciples and grand-disciples.

164. How (Brahmā) was asked by the sages of the six illustrious families about the practical application of the Vedas in sacrifices; how the sages desirous of religious rites were answered by Brahmā on being thus asked; how the sages desired for a holy region and how Brahmā, being desirous of achieving their welfare, (gave them a wheel and told them:)[1]

---

1. Verses 164-166 give the popular etymology of Naimiṣāraṇya by attributing it to the *Nemi* (felly) of a wheel set in motion by god Brahmā. The place so selected is Nimsar in U. P.

165. "This wheel has a fine nave, its form and name are divine; it has truth for its spokes; its revolution is auspicious, and it is incomparable. You follow it alertly but with self-restraint as it proceeds ahead. You will then attain what is wholesome for you.

166. The place where the rim of this wheel of law, during its motion ahead is shattered, must be regarded as holy." After saying thus to the sages Brahmā vanished from sight.

167. (It is mentioned) how Gaṅgā conceived the golden foetus and how the place acquired the name Naimiṣa. And how the sages performed the long sacrifices there and how Śaradvat was restored to life.

168. How with great faith, the sages of Naimiṣa widened the earth and set up a king whom they honoured with hospitality in accordance with the injunctions of the sacred scriptures.

169. The king who was thus pleased with their hospitality was abducted by the cruel Asura Svarbhānu[1] who disappeared with him.

170. They followed the abducted king Aila (Purūravas) and as before they saw him in the village Kalāpa[2] in the company of Gandharvas.

171. (It is mentioned) how he joined the great sages and (how) he saw the golden vessels in their sacrifice.

172. How in the twelve year-long sacrifice (King) Aila engaged in disputation and scuffle and was slain by the sages of Naimiṣa.[3]

---

1. An ancient Dānava king, son of Kaśyapa and Danu (*Mbh. Śānti* 227. 50). Ugrasena, maternal grandfather of Kṛṣṇa, was regarded as his incarnation (*id. Ādi*. 67. 12-13).

2. *Infra* Ch. 91 shows that this Kalāpa was in the Himalayas where Purūravas honey-mooned with the divine nymph Urvaśī. It is supposed that Maru and Devāpi, the last kings of Solar and Lunar dynasties, wait there as ascetics for re-establishing their kingdoms after Kali Age. It is located somewhere near Badarikāśrama—De, p. 74.

3. The death of Purūravas in his attempt to seize the gold vessels of the Naimiṣāraṇya sacrificers is recorded in *Mbh. Ādi* 75. 20-22, Bd. P. I. 1. 2. 17-23. For details vide Bd. P., Vol. I, pp. 24-25, footnote.

173. How they created Āyus, son of Aila, from within the Araṇi[1], concluded the sacrifice and served Āyus.

174. O excellent Brāhmaṇas, all this has been described as it happened. The knowledge of worldly affairs of the sages is indeed great.

175. This Purāṇa, (which is) conducive to excellent knowledge, had formerly been narrated by Brahmā. The incarnation of Rudra for the welfare of the Brāhmaṇas (has been mentioned).

176. So also the (Pāśupata) Yoga of Śiva[2] and the regions sacred to him have been glorified. How lord Śiva became blue-throated and how he manifested in the liṅga-form[3] has also been described.

177. All this was mentioned to the Brāhmaṇas by Vāyu who propounded Brahman. The recital of this Purāṇa, listening to this Purāṇa and committing it to memory in particular, is conducive to wealth, fame and longevity. It is holy and it dispels sins.

178. Now it is going to be narrated in the above order. Even lengthy narrations, if stated in a brief form, are grasped with ease. And hence the above summary. What has been indicated above in brief will be narrated in detail by me below.

179. Even he who, with the composure of mind, studies this first section would have understood the whole of this Purāṇa. There is no doubt in this.

180-181. A Brāhmaṇa, who may know the four Vedas with the Aṅgas and Upaniṣads, cannot really be regarded as having attained proficiency, if he has not thoroughly known the Purāṇas also. He should re-inforce the Veda with the Itihāsa and Purāṇa. The Veda is afraid of him who is deficient in tradition, thinking 'he will hurt me.'

---

1. According to *Mbh. Ādi.* 75.24 Āyu was the son of Purūravas and Urvaśī and was *not* created out of *Araṇi* (the wooden piece for igniting fire by attrition) as stated here. Va. P. *infra* I. 2. 2 confirms Mbh. above.

2. *Vide infra* Part I, Chs. 11, 14 and 15.

3. *Vide infra* Part I, Chs. 54 and 55.

182. Reciting frequently this chapter which has been told by Brahmā himself, one will be liberated even if he be involved in mishaps and will attain the goal of his desire.

183. This is called Purāṇa because it breathes (exists) from earliest times.[1] Even he who understands the etymological interpretation of this would be liberated from all sins.

184. Nārāyaṇa (Lord Viṣṇu) pervades the entire universe and its functions. Lord Śiva is the creator of the creator of that universe.

185. Hence listen to this gist. Lord Śiva is the supreme deity of this Purāṇa.[2] At the time of evolution he creates the universe. At the time of dissolution he withdraws it into himself.

CHAPTER TWO

A Sacrificial Session of Twelve Years

1-2. The sages who were rich in religious austerities (or who considered religious austerities as their wealth) spoke to Sūta again : "Where did the *Sattra* (sacrificial session) of those sages of miraculous deeds take place? How long did it last? How did it function? How did Vāyu (the Wind-god happen to) recount the Purāṇa to them?

3. Please narrate this in details as we are extremely eager to hear this." Thus urged, Sūta spoke (the following) auspicious words in reply.

Sūta said :

4. Listen where the wise sages performed the excellent *Sattra*, how long it continued and how it was accomplished.

---

1. A popular etymology of '*Purāṇa*'.
2. Hence Vā. P. is regarded as a Śaiva Purāṇa.

5. They performed it where, of yore, the creator of the universe desirous of creating the universe, performed the holy *Sattra* for a thousand years.

6. In that *Sattra*, Tapa was the householder (performing the sacrifice); god Brahmā assumed the office of the priest designated as 'Brahmā.' Ilā had the status of the consort (of the performer of sacrifice). The intelligent Mṛtyu (god of death) of great splendour performed the *Śāmitra* rite (of killing the sacrificial animal) in that sacrifice of those noble souls.

7. The sages performed the sacrifice for a thousand years in the place where the rim of the revolving *Dharma-cakra* (the wheel of righteousness) was shattered. Thanks to that event, that place, sanctified by the sages, became famous as Naimiṣa.

8. It is the place where the holy river Gomatī, worshipped by Siddhas and Cāraṇas, flows. There, Rohiṇī gave birth to Budha by Soma.

9. Where Śakti, the eldest son of Vasiṣṭha, was born; where Arundhatī gave birth to a hundred sons of excellent brilliance.

10. Where king Kalmāṣapāda was cursed by Śakti and where the enmity between Viśvāmitra and Vasiṣṭha had cropped up.

11. Where sage Parāśara was born of Adṛśyantī. Even as he was born, the mortification of Vasiṣṭha[1] was brought about.

12. There, at Naimiṣa, the expounders of the Vedas performed the sacrificial session. Since they performed the sacrifice at Naimiṣa, they were called Naimiṣeyas.

13. It was while the valiant king Purūravas was ruling over the earth that the sages performed the *Sattra* for twelve years.

14. We have heard that though Purūravas enjoyed the eighteen continents, surrounded by the oceans, he was never content due to his covetousness for hoarding precious stones.

---

1. **Parāśara, while in mother's womb for twelve years, became such a great Vedic scholar (*Mbh. Ādi* 176. 12-15).**

15. Urged by Devahūti, Urvaśī loved him. Accompanied by this celestial damsel, the king desired to perform a sacrifice.

16. It was during his reign that the Naimiṣeyas performed the *Sattra*. The highly refulgent foetus which Gaṅgā conceived from the Fire-god, was deposited on the mountain and it was transformed into gold.

17. Then, for promoting the welfare of the world, god Viśvakarmā, of his own accord, made of gold, the sacrificial hall (lit. the enclosure for the sacrifice) of those noble-souled sages.

18. Bṛhaspati (the preceptor of gods was) there among the (sages) of incomparable brilliance. During the course of hunting, Purūravas, the son of Ilā, happened to visit that place.

19. On seeing that great wonderful sacrificial hall of gold, his faculty of judgement (wisdom) was overwhelmed by covetousness and he tried to seize it.

20. Thereupon, the Naimiṣeyas got extremely infuriated. Urged by fate, they killed him towards the close of the night with adamantised Kuśa grass.[1]

21. Pounded by the adamant-like Kuśa grass, the king cast off his mortal body. The sages made his son, born of Urvaśī, the ruler of the Earth.

22. This king (Āyu) was the noble-souled father of Nahuṣa. He was virtuous and devoted to religion, and he behaved well with the sages. The health of that excellent person was very fine and he enjoyed a long life.

23. After mollifying the king (Āyu), the sages who were excellent among those who know Brahman, resumed their *Sattra* duly for increasing their religious merit.

24. That *Sattra* of those noble sages became as wonderful as that of the creators (of the universe) which they undertook before, with a view to create the universe.

---

1. The greed of Purūravas and his consequent death at the hands of sages is recorded in *Mbh. Ādi* 75. 20-23. Vide Bd. P. I. 1.2. 20-23 and p. 24 note 1 on it.

25. The *Sattra* was attended by Vaikhānasas, the friendly Vālakhilyas, Marīcikas and other sages who were as brilliant as the sun and fire.

26. It was attended by Pitṛs, Devas, Apsaras-s, Siddhas, Gandharvas, Nāgas, and Cāraṇas. It was equipped with the auspicious requisites in the same manner as the assembly hall of Indra by means of all these.

27. They worshipped the Devas through hymns, *Sattra*-chants and *Graha*-incantations. They worshipped the Pitṛs with the rites befitting their status. They worshipped the Gandharvas and others according to their respective position in the prescribed way.

28. The Gandharvas sang Sāman hymns; the Apsaras-s danced. They were desirous of propitiating (the invitees) in this rite.

29. The sages uttered auspicious words full of graceful expressions. Those who were versed in the philosophy of the mantras argued with one another.

30. Some disputants overcame their adversaries by fallacious arguments. The sages there were learned men, well-versed in the Sāṁkhya and Nyāya school of philosophy.

31. Brahmarākṣasas did not perpetrate any foul deeds; nor were there the Daityas who destroy the sacrifice, nor the Asuras who plunder it.

32. There was no need for expiation or imprecation. By the combination of (steady) activity, intellect and efficiency, the injunctions were carried out.

33. In this manner the intelligent sages performed the *Sattra* of twelve years' duration. Bhṛgu and other wise sages performed the Jyotiṣṭoma sacrifices separately. They paid ten thousand (coins) as fee to those returning priests.

34. After concluding the sacrifice, O Brāhmaṇas, they asked the great lord Vāyu of noble soul what I have been asked by you. Urged to describe the various dynasties of Kings, the lord spoke to them.[1]

---

1. Vāyu (the Wind-god) is the earlier interlocutor than the traditional Sūta. Cf. *Bd. P.* I. 1. 2. 36-48.

35. He (Vāyu) was a disciple of Brahmā. He could see everything directly. He had perfect control over his senses. He was endowed with the eight supernatural powers like *Aṇimā* and others.

36. He sustains all the worlds with their special characteristics of the non-human (and human) species. He perpetually flows through his seven courses (regions) as arranged.

37. The forty-nine Maruts arranged in seven groups of seven were stationed invariably in his jurisdiction. He is very powerful who could make the assemblage of three kinds of living beings. He could make embodied beings sustain through Tejas (fire).

38. He sustains bodies of living beings urging them with his five-fold activities and through the organs of sensation and activity.

39. It has been said by the learned that his source of origin was ether, attributes were sound and touch and that he was the origin of fire.

40. Lord Vāyu is the extremely active presiding deity called Vātāraṇi. He was expert in the science of language.

41. He was adept in ancient (Purāṇa) tradition. By means of sweet words full of Purāṇic contents he could delight the learned sages.

CHAPTER THREE

Origin of Creation

Sūta said :

1. Obeisance to the great God (Śiva) of supreme power and activity, the prominent one among gods, whose intelligence and brilliance is inmeasurable. Salute to him of the brilliance of thousands of suns and fire. Hail to the creator and annihilator of the universe !

2-5. I shall narrate the story that wards off the evil of the Kali age, after bowing to the Prajāpatis bowed to by all the world, to great Lords like the self-born god Brahmā, Rudra and other deities, (to) Bhṛgu, Marīci, Parameṣṭhin, Manu, (to) Rajas, Tamas (and Sattva), to Dharma, Kaśyapa, Vasiṣṭha, Dakṣa, Atri, Pulastya, Kardama, Ruci, Vivasvat, Kratu, (to) the Patriarch sage Aṅgiras, Pulaha, Cukrodhana and the group of twenty-one ordered to carry out their duty of increasing the subjects (human beings) and to those ancient, eternal sages who are accompanied by their attendants.[1] I bow to the sages, the leaders of whom are Bṛhaspati and Uśanas who shine by their firmness and fortitude. I bow to those merciful sages of auspicious conduct and penance.

6. I shall describe the excellent creation of Prajāpati (God Brahmā) embellished by Indra, gods, and the sages. It is auspicious, incomparable, sinless and pleasing to the sages and the patriarchs (Prajāpatis) of great splendour.[2]

7. The (Purāṇa) story proclaimed by the Wind-god is greater than the greatest. It describes the period from the beginning of god Brahmā's day; it describes the sages who have amply and distinctly manifested the glory of their manliness and splendour. It is spread (incorporated) in the Vedas and Smṛtis and illustrated (therein) as well.

8. It is highly delightful to the mind due to the precise construction of compounds and (the use of) appropriate variety of words. Herein is described the first activity of unmanifest nature prompted by lord Śiva.

9-10. What is mentioned as the incomprehensible cause is Brahman which is the source of origin of the Prakṛti. The individual unit is a synthesis of Ātman, the cavity of the heart, womb, eye and the body. It is immortal and imperishable. The semen comprises the sattvaguṇa, penance and is very bright. That incomprehensible eternal second Puruṣa is pervaded by Brahmā, the grandfather of the worlds.

---

1. A. adds : *Manūṁśca sarvān akhilān avasthitān*
'To all the Manus present'.
2. A. adds : *Viśuddha-vāg-buddhi-śarīra-tejasām*/
"Of extremely pure speech, intellect and bodily splendour".

11. By the mere mental conception of the great lord, Prakṛti gives birth to the eight causes for increasing the continuity of creation and to the predetermined changes in the personal soul, it (i.e. Prakṛti) being the procreator, the possessor of Rajas in abundance, bound by the cosmic time and the limits prescribed by the Vedas. (?)

12-14. (The Purāṇa describes the creation of) the Devas, Asuras, mountains, trees, oceans,[1] Manus, Patriarchs (Prajāpatis), sages, Pitṛs, twice-born castes, Piśācas, Yakṣas, Nāgas, Rākṣasas, stars, planets, constellations of stars, the sun, the night-prowling demons, months, seasons, years, nights, days, space, time, Yugas, *Ayanas*, medicinal and forest herbs, creepers, aquatic beings, Apsaras-s, animals, lightning, rivers, clouds, birds etc. In fact whatever is subtle, whatever is on the earth, whatever is stationed in the sky, whatever is mobile or immobile, whatever has motion and division (is mentioned in this Purāṇa).

15. The science of the Vedas—Ṛk, Yajus, Sāman, the Soma juice, the sacrifice—whatever is made use of and desired by Prajāpati has been mentioned.

16. (So also is described) The creation of those before that of Vaivasvata Manu—the birth of those pious ones who are bowed to by the three worlds such as the lords of gods, celestial sages, Manus and prominently intelligent (persons) who have filled in (populated) and embellished the three worlds.

17. The rebirth of Dakṣa in the world of mortals by the curse of Rudra; his residence on the Earth and the mutual curse of Śiva and Dakṣa[2] (are mentioned).

18. The revolutions of Manvantaras, the creation and dissolution of the Yugas, sages and their lineage as these happened in the primeval Yugas and would occur onward—All this is described here (in this Purāṇa).

19. Those Vyāsas who propagate the Vedas in the Dvāpara Yugas are serially described. So also the number of Kalpas, worlds and the days of Brahmā (are mentioned).

---

1. A. adds : *Gandharva-yakṣoraga-mānuṣāṇām*/
'Of Gandharvas, Yakṣas, Nāgas or reptiles and human beings'.
2. *Infra* Ch. 30. 56-67.

20. The extent of four-fold living beings, viz., birds, trees, the sweat-born insects, and animals as also of the pious heaven-dwellers, and of those who have gone to hell. Their extent is given by inference.

21. The three types of dissolution, viz. absolute, of Prakṛti (primordial nature) and periodical as also the bondage and liberation and particularly the way of worldly existence and the higher way are mentioned.

22. The position of the causes remaining in the state of Prakṛti (material cause) and their subsequent functioning, have been expounded to the sages through arguments and on the authority of sacred scriptures. O Brāhmaṇas, whatever was fully narrated factually is being recounted to you exactly. Please listen.

CHAPTER FOUR

Origin of Creation (continued)

1. On hearing that, all the sages of the Naimiṣa forest replied to Sūta with eyes excited with curiosity.

2. "You, sir, are an expert in the knowledge of different dynasties and families as you have inherited it directly from Vyāsa. Hence, please describe to us entirely the creation (etc.) of this world.

3. We wish to know the detailed '*who's who*' (lit. the genealogies) of them all, and also the diverse creation of the ancient sages, as also the primeval creation of Prajāpati".

4. On being repeatedly requested by them the noble-souled Lomaharṣaṇa, the most excellent among the good, narrated everything in detail and in due order.

Lomaharṣaṇa said :

5. The story that you have asked me to narrate is divine, charming, meaningful and destructive of sins. What is being

related by me is wonderful, full of deep meaning and in consonance with the Vedas.

6-7. He who retains this in memory, or listens to it constantly or narrates it to Brāhmaṇas and to recluses in particular, with pious mind and self-restraint, on festive occasions (or important lunar days) in holy centres and temples, enjoys a long life. By proclaiming this Purāṇa, he upholds his family and is honoured in the heaven.

8. Understand as the Purāṇa consisting of extensive sections is being recited by me word by word as it was heard (by me). It will increase the fame of you all.

9. The glorification of all meritorious persons of well-established fame is conducive to wealth, reputation, heavenly pleasure, destruction of foes and longevity.

10. Creation (of the universe, its) dissolution and re-creation, genealogy of kings, Manvantaras and the description of the families of sages—these five constitute the characteristics of a Purāṇa.[1]

11. I shall (now) recount in details the Purāṇa that was narrated by the Wind-god and is on a par with the Vedas. (I shall narrate the traditional history of) the Kalpa which is purer than any other Kalpas and is positively purer than other holy things.

12. The first section (*pāda*) called *Prakriyā* consists of the following : The Origin, dissolution, re-creation and sustenance of the world.

13. The other sections constitute the Introductory (*Upodghāta*), *Anuṣaṅga* (the central) and *Upasaṁhāra* (the conclusion). The Purāṇa is conducive to virtue, fame and longevity. It dispels all sins.

1. This verse enumerating the five characteristics of a Purāṇa is common to most Purāṇas, e.g. A. P. 1-14, Bd. P. I. 1. 37b-38, Bs. P. I. 2. 4-5, Bv. P. IV. 133. 6, GP. I. 215. 14, KP. I. 1. 12, SK. P. VII. 2. 84 and others. Amara Siṁha (5th cent. A. D.) has recorded this verse in *Amara Kośa* I. 6. 5. But "The Purāṇa Texts that have come down to us hardly conform to this definition" (*The Hist. and Culture of the Indian People*, Vol. III, p. 292). For the application of this definition to the present text *vide* Introduction.

14. Thus the four sections[1] are briefly mentioned by me. I shall describe these in detail in due order.

15-16. After making obeisance to the self-born god Brahmā, Hiraṇyagarbha (a golden-fetus, born of golden egg), who is the lord, is the first and the last Puruṣa, who is the distinguished and superior Ātman of the subjects and who governs the worlds, I shall relate in details the excellent creation without leaving anything in doubt. The creation starts with the principle of *Mahat* and ends with *Viśeṣa* (the gross body).[2] It is described in diversity of forms and characteristics with the five dimensions and six (dividing?) systems. It is presided over by Puruṣa.

17. The unmanifest primary cause is of the nature of *Sat* (existent) and *Asat* (non-existent). It is eternal. Those who meditate on the Reality call it *Pradhāna* and *Prakṛti*.

18. It is devoid of smell, colour, taste, sound and touch. It is unborn, steady, imperishable, eternal and stationed in its own Ātman.

19. It is the origin of the universe. It is the great Being, the great Brahman, the eternal. It is unmanifest and is indeed the extension of all elements.

20. It is beginningless, endless, unborn, subtle, possessed of three attributes. It is the source and the immutable one. This timeless (lit. not belonging to the present), incomprehensible, Brahman was in the beginning.

---

1. The division of Purāṇ a texts into four Pādas (as in vv. 12-14.) viz. : (1) Prakriyā, (2) Anuṣaṅga, (3) Upodghāta and (4) Upasaṁhāra is older than the *Pañca-lakṣaṇa* definition. Bd. P. is also divided into similar Pādas.

2. Purāṇas have accepted the Sāṅkhya theory of the evolution of the universe. Compare the evolution as given in AP. 17. 2-16, Bd. P. I.13.5ff, Bh. P. III.20.12-53, KP.I.2.3ff, VP. I.3.1-45. *Mahadādyam viśeṣāntam* is another common expression to state the evolution in a nutshell.

In this expression Viśeṣa indicates the differentiation amongst the five elements on the grossest plane of matter (*vide* V. S. Agrawala, *Mt.P.—A Study*, pp. 41-43). See vv. 61-62 below.

The Sāṅkhya in this text is influenced by Vedānta; see the description the Brahman in vv. 18-20 below.

21-22. All this universe which was enveloped in darkness, was pervaded by the Ātman when the Guṇas were in equilibrium. But at the time of creation Tamas reached a subsidiary state. The principle of *Mahat* appeared, due to the subsidiary state of Pradhāna, since it was presided over by the individual soul.

23. It was enveloped by the subtle and unmanifest principle of *Mahat*, which when Sattva becomes predominant, illuminates only Sattva. The mind should be understood as the *Mahat* because the mind is its cause.

24. It is born of the subtle mind, presided over by the intelligent consciousness. Dharma etc. and their various forms are the causes of the ingredients of creation. When urged by desire to create, the principle of *Mahat* performs the creation.

25. The terms *Manas*, *Mahat*, *Mati*, *Brahma*, *Pūḥ*, *Buddhi*, *Khyāti*, *Īśvara*, *Prajñā*, *Citi*, *Smṛti*, *Saṁvit*, and *Vipura* are synonymous,[1] so say the learned people.

26. Since it conceives of the fruit of the activities that multiply in a subtle way, it is called *Manas*.

27. It is termed as *Mahat* because it is born ahead of all the principles and is greater in dimension than other principles and attributes.

28. It is called *Mati* because it bears (comprehends) the measure, thinks of the division and is considered to be the Puruṣa in view of its relationship in enjoyment.

29. It is (etymologically) designated as *Brahman* because of its bigness and because it creates the beings and lifts them up from their resting place, the cosmic water.

30. It is called *Pūḥ* because it fills all the bodies by conferring benefits and makes them endowed with predetermined elements.

31. It is called *Buddhi* because through this principle, Puruṣa discriminates between the wholesome and the unwholesome and makes him advise others too.

1. Tnis tendency towards synthesis or *Samanvaya* of different schools of thought is found in other Purāṇas irrespective of their classification as Śaiva or Vaiṣṇava. The etymologies of these terms in vv. 26-39 are populist.

32. It is called *Khyāti* because re-enjoyment is felt in the awareness of this principle when (real) enjoyment is based on knowledge.

33. It is proclaimed by its attributes and is known by different names. Hence *Khyāti* has been the epithet of *Mahat*.

34. Since it knows everything directly, it is called the noble-souled *Īśvara*. It is called *Prajñā* because organs of perception are born of it.

35. It is called *Citi* because it collects the forms, knowledge etc. and the fruits of sacrificial rites for enjoyment.

36. It is declared as *Smṛti* because it is mindful of all activities and affects present, past and future.

37. It is called *Saṁvit* (derived either from √*vid* or √*vind*) as it obtains complete knowledge and hence its greatness.

38. It exists in everything and everything exists in it. Hence it is termed as *Saṁvit* by the ones possessing higher intelligence.

39. That receptacle of knowledge, (the omniscient) lord, proclaimed that knowledge arises from knowledge. *Mahat* is called *Vipura* by the learned because the *Dvandvas* (mutually clashing pairs) are covered by it.

40. Because of its being absolute controller of all worlds, it is called *Īśvaran*. It is called *Brahman* because of its bigness. It is *Bhava* because of its existence.

41. It is called *Ka* (Prajāpati) because of its knowledge of the physical body and of the soul also, due to its being absolutely one. It is *Puruṣa* because it lies in the body. It is *Svayaṁbhū* because it is self-born and because it exists from the beginning.

42. The first excellent *Tattva* (*Mahat*) has been thus explained through synonymous words by the knowers of truth and those who meditate on reality.

43. Urged by the desire for creation, *Mahat* performs creation. Its two-fold activities are conception and exertion.

44. Dharma and other principles are the ingredients of creation. *Mahat* is three-fold by virtue of the three *guṇas*, viz. *sattva*, *rajas* and *tamas*.

45. From Mahat of threefold Guṇas, is born Ego when the *rajoguṇa* is predominant. The creation of Ego is secondary and is enveloped by *Mahat*.

46. Thereafter, when the (cosmic) Ego is dominated by *tamas-guṇa*, the primary subtle element is born of the Ego characterized by *tamas*.

47. Ether is a perforated (void) extensive expanse and is characterized by the subtle element called sound and is again enveloped by the cosmic Ego (*Bhūtādi*).

48. It is reported that ether characterised by the subtle element sound created the subtle element touch. The Ego undergoing a change created the subtle element sound.

49. Wind grows powerful and is regarded as having the quality of touch. The powerful air is born of the subtle element of touch. Ether characterised by its subtle element of sound enveloped the subtle element of touch.

50. Water (consisting) of the subtle element of taste is enveloped by the subtle element of colour. Water effecting a change in the subtle element of taste created the subtle element of smell.

51. Formation of components takes place from that quality. With its particular 'smell', water with its subtle element of taste covered (the earth) consisting of the subtle element of smell.

52. The subtle elements are so called because they have specialities. This is their special characteristic. They are also called *Aviṣeṣas* because they express non-distinguishing characters. They are further called *Aviśeṣas* because they are non-quiescent, non-vehement and non-intelligent.

53. This creation of gross and subtle elements should be known (on the basis) of reciprocal activities. From the *Vaikārika* type of ego which is generated by *Sattva guṇa* and is *sāttvika* by nature, the *Vaikārika* type of creation simultaneously takes place.

54. The five organs of knowledge and the five organs of action constitute the ten efficient organs. These constitute ten (presiding) deities. The eleventh is mind. (Thus) the *Vaikārika* gods are eleven (in number).

55. Ear, skin, eye, tongue and the fifth nose are the cognitive organs for knowing sound etc.

56. Legs, anus, organ of generation, hands and the tenth organ speech are the organs of action. Their functions are movement, evacuation, pleasure seeking, manual work and speech.

57. Ether, the subtle element of which is sound, penetrates the subtle element of touch. Therefore, air consists of two attributes: sound and touch.

58. When the two attributes, viz. sound and touch penetrate the quality, 'colour', fire becomes endowed with three attributes, viz. sound, touch and colour.

59. Along with the (qualities) of sound, touch and colour it penetrated the subtle element of taste. Therefrom water characterised by taste should be known to possess four attributes.

60. The subtle element of smell entered them along with sound, touch and colour. Then (water) in conjunction with the subtle element of smell produces earth. Among all gross elements, earth alone possesses five attributes.

61. The gross elements are called *Viśeṣas* because they are quiescent, terrific and non-intelligent. These sustain one another because they penetrate one another.

62. Within earth is this entire cosmos surrounded firmly by Lokāloka. The *Viśeṣas* are perceivable by the sense organs and are limited (as they are fixed and determined).

63. The later elements attain the attributes of the former ones. Whatever characteristic is retained for a particular period is called *guṇa* (quality) for that period.

64. Having sensed smell from fire, some, out of ignorance, (may believe it) as emanating from air. It should be known that it (smell) is only in earth (i.e. it is the exclusive quality of earth). And they (the particles of earth) take resort to (i.e. are found in) air (hence its smell).

65-66. These seven extremely powerful but disparate elements were unable to create the subjects (beings) separately, without all of them being conjoined. When those great-souled (powerful) ones beginning with *Mahat* and ending with *Viśeṣas* come together, they are presided over by Puruṣa and with the blessing of the unmanifest, they create the cosmic egg.

67. Like a bubble out of water, the egg was born (suddenly) all at a time from *Viśeṣas*. What was the vast mass of water therein performed the work of Brahmā.

68. The *Kṣetrajña* designated as Brahmā (the cosmic principle of activity) woke up in the egg of Prakṛti. He is verily the first embodied being. He is called Puruṣa.

69. He is the first creator of living beings. He existed in the very beginning manifesting himself as the four-faced Hiraṇyagarbha. In the primary and the secondary creation, the *Kṣetrajña* is termed Brahmā.

70. Living beings are created along with the sense-organs which they give up at the time of dissolution. Living beings resort to bodies again in the transitional periods characterized by non-aggregation.

71. The golden Meru is the foetus of that great-souled one. The oceans constitute the embryonic liquid and the mountains, the embryonic membrane and the bones.

72. The seven worlds and this earth with the seven continents and seven oceans lie within the cosmic egg.

73. Within it are all these worlds along with thousands of very great mounts and rivers, nay, the very universe itself.

74. The moon, the sun, along with the stars, planets, the air, the Lokāloka mountain and whatever exists is included (i.e. present) in the cosmic egg.

75. The cosmic egg is enveloped externally by waters ten times its size.[1] The waters are externally surrounded by fire ten times their size.

76. Fire is externally enveloped by air ten times its size. The air is surrounded externally by ether ten times its size.

77. The air is enveloped by the ether. The ether is encircled by the cosmic Ego. The Ego is surrounded by *Mahat* (intellect) and *Mahat* (intellect) is surrounded by the unmanifest. The cosmic egg is thus surrounded by the seven coverings created by Prakṛti.

---

1. The theory of seven sheaths protecting the Cosmic Egg is another popular Purāṇic concept. Compare KP. I. 4. 42-45, Bd. P. I. 1. 3. 32 ff.

78. These eight Prakṛtis abide thus covering up mutually. Abiding at the time of creation, they swallow up one another (at the time of dissolution).

79. Thus generated mutually, they sustain one another as the sustainer and the sustained in their primary and secondary relationship.

80. The unmanifest (unconscious principle) is called *Kṣetra* and Brahmā (the conscious principle) is called *Kṣetrajña.* Thus the creation of Prakṛti is presided over by *Kṣetrajña.* It existed in the beginning without intellect. It appeared all of a sudden like lightning.

81. He who understands factually the manifestation of Brahmā, becomes endowed with fame, longevity, wealth and progeny.

82. Even if a man has renounced desires, he becomes pure-souled and attains his goal. By listening to this Purāṇa everyday one can attain pleasure and welfare.

CHAPTER FIVE

The Origin of Creation

Lomaharṣaṇa continued :

1. O Brāhmaṇas, the period of time calculated by me for the creation (of the universe) should be known as one day of the supreme Lord.

2. The night of the great Lord should also be known as entirely of the same duration. The period of creation is his day and the period of dissolution is called his night.

3. It is held that he (Brahmā) has only the day and no night. But such assumption is made just for the benefit of the world.

4-6. The subjects, the patriarchs, the seers of Vedic Mantras along with ascetics, eternally youthful sages like Sanatkumāra and others along with those who have attained salvation, the sense-organs and their objects, the subtle elements, as well as the intellect and the mind—all these stay during the day of the Lord Supreme; they are dissolved at the end of his day; at the end of the night, there is creation of the universe.

7. When the quality *Sattva* stays in itself and when the secondary creation is withdrawn, both Pradhāna and Puruṣa become similar (i.e. inactive).

8. The qualities *Tamas* and *Sattva* stay in a state of equilibrium. When there is equilibrium in the qualities mutually, it should be known as dissolution; when there is disequilibrium of the *guṇas*, it is called creation (i.e. creation takes place).

9. Just as oil abides in the gingelly seeds or ghee in milk, so does the quality *Rajas* stay unmanifest in *Sattva* and *Tamas*.

10. After remaining quiescent throughout the great night of the Lord, the creation of Prakṛti begins anew at day-break.

11. Entering the cosmic Egg, the great god caused, by his supreme Yoga, agitation in Pradhāna and Puruṣa.[1]

12. From *Pradhāna* that was being agitated, *Rajas* was produced. It is *Rajas* that causes the activity even as water causes the activity in the seeds.

13. The disequilibrium of qualities having taken effect the presiding (deities) are begotten. The three gods were created while the *guṇas* were being agitated. Those embodied gods, the souls abiding in all who have taken resort are extremely hidden.

14. The *Rajas* quality became Brahmā, *Tamas*, Fire and *Sattva* becomes Viṣṇu. Brahmā, the illuminator of *Rajas*,

---

1. *Ksobha* 'agitation' is a process of contraction and expansion which is cyclic. It is called '*Samañcana-Prasāraṇa*' in *Śat. Br.* 8. 1. 4-10 and '*Saṅkoca-Vikāsa*' in KP. I. 4. 15.

stays in the capacity of creator.[1]

15. Fire, the illuminator of *Tamas*, abides in the capacity of Kāla. Viṣṇu, the illuminator of *Sattva*, remains indifferent.

16. These alone are the three gods* and the three fires. They are mutually dependent, devoted and faithful to one another.

17. They function jointly, sustain one another; they are ever in association with one another. They subsist on one another. There is no separation among them even for a moment. They do not leave off one another.

18. Īśvara is the highest deity. Viṣṇu is greater than *Mahat*. Brahmā, with dominant *Rajas*, functions for the purpose of creation. Puruṣa is known as *Para* (the supreme) and Prakṛti as *Parā* (great).

19. He (Brahmā) functions on being presided over by Maheśvara and being urged all round. Mahat and other (creations of Prakṛti) long stationed in their respective objects due to attachment, function thereafter.

20. Due to the disequilibrium of the qualities, *Pradhāna* begins to function at the time of creation. From *Pradhāna*, which is of the nature of *Sat* and *Asat*, presided over by Īśvara, the pair Brahmā and *Buddhi* (cosmic intelligence) are born simultaneously.

21. Then the *Kṣetrajña* termed Brahmā, of the nature of *Tamas* and the unmanifest, manifests himself in the beginning, fully equipped with sense-organs for all activities.

22. He, the unmanifest endowed with intellect shines forth with brilliance. He is verily the first embodied being abiding in the capacity of a cause.

---

1. Purāṇic writers identify Guṇas with the triad of gods Brahmā, Viṣṇu and Rudra (cf. Bd. P. I. 1. 4-6 and my note on it), LP. I. 70. 77-78. In our text Agni represents *Tamas Guṇa*. But since Vedic times Rudra is identified with Agni, e.g. 1) *Tvam agne Rudro asuro maho divaḥ*/—RV. II. 1. 6, TS. 1.3.14.1; 2) *Tasmai Rudrāya namo astvagnaye*/—A. V. (Atharva Veda) VII. 87. 1.

Purāṇa writers have accepted the Sāṅkhya theory of cosmic evolution but they have added Īśvara or a supreme deity and have given a popular garb to this evolution for mass education.

**V. L.* Vedāḥ 'The Vedas'.

23. He is equipped with unobstructable knowledge and supreme lordship. He is endowed with unobstructed *dharma* and detachment.

24. The knowledge, characterised by detachment, of that lord is unimpeded. The intellect of Brahmā identifying himself with that Lord, is affected by *Dharma* and *Aiśvarya* (supremacy).

25. Whatever he wishes mentally is created out of the unmanifest naturally, due to its being controlled, due to absence of attributes (?) and due to his being the lord of Devas.

26. In the capacity of Brahmā, he becomes the four-faced creator; in the capacity of Kāla, he is the destroyer; in the capacity of Puruṣa (Viṣṇu) he is the thousand-headed lord. These are the three states of the self-born God.[1]

27. In the capacity of Brahmā, the creator, he possesses *Sattva* and *Rajas* predominantly; as destroyer (of the universe), *Rajas* and *Tamas* predominantly; and as Puruṣa (Viṣṇu), *Sattva* exclusively. Thus is the state or course of attributes of the self-born Lord.

28. In the capacity of Brahmā he creates; in the capacity of Kāla he withdraws (destroys) the worlds; in the capacity of Puruṣa he remains unconcerned. These three are the states of the Lord of subjects.

29. Brahmā has the lustre of the interior of a lotus. Kāla has the lustre of collyrium. Puruṣa is lotus-eyed. Thus is the form of the supreme soul.

30. The Lord of Yogas who out of sportiveness has different creations, activities, forms, names and functions, creates and effects changes in (different) bodies.

31. Since he functions in the world in three ways, he is called *Triguṇa*. Since he is divided into four he is glorified as *Caturvyūha* (having four manifestations).

---

1. Cf. Bd. P. I. i. 4. 18, KP. I. 2. 91-92. There, the Reality or supreme God is Mahādeva while in VP. I.2.70, it is Viṣṇu—a difference in nomenclature only. Our author emphasizes that this supreme god assumes three forms for the creation etc. of the universe.

32. He is called *Ātman*[1] because whatever he attains (*Āpnoti*), takes up (*Ādatte*) and exists (*Asti*) for the (enjoyment of) objects, that is his permanent being.

33. He is called *Ṛṣi* because he goes everywhere. He is *Viṣṇu* because he pervades everything. He has the lordship over everything. He is the lord of physical body etc.

34. He is *Bhagavān* because there are such (excellences) in him. He is *Rāga* (lord of passion) because he controls passion. He is *Para* (Supreme) because he is the cosmic being. He is *Om* because he protects (all).

35. He is *Sarvajña* (omniscient) because he knows everything. He is *Sarva* because everything originates from him. As men emerge from him, he is known as *Nārāyaṇa*.

36. He divides his self into three and acts on the three worlds. He creates, surveys (protects) and devours through the three activities. In the beginning Hiraṇyagarbha manifested himself as four-faced lord.

37. Because he is first to manifest he is called the first god. He is called *Aja* because he is not born (is self-existent). Since he protects the subjects, he is called *Prajāpati*.

38. He is called *Mahādeva* because he is the greatest deity among Devas. He is *Īśvara* because he is the lord of worlds and because he is not subject to other's control.

39. He is called *Brahmā* due to his bigness. He is called *Bhūta* because of his (eternal) existence. He is *Kṣetrajña* because he knows the unmanifest cosmic nature. He is *Vibhu* because he is omnipresent.

40. Because he lies in the subtle body (called *Pūr*) he is called *Puruṣa*. He is called *Svayaṁbhū* because he is not procreated and because he exists before the creation.

41-42. He is called *Yajña* because worship or sacrifice is offered to him. He is *Kavi* because he is omniscient. He is

---

1. The author is fond of derivations. Some of them are grammatically correct, some ingenious, but most of them are popular. Thus here *Ātman* is derived from √*āp*, √*ad*, and √*as*. Some others trace it to √*an* 'to breath', √*at* 'to move', √*vā* 'to blow' (MW. 135 a).

Kramaṇa because he is worthy of being approached and due to his patronage of castes, he is called *Āditya*, *Kapila*, *Agraja*, and *Agni*. His womb was gold and he was born of golden womb, so he is called *Hiraṇyagarbha* in this Purāṇa.

43. Even in hundreds of years, it is impossible to calculate the number of years that have elapsed since the self-born was manifested.

44. The time that has elapsed, the number of Kalpas that have passed after he had manifested is called *Para*. That much of time still remains for him. At its close, the subsidiary creation is to take place.

45. Crores and crores of Kalpas have already passed. Yet so many more still remain.

46. The Kalpa that is current now, O Brāhmaṇas, is called Vārāha. That is the first of the Kalpas now current.

47-50. It will have fourteen Manus, beginning with Svāyaṁbhuva and including those of the past, present and the future. By these rulers of men, this earth including the seven continents is to be protected along with the subjects, by means of penance. Now listen in detail. Through (the description of) one Manvantara, all the future Manvantaras, and through (the account of) one Kalpa all the past and future Kalpas (are described).[1] The future Kalpas along with the futurities and dynasties should be inferred by the intelligent one (on the basis of) the past Kalpas.

CHAPTER SIX

The Origin of Creation (*Continued*)

***Sūta said*:**

1-3. Water originated from fire. When the earth was destroyed in the fire and everything merged within (the water),

1. Cf. *Dhātā yathāpūrvam akalpayat*|
This is a strong popular belief shared by all Purāṇa writers.

when, therefore, the mobile and immobile beings were also destroyed, nothing could be known (seen) in that vast ocean of water[1]. Then Brahmā, called Nārāyaṇa, lord Brahmā of thousand eyes, thousand legs and thousand heads, the Puruṣa who is golden in complexion beyond the ken of sense organs, slept in that water.

4. Due to the preponderance of Sattva, he woke up and he beheld that the world was a void. About Nārāyaṇa they cite this verse.

5. We have heard the epithet of waters, that waters are called Nārā, and that they are minute or subtle bodies. Since he lies in waters, he is therefore called Nārāyaṇa.[2]

6. Having spent the whole period of night equal to a thousand yugas, at the close of the night, he assumed Brahmāhood for the purpose of creation.

7. Brahmā assumed the form of Vāyu[3] and moved about in the water like a glow-worm at night during the rainy season.

8-9. Then having come to know definitely that the earth lies submerged in those waters and being convinced about it by

1. *Ekārṇava*, 'the primeval watery flood' expresses the infinite unmanifest cause of the universe. Nīlakaṇṭha on HV. P. 3. 9. 1-4 calls it the *Kāraṇa Brahman* from which all life comes into being. Purāṇas believe in this doctrine and use *Mahārṇava, agādha, stabdha, salila* (HV. 3. 10. 1), *Yugānta-toya* 'Water flood at the end of Yuga' (Bh. P. III. 8. 23) as synonyms for *Ekārṇava*. This doctrine is very old and *Brahma-Vādins* (expounders of Vedas) have elaborated it to explain the process of creation and dissolution (VP. I. 2. 22).

2. The usual derivation of Nārāyaṇa in other Purāṇas also. But Bd. P. I. 4. 27 traces it to Nara : Brahmā causes the sleep (i.e. perfect rest) of Naras (men), hence he is remembered as Nārāyaṇa.

narāṇāṁ svāpanaṁ brahmā
tasmān nārāyaṇaḥ smṛtaḥ//

3. The belief regarding the assumption of the form of Vāyu for reconnaissance before assuming the form of a boar, to lift up the earth, is as old as *Tait. Br.* 1. 2. 1. 3 which says :

āpo vā idamagre salilam āsīt
tasmin prajāpatir vāyur bhūtva acarat/
sa imām apaśyat/
tām varāho bhūtvāharat/

reasoning (inference), he assumed another body as in the previous Kalpas for the lifting up of the earth. The noble soul then conceived mentally of a divine form.

10. Observing that the earth was overflowed with waters on all sides, (he thought to himself), "Oh, what great form should I assume and uplift the earth?"

11. He thought of the form of a Boar[1] charmingly comfortable in sporting about in waters. It was unassailable by living beings. It was of the nature of speech and was designated as Dharma*.

12. It had a girth of ten and a height of a hundred Yojanas. It resembled a dark blue cloud in complexion. It grunted like the rumbling of thunder-clouds.

13. It had a huge body like a mountain. Its curved fangs were white and sharp and terrible. The eyes were brilliant like lightning and fire. Its lustre was like that of the sun.

14. Its shoulders were round, plump and large. It had the lion's valiant gait. Its buttocks were stout and lifted up (well developed). It had auspicious characteristics. It was charming.

15. Assuming this large immeasurable form of a boar, Viṣṇu entered the nether regions in order to lift up the earth.

16. He was the guide for the propounders of the Vedas.[2]

---

1. The germ of Varāha incarnation as given above is in *Tait. Br.* Purāṇas have given an elaborate description of that incarnation in Bh. P. III. 13. 17-33, Mt. P. Chs. 246-248, NP. I. 4. 1-52, Bd. P. I. 1. 5. 11-23 a number of verses in which are common to our text.

**Brahman* i.e. the Veda in Bd. P. I. i. 5-11.

2. This beautiful description of the Boar-incarnation in Yajña terminology is found in other Purāṇas also. For example Bm. P. 213. 33-42, Bh. P. III. 13. 34-39. Writers on Smṛtis, Tantra and even Śaṅkara adopted it, e.g. *Viṣṇu Smṛti* 1. 3-12, Śaṅkara on *Viṣṇu Sahasranāma* 119—explanation of *Yajñāṅga*.

The comparison between Varāha and sacrifice (*yajña*) will be clear from the following attributes of the Varāha in the text e.g. 6.16b : *Agni-jihva*—Agni (fire) is the tongue of gods. Through the fire gods eat the food (offered in sacrifice). A Vedic concept—Cf. RV. IV. 57. 1

darbha-romā : The *darbha* grass spread on the altar is compared to the shaggy hair on the body of the boar.

Brahmaśirṣaḥ : Brahma is the knowledge of the Vedas—Naturally its position is the highest, viz. the head.

He had sacrifice for his chest and the firealtar (*citi*) for his face. The Fire was his tongue; the Darbha-grass was his hair and Brahma was his head. He was of great penance.

17. The day and the night constituted his eyes. The ancillaries of the Vedas were his ear ornaments. The *Ājya* (ghee offering in sacrifice) was his nose; the sacrificial ladle was his snout. The sound of the Sāman hymns was his roaring grunt.

18. Endowed with glory as he was, he was an embodiment of truth and *dharma* and was established in virtuous valour. He was engaged in expiation. He was terrible. He had the huge form with the knees of an animal.

19. His body was straightened up. The offerings of *ghṛta* constituted his Liṅga (symbol). The (sacrificial) spot was his seed. He was the great medicinal herb (incarnate for curing distress). The altar was his inner soul. Mantras were his hips. The Soma mixed with clarified butter was his blood.

20. The Vedas were his shoulders. He had the fragrance of sacrificial offering. The *Havya* (oblations for the Devas) and *Kavya* (oblations for the Pitṛs) constituted his velocity. *Prāgvaṁśa*[1] (the room accommodating the sacrificers) was his body. He was lustrous and had undergone different initiations.

21. The sacrificial fees constituted his heart. He was an all-pervading Yogin in the form of a great Sattva. He was charming with the sacrificial rites of *Upākarman*. *Pravargya* (a rite in which hot milk is poured in a vessel, thus giving rise to fumes) constituted the whorls of hair on his chest*[2].

22. His gait and paths were the different *Chandas*. The secret Upaniṣads constituted his seat. He was accompanied by his consort Chāyā. He was lofty like a jewelled peak. Having thus assumed the form of a sacrificial Boar, the lord entered the waters.

---

1. The body of Varāha was so big and spacious as to accommodate many men, as *Prāgvaṁśa* (the room in which the members of the sacrificer's family and friends stay) is spacious.

*read *Pravargyāvartabhūṣaṇaḥ* as in Bd. P. I. 1. 5. 18

2. *Pravargya-vitta-bhūṣaṇaḥ* in the text is obscure. Bd. P. I. 1. 5. 8 reads in that context *Pravargyāvarta-bhuṣaṇaḥ* which means '*Pravargya* were the whorls of hair on Varāha's chest.

23-24. He, the lord of the subjects, got at the Earth covered with the waters. He approached and lifted it quickly. He diverted the waters of the oceans in the oceans and of the rivers in the rivers. The lord, for the welfare of the worlds, lifted with his curved fangs, the Earth that had gone deep into the nether world.

25. Holding the Earth in his hands he brought it to its place. The supporter of the Earth at first mentally supported the earth and then released it.

26. Over the flood of waters, the Earth floated like an immense boat. Due to the activities of the lord, it did not sink.

27. With a desire to set up the universe, the lord lifted up the Earth. Then, he, the lotus-eyed lord, decided to divide the Earth. He levelled the Earth and created the mountains on it.

28. Formerly when the creation was burnt by the Saṁvartaka fire, all the mountains, being consumed by that fire, lay shattered and scattered all over the earth.

29. In that *Ekārṇava* (the ocean of cosmic waters) the waters (solidified by cold) and collected by wind and were placed in a scattered manner here and there (wherever they were thus deposited); they became condensed into mountains.

30. Since they became motionless after being (thus) sprinkled, they were known as *Acalas*.[1] Since they are endowed with knots and joints, they were called *Parvatas*. Since they had been swallowed and hidden (formerly), they were called *Giris*. Since they had been collected, they were called *Śiloccayas*.

31. Thus after the worlds, oceans and mountains are destroyed at the end of a Kalpa, the Maker (Creator) of the universe creates them again and again, in the beginnings of the Kalpas.

32. He again created this earth along with the ocean, seven continents and mountains, as well as the four worlds, viz. Bhūr and others. After creating the worlds, he began the creation of the subjects.

1. Note the Purāṇic etymologies of *acala, parvata, giri.*

33. Desirous of creating different species of subjects, the self-born lord Brahmā recreated the beings in the same form as they had in the previous Kalpas.[1]

34. When he was contemplating over the creation intellectually, the dark and gloomy creation manifested itself simultaneously with Pradhāna.*

35. Nescience (*Avidyā*) with five joints, viz. darkness, delusion, super-delusion, murkiness and super-murkiness**, became manifested out of the Supreme Soul.

36. While he meditated, the creation became established in five ways. Just as a lamp is covered up with a pot, the creation was enveloped by darkness. Like a lamp lighted in a pitcher illuminated within and (dark) without, it was pure but devoid of feeling.

37. Its intellect and sense organs were concealed; it consisted of vegetation and since vegetation is declared to be primary it was called primary creation.

38. On seeing that the creation did not multiply, Brahmā was dissatisfied and he went into contemplation.

39-40. When he contemplated thus the *Tiryaksrotas* (the animal world) came into being. Since this creation proceeded obliquely, it was called *Tiryaksrotas*. Predominated by *Tamas*, they were mainly ignorant. They took to wrong direction. They were self-swayed and devoted to self.

41-42. The lord saw this second creation of *Tiryak-srotas*, proud of themselves, conceited and divided into twenty-eight—eleven based on the sense organs, nine of Udaya and the eight of Tārakā and other Śaktis.

---

1. Purāṇas believe that despite the annihilation of everything at the end of a Kalpa, god Brahmā recreates the universe on the model of the previous universe. They state this succinctly as follows : *dhātā yathāpūrvam akalpayat.*

*A. reads : *Pradhyāna-samakālam* : 'simultaneously while he was meditating'.

**Com. on VP. I. 5 5 renders these as, ignorance, delusion, desire of enjoyment, anger and fear of death.

43. They were all illuminated within but covered externally. Since their activity was oblique, they were called *Tiryak-srotas*.

44. Having seen the second universe, the *Tiryaksrotas*, and having observed everything of it of that designation (nature), the Lord conceived of the (following) idea : Even as he was thinking uninterruptedly (*nityam*), the Sāttvika creation appeared (of itself, automatically).

45. This third creation was called *Ūrdhvasrotas*, consisting of beings in which the stream of life passed upwards. Since life proceeded upwards it was called *Ūrdhvasrotas*.

46. The *Ūrdhvasrotas* beings have abundance of comfort and pleasure. They are circumscribed outwardly and inwardly and are brilliant externally and internally.

47. These created beings are air etc. They are well settled after creating themselves. The *Ūrdhvasrotas* being the third (in the series of creations), that creation is known after them.

48. When gods with upward stream (the divine creation of *Ūrdhvasrotas*) were created god Brahmā was satisfied. As he was the competent Over-Lord, he thought of and created beings that would be *Sādhakas* (aspirants after spiritual power).

49. While he began contemplating, and since he was of truthful (effective) conception, the *Arvāksrotas* that could accomplish the task of creation, manifested themselves out of the unmanifest (*Avyakta*). Since the stream of life proceeded downwards, they are called *Arvāksrotas*.

50. They are characterized by the abundance of brilliance and were dominated by the attributes *Tamas*, *Sattva* and *Rajas*. Hence they have excess of misery and are continuously engaged in activities.

51. They are human beings who are enlightened externally and internally and accomplish the task of creation. Through the characteristics of *Tāraka* etc. they are of eight types.

52. These human beings are of accomplished souls. They are of the same nature as Gandharvas. Thus the creation of *Arvāksrotas* of *Tejas* (Light) has been narrated.

53. The fifth creation called *Anugraha* is of four types, through *Viparyaya* (Contrariety), *Śakti* (Power), *Tuṣṭi* (Satisfaction)

and *Siddhi* (achievement). The created beings know factually the past and the present objects.

54. The sixth creation is said to be that of beings such as *Bhūtādi*. *Bhūtādi* is characterized by contrariety and disability.

55. The first creation is of *Mahat*. It is known as *Mahat-sarga*. The second is the creation of *Tanmātras* and is called the creation of the *Bhūtas*.

56. The third creation is that of *Vikāras* (the products of Prakṛti) and is perceptible by the senses. Thus the *Prākṛta* creation took place with conscious fore-knowledge.

57. The '*Mukhya*' creation is the fourth in order. The *Mukhyas* are the immobile beings. The creation of *Tiryaksrotas* is the fifth consisting of animals.

58. The sixth creation of *Ūrdhvasrotas* consists of divine beings. The seventh creation of the *Arvāksrotas* is that of mankind.

59. The eighth creation is *Anugraha*. It is characterised by Sattva and Tamas. These (latter) five are the *Vaikṛta* creation and the (first) three are *Prākṛta*.

60-61. The ninth creation *Kaumāra* is both *Prākṛta* and *Vaikṛta*. The three *Prākṛta* creations were brought about without planning or pre-meditation. The six creations of Brahmā function intelligently. Now understand the *Anugraha Sarga* in detail.

62-63. It is of four types found in all living beings through contrariety, power, satisfaction and achievement. In the immobile beings there is *Viparyāsa* (contrariety or loss of consciousness). In the animals, there is *Śakti* (power). Human beings are *Siddhātmans* (with souls capable of achieving spiritual progress). In Devas there is *Tuṣṭi* (satisfaction).

64. There are thus the nine creations including *Prākṛtas* and *Vaikṛtas*. By their mutual combination, the types are many.

65-66. At the beginning, Brahmā created three mental sons equal to himself, viz. Sanandana, Sanaka and the intelligent Sanātana who possessed great power and enlightenment. Those (sons) of great splendour and strength renounced (the world) due to their special knowledge of *Vivarta* (the unreal appearance of the world in place of Brahman). Due to multiplicity, they were spiritually awakened. They were abandoned (by their father). Without creating any subjects they retired.

67. When they had left, Brahmā created other mental sons who could accomplish the object. They identified themselves with their position and abided till the final dissolution of the world. (Now) know them by their names :

68-70. They are water, fire, earth, air, ether, quarters, heaven, firmament, oceans, rivers, mountains, plants, the 'souls' of medicinal herbs, trees and creepers, units of time, *Lavas*, *Kāṣṭhas*, *Kalās*, *Muhūrtas*, *Sandhis* (junctions of day and night like dusk, dawn etc.), night, day, fortnights, months, *Ayanas*, years and Yugas. These are the positions with which they identify themselves.

71. The classes of society are born of his limbs : Brāhmaṇas (were created) out of his mouth; Kṣatriyas out of his arms; Vaiśyas out of his thighs; and Sūdras out of his feet.

72. The lord is beyond *Avyakta* (unmanifest Prakṛti). The Cosmic Egg is born of the unmanifest. Brahmā is born of the Cosmic Egg. The worlds are created by him.

73. Thus this first section has been narrated to you all very briefly and not in details. The whole of this Purāṇa, is briefly narrated in this first *Pāda* (quarter).

SECTION 2: UPODGHĀTA PĀDA

CHAPTER SEVEN

Transition between two Yugas (Ages)

Introductory

1. Thus this first *Pāda* (section) the main theme of which was *prakriyā* was narrated. On hearing it, Sanātana, the descendant of Kāśyapa was much delighted in mind.

2. Addressing Sūta with (appreciative) words, he asked him the subsequent narrative. "O Knower of Kalpas, please narrate to us (the events during) the period of transition between the two ages.[1]

3. We are desirous to know the difference between the two Kalpas, viz. the one that has gone and the other that is current. Let us also know the *Pratisandhi* (period of transition) between the two (Kalpas) as you are undoubtedly very intelligent."

Lomaharṣaṇa said :

4. I shall describe to you here the difference between the two Kalpas: the one that has gone and the other that is current, and the period of transition between the two.

5-6. O sages of holy rites, now understand the Manvantaras that are in the Kalpas. This auspicious Kalpa that is current now is (called the) Vāráha Kalpa. The Kalpa that has gone before this Kalpa was (known as) Sanātana. Now understand the (condition of) the interim period between that Kalpa and the present one.

---

1. Out of the five main characteristics of a Purāṇa, description of Manvantaras is one. Thus we find it in Bh. P. VIII. 1. 1-29, KP. I. 51, NP. I. 40. 17-37 and others. This chapter which textually corresponds to Bd. P. I. 2. 6 deals with Kalpas and the interim period between them.

7-8. When the previous Kalpa recedes there is a period of transition. Another Kalpa sets in again and again from Janaloka. This happens again and again when the period of transition ends, the Kalpas are cut off from each other. At the end of a Kalpa, all the rites are completely annihilated. Hence it is called the period of transition between one Kalpa and another.

9. The joints (transition) between the periods called Manvantara and Yuga are also cut off. Manvantaras function with the inter-connections of Yugas.

10. The Kalpas that have been briefly narrated in the *Prakriyā Pāda* [each Kalpa (out of them) has a *Pūrva-ardha* (earlier half) and a *Para-ardha* (later half)]. When a Kalpa elapses, its later half is followed by the earlier half of the next Kalpa.

11. The other Kalpas which follow in future are so tied with their later half. The Kalpa that is current, O Brāhmaṇas, is the first among them.

12. In it the first (half) is called *Pūrva* (*Pūrvārdha*) and the later half is called *Para*. This is the period of sustenance (of the world). The period after it is called the dissolution of the world.[1]

13-15. The Kalpa which preceded the present Kalpa was Sanātana (by name). When at the end of one thousand sets of four Yugas along with the Manvantaras, the Kalpa came to an end, then the time of the destruction (of the universe) by fire arrived:[2]

In that Kalpa the gods who used to move about in aerial chariots, constellations, planets, stars, the sun, the moon and planetary bodies (sites)—all these meritorious souls numbered twentyeight crores.

16-17. Just as (the number was 28 crores) in one Manvantara, (their number) in fourteen Manvantaras is the same.

1. At the end of a Manvantara (Manu-period), the Yuga-period connecting the two Manu-periods is not broken, but at the end of a Kalpa the Universe is annihilated.

2. The following verses describe the process of dissolution of the Universe.

Therefore their total number (in all Manvantaras) was (14× 28=) three hundred and ninetytwo crores. In the Kalpa that passed away, the number of gods moving about in aerial chariots is said as being seven hundred and eight thousand. In each Kalpa (the same number of) gods is said as possessing chariots.

18. In all the fourteen Manvantaras, there had been Devas, Pitṛs, sages and Manus in the heaven.

19-20. The sons of Manus who are their followers, the respectable Devas who receive honour and praise from the people of all castes and stages of life and those heaven-dwellers who remain in the Devaloka—all these stand on equal footing along with their associates at the time of final dissolution.

21-22. When the dissolution becomes due, the Devas residing in the three worlds realize their inevitable (fateful) turn which necessarily occurs in due course.[1] Characterized by unconcern and grief, they forsake their associated positions and fix their mind anxiously on *Maharloka*.

23. They are endowed with bodies special to *Maharloka*. All of them abound in special purity and acquire mental achievement.

24-25. They establish contact with the Brāhmaṇas, Kṣatriyas, Vaiśyas and others who have been devoted to that Kalpa. After fixing their minds on *Maharloka*, the fourteen groups of devas fix their minds on *Janaloka* too.

26. They have abundant purity and have attained mental perfection, along with the contemporaries of their Kalpa, who have attained *Maharloka*.

27. Repeating it ten times, they go to the worlds called *Svar* and *Tapas*. After staying there for ten Kalpas, they proceed to the world called *Satya*. The residents of the Kalpa go in this order.

28. Thus thousands of Yugas according to the calculations of Devas pass by when the residents go to Brahmā's world where they attain their goal of final liberation [Lit. the state from which there is no return to Saṁsāra].

---

1. Verses 21-30 describe how Devas proceed from heaven to still higher regions in the order: *Mahar→Svar→Tapas→Brahma.*

29. Except overlordship (on the world), they become equal to Brahmā in affluence, glory, form (appearance) and objects (of enjoyment of senses)[1].

30. There they stay happily due to their close contact with Brahmā. Acquiring the bliss of Brahmā, they become liberated along with Brahmā.

31. In view of the inevitability in matters pertaining to Prakṛti, they remain bound in their separateness produced at that time.

32. Just as in a wakeful stage knowledge occurs with intellectual efforts from its forms, similarly knowledge which arises in them at that time, begins to function.

33. When the differences of those whose energies are of different nature, are restrained and withdrawn, their effects and instruments (sense organs) are produced along with them.

34-35. Of those residents of Brahmaloka whose authorities are lost (destroyed) due to the manifestation of their differences and multiplicity, but who abide by their own Dharma, those Siddhas have similar characteristics, are of pure souls and unsullied. In their nature they are beyond the sense-organs and are well established in their souls.

36. After revealing itself entirely to them, Prakṛti thus seen does not function because it is not activized by Puruṣa.

37. When the creation starts again, the Prākṛtic causes join together and originate those seers of truth.

38. Here those persons who have attained liberation have not to go by the (same) path of *Saṁsāra*. There is the non-recurrence (non-existence) of these like the blazing flames of fire which has been extinguished[2].

39. When these great souls have gone up beyond the three worlds, those who have not reached Janaloka along with them from Maharloka are left behind to stay in Maharloka. They retain their body for a Kalpa.

---

1. That is the difference between a liberated soul and Brahmā; an echo of *Brahma Sūtra* IV. 4. 17-18.

2. Cf. the concept of *Brahma-nirvāṇa* in BG V. 24-26.

40. There are classes of beings from Gandharvas to Piśācas, Brāhmaṇas and other human beings, animals and birds, the immobile ones and reptiles.

41. While they (the beings mentioned in v. 40) stand there as the residents of the surface of the earth, at that time the thousand rays that emanate from the sun (getting combined and concentrated) become seven rays of the sun and each ray (out of those seven rays) becomes a sun.

42. Rising up gradually, they burn the three worlds, mobile and immobile beings, rivers and all mountains. They had already been dried up by drought and are now burnt by the suns.

43. Then all these—the mobile and immobile, both the pious and impious who are burnt by the rays of the sun, settle down and rest.

44-45. At the end of the sinful age, they go away with their bodies burnt. But they are not freed from bodies derived from their pious or impious activities. They are united with the people of Jana Loka having the same form as they have. Abounding in purity they attain mental perfection.

46. Having stayed there for the period of the night of Brahmā of unmanifest birth, they are born again as the mental sons of Brahmā, at the beginning of the creation (of the world).

47-48. When the residents of the three worlds thus function in Janaloka, and the three worlds are burnt down by the seven suns, when the earth is flooded with rain, when all abodes are scattered, the oceans, clouds and the earthly waters form a vast watery mass called '*Salila*'[1].

49. It (water) followed (one flood after another). When that enormous flood of water covered the earth (in one vast sheet of water) it is called *Arṇava* (sea).

50. The word (root)√*bhā* is used in the sense of spreading (*vyāpti*) and shining (*dipti*), as water shines and spreads. It floods on all sides and hence water is known as *Aṁbhas*.

51. The root√*Tan* means 'to cover', 'to expand.' Since waters

---

1. Verses 47-52 give the popular etymologies of *salila, arṇava, ambhas, tanu* and *nārā*. Cf. Bd. P. I. 2. 6. 51-56 for similar derivation of these words.

cover up the earth completely on all sides and expand, they are known as *Tanus*.

52. The learned say that the particle '*Aram*' denotes quickness. In the vast ocean the waters are not quick. (Hence) they are called '*Nārās*'.

53-55. At the end of a thousand Yugas, when Brahmā's day comes to an end, when, during the night everything is covered up with water, when the earth destroyed by the fire disappears in water, when the wind is calm and motionless, and darkness spreads around and there is no ray of light, Brahmā, the Lord Puruṣa who presides over all these, desires to make the apportionment of this world once again.

56. When the mobile and immobile beings are destroyed and lost in that vast ocean, Brahmā becomes (a god) endowed with a thousand i.e. innumerable feet and thousand eyes.

57. The thousand-headed Puruṣa, of golden complexion, who is beyond the ken of senses, who is Brahmā called Nārāyaṇa, goes to sleep in the water.

58. When he wakes up due to the predominance of Sattva guṇa, he sees the world a void. They cite this verse about Nārāyaṇa.

59. Waters are called Nārā. We have thus heard that the name of waters is *Tanus*. He stays there with waters coming upto his umbilicus. So he is called Nārāyaṇa.

60. In the Vedas he is called the first patriarch, the Puruṣa with good mind, thousand (i.e. inumerable) heads, thousand feet, thousand eyes, thousand faces, thousand hands[1] and devouring thousands.

61. He has the colour of *Āditya* (sun). He is the protector of the world. He is the single unprecedented and the first overpowerer of the mighty. He is the golden-wombed Puruṣa. He is the noble soul who is beyond darkness.

62. At the beginning of the Kalpas, *Rajas* predominates in him. He becomes Brahmā and creates the subjects. At the end of the Kalpas, *Tamas* predominates in him. He becomes Kāla and swallows them again.

---

1. Cf. the Purusa Sūkta (RV X. 90)

63. He who is designated as Nārāyaṇa with the Sattva Guṇa predominant, sleeps in the vast ocean. Dividing himself into three forms, he abides in the three worlds.

64-65. Through the three forms he creates, surveys and swallows them. When the mobile and immobile world is destroyed in that vast ocean, at the end of thousand sets of four Yugas, when everything is covered up with water all round, Brahmā called Nārāyaṇa sleeps in the dark, deep waters.

66. The great sages see from Maharloka, Kāla who, after swallowing four types of creation, is slumbering in the great (cosmic) ocean during the night of Brahmā.

67. The great sages like Bhṛgu and others as in seven Kalpas, so in this Kalpa, surrounded this immense being. That immense being is surrounded by the seven sages Bhṛgu and others.

68. The word '*Ṛṣi*' is derived from the root √*Ṛṣ*, 'to go'.[1] They existed from the beginning hence they are called *Ṛṣis*. The word *Mahat* indicates 'greatness'. Because they are great, they are called *Maharṣis*.

69. The sleeping Kāla was then observed by them while staying in Maharloka. In the past Kalpa there were seven sages beginning with Satya.

70. Thus, during these nights of Brahmā that had passed in thousands, the great sages (Satya and others) saw the sleeping Kāla (during the period of his slumber).

71. Brahmā is called Kāla (the destroyer) because at the beginning of a Kalpa, he fashioned fourteen forms of destruction.

72. He creates living beings at the beginning of each Kalpa again and again. He, the great lord, is both manifest and unmanifest. This entire universe is his creation.

73-74. Thus the period of transition between the two Kalpas—the one that is current and the other that has passed—has been described to you briefly. The conditions that existed in previous Kalpas have also been mentioned briefly. Now I shall explain the present Kalpa. Listen to that.

1. A correct etymology.

CHAPTER EIGHT

Four Stages of Life

Sūta said:

1. After spending a period of time equal to a thousand Yugas as his night, he assumes Brahmāhood, at the end of the night, for the purpose of creation.

2. When the mobile and immobile beings had already perished, Brahmā assumed the form of wind and moved about in the water, (enveloped) in darkness.

3-6. When the surface of the earth had been completely covered by the water, when the elements remained undivided and undifferentiated, the self-born lord, surveying everything, moved about like the glowworm at night during the rainy season.[1] Seeking a means for putting it back in position after knowing that the earth is immersed in water, he became enlightened by means of inference (as to the way) of lifting up the earth. He created another body which he recollected (as having been assumed) in the previous Kalpas.

7. On seeing the earth fully engulfed in waters, he entered the waters after assuming the form of a Boar.

8. After lifting up the earth from the waters, he deposited the waters of the oceans in the oceans; of the rivers in the rivers and of the earth on the earth. Then he collected the mountains.

9. When the previous creation was being burnt by the *Saṁvartaka*, fire of dissolution, the mountains lay destroyed and (scattered) all over the earth.

10. In that one vast ocean, the (solidified) waters tossed by wind got collected together due to cold. Wherever they were (thus) stuck (heaped) together, there they became immovable.

11. The mountains are called *Acalas* because they become motionless after being dried up and solidified. Because they have knots and joints they are called *Parvatas*. They are called

1. Cf. *Supra* 6. 7-11. A repetition of verses.

Giris because they were swallowed by waters. They are called *Śiloccayas* because they are collected.[1]

12. Then, after lifting up the earth from within the waters, the Lord established it in its position again and made division in it.

13. In each of its seven continents,[2] he made seven *Varṣas* (sub-continents). He levelled the uneven places and collected the mountains, with (heaps of) rocks.

14. There are forty(?) *Varṣas* in all the continents together. There are as many mountains also stationed at the extremities of the *Varṣas*. They were assembled there at the beginning of creation according to their nature and not otherwise.

15. The seven continents and the (seven) oceans encircle each other. They are in contiguity with each others, surrounding each other naturally.

16. Even at the outset, Brahmā created all these stations, the four worlds, viz. *Bhūḥ* etc., the sun, the moon and planets.

17-19. Formerly at the beginning of this Kalpa[3], Brahmā created the *Sthānins* (presiding deities or occupants of these posts). He created waters, fire, earth, wind, ether, heaven, elysium, quarters, oceans, rivers, mountains, the souls of medicinal herbs, the souls of trees, creepers, units of time, *Lavas*, *Kāṣṭhās*, *Kalās*, *Muhūrtas*, junctions (of night and day or twilight), night, day, fortnight, months, *Ayanas* (transits of the sun), years and yugas.

20. He created separately the abodes as well as the occupants presiding therein (who identified themselves with the

---

1. These are semantic etymologies i.e. those based on the meaning of the word. The derivations of *acala* or *giri* are understandable but others are doubtful.

2. The *Sapta-dvīpī* conception (division of the earth into seven continents) has superseded the *Catur-dvīpī* concept(division of the earth into four parts) of old Purāṇas. The figure seven was then popular. Thus the earth is divided into seven continents. Each continent has seven sub-continents; each sub-continent has seven mountain ranges (*Kula Parvatas*), seven big rivers etc. For their description *vide infra* Chapters 40-49.

3. Verses 17 ff. describe the process of re-creation of the Universe. Due to the inexorable law of Karma, every being has to re-start his or her life according to one's Karma in the new Kalpa. There is no automatic *Mokṣa* even after the complete annihilation of the Universe at the end of a Kalpa.

abodes). After creating the 'souls' for these 'posts', he created the (serial) order of Yugas.

21. They are Kṛta, Tretā, Dvāpara and Kali. In the beginning of the Kalpa, during the first Kṛtayuga, he created the subjects (beings).

22. The subjects of the previous ages who have been mentioned to you by me, were burnt by the Saṁvartaka fire then in the Kalpa that was coning to an end.

23. Those who could not reach Tapoloka, had resorted to the Janaloka. They began to function as seeds for the future creation.

24. Abiding there, in the form of seeds for the subsequent creation, they, on being let loose (scattered) serve the purpose of progeny.

25. The subjects, Devas, Pitṛs, sages and Manus are those who accomplish (the four *Puruṣārthas* viz.) virtue (Dharma), wealth (Artha), pleasure (Kāma), and salvation (Mokṣa).

26. Being endowed with Penance thereafter, they fill up (occupy) the stations. As the mental sons of Brahmā, they work as accomplished souls.

27. The created beings who have attained heaven through subversive rites are reborn (repeatedly) in every Yuga.

28. Due to the residue of the fruits of their actions, they become well-known with their souls inclined in that manner. They descend from the Janaloka due to the bondage of the Karmans.

29. It is the intention, the feelings of the mind that should be regarded as the cause, in regard to the activities. The people descend from Janaloka due to their good and bad activities (in their previous lives).

30. They take up different forms of bodies in different wombs (species) from Devas to immobile beings. They are born of one another successively.

31. Being created again and again, they pursue those activities which they had been pursuing before.

32. They pursue violent or non-violent, soft or ruthless, virtuous or evil, truthful or false activities on being urged by those previous innate feelings which appeal to them.

33. Whatever names and forms (these beings have) in the past Kalpa, they mostly receive the same in the future Kalpas.

34. They assume those very names and forms again and again. They are born in the different Kalpas with the same names and forms.

35-36. When Brahmā who was desirous of creation got his creative activity obstructed, He, of truthful contemplation, began to contemplate on the subjects. He created a thousand pairs from his mouth. With the quality of Sattva predominant, they, of good mind, were suitable for the task.

37. He created another thousand pairs from his chest. These had the quality of passion (Rajas) predominant and were fiery and impatient.

38. He created another thousand couples from his thighs. Passion (Rajas) and Ignorance (Tamas) were predominant in them. They were ambitious and aspirant.

39. He created another thousand couples from his feet. They had ignorance (Tamas) predominant in them. They were inglorious and deficient in brilliance.

40-42. The living beings born of these pairs were passionate. Being lustful, they began to copulate with one another. Thenceforward procreation from pairing originated in this Kalpa. Women did not have their menstrual courses month by month. Then they did not conceive, even when copulated. They brought forth pairs of children once at the end of life.

43. They gave birth to crooked offspring (?), when they had desire for death. From that time onward pairing originated in this Kalpa.

44. Even by contemplating once mentally, the subjects had created for them, the five objects of senses such as sound, each of which was of five characteristics in the pure form.[1]

45. In this way the previous creation by god Brahmā was through his mind (mental activity). Those who were born in his race have filled the world.

1. Verses 44-63 paint a glowing picture of the Kṛta age. They depict the ideal state of society from Purāṇic point of view—a classless society with perfect equality and full liberty.

46. The people in that age resorted to rivers, lakes, oceans and mountains. The waters in that Yuga were neither too hot nor too cold.

47. They usually took the diet of the juicy food of the earth. They moved about wherever they pleased. They had acquired mental Siddhis.

48. In that Kṛta age, there was neither virtue nor evil. The human beings were non-differentiated. They had equal longevity, happiness and beauty (form).

49. In the beginning of the Kalpa, in the Kṛta age, neither virtue (Dharma) nor evil (Adharma) existed. The people were born with their respective authority and rights.

50. The first Kṛta age consisted of four thousand divine years. They say that the period of transition consisted of four hundred divine years.

51. Even when thousands of human beings spread they had no obstruction, no clash and no order.

52. They had no fixed abode or place of resort. They wandered about mountains and oceans. They were free from sorrow. They had abundant goodness. They were happy in solitude.

53. They moved about as they pleased. They were always joyous in their minds. There were no animals, birds or reptiles then.

54. There were no trees or plants nor hellish beings born of evil. There were neither roots nor fruits nor flowers nor the seasons nor the years.

55. Time was always pleasant when peoples' desires were fulfilled. There were no extremes in heat or cold. Whatever object they desired in their minds was available everywhere and at all times.

56. Whatever juices they meditated upon, grew up from the earth. Their achievements were conducive to strength, fair complexion and destructive of ailments.

57. With their bodies requiring no decoration (or beautification), the subjects had eternal youth. Pairs of children were born from their pure mental conception.

58. They were born alike and they died together. They had similar forms and features. At that time, there was truth, absence of greed, forbearance, contentment, happiness and restraint.

59. They had no distinguishing marks in their forms and features, longevity, conduct and activity. Their actions were spontaneous and voluntary, without the intercession of intellect.

60. In the Kṛtayuga, there was no inclination towards performance of good or evil actions. There was no classification of castes or differentiation in stages of life. Nor was there intermixture of castes.

61. In their mutual dealings they behaved without being impelled by desire or hatred. All of them, had equal forms, features and longevity. There was neither superior nor inferior class of people.

62. Only those who were mostly happy and devoid of sorrow were born in the Kṛta Yuga. They were highly powerful, very strong and perpetually delighted in the mind.

63. They had neither gain nor loss; neither friends nor foes; neither likes nor dislikes, since they were devoid of desires. The objects functioned according to their minds. They neither desired to possess nor favoured one another.

64. It has been said that in the Kṛta age meditation was the highest; in Tretā it was knowledge; in Dvāpara it was sacrifice, while charity (donation) is excellent in Kali age.

65. In accordance with practice obtaining in the different ages, goodness (Sattva) predominates in Kṛta, passion (Rajas) in Tretā, passion (Rajas) and Ignorance (Tamas) in Dvāpara and only ignorance (Tamas) in the Kali Yuga.

66. As for the duration of Kṛta age, know that four thousand divine years constitute its duration.

67. The duration of eight hundred divine years constitutes its two junctions (interim periods). Then the people had longevity and suffered no pain or adversity.

68. In the Kṛta age, when the interim period (between

Kṛta and Tretā) passes off, only one fourth of the entire yuga-dharma (characterising the Kṛta age) remains.

69. When the period of junction is over at the end of the age,[1] the Dharma of the period of junction remains but one-fourth. When the Kṛta age lapses completely without any remnant, the spiritual achievement (of Kṛta age) too vanishes.

70. When the mental *Siddhi* (of Kṛta age) is lost, another comes into being in the Tretā Yuga.

71. The eight mental perfections in the beginning of the creation, mentioned by me, decline gradually and are lost.

72. In the beginning of the Kalpa, in the Kṛta age, this attainment is only mental. In all the Manvantaras in accordance with the division of the four Yugas, the attainment is due to the holy rites, due to the pursuit of the conduct of life of the respective castes and stages of life.

73. When the Kṛta age passes off thus, one-fourth of the Dharma is lost in the first junction, another one-fourth during the lapse of the main Yuga and a third one-fourth in the later junction. Thus three fourth of the power of penance, strength and longevity gets lost.

74-76. O excellent sages, when a portion of Kṛta has lapsed, then in the Tretā, another age, a portion of Kṛta remains. When that portion has also lapsed at the advent of Tretā in the beginning of Kalpa, the attainments of the remaining subjects become defunct due to efflux of time and not due to any other reason. When one attainment (Siddhi) disappears another takes its place.

77. When water becomes subtle, cloud is formed. The creation of rain showers functions through the thundering clouds.[2]

78. When the surface of the earth is drenched with rain

---

1. Verses 69-76 describe the transition between Kṛta and Tretā ages.

2. Verses 77-88 show that rain-showers, human dependance on trees (for means of subsistence, clothes, ornaments) and growing cupidity were the special features of Tretā. It is a period when men gave up their nomadic habits and began to build shelters. These settlements further developed into hamlets, villages and towns.

only once, the trees begin to manifest themselves for their abodes.

79. All the necessary objects of enjoyments emanated from them (the trees). In the beginning of Tretā, people subsisted on them (i.e. the products of trees).

80. Then after the lapse of a long time, due to their own perversity the emotions of lust and greed possessed them suddenly.

81. The menstrual flow that used to take place only at the end of life in the case of women then (in Kṛta Yuga), ceased to be so due to the power of the (new, Tretā) Yuga.

82. In their case, the menstruation began to take place every month. As a consequence thereof, they indulged in copulation the same way.

83. When the flow took this turn and when they copulated every month, the untimely menstrual flow and conception began to happen.

84. On account of their perversity and due to what was destined to happen in course of time, all the trees in their house (or which were like their houses) perished.

85. When these were destroyed, the people became excited and agitated in all their senses. They, of truthful thought, began to meditate on that mental Siddhi.

86. The trees manifested in their houses again. They yielded clothes, fruits and ornaments.

87. Invigorating honey without the bees, possessing sweet taste, scent and colour, exuded in them in every leafcup.

88. They maintained themselves with that honey at the beginning of the Tretā age. They were delighted and contented with that Siddhi. They were free from ailments.

89. As time elapsed, they were overcome with greed once again. They forcibly took possession of trees and extracted from them the nectar (of flowers) and honey.

90. Due to this misdemeanor committed by the people, the wish-yielding trees perished at some places along with honey.

91. When the period of junction remained but little, due to the passage of time, there arose extremes of climate (e.g. scorching heat and extreme cold).

92. They were terribly distressed by the extremes of biting winds and scorching sunshine. Being afflicted by these they made shelters.

93. Warding off *Dvandvas* (pairs of opposites) of heat and cold, they resorted to abodes. Formerly, they had been roaming about as they pleased, without a fixed habitation.

94. Now according to circumstances and their liking, they stayed in abodes, wildernesses, deserts, deep chasms, on hills, mountains or riversides. They resorted to fortresses, dry soils and waste lands with perpetual supply of water.

95. In order to ward off heat and cold, they made habitations in level and rugged lands in accordance with the availability and their taste.

96. Then they set up hamlets, villages and towns with due alignment and built harems too.

97-98. The measure of their length and diameter was fixed by them.[1] They built houses on this basis just as they thought fit. A unit was termed *Pradeśa*—a distance between the (extended) thumb and the (outstretched) forefinger. The distance between the thumb and the middle finger (when both are stretched) was *Tāla* and that between the thumb and the ring figer was *Gokarṇa*.

99. The distance between the thumb and the little finger (when both are stretched) was called *Vitasti*. It contained

---

1. Verses 97-102 give the units of measurement of distance as follows : The first unit '*Aṅgula*' means 'Finger-breadth'

12 Aṅgulas	=	1 Vitasti
21 Aṅgulas	=	1 Ratni
24 Aṅgulas	=	1 Hasta
2 Ratnis or 42 Aṅgulas	=	1 Kiṣku
4 Hastas or 2 Nālikās	=	1 Dhanus or Daṇḍa
2000 Dhanus or Daṇḍas	=	1 Gavyūti
8000 Dhanus or Daṇḍas	=	1 Yojana

twelve *Aṅgulas* (finger-breadths). Twenty-one *Aṅgulas* made one *Ratni* (the distance between the elbow and the closed fist).

100. Twenty-four *Aṅgulas* made one *Hasta* (hand). Two *Ratnis* or forty-two *Aṅgulas* made one *Kiṣku.*

101. Four *Hastas* or two *Nālikās* made one *Dhanus* or *Daṇḍa.* Two thousand *Dhanus* or *Daṇḍas* made one *Gavyūti.*

102. Eight thousand *Dhanus* constituted a *Yojana.* It is on the basis of the Yojana calculation that the sites were fixed then.

103. Of the four types of fortifications, three occur naturally. The fourth kind of fortress is artificial. I shall describe the mode of its construction.[1]

104. Huge mansions, lofty ramparts and fort-walls are built around. There is a principal gate called *Svastika* and there is a gynaeceum in which maidens are kept (*Kumārīpura*).

105. The (main) gate is close to a moat with flowing water current. The width of the moat is the best if (it is) eight or ten hands. Others opine that nine or eight hands (in width) is the best.

106-107. (I shall mention the dimensions) of hamlets, cities and villages and three types of forts, viz. mountains, waters (rivers) and constructed (artificially by) men. The diameter shall be half a Yojana. Its length should be one and one-eighth of a Yojana.

108-109. A city that extends to the east or north is the most excellent.[2] Its extent shall be half or one-fourth of the maximum length. It should be divided into a hypotenuse and segments and be laid out in the shape of a fan.* A city planned circularly or merely lengthwise (with little breadth) or deficient in (amenities) is not recommendable. A city set up in the form of a square with straight rows of houses in all the eight quarters is desirable.

---

1. Verses 103-107 refer to construction of forts.

2. Verses 108-117 explain the ancient ideas of town (and village) planning. The instructions about construction of roads are interesting. But crudeness or elementary nature of town planning or civil engineering shows that they are earlier than *Kauṭ. Artha Śāstra.*

3. The reading *Vyajana* from Bd. P. I. 2. 7. 107 is accepted as '*Vyañjana*', the reading here is obscure.

110. The minimum width of a dwelling is twenty-four *Hastas* and the maximum is eight hundred *Hastas*. But they praise a middle one which is neither too narrow nor too wide.

111. Important dwellings shall be constructed in a site eight hundred *Kiṣkus* wide. A hamlet has half the diameter of the city and a village is bigger than that.

112. A hamlet shall be situated a *Yojana* away from a city and a village shall be half a *Yojana* away from a hamlet. Two *Krośas* is the maximum boundary. The boundary of a field is four *Dhanus*.

113. The highway shall be twenty *Dhanus* wide. The main road in the village shall also be twenty *Dhanus* wide. But the road in the border-land shall be only ten *Dhanus* wide.

114. The main road shall be excellent if it is ten *Dhanus* wide. The movement of the traffic of people (pedestrians), horses, elephants and chariots should be without hindrance.

115. Branch roads should be four *Dhanus* wide. The roads connecting dwelling houses and side roads shall be two *Dhanus* wide.

116. The "bell-road", i.e. the main road in a village, should be four steps wide; the space between two dwellings shall consists of three steps or paces. The side roads shall be half a pace wide. The way to the sacrificial room shall be a pace wide.

117. The dust-bin shall be a pace wide. The gutters on either side of the road shall be a pace wide. They made a lay-out and built houses afterwards.

118. Thinking and recollecting again and again they began to grow trees in the places in which they stood formerly.

119. The trees had branches going upwards and apreading around. They never receded. In the same way, the branches spread in all directions (lit. obliquely) in former times.

120. They observed carefully how the branches had gone. They constructed the apartments in accordance with the growth of the branches (*śākhās*).[1] Hence they had been called *Śālās*.

---

1. Verses120-122. *Śāla* trees played an important part in construction of houses. Note the popular etymology of *Śālā*, 'an apartment' and *Prāsāda*, 'a mansion'.

121. Thus *Śālās* (apartments) became well known from branches; so also the abodes. Hence they are remembered as '*Śālās*'. Thus is explained their state of being Śālās (*Śālātva*).

122. The mind is delighted in them. They delight the mind. Hence the houses, halls and mansions are duly termed as *prāsādas*.

123. After warding off the *Dvandvas* (the pairs of mutual opposites, viz. heat and cold), they began to think of the means of their sustenance (such as agriculture). When the Kalpa-trees had perished along with the honey, they were overwhelmed by hunger and thirst and became bewildered and dejected.

124. Thereafter, in the Tretā age, a *Siddhi* (accomplishment) appeared before them. The means of agriculture that could meet their ends came as they desired.[1]

125. The waters showered (from the sky) which flowed downwards became *srotas* (river, stream). And waters flowing in ditches or excavated places are known as *Nimnagās* (down flowing).

126-127. Thus in the second creation through rain, the rivers came into being. What little of water remained on the surface of the earth thereafter, became mixed with earth and grew into plants and herbs. Plants began to put forth flowers, fruits and roots.

128. Fourteen kinds of trees and bushes which grew up in the villages and forests without ploughing or burning, put forth seasonal flowers and fruit.

129. It was in the Tretā age that vegetation manifested first and the medicinal plants appeared. The people in the Tretā age maintained themselves on the products of agriculture.

130. Then again all of them were overwhelmed with lust and greed as a result of unavoidable fate or due to the Tretā age.

---

1. Verses 124-137 show that in the Tretā Age man developed agriculture and for division of labour the society was divided into different Varṇas (Classes). The credit of introducing Agriculture is given to Brahmā.

131. They then forcibly occupied the rivers, fields, mountains, trees, clusters and medicinal plants.

132. While describing the *Prākṛta Sarga*, I have spoken about the accomplished souls. These were born as human beings according to Brahmā's plan.

133. They were quiescent, powerful, active and distressed. Then, thus functioning they were born again in the Tretā age.

134. Urged by the auspicious and inauspicious activities of the previous births they were born as Brāhmaṇas, Kṣatriyas, Vaiśyas, Śūdras and Dasyus.

135-137. Those who were truthful, non-violent, devoid of greed and self-controlled lived therein. There were others deficient in brilliance, who served these in return for the gifts they received from them. Thus there was mutual dependence. Due to their fault, the medicinal plants disappeared while they were looking on helplessly. They vanished as sand particles in handfuls.

138. The earth, due to the power of the Yuga, swallowed the fourteen kinds of plants both in villages and forests—the plants which bore fruit through flowers and flowers with leaves.

139. When these were destroyed, the people became bewildered. On being overwhelmed by hunger they approached Lord Svayaṁbhū, Prajāpati.

140-141. (It was) at the beginning of Tretā Yuga. The self-born lord Brahmā, knowing that they wanted the means of sustenance, considered what was proper by observing directly. Realising that the medicinal plants were swallowed by the earth he milked them out again (from the earth).[1]

142. Making mount Meru as the calf, he milked the earth. The earth-cow yielded the seeds on its surface.

1. This is the Purāṇic development of the ancient Vedic concept of milking the Virāj cow recorded in AV VIII, Sūkta 10. Purāṇa-writers used this motif later with Lord Brahmā, King Pṛthu as the milkers. In Mt. P. 10. 25 Vararuci became the milker and the science of Dramaturgy (*Nāṭya Veda*) was the milk.

143. The seeds grew into wild and cultivated plants yielding ripe fruits. They comprised seventeen classes.

144-146. Rice, barley, wheat, the minute gingelly seeds, the *Priyaṅgus*, *Udāras*, *Kārūṣas*, *Tinakas* (different kinds of pulse etc.), black gram, green gram, *Masūras* (a pulse), *Niṣpāvas*, horse grams, *Āḍhakis* (the pulse *cajanus Indicus spreng*), and other grams. These are the seventeen varieties of rural medicinal plants (*Grāmya oṣadhi*). Then there are fourteen kinds of plants used in sacrifices.

147. They are: rice, barley, black gram, wheat, *aṇus* (*panicum Miliaccum*), gingelly seeds, *Priyaṅgu* the seventh among them and horse-gram the eighth.

148-149. *Śyāmākas* (a variety of rice), *Nivāras* (another variety of rice), *Jartilas* (wild sesamum), *Gavedhukas*, *Kuruvindas* (a kind of barley), *Veṇuyavas* (bamboo seeds) and *Markaṭakas* (a species of grain)—these are the fourteen varieties of wild and cultivated plants. They were originally produced in the beginning of the Tretā age.

150. All these medicinal plants, trees, hedges, creepers and grasses grew in villages and forests without the fields being ploughed.

151. The seeds that were milked from the earth at the outset by the self-born god Brahmā grew into various fruits and flowers.

152-153. They grew into plants yielding seasonal flowers and fruits. When they let go (the seasonal product once) they did not grow again. The self-born Brahmā then devised for the livelihood of the people by means of agriculture.

154. From that time onwards the plants began to grow on being (ploughed and) cultivated. Thus when agriculture came into vogue the self-born lord established conventions for their mutual help.[1]

155. Those who were masters (powerful ones) had (to follow) prescribed conventions and established them (as) Kṣattriyas for the protection of others.

1. Verses 154-164 show the evolution of Varṇas or Classes in an agrarian society and the duties of each class. Verses 166-168 state the region to which pious members of these classes go.

156. Those who worship (or respect or obey) those (Kṣatriyas) are free from fear. Those who averred that Brahman is the truth and spoke according to facts (the truth) are Brāhmaṇas.

157. Those who were weak were assigned the duty of Vaiśyas. They became the cultivators of the soil. Formerly they used to destroy things in the earth. They are called Vaiśyas as they maintain their livelihood by soil and cultivation.

158. Those who were engaged in serving others, those who were lustreless and deficient in virility he called Śūdras because they bewailed their lot, were miserable and adopted crooked ways.

159. Lord Brahmā assigned their duties and virtues when the system of castes was thus established.

160. Out of delusion the people did not follow their duties. Not observing the (special) duties of castes, they clashed mutually.

161. On realising that precisely, lord Brahmā ordered strength, punishment and warfare as the means of sustenance for the Kṣatriyas.

162. The lord assigned these as the duties of Brāhmaṇas: presiding over sacrifice, teaching of the Vedas and the acceptance of monetary gifts.

163. The lord assigned breeding of cattle, trading and agriculture to the Vaiśyas. He made the practice of arts and crafts as means of livelihood and service the duties of Śūdras.

164. The duties common to the three classes—Brāhmaṇas Kṣatriyas and Vaiśyas include the performance of sacrifice, study of the Vedas and making gifts.

165. After prescribing the holy rites and duties as the means of livelihood, the lord gave them suitable regions in the other worlds achievable by means of *Siddhi*.

166. The region of the Brāhmaṇas who performed their sacred rites and duties is the world of Prajāpati. The world of Indra is the region for Kṣatriyas who flee not in battle.

167. The region of Maruts is assigned to Vaiśyas who maintain themselves as per their (ordained) duties. To the Śūdras who abide by their duty of rendering service, the region of Gandharvas is assigned.

168. These are the regions for different castes who observe their prescribed duties. When the castes were thus stabilised, he established the *Āśramas*.

169. Formerly, the Lord established the four *Āśramas*, viz. Brahmacārin (the religious student), Gṛhastha (the householder), Vānaprastha (the recluse) and Bhikṣuka (the ascetic mendicant).

170. Those who do not practise the duties assigned to their caste, they say, incurred the loss of the (fruit of) holy rites even if they maintained the activities of the *Āśramas*.

171. Brahmā established these *Āśramas* by name.[1] In order to guide them, he spoke to them about their duties, manners, restraints and observances.

172. The *Āśrama* of the householder is common to all the four castes. This stage is the very basis and support of the other three *Āśramas*. I shall explain it in order along with the observances and restraints.

173. The following are briefly the religious duties of the householders : Marriage, maintenance of the sacred fire, hospitality to guests, performance of sacrifices and continuation of the race (procreation of children).

174. The characteristic duties of a Brahmacārin are : (bearing) the staff, wearing the girdle (of *muñja* grass), sleeping on the bare ground, having matted hair, service to the preceptor and begging alms.

175. Wearing of bark garments, leaves or deer skin, diet of grains, roots, fruits or herbs (found in the forest), bathing at dawn and dusk and performing sacrifice are the characteristics of a forest-dweller.

176-177. Begging when the sound of pestles dies down, non-stealing, purity, non-negligence, refraining from sexual intercourse, mercy towards (all) beings, forebearance, absence of anger (control of temper), service to preceptors and the tenth truthfulness—This code of conduct of ten characteristics has been prescribed by the self-born god (Brahmā).

---

1. Verses 171-181 state the duties of different stages (*Āśramas*) in life. The importance of householdership (*Gṛhasthāśrama*) is duly recognised.

178. Five (of the above) are the main observances and five subsidiaries which constitute the sacred rites of the mendicant ascetic. Purity in the conduct of life, restraints, purity of the mind, counteraction of evil deeds and perfect vision—these are the five subsidiary sacred rites.

179. They say that the holy course of conduct (*dharma*) of a man of renunciation consists of meditation (samādhi), control of the mind and of the sense-organs, silence, taking of food voluntarily offered by others and endeavour for liberation (from saṁsāra).

180-181. All these stages of life have been declared by Brahmā himself for the achievement of ultimate good. Truthfulness, straightforwardness, austerities, forbearance, Yogic sacrifice preceded by control of senses, study of the Vedas and their ancillaries, sacrifices, holy observances and restraints do not bear fruit if there is fault in emotions and if one is defiled.

182. If a person is defiled in inner emotions, all his external actions never bear fruit even if he puts in his utmost effort.

183. Even if a person donates all his possessions but with an impious inner soul, he shall not be virtuous. Piety is the true cause of perfection.

184. It is said that the region attained by the persons who abide by this Dharma is that of the Devas, Pitṛs, sages and Manus.

185. There are eighty-eight thousand sages of sublimated sexuality. It is their region that is assigned to those who live with their teachers.

186. The sphere of the seven sages is the abode of heaven-dwellers. Prājāpatya (the region of Prajāpati) is the sphere of householders. The region of Brahmā is the abode for Sannyāsins. The region of immortality is the abode for the Yogins. There is no abode for those who have mental worries.

187-188. These are the regions for the people of different stages of life who abide by their allotted duties. The four paths called Devayāna have been made by Brahmā,[1] the controller of

---

1. Verses 187-189 : Purāṇic concept of Devayāna and Pitṛyāna paths after death.

the worlds in the first Manvantara on the earth. These paths lead to the region of Devas. The sun is remembered as the doorway to these paths.

189-190. Similarly the moon is the doorway to Pitṛyāna (the path of the Pitṛs). When these divisions of castes and stages of life were made but when the people did not abide by their injunctions, he evolved another mental creation from his own body which was like himself.

191. When the first Tretā age reached the middle period, gradually he began to create another mind-born progeny.

192. Then the lord created beings with (predominant) Sattva and Rajas *guṇas*. They were competent to accomplish virtue, love, wealth, liberation and their means of livelihood.

193. He created Devas, Pitṛs, sages and Manus (i.e. human beings) who were suitable for the Yuga. They have procreated these subjects as per Dharma.

194. When the subjects abided by the Dharma prescribed by the self-born lord (Brahmā) he meditated on the, mind-born beings of different forms.

195. The persons who have been mentioned to you by me, as having resorted to Janaloka became *devas* and other subjects here, when the (previous) Kalpa passed away.

196-198. While he meditated, the subjects appeared before him for creation. In the order of the Manvantaras, they are considered the first or the last. They are imbued with the knowledge of discrimination, adjuncts and topics. Endowed with efficient and inefficient activities, they are restrained by the residue of the fruit of their actions. They attain the state of *devas*, *Asuras*, *Pitṛs*, animals, birds, reptiles, trees, hellish beings and insects. He created them to be subservient to himself and his subjects.

CHAPTER NINE

Creation of Devas and Others

Sūta said :

1. Even as he was meditating, mental progeny were born of him along with those causes and effects arising out of his body. There emerged from the limbs of that intelligent Being *Kṣetrajñas* (individual souls).

2. Then, desirous of procreating the group of four living entities, Devas, Asuras, Pitṛs, and mankind, he applied himself in the water.[1]

3. Then as the self-born god Brahmā engaged himself in meditation on creation, exertion appeared on the part of the creator.

4. Then, from his loins, the Asuras were born at the outset. O Brāhmaṇas, the word *Asu* means 'the Vital Breath'. Born of that, they were called *Asuras*.[2]

5. He abandoned that body from which Asuras were created; the body so abandoned by him became night immediately as it (the abandoned body) was dominated by *Tamas*.

---

1. Verses 2-22 describe the creation of four entities of living beings, viz. Asuras, Devas, Pitṛs and human beings from various parts of god Brahmā's body at different periods, with the predominant *guṇas* of each category. They may be tabulated as follows:

Creation	*The Source : part of Brahmā's body*	*The transformation of discarded body*	*Dominant Guṇa*
1. Asuras	Loins and vital breath	Night	*Tamas*
2. Devas	Shining face	Day	Predominant *Sattva*
3. Pitṛs	Sides	Evening (Juncture of day and night)	Pure *Sattva*
4. Human beings	Mind	Moon light (but dawn)	*Rajas*

2. Vide v. 21 below. As MW 121-a notes, 'In later SK., *Sura* 'a god' has been formed from *asura* like *sita* is from *asita*'.

6. As it (the abandoned body) was dominated by Tamas, the night consisting of three watches was full of darkness. Hence the progeny of the self-born lord were enveloped by darkness at night.

7. After creating the Asuras, the lord took up another body of unmanifest nature abounding in Sattva. The lord united himself with it. While engaged with it, they say, he felt pleasure.

8. Then Devas were born from his shining face. They were so called because they were born of his refulgent face.

9. The root √*Div* means[1] 'to play'. Devas were so called because they were born of his playful (shining) body.

10. After creating Devas, the lord took up another body having only the Sāttvic attribute.

11. The lord meditated upon those sons considering them like father and created the father-like Manes from his two sides, between the juncture of day and night. Hence Pitṛs are Devas and their fatherhood[2] is due to that.

12. He abandoned the body after creating the Pitṛs. As soon as he abandoned the body, it became evening.

13. Hence day is for Devas; night is meant for the Asuras; the body (meant for) Pitṛs, evening which is between the two, is held to be important.

14. Hence Devas, Asuras, all the sages and Manus, engaged in Yogic communion, worship the middle body (i.e. the twilight time) of Brahmā.

15. Then Brahmā took up another body again. The Lord created beings with his mind, in that body consisting of Rajas.

16. Then he created mentally sons from his mind which was dominated by Rajas *guṇa*. Hence the subjects were born of his mind.

17. Having seen the subjects, he again cast off his body. The body so abandoned by him immediately became the moonlight.

---

1. Correct etymology—√*div* means both 'to play' and 'to shine'.
2. *Putratvam* would mean "His being a son unto them".

18-19. Hence the people are delighted when the moonlight comes out (and spreads). Thus these bodies abandoned by the lord instantly became night and day, the twilight and the moonlight. The three, viz. the moonlight, twilight as well as the day consist solely of the *Sattva guṇa*. The night comprises the nature of *Tamas* only; hence it has three watches.

20. Hence Devas created from the mouth are possessed of shining fraits of the day and full of delight. Since they were born during the day, they are very powerful by day.

21. Since the lord created the Asuras at night from the loins of his body, through vital breath, the night-born Asuras wield unbearable prowess during the night.

22. These alone function as the causes for the creation of Devas, Asuras, Pitṛs and human beings in the past and future Manvantaras.

23. The moonlight, the night, the day and the twilight, these four shine when illuminated. The word √*bhā* means 'to spread' and 'to shine'.[1] So say the wise scholars. The root √*bhā* is used in the sense of spreading and shining.

24. After seeing (creating?) waters, the Lord created Devas, Dānavas, human beings, Pitṛs and his other divinities.

25. After casting off that body entirely, he created another form mostly constituted of Rajas and Tamas and united himself with it.

26. Feeling hunger and thirst in darkness, he created another body. The hungry creature created by him attempted to take (possess) the waters.

27-28. Some among them declared, "We shall protect these waters". They are known as *Rākṣasas* in the world. They are wrathful souls and night-walkers. Those among them who delightedly said to one another, "We shall destroy the waters" became, due to that activity, Yakṣas and Guhyakas. They were cruel in their actions.

29. The root √*rakṣa* is considered to have the sense of protection. The root √*kṣi* is used in the sense of destroying.[2]

1. Verses 23-24 suggest the derivation of *aṁbhas* 'water' from √*bhā*.
2. Verses 27-29 give the Purāṇic etymology of '*Rākṣasa*' and '*Yakṣa*'.

30-31. On seeing them with displeasure, the hairs of that intelligent one withered. But due to heat and cold, they climbed up the Lord. As the *Vyālas* (*Vālas*—hairs) which were dropped down from my head crawled up, they became known as *Vyālas* and as they dropped down (*hīnatvāt*), they (the serpents) are called. *Ahis*.[1]

32. As they move footlessly (without foot), they are *pannagas* and they are *sarpas* as they crawl. Their abode is below in the earth under the sun and the moon.

33. The excessively terrible fiery foetus, born of his anger, entered those beings of poisonous nature—serpents who were born along with them.

34. On seeing the serpents, he became angry and out of anger he created beings of furious nature. They were very fierce goblins whose diet is flesh and who were reddish-brown in colour.

35. They were remembered as *Bhūtas* as they came into existence.[2] They were called *Piśācas* because they ate flesh. Even as he was singing words, the Gandharvas were born.

36. The root $\sqrt{}$*dhay* means 'to drink'.[3] Since they were born from drinking the (musical) words, they are known as Gandharvas.

37. When these eight classes of divine beings were created, the lord from his bodily energy created birds out of his own free will.

38. Covering up those *chandas* (wilful acts) and the birds by his age (?) and seeing them void, he created groups of winged creatures.

39. He created goats from his mouth, birds from his chest, kine from his belly and sides.

40. From his feet he created horses, elephants, Sarabhas, Gavayas, deer, camels, mules and other animals of various kinds.

---

1. Some more Purāṇic derivations : *Vyāla*<*Vāla* —'hair'; *ahi*<$\sqrt{}$*hi* but Apte derives from $\sqrt{}$*han* 'to kill ! *Hindi-Sk. Kośa* p. 134.

2. Verses 35-36 derive the words '*Bhūta*','*Piśāca*' and '*Gandharva*' from the functions they carry out.

3. *yātrarthe* in the text is incorrect. A. reads '*pānārthe*', so in Bd. P. I 2. 8. 41.

41-42. Plants or trees, fruits, and roots were born of his hair. After creating the cattle and plants thus, the lord applied himself to sacrifice. It was in the beginning of the Kalpa, in the Tretā age. Cow, goat, man,[1] sheep, horse, mule and donkey—they call these rural domestic animals. Now know about the wild animals.

43. Beasts of prey, cloven-hoofed animals, elephants, monkeys, birds constituting the fifth and the animals, mice—these were created. The seventh (in the series) were reptiles.

44. From his front mouth[2] he created the metre Gāyatrī, Varuṇa[3], *Trivṛt*[4], Soma, *Rathantara*[5], and the Agniṣṭoma among the sacrifices.

45. From his southern mouth he created the sacred hymns of (Yajurveda?), *Triṣṭubh* metre, the fifteenth *stoma*, the *Bṛhat-sāman*, and the Uktha verses.

46. From his western mouth he created the Sāman hymns, *Jagatī* metre, the fifteen hymns of praise, Vairūpya Sāman and Atirātra[6] rite.

47. From his northern mouth he created twenty-first (*stoma* hymn), the Atharvan, the Āptoryāman,[7] Anuṣṭhubh and Virāj metres.

48. In the beginning of the Kalpa, the lord created lightnings, thunderbolts, clouds, red-coloured rainbows and birds.

---

1. It seems to be the social memory of ancient human sacrifices that man is included in the list of 'domestic animals'.

2. Verses 44-47 state the creation of Vedic literature, Vedic meters and special hymns and sacrifices from the different faces of Brahmā.

3. Bd. P. I. 2. 8. 50 reads *ṛcam* (the *Ṛgveda*).

4. *Trivṛt-Soma*—a threefold *stoma* in which at first, a set of the first three verses—*Tṛcā* of RV. IX. 11 are first sung together, then the second and then the third set is sung.

5. The verses to be sung according to Sāma-music are RV VII.32. 22-23, *abhi tvā Śūra*, SV. 1. 233 (*Vedic Concordance*).

6. *Atirātra* is a form of Soma-sacrifice.

7. *Āptoryāma* is an amplification of *Atirātra* sacrifice. According to *Tāṇḍya Br*. XX. 3. 4-5, it is so called as its performance secures whatever one desires.

49. As the patriarch Brahmā created the progeny, living beings high and low were born of his limbs.

50. After creating the four classes of beings—Devas, Asuras, Pitṛs, and mankind, he next created the mobile and immobile beings.

51. He created Yakṣas, Piśācas, Gandharvas, groups or families of Apsaras-s, human beings, Kinnaras, Rākṣasas, birds, cattle, wild animals and snakes.

52. Whether changing or unchanging, stationary of mobile, these beings created and re-created, adopted those activities which they had in the previous creation.[1]

53. Violent or non-violent, soft or cruel, virtuous or evil, true or false—all these things are adopted by them as they appeal to them.

54. It is the creator who ordained diversity of forms in the great elements and their allotment to different physical bodies and the objects of different senses.

55. Some say that it is human effort and others say it is the *karma*, while still others, fatalist Brāhmaṇas, call it the destiny that decides the nature of beings.

56. Human activity and divine dispensation are decided by the nature of fruit. In fact either of the two alone does not suffice. They are inseparable from each other. Neither one is superior to the other. Neither one alone nor the two separately or collectively.

57. Persons of even vision abiding by Sattva say that the attainment of objects is due to their activities.

It is only through the words of the Vedas that the great Lord created the names and forms of living beings and the development of those that are already created.

58. He assigns names to the sages, the visions belonging to Devas and to other things that were brought forth at the end of the night.

59. Just as the indications and forms forboding the advent of seasons recur at their appropriate times, so also in the Yugas

---

1. The inexorable law of Karma is advocated in vv. 52-56, for destiny or *daiva* is the Karma of a previous birth.

the same creation appears again and again.

60. The beings of such types created by resorting to his mental power (*mānasi siddhi*) by god Brahmā born of the unmanifest, are seen manifestly at the end of (god Brahmā's) night.

61-63. Thus the living beings, the mobile and immobile came into being. But the progeny created by him did not multiply. He created some other mind-born sons equal to himself. These are known as Bhṛgu, Pulastya, Pulaha, Kratu, Aṅgiras, Marīci, Dakṣa, Atri and Vasiṣṭha. They are known in the Purāṇas as nine Brahmās. These are propounders of the Vedas and are identical with Brahmā himself.

64. Then Brahmā, the ancestor of ancients, created Rudra out of his anger, from his own self. (He created) *Saṁkalpa* and Dharma (also).

65-66. At the beginning, Brahmā created mental sons who were equal to himself, viz. Sanandana, Sanaka, the learned Sanātana and the eminent Sanatkumāra. They are eternal, independant, unattached to worldly life and hence they do not procreate.

67-68. They have the knowledge of the future. They are devoid of passions and rivalry. When they remained indifferent to the continuity of the world, the supreme lord Brahmā contemplated (angrily). Out of his anger, a person as resplendent as the sun was born. Half of his body was a man and half a woman. He was comparable to the fire in splendour.

69. "Everything has become full of lustre and equal to the sun in splendour. Divide yourself"—saying so he vanished there itself.

70. Thus addressed, the man and the woman became separate; the man divided himself into eleven parts (out of the male half).

71-72. All the (eleven) great souls were addressed by the noble being: "Try energetically and vigilantly for the totality (continuity) of the world desiring the multiplication (increase in the population) of the world, (try) for the establishment, benefit and interest of the entire world."

73. Thus addressed, they cried and ran about helter-skelter. Since they cried and ran about they are known as Rudras.

74. The three worlds including the mobile and immobile are pervaded by them. Their followers live in all the worlds.

75-77. They are the valorous lords of Gaṇas with the strength of ten thousand elephants. The highly fortunate one (the female)[1], forming half the body of Śiva, who has been mentioned to you just before, was the woman born of Brahmā's mouth. The right side of her body was fair (white) and the left black. She had been asked by Brahmā to divide herself. O Brāhmaṇas, thus requested, she bifurcated herself into black and white parts. I shall mention her names. Please listen very carefully:

78-79. Svāhā, Svadhā, Mahāvidyā, Medhā, Lakṣmī, Sarasvatī, Aparṇā, Ekaparṇā, Pāṭalā, Umā, Haimavatī, Ṣaṣṭhī, Kalyāṇī, Khyāti, Prajñā, Mahābhāgā, and Gaurī.

80. Know also in brief the universal forms assumed by the noble Lady (forms she assumed in the universe) through the formation of separate bodies:

81. Prakṛti, Niyatā, Raudrī, Durgā, Bhadrā, Pramāthinī, Kālarātri, Mahāmāya, Revatī, and Bhūtanāyikā.

82. Listen to her names at the end of Dvāpara age: Gautamī, Kauśikī, Āryā, Caṇḍī, Kātyāyanī, Satī.

83. Kumārī, Yādavī, Devī, Varadā, Kṛṣṇapiṅgalā, Barhirdhvajā, Śūladharā, Paramabrahmacāriṇī.

84. Māhendrī, Indrabhaginī, Vṛṣakanyā, Ekavāsasī, Aparājitā, Bahubhujā, Pragalbhā, Siṁhavāhinī.

85. Ekānasā, Daityahanī, Māyā, Mahiṣamardinī, Amoghā, Vindhyanilayā, Vikrāntā, Gaṇanāyikā.

86-88. These are the names of her forms that have been mentioned to you in serial order. Those persons who recite accurately the epithets of goddess Bhadrakālī as enumerated by me, will never have a failure or discomfiture. Whether in the forest, or in the outskirts, whether in the house or in the city; whether in water or on dry land, these names afford protection from tigers, robbers and thieves. One should repeat these names

1. Verses 75-85 give a list of epithets of Śakti or the female form called Bhadrakālī in v. 86. These epithets characterise the different forms of the goddess. An element of Śakti cult is found in vv. 75-91.

during mental agony and particularly in a place infested by goblins.

89. An amulet with these names should be used for children afflicted by evil planets, goblins or by evil witches, such as Pūtanā and others.

90. The great goddess is glorified as Prajñā (intellect) and as Śrī (glory). Thousands of goddesses have emerged out of these two and pervaded the universe.

91. She created *Vyavasāya* (industry) and Dharma (duty) bestowing happiness and thought in the beginning of the Kalpa. They were born of unmanifested womb.

92. Ruci was the mental son of Brahmā. He created Dakṣa from his vital breath and Marīci from his eyes.

93-94. Bhṛgu was born of his chest. He created Aṅgiras from his head and Atri from his ears. From the vital breath Udāna, he created Pulastya; from Vyāna, Pulaha; from Samāna, Vasiṣṭha and from Apāna, Kratu.

95. He created Bhadra, Nīlalohita in the form of conceit. These are the twelve sons of Brahmā born of his vital breath.

96. These are the mental sons of Brahmā. Bhṛgu and others who were created were not the expounders of the Veda.

97. They were the ancient householders. Dharma was established (and propagated) by them. These twelve create progeny along with Rudra.

98. Both Ṛbhu and Sanatkumāra sublimated sexual virility. As they were born very early before (the twelve sons), they were the eldest of all.

99. When the first ancient Kalpa was over, both of them withdrew their splendour and occupied the Vairāja region achieving (the good of) the world.

100. Both of them, practising Yogic virtue and concentrating their self in the *Ātman* maintained the *dharma* and aspiration (*kāma*) of the people by their great splendour.

101. Sanat continues to have the same form and features as at the time of his birth. So he is called Kumāra. Hence his name is mentioned Sanatkumāra.

102. Their twelve races are divine and endowed with divine attributes. Performing holy rites and multiplying the race, they are embellished by great sages.

103. Thus ends (the description of) the activity of the self-born lord in creating the worlds. The creation was born of his various organs. The creation beginning with *Mahat* and ending with *Viśeṣas* belongs to *Prakṛti* itself.

104-105. The light of the sun and the moon illuminates the world which is further embellished with planets and stars. It is surrounded by rivers, oceans, mountains, and cities of various shapes and sizes, and happy countryside. In that unmanifest Brahmavana, Brahmā spends the night.

106-108. This eternal tree of Brahmā is born of the seed of *Avyakta*. It grows up through his blessings. Intellect constitutes its branches and the sense-organs its sprout and Dharma and Adharma its flowers, happiness and sorrow its fruits. It is the source of livelihood for living beings and its root is Brahman.

109. The unmanifest which is the cause of creation is eternal and of the nature of *Sat* and *Asat*. This is the *Anugraha Sarga*, the primary creation of Brahmā.

110. The six creations *Mukhya* etc. are secondary. They exist in all the three times in Brahmā who identifies with them.

111. It is known by the learned that the creations function as causes of one another. There are two divine trees growing together, having fine leaves and sprouts and branches. Only one knows the tree of the Ātman and not the other.

112. That incomprehensible Ātman is the cause of creation of all living beings—he whose head the Brāhmaṇas eulogise as heaven; the sky as the umbilicus; the sun and the moon as the eyes; the quarters as the ears; and the earth as his feet.

113. From his mouth the Brāhmaṇas were born; from his arms the Kṣatriyas; from his thigh the Vaiśyas and from his feet the Śūdras.[1]

114. The great lord is beyond the unmanifest. The cosmic Egg is born of the unmanifest. From the cosmic Egg is born Brahmā who created the universe.

1. An echo of RV X. 90 (Puruṣa Sūkta).

CHAPTER TEN

Manvantaras

Sūta said :

1-2. When the worlds came into existence thus by the activity of Brahmā, the creator, and when the progeny did not multiply by any means, Brahmā, enveloped entirely by Tamas, became dejected. He then created intelligence which leads to a definite decision.

3. He then saw only the Tamas element moving within himself as the controlling factor. Subduing Rajas and Sattva, it was functioning.

4. Tormented by that sorrow, the Lord of the universe felt grieved. He eschewed Tamas and Rajas enveloped it.

5. The Tamas that was thus pushed out (dispelled), gave birth to a twin. Violence and sorrow were born of Adharma.* (?)

6. When the twins were born of the foot, the lord felt pleased. And he resorted to this.

7. He abandoned his body which was non-radiant. He split it into two. With one half of his body he became a man.

8. With the other half he became a woman. The woman was named Śatarūpā. Then the lord created the earth (for the support of created beings). The lord created desires also.

9. This body of Brahmā pervaded the earth and heaven by its greatness. The previous body stood enveloping the firmament.

10-11. The woman Śatarūpā who was born of half the body of the creator performed a severe penance for a million years and obtained a man of brilliant fame as her husband. He was called Manu, the first man born of god Brahmā.

12-13. Seventy-one sets of four Yugas, constitute what is called his Manvantara (reign of Manu). Having obtained Śatarūpā, not born of any womb, as his wife, he sported with her. Hence that sport is called *Rati* (sexual intercourse). The first act of coition happened in the beginning of the Kalpa.

**Śokāt* emended as *Śoko*.

14. Brahmā created Virāj[1]. That Virāj became the man (*puruṣa*). And as the king had been created mentally, he became known as Vairāja Manu.

15-16. That creation (of subjects) is called Vairāja. In that creation, Manu is the man (the progenitor of human race). Śatarūpā bore to that valorous man Vairāja two excellent sons that persons possessing sons can expect.

17. The two auspicious daughters Ākūti and Prasūti were born to Manu who gave Prasūti in marriage to Dakṣa.

18. Dakṣa should be known as *Prāṇa* (the vital breath) and Manu, *Saṅkalpa* (will, determination). Manu gave Ākūti to the patriarch Ruci.

19. Auspicious twins were born to Ākūti from Ruci, the mind-born son of Brahmā. They were Yajña and Dakṣiṇā.

20. Yajña begot of Dakṣiṇā twelve sons. They were called Yāmas, gods in the Svāyambhuva Manvantara.

21. Being born as the sons of Yajña, one of the twins (Yama), they are known as Yāmas. The two Gaṇas (groups) of Brahmā are Ajitas and Śūkas.

22. The Yāmas occupied the heaven at the outset. Hence they are called 'heaven-dwellers.' The mothers of the worlds were born of Prasūti, the daughter of Svāyambhuva Manu.

23. Lord Dakṣa begot of her twenty-four daughters. All of them were lotus-eyed and very fortunate.

24. These were wives of Yogins and Yogic mothers. The first thirteen were—Śraddhā, Lakṣmī, Dhṛti, Tuṣṭi, Puṣṭi, Medhā, Kriyā, Buddhi, Lajjā, Vapus, Śānti, Siddhi and Kīrti the thirteenth.

25. Lord Dharma took these daughters of Dakṣa as his wives. They functioned as the doorways (of creation) as ordained by Brahmā.

26-28. Besides them, the remaining younger ones were the eleven lovely-eyed daughters—Khyāti, Satī, Sambhūti, Smṛti, Prīti, Kṣamā, Sannati, Anasūyā, Ūrjā, Svāhā and Svadhā. Other great sages then accepted them. They were Rudra,

1. The author uses Vairāja, Puruṣa, Manu (and Samrāṭ) as synonyms here.

Bhṛgu, Marīci, Aṅgiras, Pulaha, Kratu, Pulastya, Atri, Vasiṣṭha, Pitṛs and Agni who took them as their wives.

29-31. He gave (in marriage) Satī to Śiva and Khyāti to Bhṛgu, Sambhūti to Marīci, Smṛti to Aṅgiras, Prīti to Pulastya, Kṣamā to Pulaha, Sannati to Kratu, Anasūyā to Atri, Ūrjā to Vasiṣṭha, Svāhā to Agni and Svadhā to Pitṛs. I shall mention the children born to them.

32. All these children were highly intelligent and very fortunate. They abide in all the Manvantaras till the final dissolution takes place.

33-36. Śraddhā (faith) gave birth to Kāma (Desire);[1] Lakṣmī to Darpa (Arrogance); Dhṛti (Firmness, self-command) to Niyama (Restraint); the son of Tuṣṭi (Satisfaction) is called Santoṣa (Contentment); Lābha (Gain) was the son of Puṣṭi (nourishment); Śruta (Learning) was the son of Medhā (intelligence). (The sons of) Kriyā (Activity) were Naya (Justice), Daṇḍa (Punishment) and Samaya (Law). Both Bodha (Knowledge) and Apramāda (Absence of errors) were the sons of Buddhi (intellect). Vinaya (Discipline) was the son of Lajjā (Bashfulness); Vyavasāya (Exertion) was the son of Vapus (body); Kṣema (welfare) was the son of Śānti (Tranquility); Sukha (pleasure) was born of Siddhi (Achievement); Yaśas (fame) was the son of Kīrti (Renown). These are the sons of Dharma.

37. Harṣa (pleasure) was the son of Kāma from the goddess Rati. Thus the progeny of Dharma resulted in happiness.

38-39. Hiṁsā (Violence) bore to Adharma (Evil) the twins Nikṛti (Wickedness) and Anṛta (Falsehood). Bhaya (Fear) and Naraka (Hell) were born of Nikṛti and Anṛta. The twins Māyā (Deceit) and Vedanā (Pain) were born to them. Bhaya begot of Māyā, Mṛtyu that takes away living beings.

40. From Raurava, Vedanā gave birth to Duḥkha (pain). From Mṛtyu were born Vyādhi, Jvara, Śoka, Krodha, and Asuyā. These were characterised by Adharma and were conducive to misery.

---

1. Verses 33-40 personify virtues and vices and state their parentage. Out of these verses 38-41 describe the *Tāmasa* creation.

41. They had no wives and no sons. They were known as Nidhanas. Thus the Tāmasa creation that checked the growth of Dharma came into being.

42. Nīla-Lohita was commanded by Brahmā to create progeny; Śiva, contemplated on his wife Satī and created sons (born of his self).[1]

43. They were neither superior nor inferior to him. They were mentally created and were equal to himself. He created thousands and thousands (such children) who were wearing elephants' hides.[2] All were equal to him in form, splendour, strength and learning. Some were reddish brown. Some had quivers. Some had matted hair.

44-51. They were tawny-coloured, equipped with quivers (for arrows); they had matted hair and were deeply red (*vilohita*) in complexion. They were green-haired. They killed with eyes (by casting a glance) and held skulls (in their hands). They were multiformed, hideous in appearance, and cosmic-formed. They rode chariots and wore coats of mail. They were virtuous and put on armours. They had hundred thousand arms. They could traverse through the heaven, firmament and the earth. They had big heads, eight fangs, two tongues and three eyes. (Some of them were) eaters of rice, (some) eaters of flesh, (some were) drinkers of ghee and (some) of Soma juice; some drank fat. They were huge-bodied and blue-black-necked and of fierce fury. They were equipped with quivers, bows, swords and leather-shields. Some were seated, some were running, some were yawning and some occupying seats. Some were teaching the Vedas; some performing Japa, practising Yoga and some studying the Vedas. Some were blazing, some showering, some shining, while some were smoking. Some were awake (enlightened), some the most enlightened, some established in Brahman and some of auspicious vision. All of them were blue-necked, thousand-eyed and nocturnal wanderers. They were invisible to all beings. They were great yogins of brilliant splendour. Some were shouting and running. Rudra created

1. Verses 42-52 describe *Raudrī Sṛṣṭi* (creation by Rudra).

2. A. reads: *Kṛtti-vāsasām* 'wearing elephants' hides'. *Kṛmi-vāsasā* in the text is obviously a misprint.

thousands of excellent gods resembling himself (Rudra) within the period of Yāma (three hours).

52. On seeing them, Brahmā said, "Do not create progeny like these. Beings equal or superior to yourself, should not be created by you. Create other offsprings. Prosperity be unto you. I am staying here (by you). You create the offsprings."

53-54. (Śiva replied), "These hideous reddish blue beings created by me in thousands and thousands are definitely comparable to myself. These gods will become Rudras of great strength. They will be known on the earth and in the sky by the name Rudra.

55. These called Śatarudra in the Veda will be worthy of sacrifices and will partake of sacrificial shares with the groups of gods.

56. They will stay till the period of dissolution, being worshipped with those Devas born of the *Chandas* (Vedas) in all the Manvantara ages."

57. Thus addressed by the intelligent Lord Śiva, the Patriarch Brahmā, replied joyfully to the terrible Rudra:

58. "O Lord, let it be as it is spoken by you. Welfare unto you." When so assented by Brahmā, everything happened accordingly.

59. Thenceforth, the lord did not create offsprings. He stood with sublimated sexual virility till the final dissolution of living beings. Since he said "I am staying", he is known as "*Sthāṇu*".

60. The following ten qualities are ever present in Śaṅkara. They are: knowledge, non-attachment, glorious prosperity, penance, truth, forbearance, firmness, creativity, self-comprehension, dominance.

61. By means of his brilliance the lord surpasses all the Devas, sages and Asuras. So he is known as Mahādeva.

62. He excels Devas by his glorious prosperity; Asuras by his strength; the sages by his knowledge; and all the Bhūtas by his Yoga.

The sages said :

63. O noble sage, explain to us the nature of the Yoga,

penance, truth, virtue and the means of perfect knowledge of the great lord.

64. We wish to hear completely all the different Dharmas comprising the Yoga of Maheśvara whereby the twice-born ones will attain Mokṣa.

Vāyu narrated :

65. Five Dharmas have been proclaimed by Rudra in the Purāṇas. They are called Māheśvarya[1] (Yoga of Maheśvara) by the Rudras of unimpaired activities.

66-67. These Dharmas are practised by Ādityas, Vasus, Sādhyas, and Aśvins, so also by all Maruts, Bhṛgus, heaven-dwellers of whom Yama, Indra are prominent and by Pitṛs, Kāla, Mṛtyu and many others.

68. The groups of sages, pure as the sky in the autumn, with all their Karmans exhausted, practise these after uniting the (individual) self with the (cosmic) self.

69. Engaged in what is wholesome and pleasing to the preceptors, and desirous of achieving what is pleasing to their preceptor, they sport about like Devas, after giving up (i.e. completing their span of) human life.

70-71. Please know in the serial order as they are being narrated, the five eternal Dharmas ordained by the great lord.

These are: *Prāṇāyāma* (Restraining of the breath), *Dhyāna* (Meditation), *Pratyāhāra* (Withdrawal of the sense-organs), *Dhāraṇā* (Steady abstration of the mind) and *Smaraṇa* (recollection).

72. I shall expound, in their particular order, their characteristics, causes and principles as explained by Rudra.

73. The restraining of the speed (span ?) of vital breath is also called Prāṇāyāma. It is of three kinds : *Manda* (slow), *Madhya* (middling) and *Uttama* (excellent).

74. Controlling the vital breath is termed Prāṇāyāma. The

---

1. Yoga of Maheśvara consisting of five Dharmas is a discussion on Yoga. The five Dharmas enumerated in vv. 70-71 below are the main stages in Pātañjala Yoga, viz. Prāṇāyāma, Dhyāna, Pratyāhāra, Dhāraṇā and the only Śaiva addition is *Smaraṇa* while Patañjali's last stage *Samādhi* is droppod.

standard span of *Prāṇāyāma* is twelve *mātrās* (mātrā = time required to pronounce a short vowel).

75. The *Manda Prāṇāyāma* has one stroke of twelve moments. The *Madhya Prāṇāyāma* has two strokes and has the span of twenty-four *mātrās*.

76. The *Uttama Prāṇāyāma* has three strokes and the *mātrās* are thirty-six. This excellent *Prāṇāyāma* produces sweat, shivering, languor and exhaustion.

77. Thus the three characteristics of *Prāṇāyāma* have been explained. Now listen to their span and other characteristics briefly.

78. A lion or an elephant or any other wild animal of the forest on being captured and tamed becomes mild and quiet.

79. Similarly though the vital breath is difficult to be controlled in case of non-self-possessed persons, it can be controlled by practice of Yoga if done regularly.

80-81. Just as a (captured) lion or an elephant becomes powerless and tamed by disciplining and lapse of time, similarly by placing the mind with the Manda (slow) type of *Prāṇāyāma*, it comes under control. Similarly the wind (life-breath) lives by being placed under mind-god (?).

82. Just as the life-breath comes under control by resorting to Yoga, similarly he can take the life-breath wherever he pleases.

83. Just as a lion or elephant which comes under control provides protection to men from other animals;

84. Just as (so ?) the wind which blows in all directions, if controlled within the body by meditation, destroys all sins in the body.

85. All the blemishes of the Brāhmaṇa who is self-controlled and engaged in *Prāṇāyāma* perish. He becomes stable in the Sattva Guṇa.

86. *Prāṇāyāma* is equal to all the penances performed and performance of (all) holy rites and observances, and the fruits accorded by all sacrifices.

87. *Prāṇāyāma* is equal to the penance and observance of the holy rite of drinking a drop of water from the tip of Kuśa grass once in a month and continuing it for a hundred years.

88. One should burn off defects of the body through *Prāṇāyāma*, sins through *Dhāraṇā*, the sensual objects through *Pratyāhāra* and ungodly qualities through *Dhyāna*.

89. Therefore, a practising Yogin should always be engaged in *Prāṇāyāma*. After purifying himself of all sins, he will attain the supreme Brahman.

CHAPTER ELEVEN

Pāśupata Yoga[1]

Vāyu said:

1-2. Sages of noble souls observe with divine vision and worship the vital breath (*Prāṇa*) by establishing themselves in penance, whether it be for a great day or a day and night or a fortnight, or a month or six months or a year or a Yuga or thousands of great Yugas.

3. Henceforth, I shall explain the purpose and particularly the benefit of Prāṇāyāma as expounded by the Lord.[2]

4. Know that the objectives of *Prāṇāyāma* are four: *Śānti*, *Praśānti*, *Prasāda* and *Dīpti* (each term is explained in the following verses).

5. Actions whether terrible in form or auspicious in nature, if performed by oneself, do bear fruits here and hereafter in due course.

6. But the quelling of evils and sins committed by parents, cousins or other relatives or a mixture of both is called *Śānti*.

1. The present chapter is important as it throws a flood of light on the Pāśupata Yoga as practised before the 10th cent. A.D. when the Vā. P. came to be finally redacted.

2. Verses 3-11 describe the purpose or objectives of Prāṇāyāma, the first Dharma in this Yoga.

7. The restraint of sins arising from covetousness is called *Praśānti*. It is a form of penance that benefits both here and hereafter.

8. Sages richly endowed with knowledge and perfect wisdom can reach the world of the sun, moon, planets and stars.

9. To the enlightened, the vision of the past, present and future is possible. It is called *Dīpti*. It is also a penance.

10. *Prasāda* is that which sublimates the five sense organs, their objects, the mind and the five vital breaths.

11. Thus the fourfold *Prāṇāyama* is the first Dharma. It should be known that it gives immediate fruit and results forthwith in composure (of mind).

12. Henceforth I shall explain the characteristics of *Prāṇāyama*, the posture and the practice of Yoga precisely.

13-18. One should utter the syllable *Om* at the outset and bow to the moon or the sun. Then he should sit in the postures of *Svastika* or *Ardhapadma*. The two knees shall be level with each other or one knee should be slightly raised. He should sit comfortably with firmness. The feet shall be brought closer. The mouth should be kept closed, the eyes half-closed, the chest raised forward. With the heels he should cover the scrotum and the penis; the head should be slightly raised, the neck be straightened. He should fix his gaze on the tip of his nose, and should not look elsewhere in any direction. He should cover Tamas by Rajas which he should envelop by Sattva. Then he should remain established in Sattva and practise Yoga with pure mind. He should then hold (control) the aggregate of his sense-organs and their objects, his mind and the five vital breaths. He shall then begin *Pratyāhāra* (withdrawing in himself these together).

19-22. He who withdraws his passion and desires as the tortoise does its limbs, becomes delighted in the self. Fixed (established) in it, he sees the Self in his self. Filling the body with air and remaining pure within and without, he shall begin the withdrawal by the process of Yoga from the navel to the throat. One winking (closing and opening of eyelids) is the period called *Kalā*. The *Prāṇāyāma* shall be held for twelve *mātrās* : *Dhāraṇā* cansists of 12 *Prāṇāyāmas*. Yoga is 2 *Dhāraṇās*. A person thus practising Yoga attains prosperity. He sees the great Self shining in his own splendour.

23. All the defects (sins) of the Brāhmaṇa who is engaged in (i.e. practices) Prāṇāyāma and is self-controled are destroyed and he becomes established in Sattva.

24. Thus, with due restriction in the diet a sage (observing silence) engaged in *Prāṇāyāma*, shall conquer Yogic stages and ascend higher and higher.

25. The great ground (i.e. stage) if not subdued (overcome) may generate many defects. It may increase delusion. Hence one cannot go to a higher stage unless the initial stage is overcome.

26. Just as water is taken up by applying force through a pipe or mechanical device, so also the Yogin should drink in the wind with effort but conquering (without incurring) exhaustion.

27-28. The wind shall be retained gradually in the umbilicus, in the heart, in the chest, in the throat, in the mouth, at the tip of the nose, in the eye, between the eyebrows and in the head. The retention of the breath a little above in the great lord is called *Dhāraṇā*. Since both the *Prāṇa* and *Apāna* are obstructed, it is called *Prāṇāyāma*.

29. It is the steadying of the mind that is called *Dhāraṇā*. The withdrawal from the sense-objects is *Pratyāhāra*.

30. When all these are combined together, accomplishment of Yoga or Siddhi takes place. The achievement is the characteristic sign of Yogic meditation. Endowed with meditation, the Yogī sees his own self as the sun and the moon.

31. If Sattva is not accomplished, the vision is not possible. If the Yoga is practised in a defective place or at the wrong time, the vision is not possible.

32-34. A Yogī should not practice concentration near fire, in the forest, over a heap of dry leaves, in a place infested with low creatures (or a crowded place), in a cremation ground, in a dilapidated cowshed, at the cross-roads (where four ways meet), in a noisy or terrifying place, near a tomb (or a Buddhist or Jain shrine) or a place full of ant-hills, near a well or a river, for these are places of disturbance. Nor should he do so when overwhelmed with hunger, displeasure or excitement. He should however practice Yoga diligently and with concentration.

35. In spite of knowing decisively these faults, if a person inadvertently engages in the practice of Yoga, the three humours in his body become deranged and put up obstacles in his path.

36. He develops sluggishness, deafness, muteness, blindness, loss of memory, old age and sickness.

37. The bodily humours of a person practising Yoga ignorantly, become virulent. Hence a Yogin should practise Yoga with pure knowledge of the mind and body.

38. If he is alert and careful in the practice of Yoga, he will not suffer from any defects. I shall explain the remedy for the defects originating from the wrong performance of *Prāṇāyāma*.

39. The enlargement of the spleen (due to the derangement of the wind humour) calms down, if the patient drinks thick, sticky gruel (while it is) very hot.

40-42. The following is the treatment for constipation. After taking in curds or gruel, the vital breath will go up. Then the 'wind knot' (a lump caused by the disturbance of the wind in the body) shall be broken up and the vital breath made to circulate in its own place. Still, if there is no improvement, the *Dhāraṇā* should be practised in the head. The practitioner of Yoga shall retain the body in the Sattva alone. For dispelling (curing) constipation this remedy should be followed.

43. At the beginning of Yogic practice if there is shaking of limbs, this treatment shall be followed. This will give him relief.

44. He shall fix firmly something in the mind and hold on to it as though observing some holy rite. If there is palpitation of the heart, the vital breath shall be retained in the cardiac region and near the throat.

45. If there is obstruction to speech, the vital breath should be retained in the organ of speech; in deafness it shall be retained in the ears. In affliction by thirst, he shall (apply) oil or ghee to the tip of the tongue by means of threads. Concentrating thus on the effect of the treatment, a Yogin achieves happiness.

46-49. In the state of consumption and leprosy, the Sāttvika breath shall be centred on the parts affected. If a part is affected by Rajas, the Yoga shall be practised with respect to that particular part. If a Brāhmaṇa practising Yoga, suffers from illness the following treatment should be pursued. His head shall be beaten with a wedge of bamboo or the wedge shall be placed on his head and beaten with a wooden stick. Thus overwhelmed by fear, he will regain consciousness. Or if he has lost consciousness he can be held with hands. After regaining consciousness he should retain *Dhāraṇā* in the head. He shall eat oily substance yet in small quantity. Thus the Yogin becomes happy.

50. When he is possessed by a non-human being, he should perform the *Dhāraṇā* of heaven, earth, wind and fire.

51. Being burnt by *Prāṇāyāma* everything comes under control. Still if it enters the body, he should ward it off.

52. Then after stupefying it with one's Yogic power, the fire of *Prāṇāyāma* be burnt over its head and it is completely perished.

53. The faults of the black serpent (i.e. ignorance) should be retained in the cavity of the heart. After keeping the worlds Mahar, Jana, Tapas and Satya in the heart, he should perform *Dhāraṇā*.

54. Drinking the *fruit* of the poison, he shall retain it but make it ineffective. He should perform *Dhāraṇā* conceiving in his mind the whole earth along with the mountains all round.

55. After placing the oceans in the heart and remembering the deities therein, he should bathe with a thousand vessels.

56. With waters upto the neck, *Dhāraṇā* shall be fixed on the head. When afflicted by the back-current of poison, he shall perform *Dhāraṇā* over all the parts of his body.

57. He shall drink in the clay from the ant-hill with the cups of the withered fallen leaves of the Arka plant. This Yogic mode of treatment is well known in the world.

58. It has been explained briefly in the manner found among the topics of Yoga. You should know the suitable traits of the Brāhmaṇa before you shall reveal it.

59. If it is revealed out of delusion to an undeserving person, the instruction proves fruitless. Hence the practice of Yoga shall not be mentioned to anybody (who is undeserving).

60. Strength, health, indifference to sensual objects, lustrous complexion, good and gentle voice, auspicious smell and less quantity of urine and faeces. These are primary signs of progress in Yoga in the body.

61. If he sees himself and the earth blazing and one entering the other, he should know that the time of accomplishment of Yoga has approached.

CHAPTER TWELVE

Evil Portents and Calamities in Yoga

Sūta said :

1. Henceforth, I shall explain how the evil portents, injuries, calamities and defects appear to a person who has realized the Truth.

2. The Yogin who is afflicted by evil may be enamoured of women, season (?) and long for human enjoyments and the fruits of learning.

3. Such an afflicted person desires to perform *Māyic* (deceptive) activities such as maintenance of sacrificial fire (*Agnihotra*), oblations in fire, performance of sacrifice, wealth and heaven.

4. If a Yogin is engaged in such religious rites, he falls a victim to Nescience (*Avidyā*). One should know that one is affected and should deliberately avoid it. If he becomes permanently devoted to Brahman, he is released from the evil effects.

5. But even though one has mastered breath-control and evils (obstructing Yoga), other evils arising from (and of the nature of) Sattva, Rajas and Tamas appear.

6. Perspicuous intellect, hearing (spiritual) voices, vision of gods and circular motion of whirling flame—these are called the signs of (attainment of) Siddhi.

7. All learning, literature, arts and other lores communicable orally as well as the essence of all learning attend upon him (for service). It is the index of his superhuman power.[1]

8. He hears words worth hearing even from the distance of a hundred Yojanas. The omniscient Yogin, even though knowing the procedure of Yoga, may become like a lunatic.

9. If the great Yogī sees Yakṣas, Rākṣasas, Gandharvas and divine beings and knows them, it is the sign of disturbance (in spiritual progress).

10. One should recognize him specifically as insane if he sees Devas, Dānavas, Sages and Pitṛs all round.

11. The Yogī, being urged by his inner soul, flounders through delusion. All his knowledge is lost when his intellect is confounded.

12. Professional activities can destroy his mental balance. If his mind is overcome (due to shock of financial loss) and urged by his inner soul, his knowledge is lost.

---

1. Verses 7-15 describe the disturbances in the path of Yogic progress. 16-25 describe the powers attained by different *Dhāraṇās*. But these Siddhis are a trap (v. 26). The gist of the remaining chapter is that a Yogī should not be attached to any exalted position—even of god Brahma himself. Then only he will be absorbed in Brahman.

13. Covering himself with a white cloth or a blanket he should quickly meditate upon the great Brahman.

14. If the inelligent Yogī desires to attain his spiritual power, he should give up (overcome) his defects caused by the (spiritual) disturbances.

15. Devas, Gandharvas, Sages, Yakṣas, Serpents and Asuras, that are involved in creating obstruction, come again and again.

16. A practising Yogin should always take light food and subdue the sense-organs. Similarly he should lie and repose in the subtle body and perform *Dhāraṇā* in the head.

17. Then, if he conquers sleep after practising Yoga, *Upasargas* in the form of vital breaths are produced in the end.

18. He should then perform *Dhāraṇās* of the earth, waters, fire, ether and the mind.

19. Then the striving (aspiring) recluse should perform *Dhāraṇā* upon his intellect. He should discard instantly whenever he sees the indications of (coming) Siddhis.

20. While he performs the *Dhāraṇā* of the earth, the earth becomes subtle. While he performs the *Dhāraṇā* of waters, the waters become subtle. Cool juices, subtle and nectar-like, begin to function.

21. While he performs the *Dhāraṇā* of fire, the subtle fire begins to function. He feels himself like fire and sees its subtle nature.

22-23. He considers himself to be wind and the universal sphere as made of that*. While he performs the *Dhāraṇā* of the ether, the subtle ether begins to function. He sees its subtle sphere and its sound begins to function.

24. While he performs the *Dhāraṇā* of the mind, the subtle mind begins to function. Through his mind he penetrates the minds of living beings; when he unites his intellect with the cosmic intellect, he understands everything perfectly.

25. The Yogin who, after knowing the seven subtle elements abandons them, attains the highest point of intellect.

---

*The same line is repeated as 23b.

26. If he identifies with any of these elements characterised by *Aiśvarya* (prosperity or mastery), he becomes entangled and thereby perishes.

27. Hence he who knows the subtle elements attached to one another and abandons them deliberately, attains the supreme lord.

28. Indeed, even the noble-souled sages of divine vision are found entangled in the subtle elements. Those are regarded as defects in them.

29. Hence no attachment should be had in regard to the subtle elements. Due to *Aiśvarya* (prosperity and glory) attachment is generated, while Brahman is called non-attached.

30. After knowing the seven subtle (elements etc.) and the excellent great god of six characteristics, he attains to the supreme Brahman.

31. Those who know the procedure, declare the (following) six characteristics of the supreme Lord. These are: omniscience, contentment, beginning-less (external knowledge), independence, never-failing power and infinite power.

32. The practising Yogin with Brahman as his permanent asset, becomes liberated from the *Upasargas*. To a Yogin who has conquered the vital breath, the *Upasargas* and passion, there remains only one *Dhāraṇā* inclusive of all desires in the external body.

33. When the twice-born fixes his mind anywhere he enters it. He enters the elements and can even shake (move) the three worlds.

34. Be means of this *Dhāraṇā*, he can abandon his body and enter another. He should determine that the Sun is the mental door of the Yoga.

35. He is called *Āditya* as he is the recipient of the activities (like taking). The Yogin who, by this procedure, becomes detached and free from the affections of the subtle elements goes beyond the sphere of Prakṛti to Rudraloka.

36. The Yogin who has attained the status of Īśvara and Guṇas becomes Brahman himself. He withdraws himself from the positions of Devas.

37-38. He should eschew from the positions of Piśācas, Rākṣasas, Gandharvas, Kubera, Indra, Soma and Prajāpati by the processes specific to these.

39. He should give up the position of Brahmā by the special *Brāhma* procedure. He should take leave of the Lord. But if he is attached thereto (to Brahmā's position), he becomes (as if) intoxicated and everything (his fall) proceeds from that.

40. Being permanently absorbed in Brahman, he should give up the aforesaid positions. Thus, being non-attached to these positions, he shall acquire the power of going anywhere (omnipresence).

CHAPTER THIRTEEN

Supreme Powers of Yoga

Vāyu said :

1. Henceforth I shall explain in detail the supreme powers of Yoga whereby the Yogin can go beyond all the worlds.

2. Eight types of powers of Yogins have been cited. Listen to these as I narrate them in order.

3-4. They are *Aṇimā*, *Laghimā*, *Mahimā*, *Prāpti*, *Prākāmya*, *Īśitva*, *Vaśitva* and *Kāmāvasāyitā*. The divine faculty that fulfils all desires is of various types.

5-8. It is (of the following types) *Sāvadya*, *Niravadya* and *Sūkṣma*. *Sāvadya* is that principle which comprises the five elements. *Niravadya* consists of the five elements as well as the sense-organs, mind and the ego. *Sūkṣma* consisting of the five elements comprises the sense-organs, mind, ego and intellect. So also the powers of omnipresence and discrimination pertaining to the Self. The combination of these three types is found in the *Sūkṣma* type alone.

9. The eightfold *Aiśvarya* too functions in the subtle elements. I shall explain its features as the lord has described.

10. In all the three worlds, among all living beings, the power of *Aṇimā* (becoming minute like an atom) is uncontrolled. It is unmanifest. It is the basis of all (powers).

11. What is stated to be inaccessible to living beings in the three worlds becomes accessible to the Yogins by virtue of this first power.

12. The second power in Yoga consists of descending (hanging down) and floating. The Yogī possessed of this power can move the fastest in all beings.

13. The ability to obtain anything in the three worlds is called *Prākāmya* (irresistible will). What is *Mahimā* also falls under this category. This is the third Yoga (Yogic power).

14. These three worlds are regarded as untraversable to all beings (except Yogins) in the three worlds. It is the Yogin who can enjoy all objects to the utmost satisfaction. He is not obstructed anywhere. Happiness and misery befall all living beings in the three worlds (but the Yogin escapes).

15. The Yogin becomes the lord of everything. In the three worlds including the mobile and immobile beings the living beings become submissive to him. They can be made to serve if he so wishes, not otherwise.

16. Where there is the supernormal power called *Kāmāvasāyitva*, by the mere will (of the Yogī), the sense-organs function or do not function according to his will.

17. Objects of senses, viz. Sound, Touch, Taste, Smell and Colour as well as the mind function or do not function just in compliance of his will.

18. He is neither born nor does he die. He is neither broken nor cut. He does not get burnt nor does he lose his sense. He is neither deficient nor attached.

19. He does not get diminished or waste away. He does not perish. He is never dejected. Anywhere he can do anything or undo it.

20. He is not characterised by smell, taste, colour, touch and sound. He is casteless, but not inferior to any caste.

21. He enjoys sensual objects but is not entangled by them. On realising the greatest and the subtlest Brahman, because of his subtlety, he attains salvation.

22. Because of salvation, he becomes all-pervading. Because he pervades (everything), he is called *Puruṣa*. Due to his subtle form, the *Puruṣa* is established in Supremacy.

23. Another characteristic of his Supremacy is the all-round subtlety. After attaining the most excellent Yoga, of unobstructed supremacy, he goes to the subtlest region, the state of Liberation.

CHAPTER FOURTEEN

Pāśupata Yoga

Vāyu continued :

1. A person who has come thus (to this stage) due to knowledge, should not perform any action due to passion. After experiencing the Rājasic and Tāmasic fruits, he becomes attached there.

2. Similarly the man who has performed meritorious actions enjoys the fruits in heaven. Fallen from that region, he is born again as a human being.

3. Brahman is therefore, supreme and subtle. Brahman is said to be eternal. One should devote oneself to Brahman as Brahman is the supreme bliss.

4. There is great exertion in performing sacrifice requiring great deal of (expenditure of) wealth. Moreover he (the sacrificer) is subject to death. Salvation therefore is the greatest bliss.

5. But he who is engaged in meditation and devoted to the sacrifice of Brahman cannot be reached even in hundreds of Manvantaras.

6. He visualizes the divine *Puruṣa* that is called the *Viśva* (all-pervading). He appears in various forms. He has feet, heads and necks everywhere (pervades the Universe). He is the Lord and the creator of the Universe. He has the cosmic fragrance, is garlanded cosmically and robed in cosmic apparel. He is the Ruler of all.

7. By means of their sense-organs people endeavour to visualize him who is the winged noble soul, the most excellent and the greatest Soul. But it is not with the eyes but with the mental concentration called Yoga that they can see the omniscient, ancient governor (Teacher) who is subtler than the subtlest, greater than the greatest, the Puruṣa of golden complexion, devoid of sense-organs.

8. They always see Puruṣa who is golden in colour, endowed with or without exterior symbols, devoid of attributes, conscious, eternal, all-pervading and pure. By means of Yoga, they see the steady light.

9. Manifested thereby He shines in his own refulgence. He is devoid of heads, feet, belly, sides and tongue, but he, though beyond the ken of senses, though still extremely subtle and alone, can see without eyes and hear without ears.

10. There is nothing that is not known to him; yet he has no intellect. He knows all, yet he is not known to the Vedas. They call him the foremost or the first Puruṣa, the great, the sentient, all-pervading and very subtle.

11. All sages call that Prakṛti, which gives birth to living beings in this world. Those who are engaged in Yoga, can visualize it mentally.

12-13. Those who are engaged in Yogic meditation on the eternal Puruṣa who is endowed with hands and feet, eyes, heads and faces (mouths), ears on all sides and who stays after permeating everything in the world (who is both immanent and transcendent) and who governs everything, does not become deluded.

14. One does not get deluded after meditating on the supreme Brahman, the Soul of all living beings, the imperishable, noble, supreme soul, the soul of all.

15-16. Just as the (presence of the) wind is to be admitted as evident through its movement in clouds, so is that of the Ātman that moves through the bodies of all. Since the Soul abides in the body, it is named Puruṣa. When the merit is exhausted due to specific Karmans he is born and re-born in the womb by the mixture of semen and blood as a result of the mixture of male and female flesh.[1]

17. Then, at the time of conception, *Kalana*, the embryo at its first stage (in the form of a drop) is formed. In due course the *Kalana* develops into bubbles.

18-19. Just as a lump of clay pressed by the wind in the potter's wheel and shaped by the hands (of the potter) attains multifarious shapes, so also the foetus united with bones and impelled by the wind becomes a human body with proper forms, features and mind.

20. The wind assembles them together. From the wind water is generated. From the water the vital breath is formed and through the vital breath the semen gets developed.

21. Thirty-three parts of blood (female contribution) and fourteen parts of the semen mixing together form only half a *Pala* (two *karśas*) and is deposited in the womb.

22. The child in the womb is covered by the five vital breaths. From the father's body he inherits his forms and features.

23. The food of the mother, drunk or licked, enters through the umbilical cord and sustains the foetus in the womb.

24. For nine months the child suffers in the body with his neck encircled by the inner vessels of its mother. His limbs are covered in disorder. He remains there for nine months. He then comes out through the vaginal passage with the head downwards.

25. Then (in his life on the earth) he commits some sinful actions and as a result he goes to the hell (after death), *Asipatravana* or *Śālmalī* where he is cut or pierced.[2]

---

1. Verses 16-25 give Purāṇic (Mediaeval) ideas on Embryology.
2. Verses 25-31 describe the tortures in hell.

26. In the hell, he is rebuked and threatened. He is forced to drink blood. These are the terrible tortures he has to undergo in Kumbhīpāka. They are very unbearable.

27. Just as waters though parted regain their normal form, so also the hellish beings though cut and broken in torturing hells regain their original form.

28. Thus the living beings become agitated and tortured through their own sins. If there is anything left over, they take other births.

29. Man must go alone to the abode of death. He must bear the punishments alone. Hence one should perform pious deeds.

30. None follows him who proceeds along the path of death. But the actions performed by him pursue him.

31. The hellish beings always cry in the abode of Yama when they are pierced or when tortures are inflicted on their bodies. Their bodies being tortured get withered up and suffer extreme pain caused by evil harassments.

32. The sin may forcibly remove everything desirable resorted to by him mentally, verbally or physically. Hence one should perform meritorious deeds.

33. In accordance with the sinful actions committed by him previously, the embodied being undergoes six types of worldly transmigrations of *Tāmasa* nature.[1]

34-35. They are : Birth as human beings; as domestic animals (*Paśu*) ; from the state of *Paśu* (he becomes) a wild animal; from that stage (he goes to) the birds; from 'bird-hood' to reptiles; from reptilehood he certainly becomes an immobile. He who has attained the immobile state evolves into a human being. He thus rotates like one propelled by the potter's wheel.

36. Thus in this migration six types of birth beginning with that as man and ending with that as plant are known as Tāmasa. He undergoes many changes there.

---

1. The life in hell and evolution through six stages upto that of man show the acceptance of the principle of redemption. No sinner is condemned to eternal hell.

37. The transmigrations beginning with Brahmā and ending with *Piśāca* are known as Sāttvika. Only in the celestial regions the embodied beings experience these.

38-39. In the world of Brahmā, there is only *Sattva*; in the world of immobile beings there is only *Tamas*. In between the two there is *Rajas*, that supports the fourteen lokas. How can he think of the great Brahman when he is distressed by pain and his vitals are being torn. It is due to the impressions of the previous pious actions that he attains human birth. Hence one should devote oneself entirely to Brahman.

CHAPTER FIFTEEN

Pāśupata Yoga (continued)

Vayū said :

1. After knowing the fourteen types of transmigrations a person overpowered by the fear of *Saṁsāra* (transmigration from birth to birth) should begin suitable action.

2. Then, being whirled round by the wheel of *Saṁsāra* he remembers (about Yoga). Thenceforth, he is always engaged in meditation in communion with the Supreme. He should start the *Yogic* practice in such a way as he would be able to visualize the Soul.

3. He is the first, the supreme light, the excellent bridge. He has grown up in living beings but this difference is not eternal.

4. Hence he who knows the procedure should worship this bridge, this Ātman, this fire with its face in every direction, abiding in the heart of living beings.

5. After sipping water once only at the beginning, with purity and with the mind concentrated on Him, he should offer

eight oblations in a serial order to the Fire that abides in the heart and should worship him silently.

6-7. The five *Āhutis* shall be offered with the following five *mantras* : *Prāṇāya Svāhā, Apānāya Svāhā, Samānāya Svāhā Udānāya Svāhā* and *Vyānāya Svāhā*. The other (three *Āhutis*) shall be offered simply with '*Svāhā*'. Then he should take food as he pleases. He should drink water once, perform *Ācamana* thrice and touch the heart.

8. He should then strengthen and satisfy himself by repeating the following mantra—"Om, Thou art the knot of the *Prāṇas*. Tou art the *Ātman*. Rudra indeed is the *Ātman*. That Rudra, the destroyer of the subjects. He is the Prāṇas of the *Ātman*.

9. You are the eldest among Devas. You are fierce, the skilful bull. You are the destroyer of death. Let this *Havis* oblation offered be propitious to us".

10-11. Saying thus he shall touch the heart, the right toe and the navel with the right hand. Touching water once again, he shall touch the chest, eyes, nose, ears, heart and the head. The *Prāṇa* and *Apāna* both are declared as two *Ātmans*.

12. Of these *Prāṇa* is the inner and *Apāna* is the external *Ātman*. *Anna* (food) is Prāṇa, and Apāna is both life and death.

13. *Anna* (food) should be known as Brahman. It is the source of origin of the people. The living beings are born through *Anna* (food). The maintenance is sought through *Anna* (food). The living beings increase through *Anna*. Hence it is called *Anna*.

14. Devas and Dānavas eat the food oblated in the (sacrificial) fire. Gandharvas, Yakṣas, Rākṣasas and Piśācas too partake of it.

CHAPTER SIXTEEN

Purity and Conduct of Life[1]

Vāyu said :

1. Henceforth I shall explain the characteristics of purity and conduct of life, the observance of which purifies the *Ātman* and leads a person to heaven after death.

2. Seeking of water for purity is the excellent state of sages. He who is not negligent in regard to these comes to no trouble.

3. Insult and honour, they say, constitute (what is called) poison and nectar. Insult is poison; honour is nectar.

4. The sage who does not err in regard to these comes to no trouble. He should remain with the preceptor for a year engaged in what is pleasing and beneficial to him.

5. He should not be negligent in the observance of vows, major (*Yamas*) or minor (*Niyamas*). After attaining supreme knowledge, he should seek permission from his preceptor and move about the earth consistently with Dharma.

6. This is the holy dictate of *Dharma*, viz. one should go along the path purified by (i.e. observed carefully by) the eyes; one should drink water filtered with a cloth; and one should utter words purified by truth i.e. state the truth only.[2]

7. It is the considered opinion that the knower of Yoga should never accept hospitality in *Śrāddhas* and *Yajñas* and that it is only thus that a Yogin becomes non-violent.

8-9. An intelligent Yogin should go out (for alms) when the fires (in the kitchen) have become smokeless[3] and have been

---

1. This chapter prescribes the rules of conduct to be followed by Pāśupata yogins. The term '*Śaucācāra*' corresponds to '*Sadācara*' in Dharma Śāstra. These are usages practised by one's ancestors (Manu) or by *Śiṣṭas* under the belief that they are part of Dharma (Kumārila). Some of the rules (as noted below) are adopted from those prescribed for saṁnyāsins. Some of the verses are adapted from Smṛtis.

2. An echo of Manu VI. 46. Cf. also Śaṅkhasmṛti. VII.7, Viṣṇu Dh. S. 96. 14-17 and KP. II. 28. 19.

3. Cf. Manu VI. 56, Śaṅkha. VII. 2.

extinguished and the people have practically taken their meals. He should not constantly beg in the same houses lest he should get insulted or people offended. It is thus without violating the code of conduct of the good, that he should carefully go out for alms.

10. First of all, he should go to the houses of only those householders who maintain good conduct. Such begging for alms is said to be an excellent means of livelihood advised to the Yogin.

11. Secondly, he should go to the abodes of modest householders who are faithful, self-controlled, learned and noble.

12. Last of all he should go to the residence of non-defiled and unfallen people. Begging for alms in the abodes of lower caste is considered mean.

13. The alms received may be gruel, butter-milk, milk, barley-water, cooked or uncooked fruits, roots, oil-cake or anything offered in accordance with the householder's ability.

14. Thus the foodstuffs conducive to the increase in Siddhis of Yogins have been proclaimed by me. Among these the most excellent is that which is received by way of alms.

15. He who begs alms in a righteous manner, is better than the person who drinks a drop of water from the tip of the *Kuśa* grass once in a month.

16. The observance of the *Cāndrāyaṇa*[1] vow is the most excellent for the Yogin. He should perform it once, twice, thrice, four times successively or as many times as he can.

17-18. Non-stealing, celibacy, non-covetousness and renunciation are the holy rites of recluses (*Bhikṣus*). The restraints (*Niyamas*) are non-violence, truthfulness; non-furiousness, ser-

1. Cāndrāyaṇa is an expiation (*Prāyaścitta*) for all lapses for which no specific penance is prescribed. It is also for accruing merits. It is so called as the intake of morsels of food increases or decreases in imitation of the course of the phases of the moon. Thus if he eats one morsel on the 1st Tithi, he is to increase one more morsel the next day eating 15 morsels on the Full Moon day. And thus he is to decrease by one morsel everyday and observe fast on the New Moon day.

vice to the preceptor, purity of body, light diet and daily study of the Vedas.

19-20. Just as an elephant is caught in the forest, is then controlled, so man with the seeds (of Karmas) as his source of birth, body as *guṇas*, is bound by Karmas. Soon he is trapped and is disciplined like a (wild) elephant. In this way, with the seeds of his Karmas having been burnt by the fire of pure knowledge, he becomes free from bondage and quiescent. He is called the liberated (soul).

21. By Vedas, by means of eulogies, all rites in a sacrifice (are performed). *Japa* is regarded more important than knowledge. Meditation free from association with attachment is better than *Jñāna*. When that is achieved, the eternal (Mokṣa) is obtained.

22. The Yogin possesses these attributes: control of sense-organs, quiescence, truthfulness, sinlessness, silence, straightforwardness towards all living beings, knowledge of things beyond the scope of sense-organs, uprightness etc. Those purified by means of knowledge have declared thus.

23. Composed in mind, absorbed in Brahma (or the Veda), un-erring and alert, pure, delighting in the *Ātman*, with senses controlled—such pure, unsullied, highly intelligent, praiseworthy (un-censurable) and pure (yogins) achieve (master) this Yoga.

CHAPTER SEVENTEEN

Attainment of the Ultimate State of Life

Vāyu said :

1-2. After passing the three (earlier) stages and reaching the ultimate (*Sannyāsa*) stage of life,[1] he shall attain the Su-

1. *Paramāśrama* is the last *āśrama*, viz. Sannyāsa. The present chapter states the rules to be followed by a Sannyāsin. We find here the echoes of Smṛtis like Manu. Cf. for example the duty of wandering (cf. Manu VI. 52), the rules of conduct (cf. Manu VI. 92). Also cf. *supra* 8. 176-178,

preme knowledge by the end of a year. Taking leave of the preceptor, he should wander over the earth. He should apply in practice that excellent essential knowledge that leads to the attainment of the knowable.

3. He who wanders remaining satisfied with the discrimination between knowledge and the knowable, will never attain the knowable even if he were to live for a thousand Kalpas.

4. Giving up contacts and attachment, subduing one's wrathfulness, subsisting on light food, he, with his sense-organs controlled, should close down all the portals of his intellect and should thus fix his mind in meditation.

5. He should always practise Yoga in uninhabited places, caves, forests or on the banks (sands) of rivers.[1]

6. He who has control over his speech, action and mind and represents each by a long staff is declared as *Tridaṇḍin*.[2]

7. Thus established, he who loves meditation, has subdued his sense-organs, gives up both auspicious and inauspicious acts. Even after abandoning this (physical) body, he is neither born nor dead from the standpoint of scriptures.

CHAPTER EIGHTEEN

Procedure of Expiation for Recluses (Saṁnyāsins)

Vāyu said :

1. Henceforth I shall explain decisively the expiations prescribed for ascetics for their (evil) actions done by them un-

---

1. *Vaikhānasa Sūtra* VIII. 9 prescribes this for a *Paramahaṁsa*. Buddhist and Jaina mendicants have similar instructions.

2. Cf.

Vāg-daṇḍo 'tha mano-daṇḍaḥ kāyadaṇḍas tathaiva ca/
yasyaite nihitā buddhau tridaṇḍīti sa ucyate//

—Manu XII. 10 also Dakṣa VII. 30.

intentionally. But people who know the subtle Dharma say that there are expiations for actions done out of lust or deliberately as well.

2. Sin is proclaimed as threefold, according as it is born of (results from) speech, mind and body both by day or night continuously. By this the whole world is bound.

3. The great Śruti declares that no man can stay without activities. In life every moment has to be spent in activity[1] for its sustenance.

4. One shall be self-possessed and un-erring. Yoga is the greatest strength. There is nothing seen to be greater than Yoga for men here. Hence, the wise who are endowed with piety praise Yoga.

5. Intelligent and resolute men transcending ignorance through knowledge, attain excellent *Aiśvarya*. Having discriminated between the greater and the lesser, they attain the highest region.

6. Expiation is prescribed for the violation of any major or minor vow ordained for the mendicant.

7. If he approaches a woman cut of lust, the expiation prescribed is that he shall perform the rite of *Sāntapana*[2] along with Prāṇāyāma.

8. He shall follow the prescribed courses (of conduct) at the end of that expiation with mental purity. He should return to the hermitage and move about carefully as a mendicant. The wise people opine that words piercing the heart[3] do not kill (?)

9. However this should not be indulged in. For this results in cruelty.

The Śruti says that there is no evil action (lasting) after a full day (i.e. day and night) (?)

1. Cf. BG III. 5

2. *Sāntapana* is generally prescribed for pollution or falling off from caste (*Jāti-bhraṁśa-kara*). It lasts for two days. One has to take *Pañca-gavya* on the first day and observe fast on the second day.

3. *marmayukta* is emended as *narmayukta* 'jocular remark' in A. The emendation deserves consideration.

10. Violence is the greatest of evil deeds created by Devas and sages. What is called wealth is the veritable external life-breath of a man. He who deprives any man of his wealth verily takes away his vital breath (life).

11-12. By committing theft a wicked person shatters off his good conduct. He falls off from his vow. After repenting for this sin, he should perform *Cāndrāyaṇa* vow for a year in accordance with the injunctions of the scriptures, says the Śruti. At the end of a year his sin will practically diminish. If he repents again he should vigilantly observe his vow of medicancy.

13. Non-violence towards all living beings, mentally, verbally and physically (shall be observed). If a mendicant injures animals or deer even unintentionally, he should perform the expiatory vow of *Kṛcchra*, *Atikṛcchra* or *Cāndrāyaṇa*.[1]

14. If due to the weakness of his organ, a recluse emits semen on seeing a woman, he should perform sixteen *Prāṇāyāmas*.

15. In the case of a Brahmāṇa who emits semen during day the observance of fast for three nights and performance of a hundred *Prāṇāyamas* are prescribed for its expiation.

16. If he has nocturnal emission of semen, he should take bath and perform twelve *Dhāraṇās*. He becomes pure in soul and free from sin by performing the *Prāṇāyāma*.

17. Daily eating at the same house, use of honey, flesh and salt as well as feasting at *Śrāddha* are forbidden for the ascetics.

18. For the violation of each of these expiatory rite consisting of *Prājāpatya* or *Kṛcchra* is prescribed. Then alone he becomes free from the sin.

---

1. *Kṛcchra* or *Prājāpatya* is a general term for several kinds of expiations. It has about 12 varieties (For details vide Kane, *HD* IV, pp. 120, 132-33).

Atikṛcchra is for purification of all sins except *Mahā-pātakas* (great sins) (Gautama 26. 22). The procedure of observing it differs with Manu XI. 213 and Yājñavalkya III. 319, the former restricting the intake of one morsel of food while the latter allowing as much food as will fill his hand (vide Kane, *HD* IV, p. 130).

19. If there is any other violation, mental, physical or verbal, he should consult expert men (for deciding suitable expiation) and act according to their injunctions.

20. A Yogin of pure intellect, looking upon a clod of earth and lump of gold alike, behaving with purity of mind towards all livings, attains the region of saintly people which is unshakable, eternal and imperishable. After reaching there, he is not born again (is liberated from *Saṁsāra*).

CHAPTER NINETEEN

Evil Omens Foreboding Death[1]

Vāyu said :

1. Henceforth I shall explain the evil omens. Know that by seeing them one can foresee one's death.

2. He who cannot see the Arundhatī star, the Pole star, the shadow of the moon and the *Mahāpatha* does not survive a year thereafter.

3. He who sees the sun bereft of rays and the fire with rays (radiating from it) will not survive the eleventh month.

4. He who vomits urine, cow-dung, gold or silver either while awake or in dream, will not survive ten months.

5. He whose feet crack either in front or at the back, or become dusty or marshy, lives only for seven months.

6. If a crow, a dove, a vulture or any other bird of prey settles on his head, he does not survive six months.

---

1. Belief in evil portents was very common in ancient India. We have a number of such references in the Mbh. (e.g. *Sabhā* 80. 28-31, *Śalya* 192. 14-21), *Rāmāyaṇa* (e. g. *Araṇya* 23. 1-7, 10-25), *Bd. P., Lalitā M.* 21. 5-20. Jaina *Ṭhāṇaṅga Sutta* 405. 8, Dharasena's *Joṇipāhuḍa* testify to the Jain belief in them. Durgadeva's *Riṭṭha-Samuccaya* of A.D. 1032 (Ed. A. S. Gopani, Singhi Jain Series 1945) shows many beliefs common to Brahmanical Purāṇas. Even today Indian masses believe in such portents.

7. He who is obstructed by rows of crows or by a dust storm, lives only for four or five months.

8. He who sees lightning without clouds, in the southern direction, or water or the rainbow (without the existence of clouds) lives only for two or three months.

9. He who does not see his reflection either in water or in a mirror or who sees his reflection without the head does not survive a month.

10. If the body smells like a corpse or like burning fat, death is imminent. He lives only for a fortnight.

11. If a biting wind seems to pierce the vulnerable points of one's body or if no sensation is experienced after touching water, death is imminent for him.

12. If he dreams that he is singing and proceeding to the south on a chariot to which bears and monkeys are yoked, it shall be known as a sign of imminent death.

13. If he dreams that he is being led to southern direction by a dark singing woman wearing black garment, he does not survive long.

14. If he dreams that he wears black rags or that his ear is broken, it shall be known as a sign of imminent death.

15. If he dreams that he is immersed in a marshy sea upto the head, he does not survive long after seeing the dream.

16. He who sees (in dream) ashes, burning coals, hair, dry river and serpents will not survive ten nights.

17. If he dreams that he is being beaten by hideous dark skinned men with weapons and stones in their hands, he dies soon.

18. If a howling vixen rushes directly at him early in the morning at sunrise, his death is imminent.

19. If he feels acute pain in the chest and morbid senstitiveness in the teeth immediately after taking bath, his death is immiment.

20. If he gasps for breath during night or day and is unable to discern the smell of a oil lamp, know that his death is imminent.

21. If he were to see the rain-bow at night and the cluster

of stars during the day, and if he is unable to see his reflection in others' eyes, he does not live long.

22. He, one of whose eyes begins to water, whose ears are dislodged from their places and whose nose becomes crooked (and curved) should be known as approaching death.

23. Death is imminent to him whose tongue is black and rough and whose face appears muddy and whose cheeks are ruddy and flattened.

24. A man who (in dream) goes to the southern direction with hair dishevelled, laughing, singing and dancing, meets with the imminent end of life.

25. He who perspires frequently, the sweat drops being like white mustard seeds, dies very soon.

26. He who in dream, goes to the south in a chariot to which camels or donkeys are yoked does not live long.[1]

27. These are two extermely ill omens, viz. he does not hear loud noise with his ears and does not see bright light with his eyes.

28. If he sees in dream that he has fallen in a ditch and that there is no door to escape through and that he is unable to stand up from the ditch, that marks the end of his life.

29. One is definitely in difficult situation if the eye moves upward without steadiness, becomes red and begins to whirl round, if the mouth becomes hot, if the umbilicus is porous and the urine is very hot.

30. If a man is directly hit during the day or night and sees the attacking man (in dream), the man so hit does not live long.

31. If a man dreams that he is entering fire but does not remember the details after waking up, that marks the end of his life.

32. Death is imminent to the man who sees his white covering cloth as red or black in dream.

33-35. A wise man should eschew fear[2] and dejection when death approaches him as indicated by the ill omens. He

1. Cf. v. 12 above.
2. Verses 33-40 advise how one should face death in a Yogic way.

should then start from his house and walk to the east or to the north. With a pure mind he should sit in a level spot isolated and devoid of crowds. He should perform *Ācamana* and sit facing north or east. He should sit in the *Svastika* posture. After bowing down to Lord Śiva he should keep his body, head and neck straight.

36. His posture is comparable to a lamp in a windless place where it is steady (not flickering)[1]. He should practise Yoga in a spot sloping to the east or north.

37. He shall perform *Dhāraṇā* in the vital breath, eyes, skin, ears, mind, intellect and chest. He shall take particular delight in keeping *Dhāraṇā* in the vital breath.

38. After realizing the advent of death and the groups (of ill omens) he shall perform Yoga-Dhāraṇās in the parts of the bodies twelve times.

39. He shall perform hundred or hundred and eight *Dhāraṇās* on the head. Without Dhāraṇās in the Yoga, the breath does not function properly (goes anywhere).

40. Then with a purity of mind, he should fill the body with *Oṁkāra*. Thus full of *Oṁkāra*, he does not perish. He becomes imperishable.

CHAPTER TWENTY

The Characteristics of Attainment of Oṁkāra

Vāyu said :

1. Henceforth, I shall explain the characteristics of *Oṁkāra* and the ways of its attainment. It consists of three *Mātrās* inclusive of vowels and a consonant.

2. The first Mātrā is *Vaidyuti*; the second is *Tāmasī* The third *Nirguṇī*, which follows the syllable (?)

---

1. Cf. yathā dipo nivātastho neṅgate sopamā smṛtā/
BG. VI. 19.

3. The *Mātrā* born of the Gāndhāra note, shall be known as Gandharvī. When employed on the head, its touch is like the touch of an ant.

4. The *Oṁkara* so directed ceases to blow (sound) in the head. The Yogin so full of *Oṁkāra* becomes imperishable in the imperishable Being.

5. The *Oṁkāra* is the bow. The *Ātman* is the arrow. Brahman is its target. It should be hit unerringly. Like the arrow, the *Ātman* shall be wholly absorbed in Brahman.[1]

6. The single-syllabled *Om* is the Brahman hidden in the cavity of the heart. This *Om* is the set of the three Vedas, three worlds, three fires, three steps of Viṣṇu and the Ṛk, Sāman and Yajur *mantras*.

7. It should be known that in fact, it consists of four *Mātrās*. The Yogin who is in communion with these will attain the *sālokya* form of salvation.

8. The letter '*A*' should be known as the phoneme (?) The letter '*U*' is *svarita* (the circumflexed note between the high and the low). The letter '*M*' is the prolated syallable. The three *Mātrās* thus termed shall be known.

9. The letter '*A*' is Bhūrloka. The letter '*U*' is Bhuvarloka. The letter '*M*' with its consonant part is Svarloka.

10. The *Oṁkāra* is a set of three worlds. Its head is the heaven. It is the entire universe. It is the region of Brahmā.

11. The region of the *Mātrās* is Rudraloka but '*A*' alone is the region of Śiva. He (the Yogin) worships that region by specific meditation.

12. Hence the devotee shall always take delight in meditation. He should worship the *Mātrā-less* syllable strenuously if he aspires for eternal region.

13. The first *Mātrā* is the short vowel; the second is long and the third is indicated as *pluta* (prolated).

14. These *Mātrās* shall be known precisely and in due order. They shall be retained as far as possible.

15. He who concentrates the sense-organs, mind and in-

---

1. Cf. *Muṇḍaka Up*. 2. 2. 4.

tellect in the *Ātman*, even if he bears only half a *Mātrā*, will attain the fruit.

16. He who worships with *Aśvamedha* every month for a hundred years, will not attain the benefit which accrues through a single *Mātrā*.

17. One can attain through a *Mātrā* that benefit which a man attains by drinking a drop of water from the tip of *Kuśa* grass, once in a month, for full hundred years.

18. One can attain through a *Mātrā* that benefit which accrues from *Iṣṭāpūrta*, from sacrifice or from truthful utterances or refraining from meat-diet.

19. One can obtain through one *Mātrā* the fruit which accrues to the warriors fighting for their master without turning away from the battlefield.

20. What one fully attains through one *Mātrā* cannot be attained through austere penance or through (performance of) sacrifices with plenty of gifts.

21. The half *Mātrā* there, which is known as prolated, shall be pursued by the Yogins who are householders.

22. This is specially the *Mātra* characterised by *Aiśvaryas* (supernormal powers). Thereby, the Yogins gain the eightfold super-power like *Aṇimā*. Hence he shall practise the Yoga thereof.

23. A Yogin who is thus in communion (with the soul) becomes pure. Having suppressed the sense-organs and conquered them, he can realize the Ātman and one who realizes his soul, gets everything (i.e. becomes omniscient).

24. The intelligent Yogin who engages (himself) in meditation, attains the knowledge of the Ṛgveda, Yajurveda, Sāmaveda and the Upaniṣadic lore through (his) Yogic knowledge.

25. Thus with all his elements (that constitute his body) dissolved, he becomes elementless. He then transmigrates to the eternal region whence there is no return.

26. After seeing it with divine sight he meditates on the four-armed, four-faced Prakṛti designated as Viśvarūpā (one manifested as the universe).

27. One goat (i.e. unborn individual soul) takes pleasure and sleeps (enjoys) with this famale goat (i.e. the unborn Prakṛti) which is beautiful, and red, white, black in complexion (i.e. consisting of the *Rajas*, *Sattva* and *Tamas guṇas*) and procreates creatures in great numbers. But the other goat (liberated soul) abandons her after enjoying her.

27 (A). The wise attain immortality after realising the reality about the primordial Prakṛti of eight syllables, of sixteen hands and feet, of four faces, of three tufts, of a single horn, who is primordial, unborn and the creator of the universe after its own form. The Brāhmaṇas who know (realize) the *Oṁkāra* are never born again (i.e. get liberated from *Saṁsāra*).

28-29. He who understands properly and again meditates upon the imperishable supreme Brahman called *Oṁkāra* leaves off the cycle of worldly existence. He becomes liberated from all ties and bondages. Undoubtedly he attains the auspicious eternal region devoid of attributes. Thus I have described to you the way for the attainment and realization of *Oṁkāra*.

30. [Prose portion] Obeisance to the lord of the worlds who has grasped the idea and knowledge of the Kalpas, and whose worship is beneficial to you. Obeisance to the attributeless, eternal Brahman to whom the lord of Yogins is devoted. One should worship him who is extremely pure and unaffected like the lotus-leaf untouched by water. *Oṁkāra* is the holiest of holy things. Consisting of syllables short and prolated, it is holy and full of sanctifying things. One shall worship *Oṁkāra* devoid of sound, touch, colour, taste and smell. Obeisance to the lord of Prakṛti, obeisance to Yogīśvara by whom has been made the fierce firmament, the earth firm and the heaven extended, by whom Elysium has been created and Ether made—the two being the abode of Devas. He has universe as (his) form. He is incomparable with *Prāṇa* and *Apāna*. He is a sacrifice and constitutes all things. The sacrifice is Veda. Veda is obeisance. Obeisance is Rudra. Hail to Rudra. Obeisance to the lord of the chiefs of Yogins. This prayer for success should be performed in the evening, morning and midday. Rudra bestows the fruits of all desires.

30. [Verse] Just as a ripe fruit is separated from the stalk

when wind blows at it, so also sin in quelled by the obeisance to Rudra.

31. The obeisance to Rudra is decisively the bestower of the fruits of all pious rites, but so is not the case with the obeisance to other Deves. He who bows to other Devas does not attain the same benefit.

32. Hence a Yogin should worship the supreme lord after taking bath thrice a day. Brahman is extensive. Brahman is tenfold extensive.

33. The lord created everything at the opportune time with Oṁkāra all round. Viṣṇu was also created by him as well as obeisance.

34. Obeisance as well as Oṁkāra eulogise the lord. *Yajña* eulogises *Oṁkāra*; obeisance eulogises *Yajña*. Rudra eulogises prayer. Hence Rudra's region is auspicious.

35. These are the secrets of the ascetics in due order. He who understands meditation attains the highest region.

CHAPTER TWENTYONE

Review of Kalpas

Sūta said :

1. Among the sages refulgent like fire, who resided in the Naimiṣa forest, there was an intelligent sage, well versed in the Vedas and was called Sāvarṇi.

2. He was very eloquent. Standing ahead of them with humility he approached Vāyu the highly majestic god who frequented that place to render favour to the *Sattra*-worshippers, and asked him.

Sāvarṇi requested :

3. O all-pervading Lord! We wish to hear from you who are the observer of everything, the legends of the Purāṇa, which are on a par with the Vedas.

4. How did lord Brahmā beget from his forehead, Lord Rudra of such a splendour, as his son ?

5. How was lord Brahmā born of a lotus? How did his son Śarva obtain the status of a Rudra?

6-7. How is it that Viṣṇu cherishes such unparalleled love towards Rudra ? There is no doubt that gods always sing. "All gods as well as *gaṇas* consist (are of the form) of Viṣṇu. There is no other goal higher that attainment of Viṣṇu". How is it that such (a great god like) Viṣṇu always pays obeisance to Bhava (Śiva) ?

Sūta said :

8. Thus addressed, Vāyu spoke to Sāvarṇi, "O Sage, an excellent question has been aptly asked by you.

9-10. Listen (attentively) as I explain in detail, how it was that Rudra became the son of Brahmā, how Brahmā was born of the lotus, how Śaṅkara became Rudra, how there is such an intense love between Viṣṇu and Rudra and why Viṣṇu always bows to Śiva. I shall explain it in due order.

11. O excellent Brāhmaṇa, after the dissolution of the last Manvantara, the seventh Kalpa called Padma came to an end. The current Kalpa is Vārāha. I shall narrate it in detail."

Sāvarṇi enquired :

12. After what period of time, does the Kalpa begin ? What is the duration of a Kalpa? Please explain to me; I am curious to know.

Vāyu replied :

13. I shall mention in due order the duration of the periods of the seven Manvantaras. Understand as I explain it briefly.

14. Two thousand eight hundred and sixtytwo crores and seventy *Niyutas* (millions) of years constitute a Kalpa. While calculating the years of half a Kalpa, this was spoken (before).

15. The multiplier and the divison too have been mentioned before. The surplus of years would be one hundred and seventyeight crores, two hundred thousand, and nine crores.

16. Upto Vaivasvata Manvantara, this should be known as the period of Kalpa according to human calculation. Half a Kalpa is multiplied by two.

17. This alone is the time limit for the seven future Kalpas. It shall be known as the view of the Lord himself.

18. The time limit is fifty-eight million and eight thousand. Another eighty-four shall be included in this.

19. The seven sages, Devas with Indra as their leader and Manu—The surplus years of this time limit should be known accordingly.

20. Thus their Manvantara-ending with human beings has been narrated. The Devas ending with Praṇava (Viṣṇu), Sādhyas, Deva-gaṇas and Viśvedevas live for the whole of the Kalpa.

21. The Kalpa that is current is called Vārāha. It consists (of the rule) of fourteen Manus beginning with Svāyaṁbhuva.

The sages said :

22. Why is the Vārāha Kalpa proclaimed by that name ? What is the reason that the Lord is glorified as *Varāha* (Boar).

23. Who is lord Varāha ? What is his origin ? What is his nature ? Why was he born ? We wish to know this.

Vāyu replied :

24-25. I shall explain all this according as I have seen and heard, (as to) how Varāha was born and what the object was (of his incarnation), how this Kalpa came to be called Vārāha, what Kalpa is and what is the conception (called Kalpa), what is the transitional period between two Kalpas.

26-27a. Bhava is proclaimed as the first Kalpa in the beginning of the world[1]. It should be known that Lord Ānanda

---

1. Verses 26-34 give the serial order of Kalpas as follows: Bhava, Bhuva, Tapas, Bhava (?), Raṁbha, Ṛtu, Kratu, Vahni, Havyavāhana, Sāvitra, Bhuva(?), Uśika, Kuśika, Gandharva, Ṛṣabha, Ṣaḍja, Mārjālīya, Madhyama, Vairājaka, Niṣāda, Pañcama, Meghavāhana, Cintaka, Ākūti, Vijñāti, Manas,

himself abides here at present (then). This was the celestial seat of Brahmā obtained (by him). It was of divine origin.

27b-34. The second Kalpa was Bhuva; the third one was called Tapas. Bhava (?) should be known as the fourth (Kalpa); the fifth was Rambha; the sixth Kalpa was Ṛtu; the seventh is remembered as Kratu; the eighth was Vahni; the ninth was Havya-vāhana; Sāvitra was the tenth Kalpa. The eleventh (Kalpa) was called Bhuva (?); the twelfth was Uśika; the thirteenth was Kuśika. The fourteenth was Gandharva when Gāndhāra as a musical note of the gamut came into existence and Gandharvas were born.[1] O Brāhmaṇas, Ṛṣabha should be known as the fifteenth Kalpa when world-enchanting note of the gamut Ṛṣabha was born. The world-fascinating (musical) note *Ṣaḍja* was the sixteenth Kalpa when six (types of men? or) sages were born. The six seasons viz.: *Śiśira* (the Winter), *Vasanta* (the Spring), the Summer, the Rainy-season, the Autumn (*Śarad*) and the *Hemanta* (the cold season in Mārgaśirṣa and Pauśa months) are the mental sons of god Brahmā. These sons born of the note *Ṣaḍja* were born in the sixteenth Kalpa. As the Lord Maheśvara was born along with those six, the musical note *Ṣaḍja* was born of him. The musical note *Ṣaḍja* is (deep and loud) like the (sound of the) ocean.

35. The seventeenth Kalpa is known as Mārjālīya[2] since

Bhāva and Bṛhat. A few more are added in the next chapter (22-9 ff). But the peculiar omission is *Vārāha Kalpa*. It is mentioned so many times elsewhere but is *not* included in this list. Similarly *Padma-Kalpa* mentioned as 7th Kalpa is not found in the list. The name of Bhava Kalpa is repeated twice. The notes of Gamut are adopted for Kalpa-names.

1. This is the translation of the emended line of the Text *Ṛṣayo yatra sambhūtāḥ svaro loka-manoharaḥ*. Births of sages and the musical notes are unrelated. So *Ṛṣayo* is emended as *Ṛṣabho* (the musical note RA or Ṛṣabha, which is also the name of the Kalpa) and *Sambhūtāḥ* is emended as '*sambhūtaḥ*. It agrees with number and gender of *Svaro loka-manoharaḥ* of the Venkateshwar Text. The line is emended as per A (Anandashrama, Poona) edition which is ch. 21 v. 34A which runs as follows :

Ṛṣabho yatra sambhūtaḥ svaro loka-manoharaḥ

The line is translated above.

2. Mārjālīya is a heap of earth to the right of the *Vedi* (altar) of the sacrifice on which sacrificial vessels are cleansed (?) or 'fond of purification' (said of Śiva) —MW 813A. But neither of the meanings is suitable here.

Mārjālīya is that activity from which the world of Brahmā is created.

36. The eighteenth Kalpa was Madhyama wherein the note of music of the gamut *Madhyama* honoured by the note of musical scale called *Dhaivata* arose in all beings from the self-born deity (Brahmā).

37. Then, the nineteenth Kalpa, was Vairājaka, where lord Vairāja, son of Brahmā, was the Manu.

38. His son was the pious, righteous Dadhīci. He, the refulgent Prajāpati, became the lord of Devas.

39. As Prajāpati Dadhīci was engaged in sacrifice, Gāyatrī was enamoured of him. From that was born the charming musical note (*Niṣāda*?) as a son to Dadhīci.

40-42. The twentieth Kalpa is glorified after him as *Niṣāda*. On seeing him (born), Prajāpati desisted from creating (beings). In order to create progeny *Niṣāda* performed a penance for one thousand divine years without taking any food and with his senses controlled (who had thus conquered his sense-organs). The refulgent Brahmā, the grandfather of the worlds, said, "sit down" as the former was standing with arms lifted up, hungry and thirsty, dejected and exhausted with penance. Since Brahmā told this quiescent son to sit down, he came to be known as *Niṣāda*,[1] the note of the gamut (endowed with *niṣāda* restfulness?).

43-45. O Brāhmaṇas, the twentyfirst Kalpa should be known as *Pañcama*. (In this) Prāṇa, Apāna, Samāna, Udāna and Vyāna (the five vital airs) were the mental sons of god Brahmā and were on par with him. The great Lord was worshipped by them with eulogistic words. As he was praised in chorus by those noble-souled ones, the fifth note (*Pañcama*) of the gamut became melodious. Hence the Kalpa became known as *Pañcama*.

46. The twenty-second Kalpa should be known as Meghavāhana when the mighty-armed Viṣṇu became a cloud and carried the hide-clad lord (Śiva) for a thousand divine years.

---

1. Fanciful derivations are given here to the names of the Kalpas. One is reminded of stories in *Brāhmaṇas* which supply such explanatory stories to derive names or terms.

47. From the mouth (of Viṣṇu) who was overwhelmed by burden and was gasping for breath, out came *Kāla* (Time) of huge dimensions, the illuminator of the world. Hence he is declared by Brāhmaṇas as Viṣṇu, the son of Kaśyapa.

48-49. The twenty-third Kalpa should be known as Cintaka. Citi was the glorious son of Prajāpati. As Brahmā was meditating on the twins—Citi and Cintā were born. Hence the Kalpa was designated as Cintaka by the self-born loıd.

50. The twenty-fourth Kalpa is called Ākūti. Ākūti and Devī were twins.

51. Since Prajāpati asked Ākūti to create progeny, he should be regarded a man, and the Kalpa was named after him.

52. The twenty-fifth Kalpa was Vijñāti. Goddess (his spouse) and Vijñāti gave birth to twins.

53. While he was meditating in mind, being desirous of a son, spiritual knowledge dawned upon him. Hence he came to be called *Vijñāti.*

54. The twenty-sixth Kalpa was Manas. Goddess Śaṅkarī gave birth to twins.

55. While he thought of the subjects and desired to create them, a conception (*Bhāvanā*) arose in his mind. Since he was created by god Brahmā for procreating the subjects, he is therefore, remembered as *Bhāvanā-Saṁbhava* due to the creation of subjects.

56. The twenty-seventh Kalpa is designated as Bhāva. Goddess Paurṇamāsī gave birth to twins.

57-58. While Brahmā, the great god (Parameṣṭhin), desirous of creating the subjects was meditating on the great Ātman Īśvara, Agni (Fire god) became a circular sphere surrounded by clusters of rays. Huge-bodied as he was, he enveloped the earth and firmament and blazed.

59-61. At the end of a thousand years, when the sphere of light was complete, he saw the sphere of the sun risen overpowering it. Since the lord sun of complete sphere invisible to (all) beings was seen by Brahmā Paraımeṣṭhin and since the Yogas, and Mantras revived and rose along with the sphere and since this was seen, the Kalpa was called Darśa.

62. Since lord Soma (the full Moon) filled up the mind of Brahmā Parameṣṭhin, it is known as Paurṇamāsī.

63. Therefore Parva days, new moon and full moon days were accepted by *Yogis* as the most important days in both the fortnights for the achievement of their interest (desired object).

64. Those (persons) of twice-born castes who perform the Darśa and Paurṇamāsa sacrifice, have never to return from the region of Brahmā (to Saṃsāra).

65-66. One who without having maintained the sacrificial fires dies or one who goes along the path of heroes (meets death on the battlefield) should stabilise his mind and repeat this Mantra[1] slowly—"O Agni, you are Rudra, Asura. You are the earth and heaven. You are Śiva. When urged, you rule over the breath. You are the sun. You sever our noose with your sword and blaze." A twice-born person should repeat this *mantra* well, within his mind. If he then enters the fire, he goes to the region of Rudra.

67. The Śruti declares that fire is the moon and the lord Kāla and Rudra, Hence he who enters fire does not return from Rudra.

68-69. The twenty-eighth Kalpa is known as *Bṛhat.* While god Brahmā, desirous of sons and procreating the subjects, mentally meditated on *Bṛhat* and *Rathantara* Sāmans, the *Bṛhat Sāman* came out with faces all round. Hence the meditators on truth call this Kalpa Bṛhat.

70. *Rathantara* shall be known as the great sphere of the sun extending to eighty-eight thousand Yojanas. Therefore the (cosmic) egg-like sphere of the sun should be known as impenetrable.

71. The *Bṛhatsāman* pierces the sphere of the sun. Brāhmaṇas of firm vows, fixing their *Ātmans* in Yoga, break through this sphere and achieve the goal. *Rathantara* includes other Kalpas collectively.

---

1. This is untraced in M. Bloomfield's *A Vedic Concordance*. Presumably it is a Purāṇic mantra.

72. Thus the spiritual philosophy of diverse nature has been narrated by me. Henceforward, I shall explain the details of Kalpas.

CHAPTER TWENTYTWO

Number of Kalpas[1]

The sages said :

1. O great sage, all this is wonderful. The secret of the Kalpas and the settlement of *mantras* have been narrated by you.

2. There is nothing in the three worlds which is not known to you. Hence please narrate in details the number of Kalpas, to us.

Vāyu said :

3. I shall explain to you the number of Kalpas precisely and what constitutes the foremost Yugas and years to the supreme god Brahmā.

4. One thousand (human) Kalpas constitute a year of god Brahmā. Eight thousand such years make a Yuga of Brahmā.

5-6. A thousand Yugas constitute a *Savana* of Prajāpati. Six thousand *Savanas* constitute the period of Brahmā's existence. I shall narrate their number later on in due course.

7. I shall now mention in order the names of other Kalpas beyond the twenty-eight Kalpas already enumerated by me, with their names.

8. Know also the names and origins of the *Mantras* in the other Kalpas beyond *Rathantara* and *Bṛhat Sāman.*

9-10. The twenty-ninth Kalpa should be known as Śveta-lohita. During the period of this Kalpa, while Brahmā was

1. The present chapter deals with the remaining Kalpas, viz. (29) Śvetalohita, (30) Rakta, (31) Pītavāsas, (32) Sita, and (33) Viśvarūpa.

One wonders how to reconcile this list with the statement in *supra* 7. 30 which limits the number of Kalpas to ten.

engaged in supreme meditation, a son of great splendour resembling the Fire-god was born to him. He had white turban, white garland and white garments and a tuft.

11. His face was dreadful, extremely fierce and very much awe-inspiring. It was reddish white. He was blazing with a refulgent body. He had a huge mouth and a white form.

12-13. On seeing him, god Brahmā, the glorious Puruṣa with faces all round and the grandfather of the world, paid obeisance to that Kumāra (youth), the supporter of the world, the omnipresent great Lord, the god of gods who was the refulgent ancient Puruṣa, the eternal universal soul of Yogins.

14. God Brahmā embraced him to his bosom—the great god (Mahādeva), the supreme soul, the ruler of all, who was newly-born (*Sadyojāta*).[1] He, then, meditated upon Brahman, knowing him, the ruler of Devas. The Lord of the world became delighted and burst into laughter.

15. Then, from his side were manifested noble-souled, white-complexioned sages refulgent with the splendour of Brahman, bedecked with white garlands and unctions (probably with holy ashes—*Bhasman*).

16. They were Sunanda, Nandaka, Viśvananda and Nandana, the noble-souled disciples by whom Brahman was then surrounded.

17. In front of him, the great sage Śveta of brilliant white complexion, endowed with great splendour was born. Nara was born of him.

18-19. All the sages, engrossed in Prāṇāyāma and absorbed (resolutely) in the realization of Brahman became absolved of sins, free from *mala* ('bondage' in Śaivism). Endowed with the splendour of Brahman, they transcend the world of god Brahmā, and go to the region of the (supreme) Brahman.

---

1. *Sadyojāta* is one of forms (also faces) of Śiva. This appeared in *Śvetalohita Kalpa*. As in his incarnations, these forms also had four sons or disciples.

Vāyu continued :

20. The thirtieth Kalpa is well-known by the name Rakta where the Being of great splendour assumed red complexion.

21. From Brahmā, the supreme god who, being desirous of a son, was engaged in meditation, a boy of great splendour was born. His body was red. He wore red garlands and garments. He was red-eyed and valorous.

22. On seeing that boy of red garments, he entered into deep meditation and realised that he was the great lord of the universe.

23. After bowing to him, Brahmā became extremely self-controlled and meditated on the Vāmadeva[1] form of Brahman.

24. The great god who was thus meditated upon by Brahmā, the Parameṣṭhin, spoke to the grandfather of the world (Brahmā, with mind full of affection.

25-26. "O most venerable god ! Inasmuch as I was visualized by you with highest devotion and Yoga of meditation while you were meditating with the desire of having a son, you who are endowed with great penance, will realize me, the supreme ruler and supporter of the world, by engaging yourself in meditation in every Kalpa." Saying so he, Śarva, burst into a boisterous laugh.

27. Then four sons of noble souls were born to him. They shone with pure intellect.

28. They were Viraja, Vivāha, Viśoka and Viśvabhāvana. They were all well-versed in the Vedas, equal to Brahmā, heroic, diligent and persevering.

29. They wore red clothes, red garlands and unguents. They had smeared red ashes over their bodies. They were ruddy-faced and red-eyed.

30-31. Those industrious, noble souls, well-versed in the Vedas, eulogising that Brahman Vāmadeva, imparted instructions in piety for showering grace on the people who desired to receive instructions from them. Then at the end of a thousand years, they re-entered Rudra, the eternal great lord.

---

1. Vāmadeva—another form of Śiva. This too had four sons listed in v. 28 below. This form appeared in the *Rakta Kalpa*.

32-33. Other excellent Brāhmaṇas practising Yoga for their communion with Vāmadeva attained the lord, as they are his devotees and attached to him. Becoming sinless and pure and attaining the splendour of Brahman, all of them reach Rudraloka whence there is no return to Saṁsāra.

CHAPTER TWENTYTHREE

Incarnations of Maheśvara

Vāyu continued :

1. The thirtyfirst Kalpa is known as Pītavāsas[1] (yellow garmented). Here, god Brahmā of great brilliance assumes a yellow complexion.

2. While Brahmā, the supreme god, was meditating with a desire for sons, a son of great splendour robed in yellow attire appeared.

3. He was a mighty-armed young man with yellow ointment applied over his limbs. He wore yellow garlands, yellow sacred-thread and yellow turban.

4. On seeing him engaged in meditation, Brahmā mentally saluted him who was the supreme lord and the creator of the universe.

5. When god Brahmā became absorbed in meditation, he saw a great hideous cow pertaining to the great god, coming out from the mouth of Maheśvara.

6. That Cow-goddess had four feet, four faces, four hands, four teats, four eyes, four horns, four curved fangs, four mouths and faces on every side. It was united with thirtytwo *Lokas*.

7. On seeing that great goddess Maheśvarī, the god of immense splendour who was bowed to by Devas, spoke :

8. "Come on. Come on," said he, eulogising her frequently by terms such as 'intellect', 'memory' and 'knowledge'.

---

1. Verses 1-19 describe the 31st Kalpa called *Pītavāsas*. God Śiva incarnated as Vāmadeva and had four disciples or sons. As the name of the Kalpa implies, yellow colour is a special feature of this Kalpa.

He got up with palms joined in reverence and addressed her thus.

9. "Enveloping the universe with Yoga, bring the whole world under (your) control. Or you will join with Rudra and become his consort. For the welfare of Brāhmaṇas, you will be the highest truth."

10-11. Then the lord of the chief of Devas gave the four-footed great goddess (Maheśvarī) to Brahmā who was meditating with a desire to have sons. Then realising by his Yogic meditation that she was the supreme goddess, Brahmā who deserves obeisance from all the world, sought refuge in her. Having meditated on the Gāyatrī pertaining to Rudra, god Brahmā became self-controlled.

12. After performing the *Japa* of Rudra Gāyatrī—the Vedic lore that was given to him and the great goddess bowed to by the people of Rudra-loka, he resorted to the great lord (Rudra) with his mind fixed on him in meditation.

13. Again remembered by him, the great lord gave him the divine Yoga, overlordship and glory, the riches of knowledge and detachment.

14-15. Then the Lord burst out into a terrific, boisterous and dazzling loud laugh. And around there appeared brilliant sons, who wore yellow garlands and yellow robes. They had yellow ointments. They had yellow heads, yellow turbans, yellow hair and yellow faces.

16-17. After staying for a thousand years, at the end of the period, these Yogic souls of pure splendour, desiring the welfare of Brāhmaṇas, took their ceremonial bath. They were endowed with piety and Yogic power. They imparted instruction in Yoga to the sages engaged in the *Sattra* of long duration and entered lord Rudra.

18-19. Even all others—those who have restrained their souls, who are engaged in meditation, who have conquered the sense organs and who have thus resorted to the lord, eschew their sins, become sinless and pure and are endowed with the splendour of Brahman. They enter lord Rudra never to be born again (in *saṁsāra*).

Vāyu said :

20. When the Kalpa of yellow colour of the self-born deity passed away, another Kalpa called *Sita*[1] began to function.

21. When the universe was turned into a single vast ocean and a thousand divine years had elapsed, the dejected Brahmā desirous of creating the subjects began to think.

22 While he was thinking and meditating with a desire for sons, the complexion of that great god turned black.

23. Then he of great splendour saw that a boy of great powers, dark in complexion and shinning with his lustre had appeared.

24. He wore dark garments, an excellent black turban, black sacred thread, black garlands and unguents and had a black head.

25. On seeing the noble-souled, immortal one with terrible *mantras*, he (Brahmā) paid homage to the dark and tawny Lord of the chief of the Devas and the universe.

26. The glorious Brahmā was engaged in *Prāṇāyāma* (breath control). With Maheśvara (the great god) in his heart, he mentally sought refuge in the Lord of ascetics absorbed in meditation. Brahmā then contemplated on Brahman as Aghora.

27. While he was thus meditating Lord Rudra burst out in a boisterous laughter.

28. Then from his sides four noble sons emerged. They were black in complexion and had black garlands and unguents.

29. They wore black garments, turbans, clothes and had black faces. They laughed aloud boisterously. They uttered great hissing sounds. They performed obeisance again and again.

30. Then they worshipped him for a thousand years by means of Yoga and at the end of that period they transferred their activities to their disciples.

---

1. Verses 20-32 describe the 32nd Kalpa called *Sita* (black). Complexion and dress suitable to the name of the Kalpa and birth of four sons after a boistrous laugh—all these are common features to other Avatāras of Śiva. The *avatāra* or form of Śiva here is *Aghora*.

31. Endowed with Yoga and by its means, they contemplated upon Śiva. They entered the region of Rudra, the lord of the universe—the region that was devoid of impurities and attributes.

32. Other Brāhmaṇas too well-versed in the injunctions who meditate upon Rudra by means of Yoga attain the eternal lord.

33. When that terrible black Kalpa elapsed, another Kalpa named *Viśvarūpa*[1] began to function.

34. After the period of dissolution was over when the mobile and immobile beings were created and when Brahmā desirous of sons began to meditate, the omnipresent Sarasvatī of great sound manifested (herself).

35-36. Brahmā who had a Yogic communion with his Ātman mentally meditated on Īśāna, the lord of all, the omnipresent, who was clad in universal garlands and robes and who wore universal sacred thread and universal turban and who had applied universal scents, who had mighty arms and had universe as his abode. Brahmā bowed to the lord.

37. To him who was thus meditating and saluting, with the words "*Oṁ* to Īśāna, O Mahādeva, obeisance be to you," the Lord Īśa (Śiva) said, "I am pleased with you. Ask what you desire."

38. Then, bowing and eulogising the lord with words, the delighted Brahmā replied with a contented mind:

39. "O lord I wish to know your universal form that pervades and rules over the universe. I wish to know who is this supreme god.

40. Who is this goddess with four feet, four faces, four horns, four mouths, four teeth and four teats?

41. How is she described as four-armed, four-eyed and pervader of the universe? What is her name? What is her Ātman? What is her prowess in activity?"

---

1. Verses 33-55 describe briefly the Viśvarūpa Kalpa. In this the Īśāna form of Śiva manifested himself and also goddess Sarasvatī—the cow called Prakṛti, the source of all the universe. As usual Śiva laughs loudly and four sons are born who follow the Yogic path for a thousand years, then enter Lord Rudra.

Maheśvara replied :

42. "Listen precisely to this holy and nourishing secret of all *mantras*. It is the great secret of the first creation.

43. The Kalpa that is current now is known as Viśvarūpa, wherein Devas, Bhava and others and twenty-six Manus (are said to have existed).

44. O Lord, this is the thirty-third Kalpa since you have occupied the position of Brahmā.

45. O great sage, O lord of devas, know that previous to your existence a hundred thousand self-born deities (i.e. Brahmās) have passed away.

46. It should be known that Ānanda (is your predecessor). In Ānanda you will be ultimately dissolved. You are of the spiritual lineage of Gālavya. By virtue of penance you have become my son.

47-48. In you are firmly established Yoga, Sāṅkhya, penance, learning, sacred precepts, rites, order, truth, Brahman, non-violence, series of generations, meditation, the body for meditation, quiescence, Vidyā and Avidyā, mind, fortitude, splendour, calmness, memory, intellect, modesty, purity, speech, contentment, nourishment, rituals, shyness and forbearance.

49. Know, O Brahmā, that this great goddess is *Prakṛti*, your mother. She possesses twenty-six attributes. She is called "thirty-two syllabled".

50-51. This venerable goddess is the mother of the self-born god. She has four faces. She is the origin of the universe. She is glorified as Prakṛti, the cow whom the meditators of the reality call *Prakṛti* and *Pradhāna*. This unborn (Goddess) is red, white and black in complexion. She is beautiful in form and creator of the universe. While I, the unborn, am intelligent knower that, the universal-formed (all-pervading) Gāyatrī, is the universal-formed cow."

52. After saying thus, the great lord laughed boisterously. Moving clapping his hands loudly he produced 'Kahākaha' sound.

53. Then from his sides divine sons of various forms were born, some with matted hair, some with shaven heads, some with tufts and some with half-shaven heads.

54-55. Those sons of great prowess worshipped the lord for a thousand divine years by means of Yoga as mentioned (before), instructed decent pupils in righteousness and Yogic practice and restraint. Thereafter, they entered Lord Rudra.

Vāyu continued :[1]

56. Then Brahmā, the grandfather of the world was struck with wonder. He resorted to the great god (Mahādeva) with heart full of devotion. He spoke the words, "O Lord ! How is this entire whiteness of yours?"

The Lord replied :

57. When it was *Śvetakalpa,* I became wholly white. I had white turban, white garlands and white garments, and was known as the auspicious.

58. My bones, flesh, hair and skin were white. My blood too was white. Hence this Kalpa came to be known as Śveta.

59. Due to my grace, the lord of Devas possessed white limbs and white blood, The Gāyatrī called Brahma Gāyatrī[2] was of white complexion.

60. O lord of Devas, I, the eternal *Sadyojāta*, stationed in the secret region, have been realised by you by means of penance. So this secret Brahman is glorified as *Sadyojāta.*

---

1. In verses 57-74 Lord Śiva recapitulates the names of the Kalpas and his appearance as follows:

N. of the Kalpa	Siva's incarnation	Special feature	Gāyatrī*
1. Śveta	Sadyojyoti	Whiteness	Brahma Gāyatrī
2. Lohita or Rakta	Vāmadeva	Redness	Rudrāṇi (Rudra Gāyatri)
3. Sita or Kṛṣṇa	Kāla or Aghora	Blackness	—
4. Viśvarūpa	Īśāna	all colours	Viśvarūpa

2. As the importance of the so-called *Gāyatrī* mantra became well-established, the Purāṇa writers (devotees of one of the trinity of gods) had a Gāyatrī Mantra pertaining to their own special deity. Thus AP 317. 7 gives the Śiva (Rudra) Gāyatrī as follows :

tan Maheśāya vidmahe, Mahādevāya dhīmahi/
tan naḥ Śivaḥ pracodayāt //

61. Hence the Brāhmaṇas who realize me hidden in secret (the heart) will approach me whence the return (to saṁsāra) is rare.

62. When I next became Lohita (red), the Kalpa too was known as Lohita through the colour assumed by me.

63. Then Gāyatrī, the cow was glorified as endowed with red flesh, bones, blood, milk, eyes, and udder.

64. Then I became Vāmadeva as my colour changed into red. By the excellence of Yoga, I was known as Vāmadeva.

65. Still, O Mighty one, I have been known by you of restrained soul as white-coloured that excels all colours. Henceforth I attained fame as Vāmadeva.

66-67. Those twice-born ones who realize my position as Vāmadeva and who realise Mother Rudrāṇī, Gāyatrī, are liberated from sins. They become free from passion. They have the splendour of Brahman. They will attain Rudrā's region from which the return is rarely possible.

68. When this Kalpa became terribly black in colour through the colour assumed by me, the Kalpa was called Kṛṣṇa.

69. There I am like Kāla (God of death). I am black and I illuminate the worlds. O Brahmā, I have been realised by you as terrible and of terrific exploit.

70. Hence to those on the earth who realise me in this terrible form, I, the eternal god shall become non-terrible and quiescent.

71. To those on the earth who realize me in universal form, I always become propitious and gentle.

72. Hence this Kalpa too is Viśvarūpa. There Sāvitrī too is Viśvarūpā (universal-formed).

73. These sons of mine art omniformed. They are mentioned to be four. Their feet are indeed worshipped by the worlds.

74. Hence too in my subjects there will be all castes and colours. The subjects shall eat all sorts of foodstuffs. They will be pure according to caste.

75. Salvation, virtue, wealth and love constitute a set of four[1]. Hence the knower and the known too will become fourfold.

---

1. Verses 75-77 speak of the sets of four (entities) such as *Arthas* (Dharma, Artha, Kāma and Mokṣa) and Yugas (Kṛta, Tretā, Dvāpara and Kali).

76. The living beings are of four categories. The stages in life are four. The feet of virtue are four. My sons are four.

77. The universe consisting of the mobile and immobile beings, exists in the four Yugas. Since it is four-fold, it becomes four-footed.

78. *Bhūr*, *Bhuvar*, *Svar*, *Mahas*, *Jana*, *Tapas* and *Śānta* are the seven regions. The region of Rudra is beyond these regions.

79. *Svar* is the third and *Mahas* is the fourth. This region is very extensive. It is the great abode of Yogins.

80. Those alone who practise Yoga, who know about it, who meditate upon it, who are in communion with it, who are free from the feeling of 'my-ness', who are devoid of egotism, lust or anger, can realize it.

81. Since you saw the four-footed Sarasvatī, all animals will be four-footed and will have four teats.

82. Since Soma charged with Mantras exuded from my mouth, O Brahmā, the soul of all living beings will drink milk contained in her breasts.

83. Hence (the milk) will be full of Soma and is designated as *Amṛta* (nectar) and hence the quadrupeds have their whiteness therefrom.

84. Since the goddess Sāvitrī, the promoter of the welfare of the world, was seen by you again as two-footed, after performing the rites, so all human beings will be two-footed and two-breasted.

85. Since this supreme goddess (Maheśvarī) of great prowess who sustains all living beings, was seen by you as the she-goat (unborn—Prakṛti) endowed with all colours, hence the universality of forms of she-goats.

86. The he-goat (or the unborn deity) of great brilliance will become universal-formed. Its semen will never be wasted. Everywhere it will have fire in its mouth. Hence the all-pervading fire is worthy of sacrifice in the form of an animal.

87. The Brāhmaṇas who have purified their souls by practising penance will see the all-pervading lord as Īśa or Śiva everywhere.

88. Being free from passion and ignorance and after aband-

oning their human bodies, they come to me once and for all and never return.

89. O Brāhmaṇas ! Thus being addressed by Rudra, Lord Brahmā, the grandfather of the world bowed down to Rudra and spoke to him again with humility and restraint.

Brahmā said :

90. O Lord Maheśvara, O chief of the lords of Devas, O omnipresent Mahādeva, these bodies of yours are revered by the people.

91. O long-armed mighty lord, of universal forms, in what Yuga will the Brāhmaṇas see you?

92. O Mahādeva ! By what *Yoga* of *Tattvas* (contemplation of true principle) or yogic meditation can your bodies be visualized by Brāhmaṇas?

The Lord replied :

93-94. Neither by penance, nor by Yoga, nor as a fruit of religious gifts, nor as a result of pilgrimage to holy places, nor by performance of sacrifices with liberal sacrificial fees, nor through the teaching of the Vedas, nor by dedicating the mind, can I be seen by human beings except through meditation.

95. The all-pervading (Viṣṇu) Nārāyaṇa, the Lord of the three worlds will be famous in this world by the name Varāha.

96. He will have four arms, four feet, four eyes, four faces, six parts, three heads and three bodies in three places (worlds). He will assume the form of sacrifice after becoming *Saṁvatsara* (year).

97-99. The four yugas, Kṛta, Tretā, Dvāpara and Kali, will be the four feet. His limbs will be the sacrifices (*Kratus*). His arms are the four Vedas; the season, the beginnings of conjunctions; the two faces are the two *Ayanas* (transits of the sun) and the eyes are four (two per face). The three heads are the three *Parva* days in the months of Phālguna, Āṣāḍha and Kārtika; three seats (in places) are the heaven, the firmament and the earth. Creation and dissolution (of the world) are described as the two stages (in his life).

100. In Vārāha Kalpa when he assumes the form of Kāla, lord Viṣṇu, Nārāyaṇa will become attainable.

101. O Lord of Devas, you will also become four-faced. People residing in Brahmaloka will worship you.

102-103. When you will see the great sage Puruṣa, Nārāyaṇa, the Lord of the Devas, lying absorbed in meditation on a float in the vast ocean (of cosmic waters), minds of both of you will be confounded by my Yogic power. Without recognizing each other at night you will be fighting with each other.

104. On seeing the worlds containing mobile and immobile beings stationed in each other's belly, you will be very much surprised and realise the truth through meditation.

105. Then you, the lotus-born Brahmā and he the lotus-navelled ancient Puruṣa (Viṣṇu) will become very famous in the Kalpa designated as Lotus (*Padma*)-Kalpa.

106. Then in the seventh Kalpa of the lord, in the Vārāha Kalpa, Viṣṇu of great splendour, Kāla the annihilator of worlds will be born as your son and known as Vaivasvata Manu.

107. In that Kalpa when the four Yugas have passed, I will be born as a great sage called Śveta having a tuft, at the end of the Yuga.[1]

108. In the beautiful peak of Himavat, on the excellent mountain Chāgala, I will be having four disciples who were excellent devotees of Śiva.

109. The four noble-souled Brāhmaṇas, masters of the Vedas, will be Śveta, (Śveta-)Śikha, Śvetāśva and Śveta-Lohitā.

110. Seeing the great goal of Brahman and fully absorbed into Brahman, they will approach and (be united with) him eternally (whence there is no return to *saṁsāra*).

111-112. Again, there will be born the patriarch Vyāsa by

1. Verses 107 ff give a list of Śiva's incarnations along with disciples (or sons). Śiva incarnates in the Kali-yuga and each incarnation has four disciples. The last Avatāra at Kāyārohaṇa in Gujarat is a historical one as we have inscriptional records about him.

For the tabulated list see Introduction : Śaivism.

name Satya[1] in the second Dvāpara age. I, known as Sutāra, will be born in the Kali age for the bliss and welfare of the people and to shower grace (on them).

113. There too my sons will be born: Dundubhi, Śatarūpa, Ṛcīka and Kratumān.

114. Attaining the Yogic power, perfect knowledge and eternal Brahman, they will go to Rudra Loka whence there can be no return (to *saṁsāra*).

115. In the third Dvāpara age, when Bhārgava is the Vyāsa, I will be born as Damana at the end of that age.

116. There also four sons will be born to me, viz. Viśoka, Vikeśa, Viśāpa and Śāpanāśana.

117. Those sons, endowed with great splendour will, by means of Yogic path, go to the region of Rudra whence there is no return.

118. In the fourth Dvāpara age, when Aṅgiras is the Vyāsa, I will be born and known as Suhotra.

119. There also four excellent sons will be born to me. They will be great ascetics, excellent Brāhmaṇas, steadfast in holy rites and endowed with Yogic souls.

120. They will be Sumukha, Durmukha, Durdama and Duratikrama. They will attain the subtle goal of Yoga and become pure. Their sins will be burnt. They too will be going along the same path.

121. In the fifth Dvāpara age, when Savitṛ will be the Vyāsa, I shall be born as a great ascetic (called) Kaṅga (Kaṅka?). I, being a Yogic soul, will perform many activities for showering grace on the world.

---

1. Vyāsa is a designation of the 'arranger' of Vedic mantras into *Saṁhitās*. He is born at the end of Dvāpara. The name of the incumbent of *Vyāsahood* is different. The list of Vyāsas is as follows:

(2) Satya, (3) Bhārgava, (4) Aṅgiras, (5) Savitṛ, (6) Mṛtyu, (7) Śatakratu (Indra), (8) Vasiṣṭha, (9) Sārasvata, (10) Tridhāman, (11) Trivṛt, (12) Śata-tejasa, (13) Dharma-Nārāyaṇa, (14) Surakṣaṇa, (15) Aruṇi, (16) Sañjaya, (17) Deva Kṛtañjaya, (18) Ṛtañjaya, (19) Bhāradvāja, (20) Vācaḥ-śravas, (21) Vācaspati, (22) Śuktāyana, (23) Tṛṇabindu, (24) Ṛkṣa, (25) Śakti, (26) Parāśara, (27) Jātukarṇya, (28) Dvaipāyana Vyāsa (Viṣṇu's incarnation).

Cf. the List of Vyāsa's in Bd. P. 35. 116-126. It differs from the same list given in KP I. 52.

122. Four blessed sons, pure in origin, free from passion, will be born to me. They will be Yogic souls, steadfast in their rites.

123. They are Sana, Sanandana, Sanātana and Ṛtu Sanatkumāra. They will be devoid of egotism and selfishness. They will approach me and cease to return to the world.

124. In the sixth revolution of the cycle of Yugas, when Lord Mṛtyu is the Vyāsa, I shall be born and will be known as Lokākṣi.

125. Four blessed disciples will be born to me. They will be divine Yogic souls, steadfast in the religious rites. Those highly fortunate ones will be highly honoured by the people.

126. They are Sudhāman, Virāja, Śaṅkha and Pādrava. All of them will be Yogic souls, great Ātmans, with their sins burnt. They too will go along the same path, to be sure.

127-128. In the seventh revolution of Yugas when Śatakratu is the Vyāsa, who formerly was lord Śatakratu of great brilliance, I will be born in the Kali age at the end of that Yuga and be known as Jaigiṣavya. I will be the most excellent of all Yogins.

129. There in that Yuga the four sons will be born to me, viz. Sārasvata, Sumedhas, Vasuvāha and Suvāhana.

130. Resorting to meditation these noble souls will go to Rudraloka.

131-132. In the eighth revolution of the Yuga-cycle when Vasiṣṭha is the Vyāsa, Kapila, Āsuri, Pañcaśikha and Vāgbali, the great Yogi, all of them will be endowed with great prowess. After obtaining (being initiated in) Maheśvara's Yoga and being absorbed in meditation, they will burn down all their sins. They will approach me (and being absorbed in me) they will never return to the world.

133. In the ninth revolution, when Sārasvata is the Vyāsa I will be born and known as Ṛṣabha. There also I shall have sons of great prowess.

134. They will be Parāśara, Gārgya, Bhārgava and Aṅgiras, noble-souled Brāhmaṇas, masters of the Vedas.

135. They will be excellent in penance and prowess. They will be capable of and experts in cursing and blessing. They too

will go in the same manner and attain the goal, through the Yogic meditation, as mentioned before.

136-137. In the tenth Dvāpara when Tridhāman is the Vyāsa, I will be born on the peak of Himavān, on the excellent mountain Bhṛgutuṅga. The peak is known so after the name of Bhṛgu.

138. There also, my sons of steadfast vows will be born. They are Balabandhu, Nirāmitra, Ketuśṛṅga and Tapodhana.

139. They will be great *yogic* souls endowed with the Yoga of meditation. With their sins burnt by penance, they will go to Rudraloka.

140. In the eleventh revolution, when Trivṛt is the Vyāsa, I shall be born at Gaṅgādvāra at the end of the Kali age.

141. My sons of loud voice known as Ugras will be born then. Endowed with great power, they will be well-behaved and well-known in the world.

142. They are Laṁbodara, Laṁba, Laṁbākṣa and Laṁbakeśaka. After attaining the Yoga of Śiva, they will go to Rudraloka. They too will attain the great goal along the same path.

143. In the twelfth revolution (of the *yuga*-cycle), the great sage Śatatejas, most excellent among poets, will be the Vyāsa.

144. At the end of the Yuga, I shall be born on the earth and be known as Atri. I shall resort to the forest called Haimaka and take to Yoga.

145. Here also my sons will be born. They will be great Yogins taking bath and smearing *Bhasma* as unguent and devoted to Rudra.

146. They are Sarvajña, Samabuddhi, Sādhya and Sarva. Devotedly engaged in Yogic meditation, they will go to Rudraloka.

147-148. When the thirteenth revolution has arrived and Dharma Nārāyaṇa is the Vyāsa, I will be born as the sage Vāli in the holy hermitage of Vālakhilyas on the mountain Gandhamādana.

149. There too my sons will be born as great ascetics (lit. who value penance as wealth), viz.: Sudhāman, Kāśyapa, Vasiṣṭha and Virajas.

150. They will be endowed with Yogic power. They will be unsullied. They will remain celibate sublimating their sexuality. Along with the same Yogic path, they will undoubtedly go (to Rudraloka).

151-152. In the fourteenth revolution when Surakṣaṇa is the Vyāsa, I will be born again at the end of the Yuga in the family of Aṅgiras, (and be called) by the name of Gautama, the excellent knower of Yoga. That forest will also become holy and be named Gautama.

153. There also, in the Kali age, my sons will be born, viz. Atri, Ugratapas, Śrāvaṇa and Sraviṣṭaka.

154. They will be great Yogic souls. They will be devoted to the Yoga of meditation. They will go along the same path and become the residents of Rudraloka.

155-157. When in due course the fifteenth revolution arrives and when in the Dvāpara age Āruṇi is the Vyāsa, I shall be a Brāhmaṇa named Vedaśiras. There Vedaśiras, the miraculous missile of the supreme Lord, will be powerful. The mountain (also) will be known as Vedaśiras. I shall be resorting to the Himavān on its excellent peak, the source of the river Sarasvatī.

158-159. There too my sons will be born, viz., Kuṇi, Kuṇibāhu, Kuśarīra and Kunetraka. Yogic souls absorbed in Brahman and of sublimated sexuality, they too will go to Rudraloka along the same path.

160. When the sixteenth revolution has arrived gradually, lord Vyāsa will be born and known as Sañjaya.

161. I too will be born and known as Gokarṇa. The forest will become holy and be known as Gokarṇa.

162. There too very powerful sons will be born to me, viz. Kāśyapa, Uśanas, Cyavana and Bṛhaspati. They too will attain the great region and go along the same path.

163. When the seventeenth revoluation has arrived in due course, Devakṛtañjaya will be the Vyāsa.

164. There too, I will be born and known as Guhāvāsin on the lofty peak of Himavat called Mahālaya. This centre of Siddhis will be very holy.

165. There too, omniscient noble-souled sons will be born to me. They will not be egotistic. They will be the knowers of Yoga and engrossed in Brahman.

166-167. They will be Utathya, Vâmadeva, Mahākāla and Mahālaya. They will have hundreds and thousands of disciples all practising meditation. In that Kalpa, all of them will be in communion with Brahman by means of meditation. Ever practising Yoga and keeping the great lord in their heart, they will step onto Mahālaya and enter the eternal Śiva.

168-169. Then at the end of the age, some other noble Ātmans too will become unsullied and pure. Attaining the holy Mahālaya, the region of the great lord, they will enable the people ten generations before and ten after, to cross the ocean of worldly existence.

170. After making everyone (of the preceding ten and succeeding ten generations) including themselves as the twenty-first, cross the great ocean (of worldly existence), they will attain, through my grace, the region of Rudra, free from (worldly) feverishness.

171-172. When the eighteenth revolution (of the cycle of Yugas) arrives, and Ṛtañjaya is the Vyāsa, I shall be born and known by the name Śikhaṇḍin on the holy peak of Himālaya, worshipped by Devas and Dānavas, where stands the mountain Śikhaṇḍin. The forest known as Śikhaṇḍin is resorted to by sages and Siddhas.

173-174. There too my sons, the ascetics will be born. These are their names: Vācaḥśravas, Ṛtīka, Śāvāsa and Dṛḍhavrata. They will be Yogic souls, very powerful and masters of the Vedas. Attaining the Yoga of Lord Śiva, they will go to Rudraloka.

175. When the nineteenth revolutation arrives, the great sage Bhāradvāja will become Vyāsa.

176. There too, I will be born and known as Jaṭāmālin, on the charming peak of the Himavat where the mountain Jaṭāyu exists.

177. There too very powerful sons will be born to me, viz. Hiraṇyanāman, Kauśilya, Kākṣīva and Kuthumi.

178. All of them will be lords of Yogic holy rites. They will observe celibacy. After attaining the Yoga of the great Lord, they will go to Rudraloka.

179-180. When in the twentieth revolution (of the cycle of yugas) Vācaḥśravas is the Vyāsa, I shall be born and known as

Aṭṭahāsin. Then men will be fond of *Aṭṭahāsas* (boisterous laughs).

181. There on the top of Himavat itself, resorted to by Siddhas and Cāraṇas, very powerful and brilliant sons will be born to me. They will be Yogic souls engrossed in meditation, regularly observing holy rites and highly Sāttvika by nature.

182. They will be Sumantu, Varvari, Subandhu and Kuśikandhara. After attaining the Yoga of the great Lord Rudra, they will go to Rudraloka.

183-184. When the twentyfirst revolution arrives in due course and when Vācaspati is the Vyāsa, I will be born and known by the name Dāruka. And the holy forest will be known as Devadāruvana.

185. There too highly powerful and brilliant sons, namely Plakṣa, Dākṣāyaṇi, Ketumālin and Baka, will be born to me.

186. They will be Yogic souls, high-minded (magnanimous), of sublimated sexuality. Resorting to supreme Yoga these sinless ones will attain the region of Rudra.

187-188. In the twentysecond revolution, when Śuklāyana is the Vyāsa, I will be born as a sage in Vārāṇasī, and known as *Bhīma* (awe-inspiring) Lāṅgalin. There devas including Indra will see me incarnated in Kali as Halāyudha (with plough-share as a weapon).

189-190. There too, righteous sons will be born to me, viz. Tulyārcis, Madhu, Piṅgākṣa and Śvetaketu. They will attain Śiva's Yoga. Engrossed in meditation, they will be free from passion. Absorbed in Brahman they will proceed to Rudraloka.

191-192. In the twentythird revolution, when Tṛṇabindu is the Vyāsa, O Brahmā, I will be born as the highly righteous son of a sage. Possessed of mighty physique, I shall be known by the name of Śveta. I will be spending my time on that excellent mountain. Hence the mountain will be known as Kālañjara.

193. There also powerful sons will be born to me, viz. Uṣija, Bṛhaduktha, Devala and Kavi. After attaining the Yoga of the Lord Rudra, they will go to Rudraloka.

194. In the twentyfourth revolution, when Ṛkṣa will be the Vyāsa, O Brahmā, in that Kali age, towards the end, I will

be born as a great Yogin by name Śūlin, in the Naimiṣa forest honoured by the Yogins.

195. There too my ascetic sons will be born, viz., Śālihotra Agniveśya, Yuvanāśva and Śaradvasu. Those sages of good religious vows, endowed with the Yogic power will attain Rudra.

196-197. When the twentyfifth revolution arrives in due course, and Śakti, son of Vasiṣṭha becomes the Vyāsa, I will be born as the lord Muṇḍīśvara with a staff (a recluse) in the city Koṭivarṣa honoured by devas.

198. There too my sons will be born in succession. They will be noble Yogic souls observing celibacy.

199. They will be Chagala, Kuṁbhakarṣāśya, Kumbha and Prabāhuka. After attaining the Yoga of the great Lord Rudra they will also go along the same path.

200. In the twentysixth revolution of the *yuga*-cycle, when Parāśara is the Vyāsa, I shall be born and known as Sahiṣṇu in the Kali age at its close, in the holy forest of Rudra.

201. There too, sons of great piety will be born to me, viz. Ulūka, Vaidyuta, Sarvaka and Aśvalāyana. After attaining the Yoga of Rudra, the great god, they will also go the same way to Rudraloka.

202-203. When the twentyseventh revolution has arrived in the course and Jātukarṇya becomes the Vyāsa, I will be born as the excellent Brāhmaṇa Somaśarman in the holy centre of Prabhāsa. I will be a Yogic soul well-known in the worlds.

204. There too the sages will be born as my sons, viz. Akṣapāda, Kaṇāda, Ulūka and Vatsa.

205. They will be noble Yogic souls, free from sin and pure in intellect. After attaining the Yoga of the great lord, they will go to Rudraloka.

206-207. When the twentyeighth revolution has arrived in due course and the glorious Viṣṇu, the great father of the worlds becomes Dvaipāyana Vyāsa, then Kṛṣṇa, the best amongst men and the chief of Yadus, by a sixth of his part, will be born of Vasudeva as Vāsudeva.

208. Then I will be a yogic soul and assume the body of a religious student to surprise the worlds, by means of Yogic Māyā.

209. On seeing a forlorn dead body (of a child) left (deserted) in a cremation ground, I, with my power of Yogic Māyā, entered (will enter) that body for the welfare of Brāhmaṇas.

210. With you Viṣṇu (as my companion), (I shall stay) in the holy cave of Meru. I shall be known by the name Nakulin, O Brahman.

211. Then it will be a centre of Siddhas called Kāyārohaṇa. It will remain famous till the earth lasts (i.e. upto the deluge).

212. There too my sons will be born as the ascetics Kuśika, Gārgya, Mitraka and Ruṣṭa.

213. They will be noble Ātmans endowed with Yogic power. They will be Brāhmaṇas, masters of the Vedas. They will be free from dirt (sin) and abstain from sexual intercourse. After attaining the Yoga of Rudra, they will go to Rudraloka and never return.

214. Thus I have mentioned incarnations from Manu to Kṛṣṇa in the twentyeight cycles of Yugas. This series of traditional accounts is very sacred and virtuous.

CHAPTER TWENTYFOUR

Hymn to Śiva[1]

Vāya said :

1. Sages know that there are four Yugas in Bhāratavarṣa.[2] There are Kṛta, Tretā, Dvāpara and Kali Yugas.

2-3. A thousand cycles of these four yugas constitute a day of god Brahmā. The seven Gaṇas (groups of gods) like Yāma and others and the fourteen Romavat groups in their

1. It is since the Rudrādhyāya in TS. IV. 5 that we find the list of epithets used as a hymn of prayer. The list of epithets went on increasing and was lastly recorded as *Sahasra-nāma*. Here we have a list of Śiva's epithets as prayer in vv. 90-164.

2. It is surprising that the cycle of Yugas should be limited to Bhāratavarṣa only.

physical bodies resort to Janaloka along with their followers. In this way, Devas go from Maharloka to Janaloka and Tapoloka.

4. When many Manvantaras pass off, the mighty devas of the Kalpa go up and attain *Sāyujya*.

5-7. When the time of withdrawal (dissolution) arrives, the fourteen Gaṇas leave Maharloka.[1] Those gods in combination with these (quit the Maharloka), when the elements and immobiles alone are left behind, when all the regions from the *Bhuvar-loka* to *Svar-loka* become void; when Devas whose duration of tenure is a Kalpa go upto Janaloka, god Brahmā then collects (all) the groups of Devas, sages and Dānavas and destroys them all through fire and showers when the Yuga comes to an end.

8. In the seventh Kalpa that has just passed off and has been described to you by me, the seven oceans joined together and formed one vast limitless (and divisionless) ocean full of darkness.

9-11. In the vast single ocean, the lord holding conch, discus and mace lay on the serpent couch. He had the colour of the cloud. He was lotus-eyed. He had a crown. He was the lord of Lakṣmī. He was Hari, the eighth Puruṣottama born of the mouth of Nārāyaṇa. He had eight arms, and a broad chest. He is the source of origin of the worlds. He was in communion with the self. Conversant with the process of Yoga, he had taken to meditation beyond the ken of thought, by his Māyā. The serpent (his couch) had a thousand hoods; its body had an unparalleled splendour and the lustre of gold.

12. While he was lying there, taking repose in the Ātman, he, the mighty Viṣṇu, created a lotus in his umbilicus just for a sport.

13. The lotus extended to a hundred Yojanas. It had the splendour of the midday-sun. It was very high supported by an adamantine stalk. It was created sportively by the powerful lord.

---

1. Verses 5-14 describe the dissolution of the universe and formation of one ocean (*Ekārṇava*) of cosmic waters with god Viṣṇu lying on the serpent couch and god Brahmā born in the lotus-flower blooming on the lotus-plant issuing from Viṣṇu's navel.

14. While lord Viṣṇu was sporting thus, the golden-coloured four-faced, wide-eyed Brahmā, unperceivable by the sense organs, and born of the golden Cosmic Egg, approached him casually.

15-16. On seeing him sporting with the fresh lotus, shining with brilliant lustre, emitting sweet smell, Brahmā worshipped him.[1] He was surprised and praising him in loud voice, he asked, "Who are you, Sir, lying in the middle of water?"

17. On hearing the auspicious words of Brahmā, Viṣṇu got up from his couch, with eyes outstretched with wonder.

18. He gave the reply, "Whatever is there (such as) the heaven, firmament, elements; but I am the master, the highest region."

19. After saying this, Viṣṇu continued, "Who are you, Sir? Where have you come from? Where have you to go again? Where is your permanent abode ?

20. Who are you, sir ? A universe-formed being? What can I do for you ?" When Viṣṇu said thus Brahmā replied:

21. "Just like you, I am the first creator Prajāpati. I am called Nārāyaṇa. Everything rests in me."

22-23. But Viṣṇu, the source of the universe, heard this with wonder. Being permitted by lord Brahmā, the creator of the worlds, the great Yogin Viṣṇu entered the mouth of Brahmā, out of curiosity. After entering he saw in the belly of Brahmā, these eighteen continents, along with oceans, and mountains, the living beings beginning with Brahmā and ending with a blade of grass, people of four castes and the eternal seven worlds.

24. On seeing all these, Viṣṇu of great renown and splendour, repeatedly exclaimed thus: "Oh, the prowess of the penance of this being !"

25. Viṣṇu wandered though different regions and different hermitages, but he could not see the end (of it) even after the expiry of one thousand years.

---

1. Verses 15ff. The meeting of Brahmā and Viṣṇu leading to their quarrel on personal superiority and the appearance of god Śiva to solve it, is the Śaivite way of establishing Rudra's greatness. Cf KP I. 9. 12-49. But here Brahmā is shown to be more magnanimous than Viṣṇu who is superior to him in knowledge about Śiva.

26. Then the Garuḍa-emblemed deity (Viṣṇu) came out of his mouth. The enemy-less (lit. one whose enemy is not born) Lord addressed Brahmā, the grandfather of the world:

27. "O Lord, O sinless one, I do not see the beginning, the middle or the end of your belly. I do not see the end of time and space."

28. After saying thus, Viṣṇu spoke again to Brahmā, "O excellent Brāhmaṇa, you too, enter my belly and see the uncomparable world within."

29. On hearing his words delightful to the mind and approving of them, Brahmā entered the belly of Viṣṇu.

30. Stationed within his body, he of unimaginable exploits, saw the same worlds. Though he wandered within he did not see the end of worlds in the body of the primordial lord.

31. On seeing that Brahmā was returning, Viṣṇu closed all the pores of his body. The lord then wished to resume his happy deep sleep in the middle of the vast ocean.

32. When Brahmā saw all the openings closed, he made his form very subtle and discovered a small opening in Viṣṇu's umbilicus.

33. Through the stalk of the lotus he came out and then resumed his own form. The four-faced lord seated in the middle of the lotus, shone with a splendour like that of the interior of the lotus.

34. In the meanwhile there arose a clash between them on the point of (individual) entirety (superiority) in the middle of the ocean.

Sūta said :

35. Then the trident-bearing Lord of unmeasurable soul, the Lord of all living beings, who was clad in gold-coloured bark garments, came where the eternal Lord Viṣṇu was lying on the couch of the (Śeṣa's) serpent's body.

36. While he was walking quickly, big drops of water kicked forcibly by his feet rose up in the sky. They were very hot and extremely chill. A violent wind also blew.

37. On seeing that mysterious phenomenon, Brahmā spoke to Viṣṇu, "The drops of water are big and hot. The lotus is

also moving terribly. Please clarify this doubt of mine. What else do you wish to do?"

38-40. On hearing these words uttered by Brahmā, the lord of unimitable activity and the destroyer of demons, thought within himself thus, "Could it be that another living being has taken abode in my umbilicus? It speaks agreeable words though it does disagreeable acts:" After thinking thus he replied, "O lord, are you agitated in that lotus ?

41. O Lord what have I done to you? Wherefore, O greatest of men, you speak to me thus, though I am your excellent friend? Speak precisely."

42. While the lord of Devas was speaking thus in accordance with the convention, lord Brahmā of lotus-like brilliant complexion, the storehouse of the Vedas, replied.

43. "O Lord, I entered your belly by your desire. Just as the worlds were seen by you in my belly, so also the worlds were seen by me in your belly.

44. O sinless one ! At the end of one thousand years, as I was returning (out of your belly), I found that due to rivalry you have closed all the openings wishing to bring me under control.

45. O blessed one, then thinking within myself, I gained an entrance through the umbilicus and came out of your navel through the lotus stalk.

46. Let there be no misgiving in your mind." On hearing these words of Brahmā, Viṣṇu spoke thus:

47. "What I shall do afterwards has been thought over by me. It was only out of sportiveness that I quickly closed the openings and not to harass you.

48. You shall not take it otherwise. You are worthy of my honour and worship. O gentle one, forgive whatever misdeed I may have committed. Hence O Lord, being urged by me, you shall get down from the lotus.

49. I cannot bear you as you are so brilliant and weighty." Then Brahmā replied, "Tell me what boon you will bestow on me if I come down from the lotus."

Viṣṇu said :

50. "O destroyer of enemies, please be my son. You will

derive great delight thereby. You are a great Yogin with truth as your asset. You are worthy of being worshipped. You are of the form of Oṁkāra.

51. O Lord of all, from now onwards you will have a white turban as your crest ornament. You will be known as *Padmayoni* (one born out of a lotus). O Brahmā, O Lord of the worlds, be my son."

52. Then Lord Brahmā accepted the boon from Viṣṇu. Pleased in his mind and without any sense of rivalry, he said, "May it be so".

53. On seeing a wonderful being approaching with the lustre of the rising sun and with a huge face, he spoke to Nārāyaṇa:

54-56. "O Viṣṇu, who is this person coming hither? He is incomprehensible with a huge mouth, curved fangs, dishevelled hair, ten arms, characterised by the trident, and faces all round with many eyes. He is the lord of the worlds, He is hideous in form. He wears a girdle of Muñja grass. His penis is lifted up. He is roaring terribly. He has great refulgence. He is a heap of splendour. He has pervaded all the quarters and heaven."

57-59. On being addressed thus, Viṣṇu spoke in reply to Brahmā, "He has been coming quickly wading through the ocean. Kicked by his feet, the whole ocean is agitated with profuse sprays of water raised in the sky. O lotus-born (god), you are being sprinkled by them. The great lotus coming out of my umbilicus is being shaken along with you by the wind exhaled through his nose. He is the eternal lord Īśa, the destroyer. Let us both eulogise the bull-bannered lord."

60-61. Then the infuriated Brahmā spoke to Viṣṇu, the illuminator of the lotus, "You do not know yourself the source of origin of all the worlds nor me Brahmā, the eternal creator of the universe. Oh ! Who is this being (called Śaṅkara) excelling us both ?"

62. On hearing the furious words of Brahmā, Viṣṇu said, "O gentle one, do not speak disparagingly of the noble Ātman.

63. The ancient Puruṣa, the lord of Māyā and Yoga is virtue (Dharma) itself. He cannot be thwarted. He is the bestower of boons. He, the eternal lord, is the cause of this universe.

64. He is the soul of all souls. He is the sole light that shines. He is god Śaṅkara himself who is sporting with childish toys.

65. As the creator of subjects his names are *Pradhāna*, *Avyaya*, the unmanifest light, Prakṛti, darkness incomprehensible. Whatsoever he may be, he is sought by ascetics, distressed with grief.

66. He is the eternal sower of the seed. You are the eternal seed. I am the eternal womb". Thus told, Brahmā, the soul of the universe, spoke to Viṣṇu again:

67. "You are the womb. I am the seed. But how is he the sower of the seed ? It behoves you to remove this subtle doubt of mine."

68. On hearing this, Viṣṇu explained to Brahmā, the sustainer of the worlds, their own origin and the origin of the worlds. He cleared the doubt of Brahmā with a suitable analogy.

69. "There is no other being greater than he or more subtle (unmanifest) than he. The region of the lord is the goal of the spiritualists. It is the abode of bliss.

70. The supreme lord has split himself into two and entered the self. He is both possessed of and devoid of attributes. His form without attributes is subtle and unmanifest.

71-72. He is the knower of Māyā (Prakṛti) and her activities; he is deep and inaccessible. His penis deposited you as the seed in my womb, in the primary stage of creation. In due course of time that seed became the huge golden egg in my womb.

73. For a thousand years, the egg was embedded in the waters. At the end of a thousand years, it was split into two by the elemental air.

74. One of the (upper) parts of the crust turned into heaven and the other (lower) into the earth. The lofty foetus became the golden mountain Meru.

75. It is from that, there woke up the golden-wombed lord (Hiraṇyagarbha) of Devas and I, the four-armed Viṣṇu.

76. Then, at the end of a thousand years, the egg was plit into two. On seeing the world a void without stars, the moon and planets, you pondered over, 'Who is here ?' Then your sons were born.

77. They are born (as your sons) again and again at the end of a thousand years—they who are the early predecessors, pleasing to look at, endowed with fire-like brilliant bodies and eyes wide like the petals of a lotus.

78. Glorious Sanatkumāra and Ṛbhu who were perpetually celibate, Sanātana, Sanaka, and Sanandana were born simultaneously. They could visualize objects even beyond the reach of sense-organs.

79. They were born with controlled mind and devoid of three distresses. They said that they would not take up the work of creation.

80-83. There is a great pain in this birth, O gentle one. It is attended by old age and sorrow. Life, death and birth occur again and again. This world is a dream. Even in heaven there are miseries. On realising the tortures of hell, the advent and the inevitability of events and seeing that Ṛbhu and Sanātana were under your control, the three sons Sanaka and others eschewed the three *guṇas* (the creative ingredients) and attaining knowledge of the illusory nature of the world, they renounced the world. When they had renounced the world you were deluded by the Māyā of Śaṅkara.

84. In this Kalpa, O sinless one, your consciousness is withdrawn and the subtle elements earth etc. remain intact (to the end of Kalpa).

85. This Māyā of the lord functioning in the world has been explained to you. That mount Meru is said to exist in Devaloka.

86-87. You will realize your greatness. You will realize your self through your own self. You shall know me the lotus-eyed one. You shall approach the lord supreme Śiva of great Yogic (power), the bestower of boons to all living beings. After approching him who is the preceptor of the universe in the form of Praṇava, you shall propitiate him by prostration. Should he be infuriated, he may burn us both by his very breath.

88. After knowing that lord of great Yogiç power I shall be strong and powerful keeping you ahead. I shall eulogise the lord who has the lustre of fire."

Sūta said:

89. Keeping Brahmā ahead, the Garuḍa-bannered deity, Viṣṇu recited this hymn (in praise of Śiva) uttering his past, present and future names of Vedic origin.

Hymn to Śiva:

90. Obeisance to you, the lord of good rites and unfathomable splendour, the lord of holy centres, the *Bījin* (sower of seeds), the trident-bearing lord.

91. Obeisance to *Ameḍhra* (one without the penis), *Ūrdhvameḍhra* (one with erected penis), *Vaikuṇṭharetas* (from whose semen Viṣṇu was born), the eldest, the superior-most, the first and the foremost.

92. Obeisance to *Havya* (one to whom *Havis* offerings are made), who is worthy of worship, to *Sadyojāta*, the impervious, the lord of wealth, the deity wearing yellow barkrobes.

93. Hail to thee, the origin of living beings like us, the lord of the materials of Vedic and glorious heroic rituals.

94. Obeisance to the lord of Yoga and Sāṁkhya, to the lord of sages of (controlled, limited) sleep.

95. Obeisance to the lord of the loud roar, lightning, thunderbolt and clouds, to the lord of oceans and continents.

96. Obeisance to the lord of mountains, of *Varṣas* (subcontinents) and of rivers flowing to the west and the east.*

97. Obeisance to the lord of medicinal herbs and trees, to the presiding deity of virtue or religion and holy rites, and to the lord of continued existence (as distinguished from *Utpatti* and *laya* or creation and destruction or death).

98. Obeisance to the lord of juices and jewels, of moments, of *Kāla* (a unit of time).

99. Salute to the lord of *nimeṣas* (winking time), of *kāṣṭhās* (1/30 of a kalā), of days, nights, fortnights and months.

100. Obeisance to the lord of seasons, of numbers of *parārdha* and to the lord of the greatest of the great.

101. Obeisance to the lord of Purāṇas, the Yugas, of the fourfold creation and to the infinite-eyed.

---

*Mallinātha, quoted in Apte's *Students' Sk. Dictionary* 278, distinguishes between *nada* and *nadī* as follows :

prāk srotaso nadyaḥ pratyak-srotaso nadāḥ narmadām vinetyāhuḥ/

102. Obeisance to the lord of agriculture and other occupations settled at the beginning of the Kalpa, to the lord of the universe, of god Brahmā and others.

103. Obeisance to the lord of lores (*vidyās*), sacred rites and of *mantras*.

104. Obeisance to the lord of *pitṛs* (manes), of *paśus* (souls bound by *pāśa*), to thee of virtuous words, and to the ancient Bull.

105. Obeisance to thee of beautiful hair, of lifted-up eyes and upward heads, to the lord of paśus, and to the Bull-emblemed god.

106. Obeisance to the lord of Prajāpatis, Siddhas, of Garuḍa, serpents and birds.

107. Obeisance to the cow-eared deity seated on the Bull, the spike-eared deity, to the chief of Rākṣasas, the incomprehensible deity of Vāraha Kalpa.

108. Obeisance to the lord of *Apsaras*-s and *Gaṇas*, waters and splendour.

109. Obeisance to the lord of Lakṣmī endowed with glory and bashful modesty, to the congeries of the weak and the strong and to the agitator of the unagitable.

110. Bow to the long-horned, single-horned, humped Bull, to the body of (great) steadiness and to the light of great splendour.

111. Obeisance to the lord of the past, present and the future, to the valorous hero of great splendour, and to one who excels others.

112. Salute to the granter of boons, the most excellent, omnipresent lord of the past, present and future.

113. Hail to thee the (lord of the) people, the penance and bestower of boons, to the deity worthy of salutes (worship). Obeisance to the lord of salvation, of the people and the hell.

114. Obeisance to Bhava, the worshipper, the worshipped and the sacrificer, one praised with loud voice, to the illuminated, the *Nirguṇa* principle.

115. Bow to the noose, the hand and the well-ornamented one. Obeisance to the one with (proper) oblations, (wrongly offered) oblations, well-offered and well-whetted one.

116. Obeisance to the *Iṣṭa, Pūrta, Agniṣṭoma, Ṛtvik, Ṛta* (order), *Satya* (truth) and the lord of living beings.

117. Salute to the member of the sacrificial council, to *Dakṣiṇā* (the monentary gift in a sacrifice) and *Avabhṛtha* (the ceremonial ablution after the sacrifice). Obeisance to the non-injurer of the worlds, the charm and medicine for the individual soul.

118. Hail to the bestower of contentment, the three-eyed sweet-scented one. To the lord of the sense organs. Obeisance to the (lord of) remedy and to the lord wearing garlands.

119. Obeisance to the universe, to the universal-formed one with eyes and faces all round and one with infinite hands and feet.

120. Obeisance to *Havya* (offerings to gods), *Kavya* (offerings to the manes) and *Havya-Kavya*. Obeisance to Siddha, *Medhya* (pure), the desired and the unchanging lord.

121-122. Hail to the great hero, terrible agitator of the unagitable, one of good intellect, the deity of good subjects, the refulgent sun. Bow again and again to *Suparṇa* (beautiful-winged one), of gold colour, to the odd-eyed, three-eyed, tawny one endowed with great strength.

123. Obeisance to the dazzler of eyes, the gentle-eyed one, to the smoke-coloured, white (coloured), black (complexioned) and the red one.

124. Bow to the adorned, the reddish brown and yellow (coloured god), one equipped with quiver. Hail to the possessor of and the one devoid of *Viśeṣas* (speciality?).

125. Obeisance to the lotus-complexioned destroyer of death and to the god of death. Salute to the dark, white, tawny and red complexioned lord.

126. Obeisance to the lovely one of the colour of cloud at dusk, to the multi-formed holding skull in the hand, to the naked and to the one with matted hair.

127. Obeisance to the incomprehensible Śarva, unslayable and excellent. Obeisance to one that supports from front and back and hail to the fire.

128. Obeisance to the great, the impassable, the obstruction and to one of tawny colour. Obeisance to one with a body as lustrous as the sun. Obeisance to one with strength and velocity.

129. Obeisance to the Pināka-bearing lord, the stretching, thriving and prosperous deity, of keen intellect and wearing Rudrākṣa. Obeisance to the naked, tufted lord.

130. Obeisance to the variegated one of variegated colours, the mysterious, the supporter of all. Obeisance to the intelligent one, the contented, non-deposited (?) lord.

131. Obeisance to the forbearing, the quiescent, with body as strong as a thunderbolt. Obeisance to the destroyer of demons, the destroyer of sacrifice, the blue-necked deity abstaining from sexual intercourse.

132. Obeisance to the slayer of enemies, the annihilator, the one holding sharp weapons. Obeisance to the rejoicing, the delighted one connected with rivers.

133. Obeisance to *Praṇava*, the lord of *Praṇava*, the bestower of happiness, the hunter of the deer, the deft and the destroyer of Dakṣa's sacrifice.

134. Hail to the spirit that is multiformed one who excels all lords, the destroyer of the cities (*Tripura*), the quiescent, sweet-scented possessor of excellent arrows.

135. Obeisance to the deity in the form of Puṣpavat, to the destroyer of Bhaga's eyes, to the excellent Kaṇāda, and the destroyer of Kāma's body.

136. Bow to the terrible wheel of the sun, the suppressor of the lord of serpents, the destroyer of Daityas, and to the one who makes divine shouts.

137. Obeisance to the god ever fond of cremation ground. Hail to the three-eyed protector of vital breaths, the wearer of the garland of skulls.

138. Salute to the god eulogised by different beings full of pleasure, to one with a (half) male and (half) female form and to the one who pleases the goddess (Umā).

139. Obeisance to you with matted hair and staff. Obeisance to the one with serpent as sacred thread, to the one habitually indulging in dance and fond of music.

140. Obeisance to Manyu (wrathful), to a habitually cool (quiescent god), to the singer of excellent songs, to the terrible god, one with bangles in the hand, to the assumer of fierce forms.

141. Obeisance to the terrible, the awe-inspiring and the suppressor of Bhaga, who is praised by the Siddhas and is highly blessed.

142. Hail to the god who laughs freely and boisterously, who roars striking (clapping) his arms, who shouts, jumps and rejoices.

143-144. Obeisance to the wonderfully mysterious, sleeping and running, staring and meditating, stretching and expanding, harassing and running, moving and sporting (god). Obeisance to the one with a pot-bellied body, to the one who shakes, to the one with a shaven head, to the one without hands.

145. Salute to the one in the guise of a mad person, to the one with tinkling ornaments, to the one with hideous dress and to the ruthless, fierce and infuriated (deity).

146. Obeisance to the incomprehensible, to the illuminated, to the brilliance beyond attributes, to the one fond of argument and to the one wearing signet jewel.

147. Hail to (the god) with child-like form, to one with unequalled qualities, to the secret Gaṇa, to the unattainable yet eternal refuge.

148. This earth, mother of the worlds, constitutes your feet resorted to by the good. Your unfathomable belly is the support of persons who have achieved Yogic power.

149. The firmament bedecked by the clusters of stars extends in your middle. The glorious garland on your chest shines like the galaxy of stars.

150-151. The ten quarters are your arms bedecked with bracelets and armlets. The expansive wide neck of yours, comparable to the cluster of blue clouds, shines gloriously bedecked with golden necklaces. Your mouth terrific with the curved fangs is unthwartable and incomparable.

152-153. How much does the turban on your head, done by garland of lotuses, shine ! The wise know that qualities like the brilliance of the sun, the beauty of the moon, the stability (and firmness) of the earth, the power of the wind, the heat in the fire, lustre in the moon, sound in (the element) ether and coolness in waters are evolved out of your excellent eternal qualities.

154-155. The following *Japa* (inaudible repetition) of the

(following) names of Śiva should be performed : *Mahāyogin* (a great Yogin), *Mahādeva* (great god), *Maheśvara* (the supreme ruler), *Pureśaya* (abiding in the city i.e. body), *Guhāvāsin* (the resident in the cavity of the heart), *Khecara* (the sky-walker), *Rajanicara* (nocturnal wanderer), *Taponidhi* (storehouse of austerities), *Guhaguru* (father or teacher of Skanda), *Nandana* (the delighter), *Nandivardhana* (increaser of delight), *Hayaśirṣa* (horse-headed), *Dharādhātṛ* (the supporter of the earth), *Vidhātṛ* (the creator), *Bhūtivāhana* (carrier or bestower of welfare),

156. *Boddhavya* (worthy of being realized), *Bodhana* (enlightener), *Netṛ* (the leader), *Dhūrvaha* (bearer of the yoke i.e. responsibility), *Duṣprakampaka* (one shaking heavily?), *Bṛhadratha* (possessor of a big chariot), *Bhīma-karman* (of terrific activity), *Bṛhatkīrti* (widely renowned) *Dhanañjaya* (winner of wealth),

157. *Ghaṇṭāpriya* (fond of bells), *Dhvajin* (having a banner), *Chatrin* (having an umbrella—a royal insignia), *patākādhvajinipati* (lord of a flag and an army), *Kavaci* (clad in a coat of mail), *Paṭṭiśin* (armed with a sharp iron club), *Śaṅkhin* (having a conch shell), *Pāśahastin* (holding a noose in hand), *Paraśubhṛt* (wielder of an axe),

158. *Agama* (mountain-like firm), *Anagha* (sinless), *Śūra* (brave), *Devarājārimardana* (slayer of the enemies of Indra). It is by propitiating you that enemies were killed in battles by us.

159. You are (such) a fire as is not satisfied by drinking all the seas. You are the abode of furiousness (but) delighted in mind. You are destroyer of Kāma (god of love) but a bestower of desired objects and a lovable one.

160. You are absorbed in Brahman, celibate, controller of sex-organs, worshipped by the good. You are the inexhaustible treasure of Vedas and sacrifice (sacrificial ritual) is ordained by you.

161. You are the sacrificial fire carrying oblations, the Vedas and prescriptions in the Vedas. When you are pleased, O Mahādeva, we too are pleased.

162. You are the lord of the eternal (beginningless), the mass of splendour, Brahmā, the creator of the worlds, the first creation. Sāṅkhyas know that you are transcendental to Prakṛti. When their meditation is over, they do not enter death.

163. The Yogins who are ever in communion with you through Yoga, eschew sensual pleasures. Other mortals who resort to you become sinless and enjoy divine pleasure.

164. Limitless is the greatness of (you) the supreme soul. Whatever we knew of the glory of the incomprehensible reality has been glorified according to our (humble) ability. Be ever and everywhere auspicious to us. Whoever you are you are so (incomprehensible). Obeisance be unto you.

CHAPTER TWENTYFIVE

Birth and Death of Madhu and Kaiṭabha

Sūta continued :

1-2. Looking at them as if drinking them in (with his eyes), the consort of Umā, with honey-like tawny eyes uneven (three) in number, the Lord, destroyer of Dakṣa's sacrifice, wielder of the Pināka bow and a battle-axe, who was surrounded by goblins, became delighted with a beaming face on hearing his eulogy.

3. On hearing their nectar-like words, the supreme Lord asked lovingly what he himself knew before.

4. "Who are you two, Sirs, of noble souls, desirous of mutual welfare, with eyes having the lustre of a lotus, and who have come together in the terrible watery expanse?"

5. After glancing at each other, they replied to him : "O lord, of what avail, is our reply ? It is already known to you. Where is infinite happiness except in your conduct as you please?"

6. The blessed lord spoke in sweet, charming words : "O Brahmā, O Viṣṇu, I am addressing you both.

7. I am delighted with your devotion of permanent nature. I honour you both; you well deserve my respect. What is the excellent boon you desire to have?"

8. When these words were spoken by him, Viṣṇu told Brahmā : "O highly blessed one, do speak out the boon wished by you".

9. "O Viṣṇu, I am desirous of having progeny. I wish to have a son who will bear my responsibility.". So spoke Lord Brahmā who coveted to have a boon granting him (such) a son.

10-12. Then Viṣṇu said to Brahmā who was desirous of progeny, "Since you wish for an incomparably valiant son who will carry out your task, you ask Lord Maheśvara, the god of gods, to be (born as your) son."

Honouring the words of Viṣṇu, god Brahmā folded his palms in reverence and humbly bowed to Lord Rudra, the bestower of boons. Desirous of a son, he addressed these (following) words in the company of Viṣṇu:

13. "O Supreme Lord, if you are so pleased with me who am desirous of a son, soul of the universe, you shall be my son or you shall grant me a son like you who will bear my burden. If you are pleased to grant me this boon, I shall not choose any other."

14. On hearing his request, the lord, the destroyer of the eyes of Bhaga, piously and undeceitfully said : "So be it".

15-16. "O *Suvrata* (one of good vows), when you will be overwhelmed by anger at the unsuccessfulness of an activity undertaken by you, I shall be born then from your forehead (as a friendly noble-souled sage Rudra), one of the eleven Rudras, the cause of the vital breaths. I shall wield a trident in my hand, and shall be accompanied by my followers."

17. After bestowing incomparable favour (boon) upon Brahmā at first, he told Viṣṇu, "I (desire to) grant you a boon too".

18. The blessed Viṣṇu replied thus: "O Lord, if you are pleased with me, it is as good as having done everything (to me). O Cloud-vehicled god, let my devotion to you be well established in you."[1]

19. The Lord, thus addressed, spoke to Viṣṇu : "O Viṣṇu, O eternal lord, listen, how I am pleased with you.

20. The entire universe, whether illuminated or unillumina-

1. Though regarded as a Śaiva Purāṇa, passages like vv. 19-29 which emphasize the identity of Śiva and Viṣṇu exercise integrative influence.

ted, mobile or immobile shall be identified with me (Rudra) and yourself (Nārāyaṇa).

21. I am the fire, you are the moon. I am the day, you are the night. I am the truth, you are the Order (*Ṛta*). You are the sacrifice, I am (its) fruit.

22. You are the knowledge, I am the object of knowledge. Performing your *Japa*, pious people (lit. performers of meritorious deeds) will enter me if you are pleased. At the end of the Yuga, there is no better goal than this (abiding with us).

23. Know yourself as Prakṛti. Know me as Puruṣa, Śiva. You are one half of my body just as I am your other half.

24. You are my left side which is dark and bears the mark of Śrīvatsa. I am your right side which is blue and red.

25. O Viṣṇu you are my heart. I am stationed in your heart. You are the doer of all activities. I am the activator.

26. So, come, hail to you, my dear cloud-coloured one, adieu". After saying this to Viṣṇu, the great Lord vanished.

27. When the lord had vanished, the delighted Viṣṇu, lord of the earth, entered water and lay on his couch.

28. Then with a delighted mind Brahmā, the lotus-born, lotus-eyed deity, resorted to his own seat in the lotus having the lustre of the interior of a lotus.

29-30. After a long lapse of time, two brothers of great strength and energy, the unrivalled Madhu and Kaiṭabha spoke to Brahmā, "You will become our prey". After saying thus both of them vanished.

31. On coming to know of their terrible intention and realising his greatness, the lotus-born deity began to gather further information.

32. As he did not know the make-up of the pericarp nor the way out, he descended to the nether regions by way of the lotus stalk. Then within the waters, he saw Viṣṇu with the deer-skin as his upper robe.

33. He then woke him up and when he woke up he said—"O Lord, I am afraid of spirits. Get up, save me. Be thou my benefactor."

34. Then, Lord Viṣṇu, the suppressor spoke, "You should not be afraid, you should not be afraid."

35. Since you have uttered at the outset, there is a danger to me from *Bhūtas* (spirits). You will therefore kill the Daityas through words *Bhū* etc."

36. Bhūr, Bhuvaḥ, Svaḥ (the earth, the firmament and the heaven) entered the self-born Lord. Having circumambulated, Brahmā returned to his (former) seat.

37. When Brahmā had gone, Lord Viṣṇu created two brothers Viṣṇu and Jiṣṇu out of his mouth, and instructed (them): "Both of you should protect Brahmā after knowing the next arrival of Madhu and Kaiṭabha."

38. Meanwhile, Madhu and Kaiṭabha assumed forms similar to those of Viṣṇu and Jiṣṇu. After assumption of similar forms, they stood in front of him facing him.

39. Then they spoke terrible words to Brahmā: "You should be the judge, while we fight."

40. Then they entered water which they paralysed by their Māyā. A tumultuous fight arose, when they fought with one another.

41. A thousand divine years elapsed as they fought. Still their pride, arrogance and eagerness for mutual fight did not subside.

42. If they had different marks, they could have been distinguished but they had similar forms. Agitated in the mind due to this similarity, Brahmā began to meditate.

43. By his divine vision he understood the distinction between them. He tied a subtle secret amulet of lotus filaments and also a girdle round their body. Then he uttered the Mantra.

44. While he uttered the Mantra, a virgin of universal form appeared there itself. The lustre of her face resembled the splendour of the lotus and the moon. The chaste lady held a lotus in her hand. On seeing her the Daityas were distressed. Their faces turned pallid due to fear.

45. In sweet voice Brahmā spoke to the virgin, "O chaste lady, tell me the truth, who you are. What are your antecedents?"

46-47. With palms joined in reverence, the virgin worshipped Brahmā and said after singing a eulogistic hymns. "Know that I am Mohinī (the enchantress), the Māyā of Viṣṇu and his messenger. O Brahmā, on being glorified by you, I came to you hurriedly." Delighted with her, Brahmā gave her a name.

48. "Since you came here as (soon as) this Mantra was uttered by me, you will be known as *Mahāvyāhṛti*[1] (the great utterance).

49. Since you appeared breaking through the head, you will be called *Sāvitrī*. Though you are born of one part (*aṁśa*) you will have many parts.

50. O auspicious-faced lady! Due to my grace, these and other minor names derived from your activities will be applicable to you."

51-22. The two demons on being afflicted thus begged for his boon. "Our death shall come in an uncovered place. We shall be born as your sons in future". Saying, "So be it", they were killed : Kaiṭabha by Viṣṇu and Madhu by Jiṣṇu.

53. Thus with a desire for the welfare of the worlds the two Daityas were killed by Brahmā, Viṣṇu and Jiṣṇu concertedly.

54. Know how Īśa (Śiva) was born as the son of Brahmā. When the fight of Madhu and Kaiṭabha with Viṣṇu and Jiṣṇu was over, Brahmā spoke to Viṣṇu:

55. "Today a hundred years have elapsed. The time has come when I shall go to my abode, terrible due to congestion and flooding".

56. At his instance, the lord effected Dissolution, making the earth devoid of immobile beings and making the mobile beings settled in Prakṛti.

57. "O Viṣṇu, O increaser of prosperity, welfare unto you. If thus the ocean has been diffused by you, tell me what I shall do for you."

58-59. "O gold-lustred, lotus-born! Listen to my words. The favour that you obtained from the lord with the desire for a son has fructified now. You have become free from indebtedness. Create four kinds of living beings or abandon the effort."

60. Getting the hint from Viṣṇu, the lotus-born deity Brahmā conceived in his mind to create the subjects. Then he performed a severe penance.

---

1. Verses 48 & 49 give popular etymology of *Mahāvyāhṛti* and *Sāvitrī*.

61. While he was performing penance thus, nothing happened. When a long time elapsed, due to grief his anger increased.

62-63. From his eyes defiled by anger, drops of tears fell. From those drops of tears, poisonous serpents manifested themselves. They had the elements of gas, bile and phlegm in their humour. They were of great strength. They were bedecked by the Svastika signs. They had scattered hairs.

64. On seeing the serpents born at the outset, Brahmā lamented. If the fruit is such, fie upon my penance. In the very beginning progeny has become destructive of the world.

65. A severe senselessness born of anger and annoyance overtook him. Due to the heat (severity) of fainting, Brahmā forsook his vital breaths (became unconscious).

66. From his body of unequalled prowess eleven souls, the Rudras, manifested themselves, crying out of pity. Since they cried, they were known as Rudras. Their Rudra designation is due to that.

67. Rudras are Prāṇas and Prāṇas are Rudras. The vital breaths are stationed in all living beings.

68. To him who was great and fierce and who had performed good actions, the trident-bearing lord gave the vital breaths. Then out of the forehead of Brahmā, there emerged a being identical with the eleven (Rudras).

69. The Lord who gave to Brahmā his vital breaths, became his son. When Brahmā was revived to life, Rudra spoke to him delightfully:

70. "O Brahmā, you may express your desire. Think of yourself and know me as your son Rudra. Bless me with your favour."

71-72. On hearing his words, mostly what he had felt in his mind, Brahmā became delighted. His eyes shone with the lustre of full-blown lotus as he returned to life. Lord Brahmā, attaining the lustre of unalloyed gold, spoke in charming majestic words :

73. "O blessed one, you delight my mind. Speak who are

you that as the embodied bliss of the universe stand divided into eleven forms."

74. Thus addressed by Lord Brahmā of infinite splendour, Rudra saluted him along with his sons and spoke.

75-76. "O Brahmā, I was requested for a boon by you along with Viṣṇu : 'O Lord, be my son, or grant me a son equal to you who would carry my burden'. Activities shall be pursued by all persons born in the universe. O Lord of Devas, cast off your gloom and create the worlds."

77. Thus addressed, Brahmā was delighted in his mind and spoke to Rudra thus:

78. "In order to help me, create the subjects along with me. You are the sower of seeds of all living beings. Hence get ready for the task." Rudra accepted the suggestion and said "yes".

79. Then Brahmā, bedecked in deerskin created the mind at first and the retentive power of living beings (?) Thereafter he created Sarasvatī, the speech in multifold forms.

80. Then he, of great lustre, created seven mental sons : Bhṛgu, Aṅgiras, Dakṣa, Pulastya, Pulaha, Kratu and Vasiṣṭha.

81. He created physical sons too, equal to himself. Pursuing their path again, the cows were born out of his mouth.

82. Brahmā, grandfather of the worlds, created the Vedas with *Oṁkāra* at the head. Then he created Devas worthy of honour and other beings as mentioned before.

83. The Lord spoke to his mind-born sons, Dakṣa and others: "Welfare unto ye. Along with Rudra you create subjects."

84. Approaching Rudra the Prajāpatis said, "O Lord, O Maheśvara, we along with you, desire to create progeny. This is what Brahmā has asked you too".

85-86. Thus addressed Lord Rudra spoke to them: "O Devas, Brahmā's sons, take the vital breaths from me. Make these sons of mine, the Brāhmaṇas, the foremost of the first born. Now you shall create, at my bidding, the seven species of people from Brahmā onward to a blade of grass. They shall be of my nature. Hail unto ye all".

87. Thus addressed by him they replied to Rudra, the trident-bearing primordial lord, "O Sir, everything will happen as you please."

88. After getting permission from lord Rudra, the Prajāpatis spoke to the noble Dakṣa, "Sir, you are the most excellent Prajāpati. Keeping you ahead and by your favour, we will create progeny."

89. Saying "So be it", Dakṣa accepted their suggestion. Desirous of progeny, he with his team, began the work of creation. When Rudra stayed (away) from creation, Brahmā took up the task.

90. When the seventh Kalpa passed Ṛbhu and Sanatkumāra were born. They settled as residents in Tapoloka. Then the Lord created mind-born sages also.

CHAPTER TWENTYSIX

Origin of Sounds[1]

Sūta said:

1. O intelligent one, wonderful are the secrets which you have truthfully spoken for blessing the worlds.

2. There I have a doubt regarding the incarnations of the trident-bearing lord. What is the reason that the great God (Mahādeva) avoids the previous Yugas and takes incarnation in the terrible Kali age (only)?

3. I wish to know how the lord took up incarnation in this Vaivasvata Manvantara.

4. There is nothing unknown to you in this or in the other world. O intelligent lord, if I deserve to hear that great account please tell me. I ask you humbly for the instruction of the devotees.

---

1. This esoteric exposition of *Oṁ*, tracing to it the creation of vowels (and consonants also) and connecting 14 Manus with the 14 vowels, shows how Purāṇic thinkers tried to emphasize the importance of *Oṁ* as the source of everything.

Lomaśa said :

5. Thus asked, Lord Vāyu of great brilliance honoured by the people and engaged in their welfare said :

6. "O son of Gādhi, what you have asked me is a great secret in the world. I shall explain everything. Please listen as I narrate this to you.

7. Formerly, when a thousand divine years had elapsed in the vast ocean of water, Brahmā, desiring to create the subjects was distressed and he began to contemplate.

8. While he was contemplating, a boy manifested himself. His body was emitting divine fragrance. He was reciting nectar-like divine Vedas.

9. He was repeating the Vedic lore that had neither sound, nor touch, nor colour nor smell nor taste and which the four-faced lord (Brahmā) had secured.

10. Then he became engrossed in meditation. After performing terrible penance, he thought within himself thrice, "Who is this ?"

11. While he was contemplating thus, an eternal (imperishable) syllable manifested itself. It was devoid of any sound, touch, form, taste or smell.

12. Then he saw his own form, the most excellect one in the worlds. Meditating upon the lord, he saw it again.

13. He saw that it was white, red, yellow and black. He looked into the colour. It was neither a woman nor a eunuch.

14. After knowing it, he contemplated over the syllable for a pretty long time. While meditating thus, the syllable came out of his throat.

15. It consisted of one single *mātrā*. Its sound was very loud. It was white in colour and very pure. That *Oṁkāra* would be the Veda. The syllable was verily Maheśvara himself.[1]

16. While the self-born Brahmā was contemplating, the red colour manifested itself. That is known as the first Veda [*Deva* in A] .

17. The Ṛgveda is the first Veda that begins with the (words) "*agnimile purohitam*" (RV1.1.1). On perceiving this

1. The identification of Oṁ, Brahman or Vedas and Śiva enhances Śiva's greatness in the minds of listeners.

Ṛk, Brahmā the creator of worlds and of great splendour thought, "What is this?"

18. While he was contemplating, the Lord, due to his power of Lordship, turned it into a syllable of two *mātrās*.

19. Then he thought of the *Akṣara* as consisting of two *Mātrās*. It manifested itself as red. The Yajur-veda was born out of it.

20. The Yajur mantra begins '*iṣetvā ūrjetvā vāyavastha devo vaḥ savitā punaḥ*' (TS 1.1.1 and 1.1.15). The Ṛgveda is declared to be (consisting) of a single *mātrā* and the Yajurveda of two *mātrās*.

21. On perceiving the Veda and the *Akṣara* of two *Mātrās*, lord Brahmā contemplated over the *Akṣara* of two *Mātrās*.

22. While he was contemplating *Oṁkāra* appeared. Then Brahmā thought over the *Akṣara Oṁkāra*.

23. Then he observed the yellow Ṛk that rose up, beginning with the words "*agna āyāhi vītaye gṛṇāno havya dātaye*". (RV VI. 16. 10, also Sāmaveda 1.1

24-26. He, the lord of great brilliance, saw the Vedas present. He contemplated over the *Akṣara* thrice during the three junctions (dawn, mid-day, and dusk). The *Akṣara* which is called Brahman the *Oṁkāra*, assumes three colours during the three *Savana* periods. Due to the contact with the three, that *Akṣara* had three colours. It was perceivable, imperceivable and manifest. It was triple, symbolizing the three heavens. It had three *Mātrās*, three worlds and three Yogas. It was eternal. Since Lord Brahmā contemplated upon that *Akṣara*, it was Brahma.

27. It had the form of the self-born (deity). It saw the lord of fourteen faces of shining splendour. After creating *Oṁkāra* at the outset, the self-born deity Brahmā became visible.

28. Then, out of the four mouths of the four-faced god came out fourteen letters—various letters and vowels. That is the refulgent initial letter. From it sixty-three letters have the letter *A* at the beginning.

29. Hence for serving a common purpose for all letters, the self-born Brahmā stood in the form of "*A*" at the outset. It was the first vowel.

30. Then from those vowels, fourteen Manus of big faces were born. They are the divine sounds in the Manvantara.

31. The letter "*A*" which has fourteen faces and which is known as Brahmā and which is equal to him is called Prajāpati. It exists in all letters.[1]

32. From the first face, Svāyaṁbhuva Manu was born. He is known as the letter "*A*" of the self-born Brahmā. Its colour is white.[2]

1. The purāṇa linguistics believes in the existence of vowel "*A*" in all letters.

2. Verses 32-49 show a crude attempt to connect the 14 Manus to the vowels as follows:

Sr. No. of Brahman's face	Letter of alphabet	Name of the Manu associated	Colour
1st Face	A	Svāyaṁbhuva	White
2nd	Ā	Svārociṣa	Yellowish white
3rd*	I	The Sun (?)—Yajurveda	
	Ī	Kṣattriya	Red
	*No Manu named for I & Ī		
4th	U	Tāmasa	Copper-coloured
5th	Ū	Cariṣṇava	Yellow
6th	Oṁ	(Vijaya?)	Tawny
7th	Ṛ	Vaivasvata	Dark
8th	Ṝ (long)	Sāvarṇī	Dark bluc
9th	Ḷ (लृ)	Dhūmra	Smoky
10th	Ḹ (लॄ)	Sāvarṇika	Similar as above
11th	E	Piśaṅga Manu	Reddish brown
12th	AI	Also Piśaṅga Manu	Reddish brown with the lustre of Bhasma
13th	O	Not named	Five colours
14th	AU	Sāvarṇi	Variegated

This tabular statement shows that

(i) The list of Manus is different from the usual list.

(ii) Names of some Manus are repeated.

(iii) Some letters e.g., I, Ī, O, Oṁ have no presiding Manus.

(iv) The Purāṇa author has foisted long Ḹ on the alphabet though no grammarian accepts it.

*Pāṇini does not recognize long Ḹ (लॄ)

33. From his second face the letter "*Ā*" was born. He is known as the Svārocisa Manu. His colour is yellowish white.

34. From his third face was born the letter "*Ī*" the most excellent of the Yajus. The sun consists of Yajus from which the Yajurveda manifested itself.

35. That Manu is known as the letter "*I*". He is valorous and of red colour. The Kṣattras (the warrior caste) function from it. Hence a Kṣattriya is red.

36. From his fourth face was born the vowel "*U*". It is copper-coloured. It is known as Tāmasa Manu.

37. From his fifth face the letter "*Ū*" was born. It is yellow in colour. It is known as Cariṣṇava Manu.

38. Then from his sixth face, Oṁkāra was born. It was tawny in colour. From the sixth was born the superior-most *Vijaya* (Victory) of great penance.

39. From his seventh face was born the vowel "*Ṛ*". It is known as Vaivasvata Manu. It is dark in colour.

40. From his eighth face emerged the (long) "*Ṝ*". Due to its dark blue colour and due to its being similar (in sibilant pronunciation ?) in Śyā-ma, it is called Sāvarṇi.

41. From his ninth face was born the ninth letter "*Ḷ*". It has the colour of the smoke and (the Manu ?) is known as "Dhūmra".

42. From his tenth face was born the letter (long) "*Ḹ*". It is similar to the lord and has a similar colour. Hence it is known as Sāvarṇika Manu.

43. From his eleventh face was born the letter "*E*". It is called 'Manu'. It is reddish brown in colour. It is known as Piśaṅga (reddish brown) Manu.

44. From his twelfth face was born the letter "*Ai*". It is reddish brown with the lustre of *Bhasma* (ashes). It is also known as Piśaṅga Manu.

45. The letter that was born from his thirteenth face was called the letter "*O*", which consisting of five colours, excels all.

46. The letter born from his fourteenth face was called the letter "*AU*". It is of variegated colours. It is known as Sāvarṇi Manu.

47. Thus the Manus, letters and colours shall be known precisely in regard to Kalpa, accent and letters.

48. The vowels are of similar colour. They are assigned to *Varṇas* due to their similarity in colour. Their logical connection or natural sequence is stated.

49. Since born in the same Kalpa, they are of the same colour, the junctions (combinations, transitions) of the Kalpas or letters occur in respect of similar entities.

50. The groups of letters are formed by their places of utterance (*sthānas*) as the distributions of castes by their professional equity. This is the practice in regard to the junctions of vowels and the transition of Kalpas.

CHAPTER TWENTYSEVEN

Names and Bodies of the Great Lord[1]

The sages said :

1. The manifestation in this Kalpa of the noble-souled supreme Lord Rudra along with the spiritually aspirant sages has been mentioned by you. Now let us hear this in detail.

Sūta narrated :

2. The origin of the primordial creation has been narrated by me briefly. Now I shall describe in detail the bodies and names of Lord Rudra.

3. The supreme Lord begot of his wives several sons in the eighth Kalpa that has passed. Now listen.

4. In the beginning of the Kalpa, while he was meditating about a son who should be his equal, there appeared in his lap

1. This chapter corresponds to Bd. P. I.2.10 and a number of verses are common to them both. The topic of this chapter—the eightfold form—*aṣṭamūrti*—of Śiva is popular in Purāṇas and classical literature.

a youth blue and red in colour. He held him who was blazing in brilliance and shouting terribly.

5. On seeing him crying suddenly Brahmā asked the child Nīlalohita,[1] "Why are you crying ?"

6. The boy said : "O grand-sire, at first give me a name".[2] "O Lord, you are named Rudra". Though he was thus told, he cried again.

7. "Why do you cry ?" Brahmā asked him again as he cried. The boy said to Brahmā, "Give me a second name".

8. "O Lord, you are Bhava by name." On being told thus he cried again. Brahmā asked Śaṅkara, "Why do you cry ?"

9. "Give me a third name", he replied to him (Brahmā). "O Lord ! You are Śiva by name", he was told. But he cried again.

10. "Why do you cry ?" asked Brahmā again as he cried. He told the self-born deity, "Give me a fourth name".

11. On being told "O Lord, you are Paśupati (the lord of Paśus-individual souls)", he cried again. As he cried again, Brahmā asked him, "Why do you cry ?"

12. When told, "Give me a fifth name", he replied, "O Lord, you are Īśa by name." On being told thus, he cried again.

13. "Why do you cry ?" Brahmā asked him as he cried. He told the Lord, "Give me a sixth name".

14. "O Lord, you are Bhīma by name". On being told thus he cried again. As he cried again Brahmā said, "Why do you cry ?"

15. "Give me a seventh name". On being told thus, he replied to him, "O Lord, you are Ugra by name". On being told thus, he cried again.

16. "Why do you cry ?" asked Brahmā as he cried. "O Lord, give me an eighth name". When he was told, "You are Mahādeva by name", he stopped (crying).

17. After obtaining these names from Brahmā, the Lord requested, "Assign bodies to these names".

---

1. The identification of Rudra and Agni is suggested by this epithet.

2. The legend of Rudra crying for a name and god Brahmā assigning a name to him and the recurrence of this granting of names for eight times is an amplification of the same story in *Satapatha Brāhmaṇa* (Ś Br.6.3.1-18).

18-19. Then the following bodies for these names were created by Brahmā. These were the sun, the earth, water, fire, air, ether, the initiated Brāhmaṇa and the moon. These (eight) have their source in Brahmā. Rudra should be worshipped and honoured in these bodies. Thus (honoured and worshipped) Rudra does not injure.[1]

20-21. Then Brahmā spoke to the lord Nīlalohita again : "To your second name declared as Bhava by me, the body shall be the waters". When this was said, the stable element of the nature of *Rasa* (the lymphatic constituent in his body) entered water. Hence water is known as *Bhava*.

22. The living beings are born of waters and purified by them (they are named *Bhavas*). Greation of beings is by means of production and purification.

23. So none shall pass urine or evacuate bowels in waters. None shall take bath in the nude or spit into water.

24. None shall indulge in sexual intercourse (in waters). None shall perform headbath. None shall look into water sportively while sailing by boat or standing still on the shore.

25. Since waters form the sacred body of Bhava, they shall nowhere be defiled. One shall avoid waters small (in quantity) or discoloured, insipid or foul smelling.

26. The ocean is the source of waters. Hence waters desire the ocean. On flowing into the ocean, waters became pure and nectarine.

27. Hence one shall not obstruct waters that desire to flow unto the ocean. Lord Bhava never injures a person who behaves with waters always thus.

28. Brahmā then spoke to the lord, "To your third name which was mentioned as Śarva,[2] let this earth be the third body."

29. When this was uttered, the firm and stable portion of the body called the bone (system) entered the earth. Hence the earth is called Śarva.

---

1. It appears that some verses are missing in this text as no mention is made of his first body. The missing verses might be corresponding to Bd. P. I.2.10.21-28.

2. There is a difference in the names—in v. 9 it is 'Śiva' while here in v. 28 it is a Śarva' as in Bd. P.

30. Therefore no wise man should leave faeces or urine in the shade or on steps. He should not pass urine on his own shadow.

31. He should evacuate the bowels after covering his head and the ground with grass. He who behaves thus to the earth is not injured by Śarva.

32-34. Then Brahmā addressed Lord Nīlalohita : 'To your fourth name designated as Īśāna by me, the wind shall be the fourth body. As soon as this was said, the wind (vital breath) which was stationed in him in five forms and is termed Prāṇa entered Vāyu. Hence Vāyu is called Īśāna. So one should not censure or revile the wind, the Lord himself, as it blows violently.

35. Then Brahmā spoke to Lord Dhūmralohita. To your fifth name Paśupati, let fire be the fifth body.

36. When this was said, Agni (Fire-god) entered the fiery element in the body. Hence Paśupati is called Agni.

37. The moon is called Soma. The group of medicinal herbs is its Ātman. Mahādeva does not kill a person who, during the full moon or the new moon day, worships the lord thus.

38. The sun protects people during the day and the moon at night. During one night (once in a month) the sun and the moon come together and that is the new moon day. One shall always be in communion with the lord on that day.

39. All this (universe) is pervaded by these bodies and names (of Rudra). The sun that moves about all alone is also called the moon*.

40. It is due to the light of the sun that the people see with their eyes. Rudra, in the resplendent form of the sun, drinks water with his rays.

41. Food and waters are eaten and drunk. The body (of Bhava) grows and flourishes by these.

42. It is his body called earth with which he sustains all people with a stable mind. It is the body called Śārvī which sustains the subjects.

---

*'Rudra' in Bd. P. I.2.10.66 is a better reading.

43. As long as the gaseous body of Īśāna is stationed in the bodies of living beings along with the functions of the vital breath, it is the vital breath of beings.

44. That which digests the food and beverages eaten and drunk, in the bellies of living beings, is called Paśupati's power. It is called the digestive power.

45. The pores within the bodies which are for facilitating the free movement of the wind, constitute the body called Bhīma.

46. The propounders of the Vedas initiated in sacrifices have their bodies in the form of Ugra. Ugra is, therefore, known as Dīkṣita (initiated Yajamāna).

47. That which conceives and contemplates and exists equally among the people is the mental body. It is known as the moon abiding among beings.

48. The moon is born again and again emerging fresh everytime. It is led[1] in accordance with their desire by Devas and Pitṛs. It is known as the great lord of nectarine nature, full of water.

49. To the first body of the lord known as Rudra[2] and symbo-

1. Bd. P.I.2.10.75 reads '*pīyate*' 'is drunk', a better reading.

2. Verses 49-60 give the names of the forms of Śiva, his abode or body allotted to him, designation of that body, name of his consort and the name of his son (s). The following tabular statement of the eight forms will clarify the above verses:

Name or Form of Śiva	Abode or Form or Body allotted	Name of the Consort	Name (s) of the Son (s)
1. Rudra	The Sun i.e. Heat or Prāṇa	Suvarcalā	Śanaiścara (Saturn)
2. Bhava	Water	Uṣā (Dhātrī in Bd. P.)	Uśanas (Venus)
3. Śarva	The earth	Vikeśī	Aṅgāraka (Mars)
4. Īśāna	The wind	Śivā	Manojava
5. Paśupati	The fire	Svāhā	Skanda
6. Bhīma	The ether (Ākāśa)	Quarters	Svarga
7. Ugra	Sacrificer (Dīkṣita)	Dīkṣā	Santāna
8. Mahādeva	The Moon	Rohiṇī	Budha (Mercury)

lized by the sun, the wife is Suvarcalā and the son is Śanaiścara (Saturn).

50. To the second body of the lord known as Bhava and symbolized by water, the wife is Uṣā and Uśanas (the planet Venus) the son.

51. To the third body of the lord known as Śarva and symbolized by the earth the wife is Vikeśī and Aṅgāraka (Mars) the son.

52. To the fourth body of the lord known as Īśāna and symbolized by the wind, the wife is Śivā and Manojava the son.

53. The body of Paśuptati which is remembered (proclaimed) as Fire by the twice-borns, has Svāhā for his wife and Skanda as the son.

54. The ether (Ākāśa) is called the body Bhīma, his sixth name. Quarters are remembered as his wives and Heaven (Svarga) as the son.

55. To the seventh body of the Lord known as Ugra and symbolized by the sacrificer, the wife is Dīkṣā (initiation) and Santāna as the son.

56-57. The eighth body of the great Lord is known as the Moon. His wife is Rohiṇī and Budha is remembered as the son. They should be saluted and bowed with respective names to each body.

58. By devotion to these bodies and the names of the Lord, viz. the Sun, the Waters, the Earth, Wind, Fire, Ether, Initiaited Priest and the Moon, the devotee attains *Sāyujya* with the Lord himself.

59. Thus the secret glory of the terrible lord has been narrated to you. Welfare be unto us the bipeds. Welfare be unto our quadrupeds.

60. Thus the origin of the bodies of Lord Mahādeva along with their designations has been recounted. Now listen to progeny of Bhṛgu.

It will be found that the abodes of the name of Nilalohita are the eight forms (*aṣṭa-mūrtis*) of Śiva which are the five *Mahābhūtas* (gross elements), Prāṇas and the mind (represented by the moon). Our Text does not give the designation of these *mūrtis* as given in the Bd. P.

CHAPTER TWENTYEIGHT

Families of Sages[1]

Sūta said :

1. Khyâti bore to Bhṛgu the holy lords Dhātṛ and Vidhātṛ living throughout the Manvantara. They were masters of happiness and misery and grant auspicious and inauspicious results to living beings.

2. Their eldest sister, the chaste goddess Śrī, the purifier of worlds, attained the auspicious lord Nārāyaṇa as her husband, and gave birth to two sons: Bala (Strength) and Utsāha (Energy).

3. Those heaven-walkers who pilot the aerial chariots of Devas and meritorious beings, were born to her as mental sons.

4-5. She had two daughters Āyati and Niyati who are remembered as the wives of Vidhātṛ and Dhātṛ. They had two sons Pāṇḍu and Mṛkaṇḍu. They were firm in religious vows, eternal and the very storehouses of the Vedic learning. Mārkaṇḍeya was born of Mṛkaṇḍu from Manasvinī.

6. Vedaśiras was his son born of Mūrdhanyā. The sons born to Vedaśiras in Pīvarī established the family line. They were known as Mārkaṇḍeyas. They were seers and masters of the Vedas.

7. Pāṇḍu begot of Puṇḍarīkā a son, Dyutimān. Two sons were born to him, viz. Dyutimanta and Sṛjavān. Their sons and grandsons had alliances with the descendants of Bhṛgu. Listen to the progeny of Marīci when the Svāyaṁbhuva Manvantara had passed.

8. Marīci's wife gave birth to a son Pūrṇamāsa. Know that these daughters too were born, viz. Kuṣṭi, Pṛṣṭi, Tviṣā and the beautiful Apaciti.

9. Pūrṇamāsā begot of Sarasvatī two sons Virajas and the righteous Parvasa.

---

1. This chapter corresponds to Bd. P. I. 2.11 even textually. It deals with the progeny of the famous seven sages such as Bhṛgu, Aṅgiras, Atri, Pulaha and others. It mentions their important descendants. The text states their (descendants') position in the Svāyaṁbhuva Manvantara.

10. Virāja's son Sudhāman was famous as learned Vairāja. The son of Sudhāman resorted to (and settled in) the eastern quarter.

11. He was the son of Gaurī and a valorous, righteous ruler of the worlds. Parvasa had great fame and he was the most excellent of all Gaṇas.

12. Parvasa begot of Parvasā two glorious sons Yajñavāma and Kāśyapa. These two righteous sons established their race.

13-14. Smṛti, the wife of Aṅgiras, gave birth to two sons and four daughters who were pious and renowned in the world. They (the daughters) were Sinivālī, Kuhū, Rākā and Anumati. The sons were two, viz. Bharatāgni and Kīrtimān.

15. Saṁhūti gave birth to Agni's (Bharatāgni's?) son, Lord Parjanya. Another Parjanya called Hiraṇyaromā was born of Marīci. He is known as the guardian of the world abiding upto the final dissolution of the world.

16. To Kīrtimān, Dhenukā bore two pious sons—Variṣṭha and Dhṛtimān. They were the most excellent of the descedants of Aṅgiras.

17-19. Their sons and grandsons who were in thousands have passed away. Anasūya gave birth to five sinless sons by Atri, and to a daughter called Śruti, the mother of Śaṅkhapada. She was the wife of Kardama, son of Pulaha, the Patriarch. The five sons of Atri are glorified (enumerated) thus: Satyanetra, Havya, Āpomūrti, Śanīśvara and the fifth was Soma. At the end of Svāyaṁbhuva Manvantara they passed away along with the Yāma gods.

20. The descendants of Atri, their sons and grandsons were in hundreds and thousands. They lived upto the end of Svāyaṁbhuva Manvantara.

21. Dattāli was the son of Pulastya by his wife Prīti. In his previous birth, in the Svāyaṁbhuva Maṇvantara, he was known as Agastya. Devabāhu was the middle and Vinīta was the third son of Pulastya.

22. Their younger sister, viz. Sadvatī was well known. She is remembered as the splended and pure wife of Agni (i.e. Bharatāgni) and mother of Parjanya.

23. The wife of Dattāli, the saintly and intelligent son of

Pulastya and Prīti brought forth many sons: Sujaṅgha and others. They became famous as Paulastyas (descendants of Pulastya).

24. Kṣamā gave birth to the sons of Pulaha. They had fiery refulgence and they established their reputation.

25. They were Kardama, Ambarīṣa, Sahiṣṇu, Ṛṣi and Dhanakapīvān. An auspicious daughter, Pīvarī, was also born.

26. Kardama's wife Śruti, daughter of Atri, gave birth to a son Śaṅkhapada and a daughter Kāmyā.

27. The glorious Śaṅkhapada was a Prajāpati and the ruler of worlds. After giving Kāmyā (in marriage) to Priyavrata, he settled in the southern region.

28. From Priyavrata, Kāmyā got ten sons equal to Svāyaṁbhuva Manu and two daughters who extended the Kṣattriya race.

29. The sons Dhanakapīvān and Sahiṣṇu became famous. So also Yaśodhārin, Kāmadeva and Sumadhyama.

30. From Ṛtu a son equal to Kratu was born and the progeny was auspicious. They did not marry and remained celibate. They were sixty thousand in number and known as Vālakhilyas.

31. They surround the sun and go ahead of Aruṇa. They will remain fellow-travellers with the sun till the universe is finally dissolved.

32. Two younger sisters were Puṇyātmā and Sumati. They were the daughters-in-law of Parvasa, son of Pūrṇamāsa.

33-34. Seven sons were born to Vasiṣṭha in Ūrjā. Their eldest sister was the slender-waisted lady Puṇḍarīkā who was the mother of Dyutimān and the wife of Pāṇḍu. Her younger brothers were seven. They were famous as Vāsiṣṭhas.

35. They were Rajas, Putra, Ardhabāhu, Savana, Adhana, Sutapas and Śukla. They are known as seven sages.

36. The famous daughter of Mārkaṇḍeya bore to Rajas a son known as Prajāpati Ketumān, a king in the western region.

37-38. Vāsiṣṭhas are known by their Gotra names. The races of the noble-souled Vāsiṣṭhas passed away in the Svāyaṁbhuva Manvantara.

Listen to the progeny of Agni.

Thus the creation of sages has been recounted along with their attendants. Henceforth, listen to the progeny of Agni in deatail and in due order.

CHAPTER TWENTYNINE

Progeny of Agni[1]

1-2. A mental son of Brahmā was the deity identifying himself with Agni (the Fire-god) in the Svāyaṁbhuva Manvantara. Svāhā bore to him three sons:[2] Pāvaka, Pāvamāna and Śuci or Śaura (solar-fire).

3. Pavamāna is the fire which is obtained after churning (the *Araṇi*). Śuci is remembered as the solar fire. Pāvaka is the fire originating from the lightning. These are their (specific) abodes.

1. In this chapter fortynine ritualistic functions of Fire are represented as so many Fire-gods and the correlation of these is arranged in a genealogical form. In fact it is a Vedic conception presented here in a popular form. Probably this formed a part of the original Purāṇa as it is found in the *Mbh. Vana* chs. 217-222, *Bd. P.* I. 2.12, *Mt. P.* 51, *VP.* I. 10. 14-17 to mention a few. V. S. Agrawal regards *Va. P.* account as the original (*Mt. P. : A study,* p. 155). Pargiter did not know the Vedic background when he condemned it as 'imaginary genealogy' (*AIHT,* p. 122) for it is no 'genealogy' at all.

2. The relations of the following fires will be clear from the following genealogical table :

Agni = Svāhā

Pavamāna (= Gārhapatya) Born of Araṇi (cf. RV. III. 29.2)	Pāvaka (= Dakṣiṇāgni) Born of water or Lightning (Vaidyuta)	Śuci (= Āhavaniya) Source The sun-god
Kavya-Vāhana (Belongs to Pitṛs)	Saha-rakṣa (Belongs to Asuras)	Havya-Vāhana (Belongs to Devas)

4. Pavamāna's son is called Kavya-vāhana. From Pāvaka was born Saharakṣa. Havyavāha was the son of Śuci.

5. Havyavāha is the fire of Devas. Kavyavāha is the fire of Pitṛs. Saharakṣa is the fire of Asuras. These are (thus) the three fires pertaining to the three (viz. Devas, Pitṛs and Asuras).

6. Their sons and grandsons are fortynine in number. I shall mention their divisions separately by (stating their) names.

7. Vaidyuta[1], the secular the fire, was the first son of Brahmā. His son Brahmaudanāgni was famous (by the name) Bharata.

8. Vaiśvānara and others were his sons. They were Mahar, Kāvya and Apāṁ-rasa. Amṛta was first churned in the Puṣkara[2] ocean by Atharvan. That Atharvan is the terrestrial fire. Dadhyaṅ[3] was Atharvan's son.

9. Atharvan shall be known as Bhṛgu and Aṅgiras as the son of Atharvan. Hence it is that the worldly fire Dadhyaṅ was Atharvan's son.

---

1. The group from Vaidyuta fire is arranged as follows :

Vaidyuta (Fire)
|
Brahmaudana or Bharata
|
Vaiśvānara — Kāvya — Apāṁ-rasa

Agni is called *Bharata* as he supplies Havya to gods. As *Śat. Br.* (I.4.2.2) explains :

eṣa agnir hi devebhyo bharati tasmād bharatagnir ityāhuḥ.

This genealogy thus identifies :

Brahmaudana=Bharata=Vaiśvānara (For details, see V. S. Agrawa *ibid* p. 158).

2. This is a reference to RVvi. 16. 12 where Agni is said to have been churned out of Puṣkara. Thus Puṣkara=Waters (*Āpo vai Puṣkaram—Śat. Br.* VI. 4. 2.2). *Śat. Br.* VII. 4.1-13 further explains that when Indra became frightened after killing Vṛtra, he resorted to waters. They (waters) offered their sap (*apāṁ rasaḥ*) to him and created a city (*pur*) for him. Hence water came to be called Puṣkara (*asmai puram akurvans tasmād puṣkaraṁ ha vai tat puṣkaram ācakṣate parokṣam.*

3. *Dadhyaṅ* is etymologically related with *dadhi* which according to *Śat. Br.* 7.5-1 is a symbol of the earth or Matter (*dadhi haivāsya lokasya rūpam*). Probably it is related to Dakṣiṇāgni.

10. Now the fire Pavamāna[1] which is remembered by the wise as *Nirmantha* (one generated by churning) should be known as *Gārhapatya* fire from whom were born two sons.

11. Śaṁsya is the *Āhavanīya* fire which is known as *Havyavāhana*. His second son is named as Śukra who is consecrated by reciting sacred Mantras.

12. *Sabhya* and *Āvasathya* were the two sons of the fire Śaṁsya. Śaṁsya *Havyavāhana* which is known as the *Āhavanīya* fire by the Brāhmaṇas loved sixteen rivers.[2]

13-14. They were Kāverī, Kṛṣṇaveṇī, Narmadā, Yamunā, Godāvarī, Vitastā, Candrabhāgā, Irāvatī, Vipāśā, Kauśikī, Śatadru, Sarayū, Sītā, Sarasvatī, Hrādinī and Pāvanī.[3]

15. He divided himself into separate sixteen parts among them and deposited himself in those *dhiṣṇis*.

16. *Dhiṣṇis* move about in the sky. Those that are born in them are called *Dhiṣṇis*. They are proclaimed as *Dhiṣṇis* as they are born in *Dhiṣṇis*.

17. Hence these sons of the rivers were born in *Dhiṣṇis*. Out of them some fires are *Viharaṇīya* (portable) and some

---

1.

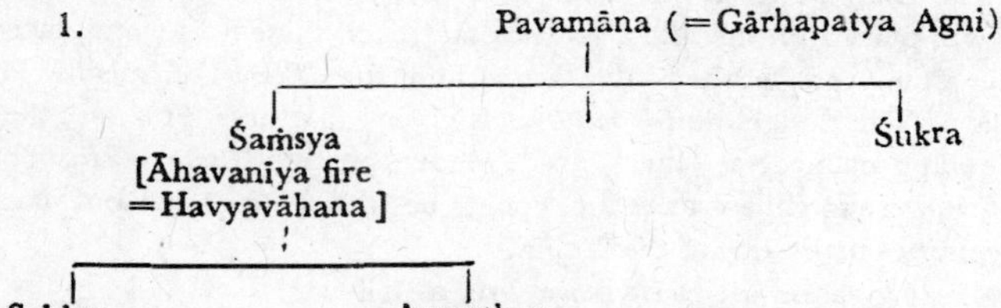

Sabhya is the fire kept burning in the recreation hall for diffusing warmth to people assembled (Medhātithi on Manu III. 185). Like the Gārhapatya fire, it is produced by friction (*Kātyāyana Śrauta Sūtra* IV. 9. 20).

Avasathya is the fire to be kept in the guest-room.

2. This is a poetic way of describing the spread of Yajña-cult. It covers the geographical area from Central Asia from the river Sītā or the Tarim (AGP 100-102) down to the Kāverī in South India. Modern political maps of India do not show India as known to Purāṇas.

3. The following are the modern names in the above list of rivers given in vv. 13-14: Kṛṣṇā-Veṇī (the Krishnā), Vitastā (the Jhelum), Candrabhāgā (the Chinab), Irāvatī (the Rāvī), Vipāśa (the Bias), Śatadru (the Sutlej), Kauśikī (the Kosī), Sītā (the Tarim—Yarkand), Hrādinī (the Brahmaputrā?), Iāvanī (the Ghaggar).

are *Upastheya* (to be worshipped at their places or spots)[1]. Listen, I shall explain them succinctly and precisely.

18. Ṛtu, Pravāhaṇa and Agnīdhra are the Dhiṣṇīs in front. Others are ordained in accordance with their seats in the order of sacrifice on the day when Soma juice is extracted.

19. Listen to the order of fires, the names of which are not mentioned before.[2] The fire Samrāṭ is the fire stationed on the second *Uttara-vedi*.

20. The Samrāṭ fire is proclaimed as eight (fold in form?). Brāhmaṇas worship them. Beneath it is the second Parṣad fire.

21. When the mantras "*Pra tadvoce nabhaḥ* (VS. 33.9?) etc. are repeated four times that fire is conceived. The fire named *Brahma-Jyoti-Vasu*[3] is spoken to have its abode in Brahmā's region.

22-23. A fire having no association with the celestial or the sacrificial fires has an abode in the cremation ground. The terrestrial fire of the ocean is said to abide in Brahmā's region. The lustrous fire Ṛtudhāmā lives in the Uduṁbara wood. (Line

---

1. The author classifies Dhiṣṇya fires into (1) *Viharaṇīya* and (2) *Upastheya*. The *Dhiṣṇyā* was a side-altar of a heap of earth covered with sand. Fire was placed on the altar. In *soma* sacrifices, these fires were placed between the altar (*Vedi*) of the Śrauta Yajña and the *Uttara-Vedi* meant for *soma* sacrifice. The designation *Upastheya* is given to these fires as they were to he approached at their fixed places on the *Uttara Vedi*. The *Viharaṇīya* fires were so called as they could be taken to any spot considered necessary on the day of the Yajña.

2. Verses 19-24 give the list of *Upastheya* fires as follows:

1. *Samrād agni* also called *Kṛśānu*.

2. Parṣad (but Mt. P. names it *Parjanya*) [Mt. P. mentions *Samūhya* fires but our text omits it].

3. *Brahma-jyotiḥ* (called *Vasudhāmā* in Mt. P.). If the reading *Vasudhāman* of *Mt. P.* 51-21 for *Vasurnāma* in our text be accepted, it would mean "The fire *Brahma-jyotiḥ* another name of which is *Vasudhāman* is in the place of the Brahman").

4. *Śāmitra* : The reading in Mt. P. (ibid) means, "The fire *Havyasūda* is also called *Śāmitra* and *Assamṛjjya*.

5. *Ajaikapāda* also called *Śālāmukhīya*.

6. *Ahirbudhnya* also called *Anuddeśya*.

The fire *Sata-dhāmā* alias *Śvarjyoti* in the list of Mt. P. is not found in our text.

3. Variations from Mt. P are noted in the notes.

repeated) the fire called Brahma-jyoti Vasu is said to be abiding in Brahmā's region.

24. Ajaikapāt is the *Upastheya* fire. Its place is in front of the sacrificial hall. Ahirbudhnya is the *Anuddeśya* (not kindled?). That fire is proclaimed as Gṛhapati.

25. All the sons of Śaṁsya fire are regarded as *Upastheya* by Brāhmaṇas.

I shall now explain the *Viharaṇiyas* and their eight sons.[1]

26. Kratu, Pravāhana and Agnīdhra are the Dhiṣṇīs there. On the day when Soma juice is extracted, they are carried to their spots.

27. The fire which is remembered as the son of Pautra, that Havya-bearer is called fire Śānti or Pracetas or Satya. It is the second fire.

28. The fire Viśvadeva is said to be at *Brahma-sthāna*. Avakṣu, the son of Acchāvāka, is conceived to be at the position of the earth (*Bhū*).

29. The powerful fire Uśīra is regarded as the son of Neṣṭhīya. The eighth fire Vyaratti is proclaimed as the son of Mārjāli (?).

30. Dhiṣṇyās are Viharaṇīyas (portable?) by Saumya (?) and another. Out of them that which is called Pāvaka is the foetus of waters.[2]

31. That fire shall be known as "*Avabhṛtha*" which is worshipped properly by oblations in the waters. The fire *Hṛcchaya* is his son, it is the fire stationed in the belly of men.

---

1. *Viharaṇīya* fires are eight in number. But their lists in our text and in the Mt. P. are different. These portable (viharaṇīya) fires are regarded as the sons of the stationary fires. The list of *Viharaṇīya* fires in our text is as follows :

1. Pravāhaṇa, 2. Śānti or Pracetas or Satya, 3. Viśvadeva, 4. Avakṣu, 5. Uśīra, 6. Vyaratti. Two more names are missing in this list, but Mt. P. 51 gives only four names and cannot supply the missing names.

2. Verses 30-35 give the following 'descendants' of the fire Pāvaka :

Pāvaka→Avabhṛtha→Hṛcchaya-→Manyumān→Saṁvartaka→Saharakṣa →Kṣāma→Kravyād.

The list of Agnis (Sons of Bṛhaspati) in *Mbh Vana* 219 though similar to this list is unsytematic and probably later. The same can be said of the list in the Mt. P. 51.

32. Manyumān, the scholarly fire, is the son of Jāṭhara (Gastric) fire. Mutually kindled that fire is the lord of living beings.

33. The son of the fire Manyumān is the terrible *Saṁvartaka* fire. That mare-faced fire stays in the ocean consuming its waters.

34. Saharakṣa is the son of the submarine fire. Saharakṣa's son Kṣāma burns human habitations.

35. The fire *Kravyāda* is his son. It consumes the dead. These are the sons i.e. descendants of the fire Pāvaka.

36. The fire Śuci, son of the Sun, was kindled by Gandharvas and Asuras by churning the *Araṇi* wood.[1]

37. Lord Āyus is the fire consecrated in the animal. Mahiman was the son of Āyus and his son was Śāvāna by name.

38. The fire that identifies (itself with it) in cooking and sacrifices is known as Savana. The son of the fire Savana was the famous Adbhuta.

39. Vivici is known as the great son of Adbhuta. It always swallows the offerings in expiatory rites of sinners.

40. Vivici's son was Arka and his sons are Anīkavān, Asṛjavān, Rakṣohā, Pitṛkṛt, Surabhi and Rukmavān. The latter abides in gold, jewels and other shining materials.

41. The fourteen fires are the progeny of the fire Śuci. These are called Vahnis. They are consecrated by reciting mantras in sacrifices.

42. In the Manvantara called Svāyaṁbhuva, in the first Sarga (creation), these fires who were *Abhimānins*, had passed away along with the Yāmas, the best of Devas.

43. In the previous Manvantara, these fires were those who identified themselves with their abodes called *Viharaṇiyas*, both sentient and non-sentient.

---

1. Verses 36-41 give the following 'descendants' of Śuci (the Son of the Sun-god):

Śuci→Āyus→Mahiman→Sāvāna (cooking as well as sacrificial fire)→ Adbhuta→Vivici→Arka.

Anīkavān | Asṛjavān | Rakṣobha | Pitṛkṛt | Surabhi | Rukmavān

Mt. P. adds Vīra as the Son of Adbhuta.

44. These (fires) were assigned to the three types of Karmas, viz. *Kāmya* (those depending on desire), *Naimittika* (occasional) and constant (*Nitya*). In the previous Manvantara they passed away along with the fair sons.

45-46. Thus the abodes and the abiders have been explained by me. Through them alone, the characteristics of the fires of the past and future Manvantaras have been enumerated. All of them are remembered as ascetics, those who performed Avabhṛtha bath, lords of subjects and luminous.

47. In the seven Manvantaras from Svārociṣa to Sāvarṇi, they shall be known through their different forms and purposes in all the Manvantaras.

48. The present fires exist with the present Devas and the future fires with the future Devas.

49. Thus the instruction about Fire-god has been imparted to you precisely. Now the account of Pitṛs (manes) will be told in detail and in due order.

CHAPTER THIRTY

The Curse of Dakṣa[1]

Sūta said :

1. Even as Brahmā was creating sons formerly in the Svāyaṁbhuva Manvantara waters,[2] human beings, Asuras and Devas were born.

2. While he thought upon Pitṛs (lit. like Pitṛs), the Pitṛs (Manes) were born. Their creation has been described before. Its details are being narrated now.

---

1. The story of the destruction of Dakṣa's sacrifice is (even textually) similar to that in *Mbh Śānti* 284 as many verses are common to both texts. But here in the introduction, we have a discussion about the concept of Time, the seasons and Pitṛs.

2. *gātrataḥ* (in Bd.P.I.2.13.1) 'From the limbs' is a better reading.

3. On seeing the creation of Devas, Asuras and human beings, god Brahmā said[1] (to himself i.e. conceived a new creation). While he thought upon Pitṛs, they were born.[2]

4. The six seasons (the spring etc.) are called the Pitṛs. The Vedic Śruti declares: "The seasons are the Pitṛ-Devas"[3]

5. In all the Manvantaras, past and future (the same is repeated). Formerly these were born in the auspicious Manvantara (called) Svāyaṁbhuva.

6. They (Pitṛs) are known by the names *Agniśvātta*[4] and *Barhiṣadas*. Those of them who were householders but did not perform *yajñas* are remembered as *Agniśvāttas*. They were not *Āhitāgnis* (who maintain regularly the sacred fire).

7. Those (of the Pitṛs) who performed sacrifices (and pressed Soma-juice) are the Pitṛs called *Soma-pīthins*. Those Pitṛs who maintained the sacred fire (while on the earth) are remembered as *Barhiṣad* Pitṛs. In the scriptures, the decision that seasons are the *Pitṛ-devas* is approved.

8-9. The months of *Madhu* and *Mādhava* (Caitra and Vaiśākha) should be known as *Rasas* (juicy); those of *Śuci* and *Śukra* (Jyeṣṭha and Āṣāḍha) are Suṣmins (lustrous). Those of *Nabhas* and *Nabhasya* (Śrāvaṇa and Bhādrapada) are cited as *jīvas*; those of *Iṣa* and *Ūrja* (Āśvina and Kārtika) are ambrosial; those of *Saha* and *Sahasya* (Mārgaśīrṣa and Pauṣa) are called *manyumān* (angry) and those of *Tapas* and *Tapasya* (Māgha and Phālguna) are terrible and cold.[5]

---

1. *abhyamanyata* (Bd. P.I.2.13.3) 'took pride in them'.

2. *upayakṣitāḥ* in the text is obscure *upapakṣataḥ*, 'from the flanks' in *op. cit.* is better. *Pa* and *ya* in Devanāgarī script are always confused.

3. The identification of seasons (*Ṛtus*) with Pitṛs is as old as *Tait. Br.* (I.4.10.8) which states:

athartavaḥ pitaraḥ prajāpatim pitṛ-yajñenāyajanta !

'Ṛtus are Pitṛs. They offered *Pitṛ-yajña* to Prajāpati, their father'. The identification of Ṛtus & Pitṛs is endorsed by Manu III. 217.

ṣaḍ ṛtūṁśca namas-kuryāt
Pitṛneva ca mantra-vit!

Also vide vv. 7, 11 below.

4. For classification of Pitṛs see *supra* ch. 1, p. 10, note 2 also.

5. The nomenclature Madhu, Mādhava etc. for modern months Caitra, Vaiśākha etc. is the orignal and older one (Kane *HD*, V. Part I, p. 668).

10. The periods of time (called seasons) are six. In them are included (periods of time called) months. These seasons are said to be sentient and insentient.

11. The seasons are the sons of Brahmā. They identify themselves with the months and fortnights as their stations.

12-13. Through the change of their abodes, these *Abhimānins* (deities who identify) will be recognizable. Day, night, month, season, tropical transits of the sun (a half year) and year constitute the abodes of the deities. Nimeṣas, Kalās, Kāṣṭhās, Muhūrtas, days and nights constitute the units of time.

14. Since these are stationed in them or since these identify with them, they are known as identifiers. I shall explain them. Understand.

15. The units of time are the *Tithis* of Parvans, the junctions; the fortnights are the halves of months: two fortnights make a month and two months constitutes a *Ṛtu* (season).

16. Three seasons constitute an *Ayana*. The two *Ayanas*, the southern and the northern, constitute a year which is a fixed period (*Sumeka*). Such are the positions of identifiers.

17. The sons of the season are five (viz. human beings, quadrupeds, birds, reptiles and trees). They are characterised by their seasonal changes.

18. Since the mobile and immobile beings are born of *Ārtavas* (seasonal changes, menstruation etc.), the seasonal changes are their fathers and seasons are grandfathers.

19. It is from *Sumeka** (fixed period of time) that beings are born and die. Hence *Sumeka* is remembered as the great-grandfather of the subjects.

20. Due to their having the same name, the same essences and the same nature, *Sthānins* (deities abiding in a particular *Sthāna* or unit of time) are declared to be identical with the *sthānas*.

21. He who is known as Prajāpati, is a year. A year is Agni. It is also called Ṛta by Brāhmaṇas.

22. Since they are born of Ṛta, the seasons are called Ṛtus.

**Vatsara* 'a year' in Bd. P. ibid. v. 21.

The months too are born of them. The Ṛtus are six in number and the five *Ārtavas* are their sons.

23. The flowering period of bipeds, quadrupeds, birds, reptiles and immovable beings is called *Kālārtava* (the seasonal change?).

24. The state of being Ṛtu and Ārtava is declared as fatherhood. Hence the seasons and Ārtavas should be known as Pitṛs.

25. Since beings are born of them through the *Ṛtu-Kāla* (period favourable for conception, the Ṛtu period), these Ārtavas are also Pitṛs—So we have heard (it reported).

26. The (deities) identifiers with Kāla (period of time) continue to stay in all Manvantaras conditioned and regulated by their identification with their positions.

27. The Pitṛs are of two types, the *Agniṣvāttas* and *Barhiṣads*. Two famous daughters were born of the Pitṛs.

28. They were Menā and Dhāriṇī both of whom supported the universe. Both of them were beautiful, propounders of the Vedas and practitioners of Yoga. Pitṛs gave both their daughters for the increase of Dharma.

29. Menā was the mind-born daughter of the *Agniṣvāttas*. Dhāriṇī was the mind-born daughter of the *Barhiṣads*.

30. The *Barhiṣads*, known as *Somapīthins* gave Dhāriṇī to Meru in marriage.

31. *Agniṣvāttas* gave Menā to Himālaya as wife. Their grandsons were known. Now listen to (the details of) the grandchildren.

32. Menā, the wife of Himavat, gave birth to Maināka and to (the river) Gaṅgā who became the wife of the briny Sea. Maināka's younger brother was Krauñca whence the continent Krauñca got its name.

33-34. Dhāriṇī, wife of Meru, gave birth to Mandara abounding in divine herbs and to three famous daughters—Velā, Niyati and the third Āyati. Āyati became the wife of Dhātṛ and Niyati was married to Vidhātṛ.

35. Their progeny are glorified (as existing) in Svāyambhuva Manvantara. Velā bore to Sāgara (the Sea) a daughter of noble qualities.

36. The daughter of the Sea called Sâvarṇā[1] became the wife of Prācīnabarhis. Savarṇā that daughter of the Sea (Samudra) (married to Prācīnabarhiṣ) gave birth to ten Pracetas who were the masters of the science of archery.

37. As a result of the curse of Śiva, Dakṣa, the son of the self-born god Brahmā, was reborn as their son[2] in the Cākṣuṣa Manvantara."

38. On hearing this, Śāṁśapāyana asked Sūta—"How was Dakṣa born in the Cākṣuṣa Manvantara formerly, as a result of the curse of Śiva? Narrate this in detail to us who ask you."

39. Thus requested, Sūta narrated the episode of Dakṣa and the occasion of Śiva's curse, after addressing Śāṁśapāyana.

40-41. Dakṣa had eight daughters whom I have already mentioned to you. He invited them from their homes and welcomed them at his house. They stayed in their father's house duly honoured. But the eldest (of them) Satī, wife of Śiva, was not invited by him out of hatred for Śiva.

42. Śiva, the son-in-law, (being) stable (enveloped in his own brilliance) never bowed to his father-in-law Dakṣa.

43. Knowing that her sisters had gone to their father's, Satī, though not invited, went to her father's house.

44. Highly infuriated (with wrath), the goddess spoke to, Dakṣa : "O Lord ! How is it that you have done this despicable act of dishonouring me by according greater honour to younger daughters ?

45. I am the eldest and the most excellent daughter. It does not behove you to be discourteous to me". Thus addressed, Dakṣa, with his eyes reddened with anger retorted :

46. "You are the most excellent of my daughters, foremost and most worthy of my respect for ever. Their husbands too are worthy of my respect always.

---

1 *Sāvarṇinā* in the text is incorrect as the next line records her name as Sāvarṇā—Sāmudrī.

2. The story of the second birth of Dakṣa is told here as in this birth Dakṣa became a descendant of Pitṛs. The story of the destruction of Dakṣa's sacrifice is found in *Mbh-Śanti* 283 and many Purāṇas like KP. I.14, 15, NP *uttara bhāga* 66 & others. Probably it is a part of social memory of some ancient conflict between Karma Mārga or Yajña cult and some Śaivite (Pāśupata?) cult or Jñāna Mārga.

47. O Satī, they are better in qualities and are more deserving than Śiva. They are good ascetics, absorbed in Brahman, righteous and great Yogins.

48. These sons-in-law of mine, viz. Vasiṣṭha, Atri, Pulastya, Aṅgiras, Pulaha, Kratu, Bhṛgu and Marīci are very great.

49. Śiva is my enemy. But you are his heart and soul, and *vice versa*. You are devoted to him. Hence I do not honour and welcome you."

50. So said Dakṣa with the deluded mind, resulting in a curse to himself and to the great sages mentioned.

51. Thus addressed, the infuriated Satī spoke to her father—"Since you insult me, who am pure in speech, mind and acts, I cast off this body, O father, born of you."

52. Then goddess Satī, dejected and infuriated due to the insult, spoke after bowing mentally to Śiva.

53. "Wherever I am reborn with another refulgent body, I, undeluded and righteous, will attain the status of the righteous wife of Śiva alone."

54. She sat there itself with her Ātman in Yogic communion. She mentally retained the *Āgneyī Dhāraṇā*.

55. Fire came out of all limbs of her body and was blown by the wind, from the *Āgneyī Dhāraṇā*. It reduced her to ashes.

56. On hearing about the death of Satī, and on understanding their conversation precisely, the trident-bearing Śiva became furious with Dakṣa and other sages.

57-58. "O Dakṣa, since for my sake pure, sinless Satī had been insulted and all other daughters were praised along with their husbands, they will die (attain Yama's region) and will be born again as persons not born of womb, when I perform another sacrifice.

59. They will be there when Brahmā will offer sour gruel in fire in the Cākṣuṣa Manvantara."

After cursing the sages he addressed Dakṣa again.

60. "There will be a king Cākṣuṣa in the family of Cākṣuṣa Manu. He will be the grandson of Prācīnabarhis and the son of Pracetas.

61. When the Cākṣuṣa Manvantara comes you will be born, by the name of Dakṣa, of Māriṣā (also Mārṣā), daughter of trees."

Dakṣa said :

62. "O evil-minded one, I will be putting up obstacles to you, there also, again and again in the rites of virtue (Dharma), wealth and love (Kāma).

63. Since you spoke cruelly of the sages for my sake, the Brāhmaṇas will never worship you in their sacrifice where they worship Devas.

64. After offering *Āhutis* (to you) they will offer water (as purification) in your rites; you will stay here (on the earth) to the end of the Yuga".

Rudra said:

65. "The earth is called the first among the worlds. At the behest of Brahmā, I shall sustain that world.

66. In this sphere the worlds and suns stand surrounded (by oceans). I support them always but not at your behest.

67. Devas are classified into four castes. They take meals together (through fire). I shall not take meals with them. They will give me meals separately". Thereafter Rudra is not worshipped with Devas. He is worshipped separately.

68. Then thus cursed angrily by Rudra of unmeasured brilliance, Dakṣa abandoned his body of Svāyambhuva Manvantara and was born among human beings.

69. After realizing the Lord, the master of all knowledge, Dakṣa worshipped him with great sacrifices along with Devas.

70. When the Vaivasvata Manvantara arrived, Himavat, king of mountains, begot of Menā, a daughter named Umā who had been Satī (in her previous birth).

71. She, being Satī formerly, now became Umā. She is the joint performer of rites with Śiva who never forsakes her as long as he wishes to remain in the Manvantaras here.

72-73. Just as Aditi is devoted to Kaśyapa, son of Marīci, Śrī is attached to Nārāyaṇa, Śacī to Indra, Kīrti to Viṣṇu, Ruci to Sūrya, and Arundhatī to Vasiṣṭha, so she was devoted to Śiva. These gentle ladies never forsake their husbands. When the cycles of Kalpas recur, they are born along with them.

74. Thus Dakṣa was born as the son of Pracetas in the Cākṣuṣa Manvantara. He was the grandson of Prācīnabarhis and the son of Pracetas.

75. It is said that as a result of Rudra's curse, he was born in Mārṣā by the tenth Pracetas in this second Manvantara.

76. All the great sages, Bhṛgu and others, were born formerly in the first Tretā Yuga. They assumed body from Varuṇa at the sacrifice of the great god.

77. Thus the mutual enmity of Dakṣa Prajāpati and Lord Śiva continued from their previous existence.

78. Hence, intense enmity should never be pursued even with enemies. Due to merits and demerits, a living being does not leave off (forget) the awareness of what was intensly conceived in the previous existence. Hence an intelligent person should use discretion in his actions.

The sages enquired :

79. O Sūta, how was the horse sacrifice of Dakṣa Prajāpati, son of Pracetas, destroyed in Vaivasvata Manvantara?.

80. How did Dakṣa propitiate the lord who was enraged at the death of Satī? We wish to know this. Please narrate this precisely.

Sūta replied :

81-82. O excellent Brāhmaṇas, formerly the lord was seated as if on a couch, on the excellent mountain Meru, bedecked by minerals, on its peak Jyotiṣka, famous in the three worlds. This peak is open to the sun and is adorned with jewels. It is immeasurable and unthwartable. It is bowed to by all the worlds.

83. Pārvatī, daughter of the Himavat, remained always by his side. The noble Ādityas and Vasus of immeasurable strength were also present.

84. Similarly, the noble Aśvins, the most excellent physicians, and king Vaiśravaṇa surrounded by the Guhyakas, were present.

85. Kubera, the lord of Yakṣas, the glorious lord residing in Kailāsa, and the great sage Uśanas worshipped him. So also Sanatkumāra and other sages.

86. Similarly the celestial sages Aṅgiras and others, Viśvāvasu Gandharva, Nārada and Parvata were present.

87. Many groups of Apsaras-s came there. Pure, pleasing, wind blew wafting different kinds of sweet smell.

88-89. The trees were in full bloom with the flowers of all seasons. The Vidyādharas, Siddhas, ascetics and other living beings (and goblins) assuming various forms began to worship the great lord Paśupati.

90. Great and terrible Rākṣasas and Piśācas were seen there assuming various forms and holding different kinds of weapons lifted up.

91-92. The attendants of the lord who were as brilliant as Fire-god stood there. Lord Nandīśvara stood in the service of the lord, wielding the blazing trident shining with its brilliance. O excellent Brāhmaṇas, Gaṅgā the excellent river, the source of all sacred waters, assumed the form of a deity and worshipped him.

93. Thus the great lord shining with his brilliance stayed there along with the celestial sages and the blessed Devas.

94. Formerly on the top of Himavat in an auspicious place near Gaṅgādvāra,[1] resorted to by the sages and Siddhas, Dakṣa began his sacrifice.

95. The Devas led by Indra gathered together and prepared to attend the sacrifice.

96. It is reported that with the permission of the Lord (Śiva), Devas who were resplendent like fire went to Gaṅgādvāra in their dazzling aerial cars.

97-98. Folding their palms in reverence, the residents of earth, sky and heaven approached Dakṣa Prajāpati, the foremost among sacrificers, who was surrounded by sages, Gandharvas and celestial damsels at Gaṅgādvāra abounding in various trees and creepers.

99. Ādityas, Vasus, Rudras, Sādhyas arrived there for their share in the sacrifice along with Maruts and Indra.

100. (Deities of the categories of) Ūṣmapās, Somapās, Ājyapās, Dhūmapās (drinkers of hot offerings, soma, ghee and smoke), the two Aśvin-gods and Pitṛs came there along with god Brahmā.

101. These and many other groups of living beings—*Jarāyujas* (viviparous animals), *Aṇḍajas* (born of eggs, birds)

---

1. The same as modern Hara(i)dwar. The actual spot of Dakṣa's sacrifice is at a distance of a kilometer from modern Haridwar.

Svedajas (insects, germs born of sweat) and *Udbhijjas* (germinating plants and trees) were present there.

102. Devas and their consorts were invoked through Mantras. Seated in their aerial chariots they shone like blazing fires.

103. On seeing them Dadhīca became angry and said, "A man incurs sin by worshipping one unworthy of worship and not worshipping one who is worthy of worship."

104. After saying thus, the sage spoke again to Dakṣa, "Why don't you invite lord Śiva who is worthy of worship?".

Dakṣa said :

105. I have so many Rudras here armed with spears and having matted hair. They stay with eleven forms. I do not know any other great god.

Dadhica said :

106. He who has invited Śiva, has invited all gods. As I do not see (regard) any other deity superior to Śaṅkara, this vast and rich sacrifice of Dakṣa will not take place.

Dakṣa said :

107. "O heroic lord, in this sacrifice, I offer unto Viṣṇu, the lord without an equal, all the *Havis* sanctified by Mantras, and invariably through the Āhavanīya fire, holding the *Havis* in a golden vessel".

108. On knowing that Devas had gone, Pārvatī, the chaste daughter of the king of mountains, spoke to Lord Śiva (her husband).

Umā said:

109. O Lord, where have these gone, led by Indra. O knower of truth, speak truly. There is my great doubt.

Maheśvara said :

110. The blessed, noble, Prajāpati Dakśa is performing a horse-sacrifice. The heaven-dwellers are going there.

Umā enquired:

111. O blessed lord, why have you not gone to this sacrifice? Wherefore is the departure thither prohibited?

Lord Śiva replied:

112. O blessed lady! All this has been done by Devas only. My share in all the sacrifices is not allotted (to me).

113. O beautiful lady! By following the traditional procedure, the Devas do not give me my due share in sacrifice.

Goddess Umā said :

114. "O Lord! You are the most brilliant among all the Devas. You excel them in good qualities. You are invincible, unthwartable by your splendour, fame and glory.

115. O blessed one, by this prohibition, I am much distressed. O sinless lord, my body heaves.

116. What indeed is the religious gift I should give or penance I should perform whereby you, my husband, shall have a share of the sacirfice—half or a third of it."

117. The unthinkable lord delightedly spoke to her who was so agitated. "O goddess of Devas, of slender belly and limbs, you do not know whether your statements are proper.

118. O large-eyed goddess ! I know that when men of good qualities speak, all of them do so attentively. But at present god Indra has fallen in delusion and the three worlds are also deluded in every respect.

119. They eulogise me in sacrifices. They sing appropriate Sāman Rathantara. In the Brahmasatra, Brāhmaṇas worship me. The Adhvaryus assign my share."

Pārvatī said :

120. "Undoubtedly my lord, though not born of Prakṛti, you either eulogise or offer self-defence in this assembly of women."

121. The Lord said: "O Goddess of Devas, I do not eulogise myself. O fair lady, O beautiful one, see and approach the person I create for the sake of my share."

122. After speaking thus to his wife, more beloved to him than his vital breath, the Lord created from his mouth a goblin that resembled the fury of fire.

123. He had a thousand heads, a thousand feet and eyes. He held a thousand iron clubs, a thousand arrows in his hands.

124. He held a conch, a discus, a mace, a blazing bow, an axe and a sword in his hands. He was terrible and awe-inspiring.

125. He was blazing with a terrible form. Half a moon constituted his crest. He was clad in a tiger-skin dripping with blood.

126. He was terrible with his curved fangs. He was whirling (?). He had wide mouth and big belly. His tongue was like lightning. His lips hung loose. His ears were long. He was inaccessible to all.

127. A thunderbolt brightened his hands. His hair shone with splendour. He was surrounded by wreaths of flames. He was bedecked in pearl-strings.

128. He blazed with brilliance like the fire of Dissolution. His gaping mouth extended upto his ears. He looked terrible all around.

129. He had great strength and spendour. He was a great Puruṣa and lord. His huge body was capable of destroying the universe. It was as huge as the clustering banyan tree. He blazed like a hundred moons blazing simultaneously or like the fire that burnt Madana.

130. He had four big mouths. His curved fangs were white and sharp-pointed. He had great splendour, fierce brilliance, and enthusiasm. He had the refulgence of a thousand fires and suns at the time of Dissolution of the world. He had the splendour of athousand moons. He resembled the Mandara mountain with all blazing medicinal herbs. He was equal to Sumeru, Kailāsa and the mountain Himavat.

131. He resembled the sun at the time of Dissolution. He had great prowess. His nose was charming. His face was big. His cheeks were fierce; eyes blazed. His face was turbid with the flames of fire.

132. He wore the hide of elephant. He was entwined by great serpents. He had a turban on. He held the moon on

the crest. In some respect he was fierce. In some respect he was mild.

133. He wore different flowers on his head. He had various kinds of scent and unguents. His limbs were decorated with different jewels. He was bedecked in ornaments.

134. He wore a shining garland of Karṇikāra flowers. Due to anger his eyes were whirling and turning. At times he danced in different postures.

135. At times he meditated with his soul in communion. At times he wiped off the gross matter. At times he sang and at times he cried over and over again.

136. He was endowed with the basic attributes of knowledge, detachment, lordship, penance, truthfulness, forbearance, fortitude, mastery and self-enlightenment.

137. He knelt on his knees on the ground. He bowed with palms joined in reverence and stood still. Then he said, "O lord of Devas, command, what work shall I do for you?"

138. The great lord spoke to him—"Destroy the sacrifice of Dakṣa". On hearing the command of the lord, the powerful Vīrabhadra bowed at the feet of the lord, bending his head.

139. Then he jumped ahead sportingly like a lion released from bondage. He considered that the sacrifice of Dakṣa was already destroyed by the fury of the goddess.

140. The great goddess, highly fierce Bhadrakālī accompanied him wrathfully to reveal her omnipresence (to all).

141. This is the infuriated lord, having his residence in the abodes of ghosts, who became known as Vīrabhadra. He dispelled the anger of the goddess.

142. From the hair pores in his body he created the chiefs of Gaṇas named Raudras. They were the followers of Rudras who possessed great prowess and exploits of Rudra.

143. They were the followers of Rudra. They had the splendour of Rudra. They started immediately in hundreds and thousands.

144. There arose tumultuous roar that filled the sky. By that loud noise, the heaven-dwellers became frightened.

145. O Brāhmaṇas, mountains crumbled, the earth shook. The Meru whirled round. The seas were agitated.

146. Fires did not blaze; the sun did not shine. Neither the planets nor the moving and fixed stars gave forth light.

147. The sages did not speak nor Devas nor Dânavas. From their aerial chariots the Gaṇas burnt everything enveloped in darkness.

148. They roared like lions. They had terrible forms and great strength. They broke everything. They uprooted the sacrificial posts.

149. They suppressed everything. They danced. Having the speed of the wind and the quickness of the mind, they ran here and there.

150. They broke the sacrificial vessels to pieces. The sacrificial altar shattered utterly, appeared like the stars fallen from the sky.

151-153. There were heaps of foodstuffs and beverages like mountains. Rivers of milk were flowing. Ghee and milk pudding formed muddy slushes. There was honey and gruel water. There were divine sugar candies, powdered like sands. Foodstuffs having all the six tastes flowed through the rivulets of jaggery, charming to the mind. There were meat dishes of several varieties. Whatever sweet foodstuffs they saw, they ate up. They squeezed the juice and licked up the lambatives. Their different faces exhibited different reactions. They rolled everywhere. They sported about assuming different forms. They seized the celestial damsels and molested them.

154. Urged by Rudra's fury, the Gaṇas as furious as Rudra himself, destroyed the sacrifice, though it was well guarded by Devas.

155. Others roared loudly terrifying all living beings. Others severed the head of sacrifice and roared.

156. Dakṣa, the skilled Prajāpati, and the lord of sacrifices began to flee through the sky in the form of a deer.

157. Vīrabhadra of incomprehensible soul then gauged his strength. He cut off the head* as he passed through the sky.

158. Dakṣa Prajāpati was confused and lost consciousness.

---

*Contrast the statement with the next verse & vv. 161, 166 etc.

He was kicked on the head by the infuriated Vīrabhadra. Being aged and weak, he fell on the ground.

159. The thirty-three crores of Devas of pure souls were bound with noose as strong as fire or lion.

160. Then Devas went to the powerful noble being and said, "O Lord Rudra, be pleased. O Lord, do not be angry with your servants".

161. Then Brahmā and other Devas and Dakṣa Prajāpati spoke with palms joined in reverence, "Please tell us who you are?".

Vīrabhadra said :

162. I am neither a Deva nor an Āditya. I have not come here to take meals, nor to visit the chiefs of Devas nor out of curiosity.

163. Know me as one come here to destroy the sacrifice. I am known as Vīrabhadra and I have come out of the fury of Rudra.

164. Bhadrakālī has come out of the fury of the goddess (Pārvatī). Sent by the lord of Devas, she has come near the sacrifice.

165. O Dakṣa, seek refuge in lord Śiva. Even his fury is better than the gift of boons from a Deva."

166. On hearing the words of Vīrabhadra, Dakṣa, the foremost of the upholders of holy rites, propitiated the trident-bearing Śiva, lord of Devas.

167-171. When the premises of the sacrifice were defiled, when the Brāhmaṇas fled, when the hideous and terrible great fire in the form of the constellation Mṛgaśiras blazed, when the servants whose faces were pierced by spears (screamed), when the uprooted sacrificial posts were scattered here and there, when the place was filled with vultures greedy of flesh rising up and flying, when the sound of hundreds of vixens by the flapping of wings (pervaded the quarters), the Lord of Devas, the conqueror of enemies, the lord having many visions, restrained his Prāṇa and Apāna strenuously in their places, directed his vision all round. Suddenly came out of the pit of fire the God of gods. His splendour was comparable to that of a thousand suns, moons and the *Saṁvartaka* fire.

172. The lord laughed loudly and said again: "O Dakṣa, you are ruined due to ignorance. I hope you are well disposed towards me now".

173-174. Smilingly he spoke again: "Tell me, what shall I do for you?" After relating what had been narrated to Devas and their preceptors, Prajāpati Dakṣa joined his palms in reverence and spoke to the lord. He was afraid, suspicious and frightened. His eyes and face were filled with tears.

175-177. "If you, my lord, are pleased, if I am your favourite, if I am to be blessed and if I am to be granted boon, I would choose this. The requisites of sacrifice are collected by me with strenuous efforts over long period. They have been swallowed, eaten, drunk, chewed, destroyed, powdered and scattered in this manner. Let them not go in vain."

178-179. "So be it", said the lord, the destroyer of the eyes of Bhaga. After receiving the boon Prajāpati Dakṣa knelt on the ground and eulogised the bull-bannered, three-eyed lord, the presiding deity of sacred rites, by his thousand and eight names.[1]

Dakṣa said:

180. "Obeisance to you, the lord of the chiefs of Devas, the destroyer of the host of the enemies of Devas. O Lord of Devas, O excellent among the immortals, O one worshipped by Devas and Dānavas.

181. O thousand-eyed one, O hideous-eyed one, O three-eyed one. O favourite of the chief of Yakṣas, you have hands, feet, eyes, mouths, heads and ears all round. You stand permeating everything in the world.

182. Obeisance to you, O pike-eared one, O large-eared one, O pot-eared one, O one residing in the sea, O elephant-eared one, O bull-eared one, O hand-eared one.

183. O hundred-bellied one, O one with hundred revolutions, O hundred-tongued one, O hundred-faced one, those who practise Gāyatrī sing about you; those who regularly worship, worship you.

1. This *Śiva-sahasra-nāma* has a number of verses common to that in *Mbh. Śānti* 284, 69-180.

184. You are the protector of Devas and Dānavas, you are Brahmā and Indra. O large-bodied one, you are the lord of the deities. Obeisance (to you), you are the upholder of the waters in the ocean.

185. Devas abide in your body as cows in the cow-shed. I see your body as the moon, fire and ocean.

186. I see you as Āditya, Viṣṇu, Brahmā and Bṛhaspati. You are the cause, becoming, being, agent and instrument.

187. You are the non-existent, the existent-cum-non-existent, the source of origin and the end of the universe. Obeisance to Bhava, Śarva, Rudra and the granter of boons.

188. Obeisance to the lord of Paśus, the destroyer of Andhaka, Trijaṭa (having matted hair in three plaits), the three-headed and the wielder of excellent trident.

189. Obeisance to *Tryaṁbaka* (three-eyed), *Trinetra* (three-eyed), the destroyer of Tripuras, *Caṇḍa* (the fierce), *Muṇḍa* (one with a shaven head), *Pracaṇḍa* (very fierce) and *Dhara* (the uplifter).

190. Obeisance to one engaged in listening to Ḍiṇḍima, Lord of *Ardhadaṇḍa*, Niṣka (body-less), Vikṛta (the deformed one).

191. Salute to *Vilohita* (ruddy), *Dhūmra* (coloured), blue-necked, Śiva, who is without a compeer.

192. Obeisance to the sun, the lord of the sun, the sun-bannered god, the lord of Pramathas, and the bull-shouldered archer.

193. Obeisance to Hiraṇyagarbha (the golden-wombed), one with golden coat of mail, the gold-crested and the lord of gold.

194. Obeisance to the destroyer of sacrifice, *Daṇḍa* (the staff), *Parṇapānapuṭa* (one having a cup of leaves for drinking); one who is eulogised, one worthy of being praised, one being eulogised.

195. Bow to *Sarva* (the all); one who subsists on non-eatable food; one who is the inner soul of all beings and who is the Hotṛ (sacrificer), to mantra, to one with a white banner on the flag-staff.

196. Obeisance to worshipper, one worthy of worship; the embodied joyous shout, one lying down, one who has lain and one who has got up.

197. Obeisance to the one who is stable; who is walking; who symbolizes a mystic sign, who is crooked, who is habitually dancing and making a musical instrument of his mouth.

198. Obeisance to the one greedy of securing presents in dances; who is engaged in songs and musical instruments, who is the eldest, the excellent and the suppressor of foes.

199. Obeisance to *Kalana* (creator), Kalpa, *Kṣaya* (complete dissolution), *Upakṣaya* (subsidiary dissolution), one laughing terribly like the Dundubhi (wardrum), cherished by Bhīmasena.

200. Obeisance to *Ugra* (the fierce one); one having ten arms and a skull in his hand; obeisance to one fond of ashes from the funeral pyre.

201. Obeisance to the terrible, the awe-inspiring one, one observing terrible rites; one of deformed chest and having tip of the tongue and the curved fangs as sharp as sword.

202. Hail to the one greedy of raw and cooked meat; one fond of *Tumba-vīṇā* (lute supported by a gourd). Bow to *vṛṣa* (the bull or holy virtue) and to *Vṛṣya* (most vigorous god), to Vṛṣṇi (the mighty) and Vṛṣaṇa (the fertilizer).

203. Bow to Kaṭaṁkaṭa (Fire-god), the fierce, the embodied one. Obeisance to Vara-Kṛṣṇa (super dark?), excellent one, the bestower of boon.

204. Obeisance to one having excellent scents, garlands and garments; the excellent and surpassing one. Obeisance to the rain, wind, shadow and sunshine.

205. Obeisance to the attached and detached, the auspicious god wearing a garland of beads. Bow to the *Saṁbhinna* (the pierced and broken?), the variegated, the hideous and isolated.

206. Hail to the god with non-terrible form and one extremely terrible, to the auspicious, quiescent and an extremely quiescent one.

207. Obeisance to the single-footed, many-eyed, single-headed one. To the old, greedy and fond of shares (in sacrifice).

208. Obeisance to the one who is worshipped with five garlands; obeisance to Pāśupata, Caṇḍa, Ghaṇṭa (equipped

with a bell) and one who has consumed the vitals with his bell (?)

209. Obeisance to one having a hundred thousand bells, one fond of a garland of bells, to the restrainer of Prāṇa, the renunciation (incarnate), and to *Hilahila* (a sport).

210. Obeisance to one who makes the "Huṁhuṁ" sound, who takes us across, who is fond of Huṁhuṁ sound. Obeisance to Śaṁbhu who is fond of mountains, trees and their fruits.

211. Obeisance to the jackal (fond of) embryo meal. Obeisance to *Tāraka* (one who takes across), *Tāra* (ferryboat), to the lord of sacrifices, the one who has fled (or rushed in).

212. Obeisance to the carrier of sacrifices, religious gifts, the goal of penance (*Tapya*) and the (scorching) Sun-god. Hail to the shore (of the ocean of Saṁsāra?) and the excellent Lord of lightnings.

213. Obeisance to the bestower of cooked food, Lord of cooked food, one born of cooked food, the thousand-headed and thousand-footed lord.

214. Obeisance to him with thousand tridents lifted up, to the thousand-eyed, one in the form of a boy, or one assuming the form of a boy.

215. Obeisance to the protector of children, one sporting with children, the pure and the enlightened, the agitator and the unwoundable.

216. Obeisance to the one whose tresses are marked by waves, the one of unbound tresses, the one abiding by six prescribed rites, the one engaged in three-fold rites.

217. Obeisance to the one who makes people of different castes and stages of life duly function separately. Obeisance to loud sound, one worthy of proclamation, who is *Kalakala* (the murmuring sound).

218. Obeisance to the one with white and reddish brown eyes, the one with black and red eyes, the one bestower of virtue, wealth, love and salvation. Obeisance to slaughter and the slaughterer.

219. Obeisance to Sāṁkhya, to the master of Sāṁkhya and Yoga. Obeisance to Rathya, Virathya and to one interested in crossroads.

220. Obeisance to the one with a deer-skin for upper garment; to the one wearing a serpent for sacred thread, O Īśāna, O destroyer of Indra. O green-haired one, obeisance be to you.

Obeisance to the sole controller of indiscrimination. Hail to you, O manifest and unmanifest lord.

221. O Kāma, bestower of desires, destroyer of the god of Love , slayer of the haughty and arrogant, *Sarva* (all in all), O bestower of all, omniscient and twilight red, obeisance be to you.

222. O powerful, mighty-armed one, and highly powerful, lustrous, great cloud, excellent-visioned great Kāla, obeisance be to you.

223. (Obeisance to) perpetual ascetic with stout and worn out limbs and matted hair, to one wearing bark garments and deer-skin, to one with matted hair resembling blazing fire and the sun, to one clad in bark garments and deer skin. Obeisance be to one resembling a thousand suns.

224. O one having hundreds of maddening revolutions, O one with tresses half filled with the waters of Gaṅgā, O Candrāvarta, Yugāvarta, Meghāvarta, obeisance be to you.

225. You are the cooked food, the creator, the bestower, and the maker of food; you are the person cooking food. Obeisance to cook and enjoyer of the cooked food.

226. O lord, you are the lord of chief of Devas and the four-fold living beings, viz. the viviparous, oviparous, the sweat-born and the germinating ones.

227. You are Brahmā, the creator of the mobile and immobile. You are their withdrawer; the foremost among the scholars of the Vedas and the knowers of Brahman.

228. Pronounders of the Vedas say that you are the very source of *Sattva guṇa*, the storehouse of waters, wind and fire; you are the Ṛg, Sāman Mantra and Oṁkāra.

229. You are the offering in sacrifice, sacrificing itself, the invocation; you are the solemn rite of oblation with words (of *mantra*). The experts in the Veda and singers of Sāman sing of you, O great God.

230. You are cited by the knowers of Brahman and

those well-versed in Kalpa and Upaniṣads, as the one consisting of Ṛg, Yajur, Sāman and Atharvan mantras.

231. The Brāhmaṇas, Kṣatriyas, Vaiśyas, Śūdras and people of inferior castes worship you alone. The clusters of clouds sing about you by their rattling and roaring thunder.

232. You are the year, seasons, months, fortnights, Kalās, Kāṣṭhās, Nimeṣas, Yugas, stars and planets.

233. You are the hump of bulls, the peak of mountains, the lion among beasts, Tārkṣya (Garuḍa) among birds, and Ananta among serpents.

234. You are the ocean of milk among oceans, bow among mechanical devices, thunderbolt among weapons, and truth among holy vows.

235. You are desire, hatred, passion, delusion, infirmity, mental control, restraint of sense organs, enterprise, fortitude, greed, love, fury, success, and failure.

236. You are the mace-bearer, the discharger of arrows, the wielder of Khaṭvāṅga, the holder of Jharjhara (drum or cymbols). You chop, pierce, strike, leak and annihilate.

237. You are the holy rite (piety) with ten characteristics. You are wealth, love, Indra, oceans, rivers, puddles and lakes.

238 You are the creeper, the winding plants, the grass and medicinal herbs; you are the animals, beasts and birds; you are the beginning of substance, activity and attributes; you are the bestower of flowers and fruits at the right time.

239. You are the beginning, end and the middle; you are the Gāyatrī and Oṁkāra *mantra*; you are green, red, black, blue, yellow and crimson.

240. You are tawny-coloured, dove-coloured, dark-blue, and gold-semened; hence you are known as having good colour.

241. You have names consisting of good letters; you are fond of gold; You are, Indra, Yama, Varuṇa, Kubera and Agni.

242. You are full-blown; you are Citra-Bhānu (fire, sun, Bhairava); you are Svarbhānu (Rāhu) and Bhānu (the Sun-god); you are the sacrifice, the sacrificial priest, the Homa, the *Huta* (what is offered in the fire), the *Prahuta* (the offering in Bhūta-yajña); you are the lord.

243. You are well-winged Brahman; you are *Śatarudriya* among *Yajurmantras*. You are the holiest among holy, the most auspicious of the auspicious.

244. You are the huge mountain, and the little one. You are the tree, the individual soul and atom. You are the Sattva, Rajas and the Tamas Guṇa; you are the creation.

245. You are (the vital airs such as) Prāṇa, Apāna, Samān, Udāna and Vyāna; you are the wink of the eyes; you are their expansion and stretching.

246. You are of red-complexioned body, wielder of a mace (*gadā*) and have curved fangs; you have a huge face and huge belly. You are white-haired and green-moustached. You have three eyes and hair lifted up.

247. You are the parts of dance, song and music; you are fond of singing and playing on instruments; you are *Matsya* (fish); you are watery, water and conducive to watery life. You are speed, time, Kali and Kāla.

248. You are improper time, propitious period and bad (famine-like) time as well as the destroyer of Kāla. You are death, decline and end and the destroyer of the earth.

249. You are the Saṁvartaka fire (annihilating the universe) and clouds of final dissolution. You are *Ghaṭa* (a duration of time), *Ghaṭika* (master of *Ghaṭa*), *Ghaṇṭika* (having small bells?), *Cūḍālolabala* (having the strength in swinging locks of hair). You are the power.

250. You are the destroyer of Brahmā; you have fiery mouth; you wield a staff; you have shaven head; you are the holder of a staff; you are the four Yugas, four Vedas, four sacrifices and crossroads (of four paths).

251. You are the knower of the four stages in life; you are the creator of the four various (classes of people); you are fond of the perishable and imperishable; you are knavish, uncountable and the lord of innumerable Gaṇas.

252. You wear the Rudrākṣa-garland and garments; you are a small mountain; you are fond of hillocks. You are the lord of artisans and the best of them. You are the originator of arts and crafts.

253. You are the destroyer of the eyes of Bhaga; you are the moon, the destroyer of the teeth of Pūṣan. You are *Gūḍhā-*

varta (the hidden eddy); you are the concealed one; you resort to hidden things.

254. You are *Tarana* (one that takes across), *Tāraka* (liberator), *Sarvabhūta-Sutaraṇa* (liberator of all living beings); you are *Dhātṛ* (creator), *Vidhātṛ* (dispenser of destiny) and the preserver of living beings; you are the supporter of all.

255. You are austerity, the Brahman, truth, celibacy, straight-forwardness, the Ātman and the maker of all living beings, the living being, the spirit, the source of everything that was, is and will be.

256. You are *Bhūḥ*, *Bhuvaḥ*, *Svar*, the origin (of the universe); you are the great Lord, *Īśāna*, the surveyor. You are the quiescent; hard to be subdued and the destroyer of teeth.

257. You are Brahmāvarta, Surāvarta, and Kāmāvarta. Obeisance be to you. You are the destroyer of Kāma's body; you are fond of the pollen powder of the Karṇikāra flower.

258. You have a moon-like face and also a terrible one. You are pleasant-faced, wry-faced, faceless, four-faced, multi-faced, and always face to face with the enemy in the battle.

259. You are gold-wombed, a big bird (a vulture) and an ocean. You are the greatest and (the most) immense being. You are the destroyer of evil, chastiser of the wicked, the wielder of the rod of punishment and fond of battles.

260. You are the best of bulls, the rider of a bull, the bull-vehicled one. You are the promulgator of Dharma, the creator of Dharma and foremost among the experts in Dharma.

261. You are the protector of the worlds and the winner (or protector) of the earth, a bestower of honour and honour incarnate; you are stable, fixed, a pillar, motionless and shaking.

262. You are unwardable, dispenser(?) of brilliant poison, unbearable, untransgressable, unsupportable, unshakable, incomprehensible, unconquerable, the victory (itself).

263. You are soft spoken (and of lovable traits), the moon, the subduer. You are chilliness and heat, an unquenchable thirst. You are the mental worries and physical ailments, the remover of ailments and diseases.

264. You are bearable, the sacrifice, the deer-hunter, the

storehouse of ailments, handless. You are having a tuft of hair. You are lotus-eyed and lotus-visioned.

265. You are a holder of the rod (of chastisement), the wielder of a staff, adorned with staff, and tonsured head. You are imbiber of poison, drinker of nectar, drinker of wine, drinker of milk and Soma juice.

266. You are the imbiber of honey, ghee and everything; you are very powerful; you are carried by a horselike bull; you are the bull (strong person), with eyes like those of a bull.

267. You are known as Vṛṣabha (a bull); you are honoured by the people; the moon and the sun are your eyes; Brahmā is your heart; you are fire and water; you are the lord achievable by pious rites.

268. O Śiva, neither Brahmā nor Viṣṇu nor the ancient sages can understand your greatness precisely.

269. Your subtle forms do not come within the ken of my vision. Protect me with them as a father does to his son.

270. The Lord is always sympathetic and favourable to his devotees. And I am always devoted to you.

271. May that lord be always my protector—the Lord who after devouring (withdrawing at the time of *Pralaya*) thousands of men, abides all alone at the bottom of the ocean.

272. Obeisance to the Yogic soul whom persons of impartial outlook, abiding by Sāttvic qualities, who have conquered their vital breaths and who are devoid of slumber, see as the brilliant light, while in Yogic communion.

273. I resort to him who lies in the middle of the expanse of water after devouring the living beings, at the close of the Yuga.

274. You enter the mouth of Rāhu, swallow the moon at night and becoming Rāhu, devour the sun too. You are the fire accompanied with Soma.

275. May the Puruṣas of the size of the thumb stationed in all embodied beings, protect me always. May they nourish me and make me flourish.

276. May the Svāhās and Svadhās reach them who have gone up from the womb and who have gone beneath. May they be appealing to them and attain them.

277. Obeisance to them all, for ever, who do not cry and who, stationed in the body, make the living beings cry. Obeisance be to them who are delighted and who delight all.

278-280. Perpetual obeisance to them, who are stationed in the ocean, in the river, in the fort, on the mountains, in the caves, at the roots of trees, in the cowpens, in the dense forests, in crossroads, in the streets, in the quadrangular courtyards, in the assemblies and in the midst of the sun and the moon, in the rays of the sun and the moon, who have gone to the netherworlds and beyond them. Perpetual obeisance to those who are subtle, gross, lean or short.

281. O Lord, you are all in all; you pervade all; you are the lord and the inner soul of all living beings. Therefore you were not invited to the sacrifice.

282. Since it is you alone who are worshipped with sacrifices with various monetary gifts and since you alone are the doer of everything, you were not invited.

283. O Lord, I was deluded by your subtle Māyā that you were not invited.

284. O Lord of Devas, be pleased with me. You alone are my refuge, my goal, my foundation. I have no other goal or resort."

285. After eulogising the great lord thus, the Prajāpati stopped. The delighted lord spoke then to Dakṣa:

286. "O Dakṣa of good rites, I am pleased with this hymn of yours; of what avail is much talk. You will come near me."

287. Then the lord of the three worlds, conversant with the appropriate use of words spoke consoling words and said again:

288. "O Dakṣa, you shall not be angry due to this hindrance. It is I, none else, who destroyed the sacrifice. You have seen that before.

289. O you of good rites, again, accept this boon from me. With your face beaming with delight, you shall listen to me with attention.

290. O Prajāpati, by my grace, you will derive the merit of a thousand Aśvamedha and a hundred Vājapeya sacrifices.

291-293. Having established the Vedas with their six ancillaries together with the Sāṁkhya and Yoga and performing penances inaccessible to Devas and Dānavas, the Pāśupata rite has been evolved by me. This rite is accompanied by objects of worship. It is evolved in secret and is unintelligible to the unintelligent. In some respects it agrees with the functions of different castes and stages of life. In some respects it is contrary to them. It is determined by the meanings of the Vedic passages. It is conducive to liberation from the bondage of individual souls. It can be followed by a person in any stage of life. It is auspicious, O Dakṣa, and it liberates one from sins.

294. O blessed one, you shall derive the benefit of this holy rite. May your mental worry be over."

295. After saying thus to Dakṣa, the valorous lord vanished along with his consort and his followers.

296. O Brāhmaṇas, after obtaining his due share as mentioned by Brahmā, the lord who was conversant with the holy rites, divided *Jvara* (fever) into many classes[1] for achieving calmness in living beings. Listen to it.

297. For elephants it is excessive pain in the head; for mountains it is bitumen; for waters it is the bluish tinge; and in serpents it is the slough.

298. It is *Khauraka* (cracks in the hoofs) for all cattle. It is barrenness for the earth. O Knower of Dharma! to the elephants it is the obstruction to vision.

299. It is the opening of pores to the horses, the splitting of the crest to the peacocks, the ailment of the eyes to the cuckoos.

300. It is splitting of the bile to the goats. It is *Himikā*[2](?) to the parrots. O Brāhmaṇa, *Śrama* (fatigue) in the tigers is their *Jvara* (fever).

301. O Omniscient lord, it is fever to the human beings. It can enter human body any time, at the time of birth or death or in between.

302. This is the brilliance of the lord that is *Jvara*. The Lord shall be worshipped, bowed and honoured by all creatures.

---

1. Cf. the kinds of *Jvara* in *Mbh. Śānti* 243.52-57

2. V.l. *hikkikā* 'inarticulate sound, cough' in *Mbh. Śānti* 283.55. The present chapter is closely similar to *Mbh Śānti.* 284 (283 as well)

303. He who reads the story of the origin of *Jvara* with undejected and concentrated mind shall be freed from the ailment. He will rejoice, attaining all joys in accordance with his desires.

304. He who narrates or listens to the hymn of praise recited by Dakṣa, attains longevity. He will never face inauspicious results.

305. Just as Śiva endowed with Yogic power is the excellent of all Devas, so also this hymn of Brahmā is the excellent of all hymns.

306. The lord shall be eulogised with devotion by those who desire fame, kingdom, happiness, prosperity, riches, longevity, wealth and learning.

307. The sick, the distressed, the indigent, the frightened, those afraid of thieves and those on the king's errand are liberated from dangers.

308. He will attain all happiness here itself. He will become the chief of Gaṇas with this body itself.

309. In a house where the lord is eulogised, neither the Yakṣas nor the Piśācas, neither the serpents nor the impediments create obstacles.

310. A celibate woman who listens to this with devotion will become the object of respect of the families both from her father's and her husband's side.

311. The affairs of the man who constantly listens to or narrates all these will become fruitful without impediments.

312. By the repeated recitation of this hymn, whatever he thinks in his mind and whatever he speaks out, will become realised.

313-314. After offering oblations to the lord, Guha, Goddess and Nandīśvara, as far as he can, practising mental control and restraint of the sense organs and united in Yogic communion, he shall repeat the names of the lord in the proper order. He will attain his desires, ambitions and enjoy pleasures. On death he will attain heaven surrounded by a thousand women.

315-316. One who performs undesirable activities or one who is defiled by sins becomes free from sins on reading the hymn of Dakṣa. After his death he is honoured by Devas and Asuras. He attains residence in the same world with the Gaṇas. Like Indra he shines while seated on a duly yoked aerial chariot. He stays permanently there till the hour of ultimate dissolution. He then becomes the attendant of Rudra.

317-319. So said the holy lord Vyāsa, son of Parāśara. This episode is a secret that shall not be divulged to anyone. After hearing this secret, even the sinners, whether they be Vaiśyas, Śūdras or women, will attain Rudraloka. The Brāhmaṇa who recounts this to the other Brāhmaṇas during Parvan days attains Rudraloka. There is no doubt about this.

CHAPTER THIRTYONE

The Race of Devas[1]

Sūta said :

1. Thus the sin-destroying story in the context of Dakṣa as told by Śiva, has been narrated to you.

2. In the context of describing the race of Pitṛs, this story has been narrated. In succession to the Pitṛs, I shall describe Devas hereafter.

3. Formerly, in the Svāyaṁbhuva Manvantara, in the beginning of the Tretā age, there were Devas known as Yāmas. They were formerly the sons of Yajña.

4. Those known as Ajitas were Brahmā's sons. Those known as Jitas and Jitajitas were the mental sons of Brahmā. They were known as Śukras.

5. There were three groups of Devas, namely (Yāma, Śukra and) Tṛptimanta. They were the chanters of the Sāmaveda and were thirty-three in all in Svāyaṁbhuva Manvantara (or born of Brahmā).

6-10. The Yāmas are twelve in number, viz. Yadu, Yayāti, Dīdhaya, Sravasa, Mati, Vibhāsa, Kratu, Prajāti, Viśata, Dyuti,

1. This chapter corresponds to Bd. P. I.2.13.87-131. In addition to Devas, the chapter discusses the nature of Time etc. in vv. 24 ff.

Vāyasa and Maṅgala. The Ajitas too are twelve in number. viz. Abhimanyu, Ugradṛṣṭi, Samaya, Śuciśravas, Kevala, Viśvarūpa, Supakṣa, Madhupa, Turīya, Nirhapu, Yukta and Grāva. The last group of twelve Devas consists of Yamina, Viśva, Devādya, Yaviṣṭha, Amṛtavān, Ajira, Vibhu, Vibhāva, Mṛlika, Didehaka, Śruti-Śṛṇa and Bṛhacchukra.

These were in the Svāyambhuva Manvantara. They were the drinkers of Soma juice. This group of Devas is called Tviṣimantas. They are virile and very strong.

11. Viśvabhuk, the first lord, was their Indra. The Asuras were their cousins and kinsmen.

12. There are eight (groups of) demi-gods, namely, Suparṇa, Yakṣa, Gandharva, Piśāca, Uraga (Reptiles), Rākṣasa, Pitṛs and Aśvinīkumāras.

13. In the Svāyambhuva Manvantara, thousands of the offsprings of these passed away. They were endowed with prowess, beauty, longevity and vigour.

14. They are not mentioned in detail so that no new topic be raised here. The creation of Svāyambhuva should be understood (as similar to) the present Manvantara.

15. The past creation should be seen through the present one, viz. Vaivasvata Manvantara in regard to progeny, gods, sages and Pitṛs.

16-18. Now know the seven sages who existed before. They were Bhṛgu, Aṅgiras, Marīci, Pulastya, Pulaha, Kratu, Atri and Vasiṣṭha. Svāyambhuva Manu had ten valient sons, viz. Agnīdhra, Atibāhu, Medhā, Medhātithi, Vasu, Jyotiṣmān, Dyutimān, Havya, Savana and Putra.

19-20. They have been mentioned by Vāyu as kings of great valour in the first Manvantara. Their families, the Asuras, Gandharvas, Yakṣas, serpents, Rākṣasas, Piśācas, human beings, Suparṇas and groups of Apsaras-s cannot be enumerated in due order, even in hundreds of years because the names are numerous in their families.

21. Those who were known by the name of Vrajakula and who were in the Svāyambhuva Manvantara, passed away as much time elapsed in the order of Ayanas, years and Yugas.

The sages asked :

22-23. Who is this lord Kāla, the annihilator of living beings? What is his source of origin? What is his beginning? What is his intrinsic essence? Who is his son? What is his eye? What is his form? What are his limbs? What is his name? Who is his Ātman? Mention these in detail as we ask you.

Sūta said :

24. May the origin of the Kāla be heard. After hearing it, may it be retained in memory. The sun is his source of origin. *Nimeṣa* is his beginning. He is called *Saṅkhyā-Cakṣu* (having Number as his eye).

25. His form is the day and night. The *Nimeṣas* are his limbs. A century constitutes his principle. Kāla is his name. He is the Prajāpati with the present, past and future as his Ātman.

26. Listen to the five divisions in which Kāla is divided by means of days, fortnights, months, seasons and *Ayanas*.

27-28. The first (year) is *Saṁvatsara*. The second (is called) *Parivatsara*. The third is *Idvatsara*. The fourth is *Anuvatsara* and the fifth is *Vatsara*. The group is called Yuga.[1] I shall explain their principle. Understand as it is being narrated.

29-30. That which is mentioned as *Kratu* (sacrifice) and *Agni* (fire) is considered as *Saṁvatsara*.[2] The fire of time which is the essence in the Sun-god is *Parivatsara*.

Soma (the moon) which is of the nature of the essence of waters, which has two movements, the bright and the dark (the bright half and the dark fortnight of the month) is *Iḍāvatsara*.

---

1. All there five names of years (Saṁvatsara, Parivatsara etc.) appear first in *Tait. S.* v. 5.7-1-13 in offering salutations to Rudra. The idea that five years constitute a *yuga* is found not only in our Purāṇa but also in *Kauṭalīya Artha-śāstra* II. 20 (*Deśakāla-māna*).

2. The identification of gods Agni etc. in vv. 29-32 is as old as *Śat. Br.* (I. 4-10.1-3) which states:

agnir vāva saṁvatsaraḥ/ādityaḥ parivatsaraḥ/candramā iḍāvatsaraḥ/vayuḥ punar anuvatsaraḥ/

In Va. P., Vāyu being the narrator, substitutes Rudra for Vāyu in v.31. The remaining verses (vv. 33 ff) give the explanation of the association of these deities with these years.

31. He who quickens (lit. warms up) the worlds with his bodies seven times seven (=49 Maruts) and who makes people to work actively (and quickly) that wind (god) is *Vatsara.*

32. He who while being born out of Brahmā, roared thrice egotistically is Rudra. That Rudra who was born red-blue (in complexion) out of them is *Vatsara*. Now I shall explain to you their essential nature. Understand it as it is being narrated.

33. Due to the contact of limbs and minor parts of the body (divisions and sub-divisions), the Ātman of Kāla is the great-grandfather. He is the source of origin of Ṛk, Sāman and Yajus. He is the lord of all the five (viz. day, fortnight etc...).

34. That (identical with) Yajus, Soma, Bhūta (elements) and Prajāpati is called *Saṁvatsara* by learned men. And what is Agni but Sūrya (the Sun-god)?

35-36. The Sun-god is the arranger of the divisions of time such as days, months, seasons, equinoxes as well as of the activities of planets, stars, of cold, heat, rain, span of life, holy rites, (but himself) is an evolute (being born of Brahmā) of kindly disposition, the son of Brahmā, the Lord protector of subjects. He is only one.* He is day, month, season and grand-sire (Brahmā).

37. He is Āditya, Savitṛ, Bhānu, the enlivener of life, honoured by Brahmā. He is called Bhāskara as he is the source of the origin and cause of destruction of all living beings and is hence designated as Bhāskara.

38. The third *Parivatsara* should be known as the presiding deity of stars. As the moon is the Lord of medicinal herbs, he is called the great-grand-father.

39. He is the life-bestower of living beings. He meets their needs and preserves them. By his rays he surveys the universe and sustains it.

40. The moon is the source of the origin of *Tithis* (days of the Lunar fortnight), junctions of *Parvans*, the Full Moon and the New Moon. He causes the night and is the Prajāpati with nectarine soul.

41-42. Hence he is fatherly soma of the nature of Ṛk,

*"He is one! he is many"—Bd. P. *ibid.* v. 125.

Yajur and Sāman. He is the propeller of all the activities of all creatures through the working of vital airs such as Prāṇa, Apāna, Samāna, Vyāna, Udāna.

43. He causes the unified and simultaneous activities of the five units of the physical body, viz. the sense-organs, the mind, the intellect, the memory and power*.

44. He is the soul of all the worlds (beings) through (his spatial forms) *Āvaha*, *Pravaha* etc. He is the creator of all. He is the *Prabhañjana* (violent wind) always energetic.

45. He is the source of origin of fire, water, earth, the sun and the moon. Hence he is Prajāpati. He is the soul of existing worlds. He is the great-grandfather.

46. When medicinal herbs decline, the Lord is worshipped by Devas, the chief of whom was Prajāpati and who seek fruits eagerly desired by them. He is worshipped (by offering *Puroḍāśa*) in three *Kapālas* (pots known as *Aṁbaka*). Hence he is called Tryaṁbaka.

47. The (Vedic metres) Gāyatrī, Triṣṭubh and Jagatī are remembered (known) by the term Tryaṁbaka. They are the sources of the origin of sacrifice.

48. It is remembered as *Tri-Kapāla* as the *Puroḍāśa* offering consecrated for (achieving) three means by the repetition of those three metrical verses united into one and through their efficacy.

49. Thus the Yuga as mentioned by the learned, is one consisting of five years. The *saṁvatsara* that has been mentioned by Brāhmaṇas as one having five-fold selves became a set of six selves with the names of Madhu (spring) and other seasons.

50. The sons of the seasons are five. Thus this creation is mentioned briefly. This wind (vital air) alone is the life of living beings.

51. The destroyer Kāla runs with the force of the current of a river with day and night for his hands. Hence he is called the wind.

52. These are the Prajāpatis (Lords of subjects) most im-

**Jalātmaka* in the text amended as *balātmaka* as *jala* is irrelevant. Bd. P. ibid. v.131 also reads *balātmaka*.

portant of all embodied beings. They are glorified as the Pitṛs of all people and the Ātmans of all the worlds.

53. The lord manifested himself by coming out of the mouth of Brahmā, as he was meditating. Hence he (the great lord) Mahādeva, the sage, the Brāhmaṇa, the soul of all living beings is the great-grandfather.

54. He, the lord of all living beings is identical with the Praṇava. The creation of the limbs (major and minor) of living beings is due to the entry of the soul (into the body).

55. Agni, *Saṁvatsara*. the sun, the moon, the wind—Lord Rudra, the soul of Kāla, the all-pervader always condenses these. It is called *Idvatsara* when it causes exhilaration and blesses the world.

56. In this universe everything is penetrated and permeated by Lord Rudra with his own brilliance, bodies and names by the relation of the supporter and the supported.

57. Hence through his prowess this second contact of welfare is the cause of supreme bliss to the worlds.

58. Since he is the cause of the general distinction existing in Devas, Pitṛs, and Kāla, he is worshipped by the learned.

59. The lord of lords, the Prajāpati of the Prajāpatis, the abode of living beings is Rudra, Nīlalohita. He revives the growth of medicinal plants declining again and again.

60. Thus the lineage of Devas cannot be enumerated due to their multiplicity. Their sons and grandsons are too many to mention.

61. He who glorifies this lineage of great Prajāpatis of noble deeds and stable renown will attain great *Siddhi*.

CHAPTER THIRTYTWO

Characteristics of Yugas

Vāyu said:

1. Henceforth I shall explain the decisive nature of *oṁkāra* as the imperishable Brahman.[1] It shall be remembered at the beginning that it consists of three letters.

2. In accordance with the letters, the presiding deities are ordained. There are Ṛk, Yajur, Sāman (Vedas), Vāyu (the Wind-god), the Fire-god and water.

3. It is from the *Akṣara* that the fourteen noble *Ātmans*, the deities of the Devas, originated.

4. Among these letters (*oṁkāra*) is omnipresent, all-permeating, the knower of all Yogas. It is lettered at the beginning, middle and the end for the bliss of the people.

5. Seven sages, Indras, Devas, as well as Pitṛs—all who are evolved out of the letter, have (really) come out of Maheśvara (Śiva), the God of gods.

6. For the benefit here and hereafter, they speak of it as the greatest region. Kāla, known as Yuga, has already been mentioned to you by me.

7. The Yugas are Kṛta, Tretā, Dvāpara and Kali. They move in cycles like a wheel.

8. Devas, being subject to the control of Kāla, felt dejected. They could not adjust to his magnitude and control.

9-10. Terrified by Kāla, the sages, Devas and Indra of great penance, restrained their speech, controlled their minds severely for a thousand years in the beginning of the Manvantara and resorted to the great lord (Śiva).

11. They said to the lord, "O great Lord! This Kāla is the lord of Devas. He has four faces and four forms. Who can comprehend him? He is too deep."

12. Then looking at Kāla of four faces, the great Lord

---

1. This chapter is a continuation of the topic of Time initiated in the previous chapter (31. 24 ff.). The introductory statement regarding 'The decisive nature of Oṁkāra' concludes with its identification with god Maheśvara.

said to Devas, "You need not be afraid. What desire of yours shall I grant You ?

13. I shall do everything for you. Your endeavour will not go in vain." Himself being the unconquerable Kāla, the lord spoke again.[1]

14. "This white face of his, seen with four tongues, is the face of Kāla and is called Kṛta Yuga. This god Brahmā, the most excellent among gods, and Vaivasvata is (this) face.

15. What I called the third—this blood-red coloured (face) with three licking tongues, is the Tretā Yuga, O Brāhmaṇas.

16. In this age the institution of sacrifice is initiated from great Lord Śiva and is worshipped in this age. The three tongues are the three fires (Gārhapatya, Āhavanīya and Dakṣiṇa). After worshipping the fires, O Brāhmaṇas, the tongue of Kāla begins to function.

17. This terrible face of reddish-tawny colour with two tongues is the Dvāpara age. I will remain two-footed in this age.

18-19. This fourth face of black colour and red eyes, the single-tongued, dark and huge, licking like a serpent again and again, is the terrible Kali age. It is terrifying to all the worlds. It is the fourth terrible face of the Kāla.

20. In this age, neither happiness nor salvation comes into being. The subjects are devoured by Kāla.

---

1. Verses 13-20 give us an interesting reification of Time. Identifying himself with Kāla, Maheśvara explains the four faces and forms of Kāla as follows : A Yuga is a face of Kāla.

Name of the Face	*Other Description*
4. Kṛta ..	Colour—white; four tongues. Identified with Brahmā and Vaivasvata Manu.
3. Tretā ..	Colour—blood-red. The three tongues are three sacrificial fires (viz. Gārhapatya, Āhavanīya and Dakṣiṇa) i.e. the institution of sacrifice was established in Tretā. Establishment of Kṣattriya Gotras.
2. Dvāpara ...	Colour—reddish tawny. Two tongues, two feet. Kṣattriyas firmly established.
1. Kali ...	Colour—black, red eyes, one tongue.

21. Brahmā shall be worshipped in the Kṛta age; in the Tretā, it is sacrifice; Viṣṇu in Dvāpara; and I in all the four ages.

22. Brahmā, Viṣṇu and sacrifice are the three parts of Kāla itself. But in all ages, the four-formed great Lord is the very Kāla itself.

23. I am the progenitor of Kāla, the initiator of Kāla.

24-25. O Excellent Devas of great power, you need not be afraid of the advent of Kali. For the welfare of the worlds, and for offering protection to the people and Devas, I shall be born (in Kali age) and be worshipped."

26. Thus addressed, Devas and the sages bowed to the Lord of the universe with bent heads. They spoke to him again.

The gods and sages enquired:

27. How is this Kāla, of great splendour, huge body, great prowess and four faces terrible to living beings?

The great Lord said:

28. "This Kāla has four forms, four fangs and four faces. For protecting the universe, he goes beyond, on all sides.

29. There is nothing impossible for him in the universe consisting of the mobile and immobile beings. Kāla creates the living beings and gradually annihilates them.

30. All are subject to the control of Kāla. Kāla is not subject to anyone. Kāla always reckons (controls) all living beings.

31. He takes seventy-one steps, as mentioned before, which constitute a Manvantara with as many cycles of the sets of four Yugas.

32. Over-stepping one, when Kāla completes a set of seventy-one steps, the Manvantara terminates."

33. Having spoken thus to Devas, sages, Pitṛs and Dānavas, the lord vanished there itself, after being bowed to by them.

34. Thus the lord creates, annihilates Devas, sages, Pitṛs and Dānavas in course of Time (Kāla) again and again.

35. Hence, due to the fear of Kāla, the great Lord is worshipped in every Manvantara by Devas, sages, Pitṛs and Dānavas.

36-37. Hence in the Kali age, a Brāhmaṇa should perform penance strenuously. The fruit of the merit of a person resorting to the great Lord is very great. Hence abandoning the heaven and descending to the earth at the advent of the terrible Kali, Devas and the sages desire to perform penance. They are engrossed in holy rites. The Lord too takes incarnation frequently in the Kali age.

38-39. Thousands of Devas, saints and kings have passed away in course of time, in Vaivasvata Manvantara. Devāpi, the king in the race of Pūru, Manu and his descendants in the family of Ikṣvāku are endowed with great Yogic strength. They wait for the change in Kāla.

40. When the Kali age terminates, and Tretā Yuga arrives, in that future Tretā Yuga along with the seven sages, the *gotras* of Kṣattriyas will be established. They are narrated.

41. The Kṣattriyas become firmly established at the end of Dvāpara, along with the sages. When Kṛta, Tretā and Dvāpara pass away, the Kali age arrives, wherein sinful men pass their time.

42. Śrutis and Smṛtis record the (completion and) passing away of the seven Manvantaras. The serial order of the termination of *yugas* is the same in all these.

43. The rise of Brāhmaṇas and Kṣatriyas is mutual along with that of the Yugas. Just as they come into existence from them, those that have come into being pass away along with them.

44. When the Kṣattriyas were exterminated by Rāma, son of Jamadagni, the widows were made unchaste by the rulers of the earth. Now I shall tell you about those that have gone to heaven. Understand.

45. They mention Aiḍa i.e. Aila (Purūravas) as the founder of Ikṣvāku race.[1] There was a line of other Kṣattriya kings on the earth.

---

1. The statements in vv 45, 46 regarding Aiḍa (i.e. Aila, Purūravas) as the founder of the Ikṣvāku race is wrong. Vide *AIHT*, pp. 145-46 for the table of Royal-Genealogies.

46-47. Ikṣvāku kings were born in the race of Aila; full hundred kings of that family were crowned; the extent of the Bhoja family of kings is twice that number. There were three hundred Kṣattriya kings divided into four lines as I have already mentioned (?)

48-49. Now hear about the kings that have gone before, as I mention about them. There were a hundred Prativindhyas,[1] a hundred Haihayas, a hundred Dhārtarāṣṭras, eighty Janamejayas, a hundred families of very powerful kings.

50. There were a hundred Paulas; Kāśi, Kuśa and others were a hundred. Śaśabindus who have gone, constitute a thousand. These performed horse-sacrifices wherein thousands and thousands (of gold coins) were given as gifts.

51. Thus, all the saintly kings who passed away in the previous Yugas, have been mentioned briefly. They cannot be mentioned in detail.

52. These have made the race of Yayāti flourish. Sustaining the worlds, these have been glorified as lustrous.

53-54. Those who hear and retain in memory their account get the five rare boons of Brahmaloka, viz. longevity, sons, wealth, fame and prosperity and they go to the region of Brahmā.

55. Four thousand years, they say, constitute the Kṛta Yuga.[2] Four hundred years oonstitute *Sandhyā* (transitional period) and four hundred years the part of *Sandhyā* (Sandhyāṁśa).

---

1. Vide Pargiter in *AIHT* p. 130. But the kings mentioned here belong to the past epoch.

2. The years mentioned in Yuga calculations are 'years of gods'. Verses 55-63 give the period of divine years of each Yuga as follows :

Name of the Yuga	*Period*	*Sandhyā*	*Sandhyāṁśa*		*Total*
1. Kṛta	4000	400	400	=	4800
2. Tretā	3000	300	300	=	3600
3. Dvāpara	2000	200	200	=	2400
4. Kali	1000	100	100	=	1200

Total period of four yugas (*Caturyugī* or Mahā-yuga) = 12,000 years.

The author identifies four parts (*pādas*) of this Purāṇa with Yugas. Thus Kṛta = *Prakriyā Pāda*, Tretā = *Anuṣaṅga Pāda*, Dvāpara = *Upodghāta Pāda*, Kali = (*Upa-*) *Saṁhāra Pāda*.

The number of years in a Mahāyuga = 12,000 years.

The number of verses in this Purāṇa = 12,000.

56. The Kṛta yuga, the *Prukriyāpāda* (the preliminary period) consists of four thousand years. Out of it, four hundred years constitute the transitional period (at the beginning and at the end of the yuga).

57. In the Tretā age the period is three thousand years with three hundred years of *Sandhyā* (twilight period) and three hundred years of *Sandhyāṁśa* (transitional period).

58. Tretā age, the *Anuṣaṅgapāda* (of the *Caturyugī*) consists of three thousand years and two thousand years period is proclaimed for Dvāpara Age.

59. The twilight period (*Sandhyā*) consists of two hundred years and the transitional period (*Sandhyāṁśa*) is of the same duration. The third *pāda* (of Caturyuga) called *Upodghātapāda* is in Dvāpara Age.

60. Persons expert in calculation opine one thousand years (as the period) of Kali age. Its *Sandhyā* period is of hundred years and *Sandhyāṁśa* period is also of a hundred years.

61. The fourth, *Saṁhāra* (*Upa-saṁhāra*) *pāda*, is stated to be in Kali Age. Four Yugas have (each of them) the twilight and transitional periods.

62-63. (This totals upto twelve thousand.) Thus learned men knew that this Purāṇa (also) consists of twelve thousand verses.

64. Just as Vedas are divided into four *Pādas*, a Yuga also has four *Pādas*. Just as god Brahmā ordained a Yuga to consist of four parts (feet), so he has ordained four parts (Pādas—feet) to this Purāṇa* as well.

---

* *Surāṇām* in the text is a misprint for *Purāṇam*, as recorded in A. Hence that reading is accepted.

CHAPTER THIRTYTHREE

Progeny of Svāyambhuva Manu[1]

Sūta said :

1. In all the Manvantaras of the past and future, equally identical persons, all of the same names and forms, are born.

2. The different Devas who are the ruler in that Manvantara, sages and human beings all (are equally identical[2]).

3. The creation of great sages has been narrated. Now know and understand the family of Svāyambhuva Manu being narrated in detail and in due order.

4-6. Svāyambhuva Manu had ten grandsons equal to himself. They were the sons of Priyavrata. This entire earth with its seven continents and various *Varṣas* was colonised by them formerly in the Svāyambhuva Manvantara in the first Tretā ages.[3] They were endowed with progeny, Yogic power, and penance and the ability to create subjects. This earth was colonised by them.

7-8. Kanyā (Kāmyā in Bd. P.), that extremely fortunate daughter of Kardama, the Prajāpati, bore to valorous Priyavrata sons endowed with progeny. She gave birth to two daughters Samrāj and Kukṣi as well as to hundred sons[4]. Among them ten brothers were very valorous and equal to Prajāpati.

9. They were Agnīdhra, Vapuṣmat, Medhā, Medhātithi, Vibhu, Jyotiṣmat, Dyutimat, Havya, Savana and Sarva.

---

1. This chapter is (even textually) similar to Bd. P.I.2.14 as both deal with the topic of the race of Priyavrata and the distribution of the continents and sub-continents among the descendants of Priyavrata.

2. This belief is shared by all Purāṇas. This chapter deals with Purāṇic cosmography. It associates the names of the continents and sub-continents of the earth with those of their respective rulers—all being the grandsons of Svāyambhuva Manu—sons of Priyavrata. Compare A.P. Ch. 107, Bh. P.V. 16.1-26, KP. I. 40, Mt. P. Chs. 112, 121, 122.

3. Tretā is the Yuga in which Kṣattriyas got established.

4. Ten sons in Bd. P.

10. Priyavrata crowned seven of them with due religious rites as kings over the seven continents.[1]

11. He made Agnīdhra the powerful lord over Jambūdvīpa and he made Medhātithi king of Plakṣa Dvīpa.

12. In the Śālmali continent, he crowned Vapuṣmat as the king. He made Jyotiṣmat ruler over Kuśa Dvīpa.

13. He granted Dyutimān the kingdom of Krauñca Dvīpa. He made Havya lord over Śāka Dvīpa.

14. He made Savana the overlord of Puṣkara. In Puṣkara Dvīpa, Savana had two sons Mahāvīta and Dhātaki. These two sons were excellent among persons endowed with sons.

15. In honour of the name of the noble soul, that continent (sub-Varṣa) [is known] as Mahāvīta. The subcontinent Dhātakī Khaṇḍa is called after the name Dhātaki.[2]

16. King Havya begot (seven) sons as the rulers of Śāka-dvīpa. They were Jalada, Kumāra, Sukumāra, Maṇīcaka, Vasu-moda, Sumodāka and the seventh son Mahādruma.[3]

17. The first sub-continent or country of (=governed by) Jalada is called Jalada; the second of (=ruled by) Kumāra is glorified as Kaumāra.

18. The third sub-continent of Sukumāra is known as Sukumāra and the fourth of Maṇīcaka is called Maṇīcaka.

---

1. The division of the earth among the sons of Priyavrata is as follows:

Name of Pripavrata's son	*Name of the Dvīpa assigned as a separate kingdom*
1. Āgnīdhra	Jambū Dvīpa
2. Vapuṣmat	Śālmala (-li)
3. Medhā	
4. Medhātithi	Plakṣa
5. Vibhu	
6. Jyotiṣmat	Kuśa
7. Dyutimat	Krauñca
8. Havya	Śāka
9. Savana	Puṣkara
10. Sarva	

2. The Sub-Divisions of Puṣkara Dvipa.

3. Verses 16-20 enumerate the Sub-Divisions of Śāka Dvipa, each named after the seven sons of Havva.

19. The fifth Varṣa of Vasumoda is called Vasumodaka and the sixth of Modāka, is glorified as Modāka.

20. The seventh of Mahādruma is named Mahādruma. All the seven countries were thus named after them.

21. Dyutimat, Lord of Krauñca Dvīpa had seven sons, viz. Kuśala, Manuga, Uṣṇa, Pīvara, Andhakāraka, Muni and Dundubhi.[1]

22. The splendid regions situated in Krauñca Dvīpa were called after the names of these (sons). The land of Uṣṇa is remembered as Uṣṇa and that of Pīvara, Pīvara.

23. Andhakāraka's land was called Andhakāra, that of Muni was Muni and that of Dundubhi, Dundubhi. These seven flourishing lands were situated in Krauñca Dvīpa.

24. These seven sons of great strength were born to Jyotiṣmat in Kuśa Dvīpa. These were Udbhida, Veṇumat, Svairatha, Lavaṇa, Dhṛti, the sixth son Prabhākara and the seventh Kapila.[2]

25-26. The first country was called after Udbhida, the second after Veṇumaṇḍala, the third after Svairathākāra, the fourth after Lavaṇa, the fifth after Dhṛtimat, the sixth after Prabhākara and the seventh Varṣa of Kapila is well-known as Kapila.

27. Thus the countries in the Kuśa Dvīpa were known after their names. The subjects therein followed the conducts befitting the stages of life.

28. The rulers of the Śālmali continent were the seven sons of Vapuṣmat. They were : Śveta, Harita, Jīmūta, Rohita, Vaidyuta, Mānasa and Suprabha.[3]

29-30. Śveta was the land of Śveta, Rohita, of Rohita. Jīmūta, of Jīmūta, Harita, of Harita, Vaidyuta, of Vaidyuta, Mānasa, of Mānasa and Suprabha, of Suprabha. All these seven were the rulers of the lands.

---

1. Verses 21-23 enumerate the sub-continents of Krauñca-dvīpa which are named after their first rulers, the sons of Dyutimat.

2. Verses 24-27 give the seven sub-divisions of Kuśa-dvīpa each named after their initial ruler, the sons of Jyotiṣmat.

3. Verses 28-30: The seven sons of Vapuṣmān, the kings of Śālmali-dvīpa gave their names to its sub-divisions, each to his special sub-division.

31. I shall describe the seven countries after Jambūdvīpa. The seven sons of Medhātithi were kings and rulers of Plakṣa-dvīpa.[1]

32-33. The eldest was Śāntabhaya, and then followed Śiśira, Sukhodaya, Ānanda, Dhruva, Kṣemaka and Śiva. The seven countries named after them were established by them in the previous Svāyaṁbhuva Manvantara.

34. The subjects in the Plakṣa-dvīpa were made to follow the conduct of life according to their respective castes and stages of life by the sons of Medhātithi residing in their respective seven countries.

35-36. In the five continents beginning with Plakṣa and ending with Śāka the sacred rite was known in accordance with the division of castes (*Varṇas*) and stages of life (*Āśramas*). Happiness, longevity, forms (beauty), strength and Dharma were all common to everyone in the five Dvīpas (continents) perpetually.

37. Understand that the Jaṁbūdvīpa is surrounded by the seven Dvīpas. Priyavrata crowned the eldest son (the son of) Kāmyā[2], Āgnīdhra of great valour as the king of Jaṁbūdvīpa.

38-40. He had nine sons equal in valour and strength to Prajāpati. The eldest was known as Nābhi; his younger brother was Kiṁpuruṣa; Harivarṣa was the third; Ilāvṛta was the fourth; Ramya was the fifth; Hariṇmat was the sixth; Kuru was the seventh; Bhadrāśva was the eighth; Ketumāla was the ninth. Undestand their lands.[3]

41-45. The father gave Nābhi the southern *Varṣa* (subcontinent) called Hima. He gave to Kimpuruṣa the *Varṣa* known as Hemakūṭa; to Harivarṣa the *Varṣa* remembered as Naiṣadha; to Ilāvṛta the central part of Sumeru. He (the father) gave to Ramya Nīla-varṣa; Śveta, which lay to the north of it, was given by the father to Hariṇmat. He gave to Kuru the

1. Verses 32-34 enumerate the seven sub-continents of Plakṣa-dvīpa each of which was named after its ruler, the son of Medhātithi.

2. *Kanyā* in the text is a misprint.

3. Verses 38-45 enumerate the nine sub-division of India as understood by the author of the Vā. P. For locations of mountains mentioned here *vide Suptā* p. 11, fn. 2.

subcontinent to the north of Śṛṅgavān. Similarly he assigned the subcontinent Mālyavat to Bhadrāśva. He assigned the subcontinent Gandhamādan to Ketumāla. Thus (he apportioned) these big subcontinents (among his sons).

46. The righteous Āgnīdhra crowned his sons in these countries in due order and then engaged himself in penance.

47. Thus, the seven continents were established by the seven sons of Priyavrata, the grandsons of Svāyaṁbhuva (Manu).

48. The eight countries beginning with Kiṁpuruṣa are very auspicious. There perfection is natural, wholly consisting of pleasure and without effort.

49. There is no calamity or misfortune, no fear of old age and death. They have neither righteousness nor unrighteousness. There are neither high born nor low born nor middling. In all those areas there are no *yuga* cycles (with their classification, duties etc.).

50. I shall now describe the lineage of Nābhi in the Hima Varṣa. Nābhi of great lustre begot of Merudevī a son (named) Ṛṣabha,[1] the best among all kings and the ancestor of all Kṣattriyas.

51. The heroic Bharata was born of Ṛṣabha. He was the eldest of his hundred sons. After crowning his son Bharata, Ṛṣabha renounced the world.

52. He entrusted the southern *Varṣa* called Hima to Bharata. Hence learned people know it by the name Bhārata Varṣa.[2]

53. Bharata's son was the scholarly and righteous Sumati. After transferring his kingdom, the royal splendour and glory to the son, Bharata entered the forest.

---

1. He is the first Tirthaṅkara of Jains. He is mentioned in Bh. P.V. Chs. 4 & 5 and in VP. II. 1.28. Brahmancial Purāṇas regard him as their own, an incarnation of Viṣṇu.

2. Jain tradition supports this Purāṇic belief. But countries are named after the major tribes that settled in that particular land e.g. Malwa, Gujarat, England. Thus the country in which the tribe called Bharatas settled was the original Bhārata.

54. His son, Tejas[1] was a lord of the subjects and conqueror of enemies. Indradyumna, the son of Taijasa, was well-known as a scholar.

55. His son was Parameṣṭhin. After his death Śobhana born in the family of Pratīhāras[2] and related to him (ascended his throne). A son known as Pratihartṛ was born to him.

56. Unnetṛ was the son of Pratihartṛ. Bhuva was his son. His son was Udgītha. Pratāvi was his son.

57. Vibhu was the son of Pratāvi. His son was Pṛthu. Nakta was Pṛthu's son and Gaya was Nakta's son.

58. Nara was the son of Gaya. Virāṭ was Nara's son. Virāṭ's son was Mahāvīrya and Dhīmat was his son.

59. Mahat was the son of Dhīmat. Bhauvana was Mahat's son. Tvaṣṭṛ was Bhauvana's son and Arija was his son.

60. Rajas was Arija's son. Śatajit was the son of Rajas. He had a hundred sons and all of them were kings.

61. Out of them Viśvajyoti was the chief. It is through them that these subjects flourished. They made this Bhārata as consisting of seven Khaṇḍas.

62. The country Bhārata was enjoyed by those born of their race, for seventyone sets of ages consisting of Kṛta, Tretā etc.

63. Along with those ages (*yugas*) which have gone, the kings of their race were hundreds and thousands in the Svāyambhuva Manvantara.

64-65. This is the creation of Svāyambhuva (Manu) by which this universe has been filled along with sages, deities, Pitṛs, Gandharvas, Rākṣasas, Yakṣas, Bhūtas, Piśācas, human beings, animals and birds. Their creation in the world revolves in cycles along with the Yugas.

---

1. Reading in A accepted as '*Tejasas tu sutaḥ*' in the text contradicts the second line thereof.

2. Bd. P. (v. 65-66) states that Pratihāra is the name of the son of Parameṣṭhin.

CHAPTER THIRTYFOUR

Geography of Jambūdvipa[1]

1. On hearing of the establishment of the people, the clever and eminent sage asked Sūta about the length and extent of the earth.

The sages enquired :

2. O holy sir, how many continents, or oceans or mountains are there? How many Varṣas(sub-continents) are there and what are the rivers in them.

3. Explain factually to us in details, the magnitude of the great elements and of the Lokāloka mountain, the circumference, the size and the course of movements of the sun and the moon.

Sūta said :

4. Henceforth I shall explain the length and extent of the earth, the number of oceans and continents in details.

5. I shall tell you how many countries (*Varṣas*) there are and what the rivers (are) therein. (Now) I shall tell you the magnitude of the great elements, the Lokāloka mountain range, the circumference, magnitude and the course of the moon and the sun.

6. There are thousands of countries and islands in the seven continents. They cannot be described in details with sufficient evidence, even in hundreds of years.

7. I shall explain the seven continents along with the moon, the sun and the planets. Men mention their extent and magnitude by guess-work.

---

1. The Vā. P. is one of the oldest Purāṇas. Though the anthor has recorded the traditional information or social memory of the places in Jambūdvipa, the information as corroborated by modren researchers shows that Purāṇic India was much wider and included modren Afghanistan and a major portion of Central Asia. The distances and the extent mentioned in terms of Yojanas are traditional (and possibly conjectural) as they often do not tally with our present knowledge.

8. One shall not make conjectures about inconceivable objects and worlds. That which is beyond Prakṛti is called eternal.

9. I shall describe to you factually Jaṁbūdvīpa consisting of nine *Varṣas*. Understand its extent and zones in Yojanas.

10-11. It extends to a hundred thousand Yojanas. It is full of different rural localities and various splendid cities. It is embellished with the (colonies of) Siddhas, Cāraṇas and Gandharvas and with mountains as well. It has mountains abounding in minerals and variegated rocks. It has many rivers rising from mountains.

12. Jaṁbūdvīpa is immense, glorious and surrounded by nine (Khaṇḍas—Zones?) inhabited by living beings. It is encircled on all sides by salt-sea.

13. All round Jaṁbūdvīpa, extending to its entire length, the six mountain systems stretch to the east.[1] They have excellent ridges. They extend to both sides plunging into the eastern and western seas.

14. The mountain Himavat is full of snow. Hemakūṭa is full of gold; Niṣadha is golden having the lustre of the midday sun.

15. The golden Meru of four colours is known as the highest.[2] Leaping up in symmetrical shapes on all sides it rises up.

16. On its sides it has various colours. It is endowed with the attributes of Prajāpati. It is born of the umbilical knot of Brahmā, of unmanifest origin.

17. It is white on the east, hence its Brāhmaṇahood. It is yellow on the south, hence its Vaiśyahood.

---

1. These are called *Varṣa parvatas* as they divide one *Varṣa* (sub-continent or country) from another. For their location and modern name *vide Supra* Ch. 1, p. 11, note 2.

2. Verses 15-23 describe the pivotal mount Meru. About its shape and size there is a consenus among Purāṇas like KP, Mt. P., Bd. P., Mk. P. M. Ali (*AGP*, pp. 47-50) points out that Persians, Greeks, Chinese, Jews and Arabs confirm the traditional nodality of Meru. After discussing the problems, he shows that Mt. Meru of Purāṇas is identical with the Pamirs in Central Asia.

For a diagrammatic representation of Jaṁhū-dvīpa and its cross section *vide* Fig. 4 on *AGP*, p. 65.

18. On the west it is black like the aloe leaf. It is very hard, and renders services to many.

19. Its northern side has a natural red colour. Hence its Kṣattriya-hood. Thus all its colours are described. Its manifest characteristic are described according to its colour and effects.

20-21. The Nīla mountain is full of *Lapis lazuli*; Śvetasṛṅga, full of gold; Śṛṅgavān is of gold but variegated in colour like peacock feathers. These lordly mountains are resorted to by Cāraṇas and Siddhas. Their inner girth is said to be nine thousand (Yojanas).

22. It is in the centre of Ilāvṛta which surrounds it. It extends to nine thousand Yojanas. In the centre of the Meru, there is a smokeless fire.

23. The southern and the northern halves of Meru come together like the middle of the sacrificial altar. The seven mountain systems of the seven countries (Varṣas) are two thousand Yojanas long and as much high.

24-27. Their length is said to be similar to that of Jaṁbūdvīpa. The two middling mountains, Nīla and Niṣadha are a hundred thousand Yojanas in length; the other (four mountains) are shorter (in length) than these. (They are) Śveta, Hemakūṭa, Himavān, and Śṛṅgavān. Out of these mountains Śveta and Hemakūṭa are each ninety thousand Yojanas long. (Mountains Himavān and Śṛṅgavān) are each eighty thousand in length. There are *Janapadas* (territories) in between them. The *Varṣas* are seven in number. They are encircled by mountains that are difficult to cross on account of steep precipices. They are criss-crossed by different rivers. It was impossible to travel from one *Varṣa* to another (lit. they were mutually unapproachable). Animals of different species live in them.

28. This *Varṣa* deriving its name from Himavat is well known by the name Bhārata. Hemakūṭa is beyond this. It is remembered by the name Kiṁpuruṣa.

29. Naiṣadha (*Varṣa* is beyond) Hemakūṭa. It is called Harivarṣa. Ilāvṛta is beyond Harivarṣa (with Meru in the middle).

30. Nīla is beyond Ilāvṛta and is well-known by the name Ramyaka. Beyond Ramyaka is Śveta and is well known as

Hiraṇmaya. The Śṛṅgavat is beyond Hiraṇmaya and it is remembered as Kuru.

31. The two sub-continents in the south and north should be known as situated in the form of a bow. Four others are situated lengthwise and the middle one is Ilāvṛta.[1]

32. Vedyardha which is on the hitherside of Niṣadha is known as southern Vedyardha and that which is beyond the Nīlavān is the northern Vedyardha. On the southern side of Vedyardha there are three *Varṣas* and three on the northern side.

33a. Meru should be known as standing in between them and Ilāvṛta is in the middle of Meru.

33b-34. To the south of the Nīla and to the north of Niṣadha, there is a great mountain stretching to the north named Mālyavān.

It stretches a thousand Yojanas from Nīla to Niṣadha. It is glorified as one thirtyfour thousand Yojanas in extent.

35. The mountain Gandhamādana should be known as situated to its west. In length and extent it is reputed to be like Mālyavān.[2]

---

1. This is the seven-continent concept of the earth in the Purāṇas. It may be diagrammatically represented as follows :

NORTH

Uttara-Kuru Varṣa	—	Mt. Śṛṅgavān
Hiraṇmaya Varṣa	—	Mt. Śveta
Ramyaka Varṣa	—	Mt. Nīla
Ilāvṛta Varṣa Mt. Meru Ilāvṛta Varṣa		
Hari Varṣa	—	Mt. Niṣadha
Kiṁpuruṣa Varṣa	—	Mt. Hemakūṭa
Bhārata or Haimavata Varṣa	—	Mt. Himavat or Himālaya

SOUTH

Does the bow-like formation of these Varṣas suggest the spherical shape of the earth?

2. The Purāṇas differ about the location of these mountains. But here Mt. Mālyavān due to its association with Gandhamādana and Meru may be identified with the Sarikol range, as Gandhamādana was the northern ridge of the great Hindukush arch with its northern extension, the Khwaja Mahammad (*AGP*, pp. 58-59).

Meru, the golden mountain, is in the middle of two cirdes. That golden mountain has four colours. It is symmetrical and very lofty.

36. In between the two, there is the four-coloured, golden, four-cornered, lofty, excellent mountain Meru. From the unmanifest, the elements of water etc. are born.

37. From the unmanifest the great lotus of the earth is evolved. Its pericarp is the four-cornered Meru that is five times great.

38-39. O excellent Brāhmaṇas, then all the deities were born. The noble Puruṣottama was born with his *Ātman* purified by merits earned through many Kalpas previously. Then there was born Mahādeva, the great Yogin, the great lord who is elderly to the universe which he pervades, and who is infinite and formless.

40. He has no form evolved out of Prakṛti, that is to say no form of flesh, fat or bone; with his Yogic power and lordly nature, he pervades the universe.

41. From him as the cause, was born the eternal lotus of the worlds. As the natural sequence of time, it occurred at the advent of the Kalpa (?)

42. In that lotus was born the four-faced lord of Devas, Brahmā, the chief of Prajāpatis, the lord of the universe.

43. His creation is the seed of the lotus precisely. The whole of it, along with the creation of the subjects, is mentioned here in detail.

44. The lotus that was fashioned by Viṣṇu grew from his umbilicus. The earth along with the forests and the trees was evolved in the shape of a lotus.

45. O Brāhmaṇas, listen to the detailed description of this lotus of the universe and its divisions in due order.

46. The four famous great continents are stationed on the petals.[1] The powerful Meru is stationed on the pericarp.

1. Verses 46 ff explain the four-continent (*Catur-dvīpī*) concept of the earth. It regards Meru as the pericarp of the Earth-lotus with four *dvīpas* as petals, one in each direction. Four-directionwise concept was naturally earlier and is found in Mbh. VI., 6.12-13, VP. II. 2. 39 ff and in early Buddhist works (see Childers, *Pali-Eng. Dictionary*; S. V. Mahādipo and Malalsekera, *Dict. Pali. Prop. Names*—Jambūdīpa).

47-48. Of its sides of different colours the eastern side is white; the southern is yellow; the western is black; and the northern is red. With variegated colours shining brightly, Meru is established like a king.

49. It is as refulgent as the midday sun or the smokeless fire. It is eightyfour thousand Yojanas in height.

50. Its depth below the surface of the earth is sixteen thousand Yojanas and at its base it extends also as much. It is situated like an arrow pointing to the east. Its diameter at the summit is thirtytwo thousand Yojanas.

51. Its girth all round is thrice its lateral extent. The spherical curvature is half of it. It lies in three angles.

52. Its extent all round is forty thousand Yojanas. In the angular calculation, it will be eight thousand more.

53. In the quadrangular calculation the girth is fortyeight thousand Yojanas.

54. That mountain is extremely rich in divine medicinal herbs. It is encircled by auspicious golden worlds.

55. All the groups of Devas, Gandharvas, Uragas, Rākṣasas and splendid Apsaras-s, are seen on that lordly mountain.[1]

56. That Meru, the purifier of living beings, is encircled by worlds. Four lands are established on its different sides.[2]

57. They are Bhadrāśva (to the east), Bhārata (in the south), Ketumāla in the west, and the Kurus in the north.

---

1. *Śailarājaiḥ* is emended as *Śailarāje* as in A.
2. Verses 56-57 state in a nutshell the *Catur-dvīpī* concept as follows :—

NORTH
(Uttara) Kuru
,,
|
West : Ketumāla——| Mt. Meru |——Bhadrāśva : *East*
|
Bhārata
SOUTH

Early Buddhists show the same distribution though they substitute Pūrva-Videha for Bhadrāśva and Apara Godāna (Pali—*Goyāna*) for Ketumāla. For a discussion of these names vide D.C. Sircar, GAM, I, pp. 19 ff and CGEIL—*Cosmography and Geography in Early Indian Literature* pp. 38-43.

They (Kurus) are the resorts of those who perform pious deeds.

58. The pericarp of that lotus is spherical all round extending to ninety-six thousand Yojanas. The internal measurement is eighty-four thousand Yojanas.

59. Its filaments extend to three hundred thousand Yojanas in all directions.

60. It has four petals to the four quarters, a hundred thousand Yojanas in length and eighty thousand in width.

61. Listen attentively to the description of what I had called before the pericarp and know it briefly.

62. Atri[1] thought it has a hundred angles or corners; sage Bhṛgu, one thousand. According to Sāvarṇi; it is octangular, and a quadrangle according to Bhāguri.

63. Vārṣāyaṇi opines that it is four-sided; Gālava thinks it has the shape of a saucer; Gārgya regards it as twisted braided hair; while Kroṣṭaki conjectures it to be spherical.

64. Each of these sages knew only that side of this lordly mountain which was near him. Only Brahmā knows the entire range.

65-66. Know that Meru, the most excellent of mountains, is full of gems and jewels. It has various colours and lustres. It is golden and refulgent like Aruṇa. It is very attractive. It has a thousand knots and ridges, where water flows. It is like a lotus with a thousand petals.

67-70. It is full of columns studded with gems and jewels. It has altars decorated with diverse jewels. Festoons of corals and golden pieces adorn it. On festival occasions hundreds of glorious heaven-dwellers moving about on aerial chariots, illuminate all its sides with their lustre. The abodes for Devas are laid in thousands of its beautiful ridges. The four-faced lord of Devas, Brahmā, the most excellent among those who know Brahman and the leader of heaven-dwellers, occupies its upper surface.[2]

---

1. Verses 62-63 show the confusion of pre-Vā P. geographers about Meru. The author of Vā. P. is not much wiser or reliable here.

2. In order to justify the identification of Meru with heaven or Svarga in vv. 94-96 below, we are told how the assembly halls of Gods are

71-72. The various quarters set up on the mountain contain thousands of great Devas capable of bestowing desired fruits. They have occupied the great regions there. Here is a glorious assembly-hall of Brahmā, resorted to by several Brahmanical sages. It is known as Manovatī in all the worlds.

73. The great aerial chariot of lord Īśāna, having the brilliance of a thousand suns, is there proclaiming its own glory.

74. Devas and sages (stay there) near Brahmā. The mass of splendour (god Brahmā?) is glorified there. I shall describe it to you now.

75. The glorious lord of riches, the thousand-eyed Indra, stays here honoured by Devas and the celestial sages of great Yogic prowess.

76. Here alone is the region of lord Indra, the great monarch, the lord of the worlds. It is as refulgent as the sun. It is bowed to by all Siddhas.

77. Here is the region of Indra endowed with the highest prosperity of the world. It is brightened by the excellent immortal Devas and is ever resorted to by them.

78-80. In the second inner ridge, in the intermediate point between the east and the south, is the famous splendid assembly-

---

located on the different ridges of Meru. God Brahmā, being the greatest of gods, is on a higher plane with his assembly hall Manovatī.

The direction-wise distribution of gods and their assemblies given in vv. 75-92 is as follows :

Direction of the Ridge		*Name of the presiding god*	*Name of his Assembly Hall*
I.	East	Indra	—
II.	South-East	Agni (Fire-god)	Tejovatī
III.	South (?)	Vaivasvata (Yama)	Susaṁyamā
IV.	?	Nairṛtya	Kṛṣṇāṅganā
V.	West (?)	Varuṇa	Śubhavatī
VI.	North-West	Vāyu	Gandhavatī
VII.	North ?	The Moon	Mahodayā Vibhāvarī in *infra* 50.90
VIII.	?	Īśāna	Yaśovatī

The list of the lords of directions as given here in Va. P. is different from the traditional one. The list quoted from Amarakośa (in Apte's Sk. Dictionary) substitutes Kubera for the Moon while Mbh V. 16.27 excludes Indra and Agni and includes both Kubera and Soma.

hall that shines like fire. It is very beautiful and lustrous, inlaid with metals of diverse colours. The ground is paved with various gems. It has several pillars made of gold and rising high. There are many gem-studded platforms, secret and hidden excellent apartments on either side. This famous spacious aerial chariot is refulgent and fire-like.

81-82. That alone is the great assembly-hall of the Fire-god. It is called Tejovatī. The Fire-god Vibhāvasu, the most excellent (among Devas) and the mouth of all celestial deities, endowed with thousands of leaping flames, is eulogised by Devas and sages, who perform *Homas* too.

83-84. The Fire-god is the intermediary and a distinguished deity of Brāhmaṇas. Though he is indivisible, his splendour is shared by all. He, the lord of splendour, assumes various forms. His diversity both as the cause and effect is perceptible through concentrated mind.

85. That Fire-god is respectfully bowed to by noble Siddhas, blessed sages, knowers of the world and worldly affairs and those who assimilate his prowess and exploits.

86. In the third inner ridge is a great assembly-hall of Vaivasvata (god of death). It is known as Susaṁyamā.

87. In the fourth inner ridge is the great assembly-hall of the intelligent lord Nairṛtya of squint-eyes. The hall is named Kṛṣṇāṅganā.

88. Similarly in the fifth inner ridge there is a great assembly hall of Varuṇa, lord of waters and son of the sun. This hall is named Śubhavatī.

89. In the northern quarter beyond that, in the sixth inner ridge, there is the great assembly-hall of Vāyu. It excels all in good qualities. It is called Gandhavatī.

90. In the seventh inner ridge, there is the assembly-hall of the Moon, lord of the stars. It has raised platforms and altars of brilliant *lapis lazuli*. This hall is called Mahodayā.

91. So also in the eighth inner ridge there is a great assembly-hall of Īśāna. It is named Yaśovatī. It has the lustre of the molten gold.

92. These splendid assembly-halls are situated in the eight quarters. They belong to the eight chief Devas, Indra and others.

93. They are resorted to by the sages, Devas, Gandharvas, Apsaras-s and serpents, who come for worship.

94-96. What is known and called by the synonyms of heaven, viz. Nākapṛṣṭha, Diva and Svarga, by those who know the Vedas and their ancillaries is this. It is here where Devas live. It is so said in the Vedas. One attains this Devaloka by various observances, restraints, sacrifices or different sorts of meritorious deeds. It is called Svarga also.

CHAPTER THIRTYFIVE

Jambū-dvipa (contd.)

Sūta said :

1. What is described as the root of the pericarp[1] is seventy thousand Yojanas beneath.

2. It is heard that a sphere of fortyeight thousand Yojanas encompassed by the lord of mountains is what is called *Merumūla* (Root of Meru).

3. In all the quarters, there are boundary mountains, the loftiest among thousands of mountains.

4-6. They are beautified by hedges, caves, rivers and rivulets. They have many ridges like huge mansions shining with flowers. Their sides are beautified by minerals. Their flanks are decorated by clusters of flowers. Their peaks are golden brown. Many streams flow over them. All these mountains are richly decorated with gems. There are inimitable bowers with hundreds of birds resorting to them. Lions, tigers, *Sarabhas* (a mythological eight-footed animal), Camarī deer and elephants live there. They (boundary mountains) are bounded by mountain (ranges) of various shapes and colours.

1. This is a continuation of the description of Mt. Meru. The author is recording his hearsay information—social memory. Modern geographers try to identify the mountains, rivers etc., in Purāṇas, many times without success.

7. Each of the ten mountains is marked by the sun, lion and the black deer. They have three streams (?) flowing in and out.

8. To the east of Meru are the two mountains Jaṭhara[1] and Devakūṭa which run north to south and stretch upto the Nīla and Niṣadha mountains.

9. The Kailāsa and the Himavat are to the south and north. Extending to the east and the west, they enter the sea.

10. O excellent Brāhmaṇas, now I shall tell you the diameter of Meru, the mountain of gold.

11. Meru has four great ranges (legs) in all the four quarters. Held by them, the earth with her seven continents does not move.

12. Their extent is ten thousand Yojanas. They shine with many gems and jewels of Devas, Yakṣas and Gandharvas who reside there. Many rivulets flow from their rocky declivity and their beautiful caves.

13. The table-lands of diverse colours and features shine with the clusters of flowers blooming around the slopes and ridges, abounding in red arsenic mines and yellow orpiment.

14. The caves all round shine in diverse colours with gems and gold. The place abounds in vermilion, gold and minerals.

15. They are decorated in corals set in variegated shapes and sizes of gold. There are abodes of Siddhas with hundreds of joints (storeys?) which are beautiful and delightful. They are dazzling all around with majestic palatial aerial chariots.

16. To the east is the Mandara,[2] to the west, the Vipula and to the north, the Supārśva.

17. On thousands of their peaks, there are platforms of diamonds and *Lapis lazuli*, with trees of thousands of branches. With firm roots, they are well-established.

---

1. Jaṭhara and Devakūṭa are the Kuruk-Tagh and Altin Tagh (Nanshang—Tsing-ling) mountains of Sinkiang (AGP 99-100).

2. The Pamirs if taken as Meru, Supārśva is located in Kirghistan. Mandara is not the hill in the Banka sub-division of the Bhagalpur district (Bihar) as given by De 124, but the Sarikol range (N. China) (AGP 101), and Vipula is in Ketumāla (see p. 248, note 2). The identification of Mandara with Ptolemy's Maiandros is doubtful.

18. They have thickly grown smooth dark leaves, with large fruits and flowers. They cover the ground with shade. They are very lofty.

19. Four great trees which are the land-marks of the continent, have grown there. They are resorted to by Siddhas, Yakṣas and Gandharvas.

20. On the peak of mountain Mandara, there is a great tree *Keturāṭ* (the king of banners) with hanging branches. There is a *Kandara* tree also.

21. It is splendid with excessive fragrant, full-blown flowers as big as a pitcher, with filaments spread out. They bloom in all seasons.

22. Wafted by the gentle wind, the fragrance fills up the quarters to more than a thousand Yojanas around.

23-25. O Brāhmaṇas, the continent Bhadrāśva[1] is well-known as *Varaketu.* Here Viṣṇu is directly worshipped by groups of Siddhas. Formerly Hari (Indra), the most excellent among Devas, riding a white horse and accompanied by a group of Rudras, travelled over the entire continent. O leaders of Brāhmaṇas, the continent is, therefore called Bhadrāśva.

26. There is a Jambū tree (Rose Apple) on the top of the southern mountain. It is resorted to by Devas. It ever blooms and bears fruits. It shines with garlands of flowers.

27. Its roots and branches are very extensive. Its branches are of pleasing colours. The tree is always bedecked with fresh flowers, fruits and branches.

28. The sweet and soft fruits of huge size falling on the peak of the mountain are nectar-like in taste.

29. From the table-land on the top of this excellent mountain, flows the river Jambū with currents of honey.

30. Gold known as Jāmbūnada, with the lustre of burning fire, is formed here. It is the incomparable ornament of Devas and the destroyer of sins.

31. Devas, Dānavas, Gandharvas, Yakṣas, Rākṣasas and Pannagas (serpents) drink the honey, the juice exuding from the Jambū tree which is as sweet as nectar.

---

1. Bhadrāśva is the Tarim-Hwango-Ho basin or North China (AGP 64, 65, 73).

32. That eternal Jaṁbū tree which is well-known in the world is the landmark in the southern continent.[1] The continent is called Jaṁbūdvīpa after its name.

33. A great Aśvattha tree grows on the peak of the great western mountain Vipula.[2]

34. It has hanging garlands, and golden platforms set with gems. Its trunk and branches are very lofty. It is the abode of many living beings. It abounds in good qualities.

35. That tree is the landmark of the people of Ketumāla. It is embellished with auspicious fruits growing in all seasons. They are of the size of big pots and very pleasing. The tree is resorted to by Devas and Gandharvas.

36. How the continent came to be known as Ketumāla, O great Brāhmaṇas, hear. I shall tell you the etymology of the name.

37-38. After the churning of the milk ocean the Daityas were defeated; on being pressed in the tumult of the battle, when the trees shook, a garland wreathed by the thousand-eyed lord Indra was put round the trunk of that Aśvattha tree (as a form of worship).

39. It still retains its excessive fragrance. It never fades. It bestows all desires. That blessed garland is worshipped by Siddhas and Cāraṇas.

40. The garland, as it were a flag-staff bestowed by Indra, shines in a divine way. Blown by the wind, it wafts pleasing fragrance.

41. Symbolised with the two names (Ketu and Mālā) joined together, the continent is known as Ketumāla.[3] It lies in the western region. It is very extensive, well known here as well as in the heaven.

---

1. It appears that certain climatic zones favourable for the growth of some typical trees are regarded as 'continents'. Thus *Jaṁbūdvīpa* has *Jaṁbū* (Rose-apple) as its representative tree implying the climatic zone (and other condition) conducive to its growth.

2. This is located in Ketumāla. Ketumāla is bounded on the south by Niṣadha (Hindukush-Kunlun), in the north by Nila (Zarafshan—Tien Shan), on the west by the (Caspian) Sea—the 'Western Sea' of Purāṇas, and on the north by the Turan desert (AGP, 88).

3. A popular etymology.

42. On the northern peak of the mountain Supārśva, a great fig tree grows up with extensive branches. It covers an area of many Yojanas.

43. It is resorted to by Siddhas and Cāraṇas. From its branches clusters of garlands of sweet fragrance hang loose. It shines with them.

44. This tree is the landmark of the northern Kuru country. It shines with fruits full of honey. The fruits resemble the coral cup.

45. Seven mental sons of Brahmā, the blessed younger brothers of Sanatkumāra, stay there. They are known as Kurus.

46. They attained (spiritual) knowledge in that region. They are characterised by piety and good qualities. They are of meritorious fame. This eternal, imperishable, great region has been attained by them.

47. This continent has derived its name from those seven great souls. The northern Kurus[1] are famous here and in the heaven for ever.

CHAPTER THIRTYSIX

(Geographical) Arrangement of the World

Sūta said :

I shall explain in due order the adjuncts of the four leading mountains. They are very charming at all times and seasons.

2. The place abounds in *Sārikās* (the bird *Turdus Salica*), peacocks, inebriated *Cakoras*, parrots, kingly bees and leopards all round.

3-4. The spots are everywhere charming with the melodious sounds of the *Jīvaṁjīvaka* (Cakora) birds, the sounds of *Hemakas* (?), the cooing notes of inebriated cuckoos and the bleating sounds

1. M. Ali identifies Uttara Kuru with Western Siberian Region including the basins of the river Irtysh, the Op and the Tobol (AGP. p. 85).

of goats. There are the charming sounds of the golden swans, sparrows and other pleasing chirping sounds.

5. The forest regions appear to be singing with the sweet humming sounds of the excessively lazy and intoxicated bees. They are resorted to by Kinnaras in some places.

6. The trees, shaken by the gentle winds, rain flowers there. They shine with their charming tender sprouts.

7. They are equipped with bunches and clusters of flowers and copper-coloured tender sprouts swinging gently due to the mild wind.

8. O excellent Brāhmaṇas, hundreds of shining pebbles and diverse minerals get mixed with the barks of trees and rinds of fruits scattered splendidly.

9-10. There are four divine play-grounds. They are splendid and charming. They are resorted to by Devas, Dānavas, Gandharvas, Yakṣas, Rākṣasas, Nāgas, Siddhas and Apsaras-s. Listen to their names.

11. On the eastern side is the forest named Caitraratha, on the southern (mountain), the forest Nandana, on the western (mountain), the forest Vaibhrāja and on the northern mountain, the forest of Savitṛ (the Sun-god).

12. In these great forests (parks) charming adjuncts are fitted in due order. Here birds chirp melodiously.

13. Extensive holy centres and great sanctifying gardens are the residences of great Nāgas and those are resorted to by noble souls.

14. Sweet and pure waters are auspicious and very pleasing. They are drunk by Siddhas, Devas and Asuras.

15. There are four great lakes shining with lotuses and lilies, with huge leaves, charming, fragrant and full-blown. These are umbrella-like in appearance and size. I shall mention their names.

16. On the east is the lake Aruṇoda;[1] in the south is the

1. The lake Aruṇoda is the Kara Kul which lies on the north-eastern corner (here called 'The East') of the Pamirs (Meru) near the source of Kizil-Su or the Sītā river (AGP. 101). The Mānasa is well-known. Sitoda is Victoria (in Pamirs) and Mahābhadra is Son Kul (AGP. 201).

Mānasa lake; on the west is the Sitoda and on the north, Mahābhadra.

17. The mountains to the east of Aruṇoda are being narrated by me in detail. Please hear.

18-20. On the east of Mandara are the mountains Śītānta,[1] Kumuñja, the excellent mountain Suvīra, Vikaṅka, Maṇiśila, Vṛṣabha the best of mountains, Mahānīla, Rucaka, Sabindu Mandara, Veṇumān, Sumedha, Niṣadha, Deva-Śaila and others. They are the abodes of Siddhas.

21. Understand that these great mountains lie on the south side of the Mānasa lake. Listen to their names as narrated by me.

22-25. The excellent mountains Triśikhara, Śiśira, Kaliṅga, Pataṅga, Rucaka, Sānumān, Tāmrābha, Viśākha, Śvetodara, Samūla, Viṣadhāra, mount Ratnadhāra, Ekaśṛṅga, Mahāmūla, Gajaśaila, Piśācaka, Pañcaśaila, Kailāsa and the excellent mountain Himavat lie on the southern side of Meru of divine splendour. These are excellent mountains of godly nature.

26. O excellent Brāhmaṇas, I shall mention in due order, those excellent great mountains which lie on the western side of lake Sitoda.

27-29. Suvakṣas,[2] Śikhiśaila, Kāla, Vaidūrya, Kapila, Piṅgala, Rudra, Surasa, Mahācala, Kumuda, Madhuman, Añjanīmukuṭa, Kṛṣṇa, Pāṇḍara, Sahasraśikhara, Pāriyātra and Triśṛṅga. These are the leading mountains in the western region.

30. I shall name in due order, as before, the mountains on the north of the glorious lake Mahābhadra.[3]

---

1. The Kashghar range, the last longitudinal range of the Pamir region. It is a climatic barrier separating the cold plateau on its west. Hence its name Śitānta. Kumuñja is an offshoot of the Tien Shan. Mt. Vikaṅka (Kungur), Maṇiśila (Mustagh range)—these mountains are associated in a way to the river Sītā (Kizil-Su).

2. In this list, Triśṛṅga is a cluster of three peaks, viz. Vashan Tagh, Khan Thag and Chimtarga, all within a radius a radius of three miles. Añjani corresponds to the spurs of the Hissar range. (AGP. 93).

3. C of the list of mauntains, north of the lake Mahābhadra (lake Son Kul) the following mountains are identifiable: Vṛṣabha, Śataśṛṅga etc. (Chatkal Range), Nila (Tien-Shan). Nāga (Śaila) is the Farghana

31-32. Śaṅkukūṭa, Mahāśaila, Vṛṣabha, Haṁsa, Nāga, Kapila, Indraśaila, Sānumān, Nīla, Kanakaśṛṅga, Śataśṛṅga, Puṣpaka, Meghaśaila, the excellent mountain Virāja and the leading mount Jārudhi. These are the mountains on the north.

33. Understand the valleys and canyons and lakes in the inter-spaces of these chief mountains.

CHAPTER THIRTYSEVEN

Arrangement of the World (Valleys and Lakes)[1]

Sūta said :

1. The valleys between Śītānta and Kumuñja[2] ranges are noisy with birds and resorted to by innumerable creatures.

2. They are three hundred Yojanas in length and one hundred Yojanas in breadth. There is an excellent lake with sweet and pure water.

3. The lake extends over the full length of the valley which

(i.e. former Kugart) range. Most of the mountains mentioned are thus traceable (vide GAP. p. 79-80). Jārudhi (Mt. Ula Tau) is the last mountain in this series of ranges.

1. This chapter describes three important oases on the margin of the Tarim basin where the rivers Kizil-su (Sitā), Yarkanda and Akṣu enter the sandy belt of the basin. The valley described in vv 1-15 is the Kashgar oasis, the one described in vv 16-22 is the Yarkand oasis and the last 'Palm forest' in vv 23-25 is in and about the Akṣu. The poetic description of these oases associating them with gods, goddesses and sages is no exaggeration as the cities of Kashgar, Yarkand, Akṣu (and Khotan) have been praised by ancient and mediaeval travellers, for their affluence, beauty and administration. Remarks M Ali, "It is no wonder that the Puranics honoured these 'Paradises' (advanced beautiful oases in the midst of deserts) by associating them with goddess Lakṣmī, god Kāśyapa and Lord Indra to keep fresh in their memories the beauties of the land which was under their influence for a long time" (AGP p. 104).

2. The Kashgar oasis located between Mt. Śitānta (Kashghar range) and Kumuñja (an offshoot of Mt. Tien-shan).

is embellished with white lotuses of sweet fragrance and great red lotuses of hundreds and thousands of petals.

4. Great and unapproachable snakes of huge bodies are found there. The auspicious water is used by Devas, Dānavas and Gandharvas.

5. The sacred lake called Śrīsaras is famous here and in heaven. It is filled with clear water. It is a worthy refuge for all embodied beings.

6. In the middle of the vast expanse of lotuses there is a lotus which has a crore petals spread on all sides. It has the lustre of the midday sun.

7. It is always open and full blown. It never withers. It is tremulous and circular. It has many charming filaments. It is resonant with the buzzing sound of inebriated bees.

8. The goddess Lakṣmī herself always abides in that lotus. Undoubtedly, the lotus is the abode of Lakṣmī in an embodied form.

9. On the eastern side of the lake resorted to by Siddhas, there is a charming Bilva forest which is full of flowers, and fruits.

10-12. It is a hundred Yojanas in breadth and three hundred Yojanas in length. It is full of thousands of large trees with big trunks and extensive branches and tops half a Yojan in height. The ground is littered with sweet smelling fruits as sweet as nectar, as huge as war-drums, some golden, some green, some pale, some white in colour, all falling down and shattering themselves.

13. It is known as Śrīvana. It is resorted to by Kinnaras, Yakṣas and Mahānāgas (big serpents).

14. It is resorted to by Siddhas who subsist on Bilva fruits. Various groups of living beings (or goblins—*Bhūtas*) always reside in it.

15. The goddess Lakṣmī herself dwells there perpetually. She is worshipped by (groups of) Siddhas.

16-17. In the midst of the leading mountain Vikaṅka and Maṇiśaila, there is an extensive Campaka forest,[1] one hundred

1. This Campaka forest is located between Vikaṅka (Kungur) and Maṇiśaila. It corresponds to the Yarkand oasis.

Yojanas wide and two hundred Yojanas long. It is resorted to by Siddhas and Cāraṇas surrounded by rich and glorious crop of flowers. It appears to be glowing as if it were on fire.

18. That forest appears to be yellow with trees with huge trunks and branches blooming with flowers and tops spread about half a Krośa upwards.

19-20. The flowers measure two *Hastas* (cubits) in girth and three *Hastas* in length. Their pale yellow filaments contain pollen powder resembling red arsenic. They are always in bloom and sweet smelling. The forest shines with these flowers. It is resonant with the humming of inebriated bees.

21. It is resorted to by Dānavas, Devas, Gandharvas, Yakṣas, Rākṣasas, Kinnaras, Apsaras-s and big serpents.

22-23. Here is also the hermitage of the holy Lord Kaśyapa Prajāpati, where Siddhas and Sādhyas are found in large numbers and is (as if) decorated with the sound of Vedic recitations. In the midst of the mountains Mahānīla and Kumuñja,[1] on the banks of the great river Sukhā, resorted to by Siddhas, there is a charming palm forest fifty Yojanas in length and thirty Yojanas in width, with the top reaching a height of half *Krośa.*

24. The Kumuda and Añjana trees have great roots and are very strong. They cluster together without any interstices between them. They are firm, great and circular in shape. Their smell and juice are sweet. This forest is inhabited by Siddhas.

25. It is the abode of the auspicious (type of elephants called *Bhadra*) Airāvata, the Lord of elephants of the great Indra. It is well known in all the worlds.

26-27. To the north of the mountain Veṇumān and Sumedha[2], there is a big stretch of Dūrvā grass, a thousand Yojanas long and a hundred Yojanas wide, devoid of trees, hedges, creepers, winding plants and all kinds of animals.

---

1. This is the Akṣu oasis located at the foot of the Tien-shan. The ancient city of Akṣu (and Khotan) has been described highly by ancient and mediaeval travellers.

2. Identified with the Taklamakan desert, the core of the Tarim basin—the Dead Heart of Asia (AGP 104).

28-29. Similarly, north of the mountains Niṣadha and Deva, there is a big rocky piece of land, a thousand Yojanas long and a hundred Yojanas wide. The ground is devoid of trees and creepers although it is moistened with ankle deep water.[1]

30. Thus, in due order, O leading Brāhmaṇas, are described the valleys between the mountains. They are to the east of Meru and are of various shapes and sizes.

CHAPTER THIRTYEIGHT

Valleys between Mountains

Sūta said :

1. I shall now describe the valleys of the southern quarter, frequented by the Siddhas. Listen to them in due order.

2-3. In the midst of the leading mountain Śiśira and Pataṅga, there is the charming forest of Udumbara.[2] Its ground is gloriously smooth and polished. The creepers there embrace (twine round) the trees. It shines with huge trees with lofty tops. It is resorted to by the flocks of birds.

4. The glittering forest shines with ripe fruits as big as great pitchers. They are ripe, coral-coloured, charming and full of honey.

5. Siddhas, Yakṣas, Gandharvas, Kinnaras, Serpents and jolly Vidyādharas subsist themselves perpetually on them.

6. There, the rivers contain ample water, clear and sweet. There are lakes all round with tasty pure water.

7. There is a charming hermitage of the holy lord Kardama Prajāpati, where Devas live. All around, it is surrounded

1. M. Ali locates this region to the outer slopes of Mt. Kunlun and the subjacent range, the Altin Tagh. The region is on the southern border of the Tarim basin.

2. Śiśira and Pataṅga—mountains to the south of the Mānasa Lake—CGEIL p. 45.

by forests of variegated colours. It is circular extending to a hundred Yojanas.

8-11. Between the mountains Tâmravarṇa and Pataṅga, there is a highly sacred lake, a hundred Yojanas wide and two hundred Yojanas long. It is beautified with white lotuses as refulgent as the midday sun and full-blown red big lotuses with thousand petals. The water therein shines with sweet-smelling, blooming, red and blue lilies with the honey bees resting within. The lake is resorted to by Devas, Dānavas and great serpents. It is decorated with clusters of blue lotus flowers.

12. There is a country within, a hundred Yojanas long and thirty Yojanas wide. It is embellished with red minerals.

13-15. There is a flourishing city with beautiful ramparts and high archways. It is teeming with men and women. The houses have turrets with stable sloping roofs studded diversely and separately with jewels. The grounds are paved with gem-slabs of various colours. There are bed-coverings smooth and variegated. There are rows of mansions excellent and lofty. Such a beautiful city of Vidyādharas splendidly shines there.

16. The famous lord of Vidyādharas, Puloman, is there. His dress and features are variegated. He wears garlands. His lustre resembles the splendour of Lord Indra.

17. He is the emperor of thousands of resplendent Vidyādharas having the splendour comparable to the sun, wearing variegated dresses.

18-19. Between the great mountain Viśākha and Pataṅga, on the eastern bank of the lake Tâmravarṇa is the famous mango grove. It is hit by the five arrows of the Cupid. The trees have splendid boughs. They shine in various colours, bearing fruits in all seasons. The grove is flourishing and prosperous.

20. The fruits are golden in colour and very tasty. They are sweet-smelling and of the size of big pitchers. They spread their branches on all sides thickly.

21. Gandharvas, Kinnaras, Yakṣas, Nāgas and Vidyādharas drink the sweet ambrosial juice of the mango fruits.

22. The exhilarations of those who drink the mango juice merrily and are thus delighted and nourished, are heard in the great forest.

23-24. O Brāhmaṇas, between the lordly mountain Sṛmūla and Vasudhāra, there is a Bilvasthalī, fifty Yojanas long and thirty Yojanas wide. It is a level land sweet-smelling and flourishing. It is lovely due to the presence of birds. It is pure. The trees bear fruits which are hanging very low.

25. The soil on the ground is wet and damp with the shattering and shattered sweet Bilva fruits resembling coral (in colour) and comparatively large.

26. Yakṣas, Gandharvas, Kinnaras, Siddhas and Nāgas mostly eating only the Bilva fruits, live in that natural region.

27-28. In between Vasudhāra and Ratnadhāra is the beautiful fragrant forest of *Kiṁśuka* (*Butea frondosa*) a hundred Yojanas long and thirty Yojanas wide, where the trees always bloom. With the rich growth of flowers, it seems to be blazing all round.

29. By its divine fragrance the whole region is sweetened upto a hundred Yojanas in the forests all round.

30. That beautiful forest of *Kiṁśuka* trees is resorted to by Siddhas, Cāraṇas and Apsaras-s. It is bedecked with various water-sheds.

31. There is a great brilliant abode of lord Āditya there. Every month Prajāpati Sūrya descends there.

32. There, multitudes of Siddhas bow to the thousand-rayed excellent lord Sun who is honoured by all the worlds and who is the creator of Time.

33-34. In between the mountains of Pañcakūṭa and Kailāsa is an impassable land, a hundred Yojanas long and thirty-six Yojanas wide. Small animals cannot live there. It is as white as a swan all round. No animal can cross it. It is awe-inspiring.

35. Thus the valleys in the southern tract have been enumerated in due order, wholly. They are resorted to by the groups of Siddhas.

36. O excellent Brāhmaṇas ! Now listen to the description of the valleys which are located on the west.

37. In the central part between Suvakṣa and Śikhiśaila mountains, is a rocky and stony stretch of land extending to one hundred Yojanas on all sides.[1]

---

1. Verses 37-44: This is the Kulyab region in Tajikistan (USSR). Near

38. It is alway hot. People are afraid of touching that surface. It produces horripilation. It is inaccessible to creatures. It is terrible even to gods.

39. In the central part of that rocky surface, the zone of which is thirty Yojanas, there is a terrible abode of the Fire-god where thousands of flames are thrown out.

40. There the Fire-god is always burning without any fuel. He blazes there perpetually.

41. That *Saṁvartaka* (the fire that ultimately destroys the world) blazes there eternally. As tutelary deity it receives its share in the sacrifice.

42. Between the two great mountains there is an auspicious pond of Devas (Deva-vāpī[1]?). There is a tract (of land) of ten Yojanas known as Mātuliṅga.

43. That great region is wholly splendid with ripe fruits of golden lustre and juice sweet as honey.

44. The holy hermitage of Bṛhaspati is there. It is resorted to by saints. It gives pleasure and fulfils desires.

45. There is the valley between two great mountains Kumuda and Añjana. It is called Kesara[2] and it covers several Yojanas and is abounding in Bakula trees.

46-47. The forest shines with spotted and brindled flowers blooming in every season. These flowers are two *Hastas* (cubits) in length and three *Hastas* in girth. They have the colours of

---

Kulyab two mountains Devāpi (Hoja Sartis) and Caya are the biggest salt cupolas and as such have sub-terranean gas. "Scientific investigation has shown that the Kulyab district is one of the biggest gas bearing districts in Tajikistan", States P. Luknitsky in *Soviet Tajikistan*, p. 209. The Āśrama of Bṛhaspati is probably modern Kulyab—AGP 93-95.

The subterranean gas explains the phenomenon in vv. 38-41 attributed to Saṁvartaka fire by the Purāṇa writer.

1. The text *Devā vāpi* is obscure. *Deva-vāpī* which also suits the metre and meaning, is a conjectural emendation.

2. Verses 45-48: This valley between mountains Kumuda and Añjana (i.e. modern Rangan Tau Range and the southern longitudinal spurs of the Hissar Range) was famous for the production of saffron (*Kesara*). In the Middle Ages the two areas—Shuman (mod. Dushambe) and Veshagird (mod. Foyzabad on the Illaq) in this valley were famous for production of saffron. M. Ali suggests that the Viṣṇu temple (in v. 48) is the Anzob peak of the Hissar Range—AGP 95.

lunar rays. They are full-blown. They are resonant with the humming sounds of inebriated bees. They are charming and fragrant with honey, ghee and pollen-powder.

48. The great resplendent temple of Viṣṇu, the leader of the Devas, is there. It is well-known in three worlds and respected by all.

49-50. In the middle of the excellent mountains Kṛṣṇa and Pāṇḍura, there is a single tract of smooth rocky land ninety Yojanas in length and thirty Yojanas in width.[1] It is devoid of trees and creepers. There walking is easy and pleasurable because the surface is nowhere uneven.

51. In the middle there is a charming grove of land-lotuses. It is decorated with full-blown lotuses of thousand petals of the size of huge umbrellas.

52-54. That extensive grove of land-lotuses is frequented by Yakṣas, Gandharvas, and resorted to by Siddhas and Cāraṇas. Hovering round these flowers, the inebriated honey bees hum and buzz. Kinnaras with voices of sweet and choked throats sing the glory of the flowers. There are white lotuses of charming appearance, fragrant hundred-petalled lilies and full blown flowers with blue petals.

55-57. In the midst of that lotus-grove, there is a Nyagrodha tree extending over an area of five Yojanas. It has stout trunk and various steps of ascent (several branches). There, the glorious moon-lustred lord Viṣṇu is worshipped by Yakṣas, Gandharvas and Vidyādharas. The lord has a thousand faces. He is the destroyer of the enemies of Devas. He wears blue clothes. His face resembles the full moon. He wears the garland of lotuses. He is blessed and ever victorious.

58. In that abode the immortal Viṣṇu himself is worshipped by Siddhas and Cāraṇas with different lotuses as presents.

59. That place is known in all the world as the home of Ananta (*Ananta-Sadas*). It is brightened with garlands of lotuses and other flowers suspended there-in.

60-61. In the central part of Sahasra-śikhara and Kumuda[2]

1. Verses 49-59 describes the basin of the lower Surkhan. The *Ananta-Sadas* (the home of Ananta) in v.59 is somewhere near modern Termez (AGP 95).

2. This peak is the snowcovered peak Bazzengi (16456 feet) at the meeting place of the Hissar and Zarafshan ranges (Kumuda and Sahasra-Śikhara)—AGP 96.

there is a peak, an arrow's range high, fifty Yojanas long and thirty Yojanas wide. It is resorted to by various birds. It abounds in tall trees all round, dripping with honey and bearing fruits as big as an elephant. They are sweet-smelling and most delicious.

62. The highly meritorious and well-known hermitage of Śukra of holy rites is there. It is resplendent and resorted to by multitudes of sages and gods.

63. Between mountains Śaṅkukūṭa and Vṛṣabha, there is a beautiful region of Parūṣaka (*Grewia Asiatica* ?) which extends to many Yojanas.

64. The ground is moistened with the fruits of Parūṣas fallen from their stalks. They are as big as Bilvas. They are auspicious, sweet and fragrant.

65. Kinnaras, serpents and Saints live in that region. They are elated by the juice of Parūṣaka. The Cāraṇas thereof are highly honoured.

66-67. In the middle of Kapiñjala and Nāga mountains, there is a beautiful region two hundred Yojanas long and a hundred Yojanas wide. It is decorated with various forests and endowed with various flowers and fruits. It is resorted to by Kinnaras and Uragas (serpents).

68-70. There are charming groves of grapes, Nāga-leaves, Kharjūras, blue Aśoka groves, tasty pomegranates, Akṣoṭaka (walnuts), Atasī (linseed), Tilaka, gingelly seeds and plantain groves. There are small plots of tasty Badarī fruits. They are auspicious regions brightened by rivers full of tasty, cool water.

71. The ground between the mountains Puṣpaka and Mahāmegha is a hundred Yojanas long and sixty Yojanas wide.

72. That is a level land like the palm of the hand, firm, thick and white. It is devoid of trees, hedges, creepers and grass.

73. It is devoid of animals too. It is a forest region, terrible and horripilating.

74. There are great lakes, great trees, great forests all round.

75. This region of lakes and forests is the abode of Prajāpati. There is no end to the number of minor lakes there.

76. The lakes, chasms, forests and regions are of various sizes—ten, twelve, seven, eight, twenty or thirty Yojanas.

77. Some of them are dark and terrible. The caves of the mountains are never touched by the rays of the sun. They are always cold and inaccessible.

78. O Excellent Brāhmaṇas, there are lakes with hot water within the mountains, hundreds and thousands in number.

CHAPTER THIRTYNINE

Abodes of Devas

Sūta said :

1. Henceforth I shall tell you about the excellent abodes of Devas situated on different mountains.

2-10. The forest of sport of Mahendra is on the great mountain Śītānta. The forest is endowed with all desirable qualities. The mountain contains many belly-like caves, which are the abodes (of Devas). The mountain is very extensive with hundreds of variegated minerals and jewel mines. It is the abode of animals of good qualities. Its ridges and slopes are laden with flowers where the bees hum and buzz. It is decorated with the assemblage of gold pieces veriegated with valuable jewels. The slopes hum with the buzzing sound of bees. There are corals mixed with gold. The ridges are covered with flowers where the bees hum. There are hanging creepers of various colours. Hundreds of minerals are spread over the peaks and precipices. Gems of different colours along with flowers decorate the mountain. There are fountains and springs of pure and tasty water. It is embellished with many hedges abounding in flowers. It is beautified with streamlets wherein flowery rafts float. The inner crevasses of the mountain are frequented by Kinnaras. There are many caves and cavities frequented by Yakṣas and Gandharvas. Some of them are comfortably resorted to and some are dense and impassable. Many animals frequent it. Good potable water is abundant. The mountain is embellished with trees bearing various fruits and flowers.

11. The great Pārijāta forest of the king of Devas is also there. It is well—known in the three worlds and is praised in song as can be ascertained from reports.

12. By means of the excessively fragrant and charming flowers blazing like the midday sun, the excellent mountain is illuminated as it were all around.

13. The wind blowing from that forest wafts the fragrance of Pārijāta flowers full hundred Yojanas.

14-15. The tanks therein are adorned with blue lotuses resembling *lapis lazuli* with golden and diamond-like filaments, possessed of fragrance and resonant with the buzzing of bees. There are full-blown, hundred-petalled, charming, large-leafed red lotuses also.

16. Thousands of fishes shine within the waters with unwinking eyes and decorated with golden gems.

17. With tortoises richly embellished with gold and occupying many positions, the water gets splashed all round and shines well.

18-19. That beautiful forest of the intelligent thousand-eyed Indra is beautified by birds of different colours and of gem-like hairs emerging out of their bodies. The birds have gemset beaks decorated with flowers of good colours; They are always elated while they fly all around chirping sweet attractive sounds.

20. Hence that forest of sport has become a resort of perpetual pleasure, by the sounds of the elated bees and the chirpings of the birds.

21-22. The forest is full of monkeys of variegated colour and gem-like hairs. It abounds in the animals of various types, colours and shapes. The mountains have glorious golden sides set with gems and pearls. Their peaks too are set in gems.

23. The tender creepers and the Pārijāta trees, when gently shaken by the mild wind, make a shower of flowers.

24. O Brāhmaṇas, when gemset couches and seats are laid all round the playing grounds, the forest looks very splendid. There the sun is neither hot nor cold. He is of equable nature. The climate is always temperate.

25. The wind blowing in the months of spring is rendered fragrant by various flowers and produces excessive elation. It

dispels fatigue caused by exertion and gives pleasure by its mere contact.

26-27. In that splendid forest of Indra Devas, Dānavas, Pannagas, Yakṣas, Rākṣasas, Guhyakas, Gandharvas of unmeasured splendour, Vidyādharas, Siddhas and Kinnaras are joyous. Groups of Apsaras-s too are engaged in sports.

28. On the eastern side of that royal mountain is the lordly mountain of Kumuñja with many streams and caves.

29. On the summit abounding in variegated minerals, there are eight big cities of noble-souled Dānavas.

30. The abode of Rākṣasas crowded with men and women is situated on the mountain Vajraka with many peaks and caves.

31. These terrible Rākṣasas known as Nīlakas can assume forms as they please. They are endowed with great strength and exploit. They live there for ever.

32. On the great mountain Mahānīla, there are fifteen famous cities of the horse-faced Kinnaras.

33. Devasena, strong as Indra, is a powerful ruler. There the fifteen Kinnara kings are very haughty.

34. The great mountain is decorated with the enclosed settlements which have golden flanks mostly and which possess people of different races.

35. Hundreds of great Uragas (serpents) live there under the control of Garuḍas. They are terrible, fiery and inaccessible and of venomous sight.

36. In the great mountain Sunāga, there are thousands of abodes of Daityas. These consist of mansions and palaces with huge ramparts and archways.

37. On the great mountain Veṇumanta, there are three cities of Vidyādharas, fifty Yojanas long and thirty Yojanas in breadth.

38. The rulers of the Vidyādharas, there, as valorous as Indra, are Ulūka, Romaśa and Mahānetra.

39-40. On the top of the great peak Vaikaṅka with caves and rivulets within, there lives Sugrīva, the fierce and powerful, the unthwartable enemy of serpents and the son of Garuḍa with the great speed of the wind. This peak is of variegated colours due to jewels and minerals.

41. The whole of that mountain is teeming with birds which destroy serpents. They are of huge size, valorous and powerful.

42. Śiva, the Lord of Yogins and Bhūtas, whose emblem is the Bull, lives on the mountain Karañja.

43. All round the ridges and slopes are scattered the Bhūtas, the unassailable Pramathas, with diverse dresses and features.

44. They say that the eight illustrious abodes of the eight Vasus, the noble souls of unmeasured power, are situated on the mountain Vasudhāra.

45. The seven holy hermitages of the seven sages and the abodes of the Siddhas are on the mountain Ratnadhātu.

46. The abode of the four-faced lord, the great Prajāpati (Brahmā) is on the excellent mountain Hemaśṛṅga. It is revered by all living beings.

47. On mountain Gajaśaila, holy lord Rudras rejoice for ever along with (the groups of) Bhūtas. They are respected by all living beings.

48-49. The constructed abodes of Ādityas, Vasus and Rudras of unlimited splendour are on the great mountain Sumegha which resembles a cloud and is richly endowed with minerals. The mountain is beautified with many caves, bunds and hedges. The charming mansions of the Aśvin gods too are there.

50. The abodes of Devas have been established by Siddhas on the excellent mountain. Yakṣas, Gandharvas and Kinnaras, are engaged in worship there for ever.

51. On the excellent mountain Hemakakṣa is the prosperous Gandharva city Aśītyā as refulgent as the celestial Amarāvatī. It has great ramparts and archways.

52. The Siddhas are known as *Apattanas* (city-less). Gandharvas are of fighting nature. Their ruler is Kapiñjala, the king of kings.

53. The abodes of Rākṣasas are on Anala. Dānavas live on Pañcakūṭa. They are inimical to Devas. They are powerful and valorous.

54. On the Śataśṛṅga mountain are the hundred cities of Yakṣas of unmeasured valour. The excellent city of Takṣaka, son of Kadru, is on the Tāmrābha mountain.

55. The great mansion of Guha, fond of residing in a cave

is on the excellent mountain Viśākha, auspicious with various bunds and caves.

56. There is the city of noble Sunābha, son of Garuḍa on the mountain Śvetodara, embellished with great mansions.

57. There is a mansion embellished with palaces on the excellent mountain Piśācaka. That is the great abode of Kubera, frequented by Yakṣas and Gandharvas.

58. Lord Hari is revered by all living beings on Harikūṭa. By the influence of the lord, this mountain shines with great refulgence.

59. The abodes of Kinnaras are on the mountain Kumuda. The Nāgas (and their tribe) live on the Añjana mountain. The cities of Gandharvas, with many mansions, are on the mountain Kṛṣṇa.

60. On the beautifully peaked Pāṇḍura, with ramparts and archways the city of Vidyādharas is situated. It has a series of big houses.

61. On the mountain Sahasra-śikhara, there are thousand cities of Daityas of fierce activities, wearing gold necklaces.

62. There are residences of Pannagas (serpents) on the Mukuṭa mountain and multitudes of sages always live happily on Puṣpaka mount.

63. On the excellent mountain Supakṣa, there are four mansions of Vaivasvata (Yama), Soma, Vāyu and the king of serpents.

64. In their respective places, their respective gods are highly worshipped by Gandharvas, Kinnaras, Yakṣas, Nāgas (serpents) and excellent Vidyādharas and Siddhas.

CHAPTER FORTY

Boundary and the Limits of Mount Devakūṭa

Sūta said :

1-2. Know that the place of birth of the intelligent Suparṇa (Garuḍa), son of Vinatā, extends to a hundred Yojanas all round. It is embellished with a great mansion on the extensive peak of the excellent boundary-mountain Devakūṭa.

3. (It is resorted to) by many multitudes of swift, valorous big birds. They are of perfect vigour, enemies and suppressors of serpents.

4. There is the first mansion of the noble king of birds who has the velocity of the wind and residence in Śālmalī Dvīpa.

5-7. On the seven southern peaks of its charming hill, there are seven cities of Gandharvas where men and women live. They are forty Yojanas in length and thirty Yojanas in breadth. The golden ramparts and archways rise up. They are built by Devas and beautified with a series of great mansions. They resemble clouds at dusk. The peaks are of variegated shapes and colours. They are prosperous.

8. There are very powerful and valorous Āgneya Gandharvas. They are the brilliant followers of Kubera. These are their excellent mansions.

9-10. On the northern peaks of the lofty mountain Bhuvana, there is a city teeming with serpents. It is full of mansions and palaces and is beautified with gardens and parks. It has great ramparts and archways. The interior of the parks is rendered pleasant by the sound of hundreds of musical instruments.

11. Know that there is on the mount Devakūṭa the city of Saiṁhikeyas, the enemies of gods. It is unassailable by enemies. Its outer wall measures thirty Yojanas. It is frequented by Siddhas and divine sages.

12-15. O Brāhmaṇa, there on the charming ridge of Devakūṭa is founded the invincible and inaccessible city of the demons known as Kālakeyas. It looks like a cluster of clouds. It is well-known as Sunāsa. It is on the next boundary mountain. It has a series of great mansions of different colours. It is decorated in various ways with gold and precious stones. Its streets are broad. It is full of joy, auspiciousness and teeming with men and women. Its ramparts and archways are very high. The city is hundred Yojanas in length and sixty Yojanas in breadth.

16-17. On the southern peak of the same mountain, there is the jolly big city of Autkaca Rākṣasas. They are joyful, well-nourished, proud and can assume any form at will. The city is sixty-two Yojanas in length and twenty Yojanas in breadth. Its ramparts and archways are made of gold.

18-20. On the central peak of the mountain Devakūṭa, there is the famous resplendent temple (abode) of the noble-souled, three-eyed god Mahādeva, known in all the worlds as Bhūtavaṭa. It is the resort of various groups of *Bhūtas* (goblins). It is built of smooth and splendid pieces of gold and precious stones. There are trees of hundreds and thousands of branches with many off-shoots and overgrowths. The leaves are very smooth and splendid. There is a perpetual thick shade. The trees have their roots deep into the earth bearing vast trunks. The place is a circular zone extending to ten Yojanas.

21-24. The city is full of Bhūtas (people) fierce, valorous, and with terrible faces like those of boars, elephants, lions, bears, mules, vultures, owls, rams, goats and camels. They are hideous and stout with long hairs, both on the heads and bodies. They have various complexions and features. They congregate into groups and worship the lord of Bhūtas (Śiva) by playing drums, *Jharjhara*, *Bherī*, *Paṭaha*, *Ḍiṇḍima*, *Gomukha* and conches.

25-26. With the jingling sounds of instruments and high pitched vocal music, the leading Gaṇas are hectically engaged in worship. The Pramathas, the enemy of the Tripuras too, are engaged in sports. Here lord Śiva, the benefactor of the worlds is worshipped by Siddhas, Devas, sages, Gandharvas, Yakṣas and Nāgas.

CHAPTER FORTYONE

Description of Kailāsa[1]

Sūta said :

1. Kailāsa is the abode of the devotees of the lord who are of meritorious souls. It has isolated, charming summits. It is full of vegetation. It has the lustre of the conch.

---

1. This is a poetic description of the peak near Lake Mānasa and not of the trans-Himalayan Kailasa range. The climatic conditions of those days seem favourable for vegetation and human habitation.

2-4. In the central ridge, as beautiful as Kunda flower, there is the invincible city of the noble-souled Kubera,[1] the presiding deity of wealth. It is a hundred Yojanas in length and fifty Yojanas in breadth. It is beautified with a series of big mansions, set in diverse ways in gold and silver. It is very extensive, affluent and joyful.

5. There is a charming assembly-hall in the centre, embellished with variegated pieces of gold. It is known as *Vipulā* because it abounds in archways and pillars.

6. The aerial chariot Puṣpaka, decorated in jewels, is there. It is very charming and endowed with all desirable qualities.

7. As quick as the mind, it can reach any desired goal. It is decorated with clusters of gold pieces. It is the vehicle of Kubera, king of Yakṣas.

8. Lord Kubera the companion of Mahādeva lives there. He is the king of Yakṣas revered and honoured by all living beings.

9. Kubera, excellent among Devas, lives there along with Apsaras-s, Yakṣas, Gandharvas, Siddhas and Cāraṇas.

10-11. Here the Lord of Wealth has eight treasures:[2] Padma, Mahāpadma, Makara, Kacchapa, Kumuda, Śaṅkha, Nīla and Nandana. These being inexhaustible, divine great Treasures hoarding jewels are kept in the assembly-hall.

12. Similarly this mount Kailāsa is the abode of Indra, Agni, Yama, Devas and Apsaras-s where Kubera, the Lord of Yakṣas, is the ruler.

13. The attendants of Devas first pay their respects to the king of Yakṣas and then proceed to their respective lords.

14-17. The great and charming water-reservoir 'Mandākinī'[3] is there. It has abundance of water. Its embankment has steps plated with gold and studded with gems. There are

---

1. This city is Alakā immortalised by Kālidāsa in the *Meghadūta*. The city was either on or near the Kailāsa peak.

2. This list agrees with that in Mt. Purāṇa (SKD. 982 b). But normally nine treasures of Kubera are enumerated (MW 548 C). *Kharva* from the list in MW is not mentioned here. The geographer M. Ali regards these 'Treasure-houses' as the minor peaks of Kailāsa (AGP 57).

3. Verses 14-18 show the author's familarity with this topography.

golden lotuses with sweet smell, touch etc., great blue lotuses with leaves and petals as blue as *lapis lazuli*. The reservoir is beautified with lilies and lotuses of great fragrance. It appears splendid with the womenfolk of Yakṣas, Gandharvas and Apsaras-s. The waters of the reservoir are used by Devas, Dānavas, Gandharvas, Yakṣas, Rākṣasas and Pannagas (serpents).

18. Then, there are excellent rivers, the Nandā and the Alakanandā. These rivers are endowed with excellent qualities and are used by celestial sages.

19-20. On the eastern peak of this lordly mountain,[1] there are ten famous cities of Gandharvas endowed with prosperity. They are one thousand Yojanas in length and thirty Yojanas in breadth. They are decorated with a series of great mansions.

21. There are ten Gandharva kings as valorous as the blazing fires. They are named as Subāhu, Harikeśa, Citrasena, Jara and others.

22-23. On the western peak of Kailāsa, as lustrous as the Kunda flower, is the abode of each of the Yakṣas, eight Yojanas in length and forty in breadth. The place is resorted to by Siddhas and celestial sages. It abounds in various minerals and has long rows of lofty mansions.

24. There are thirty rich and flourishing abodes of Mahāyakṣas that are joyous and prosperous all round.

25. Thirty prosperous kings of Yakṣas (e.g.) Mahāmāli, Sunetra, Maṇivara and others rule over there.

26. Thus have I mentioned Yakṣas as lustrous as Vāyu and Agni, whose ruler is the prosperous lord Kubera.

27-28. South of Himavat, stretching from the eastern to the western sea,[2] hundreds of cities of Kinnaras are established on the ridges abounding in hedges, bushes, fountains, caves and precipices.

---

1. Verses 19-25: It appears that in those days people were fond of hills. The eastern region of Kailāsa still has a lot of sunshine, more fertile soil than its western region (AGP 57-58).

2. Verse 27 gives a poetic yet accurate information about the Himālayan region, viz. location of the Himālaya to the south of the Kailāsa range, its extension from sea to sea, having a large number of peaks, tracts and lower cultural level of inhabitants, though a great number of hermitages were there (AGP 58).

29. In the bosom of the lord of mountains with many peaks, men and women rejoice. The place is full of delighted and well-nourished people.

30. There are a hundred kings for these bright and powerful people. They are Druma, Sugrīvasainya, Bhagadatta and others.

31. It was here that the marriage of Rudra with the great goddess Umā took place. It was here that she, the great goddess, performed penance.

32. It was here that Rudra sported as a hunter. It was from here that the couple surveyed Jambūdvīpa.

33. The play-grounds of Rudra abounding in flowers of manifold colours and fruits of various shapes and sizes are here. These, with the different groups of living beings, are delightful.

34. It is the place where the beautiful Kinnara maidens, the slender-bellied, bright-eyed, joyous dwellers of the mountain caves sport about.

35. Similarly it is here that the long-eyed Yakṣas, groups of Apsaras-s and Gandharvas of charming physique move about with pleasure.

36. The famous garden of Umā is also there. It was here that Śiva assumed the form of half-man and half-woman.

37. Śaravaṇa where the six-faced Kārttikeya was born and whence enthusiastically he started to the Krauñca forest, is also there.

38. Here itself is the chariot of Kārttikeya with lions yoked, which has a flagstaff and banners, and which sparkles with clusters of tinkling bells.

39. It was here on the ridge of the Krauñca mountain where there are flower bushes of various colours, that Skanda, the destroyer of foes of Devas discharged his spear (*śakti*).

40. It was here that Guha, brilliant as the twelve suns, the enemy of Daityas, was crowned as the commander-in-chief of the army by the excellent Devas including Indra and Viṣṇu.

41. O Brāhmaṇas, these and other spots and abodes associated with Kumāra and abounding in living beings are also there.

42. Similarly, on the auspicious summit of Himavat abounding in living beings, there is a play-ground called Pāṇḍuśilā, of the destroyer of Krauñca.

43. On its beautiful eastern ridge is the residence of Siddhas. It is known as Kalāpagrāma.

44-47. There are hundreds and thousands of hermitages of the sages Mṛkaṇḍa, Vasiṣṭha, Bharata, Nala, Viśvāmitra, Uddālaka and others, of severe penance and purified souls, on the mountain Himavat. This excellent mountain, the abode of many Siddhas, is decorated by their temples and holy spots. Yakṣas and Gandharvas move about here and there. Several groups of Mlecchas too live there. It abounds in mines of jewels. It is resorted to by different animals. It is the source of origin of thousands of rivers.

48. O Brāhmaṇas, now listen to the special features of the western lofty mountain Niṣadha[1], as it is being narrated wholly and precisely.

49. On the extensive central summit embellished with gold and minerals is the brightly illuminated abode of Viṣṇu. It is resorted to by multitudes of Siddhas, sages, Gandharvas and crowds of Yakṣas, Apsaras-s.

50. There the great lord, the yellow-robed Viṣṇu, the bestower of boons, the eternal maker of the worlds, is served by Siddhas.

51-54. On its interior peak embellished with different minerals, on the ridge of the Niṣadha mountain where the rocky surface is smooth and charming, is the delightful city of Rākṣasas (called) Ulaṅghis. The city extends to thirty Yojanas. There are series of gardens there. The city cannot be thwarted by enemies. It is full of (Rākṣasas) as cruel as poisonous snakes.

The palaces have golden turrets and pinnacles. The archways are made of molten gold. There are hundreds of lofty buildings with sloping roofs, in the main streets and thorough-fares.

The mansions and palaces (in it) are incomparable. They are embellished with pieces of molten gold. It is very extensive and always joyous.

---

1. The southern ridge of the Hindukush which merged into Northern Karakorum and the Kunlun (AGP 58-59).

55. South of the same mountain with many abodes of Daityas, there is an inaccessible city within the (belly of) the mountain, with only a cave as the main entrance.

56. Similarly, on the western peak, on a lofty rock of Pārijāta, there are flourishing cities of Devas, Dānavas and Nāgas.

57. On the great ridge of the mountain, there is the rock called Somaśilā where the moon descends on Parvan days.

58. The sages, Kinnaras and Gandharvas worship the glorious lord of stars, dispeller of darkness, the praiseworthy (uncensured) lord, the moon.

59. North of the same mountain, there is the spot known as Brahmapārśva. It is the abode of Brahmā, lord of Devas, It is well-known in heaven.

60. Siddhas, Yakṣas, Gandharvas and Dānavas worship the self-born lord with sacrifices, worships and prostrations.

61. Similarly, the abode of the Fire-god is famous in all the worlds. There the embodied god Fire is worshipped by Siddhas and Cāraṇas.

62. Similarly, on the excellent mountain Triśṛṅga, to the north, is the city Hemacarita, well-known in the three worlds. This mountain is frequented by sages and Siddhas. It is the abode of different living beings.

63. There are three abodes of the three chief deities. O Brāhmaṇas, the abode of Nārāyaṇa is on the eastern peak, that of Brahmā is in the middle and that of Śiva is on the west.

64. These mighty lords of Devas, worthy of worship, are revered by Daityas, Dānavas, Gandharvas, Yakṣas, Rākṣasas and Nāgas.

65. Here and there, on the excellent mountain Triśṛṅga and adjoining places, are the beautiful cities of Yakṣas, Gandharvas and Nāgas.

66-67. Similarly, to the north, on the divine mountain Jārudhi, which abounds in peaks and which is resorted to by Siddhas and sages, are the cities of Yakṣas, Kinnaras, Gandharvas, Nāgas, Rākṣasas and Daityas in hundreds and thouands.

68-72. On the central summit of that mountain resorted to by Siddhas, Devas and sages, embellished by jewels and minerals, there is a circular zone of thirty Yojanas. It looks splendid with expanses of full-blown lotuses, lilies, *Saugandhika* grass (or white water-lilies), night lotuses (opening at moon-rise). It is resounded with the chirping of and is beautified by birds. It is the haunt of various animals, beasts and birds. It is crowded with swans and ducks and is resorted to by inebriated bees. The place abounds in sweet, pure water used by Siddhas. There is a sacred lake called Ānaṇḍajala.

73. The fierce lord of Nāgas, invincible Caṇḍa, with a hundred heads, the blessed one marked by Viṣṇu's discus, resides here. There eight wonderful mountains are known as Devaparvatas.

74-77. Thus, the earth is full of cities, abodes, excellent and sacred lakes of holy waters, silver and jewel mountains having the lustre of gems, mountains of yellow orpiment, vermilion and gold, vast expanses of pure red arsenic shining in their red hue, and mountains of precious stones with minerals of variegated colours. There are very extensive mountains with the rivers, caves, ridges and precipices of variegated colours and many shapes.

78-79. These mountains are the abodes of Daityas, Rākṣasas, saints, Kinnaras, serpents, Gandharvas of wonderful features, Siddhas, Cāraṇas. These are resorted to by Gandharvas and divine damsels. They are extensive and are inhabited by meritorious persons. They appear like filaments of lotuses.

80. The circle of mountains of the Meru (region) is known as the Siddhaloka. It has various resorts for shelter. Meritorious persons frequent the place.

81. The images of Siddhas of no fierce activities, stand in the middle. That place (also) is known as heaven. Its order is thus stated.

82-83. This earth is declared as having four Dvīpas. It is inhabited by people of all castes, statures, complexions and powers. They partake of different kinds of food and beverages. They wear different sorts of dress and ornaments. They have different emotional reactions.

84-85. The four big continents inhabited by many castes are known as Bhadra, Bhārata, Western Ketumāla (i.e. Ketumāla to the western side) and the Northern Kuru. They are the abodes of meritorious people. O Brāhmaṇa, this earth, in the shape of a lotus, and divided into four continents and many sub-continents, has thus been described by me.

86. This wide earth along with the interspersed continents, mountains, forests, and groves is called *Padmā* (lotus-shaped). It is very extensive.

87-89. The worlds of Brahmā, Devas, Asuras and human beings are three. That which is heated by the moon and the sun is known as the world (the earth). It has the qualities of smell, colour, taste, sound and touch. This lotus-shaped universe is known as Lotus in the Vedas. This is the accepted order in the Purāṇas as well.

CHAPTER FORTYTWO

The Divine Rivers

Sūta said :

1. The divine rivers of holy waters have sprung from excellent lakes.[1] These have great volume of waters. Listen to them in due order.

2. What is called the moon (Soma) of the ocean of the firmament, the support of all living beings, is the reservoir of nectar for Devas.

---

1. Purāṇa writers believed in the following notions about river systems in general :

1. A river normally originates from a lake either overground or underground and is associated with a mountain.
2. A river can penetrate through sub-terranean channels, mountain ranges and can flow in more than one current if intervened by ridges.
3. A river along with tributaries is treated as one single river.

3. The celestial river of sacred waters springs from it (the reservoir or nectar). That river of clear transparent water flows through the sky through the seventh path of the wind.[1]

4. It turns back on reaching the mass of brilliance. It is resorted to by luminary bodies. It extends to the full length of the sky, with thousands of crores of stars.

5. While the lordly elephant of lord Indra moves about in the firmament, he sportively agitates the water within it.

6. When Siddhas pass through the sky in their aerial chariots (great many in number), they have a sip in the sacred and healing water of this river.

7. Just as the sun revolves everyday, so this river urged by the wind, flows through various places.

8. It extends to eighty-four Yojanas allround. It circumambulates the Meru with great velocity.

9. The water currents are split by the fiery wind and the river falls upon the four northern peaks of Meru.

10. After emerging on the excellent sides of ridges of these peaks of Meru, the waters, divided into four, flow thus.

11. After flowing through the supportless firmament for sixty thousand Yojanas, the glorious river falls through the four sides of Meru.[2]

12. This splendid, sacred river flowing through the four bases (feet) of Meru, falls again on the eastern Mandara.

13-15. The eastern branch of the river flows over the Mandara which is the abode of Devas and all the groups of Siddhas, which has many rivulets, caves, golden and variegated lands, ridges. It flows with the crystal clear water that subdues the arrogance and valour of the side-bunds. It flows round the beautiful Caitraratha overflowing the path. This river of the firmament then enters the excellent lake Aruṇoda (Kara Kul, NE Pamirs).

---

1. Verses 3-11: This poetic synthesis of the heavenly Gaṅgā (Galaxy) as the source of glaciers and rivers of Asia is repeated in other Purāṇas like Bd. P., Mt. P.

2. Though the river system described in the remaining part of the chapter is the traditional knowledge of the Purāṇa writers, it was to a great extent correct and reliable (vide AGP. Ch. iv 'The river system of Purāṇas').

16. After coming out from Aruṇoda, the gently-flowing river falls on the mountain Śītānta (Kashghar range) abounding in beautiful fountains. This mountain is the abode of (multitudes) of Siddhas.

17. The sacred and excellent river is called Sītā. Being held within the various groves and bushes, it is further divided into several branches.

18. From the peek of Śītānta,[1] it falls on the mountain Sukuñja.[1] From that mountain, it falls on the the mountain Sumañjasa.[1]

19. Therefrom it falls on the mount Mālyavān[2] and comes to Vaikaṅka and from Vaikaṅka it passes to Maṇiparvata and then falls on the mountain Ṛṣabha full of caves.

20. Piercing through thousands of mountains thus, the river falls on the mountain Jaṭhara resorted to by Siddhas.

21. From there the river again falls on the Devakūṭa mountain, the lower part of which extends upto the sea. In this way, the river gradually reaches the plains.

22-24. Thus flooding through thousands of valleys, hundreds of mountains, strange forests, a variety of lakes, the river, creating eddies in its expanses and joined by thousands of tributaries, flows over the great eastern continent[3] Bhadrāśva and falls into the eastern sea.

25-26. The river (Alakanandā) that flows over Gandhamādana, the lord of mountains in the south, has many waterfalls and splashes waves and ripples in various ways. It then irrigates the Nandana park, the pleasant resort of Devas. This blessed river then circumambulates the forests of Gandhamādana.

27. It is known in the worlds as the Alakanandā. It enters the northern lake Mānasa which is as clear as the minds of Devas.

28. From the Mānasa lake, the river flows to the beautiful Triśikhara, the lord of mountains. From the summit of the mountain Trikūṭa, it falls on the peak of Kaliṅga (?) mountain.

---

1. Offshoots of Tien Shan mountains.
2. Modern Mustagh Ata.
3. The Hwang Ho of China was believed to be the eastern extension of the Sitā.

29-30. Falling from the peak of Kaliṅga, it flows on to the mountain Rucaka. From there it flows to Niṣadha and then to Tāmrābha. Falling from the peak of Tāmrābha, it flows to mount Śvetodara, thence to the lordly mountain Sumūla and then to the mountain Vasudhāra.

31. From there it flows to Hemakūṭa and thence to Devaśṛṅga, thereafter it flows to Mahāśaila and then to Piśācaka mountain.

32. From the excellent mountain Piśācaka, it flows to Pañcakūṭa and from Pañcakūṭa to Kailāsa, the mountain residence of Devas.

33. Whirling about in its bowels of caves and ridges, it falls on the excellent mountain Himavat.

34-35. Piercing through thousands of mountains thus, it flows quickly irrigating hundreds of land surfaces. Then it flows through thousands of forests and hundreds of caves and falls into the southern sea.

36-37. This river is one Yojana in breadth; it is hidden in the bowels of the peaks of mountain. It is held on head by noble-souled Śaṅkara, lord of Devas. It is sanctifying, O leading Brāhmaṇa. It quells even terrible sins. By virtue of the contact with the body of lord Śaṅkara, the great river has its waters rendered doubly sanctimonious in all the worlds.

38-40. From all round that mountain Himavat, through its many openings, thousands of rivers spring forth. They are known by other names. The river Gaṅgā is resorted to by Siddhas and its waters are drunk by Rudras, Sādhyas, Anilas and Ādityas. Blessed are the lands through which this great and reputed river flows.

41. Now I shall describe the western side of Meru mountain which is holy and contains several mines of precious stones and which is resorted to by pious persons.

42-45. Meru, the lord of mountains, is very massive with large bowels and caves. Its central region is embellished with table-lands, ridges and bushy growths. The water of this river is used by Devas and the river is held by the three-eyed deity. Urged by the wind, it flows far and wide, and whirls again like a creeper. It falls from the peak of Meru. Its water is used by many living beings. It is pure like the spotless silk and is splashed extensively. This river of the firmament resorted to by Siddhas and Cāraṇas on its peak, circumambulates the mountain and goes ahead.

46-47. This blessed river of many flowers and fruits irrigates the great forests of Devabhrāja, Mahābhrāja and Vaibhrāja. Decorated by various forests and circumambulating the mountain, it enters the western lake of pure waters, Sitoda.

48-49. From Sitoda is goes to mount Supakṣa. Again this river of holy clear water which is used by divine sages, falls from the peak of Supakṣa. Thence this river of blessed waters falls on the Śikhi mountain.

50-53. (The river flows from one mountain to another:)

Thereafter the river flows from mountain Śikhi to mount Kaṅka, thence to Vaidūrya, then to mount Kapila and thence to Gandhamādana. From that excellent mountain it flows to Piñjara, the splendid mountain; from Piñjara it flows to Sarasa and from there it flows to Kumudācala mountain.

It flows to the mountains Madhumān, Jana, Mukuṭa. From the peak of Mukuṭa, it flows to the great mountain Kṛṣṇa, from Kṛṣṇa it flows to the great mountain Śveta, served by (other) great mountains. From Śveta it ultimately comes down to thousand-peaked Śailendra, the lord of mountains.

54. With its waters augmented by tributaries, this auspicious river denudes thousands of mountains. It then flows at full speed and falls on the great mountain Pāriyātra.

55-57. It glides among fountains, streams, caves and ridges. With numerous waves, it wanders through its many bowels. Its current is impeded by several rocks and boulders accidentally falling therein and its waters are split in various ways. It descends on the plains (the earth). The blessed river then irrigates the great continent Ketumāla, populated by Mleccha tribes, and falls into the western sea.

58-60. The great river flows through the supportless auspicious firmament for a distance of sixty thousand Yojanas, throwing cascades of water like a garland being scattered. It falls from the peak of Meru, its waters being urged by the wind. Being cast in the sky, it takes a curved (circle-like body). It falls at the foot of Meru on the northern mountain Supārśva which is inhabited by living beings and whose flanks are variegated due to brilliant colours.

61-64. Then it drops from the ridges of the peaks resorted to by Devas and sages, with its waters scattered by flowery rafts. The blessed river irrigates and circumambulates the forest of the Sun-god which is the sylvan place of origin of variegated jewels. It then falls into the sacred lake Mahābhadra resorted to by blessed people. The beneficent white river is called Bhadrasomā. It flows rapidly and its shores are far apart. The great and holy river Mahābhadrā flows thereafter.

65. Flowing rapidly with many rivulets flowing into it, and dashing against many bunds, the river falls on the ridges of Śaṅkhakūṭa.

66. Falling down the ridges of Śaṅkhakūṭa, it proceeds to Vṛṣa Parvata. From Vṛṣa Parvata, it flows then to Vatsagiri and then to Nāgaśaila.

67-71. From Nāgaśaila, it reaches the excellent mountain Nīla, the Varṣa mountain. From Nīla, it flows to Kapiñjala, and then the river flows to Indranīla, thereafter it flows to Mahānīla, and Hemaśṛṅga. From Hemaśṛṅga it flows to Śveta, and from Śveta to Sunāga. From Sunāga, it flows to Śataśṛṅga. Then the great river flows from Śataśṛṅga to the flower-carpeted Puṣkara. From Puṣkara to Dvirāja, the great mountain of great strength (*Sumahābala*). From there, it flows to Varāha Parvata and the mountain Mayūra. From the mountain Mayūra the rapid river flows to Ekaśikhara bedecked with caves and crevasses, and then to the peak of the Jārudhi mountain.

72. After piercing (forcing its way) through thousands of mountains thus, the great river reaches Triśṛṅga, the boundary mountain with many peaks.

73-74. Falling from the ridges of Triśṛṅga inhabited by blessed people this river of pure water falls off the ridges of Meru, and urged by the wind flows to the excellent mountain Viruddha. After irrigating the mountain the river flows into the western ocean.

75-77. On the wonderful great foot of Meru inhabited by living beings, on the northern mountain Supārśva whose sides are the sources of gold, the river falls into the bowels of caves, into various divisions and descends to the earth with wonderful flowery rafts. Irrigating the Northern Kuru region, the delightful auspicious river runs through the middle of the continent and flows into the northern ocean.

78. In this way the four great rivers of pure waters, falling down the ridges of great mountains, flow into the four directions.

79. Thus the earth of vast expanse I have almost explained to you. It is surrounded on all sides by Meru and other mountains.

80. The earth has four great continents, four forests of sports, four great trees as the four land-marks and four excellent lakes.

81. It has four great mountains and has four serpents for support, eight superior mountains and eight inferior.

CHAPTER FORTYTHREE

Description of Bhadrāśva

Sūta said:

1-3. Near Gandhamādana there is a large and bulky boulder above, thirty-four thousand Yojanas long, and thirty-two thousand Yojanas wide, east to west. The residents of this area perform auspicious rites. They are well-known as Ketumālas. The men are black in complexion. They are vigorous and powerful. The women have the lustrous complexion of the petals of a lotus. All of them have pleasing appearances.

4. There is a great divine Panasa (Jack-fruit) tree there. It has six tastes. It is the son of Brahmā, capable of moving about according to its pleasure. It has the speed of mind. It is veritable Īśvara himself. Imbibing its juice, the people there live for ten thousand years.

5. On the eastern side of Mālyavat, there is another big boulder. In length and width, it is like the former one.

6. The people of the area are called Bhadrāśvas. They remain always joyous in mind. There is a splendid forest of huge trees called *Kālāmra* (black mangoes).

7. The men are fair-complexioned, vigorous and powerful. The women are charming and comely in appearance, with the hue and lustre of lilies.

8. They have the complexion and lustre of the moon and their faces resemble the full moon. Their bodies are as cool as the moon. They have the fragrance of lotuses.

9. Their span of life is ten thousand years. They are free from ailments. Imbibing the juice of the black mangoes, they enjoy perpetual youth.

The sages said :

10. The magnitude, lustre and the span of life of the people of all the four great continents have been explained precisely and succinctly, but not in detail.

Sūta said :

11. O Sages of enhancing reputation ! The characteristics of the people of Bhadrāśva mentioned by me are what have been cited by earlier Siddhas. Now listen to them in detail.

12-13. I shall narrate fully and in detail what I have seen and heard, of the five principal mountain ranges, countries and rivers which surround the famous Devakūṭa mountain.

14. The five principal mountains are Śaivāla, Varṇamālāgra, the excellent mountain Korañja, Śvetavarṇa and Nīla.

15. There are hundreds, thousands and crores of small mountains besides, which are offshoots of these five ranges.

16. (In and near these mountains) there are many lands and countries where a great variety of people live, which abound in various types of animals and which are looked after by many kings.

17. The lands are occupied by prosperous leading men of well-known names and valour. They are splendid and worthy of being glorified.

18. Many kingdoms are established between the mountains in the lands whether plain or rugged and uneven. Their names are as follows :

19-23. Sumaṅgalas, Śuddhas, Candrakāntas, Sunandanas, Vrajakas, Nīlaśaileyas, Sauvīras, Vijayasthalas, Mahāsthalas,

Sukāmas, Mahākeśas, Sumūrdhajas, Vātaraṁhas, Sopasaṅgas, Parivāyas, Parācakas, Saṁbhavaktras, Mahānetras, Śaivālas, Stanapas, Kumudas, Śākamuṇḍas, Urahsaṁkīrṇas, Bhaumakas, Sodakas, Vatsakas, Vārāhas, Hāravāmakas, Śaṅkhas, Bhāvisandras, Uttaras, Haimabhaumakas, Kṛṣṇabhaumas, Subhaumas and Mahābhaumas. These and other lands and countries are very famous.[1]

24. They drink from the holy river Mahāgaṅgā[2] which was, in the beginning, known in the three worlds as Śītā bearing down volumes of cold water.

25-31. The other rivers are Haṁsavasati, Mahācakrā, Cakrā, Vaktrā, Kañcī, the excellent river Surasā, Śākhāvatī, Indranadī, Meghā, Maṅgāravāhinī, Kāverī, Haritoyā, Somāvartā, Śatahradā, Vanamālā, Vasumatī, Paṁpā, Paṁpāvatī, Suvarṇā, Pañcavarṇā, the holy Vapuṣmatī, Maṇivaprā, Suvaprā, Brahmabhāgā, Śilāśinī, Kṛṣṇatoyā, Puṇyodā, the auspicious Nāgapadī, Śaivālinī, Maṇitaṭā, Kṣārodā, Aruṇāvatī, Viṣṇupadī, Mahāpuṇyā, Mahānadī, Hiraṇyavāhinī, Nīlā, Skandamālā, Surāvatī, Vāmodā, Patākā, Vetālī and Mahānadī Gaṅgā and these rivers are glorified as the heroines (important rivers). Besides there are other rivers small and innumerable—hundreds and thousands.

32. Thus the holy rivers in the eastern continent have been enumerated to you. A person becomes sanctified by merely enumerating them.

33. The kingdom is flourishing and prosperous. It consists of many provinces where trees and forests grow in abundance. These are encircled by many hills.

34. It is teeming with groups of men and women. The kingdom is auspicious and joyous. People are governed by many kings. They are rich in money and foodgrains. There are many mines of jewels, glorified in many ways.

35. In that country, men are said to be lustrous in comple-

1. Verses 35ff: These seem to be provinces in China as the people, thereof are 'gold-complexioned'.

2. This is the Hwang Ho river of China. The Purāṇic belief that the Sitā (which flows to the western sea) has emerged in the east in Bhadrāśva through underground channels is shared by Chinese, Arabs and Persians (AGP 102).

xion like gold and conch-shell.[1] They are big-bodied, extremely vigorous like bulls.

36. They can meet, talk and associate with Devas and occupy the same seats with them.

37. Their span of life is ten thousand years. There is no difference of Dharma and Adharma among them (all people are equal). They are naturally truthful and non-violent.

38. Everyday they perform sacrifices, worships and obeisance with devotion to Lord Śaṅkara and Gaurī, the great Vaiṣṇavī (Śakti).

CHAPTER FOURTYFOUR

Description of Ketumāla

Sūta said :

1. The natural characteristics of the Bhadrāśvas have been narrated precisely. Now Listen to a detailed description of Ketumāla.[2]

2-3. It behoves you to hear in detail the description of the seven principal mountain ranges, countries and rivers in particular, situated in all the quarters to the west of the western lordly mountain Niṣadha.

4. The seven ranges of *Kulaparvatas* are Viśāla, Kaṁbala, Kṛṣṇa, Jayanta, Hariparvata, Aśoka and Vardhamāna.

5. There are other hills by hundreds, thousands and crores of other massive and extensive mountains, the offshoots of the seven ranges of *Kulaparvatas*.

---

1. Verses 35-38 describe the people of Bhadrāśva (N. China, Sinkiang).

2. Roughly Ketumāla corresponds to old Bactria, the basin of the Oxus. The latitudinal range Niṣadha (i.e. Hindukush-Kunlun) is to its south and the Nila (Zarafshan-Tien shan) range is to the north and to the west is the Western Sea (the Caspian). For the mountains, valleys, settlements on mountains and the rivers of Ketumāla *vide supra* chs. 36,38,39,42.

6. In and near them, there are lands and kingdoms where people of various castes and creeds dwell and which are governed by many rulers.

7. They are famous on the earth, well-known by their names and valour. They are embellished (as it were) by the praises of their exploits (sung) by the people of the country they occupy.

8. Their kingdoms are established on even and uneven lands among mountains. They are known by their own respective and varied names.

9-15. The nationalities are:[1] Gomanuṣya, Kopataka, Tatsukhas, Bhramara, Yūtha, Māheya, Acalakūṭaka, Sumaula, Stāvaka, Krauñca, Kṛṣṇāṅga, Maṇipuñjaka, Kūṭakambala, Mauṣīya, Samudrāntaraka, Karambhava, Kuca, Śveta, Suvarṇakaṭaka, Śubha, Śvetāṅga, Kṛṣṇapāda, Viha, Kapilakarṇikā, Atyākarālā, Gojvālā, Hīnāna, Vanapātaka, Mahiṣa, Kumudābha, Karavāṭa, Sahotkaca, Śukanāsas, Mahānāsa, Vanāsa, Gajabhūmika, Karañja, Mañjama, Vāha, Kiṣkindī, Pāṇḍubhūmika, Kubera, Dhūmaja, Jaṅga, Vaṅga, Rājīva, Kokila, Vācāṅga, Mahāṅga, Madhaureya, Surecaka, Pittala, Kācala, Śravaṇa, Mattakāśika, Godāva, Bakula, Vāṅga, Vaṅgaka, Modaka and Kalā.

16. These blessed people drink the holy waters of the river Suvaprā resorted to by Nāgas.

17-23. They also drink the waters of the rivers Kambalā, Tāmasī, Śyāmā, Sumedhā, Bakulā, Vikīrṇā, Śikhimālā, Darbhāvatī, Bhadrā, Śukanadī, Palāśā, Bhīmā, Prabhañjanā, Kāñcī, Kuśāvatī, Dakṣā, Śākavatī, Puṇyodā, Candrāvatī, Sumūlā, Ṛṣabhā, Samudramālā, Campāvatī, Ekākṣā, Puṣkalā, Vāhā, Suvarṇā, Nandinī, Kālindī, Bhāratī, Sītodā, Pātikā, Brāhmī, Viśālā, Pīvarī, Kumbhakārī, Ruṣā, Mahiṣī, Mānuṣī and Daṇḍā. These are excellent rivers frequented by Devas, Siddhas and sages. Their waters are holy and auspicious and they dispel sins.

24. The land is flourishing with various countries. It is beautified by great rivers. It is full of many gems and jewels. It is perpetually rejoicing and splendid.

---

1. Some of the nationalities or sub-regions mentioned in vv. 9-15 are identified with their mediaeval names as follows:

Gomanuṣya (Gonaridh), Kapotaka (Murghab), Karambhava (Karmina), Kuca (Kuz-Panjdeb)—(AGP 98).

25. The whole continent is prosperous with wealth, food-grains, and other articles and abodes of human beings spread all around. This is the abode of pious persons. Thus the natural characteristics of Ketumāla have been narrated to you.

CHAPTER FORTYFIVE

Description of Bhāratavarṣa

Śaṁśapāyana said :

1. O holy lord, the two continents in the east and the west have been narrated to us. Now tell us about the people dwelling in the northern and southern continents as well as those on the mountains.

Sūta said :

2. South of the Śveta mountain and north of the Nīla, there is a sub-continent called Ramaṇaka[1] where human beings are born.

3. Animals (thereof) fulfill desires in all seasons. People are free from the stink of old age (They do not become senile or decrepit). They are a good-looking people descended from a noble, fair-complexioned race.

4. There is a great divine *Nyagrodha* tree (the Indian fig tree) called Rohiṇa. The people subsist on the juice of its fruit.

5. Those excellent people are always delightful and happy. They live for eleven thousand five hundred years.

6. To the north of the Śveta and to the south of the mountain called Śṛṅgavān, there is a sub-continent called Hiraṇyata[2] (*Hiraṇvat* in A) where a river Hairaṇyatī (*Hairaṇvatī* in A) flows.

---

1. Identified with ancient Sogdiana (AGP 83-84).

2. This Varṣa is closely associated with the river Hiraṇvatī (mod. Zarafshan). Both forms of the name mean 'possessor or scatterer of gold'. Due to its association with this river, this Varṣa must be presumed to be adjacent to Sogdiana—AGP 84-85.

7. Very strong and brilliant men are born there who are Sattvic in quality, bestower of desires in all seasons. They are rich and comely in appearance.

8. These people of unlimited splendour live upto twelve thousand five hundred years.

9. In that country there is the great *Lakuca* tree (Bread-fruit tree) yielding six tastes. Men maintain themselves on the juice of its fruits.

10. There the Śṛṅgavān mountain has three great and lofty peaks. Out of them one is full (lit. consists) of diamonds, the second, of gold and the third, full of all kinds of precious stones. They are embellished with mansions.

11. On the southern shore of the northern sea is the holy country of the Kurus[1] which is resorted to by the Siddhas.

12. The trees there provide sweet fruits and flowers throughout the year. They put forth clothes and ornaments along with fruits.

13. Many are the charming trees that bear fruits desired by all. They exude excellent honey of exquisite taste, colour and fragrance.

14. There are other charming trees called *Kṣirin*. They always yield milk like nectar yet presenting six types of tastes.

15. The entire ground is full of jewels, even the fine sand being gold which is pleasant to touch. It is auspicious, free from impurities and thorns.

16. Descending from the world of Devas, people are born as auspicious men. They are born in fair complexioned families and have perpetual youth.

17. The charming women give birth to twins who imbibe the nectarine juice of the *Kṣirin* (milk-yielding) tree.

18. The twins are born simultaneously and grow up together. They are of similar forms, traits and conduct of life. They also die together.

19. Like the couples of Cakravāka birds, they are affectionate to each other. They enjoy life, not knowing disease, sorrow or suffering.

---

1. Kuru or Uttara-Kuru as described here and in other Purāṇas includes the basin of rivers Irtysh, Obe, Tobol i.e. modern western Siberia—AGP 84-85.

20. They have great vigour and vitality. They live upto fourteen thousand five hundred years. They never resort to others' women.

21. North of Jārudhi, the king of mountains, are the northern Kurus. The land is glorified in all directions. Now listen to its detailed description.

22-23. There are two lofty *Kula-Parvatas*, Candrakānta and Sūryakānta.[1] They are embellished by many caves, crevasses, cavities and rivulets; they possess many bushes and hedges. They are decorated with minerals of various colours. They contain many kinds of metals; they are adorned with all kinds of mineral ores. They have trees with perpetual fruits, flowers and roots; they are resorted to by Siddhas and Cāraṇas.

24-25. The whole of that country is pervaded by hundreds of their peaks and ridges. The great river Bhadrasomā[2] flows in between the two mountains, Candrakānta and Sūryakānta.

26. There are thousands of other rivers with pure and tasty water, sufficient for the Kuru people for drinking.

27. Similarly there are thousands of great rivers flowing with milk, honey, butter and the intoxicant beverage Maireya.

28. There are hundreds of pools full of curds. There is a huge mountain rich in tasty food, nectarine, ripe fruits of different kinds.

29. There are roots and fruits of sweet fragrance, taste and colour. Their fragrance can be smelt from a distance of five Yojanas.

30. There are thousands of flowers of different colours and shapes, large, pleasant and conducive to welfare.

31. There are forests of Tamāla, Aguru and sandal-wood pleasant to touch and rich in fragrance, colour and taste.

32. The forests are in full bloom. Bees hum and hover round. The forests abound in pleasant trees, hedges and creepers.

33. O excellent Brāhmaṇa, there are thousands of lakes abounding in lotuses and lilies wherein bees hum and birds chirp.

---

1. Identified with mod. Tarbagatai and Jingar—Ala Tau mountains.

2. Mod. Irtysh river.

34-35. There are many charming grounds of sports affording pleasure in all the seasons. There foodstuffs, garlands, unguents, beds, seats and other articles of enjoyment are ever available. Birds of beautiful shape and variegated colours chirp there.

36. The grounds of sports are flourishing and richly embellished in gold and jewels. There are bowers and grottos of plantain and other trees as well as rocks.

37. There are thousands of bowers of creepers all around. They are very pleasant. There are hundreds of underground houses as lustrous and pure as conch shells.

38. The windows are made of gold adorned with a network of diamonds. They are very large and of various sizes with wonderful workmanship in gold and gems.

39. There are thousands of excellent trees. The clothes are of various shapes (and fashions). They are of fine texture and very pleasant (to the sight).

40. There are various musical instruments like *Mṛdaṅga, Veṇu,* flute, *Paṇava* which are widely used. There are hundreds and thousands of Kalpa trees bearing fruits.

41. There are parks of that description everywhere and so are the cities all over (the Kurus). The whole land is joyous, full of men and women. The wind blows wafting the fragrance of different flowers.

42. That country is always the abode of happiness, providing relief from fatigue. There, the gods descend from heaven in the shape of human beings and take their birth. Thus this excellent land is heaven itself, (maybe) even better than that.

43. The men living on the eastern ridge of the Candrakānta mount are dark in colour, while those on Sūryakānta are dark as well as fair. They are excellent and happy.

44. In that land, there are excellent men, strong and valorous like the Devas. They always enjoy themselves as much as they please. They look very refulgent.

45. They are bedecked in bangles, bracelets, shoulderlets, necklaces and earrings. They wear garlands of various colours and coronets. Their upper garments and clothes are of various colours.

46. They never grow old. They have perpetual youth. They are fond, affectionate and comely in appearance. They live upto many thousand years.

47. They do not procreate nor do they decline in numbers. Pairs are born of the tree unlike each other but befitting each other.

48-49. The riches are common to all. They do not have the sense of possession. There is no virtue, no vice, no sickness, no old age, no mental confusion, no feeling of exhaustion. On completing their full length of time, they disappear like bubbles of water.

50. They are extremely happy, devoid of all miseries. Being passionately attached, they do not observe (the restrictions of) Dharma. For Dharma grows from misery.

51-52. To the southern side of Northern Kurus, there is the famous country called Candradvīpa[1] shaped like the disc of the moon. It is at a distance of five thousand Yojanas beyond the region of gods. (Being a seaside land) it is ever decorated with garlands of sea waves and is resonant with many sounds.

53-55. It extends to one thousand Yojanas in area and is full of fruits and flowers. It is fertile and flourishing. It is one hundred Yojanas in breadth and so much in height. There is an excellent mountain Kumudaprabha in its centre, inhabited by Siddhas and Cāraṇas. It has various gems equal in lustre to the moon. These have all good traits and shine in their lunar shape. There are lilies of diverse colours, parks and gardens of variegated hues. There are many rivulets and caves. It is decorated with great ridges, precipices, crevasses and bushy hedges.

56. The excellent river of many waves, Candrāvartā flows from this mountain. It is full of pure and holy water, bright like the moon's rays.

57. There is the excellent abode of the moon, the lord of stars. The moon, the lord of planets, always resides there.

58. There is a famous mountain known by the name of the moon. The great land called Candradvīpa is famous both in this world as well as in heaven.

1. The Tuva region in southern Siberia where the river Yenisi flows.

59. All the people here shine like the moon. They resemble the moon, with their faces shining like the moon. They are free from dirt and consider the moon their deity.

60. The people there, are very virtuous, gentle, truthful and brilliant. Their conduct is good and their span of life extends to a thousand years.

61-62. To the west of this western continent is the land called Bhadrākara four thousand Yojanas from the ocean. It is a circular zone ten thousand Yojanas in diameter. It looks splendid with different kinds of flowers.

63. The place is rich and abounds in foodgrains. It is ruled over by many kings. It is joyous, prosperous and beautiful on account of the great mountains.

64. There is a very splendid seat of Vāyu there, embellished with various jewels. There, the embodied form of Vāyu is worshipped always on *Parvan* days.

65-66. The people living there have golden complexion. They are bedecked in gold. They are as refulgent as the immortal Devas. Their garments and garlands are of variegated colour. They are blessed, vigorous, joyous and truthful. They live upto five hundred years. They consider Vāyu their deity.

Sūta said :

67. These are the natural characteristics of the countries in Bhārata as seen by the knowers of the supreme truth. What else shall I narrate to you ?

68. When this was said by the intelligent son of Sūta, the sages eager to listen to the sequal asked him thereafter.

The Sages said :

69-71. O excellent one, it is in this Bhārata country that the fourteen Manus, Svāyaṁbhuva and others, are born at the time of the creation of subjects. We wish to know this further. Please narrate.

On hearing their words Sūta Lomaharṣaṇa, well-versed in the Purāṇas and of pious mind, described this in detail to the sages of purified souls.

Sūta said :

72. The natural traits of the Kurus have been precisely recounted. Now I shall mention the features of Bhārata.[1] Understand them.

73-74. O excellent Brāhmaṇas, in the sacred centre to the south of the southern mountain Himavat, extending from east to west is the Bhārata sub-continent. It behoves you to listen now to the details of the countries in the Bhārata Varṣa and of the people there.

75. With its diverse features giving rise to auspicious and inauspicious results, this sub-continent is in the middle, to the north of the ocean and to the south of Himavat.

76. Since the country (*Varṣa*) is called Bhārata the people are Bhāratīs. Since Manu ruled over the people, he is called Bharata.[2] Etymoligically derived thus the Varṣa (country) is called Bhārata.

77. It is from here alone that one goes to heaven or attains salvation.[3] The middle course—heaven as well as the end, the final emancipation—is attained from here. Rituals for human beings are not ordained anywhere else on earth.

78. There are stated to be nine divisions of this Bhārata Varṣa.[4] Being separated by oceans, they are mutually inaccessible.

---

1. The description of Bhārata is repeated in other Purāṇas also e.g. AP. 118, Bd.P. I.2.16, VP.II.3.

2. This etymological explanation of 'Bhārata' attributing its credit to Manu who is called 'Bharata' due to his act of maintaining (and feeding) the people, supersedes the Jaina tradition which attributes it to Bharata, the son of Tīrthaṅkara Vṛ(Ṛ)ṣabha.

3. Due to this special importance of Bhārata, it is called *Karma-bhūmi*. Cf. Bd.P.I.2.16.7, Bm.P.27.2, Mk.P. 55. 21-22, Mt.P. 114. 6-7, *Siddhānta Śīromaṇi* III.41.

4. Cf. Mk. P. 57.5, Mt.P. 113.7-9. The names of the nine regional divisions of Bhārata Varṣa indicate a period when Hindu culture was assimilated by countries in South and South-East Asia. There are differences among scholars about their identification from the days of Al Biruni to De, M.Ali and V.S. Agrawala. Thus Indradvīpa is identified with Madhyadeśa (Al Biruni), region between Laṅkā and Mahendra Hills (Abul Fazl in *Ain-e-Akbarī*), Burma (Majumdar), Andamans (V. S. Agrawala), Trans-Brahma-

79-81. They are Indradvīpa, Kaseru, Tāmravarṇa, Gabhastimān, Nāgadvīpa, Saumya, Gandharva and Vāruṇa. This Bhārata, the ninth among them, is surrounded by the sea. From south to north it extends to a thousand Yojanas, from Kumārī to the source of Gaṅgā. Sideways in the north it extends to nine thousand Yojanas.

82. On the eastern boundary are Kirātas and Yavanas at the western boundary.

83. Within it dwell Brāhmaṇas, Kṣattriyas and Vaiśyas attending to sacrifices, war and trade respectively. The Śūdras live in different parts.

84. There are mutual dealings among these based on virtue, wealth and love. The different castes are engaged in their own functions.

85. People perform the duties of the five stages of life, the fifth being that of *Saṅkalpa*. They possess the human tendency to endeavour to attain heaven and salvation.

86. He who conquers this ninth Dvīpa entirely, along with the countries extending sideways, is declared an emperor (*Samrāṭ*).

87. He who conquers this world is remembered as Samrāṭ, the conquerer of Antarikṣa as *Virāṭ*, while the conquerer of the other world is called *Svarāṭ*[1]. I shall explain this later on.

88. There are seven great mountain systems with excellent knot-like ridges in this Varṣa. They are Mahendra, Malaya,

---

Putra region (M.Ali). These are mere speculations of scholars. After discussing the regional classification (AGP 126-132), M.Ali comes to the following conclusion:

Indradvīpa = the trans-Brahmaputra region.

Kaseru = The coastal plain between the deltas of Godāvarī and Mahānadi.

Tāmravarṇa = The sector of Indian Peninsula south of Kāverī.

Gabhastimān = The hilly belt between Narmadā and Godāvarī.

Saumya = The coastal belt west of Indus.

Gandharva = The trans-Indus region.

Vāruṇa = The western coast of India.

1. The precise meaning of terms *Samrāṭ*, *Virāṭ* and *Svarāṭ* is worth noting.

A farfetched interpretation of this verse is suggested as follows: "This region is known as monarchical, Antarikṣa as non-monarchical (*vi-rāṭ*) and other region as self-governing (*sva-rāṭ*)".

Sahya, Śuktimān, Ṛkṣaparvata, Vindhya and Pāriyātra.[1]

89. There are other thousands of mountains adjacent to these. They are endowed with all qualities, and have broad and variegated summits.

90-92. The chief of them[2] are the excellent mountain Mandara, Vaihāra, Dardura, Kolāhala, Surasa, Maināka, Vaidyuta, Pātandhama, Pāṇḍura, Gantuprastha, Kṛṣṇagiri, Godhana, Puṣpagiri, Ujjayanta, Raivataka, Śrīparvata, Kāru and Kūṭaśaila.

93. There are other smaller mountains with thin population. The land strips between them have a mixed population consisting of Āryas and Mlecchas.

94-96. The rivers rising from the foot of Himavat,[3] of which those people drink the water are : Gaṅgā, Sindhu, Sarasvatī, Śatadru, Candrabhāgā, Yamunā, Sarayū, Irāvatī, Vitastā, Vipāśā, Devikā, Kuhū, Gomatī, Dhūtapāpā, Bāhudā, Dṛṣadvatī, Kauśikī, Tṛtīyā, Niścīrā, Gaṇḍakī, Ikṣu and Lohitā.

---

1. Out of these mountain systems, Mahendra, Malaya and Sahya ranges are well-known. The Vindhya of the Purāṇas includes the Satpura range, south of the Narmadā. According to De (p. 196) Śuktimān is that portion of the Vindhya range joining Pāriyātra and Ṛkṣa mountains including the hills of Gondwan and Chhota Nagpur. But M. Ali in the topographical Map of Bhārata, shows it as a ring of ranges encircling the Mahānadi basin, very nearly coinciding with Purāṇic Dakṣiṇa Kosala (mod. Mahakosal area in MP).

The Pāriyātra mountain is a ring of ranges north of Narmadā, nearly encircling the catchment area of Chambal and Betwa and thus corresponds to the Aravallis and (modern) Western Vindhya.

The Ṛkṣa mountain represents the modern Vindhya from the source of Sonar to the eastern ranges marking the catchment area of the river Śoṇa (AGP 112-113).

2. Mandara=A portion of Himālaya to the east of Sumeru in Garhwal (De, p.124- 25).

3. The mountain ranges described in note 1 above are watersheds which bound wholly or partly the catchment areas of important rivers in India.

It is significant that the names and order or enumeration is practically the same as in Mt.P. and Bd.P.

Here is the list of rivers rising from Himālaya. The modern names are given in brackets:

97-98. The rivers issuing from Pāriyātra[1] are: Vedasmṛti, Vadavatī, Vṛtraghnī, Sindhu, Varṇāśā, Candanā, Satīrā, Mahatī, Parā, Carmaṇvatī, Vidiśā, Vetravatī, Śiprā and Avantī.

99-101. The rivers originating from Ṛkṣaāda and having crystal-clear water are: The great Nada Śoṇa, Narmadā, Sumahādrumā, Mandākinī, Daśārṇā, Citrakūṭā, Tamasā, Pippalā, Śroṇī, Karatoyā, Piśācikā, Nīlotpalā, Vipāśā, Jambulā, Vāluvāhinī, Siterajā, Śuktimatī, Makruṇā, and Tridivā.

102-103. The auspicious rivers of holy waters issuing from the slopes of the Vindhya mountains[2] are: Tāpī, Payoṣṇī, Nirvindhyā, Madrā, Niṣadhā, Veṇyā, Vaitaraṇī, Śitibāhu, Kumudvatī, Toyā, Mahāgaurī, Durgā and Antaśilā.

Śatadru (Sutlej), Candrabhāgā (Chenab), Irāvatī (Ravi), Vitastā (Jhelum), Vipāśā (Beas), Devikā (Deeg, a tributary of Ravi), Kuhū (Kabul), Dhūtapāpā (Śāradā, with its headstreams), Bāhudā (Rapti), Dṛṣadvatī (Chitang, a tributary of Ghaggar), Kauśikī (Kosi with its three headwaters), Lohitā (Brahmaputra).

1. Pāripātra is a variation of Pāriyātra. The modern names of these rivers are mentioned in the brackets:

Vedasmṛti (Banās), Vedavatī (Berach), Vṛtraghnī (Bāṇgaṅgā—Utangan). These were big, perennial rivers of ancient Matsyadeśa (now a part of M.P.)

Varṇāśā is W.Banas which flows west of Aravallis, Nandanā (Sābarmati); Sadānīrā (Sarasvatī) is probably the correct name for Satira. Pārā (Pārbatī), Carmaṇvatī (Chambal), Vidiśā (Bes), Vetravatī (Betwa).

The names of Purāṇic mountain ranges are so mixed in modern times thatsome rivers are attributed to both.

Śoṇa, Mahānada and Narmadā do not rise in Purāṇic Ṛkṣa Parvata. Rivers from Mandākinī onwards are from Bundelkhand (M.P.). The modern names of the rivers are juxtaposed in brackets:

Daśārṇā (Dhasan), Tamasā (Tons); Pippalā and Śroni (Śyenā in Bd.P.) seems to be one river, viz. Pippali-Śyeni as in Mt.P. (mod. name: (Paiśunī).

Vipāśā is probably Viśālā as in Bd.P. It is Bewas near Sagar in M.P.

Jambūlā (Jammi) a tributary of Betwa, Śuktimatī (Ken) (AGP 118-119).

2. As stated above, Purāṇic writers include even the Satpura hills in the Vindhya ranges.

The modern names of the rivers are given in brackets:

104. The rivers of the southern land rising from the slopes of Sahya mountains are the Godāvarī, Bhīmarathī, Kṛṣṇāvaiṇī, Vañjulā, Tuṅgabhadrā, Suprayogā and Kāverī.

105. The rivers issuing from the Malaya mountains[1] are Kṛtamālā, Tāmravarṇā, Puṣpajātī and Utpalavatī. All of them are very splendid. Their waters are very cool.

106. The rivers originating from Mahendra mountains[2] are Trisāmā, Ṛtukulyā, Ikṣulā, Tridivā, Lāṅgūlinī and Vaṁśadharā.

107. The rivers issuing from the mountain Śuktimān[3] are Ṛṣikā, Sukumārī, Mandagā, Mandavāhinī, Kūpā and Palāśinī.

108. All of them are sacred like Sarasvatī. All of them flowing into the sea are (holy like) Gaṅgā. These are the mothers of the world and are declared as removers of the sins of the world.

Tāpi (Tapti or Tāpi), Payoṣṇi (Pain-ganga—De, p. 150), Nirvindhyā between Ujjain and Vetravati (in *Meghadūta*) (mod. Newuj), Niṣadhā (Sind, on this Narwar, the capital of Niṣadhas was located).

Venyā (Van-gaṅgā), Vaitaraṇi (Baitaraṇi), Kumudvatī (Suvarnarekhā), Toyā (Brāhmaṇi), Mahāgauri (Damodara). *Durgā* (difficult to cross) and *anta-śilā* (full of rocks) are probably the adjectives of that wild river—AGP 120-121.

Most of the rivers are known by their old names with a few modifications such as Bhimarathi (Bhīmā), Kṛṣṇā-vaiṇi (also in inscriptions for mod. Kṛṣṇā), Vaṅgulā (Manjirā), Suprayogā (Vedavati).

1. The modern names are bracketed:

Kṛtamālā (Vai-gai), Tāmravarṇā (Oparṇi), Puṣpajāti (Pambiar), Utpalavati (Periyar)—AGP 122-123.

2. Modern names of these and explanatory remarks are siven in the brackets.

Trisamā (the three headwaters of the Ṛṣikulyā, viz. Ghod-hada, Bhagava and Patana, have this collective name); Ṛtukulyā is Ṛṣikulyā (repeated under rivers from the Śuktimān)

Tridivā (a collective name for Vegavatī, Nāgavatī and Suvarṇamukhi—the three headwaters of Lāṅgūlinī, mod. Langulia).

3. Modern names of these rivers are brackated.

Ṛṣikā (probably Ṛṣrikulyā mentioned above); Sukumārī (Suktel, joins the Mahānadi near Sonpur, Orissa), Mandagā (Mand), Manda-vāhinī (-gāminī in Bd.P., Mahānadī proper), Kūpā (Krpā in Bd.P., Arpā), Palaśinī (Jonk in Raipur Dist. in M.P.)

109-111. The branches and tributaries of these rivers are hundreds and thousands. The countries in Central Region (Madhyadeśa)[1] are chiefly Kurupāñcālas, Śālvas, Jāṅgalas, Śūrasenas, Bhadrakāras, Bodhas, Śatapatheśvaras, Vatsas, Kisaṣṇas, Kulyas, Kuntalas, Kāśikosalas, Tilaṅgas in the borderland, Magadhas and Vṛkas.

112. Now along the northern half of Sahya mountains where the river Godāvarī flows is the most delightful region within the whole of this earth.

113-114. There is a heavenly city named Govardhana.[2] It was built by the king of Devas for Rāma's spouse. Trees and herbs were planted by the sage Bhāradvāja for the sake of Rāma's spouse. He made this delightful wooded tract the private part of the palace.

115-119. The colonies of Kṣattriyas[3] are Vāhlīkas, Vāḍhadhānas, Ābhīras, Kālatoyakas, Aparītas, Śūdras, Pahlavas,

---

1. At the time of the final redaction of the Purāṇa, the following parts of India were included in "Madhyadeśa". These are originally the names of the tribes applied to the land where they were then settled:

Kurus—Between Ghaggar in the west and Gaṅgā in the east and with forest belt on the south and the north.

Pāñcālas—Co-terminus with modern Rohilkhand with the central portion of the Gaṅgā-Yamunā doab added to it.

Śālvas—Near Kurukṣetra to the west of Matsyadeśa. De thinks that it comprised some parts of former Jodhpur, Jaipur and Alwar states (De p. 175).

Jāṅgalas—Generally associated with Kurus as "Kurujāṅgala". Probably, it occupied the NE part of Kurus (AGP 135).

Bhadrakāras and Bodhas along with Śālvas occupied the borderland of the Madhyadeśa of Purāṇas.

2. Now a village in Nasik district of Maharashtra. Formerly it was an important centre of learning. Brāhmaṇas coming from that place formed a sub-caste 'Govardhana Brāhmaṇas". It is mentioned several times in the famous Nasik inscription of Uṣavadāta (100 B.C.) (*Epigraphica Indica* VIII, p. 78).

3. Generally realms or countries are named after the names of tribes or peoples who colonise them. The identification of these realms is based on AGP pp. 137-147. D.C. Sircar's GAMI is also referred to and only the page no. is mentioned.

(1) The Vā (Bā) hlikas=People of Balistan region covered by the Bolon, Nari and Gokh rivers. It coincided with former British Baluchistan. But according to D.C. Sircar (p. 32) it is Balkh (N. Afghanistan).

Carmakhaṇḍikas, Gāndhāras, Yavanas, Sindhus, Sauvīras, Bhadrakas, Śakas, Hradas, Kulindas, Paritas, Hārapūrikas, Ramaṭas, Raddhakaṭakas, Kekayas and Daśamānikas. The tribes of Vaiśyas and Śudras are : Kāmbojas, Daradas, Barbaras, Priyalaukikas, Pīnas, Tuṣāras, Pahlavas, Bāhyatodaras, Ātreyas, Bharadvājas, Prasthalas, Kaserukas, Laṁpākas, Stanapas, Pīḍikas and Juhuḍas.

120. Apagas, Alimadras, Tomaras, Haṁsamārgas, Kāśmīras and Taṅganas are the tribes of Kirātas.

121. These along with Cūlikas, Āhukas and Pūrṇadarvas are the northern peoples. Now hear from me the people in the East.

122-123. People in the east :[1] Andhravākas, Sujarakas,

---

(2) The Vāḍhadhānas (Vātadhānas)=Prob. Waziristan. But in Sircar (p. 32) the Panjab-Rajastan region.

(3) The Ābhīras=South of Sauvīra but east of the Indus=Western part of Hyderabad dist., Sind.

(4) The Kālatoyakas=Residents of Kalat region in Baluchistan.

(5) The Pahlavas=The region adjoining the Hingol valley on the Parikan river. They included Vaiśyas and Śudras as well.

(6) The Carmakhaṇḍikas=At the mouth of the river Hab and the Churma island.

(7) The Gandharas=Kandahar-lower Kabul valley.

(8) The Yavanas=Ionians, Greeks.

(9-10) The Sindhus and Sauvīras=Though usually linked together, they are different regions. Sauvīra coincides with Rohri-Khairpur region of Sind and the remaining portion is Sindhus.

(11) The Śakas=Scythians.

(12) The Ku(Pu)lindas=Kunets of Kulu. But formerly they extended to Saharanpur and Ambala (Sircar, 33).

(13) The Kekayas=People of the country between the Beas and the Sutlej.

(14) The Kambojas=People from Kafirstan who colonised the Kunar basin.

(15) The Daradas=The same ancient tribe living in the valley of the Kisenganga in Kashmir.

(16) The Barbaras=People migrated from Barbary or North Africa.

(17) The Tuṣāras=Tokharians in N. Afghanistan, but people on the Tochi according to AGP 142.

(18) The Lampakas=Lamghans associated with upper Kabul.

1. The ancient tribes and their locations from Eastern India are identified as follows:

Antargiris, Bahirgiris, Pravaṅgas, Vaṅgeyas, Māladas, Mālavartins, Brahmottaras, Pravijayas, Bhārgavas, Geyamarthakas, Prāgjyotiṣas, Muṇḍas, Videhas, Tām(r)aliptakas, Mālas, Magadhas and Govindas are the counties in the east.

124-131. Now the other people who dwell in the southern region[1] are: Pāṇḍyas, Keralas, Caulyas (Colas), Kulyas, Setukas,

---

Antargiri=Rajmahal hills in Santhal Pargana, Bengal (De 8). But Sircar locates Antargiri and Bahirgiri towards the north of Assam.

Vaṅgeyas=Bengal proper—the deltaic triangle between Bhāgirathī-Hooghly (the main outlet of Gaṅgā in ancient times) and Padmā (AGP 151).

Māladas—A Part of the district of Shahabad—the site of Viśvāmitra's Āśrama in Buxar (De, 100); Malda district of Bengal, Rajashahi and West Dinajpur of Bengal (AGP, p. 151).

The Bhārgavas=Probably the same as Bhargava-Aṅgaya (in AGP, p. 152) i.e. the Yamuna-Meghna Doab.

The Prāgjyotiṣas=Kāmarūpa Dist. in Assam.

The Muṇḍas=Chhota Nagpur, especially the Ranchi district (De, p. 134).

The Videhas=Tirhut country between the Kosi and the Gandak to the north of the Ganga (De, p. 35).

The Tāmraliptakas—Tamluk in Midnapur district including Kontai (De, p. 203) (AGP, p. 152).

The Mālas (The Mallas in Bd.P.)—The country round the Parasnath Hills (Part of Hazaribagh and Manbhum Districts). The Mallas were at Pāvā and Kuśinagara at the time of the Buddha (De, p. 123).

The Magadhas=South Bihar.

The Govindas or Gonarda (in Bd.P., Mt.P.)=De (p. 71) identifies it with Gonda in Oudh.

1. The following identifications are based on De, (page no. indicated in notes) and Sircar (GAMI).

The Pāṇḍyas—Modern districts of Tinnevelly and Madura in Tamil Nadu (p. 147).

The Caulas (Colas)=The Coromandal coast to the south of the Pennar including Tanjor (p. 151).

The Setukas=People of Setubandha, Rameshwar (Sircar p. 38).

The Mūṣikas=Travancore on the Malbar coast (p. 134). But Sircar (p. 36) suggests people living on the Muri river (in Nellore and Guntur dists., A.P.)

The Vanavāsikas=Banwasi in North Kanara Dist. Karnatak (CGEIL p. 79). The Kingdom of the ancient Kadamba dynasties.

The Mahārāṣṭras=Roughly identified with Marathi speaking people.

The Mahiṣakas=Southern Mysore (p. 120), also Sircar (p. 39).

The Kaliṅgas=South Orissa (Puri and Ganjam Districts)—Sircar (p. 39).

Mūṣikas, Kumanas, Vanavāsikas, Mahārāṣṭras, Māhiṣakas, Kaliṅgas, Ābhīras, Caiṣikas, excellent Āṭavyas, Pulindras, Vindhyamūlikas, Paunikas, Maunikas, Aṣmakas, Bhogavardhanas, Nairṇikas, Kuntalas, Āndhras, Udbhidas, Nalakālikas.

Now hear from me the names of other people : Śūrpākāras, Kolavanas, Durgas, Kālītakas, Puleyas, Surālas, Rūpasas, Tāpasas, Turasitas, all the Parakṣaras, Nāsikyas and others; those lands in the valley of Narmadā[1], viz. : Bhānukacchas, Samas, Heyas, Sahasas, Śāśvatas, Kacchīyas, Surāṣṭras, Ānartas, Ānartas, Arbudas and Saṁparītas. Now listen to the residents of the Vindhya mountains.[2]

The Ābhīras=South-eastern portion of Gujarat about the mouth of the Narmada (Sircar, p. 1).

The Pulindras (also Pulindas)=Region between the Pranahita and Bandia rivers, both tributaries of the Godavari.

The Paunikas or Paurikas=A small territory occupying the valley of the Pūrṇā, a tributary of the Godāvarī.

The Āśmakas=Aurangabad district and Bodhana country round about in Nizamabad Dist. (Sircar, p. 40).

The Bhojavardhanas=The valley of the upper Pūrnā river below the Sahyadri. Bhokardan about 30 miles from Ajanta (Sircar, p. 40).

The Kuntalas=The southern Maharashtra and northern Canara Dist.

The Āndhras=Not the present big state in south India. Region comprising Krishna and Guntur district of Andhra Pradesh together with its neighbouring area (CGEIL p. 80).

1. Some identifications proposed:

The Kacchast=Cutch, now in Gujarat state.

The Surāṣṭras=Saurashtra (former Kathiawad) now in Gujarat.

The Ānartas=Gujarat and a part of Malwa (De, p. 8).

The Arbudas=The country around Mt. Abu (De, p. 16).

2. The Mālavas=Though Malavas settled in Avanti (around Ujjain) finally and gave their name to the ancient Avanti deśa, it is possible that they were in south Marwar (in Rajasthan) at the time of this Purāṇa.

The Kāruṣas=The country around Reva (De, p. 95).

The Mekalas=Country around Amarkantak, the source of the Narmada

The Utkalas=Orissa.

The Daśārṇas=Modern eastern Malwa (Sircar, p. 43).

The Bhojas=Country around Bhilwara in the Chambal basin (AGP, p. 159). Sircar identifies them with the people of Vidarbha who founded a kingdom in Goa (p. 43).

The Kiṣkindhakas—Sircar identifies it with modern Kalyanpur, south of Udaipur Division (p. 43)-

132-134. Mālavas, Karūṣas, Mekalas, Utkalas, Uttamarṇas Daśārṇas, Bhojas, Kiṣkindhakas, Tosalas, Kosalas, Traipuras, Vaidikas, Tumuras, Tumburas, Ṣaṭsuras, Niṣadhas, Anupas, Tuṇḍikeras, Vītihotras, Avantis. These are the kingdoms on the Vindhya mountains.

135-137. Now I shall mention mountainous territories.[1] These are : Nigarharas, Haṁsamārgas, Kṣupaṇas, Taṅgaṇas, Khasas, Kuśaprāvaraṇas, Hūṇas, Darvas, Hūdakas, Trigartas, Mālavas, Kirātas and Tāmasas. The learned know of four ages in this Bhārata, viz. Kṛta, Tretā, Dvāpara and Kali. I shall explain their natural features later.

The Tosalas=The southern part of Kosala or Gondwan District around Tosali (mod. Dhanti) in Puri District (De, p. 43).

The Kosalas=Sircar identifies this with Dakṣiṇa (Southern) Kosala—modern Raipur, Bilaspur and Sambalpur region (p. 43).

The Traipuras=The region around Tewar. This covers present Jabalpur, parts of Mandla and Narasimhapur Districts.

The Vaidikas=A misprint for Vaidiśas: Eastern Malwa with Vidiśā or Bhilasa as the capital (p. 43).

The Tumuras=Modern Tumain in Guna Dist., M.P.—(Sircar, p. 44).

The Niṣadhas=Marwar with Narwar as its capital (ibid).

The Anupas=South Malwa country about Nimar (De, p. 8).

The Tuṇḍikeras=The Narmada basin around the town Sainkheda (AGP 161).

The Vitihotras=The country around Satwar 30 miles north-west of Harda. It is bounded on the north-east and west by the Vindhyas and by the Narmadā in the south.

The Avantis=The country around Ujjain.

1. Sircar identifies some as follows:

The Haṁsa-mārgas=People of Hunza in N-W Kashmir (p. 45.)

The Khasas=Mod. Khakkas. They lived in Kashmir.

The Trigartas=Modern Jalandhar region (Panjab).

The Kirātas=Himalayan Mountaineers.

CHAPTER FORTYSIX

Description of Kiṁpuruṣa Varṣa

Sūta said :

1. On hearing this and desirous of hearing further, the delighted sages asked Lomaharṣaṇa:

The Sages said :

2-3. The sub-continent of Bhārata has been described by you. Now describe the Kiṁpuruṣa[1] and Hari Varṣas.[2] Thus requested by the Brāhmaṇas, Lomaharṣaṇa replied suitably this question as follows (lit. in the manner indicated in this Purāṇa).

Sūta said :

4. Please listen, O Brāhmaṇas, to what you are pleased to hear. In the Kiṁpuruṣa country, there is a big grove of Plakṣa trees comparable to the Nandana forest.

5. The span of life in the Kiṁpuruṣa land is said to be ten thousand years. The men are gold-complexioned and the women resemble Apsaras-s.

6. They do not suffer from ailments; they are devoid of sorrows; they are pure in mind; they possess the lustre of molten gold.

7. In this holy country Kiṁpuruṣa, there is a fig tree exuding honey. All the inhabitants of Kiṁpuruṣa Varṣa drink its excellent juice.

8. Adjoining Kiṁpuruṣa, there is Harivarṣa where the people are yellow as gold in complexion.

9. All the people there are descended from Devaloka and have divine forms. In Harivarṣa, all people quaff the splendid juice of sugarcane.

---

1. Kiṁpuruṣa Varṣa a mythical land—GAMI, p. 366; Kiṁpuruṣa deśa—Nepal (De, 100).

2. Hari-Varṣa—mythical territory (GAMI, p. 559); the western Tibet (De, p. 74).

10. They live joyously upto eleven thousand years. They remain delighted in their minds. Old age does not afflict them, nor do the people get decrepit or senile.

11. In the central sub-continent Ilāvṛta[1] which I have mentioned before, the sun does not blaze fiercely and men do not get aged (pre-maturely).

12. In Ilāvṛta the moon, the sun and the stars are dim. Men have the colour, lustre and fragrance of the lotus flower. Their eyes are as wide as the lotus leaf.

13. They feed on the juice of Jaṁbū fruit. They neither grow aged nor decay. They have fragrance. They are cultured and polished. They enjoy pleasures as the fruit of their auspicious rites.

14. They are fallen from Devaloka. They are non-senile and deathless. These excellent men live for thirteen thousand years.

15-16. In the sub-continent Ilāvṛta, they live the full span of life. The sub-continent is twenty six thousand Yojanas in length and nine thousand Yojanas in breadth around Meru. It is fashioned like a saucer.

17. Nine thousand Yojanas to the west of Meru lies the mountain Gandhamādana, thirtyfour thousand Yojanas long.

18. To the north and south, it stretches upto Nīla and Niṣadha mountains. Its height is forty thousand Yojanas. It penetrated downwards to a thousand Yojanas.

19. The mountain Mālyavān lies in the east. Its magnitude has already been mentioned. It is to the south of Nīla and to the north of Niṣadha. The great mountain Meru of extensive magnitude lies in the centre of these mountains, which seem to penetrate it.

20-22. Its extent is hundred thousand Yojanas since the ocean is circular and since it sanctifies the zone of the earth. Measurements are reduced in rectangular areas when they are undemarcated. Coming to the middle they split (?)

23. A river of Jaṁbū juice resembling liquified collyrium flows from the south of Meru to the north of Niṣadha.

---

1. Ilāvṛta—The country surrounding the Pamirs (AGP, p. 32, fig 2).

24-26. There is an everlasting Jaṁbū tree called Sudarśana. It blooms and bears fruits perpetually. It is resorted to by Siddhas and Cāraṇas. It is the biggest tree in Jaṁbūdvīpa, a hundred thousand Yojanas high. This lordly tree touches heaven. The length of the fruit is eight hundred and sixty one *Aratnis*. This is determined by sages who know the truth.

27. When the fruits fall on the ground, they make a loud noise. The juice of the Jaṁbū fruits develops into a flowing river.

28. The river passes around Meru and then enters *Jaṁbū mūla* and the people there drink of it. They are delighted and surrounded by the tasty Jaṁbū fruits.

29. Imbibing the juice they conquer old age. Certainly they never fall sick or die.

30. The gold called Jāṁbūnada which Devas wear as ornaments is found there. It appears as splendid as the glow-worm.

31. The splendid juice of the fruits of all *Varṣa*-trees (Jaṁbū) strengthens the people (of the continent). It is the gold that is used for ornaments of Devas.

32. Their excretions (faeces and urine) are scattered all round. Thanks to the blessings of the Lord, the earth absorbs the refuge and the dead bodies.

33. The Rākṣasas, Piśācas and Yakṣas reside on Himavat. The Gandharvas and Apsaras-s live on mountain Hemakūṭa.

34. The Nāgas including Śeṣa, Vāsuki and Takṣaka live on Niṣadha. The thirtythree groups of Devas, the Yājñikas, wander over the great Meru. On the Nīla, full of lapis lazuli, Siddhas and Brahmarṣis live.

35. The mountain Śveta is the abode of Daityas and Dānavas. The mountain Śṛṅgavān is the place which the Pitṛs frequent.

36. Thus the mobile and immboile beings have settled in the nine continents in their respective places.

37. The population of Devas and human beings is too enormous to be enumerated. It should be accepted with faith by those who wish to know it (by experience).

CHAPTER FORTYSEVEN

Descent of the Gaṅgā

Sūta said:

1. The mountain Kailāsa[1] is on the left of Himavat. Here lives the prosperous Kubera along with the Rākṣasas. The ruler of Alakā rejoices in the company of Apsaras-s.

2-3. Splendid, auspicious, cool water flows from the foot of Kailāsa into a lake called Manda. It is full of lilies and is sparkling like autumnal clouds. From that (lake) proceeds the auspicious, heavenly river Mandākinī.[2] On its bank stands a great celestial forest called Nandana.

4-5. To the north-east of Kailāsa, there is a mountain called Candraprabha near mount Suvarṇa which abounds in celestial animals, medicinal herbs and minerals for the use of Devas. The mountain Candraprabha[3] is like a pure jewel. There is a divine lake Acchoda at its foot.

6. From that lake rises the divine river Acchodā. On its banks there is a great, sacred forest Caitraratha.

7. Maṇibhadra, a general of Yakṣas, lives on that mountain along with his attendants. He is surrounded by his retinue of fierce Guhyakas.

8. The holy river Mandākinī and the river Acchodā flow into the great ocean through this zone of the earth.

9-11. South-east of Kailāsa, there is the great mountain Lohita. It is brilliant like the sun and has peaks of gold. It is adjacent to the heavenly mountain Piśaṅga that abounds in red arsenic. It is full of auspicious animals and medicinal herbs. At the foot of the mountain (Lohita), there is a great divine lake called Lohita, from which flows the great auspicious water

---

1. The description of Kailāṣa here, though poetic, shows that the Purāṇa writer was conversant with the topographical features of the Mānasa Sarovar basin—AGP 55-58.

2. Probably this is the river Umā and the Zhong Chhu which flows through Gaurī Kuṇḍa on the eastern flank of mount Kailāsa into the Rākṣasa Tāl (the twin lake of the Mānasa Sarovar)—AGP 65.

3. Probably the Surange La, the NE range of Kailāsa from which water flows into Lake Kongys Tso or Lake Gounche—AGP 65.

(river) called Lauhitya.[1] On its bank there is a great divine forest of gods, called Viśoka.

12. On that excellent mountain there lives the self-controlled Maṇivara Yakṣa, along with his retinue of righteous Guhyakas.

13-14. The great mountain Vaidyuta[2] consisting of variegated minerals and metals lies near the Añjana mountain born of the body of the demon Vṛtra. It has three peaks and it abounds in ferocious animals and medicinal herbs. It is on the southern side of Kailāsa. At the foot of the mountain Vaidyuta, there is the holy lake Mānasa where Siddhas live.

15. From that lake rises the sacred Sarayū that sanctifies the worlds. The divine forest on its bank is very famous by the name Vaibhrāja.

16. The Rākṣasa Brahmapāta, an attendant of Kubera and son of Prahetṛ lives there. He has infinite valour (yet) he is self-controlled. He is surrounded by hundreds of Yātudhānas capable of traversing aerial regions.

17-19. To the west of Kailāsa, there is the excellent mountain Aruṇa.[3] It is full of important animals, medicinal herbs, gold and other minerals. Nearby is the mountain Muñjavat, a glorious mountain resembling clouds. This is a favourite haunt of the great Lord Śaṅkara. It is surrounded by clusters of rocks, pure and golden. It appears (as if) to brush the heaven with its hundreds of golden peaks. This great divine mountain is snow-capped and inaccessible.

20-21. On this mountain lives Lord Dhūmra-Lohita,[4] the king of mountains. At its foot there is the lake Śailoda[5] from

---

1. This is the Brahmaputrā. From a small lake at the foot of the mountain, the Brahmaputrā enters Tamchok Khambah, the headwater of the Brahmaputrā—AGP 66.

2. This is the peak Gurla Mandhata, since lake Mānasa Sarovar lies below its northern face and the river Karnālī (Map Chhu of Tibetans), a major tributary of the Sarayū, rises here—AGP 66.

3. This is the Ladakh or Leh range (*Ibid*).

4. According to M.Ali, it is the Nanga Parbat (for details vide AGP 66-67).

5. M.Ali identifies lake Śailoda with the Wular lake which once occupied the whole of Kashmir—AGP 67.

which flows the heavenly river Śailodā. Between the rivers Cakṣus and Śītā (Sītā), it enters the sea.

22-23. The famous divine forest Surabhi lies on its banks. North of Kailāsa there lies a mountain Gaura by name, which is the resort of auspicious beings and abounds in medicinal herbs and yellow orpiment. It is a splendid bejewelled mountain having golden peaks.

24. At the foot of the mountain, there is a splendid lake called Bindusaras.[1] Even its sands are of gold. It was to this lake that Bhagīratha came.

25. For the sake of the river Gaṅgā, that saintly king lived there for many years (thinking to himself:) "My ancestors will go to heaven, if they are bathed in the waters of the Gaṅgā."

26. The goddess Gaṅgā (lit. a river flowing through three paths, viz. the heaven, the earth and the nether-world)[2] was first initiated there. Rising from the foot of Soma mountain, she divides herself in seven streams.

27. There the sacrificial posts are made of precious stones. The *citis* (oblong quadrilateral sacrificial pits) are golden. It was after performing a sacrifice there that Indra along with attending Devas attained to Śiva.

28. The innumerable stars of the milky way in the clear sky, which look very close to each other and glitter brightly at night are nothing but the goddess Gaṅgā.

29. Having flowed through the sky and the heaven, the Gaṅgā came down upon the earth. When she fell down on the head of Śiva, he held (up) her with his Yogic Māyā power.

30. As the river became furious, some drops (of her water) fell an the earth and created a lake of drops and hence came to be known as Bindusaras.

---

1. The name is explained in two ways:

(i) A collection of drops of water. The basin between mountain Aling Kangri and Kailāsa Tanglha is dotted with innumerable small and large lakes.

(ii) A lake of frozen particles of snow. In the past the basin Aling Kangri and Kailāsa Tanglha was an extensive snowfield.

2. Verses 26-40 describe the natural phenomenon called descent of the Gaṅgā. The term *Tripathagā* indicates the three stages in the descent of the

31-33. It is reported that when (the flow of) the goddess Gaṅgā was checked by Śiva smilingly, she planned in her mind of sweeping away god Śiva: "I will cut my way (to Pātāla) and carry off Śaṅkara along with my current". On coming to know the wicked design Lord Śiva intended to keep her in obscurity in his body (head). Realizing the cruel intention of the river, he confined her on his head, as she fell down with force on the earth

34-35. At the same time Lord Śiva saw before him King Bhagīratha who had grown emaciated, and a veritable network of (visible) veins and whose sense-organs were not functioning well due to hunger. The Lord thought to himself, "I have been propitiated by him (this king) earlier for this river." Becoming aware of the boon granted to him earlier, he controlled his anger (against the river).

36. On hearing the request of God Brahmā to keep up his promise, the Lord released the river held up by him by his prowess, for the sake of Bhagīratha by whose severe penance he felt satisfied.

37-39. As the river was being released, the flow of the river started in seven currents. Three of them flowed to the east and three to the west. The entire course of the river Gaṅgā was divided into seven parts. Nalinī, Hrādinī and Pāvanī[1] flowed to the east. Sītā, Cakṣu and Sindhu flowed to the west. The seventh current led by Bhagīratha flowed to the south.

40. Hence it is known as the Bhāgīrathī. That river entered

Gaṅgā, viz. (i) the Milky Way in the sky, (ii) Snowy or Glacial Gaṅgā and (iii) the Fluvial Gaṅgā. Out of these Ākāśa-Gaṅgā is a poetic name for the Milky Way (v. 28). The confinement of the Gaṅgā in the matted hair of god Śiva (vv. 29-33) is the glacial stage and the release of Gaṅgā (v. 36) indicates the melting of the snowfields and glaciers. M. Ali depicts the whole process graphically (*op.cit.* pp. 63-64) but he does not explain the role of Bhagīratha in this descent. Did he manage through his engineers to divert that river to India in the south?

1. M. Ali (*op. cit.* p. 69) identifies Nalinī, Hrādinī and Pāvanī—the east-flowing rivers with Yangtse, Mekong and Salween, the rivers flowing to the west, viz. Sītā, Cakṣus and Sindhu with Yarkand, Shyok and Indus while the southern river Bhāgīrathī is the Gaṅgā. De, however, identifies Sītā with Jaxartes (p. 181) and Cakṣus with Oxus or Amudariya (p. 43).

the salt ocean. All these (seven currents) offer devotion to the Varṣa called Hima.

41-43. These seven streams issuing from the Bindu lake sanctify several countries mainly occupied by Mlecchas and approach a place where Indra showers the rain. They are as follows: Sirindhras, Kuntalas, Cīnas, Barbaras. Yavasas, Druhas, Ruṣāṇas, Kuṇindas and Aṅgalokavaras. The river Sītā divides the desert of Sindhu into two and flows into the western ocean.

44. The river Cakṣu flows through these countries: Cīnamarus (Chinese desert ?), Naṅgaṇas, Sarvamūlikas, Sādhras, Tuṣāras, Taṁpākas, Pahlavas, Daradas, and Śakas. It then falls into the ocean.

45-49. The Gaṅgā sanctifies the auspicious Aryan countries: Daradas, Kāśmīras, Gāndhāras, Varapas, Hradas, Śivapauras, Indrahāsas, Vedātiṣ, Visarjayas, Saindhavas, Randhrakarakas, Bhramaras, Ābhīras, Rohakas, Śunāmukhas, Ūrdhvamanus, the places frequented by Siddhas and Cāraṇas, Gandharvas, Yakṣas, Rākṣasas, Vidyādharas and Uragas (Serpents), Kalāpa-grāmakas, Pāradas, Sīgaṇas, Khasas, Kirātas, Pulindas, Kurus, Bharatas, Pañcālas, Kāśi, Mātsyas, Magadhas, Aṅgas, Brahmottaras, Vaṅgas and Tām (r) aliptas.

50. Obstructed by the Vindhya mountain, it falls into the southern sea. The holy river Āhlādinī (one of its eastern branches) flows to the east.

51-55. It inundates the habitations of the Niṣādas, Dhīvaras, Ṛśikas, Nīlamukhas, Keralas, Uṣṭrakarṇas, Kirātas, Kālodaras, Vivarṇas. Then it vanishes into the expanse of the sea towards the east. The branch Pāvanī also flows to the east sanctifying Apathas, Indradyumna lake, Kharapathas, Indraśaṅkupathas, the middle of the garden Maskara and Kuthaprāvaraṇa. Near Indradvīpa, it enters the salt ocean.

56-58. The branch Nalinī flows to the east sanctifying the Tomaras, Haṁsamārgas and Hūhukas. Rising in the eastern lands and piercing through mountains in several places, it reaches Karṇaprāvaraṇas and Aśvamukhas. After passing through the desert mountains, it reaches Vidyādharas. It flows into the great ocean at the Nemimaṇḍala Koṣṭha.

59. The branches and tributaries of these rivers are

hundreds and thousands. They fall into the ocean as the water is showered by Indra.

60. On the banks of the river Vasvokasā, on the peak Hariśṛṅga famous for its fragrant waters, lives the scholar Kauberaka of self-control.

61. Yajñopeta, Sumahān, Amitaujas and Suvikrama are his attendants. They are on par with him. Kauberaka is surrounded by scholarly Brahma-rākṣasas of the family of Agastya.

62. The prosperity of the inhabitants of mountains should be known thus. Through mutual cooperation their prosperity arising from Dharma (Virtue), Artha (Wealth) and Kāma (Love) becomes doubled.

63. Behind Hemakūṭa there is the lake Sāyana.[1] The rivers Manasvinī and Jyotiṣmatī emerge from this lake.

64. They flow into the eastern and western oceans respectively. On the excellent mountain Niṣadha is the lake Viṣṇupada.[2]

65. The two rivers, Gāndharvī and Nanvalī rise from it. There is a great eddy called Candraprabha rising to the west of Meru.

66. The holy river of Jaṁbū juice, the source of the splendid gold (called Jāṁbūnada) flows from here. The lake Payoda,[3] as splendid as the white lotus, is on the mount Nīla.

67. It is from this lake that the rivers Puṇḍarīkā and Payodā have their source. The holy lake Uttara-mānasa rises from mount Śveta.

68-69. The two rivers Jyotsnā and Mṛgakāntā rise from this (lake). The holy lake known as Rudrakānta is[4] full of

1. This lake known as Nāga in other Purāṇas is the Lake 'Naktso' which with Pangong Tso forms an extensive water sheet—AGP 71.

2. Now known as Lake Chakmaktin, the source of the Wakhan river which flows west in the land of Gandharvas. It is in the Wakhan region that mounts Meru and Niṣadha come closer to each other—AGP 71.

3. M. Ali identifies this with the Kara Kul of northern Pamirs. It is a twin lake mentioned as Payoda and Puṇḍarīka (like lakes Mānasa Sarovar and Rākṣasa Tāl in the South Kailasa region). Hence this twin lake Kara Kul is aptly called Uttara Mānasa.

4. M. Ali believes that the lakes in vv. 68-70 were in Siberia—AGP 72.

honey and lotuses and is agitated by fishes and birds. It abounds in wish-yielding trees. It is pleasant and sweet like honey. It is reported that it is created by Śiva.

70. There are twelve famous lakes full of lotuses, fishes and birds. They are named as Rudrājayas and they are (big) like seas.

71. From these lakes there emerge the rivers Śāntā and Mādhvī. There is no rainfall in the Kiṁpuruṣa continent.

72-73. Excellent rivers flow here with waters from the subterranean regions. These blessed rivers flow through the mountains Ṛṣabha, Dundubhi, Dhūmra and Mahāgiri, to the east and fall into the briny sea. Others flow to the north over the mountains Candrakaṅka, Prāṇa, Mahān and Agni and merge into the great ocean.

74. The mountains Somaka, Varāha and Nārada extend to the west upto the briny sea.

75-76. The great mountains Cakra, Balāhaka and Maināka extend to the southern ocean. In between Candra and Maināka, to the south, there is the great fire Saṁvartaka which consumes the waters of the ocean. It is known as Aurva and Vaḍavāmukha.

77-78. The twelve mountains entered the ocean because they feared Mahendra who would have cut off their wings. What is seen reflected in the form of a black hare on the white (orb of the) moon is the replica of Bhāratavarṣa divided into nine regions. It is seen in the moon that rises here and not elsewhere.

79-80. These countries become more and more flourishing in respect of good qualities, health, longevity and magnitude based on virtue, love and wealth. Different kinds and castes of people and other living beings endowed with good qualities live in the different countries. Thus the Earth holds the entire universe.

CHAPTER FORTYEIGHT

Countries of the Jaṁbūdvīpa

Sūta said :

1-4. Know that there is an ocean ten thousand Yojanas in extent to the south of Bhārata. There is a country in it three thousand Yojanas long and one-third of it in breadth. It abounds in fruits and flowers. The regional mountain (*Kula-parvata*) thereof is Vidyutvān,[1] the innumerable peaks of which embellish the land. There are thousands of rivers there, with clean and tasty water. The lakes contain pure water.

5-7. In the many long and wide caves, and crevasses of that mountain there are many prosperous jolly men and women of various shapes and features. In the many spacious and long and wide cavities (valleys?) are established hundreds and thousands of cities built into the mountain. These houses are joined to one another and have only a door each.

8. The subjects thereof have long beards and moustache. They are black and shining like clouds. They have the maximum life span of eighty years.

9. They eat fruits and roots and live like monkeys. Like cattle, they follow promiscuous, unconcealed sexual habits. They are devoid of bodily and mental purity and they have no fixed rules or conventions.

10. That continent is full of worthless men. Similarly other countries and islets shall be known in due order.

11-14. The groups of islands known as Peacock islands are extending to twenty, thirty, fifty, sixty, eighty and hundred Yojanas. There are a few, extending to a thousand Yojanas. They are long, wide and full of various living beings. Besides Jaṁbū-dvīpa there are six islands. These islands are famous all over the earth for their mines of gems and precious stones. They are known as Aṅga, Yama, Malaya, Śaṅkha, Kuśa and Varāha[2] islands.

---

1. The Vidyutvān mountain is obviously the Arakan Yoma of Burma. The islands dotting the Arakan coast are mentioned in vv. 11-12—AGP 178-179.

2. These are the lands around India.

15. Know ye that the Aṅga Dvīpa[1] comprises islands, and many people of the Mleccha tribes live there. That continent is very large.

16. There are mines of gems, corals and gold in that land here. It is variegated with rivers, mountains and forests. It resembles the vast expanse of the briny sea.

17-18. There is a mountain called Cakragiri full of many rivulets and caves. The caves afford shelter to various living beings. That great mountain spreads on to many places in the Nāga land with its extremities reaching the lord of rivers, the abode of serpents (ocean).

19. What is called Yamadvīpa[2] is also full of mines of gems. There is a mountain called Dyutimān, embellished with minerals and is the source of many rivers and gold (mines).

20-21. Similarly, the Malaya Dvīpa[3] is also surrounded by the ocean. It is the source of gems, jewels and gold. It is very prosperous. It is the place of origin of sandalwood and is surrounded by gulfs (*lit.* seas). Many kinds of Mleccha tribes live there. There are many rivers and mountains.

22. The glorious mountain Malaya is the source of origin of silver. This excellent moutain is famous as Mahāmalaya.

23. It is known as the second Mandara mountain. The abode of Agastya, bowed to by Devas and Asuras, is also there.

24-25. There is another mountain Kañcanapāda which is a second Malaya. There are many hermitages there, resorted to by pious persons and full of hedges of grass and Soma plants. It abounds in flowers and fruits of all kinds. It excels even the heaven. On festive occasions, on all Parvan days, heaven descends to that place.

26-28. There is a great city Laṅkā on the beautiful ridge and peak of the mountain Trikūṭa decorated with different

---

1. Verses 16-18 describe Aṅga-dvīpa. Ali identifies it with the Malaya Peninsula due to pointers such as Mleccha population, gold, corals (AGP 179).

2. Yama-dvīpa is tentatively traced to Sumatra, Malaya, and Java.

3. M. Ali identifies it with the southernmost peninsular India—AGP 179-180.

minerals. The mountain is many Yojanas in height. Its variegated precipices and caves resemble houses. The city has gold ramparts and archways. There are many mansions and palaces with turrets and gables of variegated colour. It is a hundred Yojanas long and thirty Yojanas broad. It is flourishing and the people there are happy and gay.

29. It is the abode of noble Rākṣasas who can assume various forms as they please. Know that to be the habitation of the enemies of Devas, proud of their strength. Free from all harassments, this city is inaccessible to human beings.

30. In that island, on the eastern shore of the sea there is Gokarṇa, the great shrine of Śaṅkara.

31. Śaṅkhadvīpa[1] is ruled as a single kingdom extending to a hundred Yojanas. It is the abode of many Mleccha tribes.

32. The mountain Śaṅkhagiri has the lustre of white conch-shell. It is sacred and is the source of many gems. It is resorted to by pious persons.

33. From this mountain rises the holy river Śankhanāgā. Śaṅkhamukha, king of Nāgas, has his abode there.

34. Similarly, the Kumūdadvīpa[2] is brightened by variegated flowers. Full of many villages, it is the source of many gems and jewels.

35. There the blessed sister of Mahādeva, named Kumudā, the destroyer of evil persons, is worshipped by the people.

36-38. Similarly in the island called Varāha[3], there is a beautiful mountain known as Varāha containing many caves, crevasses and rivulets. The island is densely populated by different Mleccha tribes and people of different castes. There are many habitations and cities flourishing and prosperous with wealth and foodgrains. It is full of righteous people. The rivers, mountains and forests thereof contain various kinds of fruits and flowers of various colours.

---

1. Śaṅkha-dvīpa is Zangistan of Arab geographers. It represents a part of the eastern shore of Africa from Abyssinia to Madagascar.

2. Kumuda-dvīpa or Kuśadvīpa identifiable with western Asia, Arabian Peninsula—AGP 183.

3. Varāha-dvīpa is identifiable with 'Horn of Africa'. Scholars differ about these identifications.

39. A great river known as Vārāhī emerges from that mountain. Its waters are tasty. There are holy centres on its banks. This river is bestower of bliss.

40. O Brāhmaṇa, the people bow to Viṣṇu the powerful deity in the form of a Boar. They do not honour any other god.

41. Thus the six southern islands of the Bhārata country have been described in detail.

42. In this single Bhārata there are many islands separated by the ocean. They have been divided into various parts.

43. Thus have been described in details the four great continents adorned with islands interspersed in between as well as Jaṁbūdvīpa together with its adjacent islands.

CHAPTER FORTYNINE

Description of Plakṣa Dvipa and other Dvipas

Sūta said :

1. O excellent Brāhmaṇas, I shall describe the Plakṣa-dvīpa[1] precisely but succinctly. Listen to it as I narrate it exactly.

2. Its extent is twice that of Jaṁbūdvīpa. Its circumference (perimeter) is thrice its breadth. This briny sea is surrounded by that continent.

3. The people over there are righteous and have a great longevity. There is neither famine nor fear of old age and ailments.

---

1. The dvīpa derives its name from Plakṣa tree (a fig tree) (v. 26). It indicates Mediterranean climate V.V. Iyer identifies Plakṣa with Greece and adjoining lands in 'The Seven Dvipas of the Purāṇas', *Quarterly Journ. of Mythic Society* (London) XV. 62. 75. M. Ali identifies it 'without hesitation' as the basin of the Mediterranean (AGP 41). Placia, a town in Mysia is traceable to Plakṣa.

4. There are seven mountains and seven rivers there also. They are splendid sources of precious stones. I shall mention their names.

5. In the seven continents, Plakṣa and others, there are seven great and steep mountains established in all directions.

6. I shall first mention the seven great mountains in the Plakṣa Dvīpa. The first is Gomedaka resembling a cloud. The country too is named Gomedaka after the name of this mountain.

7. The second mountain named Candra is full of medicinal herbs. For the preparation of *Amṛta* (nectar) (gods) Aśvinī Kumāras planted the medicinal herbs here.

8. The third is named Nārada. It is an impassable mountain of great height. It was on this mountain that the sages Nārada and Parvata were born.

9. The fourth mountain is called Dundubhi. On this mountain, formerly a drum was beaten by the Devas, the sound of which killed living beings. The Śālmala tree by its drum Rajjudāra full of ropes slays the Asuras.

10. The fifth is named Somaka where the nectar was collected formerly by Devas. It was taken away by Garuḍa for his mother.

11. The sixth is named Sumanas and also Ṛṣabha. The demon Hiraṇyākṣa was killed by Varāha on this mountain.

12. The seventh mountain is Vaibhrāja. It is great and glittering like crystal. Since it shines with rays, it is known as Vaibhrāja.

13-14. I shall mention the names of the countries of these mountains in due order. The first country is Gomeda. It is a peaceful country (where fear is quelled.) The country of Candra is Śikhara; that of Nārada is Sukhodaya; that of Dundubhi is Ānanda; that of Somaka is Śiva; that of Kṣemaka is Ṛṣabha; and that of Vaibhrāja is Dhruva.

15. In these countries Devas, Gandharvas, Siddhas, and Cāraṇas reside, and are seen playing about.

16. The rivers flowing into the sea, in this continent, are seven, one for each country. I shall mention the names of these rivers known as the seven Gaṅgās.

17. These rivers along with thousands of their tributaries flow (towards the ocean). They are always in flood with abundant water, as the rain-god Indra showers (rains) profusely.

18-19. The people in these realms drink from these rivers and are delighted. The seven rivers are Śubhā, Śāntavahā, Pramodā, Śivā, Ānandā, Dhruvā and Kṣemakā. There the people are righteous. They observe the duties and rules of their castes and stages of life.

20. They are all free from ailments. They are strong and never suffer from illness. Among them there is no (influence of) *Utsarpiṇi* (evolutionary) and *Avasarpiṇī*[1] (involutionary) eras.

21. There is no division of time based on the peculiarities of the four Yugas. The condition of Tretā Yuga is perpetually prevailing there.

22. In the five continents beginning with Plakṣa, the activities of the seasons accord with those of the (particular) continent.

23. The people live for five thousand years. They are handsome, well-dressed, strong, and free from sickness.

24. In the continents beginning with Plakṣa and ending with Śāka, happiness, longevity, strength, beauty, health and virtue are exquisite.

25. Plakṣadvīpa is large and glorious. It abounds in riches and foodgrains. It is endowed with divine medicinal herbs and fruits. It has many kinds of plants and herbs.

26. There are thousands of domestic and wild animals there. O excellent Brāhmaṇas, the details of Plakṣa Dvīpa are covered by the details of Jambū Dvīpa. (Just as Jambū Dvīpa is named after Jambū tree) Plakṣa Dvīpa derives its name from the Plakṣa tree thereof.

27-28. The deity (Śiva) is worshipped in the centre of this continent. The continent is surrounded by the sea of sugarcane-juice. Thus the situation of Plakṣa Dvīpa with its extensiveness (etc.) has been explained. Now listen to the description of Śālmala Dvīpa in brief and in due order.

---

1. This Purāṇa uses the Jaina terms '*Utsarpiṇī*' and '*Avasarpiṇī* for time cycles, the former indicating 'ascending time cycle' and the latter 'descending one' (MW, p. 105).

29. The third among the Dvīpas is the excellent Dvīpa Śālmala.[1] The ocean of sugarcane juice is encircled by the Śālmala Dvīpa. It is twice Plakṣa Dvīpa in extent.

30. There also, in its countries, there are seven mountains and rivers. They should be known as sources of precious stones.

31. The first mountain is named Kumuda. It is as refulgent as the sun. Its peaks are rocky and abound in all minerals.

32. The second mountain there is famous by the name Unnata. It envelops the heaven by its peaks, full of yellow orpiment.

33. The third mountain thereof is known as Balāhaka. With its peaks of collyrium, it stands enveloping the sky.

34. The fourth is named Droṇa[2] where the strong medicinal herbs *Viśalyakaraṇī* (remover of darts or splinters) and *Mṛtasañjīvanī* (that which re-suscitates the dead) are found.

35. The fifth mountain is Kaṅka of excessive height. It is covered with trees and creepers endowed with divine flowers and fruits.

36. The sixth mountain is Mahiṣa resembling clouds. A fire, born of water and known as Mahiṣa, exists there.

37. The seventh mountain is called Kakudman. Indra himself showers innumerable gems there. This is the procedure to be performed in Prājāpatya rite in honour of Prajāpati.

38. There are seven mountains in the Śālmala Dvīpa. They are bedecked in jewels. I shall now describe the seven auspicious countries (*Varṣas*) associated with them. The first (*Varṣa*) is Śveta connected with mount Kumuda, and the second is Lohita connected with Mt. Unnata.

39-40. The Varṣa associated with Balāhaka and Jīmūta and that with Droṇa is Harita, that of Kaṅka is Vaidyuta, that of Mahiṣa and that of Kakuda is Suprabha. These are the seven countries and their seven mountains. Now know the rivers there.

---

1. From its description in vv. 29-45, M. Ali identifies it with tropical Africa bordering on the Indian Ocean, including Madagascar—AGP 45.

2. Mount Droṇa is noted for its medicinal plants. VR vi. 50.31 locates it in Kṣīrasāgara. De (p.58) identifies it with mount Doonagiri in Kumaun while it is located here in the Śālmaladvīpa (land of silk cotton trees).

41. Pāni, Toyā, Vitṛṣṇā, Candrā, Śukrā, Vimocanī and the seventh (river) Nivṛtti are the rivers of their respective countries.

42. There are hundreds and thousands of adjacent rivers which cannot be enumerated. They are to be believed (taken for granted) by one who wishes to know them.

43-44. Thus the locus of Śālmala Dvīpa has been described to you. Like the great Plakṣa tree in Plakṣa Dvīpa, there is a Śālmali (silk-cotton) tree in the middle of the Dvīpa which is named after it. It is surrounded by the ocean of wine equal to Śālmala (dvīpa) in extent.

45. O knowers of Dharma, now listen to the description of the people in the northern continents. Understand as I relate to you in accordance with what I have heard.

46. I shall describe the fourth continent Kuśa Dvīpa[1] succinctly. The ocean of wine is surrounded on all sides by this continent (Kuśa).

47. It is twice the extent of Śālmala. There are seven mountains there. Listen as they are being described to you.

48-50. The first mountain in the Kuśa Dvīpa is known as Vidrumoccaya; the second is Hema; the third is Dyutimān, a mountain resembling clouds; the fourth is Puṣpavān; the fifth is Kuśeśaya; the sixth is Hari; and the seventh is Mandara. The word *Manda* means waters and *Mandara* means that which splits the waters.

51-52. The distance between these mountains is twice their magnitude. The first country is Udbhida; the second is Veṇumaṇḍala; the third is Svairathākāra; the fourth is Lavaṇa; the fifth is Dhṛtimat; the sixth is Prabhākara; and the seventh is Kapila. These are the seven countries and mountains.

53. In these *Varṣas* Devas, Gandharvas, Prabhas, Prajāpatis are seen residing and sporting about.

54. In these countries there are neither robbers nor Mlecchas. The people are mostly fair in complexion. They die according to seniority in age.

---

1. After detailing the main features of Kuśadvīpa, M. Ali identifies it with tropical grasslands such as Iran, Iraq and the fringing lands of the hot desert (AGP 40-41).

55. Here also are the seven rivers which are auspicious and which dispel sins. The chief of them are Pavitrā, Śantati, Dyutigarbhā and Mahī.

56. Hundreds and thousand of others are known as their branches. They flow on as Indra showers in plenty.

57. The Kuśa Dvīpa is surrounded by the ocean of ghee. In extent it is equal to Kuśa Dvīpa.

58. Thus the position of Kuśadvīpa has been described to you. Now I shall explain the extent of Krauñca Dvīpa.[1]

59. It is remembered to have twice the area of Kuśa Dvīpa. The ocean of ghee is encircled by this continent.

60. In this continent the chief mountain is Krauñca. The next after Krauñca is Vāmana and the next after Vāmana is Andhakāra.

61. After Andhakāra comes Divāvṛt. After Divāvṛt comes Divinda.

62. After Divinda is the great mountain Puṇḍarīka. After Puṇḍarīka is the mountain Dundubhisvana.

63. These are seven bejewelled mountains of Krauñca Dvīpa. They abound in fruit trees and a number of creepers.

64. The Varṣa mountains are twice in height as compared with the previous ones. Now I shall mention the names of the Varṣas. Listen and understand them.

65-66. The main land-tract of the Krauñca mountain is Kuśalin; that of Vāmana is Manonuga. Beyond Manonuga is the third land tract Uṣṇa. Beyond Uṣṇa is Prāvaraka and beyond Prāvaraka is Andhakāra. Beyond Andhakāra is Muni Deśa.

67. Beyond Muni Deśa is Dundubhisvana full of Siddhas and Cāraṇas. There the people are mostly fair in complexion.

68. There also the rivers are seven in number one for each country. They are Gaurī, Kumudvatī, Sandhyā, Rātri, Manojavā, Khyāti and Punḍarīkā. These seven appear as Gaṅgā divided into seven rivers.

69. Other rivers flow into these or nearby and meet the ocean. They are large and flow with great volume of water.

---

1. M. Ali examines the description of this Dvīpa from different sources and identifies it with the basin of the Black Sea (AGP, 45-46).

70. The glorious Krauñca Dvīpa is surrounded by the ocean of whey which is equal to Krauñcadvīpa in extent.

71-72. Thus Plakṣa and other continents have been briefly described to you. It is impossible to describe the growth, decay (creation and annihilation) and other details of these continents even in hundreds of years.

73. I shall henceforth explain the features of the entire Śāka Dvīpa[1] exactly as they are. Listen as I recount them precisely.

74. Its extent is twice that of Krauñca Dvīpa. It encircles the ocean of whey.

75. All the countries there are very sacred. People die only after a long life. There is neither famine nor fear of old age and sickness.

76. There also are seven bejewelled mountains which as well as the rivers are the sources of gems and precious stones. Listen to their names.

77. The first mountain, called Udaya, extends to the east. It is golden and is the abode of divine sages and Gandharvas. Hence it is like Meru.

78-79. Clouds rise and pass pouring down showers. There is a great mountain Jaladhāra where Indra showers plenty of water. There in the rainy season people get ample showers.

80. There is mountain Raivataka raised by god Brahmā. It is here that the Star Revatī is always established in the heavens.

81. Beyond that there is a very great mountain called Śyāma. It was due to it that people got dark complexion from the outset.

82. Next is the massive mountain Astagiri, full of silver. The next mountain is Ambikeya, an impassable snowclad mountain.

83. Next to Ambikeya is Ramya where all medicinal herbs grow. It is called Kesarī and the winds blow on it.

---

1. M. Ali identifies this with the monsoon lands of Asia where teak abounds, viz. Malaya, Siam, Indi-China (AGP 39), while De (pp. 172-173) identifies it with Tartary including Turkestan in central Asia.

84-86. Listen to the names of the countries of these mountains in due order. The country (*Varṣa*) of the mountain Udaya is Udaya well known as Jalada. The second Varṣa, that of Jaladhāra is Sukumāra; that of Raivata is Kaumāra; that of Śyāma is Maṇīcaka; the splendid Varṣa of Asta is Kusumottara; of Ambikeya is Modaka; and that of Kesaras is Mahādruma.

87. The extent, magnitude, length and breadth of this continent are as those of Śāka dvīpa (?) A great tree called Śāka (teak) grows in its centre and is worshipped by the people.

88. Devas, Gandharvas, Siddhas and Cāraṇas are visible and play about here in the midst of people.

89. The people (in the countries thereof) are virtuous and observe (the distinctive rules of) their respective four castes (*Varṇas*). There are seven rivers flowing to the sea, one in each Varṣa and these seven rivers are remembered as the seven streams of Gaṅgā.

90-91. The first river is known by the names Sukumārī, Gaṅgā, Śivajalā; and Anutaptā, the second is known as Kumārī, Siddhā and Satī; the third is designated as Nandā and Pārvatī.

92. The fourth is Śivetikā which is also remembered as Tridivā; the fifth is known as Ikṣu as well as Kratu.

93. These seven great Gaṇgās of auspicious waters sanctify all the people residing in Śāka dvīpa every year.

94. There are thousands of others rivers joining them. They have abundant of waters since Indra showers rain profusely.

95. It is impossible to enumerate their names and magnitudes. These excellents river are very holy. The joyous people drink from them.

96-97. O Śaṁśapāyana, this continent is very extensive. It is like a wheel, covered by rivers and cloud-like mountains wonderful and variegated with minerals and decorated with jewels and corals. The cities are of various shapes. They abound in flourishing and prosperous people.

98. The continent is full of trees laden with. flowers and fruits. It is flourishing with wealth and foodgrains. It is surrounded by the ocean of milk equal in size to it.

99-100. The land-tracts amongst those mountains are seven in number. They are holy and splendid. The people thereof abide by the rules of castes and stages of life and admit no mixture of castes or stages of life. Since they do not swerve from the path of virtue, they are invariably happy.

101. They are neither greedy nor deceptive and neither jealous nor malicious. There is no loss of fortitude nor adverse results. Everything is natural with them.

102. No tax is raised. No punishment is meted out. There is none to punish. They know of virtue by natural righteousness. They protect one another.

103. This much and no more can be mentioned about the residents of this continent.

I shall now describe the seventh continent Puṣkara. Please listen.

104. The ocean of milk is surrounded by Puṣkara Dvīpa,[1] which is twice the Śāka Dvīpa in extent.

105. There is only one glorious mountain called Mahāśila having lofty peaks full of variegated jewels.

106. This great mountain with wonderful and variegated ridges and precipices stands in the eastern half of the Dvīpa. Its circumference is twentyfive thousand Yojanas.

107-109. Its height is thirty-four thousand Yojanas. The excellent Mānasa mountain encircles half this Dvīpa. It stands on the seashore looking like the newly risen moon. Its height is fifty thousand Yojanas. Its girth too is so much. This mountain Mānasa is on the western half of the Dvīpa.

110. In fact the two mountains constitute but a single mountain with peaks and ridges divided into two. It is surrounded by the ocean of fresh water.

111-112. The whole mountain-range spreads over the full extent of Puṣkara Dvīpa. There are two holy and splendid provinces in that Dvīpa on either side of the mountain Mānasa. The Mahāvīta Varṣa is exterior to the mountain while Dhātakī is the interior.

113. The people there live upto ten thousand years with splendid health and happiness. They have attained mental Siddhis.

---

1. M. Ali identifies Puṣkara Dvīpa with Japan, Manchuria and south-eastern Siberia (AGP 42), while De (p. 163) regards it as the portion of Central Asia north of the Oxus (including western Tartary). He regards Puskara as the Sanskritisation of Bhushkara or Bokhara.

114. In the two countries (*Varṣas*) the forms and features and the span of life are similar. There is no distinction of high and low among them. In appearance and conduct of life all of them are equal.

115. None defrauds (anyone); none is jealous. There are neither thieves nor fear nor imprisonment nor punishment, nor greed nor illegal acceptance of gifts.

116. There is neither truth nor falsehood nor virtue nor evil nor the rules of caste nor the stages of life. There is no trade, no cattle breeding, no business enterprise.

117. The lore of the three Vedas, the system of civil and military administrarion, acts of service to others in return for payment, wounding others with harsh words or sharp implements—these are absent in the two Varṣas of Puṣkara.

118. There are no rivers, no rainfall, neither bitter cold nor oppressive heat, no vegetation, no water, no mountains, no rivulets.

119-120. The season is perpetually the same as in Northern Kurus. The people are happy, devoid of old age and exhaustion. This is the condition in Dhātakī and Mahāvīta countries. Thus the entire situation in Puṣkara Dvīpa has been nararted.

121. Puṣkara is surrounded by the ocean of sweet water equal in extent to that continent.

122. The seven continents are encircled by the seven oceans. The ocean immediately adjacent to a continent encircles it.

123. The relative increase in the size of the continents and oceans should be known thus. Since they have abundant increase of waters, the oceans are called *Samudras*.

124. Since in the land-tracts the four groups of people and sages live, they are called Varṣas. They afford happiness to the people.

125. The word *Ṛṣi* is derived from the root √*Ṛṣ*. The root √*Vṛṣ* means the continuance of energy. Since the land-tracts afford continuance of energy they have the designation *Varṣa*.[1]

126. In the bright half, when the moon waxes, there is

1. A Popular etymology of *Varṣa*—'a continent'.

high tide in the ocean. When the moon wanes in the dark half and sets there is low tide.

127. In the bright fortnight, the ocean gets filled with water by itself. In the dark fortnight, the ocean recedes by itself.

128. Just as water in a cooking pot boils up by its contact with fire, similarly water in the vast ocean swells in quantity and magnitude.

129. The increase and decrease of water is of fixed quantity, neither more nor less in the bright and dark fortnights at the rise and setting of the moon. The increase and decrease in the ocean again is the result of the waxing and the waning of the moon.

130. It is observed that the increase and decrease of (the level of water in) the ocean is upto five hundred and ten *aṅgulas*. This (increase and decrease) is seen (occurring) on the parvan days.

131. The term *dvīpa* (island) is so called on account of waters being on either side.[1] They are surrounded on all sides. As it is a store-house of waters, the ocean is called *Udadhi*.

132. Mountains without knots and peaks are *Giris*. Those with knots are *Parvatas*. Hence in the Plakṣa Dvīpa, Gomeda, having knots is called a *Parvata*.

133. The great Śālmali (silk-cotton) tree is worshipped in the Śālmala Dvīpa. In the Kuśa Dvīpa, a stump of Kuśa grass is worshipped. Hence the continent is called by its name (viz. Kuśa).

134. In the Krauñca Dvīpa, the mountain Krauñca stands in its centre. The tree in Śāka Dvipa is *Śāka* (teak). (Hence) the *dvīpa* (continent) is named after it.

135. In the Puṣkara Dvīpa, the Nyagrodha tree is worshipped by the people. The great lord in Puṣkara is Brahmā, the lord of the three worlds.

136. Brahmā, the Prajāpati, lives there along with Sādhyas. The Devas numbering thirtythree, along with sages worship him. The most excellent of the Devas is worshipped there.

1. Verses 131-105 give explanatory etymologies of *dvīpa* 'an island', *udadhi* 'Sea', *giri*, *parvata* 'a mountain' and explain the names of Dvipas.

137-138. Various gems and precious stones are obtained in Jaṁbū Dvīpa. In all these continents people observe truth, celibacy and self-control. Thereby, their health and span of life is increased twofold.

139. In the above-mentioned two sub-continents of Puṣkara Dvīpa, god Brahmā himself protects the subjects who are (as if) adorned with good people.

140. The supreme ruler Brahmā, the lord of three worlds, holds the rod (*Daṇḍa*) of chastisement (to govern them). He is their lord, Viṣṇu, Śiva, father and grandfather.

141. (Their) food comes to them automatically without any effort on their part. The people always take that nutritious food of six tastes.

142. The great ocean of sweet water encircles the Puṣkara Dvīpa on all sides.

143. There is a great world beyond it. The ground is golden and flat as if it is a single slab. It is twice (?) in extent.

144. Beyond that there is a mountain. At the end of the boundary, there is a circular horizon. It is both lighted (on the hither-part) and dark (on the rest). It is called *Lokāloka.*

145. Its height is ten thousand Yojanas. Its hitherward side is bright and its side beyond is dim (dark).

146. Its breadth is as much (as its height). It can rise above the earth (to any height) according to its will.

The word '*loka*' in '*āloka*' is understood in the sense of illumination (the bright interior side) and indicates the world. And '*Nirāloka*' is the dark, external side.

147. The illuminated part extends to (the world or the area where people live). Beyond that, it is surrounded by water. The *Nirāloka* (the dark part and portion beyond) covers he Cosmic Egg.

148-149. Within the Cosmic Egg there are the worlds, viz. Bhūr i.e. the earth consisting of seven continents, Bhuvar, Svar, Mahar, Jana, Tapas and Satya. This much constitutes the world which can be known. Beyond that, there is the end of the world.

150-151. The cosmos is shaped like the new moon on the western horizon (at the beginning of the bright half) when the sun is in the Aquarius Zodiac.

There are thousands of crores Cosmic Eggs like this, above, below and on all sides. They are caused and pervaded by the seven effects of Prakṛti (viz. the elements, *Mahat* and *Bhūtādi*).

152. They support one another. The later is ten times bigger than the former. They are caused and pervaded by one another.[1]

153. All round this Cosmic Egg, there is a 'solid' sea. With its waters it holds the Cosmic Egg.

154. Outside the solid water, on all its sides and above, the 'solid' fire holds and supports it.

155. The fire stands like an iron ball circular and globular in shape. It is supported and held all round by solid wind. The solid wind supports the ether as well.

156. *Bhūtādi* (Cosmic Ego) holds and supports the Ether. *Mahat* (Cosmic Intellect) supports the Cosmic Ego and is itself pervaded and supported by the infinite Unmanifest (*Prakṛti*).

157. The infinite Unmanifest (*Prakṛti*) is subtle and divided into ten. It is infinite, immobile (with no Soul). It has neither beginning nor end.

158. It is beyond everything. It is terrible. It has no support. It is free from ailments. It is many thousand Yojanas in distance. It is covered with darkness (*Tamas*).

159. It is darkness itself. It is devoid of light. It is unlimited. It does not occupy space. Even Devas cannot comprehend it. It is devoid of activity.

160. There is a great, famous, refulgent shrine of Śiva at the end of darkness and the Ether and hence at the very border. It is well-known for its splendour.

161. They say that spot is inaccessible even to Devas. It lies in the premises of the great lord of Devas.

162. In the universe, the worlds getting the light and heat of the sun and the moon, are called *Lokas*. There is no doubt about this.

---

1. Verses 152ff give the Purāṇic concept of the seven protective 'sheaths' round the universe (Brahmāṇḍa)? The influence of Sāṅkhya categories is obvious.

163. There are seven worlds beneath and seven above the Earth. O Brāhmaṇas, there are seven pathways of the wind and god Brahmā's abode.

164. From Pātāla to heaven there is a fivefold course. This is the extent of the Universe. This is the ocean of the worldly existence.

165. The activity of the Universe with neither beginning nor end goes on like this arising from different types and groups of people. This unsteady activity of the Universe is really wonderful.

166. The physical creation of this is very extensive. It cannot be comprehended even by the blessed Siddhas who know things even beyond the scope of sense-organs.

167-168. O excellent Brāhmaṇas! There is no limit, decline or end to the magnitude of (the elements, viz.) Earth, Water, Fire, Wind, *Mahat*, *Tamas*, the infinite, omnipresent Lord Īśvara. While enumerating the names of the Lord (Śiva), I have mentioned this before.

169. The Lord who is called by the name Śiva has been glorified to you. He pervades everything and is worshipped in all places.

170. He is worshipped on the earth, in rasātala, ether, wind, fire, seas and heaven. There is no doubt in this.

171. He is to be realized through penance as the Lord of great splendor. This great God, the great Yogin has divided himself in various forms. He, the Lord of the worlds, is worshipped in various ways in all the worlds.

172. Thus the worlds orginating from one another support one another by the relationship of the supporter and the supported or as the effects of their cause.

173. The elements earth etc. are the evolutes covered up by one another. They enter into one another, the lesser into the greater.

174. Since they penetrate one another, they have attained stability. Formerly they were without special features. But by intermingling they became possessed of speciality. The earth, fire and the wind, these three are separately and accurately ascertained.

175. Their accurate ascertainment is specially noticed by the decline in attributes and essence. The accurate determination of the rest is not observable due to their subtleness.

176. *Āloka* is beyond all the *Bhūtas* (elements). They are discernible separately only in the illuminated Ether (*Ākāśa*).

177. Just as in a big vessel smaller vessels are placed and are mutually supported by it though separate from each other, similarly the separateness of the elements is internal within the illuminated Ether (Ākāśa).

178. All these four elements are consecutively bigger, the later bigger than the former. The creation can function as long as the elements exist.

179. The perfection (creation) of creatures is regarded as being within (i.e. based on) *Bhūtas* (elements). The creation of effects cannot take place without *Bhūtas.*

180. The *Bhūtas* being of the nature of effects are restricted. The entities e.g. the *Mahat* (Cosmic Intellegence etc.) are of the nature of causes.

181. Thus, O Brāhmaṇas, the arrangement of this earth with seven continents and oceans has been explained to you along with their divisions precisely as they are.

182-183. The cosmic form of *Pradhāna* (the Unmanifest Nature) which has been described (lit. enumerated) to you by its extents and zones, is only a partial modification. Its cosmic form is the abode of the Lord to whom belongs the whole Universe. In this way, the elements have interpenetrated each other.

184. Only this much of established arrangement (of the Universe) can be explained by me. O King, only this much need be heard in regard to the constitution and arrangement of the world.

185. The seven *Prakṛtis* support one another. There are many *Prakṛtis* above and below and on all sides. I shall explain them to a little extent.

186. O excellent Brāhmaṇas, now I shall describe the position of the luminaries, the boundaries, the horizon and sub-horizon of the earth.

CHAPTER FIFTY

The Nether-worlds : Manifestation of the Luminaries*

1. Understand the magnitude of the earth below and above. The earth, wind, sky, water and the fifth (element) fire are proclaimed as infinite primary elements which are all-pervading.

2-3. The earth is the mother of all beings. It is called *Dharā* as it sustains all animals and living beings. It is spread over with various countries and is teeming with many towns and abodes. It has many (big) rivers, rivulets and mountains. It is crowded with all classes of people. (Hence) this extremely extensive goddess earth is praised as infinite.

4-5. Water is present in rivers, oceans, small receptacles such as ponds or puddles, mountains, firmament and the bowels of the earth. Hence water should be regarded as infinite. Similarly, the element of fire pervades all the worlds. It is said to be infinite, all-pervasive and born of everything.

---

*The Cosmic Egg is supposed to consist of fourteen worlds arranged vertically as follows :

I. The Upper Regions: Satya Loka
↓
Tapo Loka
↓
Jana Loka
↓
Mahar Loka
↓
Svar Loka
↓
Bhuvar Loka
↓
II. The Middle Region : The Earth (Bhūr-loka)
↓
III. The Lower Regions or Nether Worlds: Atala
↓
Sutala
↓
Vitala
↓
Gabhastala
↓
Mahātala
↓
Śrītala
↓
Pātāla

6. Similarly, the firmament is well-known as supportless, charming, the support (accommodater) of various things and infinite. The wind is born of the Ether.

7. Waters lie within the earth and the earth is established over waters. The sky is above, the earth is below (it) and again waters are underneath.

8. In this way there is no end to the evolutes of the *Bhūtas*. They are infinite. Know that this has been decisively mentioned by gods formerly.

9. The sequence should be known thus. First the earth, then the water and the sky thereafter. This order prevails upto the seventh world—Rasātala.

10. The nether world extends[1] to ten thousand Yojanas at each rung. Each of these rungs has been explained in detail by the sages.

11. The first rung is Atala, below that is Sutala. The widely extensive Vitala is below that.

12. Thereafter come Gabhastala, Mahātala, Śrītala and Pātāla is known as the seventh.

13-14. The ground surface of the first (nether-world) is black; of the second, pale white; of the third, red; of the fourth, yellow; of the fifth, sandy, gravel-covered; of the sixth, rocky; and of the seventh, golden.

15-19. In the first nether-world, there stands the palace of the lord of Asuras, Namuci, the enemy of Indra. The following abodes too are in the first nether-world, viz. the abode of Mahānāda, the city of Śaṅkukarṇa, the palace of Kabandha, Niṣ-

1. Verses 10-44 describe the Nether-worlds. Their main features are tabulated below:

Name of the Nether world	*Ground Surface*	*Kings*
Atala	Black	Namuci
Sutala	Pale White	Mahājambha
Vitala	Red	Prahrāda and Anuhrāda
Gabhastala	Yellow	Kālanemi
Mahātala	Sandy	Virocana
Śrītala	Rocky	Kesari
Pātāla	Golden	Bali

kulāda's town fully inhabited by delighted (jolly) people, the abode of the demon Bhīma, the mansion of Śūladanta, the city of Lohitākṣas and Kaliṅgas, the town of Śvāpada, the city of Dhanañjaya and of the noble-souled Nāgendra* (Lord of Serpents), the city of Kāliya, the serpent and that of Kalasa. Thus it should be known undoubtedly that there are thousands of cities (and abodes) of Serpents, Dāṇavas and Rākṣasas in the first nether-world with black-soil.

20-24. In the second Nether-world (Su)Tala, O Brāhmaṇas, there are the abodes of the following: the city of the first lord of the Daityas and Rākṣasas (namely) of Mahājaṁbha; the palaces of Hayagrīva, Kṛṣṇa and Nikuṁbha; the cities of the (demon) named Śaṅkha and that of Gomukha, demon Nīla, Megha, Krathana and Kurupāda; the abode of Mahoṣṇīṣa; the city of Kaṁbala, the serpent and that of Aśvatara and the city of Takṣaka, the noble-souled son of Kadru.

Thus, O Brāhmaṇas, there are thousands of cities belonging to Serpents, Dānavas and Rākṣasas in the second Nether-world of pale-white coloured soil. There is no doubt about this.

25-30. In the third Nether-world, there stands the famous city of the noble-souled Daitya king Prahrāda and Anuhrāda; the city of (the Daitya) named Tāraka; the city of Triśiras; the demon Śiśumāra's city full of commotion, due to the gay, well-nourished citizens; the palace of Cyavana, the Rākṣasa; of Kumbhila and Khara; the city of the ruthless Virādha of fire-emitting mouth; the city of Hemaka, the Serpent and that of Pāṇḍuraka and Maṇimantra; the palace of Kapila and that of Nanda, the Lord of Serpents and of Viśāla.

Thus there are undoubtedly thousands of cities of serpents, Dānavas and Rākṣasas, O Brāhmaṇas, in the third Nether-world with yellow soil.

31-33. In the fourth Nether-world is the city of Kālanemi the lion among Daityas, that of the noble-souled Gajakarṇa, the city of Kuñjara, the vast and extensive city of Sumāli the leading Rākṣasa, the abode of Muñja, Lokanātha and Vṛkavaktra and the city of Vainateya. The latter city extends to

*'Māhendra' in the text is a misprint.

many thousand of Yojanas and that is crowded with many birds. All these are in the fourth Nether-world.

34-37. In the fifth Nether-world that is covered with sand and full of gravel extending to many Yojanas, there is the city of the intelligent Daitya chief Virocana, the lion among Daityas, the abodes of Vaidūrya, Agnijihva and that of Hiraṇyākṣa, the city of the intelligent Vidyujjihva, the lord of Rākṣasas, the city of Mahāmegha, that of Mālin, the leading Rākṣasa, the city of the serpent Karmāra and those of Svastika and Jaya.

Thus there are thousands of cities of the serpents, Dānavas and the Rākṣasas in the fifth Nether-world full of gravel. This should be known [as the situation] for ever.

38-40. In the sixth Nether-world, there is the excellent city of Kesari, the lord of the Daityas, the cities of Suparvan, Suloman and Mahiṣa, and the city of the noble-souled Utkrośa, the leading Rākṣasa. It is there that Śataśīrṣa the son of Suramā, lives joyfully. The king of serpents named Vāsuki, the son of Kaśyapa (stays there).

Thus there are thousands of cities of the serpents, Dānavas and the Rākṣasas in the famous sixth Nether-world, Rasātala, with rocky ground.

41. It should be known that the city of Bali is in the seventh and the last Nether-world, Pātāla. It is beyond every world. It is gay and full of men and women.

42. It is full of Asuras, serpents and teeming with haughty enemies of the Devas. There itself is the great city of Mucukunda, the Daitya.

43. It is teeming with innumerable great cities of Daityas, full of bustle and commotion and thousands of the rich and prosperous city of the serpents.

44. It is crowded with great rising (flourishing) cities of Daityas and Dānavas and the many flourishing abodes of Rākṣasas.

45-53. O leading Brāhmaṇas, at the (lowest) extremity of Pātāla extending to many Yojanas, lives the excessively brilliant Śeṣa, king of all serpents. His eyes resemble a red lotus. He is noble-souled, free from death and old age. His complexion is white as the interior of a shining conch-shell. He wears blue garments. His arms are mighty. His body is large and expansive.

He is brilliant and powerful. He wears garlands of various colours. He has a thousand faces (hoods) as bright and sparkling as the gold-peaked mountain. He shines with ear-rings. He appears like mount Kailāsa encircled by ringlets of blazing flames due to his tongues emitting the lustre of blazing fire with leaping flames. With a splendid halo round him and two thousand sparkling eyes as lustrous as the rising sun, he shines gloriously. He has the colour of the moon and the Kunda flower. His string of beads shines like a cluster of midday suns on the top of Śveta mountain.

He is brilliant and terrible with his matted hair. While lying down or sitting, he appears like a mountain with a thousand peaks sprawling over the Earth. He is the excessively refulgent lord of Nāgas and is attended by blessed Nāgas of great strength and huge bodies. He is the Śakti of Viṣṇu in the form of a Serpent. That is the final established boundary (of Nether-worlds).

54. Thus the seven Nether-worlds that could be discussed have been recounted. They are always inhabited by Devas, Asuras, great Serpents, and Rākṣasas.

55. Beyond this is total absence of light. It cannot be traversed by Siddhas and Sādhus (good people or sages). It is unknown even to Devas and is traffic (life)-less.

56. O excellent Brāhmaṇas, thus is the grandeur of earth, fire, water, wind and ether described by the sages. There is no doubt about this.

57. I shall now describe the rotation of the sun and the moon.[1] These are stationed in the ether along with their discs and shine with their lustre as long as they move.

58-59. The extent of the earth is half of the extent of the seven oceans and continents (?). The sun and the moon illumi-

---

1. This is a new section dealing with Purāṇic astronomy. Bd. P. has given a separate chapter (I.2.21) to this and the text corresponds to our text to a great extent.

These Purāṇic astronomical ideas—the position, size, movements of the stars etc. are of the pre-telescope age and unacceptable to-day. They are found in other Purāṇas also, e.g. Bh. P. V. Chs. 21-24, Mt. P. Chs. 124-128, VP. II. Chs. 8-12.

nate the earth on its globular outer surface to the extent of the magnitude of its outer circumference. The magnitude of this outer circumference is equal to the extent of the firmament.

60. Revolving all round, the Sun illuminates and protects the three worlds. Hence on account of illumination and protection, he is called '*Ravi*'. The root $\sqrt{}$*av* means 'illumination' (and protection).[1]

61. Now I shall mention the magnitude of the moon and the sun. The word *Mahī* is derived from $\sqrt{}$*Mah* 'to celebrate'. The word denotes the celebrated Bhārata Varṣa.

62. The extent of Bhārata is equal to the extent of the vastly extensive disc of the sun. Now listen to the number of Yojanas it covers.

63. The extent of the sun is nine thousand Yojanas. The girth or the extent of its disc is thrice its diameter. The lunar disc is twice the solar disc (in diameter as well as girth).

64-65. Now I shall recount the extent of the earth in Yojanas. The extent and girth (circumference) of the earth consisting of seven continents has been reckoned in proper measure in the Purāṇas. I shall recount that after enumerating the current *Abhimānins* (Deities etc. who preside or have the sense of possession etc.).

66. Those *Abhimānins* who have gone were on a par with the current ones. The Devas who have gone are on a par with the current ones in forms and names.

67. Hence, I shall describe the surface of the earth through the current Devas. (I shall recount) the situation of the heavenly world entirely through the current (Devas).

68. The entire earth is known as fifty crores (of Yojanas) in extent. From the middle of Meru on all four sides is half of it.

69-70. Half the extent of the earth is stated in terms of Yojanas. The extent of the earth towards all the sides (quarters) from the middle of Meru is said to be eleven crores and eighty-nine lakhs (of Yojanas) and fifty thousand[2]).

1. A popular etymology : *ravi* is normally traced to $\sqrt{}$*ru* according to Uṇādi IV. 138.

2. It is considered as the radius of the circular zone.

71-72. Understand the entire extent of the earth in terms of Yojanas. The extent over the four quarters is calculated as three crores one hundred and seventy-nine thousand. This extent of the earth includes seven continents and oceans.

73-74. The sphere at the extremity is thrice this in extent. On being calculated thus the spherical zone of the extremity of the earth has the overall area of eleven crores one hundred and thirty-seven thousand Yojanas. Thus the measurement upto the extremity of the earth has been specified.

75. The outer surface of the globular sphere of the earth is co-extensive with the sphere of the stars in the firmament.

76. In regard to the magnitude of the outer surface the firmament is equal to the earth. The same is the measure of all the seven worlds.

77-78. The worlds are situated above one another spreading like an umbrella with their outer spheres. They are all populated. Thus the cauldron of the Cosmic Egg has been explained.

79. It is within the Cosmic Egg that the earth with its seven continents and seven worlds, viz. Bhūr, Bhuvaḥ, Svaḥ, Mahar, Jana, Tapas and Satya is stationed.

80-81. These seven worlds shaped in the form of umbrellas are severally supported by their own subtle outer coverings, which are ten times bigger in order. They are created with specific attributes and they support the seven worlds.

82. All round this Cosmic Egg there is a solid ocean. The entire sphere of the earth is supported by the solid water.[1]

83-85. Beyond the solid ocean is the solid fire by which the sphere of the world is supported. Beyond and outside the solid fire is the sphere of solid wind that covers the earth on all sides round and above. Beyond the solid wind is the firmament which is surrounded by Cosmic Ego entirely. That Ego is surrounded by Mahat (the Great Principle or Intellect) which again is surrounded by the infinite Unmanifest Prakṛti of unchanging form.

86. I shall enumerate in order the cities of the guardians

---

1. This Purāṅic concept of seven protective sheaths of our Cosmic Egg shows the influence of Sāṅkhya *Tattvas*.

of the worlds.[1] The proof of the movements of the luminary bodies will also be mentioned.

87. To the east of Meru and above Mānasa is the holy city of Mahendra abounding in all essential riches and richly inlaid with gold.

88. To the south of Meru and above Mānasa lives Yama, son of Vivasvān, in his city Saṁyamana.

89. To the west of Meru and above Mānasa is the charming city of the intelligent Varuṇa. It is called Sukhā.

90. To the north of Meru and above Mānasa is the city Vibhāvarī of Soma (the moon) which is comparable to the city of Mahendra.

91. Above Mānasa in all the four quarters the guardians of the worlds are stationed for the establishment of virtue (Dharma) and protection of the worlds.

92. Understand the solar movement when the sun reaches south during the southern transit all round above the guardians of the worlds.

93. In his transit to the south, the sun moves fast like a discharged arrow. It takes the group of luminary bodies with it and revolves always.

94. When the sun is in the mid-horizon in Amarāvatī, it is called sunrise in the city of Saṁyamana of the son of Vivasvat.

95. Then it is midnight in Sukhā. When the sun is in mid-horizon (in Saṁyamana) the sun is seen rising in Sukhā, the city of Varuṇa.

96. When it is midnight at Vibhāvarī, it is sunset in Amarāvatī, the city of Mahendra. To the people of the south-east (or south and the east) it is afternoon.

97. What is (when it is) the forenoon of the people of the southern and western countries it is the late night to the people in the northern territories.

98. It is early in the night for the territories that are in the north and east. Similarly (the following is the situation) when the sun shines in the abodes of the north, during the northern transit.

1. Compare *Supra* p. 242 note 2.

99. When the sun is in midday in Sukhā, the city of Varuṇa, it rises in Vibhāvarī, the city of Soma.

100-101. It is midnight in Amarāvatī and the sun sets in the city of Yama. Then the sun is in midday in Vibhā, the city of Soma. When the sun rises in Amarāvatī, it is midnight in Saṁyamanā and the sun sets in the city of Varuṇa.

102. Making the stars (and planets) whirl and revolving itself like a firebrand, the sun sets and then rises quickly.

103. Thus the sun moves in the four continents ending with the southern one. It rises and sets again and again.

104. The sun gives warmth to two abodes of Devas in the forenoon and two in the afternoon. With its rays alone it heats one of them during midday.

105. After rising the sun blazes with its rays of increasing heat till midday. Thereafter with its rays of decreasing heat it sets.

106. The eastern and western direction is determined by sunrise and sunset. While the sun blazes in front (its heat is felt) behind as well and on sides also.

107. Where the sun appears rising, it is known as sunrise to the people thereof; (while) where the sun vanishes, it is called sunset in regard to the people there.

108. Due to the far distant position of the sun and being covered up by the line (horizon) of the earth, its rays become invisible (being obstructed from sight). Hence it is not seen at night.

109. The appearance of the planets, stars and the sun as well as their rising and setting should be known by the magnitude of their height.

110. Fire and water have white lustre and the earth has black shadow. Since the sun is at a great distance at the time of rising, it appears to be without rays. Since it is without rays, it has the red lustre, and the absence of heat is due to its redness.

111. Wherever the sun is seen to be stationed on the line (of horizon) it is seen a thousand Yojanas above.

112. When the sun sets, the brilliance of the sun partially enters fires. Hence fire shines more brilliantly at night, even from a distance.

113. When the sun rises again, the brilliance of fire enters the sun. This together with the brilliance left in the sun at the time of sunset, makes it all the more brilliant. So the sun blazes during the day.

114. The light and heat of the sun and fire getting mixed together nourish people during day and night.

115. In the northern and southern halves of the earth, when the sun rises, night enters waters. Hence, during day waters are copper-coloured as a result of the entry of night.

116. When the sun sets, day enters waters. Hence during night, water appears white and bright as a result of the entry of day.

117. In this manner, in the southern and northern halves of the earth, day and night enter waters at the time of sunset and sunrise.

118. Day is the time when there is sunlight and night is the time when there is darkness. Hence, night is established (independently) due to this, while day is dependent on the sun.

119. When the sun passes through the middle of the sky, it traverses one-thirtieth of the diameter of the earth in a *Muhūrta* (forty-eight minutes).

120-121. In regard to the distance traversed in Yojanas, know that it is three million one hundred and fifty thousand in full. This is the distance traversed by the sun in one *Muhūrta*.

122-124. Traversing thus the sun reaches the southern-most limit in the month of Māgha and moves about there. The distance traversed by the sun during a day and a night is nine crores and fortyfive hundred thousand Yojanas.

125-126. When the sun returns from the south and traverses the equinox, it goes to the quarters north of the ocean of milk. Know the distance in Yojanas, of the zone traversed during the transit in the equinox. It is thirty million and eighty-one hundred thousand Yojanas.

127. When the sun, while traversing in the north, is in the (constellation) Śravaṇa, it traverses the northern regions of the sixth continent (called) Śāka-dvīpa.

128-129. The extent of the zone in the northern quarter in Yojanas as calculated by the Brāhmaṇas is one crore eight million and fiftyeight Yojanas.

130. The northern orbit is called Nāgavīthī[1] and the southern one is called Ajavīthī. When the sun rises in the constellations Mūla, Pūrvāṣāḍhā and Uttarāṣāḍhā it is called Ajavīthī. When the sun rises during the rise of the three stars after Abhijit (i.e. Aśvinī, Bharaṇī and Kṛttikā) it is called Nāgavīthī.

131-132. I shall mention the distance in Yojanas between these two quarters. This distance is three million one hundred and three thousand three hundred and thirtythree Yojanas.

133. Now I shall mention the distance between the southern cardinal points and meridians in Yojanas. Understand it.

134-135a. The external and internal distances between the two quarters and meridians are seven million and one hundred and seventyfive Yojanas.

135b-136a. During Uttarāyaṇa (the northern transit of the sun) the sun goes round the internal zones. During Dakṣiṇāyana (the southern transit) the sun goes round the external zones. This is the usual order.

136b-137. In the north there are one hundred and eighty zones. In the south also the sun traverses that much. Know the distance of the Maṇḍala (zone) in Yojanas.

138-139. The magnitude of this zone is twentyone thousand two hundred and twentyone Yojanas. This is the measurement of the zone calculated in Yojanas.

140. The diameter of the zone is laid obliquely. Everyday the sun traverses those (zones) in due order.

141. Just as the outer rim of the potter's wheel comes back (revolves) quickly, so also the sun returns quickly during its southern transit.

142. Within a short time, therefore, the sun traverses the extensive earth. Within twelve Muhūrtas it traverses quickly from the south to to the north.

---

1. According to Varāhamihira's *Bṛhat-Saṁhitā*, Vithī is a particular division of the planetary sphere comprising of three asterisms. Thus Nāgavīthī is constituted of asterisms Aśvinī, Bharaṇī and Kṛttikā while Ajavīthī is formed of Mūla; Pūrvāṣāḍhā and Uttarāṣāḍhā.

143. The sun passes through thirteen and a half constellations of stars during the day. During the night in eighteen Muhūrtas it passes through as many (i.e. thirteen and a half) of stars.

144. Just as the central region of the potters wheel moves slowly, so also in the course of the northern transit the sun moves slowly.

145. The sun passes through thirteen and a half stars. Hence it covers less extent of the earth in longer time.

146. In the later part of the northern transit, a day has the duration of eighteen Muhūrtas. Then also the sun proceeds very slowly.

147. The sun passes through thirteen and a half stars during half the time (i.e. the day time). During night, it passes through as many stars in the course of eighteen Muhūrtas.

148. Just as a ball of clay placed on the middle of the wheel whirls slowly, so also does the Pole Star.

149. They say that day and night together constitute thirty Muhūrtas. The whirling Pole between the two quarters revolves in a circle.

150. Just as the nave of the potter's wheel remains there only, similarly it should be known that the Pole Star whirls there only (without changing its place).

151. Thus the rotation of the sun in a circle between the two quarters is slow during day and fast during night.

152. During the northern transit, the movement of the moon (?) is slow during day and fast during night.

153. During the southern transit the sun's movement is fast during day and slow during night.

154. Dividing nights and days thus by its special diverse movements, the sun traverses the path by its even (regular) and uneven (irregular) movement.

155. Agastya (the star Canopus) traverses quickly over the guardians of the worlds stationed in the four quarters over the mountain Lokāloka. He divides days and nights by diverse movements.

156. He is the protector of the worlds to the south of Nāga-

vīthī and north of Lokāloka[1] and outside the path of Vaiśvānara.

157. There is as much of sunlight at the sides, behind and all round Lokāloka as there is on its top in front.

158. This mountain is above ten thousand Yojanas in height. It is partly bright and partly unilluminated. It is circular all round.

159. The stars, the moon, the sun and planets shine within the internal part of mount Lokāloka.

160. The world is only so far and no further. Beyond this there is darkness. The Lokāloka is single but Nirālokas (the darker sides) are numerous.

161. Since the sun in its circular movement unites the Lokāloka, the wise call the inter-space between Uṣā and Vyuṣṭi by the name Sandhyā. Uṣā is night and Vyuṣṭi is day.

162. A curse was cast on the wicked demons who were bent on devouring the sun at the time of twilight that they would have imperishability of bodies but they would be made to die (everyday).

163. Three crores of demons who are well-known as Mandehas seek everyday the rise of the sun. The wicked ones harass and desire to devour the blazing sun.

164-165. Then there was a terrific fight between them and the sun. The excellent Brāhmaṇas, Devas and Brahmā who had been performing the worship of Sandhyā sprinkled the holy water sanctified by Oṁkāra and Gāyatrī. As the water became adamantine, the Daityas were burnt.

166. Then the sun of great splendour, excessive lustre and valour rises up a hundred thousand Yojanas.

167. Then goes forth the Lord (the Sun-god) with his brilliant rays. He is surrounded by Brāhmaṇas and Vālakhilya Sages who have achieved their object (of protecting the Sun).

168. Fifteen *Nimeṣas* (winking time of the eye) make one *Kāṣṭhā*, thirty *Kāṣṭhās* make one *Kalā*; thirty *Kalās* make a

---

1. This is a mythical mountain encircling the world. The area within its circle is lighted (that gets light) while on the other side of this dividing mountain, there is utter darkness.

Muhūrta and thirty *Muhūrtas* make (a full day consisting of) a night and a day.

169. There is increase and decrease in the length of day by a few parts. But whether (it) is increased or decreased, the duration of twilight remains constant one *Muhūrta*.

170. The three *Muhūrtas* from the time when the sun rises from the horizon constitute the *Prātastana* (early morning) period which is one-fifth part of day.[1]

171. The period of three *Muhūrtas* from the early morning is called *Saṅgava* (forenoon). The period of three *Muhūrtas* after forenoon is called *Madhyāhna* (midday).

172-173. The period of three *Muhūrtas* from midday is called *Aparāhṇa* (afternoon).

The period of three *Muhūrtas* from afternoon is called *Sāyāhna*. There are only three (sacred?) Muhūrtas out (of a day) of fifteen Muhūrtas.

174. When the sun is in the equinox, day and the night each consists of fifteen Muhūrtas.

175. During the transit of the sun to the north and south the duration of day increases and decreases accordingly. Day swallowst night and night swallows day.

176. The equinox occurs between autumn and spring. The moon attains his seven[2] (?) Kalās during the day and the night.

177. Fifteen days make one Pakṣa (half of a month). Two halves make one month and two months make a *Ṛtu* (season). Three *Ṛtus* (seasons) make one *Ayana* and two *Ayanas* make a year.

178. The unit of time constituted by fifteen *Nimeṣas* is *Kāṣṭhā*. Thirty *Kāṣṭhās* make a *Kalā*. It consists of one hundred and sixty *Mātrās*.

179. The unit of time *Calā*[3] (*Kalā*?) is thus defined. It consists of ninetynine, thirty, thirtysix, sixtytwo or twenty-three Mātrās (Defective Verse).

---

1. Verses 170-173 give the five divisions of day, each consisting of three *Muhūrtas* in duration.

2. *Samam* 'equal number of Kalās' in Bd. P. I. 2.21.124.

3. A misprint for *Kalā*.

180. Forty thousand and eight hundred and seventy *Mātrās* make the unit of time called *Vidyuti.*[1] To be precise, it is ninety (instead of seventy).

181. In *Vaidhasaṁyuga* (?) they say that there are only four hundred *Mātrās* in a *Vidyuti*. This is known as *Carāṁśa*. The cause is Nālikā [Ghaṭikā = 24 minutes].

182. The five units of time, Saṁvatsara etc., have four alternative calculations.[2] The fixation[3] of Yuga is decisively done on this basis in all the units of time.

183. The first year is *Saṁvatsara*; the second is *Parivatsara*; the third is *Idvatsara*; the fourth is *Anuvatsara*; the fifth is *Vatsara*. Thus the various units of time are termed.

184-185. Twenty hundreds of *Parvans* (i.e. a thousand months) constitute a Yuga of the sun. These eighteen plus thirty (i.e. 48) Yugas make one *Udaya* of the sun. Thirty *Ṛtus* of the sun make ten *Ayanas*. Three thousand five hundred *Ayanas* make sixty months of the sun.

186. Thirty days and nights make one month of the sun. Sixtyone days and nights make one Danu.

187. One hundred and eightythree days constitute the time of one transit of the sun over the world.

188. The four types of calculation, viz. *Saura* (solar), *Saumya* (lunar) *Nākṣatra* (stellar) and *Sāvana* (sacrificial) should be clearly understood.

---

1. A new unit of time. In Bd. P. I. 221. 126-29 it is *Vidyut*. Its duration is not clear.

2. *Vide* verse 188 below. The calculation systems were: *Saura* (based on the sun, solar), *Saumya* (the lunar), *Nākṣatra* (stellar), *Sāvana* [relating to the three soma libations per day corresponding to the solar time (day, month etc.)] —MW 1210.

3. The Purāṇa records the age-old tradition that the Yuga period consists of five years. In Vedic times a Yuga was a period of five years and the names of those five years (with a slight variation in the name Idavatsara, viz. Ida-or Idu-vatsara) are the same as recorded here (*vide* Tai. S. V. 7. 1-3; Vāj. S. 27. 45; Atharva VI. 55. 3). Tai. Br. I.4.10.1 identifies Saṁvatsara, Parivatsara etc. with gods Agni, Āditya etc.

Kauṭilya in *Arthaśāstra* II. Ch. 20, declares: "A Yuga consists of five years", the same as in this Purāṇa.

189. There is a mountain Śṛṅgavān to the north of Śveta. Its three peaks appear to touch the sky.

190. Due to these peaks the mountain is known as Śṛṅgavān. The single path (leading to it), its extent and girth have been already mentioned.

191. Its eastern peak in the middle is golden. The southern peak consists of silver. It has crystalline lustre.

192. The excellent peak in the north consists of precious stones and jewels. Thus with the three peaks the mountain is well known as Śṛṅgavān.

193. Betwixt autumn and spring, the sun proceeds with medium velocity, neither fast nor slow. It reaches that peak of the mountain which is near the equinoctical line. The Dispeller of darkness, i.e. the sun, makes the night equal to the day.

194. Divine green-coloured horses are yoked to his great chariot. They appear (shining) as though they are smeared with the (solar) rays red like lotus.

195. During the *Meṣa* and *Tulā* zodiacal transit of the sun days and nights contain fifteen *Muhūrtas* beginning with sunrise.

196. When the sun is in the first quarter of the constellation Kṛttikā (Pleiades), the moon is known to be in the fourth part of the constellation Viśākhā.

197. When the sun traverses through the third part of Viśākhā, know that the moon has occupied the top of Kṛttikā.

198. The sages call that as equinox. Equinox shall be known through the (position of the) sun and the time through (that of) the moon.

199. When days and nights are equal it is equinox. During equinoctical transit oblations to the Pitṛs and charitable gifts to the Brāhmaṇas should be made. Brāhmaṇas are the mouths of Devas.

200. In view of the differences due to *Kalās*, *Kāṣṭhās* and *Muhūrtas*, the night of short duration and intercalary month occur. The full moon is of two types: Rākā and

Anumati[1]. The new moon too is of two types: Sinīvālī and Kuhū.[2]

201. The six months, viz. Māgha, Phālguna, Caitra, Vaiśākha, Jyeṣṭha and Āṣāḍha are the months of *Uttarāyaṇa* (northern transit of the sun). The six months, viz. Śrāvaṇa, Bhādrapada, Āśvina, Kārttika, Mārgaśirṣa and Pauṣa are the months of *Dakṣiṇāyana* (southern transit of the sun).

202. These months make a year. The five years are the sons of Brahmā. *Ṛtus* are born of them. These are their parts.

203. Hence the New Moon Day (Amāvāsyā) is known as the leader of the Parvans. More than that the equinox should be known as favourable to Devas and Pitṛs.

204. After knowing this, a man should not get deluded regarding rites concerning Devas and Pitṛs. Hence equinox is remembered as all-pervasive by the people.

205. The worlds (*Lokas*) should be known (to exist) as far as light (the space illuminated by the sun) extends. The end of the world is also called *Loka* (of the Lokāloka mountain). The guardians of the worlds are stationed there in the middle of the Loklāoka mountain.

206. They (the Lokapālas) are the four noble souls who stay till the final dissolution of the world. They are Vairāja of good (brilliant) splendour, Kardama of good and merciful disposition, Parjanya of golden hair, and Ketumān of fixed determination.

207. The guardians of the worlds are stationed in the four quarters in Lokāloka, free from *Dvandvas* (mutually clashing opposites), devoid of arrogance, without an attendant, and absolutely uncontrolled by anyone else.

208. The path that is to the north of Agastya, south of Ajavīthī and outside the path of Vaiśvānara is called *Pitṛyāna*.

---

1. According to Nirukta XI-29, Paurṇamāsi (the full moon day) when mixed with the 14th Tithi, is *Anumati* and when mixed with the 1st day of the next (i.e. dark) fortnight is *Rākā*.

2. When Amāvāsyā (the new maon day) is mixed with the 14th Tithi, it is *Sinīvālī* and when mixed with the 1st Tithi of the next (i.e. bright) fortnight it is *Kuhū*.

209. Stationed there in the path of *Pitṛyāna* are the sages blessed with progeny who perform Agnihotras and who perpetuate the lineage of the world.

210. Desirous of the welfare of the worlds, they bless the activities of living beings and begin the activities of Ṛtviks. Theirs is the southern path.

211. In every Yuga they re-establish Dharma that has gone astray (being rudely shocked and shaken) by their progeny, penance, adherence to the bound of decency and persuit of learning.

212. The earlier ones on their death are reborn in the houses of the later ones. This series of births and deaths makes them live upto the hour of final dissolution of the universe.

213-215. There are eighty thousand householder-sages resorting to the path south of the sun. They stay there as long as the moon and the stars exist. In view of their worldly activities, the creation of living beings, natural desires and hatred, sexual intercourse and other sorts of enjoyments of pleasures as well as due to other causes, the Siddhas have resorted to cremation grounds. These sages, desirous of progeny, were born in the Dvāpara age.

216. The path north of Nāgavīthī and south of the Sapta Ṛṣis (Great Bear) is Devayāna, the northern path of the sun.

217. The Siddhas residing there are unsullied and celibate. They hate sexual intercourse. They have conquered death.

218. These *Ūrdhvaretas* sages (who have sublimated their sexual desire) are eighty thousand in number. They have resorted to the northern path of the sun and stay there till the final dissolution overtakes the universe.

219. In view of these pious causes they have attained deathlessness that will last as far as the final dissolution of the *Bhūtas* (elements). Deathlessness is predicated of those who survive till final dissolution.

220. This is the period (of life) till the three worlds last, for sages who do not return to the path of Saṁsāra. Others of

sublimated sexual urge are sinners as well as meritorious ones on account of their (sins of) murdering a Brāhmaṇa or the performance of the Aśvamedha (Horse sacrifice). The Ūrdhvaretas sages pass away at the end of the annihilation of all living beings.

221-222. To the north and above the world of sages, where Dhruva is said to be present, is the divine shining region of Viṣṇu. On reaching that region none is affected by sorrow or pain. It is the greatest region of Viṣṇu where Dharma, Dhruva and other Sādhakas of the world stay.

CHAPTER FIFTYONE*

Movements of the Luminary Bodies

Sūta said :

1. While narrating the details of Svāyaṁbhuva Manvantara, events of past and future have been narrated. Now I shall recount them in their proper order.

2. On hearing this, the sages asked Lomaharṣaṇa about the movements of the sun, the moon and the planets.

The Sages enquired :

3. How do these luminary bodies revolve in the firmament ? They all move in circular orbits and laterally. Still they do not collide with one another. Who makes them revolve ? Or do they revolve of their own accord ?

4. O excellent one, we wish to know this. Narrate it to us. This is a matter that deludes living beings. We have a desire to hear about this.

Sūta said :

5. Listen to and know this wonderful thing which though very clear and visible, deludes people.

6. It is Dhruva, son of Uttānapāda, who is stationed at the tail-end of what appears like the Gangetic porpoise with tails

*This chapter corresponds to Bd. P. I. 2.22.

towards the four quarters in the sky.[1] He has become the pivotal peg in the sky.

7. It revolves itself and makes the sun and the moon revolve along with the planets. While it revolves like a wheel, the stars follow it.

8-10. The group of stars moves at the will of Dhruva.[2] The sun, the moon, the fixed and moving stars and the planets are bound to Dhruva through the bonds in the form of groups of winds. It is from Dhruva that their combination, difference, seasonal movement, rising and setting, portentious phenomena, southern and northern transit, the equinoxes and colours begin to function.

11. Rain, heat, snow, night, twilight, day and the auspicious and inauspicious events befalling the subjects—everything begins to function from Dhruva.

12. The sun covers the stars etc. activised by Dhruva and stands by. Hence his rays are illuminated. The sun is the deadly fire (that ends the world).

13. O Brāhmaṇas, in the course of his revolution, the sun brightens the quarters by his brilliance. With the mass of his rays in the company of the wind all round, O excellent Brāhmaṇas, the sun takes up the waters of the universe.

14. The water drunk in by the sun gets transferred to the moon from the solar fire. Through the Nāḍis (tubular veins) full of wind the activity of sustaining the worlds begins.

15. What exudes from the moon, the sun receives at its tips. When the wind blows the clouds let it shower on the earth.

16. Thus the water is poured and it falls again and again. The same water assumes various shapes.[3]

17. For the up-keep of the living beings, Māyā has been created. The three worlds including the mobile and immobile beings are pervaded by this Māyā.

---

1. Cf. Bh. P. V. 23.4.7 and Bd. P. I.2.22.6.
2. Bh. P.V. 23.2 attributes this driving power to Kāla (Time).
3. This belief in indestructibility of water is surprisingly modern, though the concept of water-cycle is archaic.

18. The sun is the lord of the universe; he is the creator of the worlds; he is the thousand-rayed lord; he is the lord of the subjects; he is the sustainer of the world; he is lord Viṣṇu himself.

19. The water of the worlds has exuded from the moon in the sky. The universe is, therefore, supported by the moon. This fact has now been declared.

20. The hot rays emanate from the sun; the cool rays from the moon. These two powerful hot and cool rays sustain the universe.

21. The holy Gaṅgā with pure waters has the moon for support. O excellent Brāhmaṇas, the great rivers have the son of the moon as their leader.

22-23. Water is present in the bodies of living beings. When the bodies of the mobile and immobile beings burn, the water becomes vapour and rises on all sides. Thereby clouds arise and they are the receptacles of water. The brilliance of the sun takes up the water from the living beings through the rays.

24. The rays take the waters from the ocean through the wind. The revolving sun imparts water to the clouds by means of his white rays in the proper seasons.

25. When blown by the wind, the water drips from the clouds. The clouds scatter showers for the benefit of living beings when they are blown by the winds in all directions.

26. The clouds shower for six months in order to nourish and develop all living beings. They produce the rumbling sound of thunder arising from the wind and brilliant lightning arising from the fire.

27. The root √*mih* means 'to exude', 'to sprinkle'. Since the clouds exude water, they are called *Megha*. That from which water does not fall off they call *Abhra*.[1]

28. Clouds arise in three ways. Their source of origin are three. The types of clouds are *Āgneyas*, *Brahmajas* and *Pakṣajas*.[2]

---

1. *Abhra* from √*bhraṁś* is a fanciful derivation. It is usually derived from √*abhr* 'to wander about' + suffix *ac* (i.e. *a*) or from *ap* + √*bhṛ* + suffix a.

2. Verses 21-52 give a pseudo-scientific classification of clouds by ancient Indians. It contains some interesting poetic flashes of imagination.

Thus the three types of clouds have been narrated. I shall mention their mode of origin.

29. Clouds arising from the waters of ocean are *Āgneyas*. They function therefrom. Chilliness and winds on a cloudy day are their attributes.

30. They assume the shapes of buffaloes, boars and elephants in their rut. They roam about and sport very near the earth.

31. The clouds are called *Jimūtas* since they are the source of living beings. They do not have the attributes of thunder. They hang down due to the water-content in them.

32. These clouds are huge and silent. They follow the current of the wind submissively. They shower water within a half to one Krośa (from the earth).

33. They shower on the tops and ridges of mountains and sport. They pierce the wombs of the flocks of the white cranes. They make them conceive.

34. The types of clouds called *Brahmajas* are born of the breath of Brahmā. They have the attribute of lightning. They are fond of rumbling sounds. They thunder.

35. Due to their loud report the earth gets a thrill. Like a queen crowned by a king earth attains youth once again. Being the cause of the birth of the living beings, the earth endears itself to the clouds.

36. The birth of living beings is from these clouds called *Jimūtas*. These clouds resort to the second layer of wind called *Pravaha*.

37. These clouds shower from a distance of a Yojana, half a Yojana or one-fourth of a Yojana from the earth. They rain in continuous torrents.

38. The wings of the powerful mountains who could go as per their will and pleasure, had grown very large. Indra cut them off for the (welfare of all) living beings.

39. These clouds are called *Puṣkaras*. They are huge and they are exhilarated with their waters. For that reason they are called *Puṣkarāvartakas* (revolving Puṣkaras).

40. They assume different forms. They are very terrible.

The winds viz. *Āvaha, Pravaha, Vivaha, Udvaha, Saṁvaha* and *Parivaha* are cloud-bearing. They are winds of different types with different functions.

They pour forth showers at the end of Kalpas. They control the Saṁvartaka fire.

41. The third type of clouds mentioned before shower at the close of the Yugas. They assume many forms and fill the surface of the earth. They resort to the wind called *Paravāha* and conclude a Kalpa.

42. All the clouds are reputed to have been born of the same Cosmic Egg-shell of Prākṛta form from which the self-born four-faced Brahmā was born.

43. It is the smoke that makes them all fully developed without any difference. The most excellent among them is *Parjanya*. And there are four elephants of the quarters.

44. Elephants, mountains and clouds along with serpents belong to one and the same family, though they are severally manifested, since water is known as the source of (their) origin.

45. During Hemanta (early winter) *Parjanya* and the elephants of the quarters born of chilliness shower snow (drops) for making the corn flourish.

46. The great wind called *Parivaha* is their support. It is that lordly wind which sustains the Gaṅgā that flows through the sky. It is the sacred, heavenly river, flooded over with water, stationed in the heavenly path like the divine Lore (Vidyā).

47. The elephants of the quarters spray all round drops of water from the Gaṅgā by means of their huge trunks. That (spray of water) is called the hoarfrost.

48. The mountain to the south of Meru is Hemakūṭa. There is a city called Puṇḍra to the south of this mountain and to the north of Himālaya.

49-50. The rain arising from this shower of mist, falls on this mountain. The wind Āvaha blowing from Himavat brings drops of mist with it and sprinkles them over the great mountain. The remnant of the shower crosses Himālaya and comes here thereafter in order to make the western region flourish.

51. The two types of clouds that make the regions flourish have been already described. The sun alone is mentioned as the maker of showers.

52. Controlled by Dhruva, the sun causes the rainfall through these two (types) of clouds. The wind encompassed by Dhruva withdraws the rain.

53. The wind starts from the planet sun and traverses the entire stellar zone. At the end of the day it enters the sun encompassed by Dhruva.

54. Now listen to the description of the Sun's Chariot.[1] It has one wheel with five spokes and three naves.

55. The Lord Sun goes ahead on his Chariot that has golden wheel, that is very powerful, that has knotty joints, that has six-fold rim and one felly, which dispells darkness on the way.

56. Its width is ten thousand Yojanas. Its length from the middle (cockpit) to the shaft is twice of it (twenty thousand Yojanas).

57. This Chariot had been made by Brahmā for some specific purpose. It is divine and golden. Swift horses have been yoked to it.

58. It is the Vedic metres that have assumed the forms of the horses. It is stationed in the sphere of Śukra (Venus). It has the characteristics similar to those of Varuṇa's chariot. In this shining Chariot the Sun traverses the sky.

59. These parts of the Chariot of the Sun are fashioned out of the parts of the year in due order.

60. The day is the nave of the wheel. The Chariot has one wheel. The spokes are the five seasons and the rim is the sixth season.

61. The year is the inner seat of the Chariot; the two *Ayanas* are the two shafts; the *Mnhūrtas* are the fastening ropes and the *Kalās* are the pins of the yoke.

62. The *Kāṣṭhās* constitute its nose and the *Kṣaṇas* (moments) make up the shaft; the *Nimeṣas* are the axle-trees and the *Lavas* make up the poles.

63. The night is the frontal fender; *Dharma* is its highly rising banner. *Artha* and *Kāma* are the two tips of the pole and axle.

---

1. Verses 54 ff. give a symbolic description of the Chariot of the Sun.

64-65. The seven Vedic metres, viz. Gāyatrī, Triṣṭup, Anuṣṭup, Jagatī, Paṅkti, Bṛhatī and Uṣṇik, have assumed the forms of horses and bear the burden. The wheel is fixed to the axle and the axle is fastened to Dhruva.

66. The axle turns along with the wheel; Dhruva turns along with the axle. Urged by Dhruva the axle turns along with the wheel.

67. This is the description of the peculiar construction of the chariot. By means of the parts joined together a shining chariot is fashioned out.

68-69. With that the lord Sun moves quickly in the heaven. There are two reins of the chariot tied to the tips of the pole and the axle. Propelled by Dhruva the chariot moves in the sky in a circular fashion.

70. Handled by Dhruva the tips of the pole and the axle on the right side of the chariot appear like white reins in a chariot of two wheels.

71. The two rays (reins) follow the whirling Dhruva. The tips of the pole and axle of the chariot are wind-waves.

72-73. Just as the rope tied to a peg revolves in all directions, so the two rays (reins) shrink in the zones in the Uttarāyaṇa. They increase in the Dakṣiṇāyana. The two reins handled by Dhruva lead the Sun.

74. When these are dragged by Dhruva, the Sun takes the internal revolutions.

75-76. The Sun thus traverses the one hundred and eighty circular zones of the two quarters. When the reins are released by Dhruva, it revolves round the external zones. Encircling them the Sun moves fast round the zones.

CHAPTER FIFTYTWO

Movement of Dhruva

Sūta said :

1. That chariot is occupied by the Devas, Ādityas, Sages, Gandharvas, Apsaras-s, Grāmaṇis (Yakṣas), Serpents and Rākṣasas[1].

2-5. The following reside in the Sun in succession for a period of two months each[2]. Among them (gods) Dhātṛ, Aryamā, (sages) Pulastya, Pulaha the Prajāpati, the Serpents (Nāgas) Vāsuki and Saṅkīrṇāra, (Gandharvas) Tuṁburu and Nārada, the foremost among the singing Gandharvas, the Apsaras-s Kratusthalī and Puñjikasthalī, Grāmaṇīs or Yakṣas Rathakṛcchra, Taporya[3] (?), Rākṣasas and Yātudhānas Heti and Praheti—these reside in the Sun during the months of Madhu and Mādhava[4] (i. e. Caitra and Vaiśākha). [These are the months in the season Vasanta (the Spring)]

---

1. The sublime concept of the Solar Chariot is based on Vāj.S. 15.15-19. Here Devas, Sages and Gandharvas represent light and immortality—the actinic portion of the Solar Spectra. The Serpents, Grāmaṇis (Yakṣas) and Rākṣasas signify heat or death, the thermal field of the Spectra. This Heptad of the Sun signifies the mutual difference in the different "wavelengths" of the seven colours. This may be regarded as Purāṇic VIBGYOR.

2. Verses 2-26 enumerate the names of the different Devas, Sages etc.—the heptad who occupy the Solar Chariot every two months. These verses are common to other Purāṇas such as the Mt. P. Ch. 125, Bd. P. I.2. 23.2.24. The Vedic names of these occupants of the Chariot are somewhat different.

3. 'Rathaujas' in Bd. P. I.2.23.2-5.

4. The following are the names of modern months for the old ones.

Old names	*New names*
Madhu	Caitra
Mādhava	Vaiśākha
Śuci	Jyeṣṭha
Śukra	Āṣāḍha
Nabhas	Śrāvaṇa
Nabhasya	Bhādrapada
Iṣa	Āśvina
Ūrja	Kārtika
Saha	Mārgaśirṣa
Sahasya	Pauṣa

6-8. During the months of Śuci and Śukra (i.e. Jyeṣṭha and Āṣāḍha), the months of the season grīṣma (summer), the following reside in the Sun: (gods) Mitra, Varuṇa; (sages) Atri, Vasiṣṭha; (Nāgas) Takṣaka, Raṁbha; (Apsaras-s) Menakā, Sahajanyā; Gandharvas Hahā and Huhū; Grāmaṇīs (Yakṣas) Rathasvana and Rathacitra; and Yātudhānas (Demons) Pauruṣeya and Dhava (Vadha in Bd. P.).

9-11. Then during the months of Nabhas and Nabhasya (i.e. Śrāvaṇa and Bhādrapada) the (following) other deities reside in the Sun : (gods) Indra and Vivasvān. So also (sages) Aṅgiras, Bhṛgu; the two Nāgas Elāparṇa and Śaṅkhapāla; (Gandharvas) Viśvāvasu and Ugrasena, Prātaḥ and Aruṇa; Apsaras-s Pramlocā and Nimlocā; the Yātudhāna Vyāghra; and the Nāga Śveta.

12-15. During the autumn, in the months of Iṣa and Ūrja (i.e. Āśvina and Kārttika) noble sages and deities occupy the Sun: (gods) Parjanya and Pūṣan; (sages) Bhāradvāja and Gautama; Gandharvas Viśvāvasu and Surabhi; the two Apsaras-s of auspicious characteristics Viśvācī and Ghṛtācī; the famous Serpents Airāvata and Dhanañjaya; the leaders of armies and Grāmaṇīs Senajit and Suṣeṇa; and the two Yātudhānas Āpa and Vāta.

16-19. During the two months of Saha and Sahasya (i.e. Mārgaśīrṣa and Pauṣa), the two months of early winter, the following reside in the Sun: (gods) Aṁśa and Bhaga; the sages Kāśyapa and Ṛtu; the two Senānīs and Grāmaṇīs Tārkṣya and Ariṣṭanemi; the two fierce Yātudhānas Vidyut and Sphūrja; and the Nāgas Mahāpadma and Karkoṭaka; the two Gandharvas Citrasena and Ūrṇāyu; and the splendid Apsaras-s Urvaśī and Vipracitti.

20-23. During the two months of late winter the following reside in the Sun for two months: (gods) Tvaṣṭṛ and Viṣṇu; (the sages) Jamadagni and Viśvāmitra; the two Serpents Kambala and Aśvatara, the sons of Kadru; the two Gandharvas

---

Tapas	Māgha
Tapasya	Phālguna

The new year begins in Māgha according to this Purāṇa and Bd. P. (I.2.21.151).

Dhṛtarāṣṭra and Sūryavarcas; the two Apsaras-s Tilottamā and splendid Raṁbhā; the world-famous Grāmaṇīs; Ṛtajit and Satyajit; and the Rākṣasas Brahmopeta and Yajñopeta.

24. The twelve sets of seven deities (heptads) identifyng themselves with their place of residence augment the excellent splendour of the Sun with their extra refulgence.

25. With well-known hymns of prayer the sages eulogise the Sun. Gandharvas and Apsaras-s attend upon him with dance and music.

26. The Grāmaṇīs, Yakṣas and Bhūtas collect hideous and terrible things. The Serpents bear the Sun and the Yātudhānas follow him. Worshipping the Sun from the time of rising, the sages Vālakhilyas lead him to the mountain of Sunset.

27-28. The Sun blazes with his brilliance and in accordance with the prowess, penance, Yogic power, truthfulness, righteousness and strength of these deities. These stay with the Sun for (a period of) two months.

29. They are the (sets of seven): the Sages, Devas, Gandharvas Serpents, groups of Apsaras-s, Grāmaṇīs and most of the Yakṣas and Yātudhānas.

30. On being glorified, these blaze, rain, shine, blow, create, and dispel the inauspicious demerits of living beings.

31. They remove the auspicious merit of the wicked people and in some cases remove the sins of mobile beings.

32. They are seated in the celestial aerial chariot. They go as they please. They have the velocity of the wind. They revolve along with the Sun and follow him throughout the day.

33. Showering rains, blazing and delighting people, they protect living beings till the end of Manvantara.

34. This position of the deities (who identify themselves with it) exists in all the Manvantaras in the same manner whether past, present or future.

35. These sets of seven reside in the Sun and the space around him in all the fourteen Manvantaras and creations.

36. In accordance with the seasons, the Sun changes his rays, releasing heat in the summer, mist and fog in the winter and rain during the rainy season and demarcates day and night. He (thus) propitiates Devas, Pitṛs and human beings.

37. By means of the ray (Suṣumṇa), the Sun develops the Moon in the bright half (of the month) day by day and it is complete (full on the full-moon days). Devas imbibe its nectar during the dark half. Thus he propitiates Devas with the nectar.

38. After being sucked thus, the moon has only two Kalās (digits) left. Pitṛs take it as Kavya offering. Devas and Saumyas consider it as nectar and drink it.

39. Men conquer (satisfy) hunger by means of foodstuffs, beverages and medicinal herbs developed by means of rains, with water lifted up and released as rain-showers by means of his rays by the Sun.

40. For half a month Devas are propitiated through nectar. For half a month Pitṛs are propitiated by Svadhā food. The Sun sustains human beings perpetually through food. The Sun sustains them through his rays.

41. The Sun moves ahead in his chariot of green horses. Through his rays he takes up waters. At the time of their release he discharges them. Thus the Sun sustains the mobile and immobile beings perpetually.

42. He is carried by green horses. By means of his thousands of rays he drinks water. While being carried by green horses he showers it again.

43. Thus the Sun moves ahead quickly in his celestial sphere by means of his single-wheeled chariot dragged by the unimpaired gentle horses.

44. In the course of a day and night he traverses over the world of seven continents and oceans by means of his single-wheeled chariot dragged by the seven horses.

45. The Vedic metres that have assumed the form of horses are yoked to the chariot near the wheel. They can assume any form they please. They are yoked but once. They have the unlimited speed of the mind.

46. They (are accompanied) by tawny coloured masters expounding the Brahman (or the Vedas). They cover one hundred and eighty zones within one year.

47. They are yoked in the beginning of the Kalpa. They continue their journey till the final dissolution. They traverse the

external and the internal zones day by day. Surrounded by Vālakhilyas they wander day and night.

48. The Sun is eulogised by the sages through well-known words of prayer. He is served by Gandharvas and Apsaras-s by means of songs and dances. The lord of the heaven, the Sun thus traverses by means of his horses.

49. The Moon too moves among the stars that stay in the pathway of heaven (vīthī). The increase and decrease of its rays are similar to the increase and decrease of the Sun.

50-51. The chariot of the Moon has three wheels.[1] The horses are tied in pairs on either side. The chariot along with the horses and the charioteer has come out of the womb of the waters. The three wheels have a hundred spokes. Excellent white horses have been yoked thereto. They are ten in number. They are slender and divine. They are unimpeded and have the velocity of the mind. They are yoked but once (in the beginning of the Kalpa) and they travel till the end of the Yugas.

52. A white serpent acts as the rein in that chariot. All the horses are of the same colour. They carry the conch-coloured Moon.

53-54. The names of the ten horses are—Yāyu, Trimanas, Vṛṣa, Rājīvala, Haya, Vāma, Turaṇya, Haṁsa, Vyomin and Mṛga. They carry the Moon till the close of the day (?)

55-57. The gentle Moon goes ahead surrounded by Devas and Pitṛs. In the beginning of the bright half when the Sun is in front, the interior of the city of the Moon is filled duly everyday. The Sun develops the Moon drunk by Devas in the declining fortnight. The Moon is drunk for fifteen days and the Sun replenishes one part everyday. Nourished by Suṣumna the white digits flourish.

58. They decline and decrease in the dark half and develop and nourish in the bright half. Thus the body of the Moon is developed fully by the vigour of the Sun.

59. Developing gradually in the bright half day by day, the Moon attains completion on the full moon day.

---

1. Verses 50-83 describe chariots etc. of other planets like the Moon, Mercury (Budha) and others.

60. Beginning with the second day in the dark half and ending with the fourteenth day Devas drink the watery wine, the nectar of the Moon that is essentially made up of water and that by nature consists of tasty essence.

61-62. By the brilliance of the Sun the nectar is collected and prepared in the course of a fortnight. On the full moon night Devas, Pitṛs and the Sages attend the Moon facing the Sun.

63. The digits being drunk decline gradually in the dark half and become refilled in the bright half.

64. When days pass on gradually Devas drink the Moon for half a month until the new-moon day and go away. On the new-moon day Pitṛs resort to the Moon.

65. When the fifteenth part of the digits is left over in the later part of the day, that part is used up by the groups of Pitṛs.

66. The remaining digit is drunk by Pitṛs during the period of two Kalās. From the lunar rays the nectar of Svadhā comes out on the new-moon night. They drink the nectar and remain content for a month. They attain immortality.

67. All these (following) are Pitṛs: Saumyas, Barhiṣads, Agniṣvāttas and Kavyas.

68. The years, which are enumerated by Brāhmaṇas as five, are Kavyas. Saumyas should be known as *Ṛtus* (Seasons) and Barhiṣads are remembered as *Māsas* (Months). Agniṣvāttas are *Ārtavas* (Fertility period?) and these are the creations of the Pitṛs, O Brāhmaṇas.

69-71. When the digit is being drunk by Pitṛs on the fifteenth night i.e. Amāvāsyā, the last digit is left and it is refilled. The increase and decrease of the Moon are on the sixteenth day (at the beginning of each next half). Thus the increase and the decrease of the Moon are caused by the Sun. I shall now mention the increase and decrease of the stars and planets; and also describe the chariot of Rāhu later.

72. The chariot of the son of the Moon (Budha, Mercury) is bright, full of watery splendour. It is yoked with eight tawny horses and can move as fast as the wind.

73. The chariot resembles cloud. It has the frontal

fender and the axle-tree at the bottom. The charioteer is divine and great. It has all the fittings, banner and flag-staff.

74-75. The chariot of Bhārgava (Venus) is glorious. In refulgence it resembles the Sun. It is yoked with excellent horses born of the earth and having various colours. They are white (tawny), brown, blue, yellow, red, black, green, spotted and variegated. All the ten are highly blessed. They are not lean. They have the speed of the wind.

76. The chariot of Mars is glorious and golden. It is yoked with eight red, unimpeded horses. They are born of fire, and they can go everywhere. (Mars) traverses the signs of zodiac in straight, curved and circular lines.

77. Then the scholarly preceptor of Devas, Bṛhaspati (Jupiter) of the family of Aṅgiras, moves ahead in his golden chariot yoked with red horses.

78. Eight horses as speedy, as the wind and divine in nature, are yoked to it. In a constellation this planet stays for a year; then he traverses quickly.

79. Śanaiścara (Saturn) rides in a chariot made of black iron and traverses slowly. His horses are variegated in colour. They are born of the ether.

80. Rāhu's chariot is of Tāmasic nature (dark-coloured). Eight black horses, as speedy as the mind, are yoked to it.

81. Leaving the Sun, Rāhu rushes at the Moon during the lunar *Parvan* (i.e. the Full-Moon). Leaving the Moon it rushes at the Sun during the solar *Parvan* (i.e. the New-Moon day).

82. Horses yoked to the chariot of Ketu are eight. They are as speedy as the wind. They have the colour like smoke from burning straw. They are strong. They are tawny (and variegated in colour) like donkeys.

83. These horses of the planets I have explained along with their chariots. They are fastened to Dhruva by gaseous rays.

84. Being fastened by invisible gaseous rays, these (planets) being whirled, revolve in an orderly manner.

85. Being bound to Dhruva, the Moon, the Sun and the planets move about in the firmament. The planetary system united to Dhruva follows it as it whirls.

86. Just as a boat is carried along by the water in a river, so the abodes of Devas are carried by the gaseous rays. Hence all the groups of Devas are seen in the firmament by everyone.

87. There are as many gaseous rays as there are stars. They are tied to Dhruva. They whirl Dhruva and whirl by themselves.

88. Just as oil-crushers whirl and cause the wheel (of an oil-mill) to whirl, so also do the luminaries fixed (to Dhruva) on all sides by gaseous rays (bonds).

89. They move about like a fire-brand on being urged by the whirling wind. Since the wind bears the luminary bodies, it is called *Pravaha.*

90. Thus the cluster of the luminary bodies united to Dhruva traverses the firmament. The Gangetic porpoise-like appearance in the sky made up of the stars is Dhruva. If it is seen in the night, the sin committed during the day is quelled.

91. Persons looking at Dhruva regularly live for as many years, or even more, as there are stars in the "Gangetic porpoise" in the firmament.[1]

92. This permanent Gangetic porpoise shall be realised in its various divisions. Its upper jaw is known as Uttānapāda.

93. Its lower jaw is Yajña. Dharma resorts to the top of its head. Nārāyaṇa abides in its heart and Aśvins stay in its forelegs.

94. Varuṇa and Aryaman are its hind thighs. Saṁvatsara is its penis and Mitra resorts to its anus.

95. In its tail are Agni, Mahendra, Marīci, Kaśyapa and Dhruva. The four stars (?) and the Gangetic porpoise do not set.

96. The stars, Moon, Sun, planets and constellations stay in the sky with face up or in front. They are in the form of a wheel.

97. These are presided over by Dhruva. They circumambulate Dhruva which acts like the pivotal peg in the firmament.

---

1. Verses 91-95 describe the heavenly Gangetic porpoise with various stars forming parts of its body.

98. Among Dhruva, Agni and Kaśyapa Dhruva is the most excellent. It alone whirls round at the top of the mountain Meru.

99. With its face downwards it attracts the group of luminaries. Looking at Meru, it circumambulates it.

CHAPTER FIFTYTHREE

Arrangement of Luminaries

Śāṁśapāyana said :

1. Hearing this the sages became doubtful. They asked Lomaharṣaṇa again for its clarification.

The Sages said :

2. Sir, you have mentioned the famous abodes of Devas. How are these abodes ? How are these luminaries ? Please describe.

3. Please say everything precisely about luminaries.

On hearing their words the pious *Sūta said*:

4. I shall explain to you what has been mentioned by great intellectuals of perfect knowledge, in connection with the origin of the Sun, the Moon, how the Moon and the Sun are the abodes of gods.

5. Now I shall mention the origin of three fires[1]: celestial, elemental (atmospheric) and terrestrial.

6. When the great night came (lit. dawned) on Brahmā, born of the Unmanifest, the universe became undefined and enveloped by nocturnal darkness.

1. Vedic Aryans regarded Agni (Fire-god) as a great deity and it was given designations according to its functions. Purāṇas amplified the tradition and attributed cosmic functions in verses 5-18. Heating being the common factor between the Sun and fire, they are in a way identified. The credit of creating seasons through the rays of the Sun is given to Fire-god also.

7. Only four elements were there. That which blazed at first is called terrestrial fire. The fire that blazes in the Sun is called *Śuci* (celestial).

8. I shall now mention the characteristics of the fire called *Vaidyuta* (atmospheric) fire. Three fires—Vaidyuta (lightning), Jāṭhara (gastric) and Saura (solar) are born of the womb of waters. Hence by drinking water the Sun blazes in the sky with his rays.

9. The fire from lightning that burns trees cannot be quelled by water. Nor the fire in human bellies can be quenched by it.

10. The fire existing in the belly is full of rays. It is a great fire. The diffused light of the Sun devoid of heat is white and spreads everywhere.

11. It partially (with its quarter part) enters the fire at night, when the Sun sets. So the fire is seen blazing from a distance.

12. The heat of the fire permeates the Sun when he rises again. With a quarter of the heat the terrestrial fire blazes forth.

13. The light and heat of the Sun and fire develop by day and night, thanks to this mutual permeation.

14. In the northern or southern hemisphere, when the Sun rises, the night enters the water. Hence the water becomes copper-coloured during the day, because of the entry of the night.

15. When this Sun sets again, the day enters the water. So during the night the water sparkles due to the entry of day.

16. In this manner, in the southern and northern hemispheres, at the time of sunrise and sunset, the day and the night enter the waters.

17. That which blazes in the Sun drinking the waters through the rays is the celestial fire mixed with the terrestrial one.

18-19. The celestial fire of a thousand rays is circular and shaped like a jar. With its thousand rays it takes up the water of the rivers, oceans, wells, desert lands, both mobile, i.e. flowing, and stationary. The Sun of golden form has a thousand rays that exude rain, chillness and heat.

20. Four hundred of those rays having variegated forms shower rain. The rays that generate rain are called Vandanās, Vandyās, Ṛtanās, Nūtanās and Amṛtās.

21. Apart from these, there are three hundred rays that exude chilliness. These are called Dṛśyās, Medhyās, Vāhyās and Hrādinīs.

22-23. These are called Candrās. All these rays are yellow-coloured.

The rays that generate hot energy are Śuklās, Kakubhs, Gaus and Viśvabhṛts. They are also three hundred. All of them are white. With these the Sun sustains human beings, Pitṛs and Devas alike.

24. He gratifies human beings through medicinal herbs; the Pitṛs by means of Svadhā; and Devas by means of nectar.

25. During spring and the summer he blazes with the three hundred rays. During rains and autumn he generates rain by the four (hundred rays).

26. The Sun creates mist and fog by means of the three (hundred rays) during early and late winter. He deposits energy on the medicinal herbs. By means of Svadhā he propitiates Pitṛs. By means of nectar of three varieties he bestows immortality.

27. Thus thousand rays of the Sun achieve the purpose of the worlds. They differ according to the season by exuding water, chilliness and heat.

28. Thus the bright and sparkling solar zone is described. It is the support and source of origin of the stars, planents and the Moon. All these, the stars, the Moon and the planets should be known to have originated from the Sun.

29. The Moon is the lord of stars; the Sun is the king of planets. The remaining five planets are known as Īśvaras having forms as they please.

30. It is said that the fire is Sun and (the source of) water is the Moon. Now listen to the source of other planets as explained in detail.

31. The commander-in-chief of the army of Devas, Skanda, is said to be the origin of Aṅgāraka (Mars). Those who have perfect knowledge know that Nārāyaṇa is the origin of Lord Budha.

32. Lord Rudra himself who is the prototype of Dharma, the son of Vivasvat, in the world, is the origin of the great planet Saturn, the slowest of all planets. He is the most excellent among Brāhmaṇas.

33. The two great planets with bright rays are Śukra (Venus) and Bṛhaspati (Jupiter), the preceptors of Asuras and Devas. They are the sons of Prajāpati.

34. There is no doubt that the entire universe, all the worlds including Devas, Asuras and human beings, have their roots in the Sun.

35. It is his universal splendour, O leading Brāhmaṇas, that shines as the refulgence of all heaven-dwellers such as Rudra, Indra, Viṣṇu and the Moon.

36. He is the Ātman of all, the lord of all the worlds. He is the primordial great deity. Everything originates from him and merges in him.

37. O Brāhmaṇas, the creation and dissolution of the worlds arose from the Sun formerly. The Universe is known as a planet. The Sun is the most excellent and refulgent planet.

38. From him are born again and again and into him merge after death, all the moments, Muhūrtas, days, nights, fortnights, months, seasons, years, sets of five years and Yugas.

39. Their time-calculation is impossible without the Sun. Without time there is no sacred scripture, no initiation, and no daily routine.

40. Without him how can the seasons be named and classified? How can the foodgrains and plants grow? How can there be medicinal herbs of good quality?

41. Without the Sun, the thief of water, the scorcher of the Universe, all the affairs of Devas here and in heaven cannot go on.

42. O excellent Brāhmaṇas, he alone is Kāla (Time) and fire. He is the twelve-souled Prajāpati. He blazes the three worlds including mobile and immobile beings.

43. He alone is a mass of splendour. He is the entire world and benefactor of all the worlds. Resorting to the uppermost path of Vāyu, he blazes this Universe by means of his splendour at the sides, above and below.

44. Seven among the thousand rays of the Sun already mentioned by me are the most excellent. They are the causes of the planets.[1]

45. They are—Suṣumna, Harikeśa, Viśvakarman, Viśvaśravas, Sampadvasu, Arvāvasu and Svarāṭ.

46. The Sun's ray called Suṣumna develops the declining Moon. It is said to be exerting power laterally and from above.

47. The ray Harikeśa is said to be the primordial cause of the stars. It spreads forward. Towards the south the ray Viśvakarman makes Budha.

48. The next ray called Viśvaśravas is the source of Śukra (Venus). The ray Sampadvasu is the cause of Lohita (Mars).

49. The sixth ray Arvāvasu is the source of origin of Bṛhaspati (Jupiter). The ray Svarāṭ develops Śanaiścara (Saturn).

50. Thus all the planets, stars and constellations flourish by the energy of the Sun. The entire Universe too flourishes thereby. The *Nakṣatra-hood* (i.e. the term Nakṣatra) is so called due to (fact that) they do not decline.[2]

51. The Sun too is a Nakṣatra because he falls into their Kṣetras (spheres) and then by means of his rays he takes them up.

52. The constellations (*Tārakas*) are so called because they have crossed (the ocean of existence) by means of merit, because they resort to the planets at the end of their pious actions. They are called *Tārakas* because they enable others to cross (the ocean of existence) and because they are sparkling.

---

1. Verses 45-49 trace the origin of planets to the specific rays of the Sun.

2. Our author gives popular etymologies which are not tenable, e.g. in vv. 51-55 we have derivations as follows :

   (1) *Nakṣatra* 'a Star' traced to $\sqrt{}$*kṣi*, 'to get diminished'. 'That which does not get diminished' (*na kṣīyate*) is *Nakṣatra* but grammatically, it is from $\sqrt{}$*nakṣ* 'to go' + *tran* (uṇādi). *Āditya* is normally derived as *Aditi* + *ṇya* (=ya), 'the son of Aditi' but our author traces it to *ā* + *dā* 'to take away'.

53. The Sun is called Āditya, because it always removes (lit. takes away $\sqrt{}$*ā-dā*) darkness of the night both celestial and terrestrial. He is great by his refulgence.

54. The root $\sqrt{}$*su* means 'to throb' and 'to exude.' Since it diffuses light and exudes water it is called "*Savitṛ*".

55. The root $\sqrt{}$*cad* which gives the word 'Candra' has many meanings: 'to delight,' 'to sparkle', 'to act as nectar' and 'to be cool.'

56-57. The divine and sparkling orbs of the Sun and the Moon are in the sky. They sparkle like blazing fire. They are auspicious and they resemble a circular jar. The orb of the Moon is of solid water and the orb of the Sun is of solid refulgence.

58. Devas resorting to the stars, the Sun and the planets enter these spots in all the Manvantaras.

59. These abodes of Devas are named after them. The Sun enters the abode *Saura*; the Moon enters the abode *Saumya*.

60. The valorous sixteen-rayed Śukra (Venus) enters the abode *Śaukra*. Bṛhaspati (Jupiter) enters the abode *Bṛhat*; Lohita (Mars) enters the abode *Lauhita*; Śanaiścara (Saturn) enters the abode *Śānaiścara*.

61. The planets are brightly illuminated due to their contact with the rays of the Sun.[1] The diameter of the Sun is nine thousand Yojanas.

62. The girth of the Sun is three times its diameter. The width of the Moon is twice that of the Sun.

63. Equal to them, Svarbhānu (Rāhu) goes beneath. The planet Rāhu is created in globular form out of the shadow of the earth.

64-65. The dark abode of Svarbhānu is fashioned out of darkness. During full moon days he comes out of the Sun and goes to the Moon. From the Moon he goes to the Sun (during the new-moon days) and again he goes to the Moon. He dispels (the brilliance of) the heaven with his refulgence and is, therefore, called Svarbhānu.

66. The magnitude of the diameter and girth of Bhārgava (Venus) is one sixteenth of that of the Moon.

1. Scientifically correct observation but the rest (vv. 62-102) is imaginary.

67. Bṛhaspati (Jupiter) is three-fourths of the planet Venus in size. Kuja (Mars) and Saura (Saturn) are three-fourths of Jupiter in the size. Budha (Mercury) is three-fourths of each of them in width and girth.

68. (Heavenly) bodies, and constellations seen in the sky are equal to Mercury in width and girth.

69-70. One conversant with reality should know that the stars are usually in conjunction with the Moon. The stars and constellations differ from one another by five hundred, four hundred, three hundred and two hundred Yojanas as well. The spheres of the stars are lesser than the earlier ones. There is no star smaller than the ones with one and a half Yojanas.

71. The three planets Saturn, Mars and Jupiter, move far above the other planets. They go slowly and their movements are crooked as well.

72. The four great planets—the Sun, Moon, Mercury and Venus, have their orbits below. They move swiftly.

73. There are crores of constellations and as many stars too. The way (orbit) of the stars is well arranged through the control of *Vithis*.

74. In the order of his transit, the movement of the Sun is either above or below. When the Moon is in the northern sphere during Parvans, Budha and Svarbhānu occupy their own abodes.

75. The stars occupy their own abodes. These luminaries are the abodes of pious persons.

76. The abodes are created by the Self-born Deity at the beginning of the Kalpa. They stay upto the dissolution of all living beings.

77. These are the abodes of the deities in all Manvantaras. These deities identify themselves with these abodes and stay till the final dissolution.

78. The abodes of those who have gone have vanished. The abodes of the future Devas and Asuras will be created along with them. The present groups of Devas stay in those abodes.

79. In this Manvantara, the planets reside in aerial cars. In the Vaivasvata Manvantara the Sun is born of Aditi and is called Vivasvat.

80. Tviṣimat, the son of Dharma, known as Vasu is the lord Moon. The lord Śukra, king of Asuras, is known as Bhārgava (Venus).

81. The excessively refulgent lord Bṛhaspati, son of Aṅgiras, is the preceptor of Devas. Budha is charming and is known as the son of Tviṣi.

82. Agni was alternatively born as the youthful lord of Lohita (Mars). The daughters of Dakṣa resort to the stars and constellations.

83. Svarbhānu is the son of Siṁhikā, who, being a demon, harasses all living creatures. Thus the deities identifying themselves with the Moon, the Sun, planents and stars have been recounted.

84. Thus the abodes and their resident deities are mentioned. The abode of the thousand-rayed Sun is full of fire and sparkling.

85. The abode of the thousand-rayed Moon is full of water and sparkling white. The abode of the five-rayed charming planet Budha is dark in colour.

86. The abode of the sixteen-rayed Venus is full of water. The abode of the nine-rayed Mars is full of water and red in colour.

87. The abode of the twelve-rayed Bṛhaspati is big and green. It is full of water. The abode of the light-rayed Saturn is dark in colour. It is full of water.

88. The abode of Svarbhānu is dark. It is the abode harassing all living beings. The constellations are single-rayed and full of water.

89. They are the abodes of persons of pious fame. They are bright and white in colour. They are of the nature of solid water. They are created in the beginning of the Kalpa in accordance with the Vedas.

90-91. Because of his loftiness, the Sun is seen quickly by his bright rays. The Sun stationed in the *Nāgavīthi*, the path of southern transit, is encompassed by the line of the Earth during full moon and new moon days. He is not seen at the usual time and he sets early.

92. Hence, the Moon stationed in northern path is not

invariably seen during the new moon day in the southern path.

93. By virtue of the movement of luminaries, the Sun and the Moon rise and set at the same time during the equinox.

94. In the northern pathways, they rise and set at different times. During the new moon and full moon days they follow the circle of luminaries.

95. When the Sun is stationed in the southern path, he moves beneath the planets.

96. Making his orb extensive, the Moon traverses the orbit above (the Sun). The entire multitude of stars moves above the Moon.

97. Mercury is above the stars; Jupiter is above Mercury; Saturn is above Jupiter; and still above is the zone of Seven Sages (Great Bear). Dhruva (Pole Star) is above the Seven Sages.

98. The intermediate distances between the stars and the planets are above two hundred thousand Yojanas and vary in individual cases (obscure Text).

99. The planets, the Sun and the Moon come into contact with the stars everyday in the sky by their divine splendour and they separate also in the due order.

100. The Sun, stars and the planets may be either below or above or in the middle. When they come together or separate from one another, people see them simultaneously.

101. They stay in juxtaposition with one another coming into mutual contact. But their communion is free from intermixture.

102-103. Thus I have described to you the position of the luminaries on the earth and that also of the continents, oceans, mountains, sub-continents and rivers where they are situated*. These self-same planets formerly originated from the stars.

104. Vivasvān, the son of Aditi, the first among the planets, ie. the Sun-god, was born under the constellation Viśākhā in the Cākṣuṣa Manvantara.

105. The brilliant Moon-god Viśvāvasu, the son of Dharma,

---

*Bd. P. reads: *Ye ca teṣu vasanti vai*: 'Those who stay in them'.

the cool-rayed maker of nights, was born under (the costellation) Kṛttikā.

106. After the Sun, Śukra (Venus), son of Bhṛgu, endowed with sixteen rays, who is next to the Sun is the most excellent among constellations and planets. He is born in the constellation Tiṣya (Puṣya).

107. The planet Bṛhaspati (Jupiter) of twelve fiery flames, who is the son of Aṅgiras and is the preceptor of the universe was born under the constellation Phālgunī (Pūrvā Phālgunī in Bd. P).

108. It is reported that the nine-rayed, red-bodied planet (Mars), son of Prajāpati, is born under the constellation Pūrvāṣāḍhā.

109. The seven-rayed planet, Saturn, son of the Sun, is born under the constellation Revatī. The planets harassing the Sun and the Moon are born under the constellation Rohiṇī.

110. These stars and planets beginning with Śukra (Venus) should be comprehended (properly) because they attain evil propensities when the constellation of nativity is afflicted. They are affected by that defect (and are redeemed) due to devotion to the planets.

111. Āditya (the Sun) is called the first among these planets. Among the stellar planets Śukra is the first. Among the comets (Ketu) is the first.

112. Dhruva (Pole Star) is the pivotal peg among the planets divided in the four quarters. Among the stars, Śraviṣṭhā (Dhaniṣṭhā) is the most excellent; among the *Ayanas* (Transits) the Uttarāyaṇa (northern transit) is the most excellent.

113. Among the five years the first is Saṁvatsara; among the seasons Śiśira (late winter) is the first; among months Māgha is the first.*

114. Among the fortnights the bright half is excellent; among the Tithis (days of the lunar fortnight) *Pratipat* (the first day) is excellent; in the divisions of days and nights day is declared excellent.

---

*This shows that new year began in Māgha.

115. Among the Muhūrtas, the first is excellent. It has Rudra for its deity. *Nimeṣa* (the time taken in the winking of the eyes) is excellent among the units of time. So is the opinion of those who know Time.

116. Beginning with Śraviṣṭhā (Dhaniṣṭhā) and ending with Śravaṇa there shall be the Yuga of five years. As a result of the rotation of the Sun, it revolves like a wheel.

117. Hence the Sun is remembered as Kāla (Time). Know that he is the Īśvara (Lord), the activiser of the four types of living beings and their destroyer as well.

118. Thus, this is the regulated arrangement of luminaries as a decisive feature of the affairs of the world. It is evolved by the Lord for the regular functioning of the world.

119. It is born of Śravaṇa and consolidated in Dhruva. It extends all round in the form of a circle.*

120. It was told (ordained) so intelligently at the beginning of Kalpa by the Lord. He is the supporter and the *Abhimānin* (the identifier) with all. He is the Soul of luminary bodies. He is the cosmic form, a miraculous transformation of *Pradhāna*.

121. The movement of the luminaries among human beings cannot be precisely observed by the physical eye, nor can it be narrated exactly by anyone.

122. By means of scriptures, inference, perception and reasoning, after scrutinizing intelligently and carefully, a learned man should entertain sufficient faith in it.

123. O excellent among intelligent beings, these five functions are the means for ascertaining the true positions of the luminary bodies, viz. the eye, scriptures, water, written documents and mathematical calculations.

**Vṛkṣākāra* is probabaly a misprint for *Vṛttākāra* as in Bd. P. I.2.24.148.

CHAPTER FIFTYFOUR

Hymn to Nīlakaṇṭha

The Sages said :

1. O excessively refulgent sage, in which land has this holy and excellent incident happened in regard to persons progressing in Brahman ? At what time? Narrate this exactly in the manner it happened.

Sūta said :

2-3. O excellent Brāhmaṇas of pure rites, I shall narrate what had been heard by me before, when it was being narrated by Vāyu, the very breath of the Universe, at the sacrifice lasting for a thousand years. It refers to how the throat of Śiva, the lord of Devas, attained blueness.[1]

4-5. On the north of the king of mountains Himavat, there are lakes, rivers and eddies, where in sacred parks, holy centres, temples, high peaks of mountains, caves and gardens noble sages of pure rites and devotion eulogise the great Lord in due manner.

6. By means of Ṛk, Yajus and Sāman Mantras, dances, songs and worships, by Oṁkāra and obeisance they always worship Śiva.

7-9 The (heavenly) luminaries had come up. The Sun had reached the middle of the sky, the sages who had been performing sacred rites and discussing the holy story were so exhausted as to feel that life just clung to them. Then Vāyu said, "Obeisance to the blue-necked !" On hearing that the eighty-eight thousand sages of sublimated sexuality, who were known as Vālakhilyas, whose souls had been purified and who had performed holy rites, who were constant devotees of the Sun and whose diet was cofined to wind, leaves and water, asked the Wind-god :

---

1. The popular legend attributing the blue colour of Śiva's throat to the drinking of Kālakūṭa poison appears in the *Mbh. Ādi.* 11.41.43 and in other Purāṇas. The text of this chapter in vv. 10 ff. corresponds to Bd. P. I. 2.25.6 ff.

The Sages said :

10-11. O excellent Vāyu, what has been uttered by you as Nīlakaṇṭha is a great secret. It is the holiest of all sacred things. O most excellent one among pious persons, O Wind-god, we wish to hear about it by your favour, what made the throat of the lord of Aṁbikā blue !

12. We wish to hear it particularly from your mouth. Whatever is uttered by you, whatsoever words come out of your mouth are full of meanings.

13. When breath touches the proper place of articulation, then the activity of speech begins. Knowledge at the outset and desire afterwards gets activated from you, O Vāyu.

14. If you are motionless, the functions of sound cease. Where speech has ceased, the sustenance of body becomes difficult.

15. Even there, there is your excellence, O Vāyu, you are all-pervasive. O Wind-god, there is no god other than you who is all-pervasive.

16. O Vāyu, this world of living beings is directly visible to you from everywhere. You know the lord of speeches, Īśvara, the leader (controller) of the mind.

17. Tell us how was the deformity of the neck of Śiva brought about ?

On hearing the words of the sages of pious souls, Vāyu who possessed great brilliance and was honoured by the entire world, replied to them :

Vāyu said :

18. Formerly, in the Kṛtayuga there was a Brāhmaṇa Vasiṣṭha. He was a mental son of Brahmā. He was a righteous soul interested (expert) in deciding the (meaning of the) Vedas.

19-21. He asked Kārttikeya whose excellent vehicle was the peacock and who stole collyrium from the eyes of the womenfolk of Mahiṣa (i.e. made them widows by killing Mahiṣāsura), a great soul. His voice resembled the thundering sound of the clouds. He assumed the guise of a boy to delight the mind of Umā. He had killed Krauñca and delighted the heart of Pārvatī. Vasiṣṭha devoutly asked Kārttikeya of great power:

Vasiṣṭha said :

22. "Obeisance to you, O son of Hara; salute to you, O one born of the womb of Umā; Hail to you, O one born of the womb of Agni. Bow to you, O one born of the womb of Gaṅgā.

23. Obeisance to you, O one born of Śara (grove). Obeisance to you, O son of Kṛttikās; salute to you O twelve-eyed lord; obeisance to you, O six-faced god.

24. Obeisance to you, having Śakti in your hand, and a divine bell or a flag staff".

After eulogising Mahāsena he asked the Peacock-vehicled Lord thus:

25. "What is this auspicious colour as bright as collyrium, on the throat of Lord Śiva, which is lustrous as the Kunda flower or the Moon? How did it happen?

26. Please narrate this to me who am a faithful devotee with self-control. I request you, O blessed one. It behoves you to narrate the holy auspicious story quelling sins, for my pleasure."

27. On hearing the words of noble-souled Vasiṣṭha, Kārttikeya, the lord of great splendour, the destroyer of the armies of the enemies of Suras replied :

28. "Listen to the words as narrated by me, O excellent one among eloquent persons. (I am repeating) what has been heard by me formerly as I sat on the lap of Umā.

29. O great sage, this is the dialogue between the great Ātman Śiva and Pārvatī. I shall narrate it to you (for your delight).

30-43. On the beautiful peak of Kailāsa Lord Śiva who had destroyed Madana (god of love) was comfortably seated on a charming golden rocky slab embellished with pearls, jewels and gems. The peak of the mountain appeared wonderful with variegated minerals. It was over-grown with many trees and creepers. It was beautified by the Cakravāka birds. It was resonant with the humming of the bees and the continuous sound of waterfalls. The interior of the caves was resounded with the sounds of inebriated Krauñca birds and peacocks. The peak was full of Apsaras-s, Kinnaras and Jīvañjīvaka birds. It was beautified by Jāti creepers. It was sweetened with the cooings of cuckoos. It was resorted to by Siddhas and Cāraṇas. The sound of the celestial cow Saurabheyī spread everywhere. The place beneath was resonant with the rumbling sounds of clouds. The caves were full of the trumpeting of the elephants frightened on seeing Vināyaka. (It was filled) with the sounds of musical instruments like Vīṇā (Lute) and others, fascinating to the ears. It was resorted to by the bevies of ladies swinging in *Hindolas* (swings). It was echoing (with) the tinkling sound of bells fitted to the flag-staff. (It was full of sounds) with musical (wind) instruments and drums and the stroking (of arms) by powerful people. The sounds filled all the houses there. In some places the attendants of Mahādeva were laughing boisterously. Their faces were hideous and terrible. Different odours emitted from their bodies. They sported about here and there in the steps leading to the place embedded with gems, crystal and diamonds. The Lord of Bhūtas was surrounded by his attendants whose faces resembled those of tigers, lions, elephants, horses, fierce cats and foxes. Some were short, some tall, some lean, some stout; some had protruding bellies; some had pot-bellies. The calves of some were short; the lips of some hung loose; the calves of others were as big as the palmyra; the ears of some were like those of a cow; some had a single ear; some had long ears; some had no ear at all. Some had many legs. Some had great legs. Some had only a single foot. Some had no foot at all. Some had many heads. Some had huge heads. Some had a single head. Some had no head at all. Some had many eyes. Some had large eyes. Some had a single eye. Some had no eye at all. The Lord was surrounded by great Yogins as his attendants. The daughter of the Lord of mountains spoke thus to the Lord :

The Goddess said :

44-45. "O lord, lord of past and future creations, O bull-emblemed one, O Mahādeva, there is something resembling a dark cloud shining on your throat. It is neither too bright nor too clear. It resembles the heap of blue collyrium. O destroyer of Kāma's body, O lord, what is this that shines on your throat ?

46. What is the cause of this blue tinge ? What is the reason for the blueness of your throat, O lord. Please narrate this duly to me. I am interested in it".

47. On hearing these words of Pārvatī, Śiva, the consort of Pārvatī, narrated the auspicious story.

48. "Formerly when the ocean of milk was being churned for extracting Amṛta, by Devas and Dānavas, the poison as lustrous as the deadly fire, rose up in front.

49. O splendid-faced lady, on seeing it the groups of Devas and Daityas became pale-faced and dejected. They approached god Brahmā.

50. On seeing the groups of Devas frightened, Brahmā of excessive lustre spoke: "O blessed ones, why are you frightened ? Why are you dejected in mind ?

51. O excellent gods ! Eightfold *Aiśvarya* (Lordship and prosperity) has been assigned to you by me. By whom were you deprived of that *Aiśvarya* ?

52. You are the lords of the three worlds. You are free from ailments and worries. Among my creations there is no one who dares flout my behests.

53. You move about on aerial chariots as you please. You are capable of activising people in spiritual, physical and godly rites and assign the fruits thereof.

54. Hence, wherefore are you frightened like the deer harassed by lions ? What is your affliction ? Whereby is your helplessness and distress ? What is the source of your fear ? You narrate all this precisely and immediately".

55. On hearing the words of Brahmā, the great Ātman, the leaders of Devas, Daityas and Dānavas spoke thus in the company of sages :

56. "When the ocean was being churned by the noble Devas and Asuras, the poison resembling serpents, bees and blue clouds appeared before us. It was terrible and bright as the fire at dissolution of the Universe.

57. It has come up like Black Death; it has the splendour of the sun at the close of Yugas; it has the refulgence of the sun about to destroy the three worlds; it sparkles all round.

58. Viṣṇu whose complexion was fair and reddish has been burnt by the poison that rises with lustre of black fire. He has turned black (in complexion).

59. On seeing the whitish red-complexioned Janārdana rendered black, all of us got frightened. We seek refuge in you".

60. On hearing the words of Devas and Asuras, (Brahmā) of great splendour replied, desiring the welfare of the worlds:

61-62. "O ye Devas, sages and saints, all of you listen. The poison, resembling black fire, that rose up when the great ocean was being churned is known as Kālakūṭa. Even as it rose up, (Viṣṇu) was rendered black.

63. Neither Viṣṇu nor I nor the leading Devas can bear the brunt of that poison, excepting Śiva."

64. After saying this, the lotus-born Brahmā, grandfather of the worlds, the deity who has the lustre of the interior of the lotus and he who is not born of a womb, began to pray :

65. "O Virūpākṣa, obeisance to you of many eyes, who wields Pināka bow and thunderbolt in the hands.[1]

66. Obeisance to you, Lord of the three worlds. Hail to you, Lord of living beings, the destroyer of Asuras, the three-eyed sage.

67. Obeisance to you who are Brahmā, Rudra and Viṣṇu. Bow to you (the deity of) Sāṁkhya and Yoga and (to you) who are the aggregate of *Bhūtas*.

68. Obeisance to you, the destroyer of (the body) of Kāma, the slayer of Kāla. Hail to you, Rudra, the Lord and god of Devas.

69. (Obeisance to you) with matted hair, terrible (yet) propititious, bearer of a skull, the multiformed (yet) single-formed Śiva, the bestower of boons.

70. Obeisance to you, the destroyer of Tripuras, the lord of Mothers and worthy of respect. Obeisance to you the enlightened, pure, liberated and absolute one.

71. Obeisance to you, the lord holding lotus in the hand, the quarter-clad, the tufted lord, the maker of three worlds. Bow to Candra and Varuṇa.

72. Obeisance to you, the foremost of the fierce, the sage, of many eyes, possessed of Rajas, Sattva and Tamas and to one of unmanifest source of origin.

---

1. This eulogy is practically a string of names or adjectives. Śiva is equated with Para-Brahman & the highest encomium is offered to him. We find Śiva so glorified in Tait. Saṁ. IV. 5 (Rudrādhyāya). It can be claimed as a source of Purāṇic *Sahasra-nāmas*.

73. Obeisance to the eternal, non-eternal and eternal-cum-non-eternal one; to the manifest, unmanifest and manifest-cum-unmanifest.

74. Obeisance to the comprehensible, incomprehensible and comphrehensible-cum-incomprehensible one, to the Deity quelling the distress of devotees. Obeisance to you who are Nara-Nārāyaṇa.[1]

75. Obeisance to you the lover of Umā, obeisance to Śarva; obeisance to you, the deity marked by Nandicakra; obeisance to you who are fortnight, month and half a month; obeisance to you who are *Saṁvatsara*.

76. Hail to you, the multi-formed, shaven-headed, staff-bearing, armoured god. Obeisance to the bearer of a skull, the quarter-clad (naked), tuft-bearing god.

77. Obeisance to you with flagstaff and chariot. Obeisance to you the self-controlled and the celibate. Obeisance to you who are Ṛk, Yajus and Sāman. Obeisance to you O god, of such activities as these".

Śrī Mahādeva said :

78. Thus I had been eulogised by Devas who bowed to me, O splendid-faced lady.

79. "On realising my devotion, the lord of Devas whose hair and tresses are flooded with Gaṅgā water still remains subtle. Thanks to the surpassing Yogic power, he is inconceivable. He remains invisible like the moon that has been hidden (by the clouds)."

80. Thus I had been eulogised by lord Brahmā, the creator of the Universe, by means of diverse hymns taken from the Vedas and Vedāṅgas.

81. Then I became delighted with Brahmā, the great and noble Ātman. After that I spoke to him in subtle words.

82. "O lord, lord of past and future, lord of the worlds, lord of the Universe, O Brahmā of good rites, what shall I do for you?"

---

1. Purāṇas try to synthesize Vaiṣṇavism and Śaivism by identifying Śiva with Viṣṇu.

83. On hearing my words, the lotus-eyed Brahmā replied: "O Īśvara, O lord of the past, present and future, may this be listened.

84-85. O lotus-eyed lord, when the ocean was being churned by Devas and Asuras, the terrible poison, resembling a cloud, shining like a blue cloud, having the lustre of the Saṁvarta fire, refulgent like the sun at the end of the Yugas, appeared in front like the Black Death.

86. It has the brilliance of the sun capable of destroying the three worlds. It sparkles all round. The poison having the lustre of deadly fire has risen in front.

87. On seeing it we are much frightened and agitated. O Mahādeva, desiring the welfare of the worlds, you will please drink it. O Sir, you are the enjoyer of the most splendid, you are the excellent lord.

88. O Mahādeva, excepting you, there is no one to endure the poison. No other person is sung about (=glorified) as capable of it, in the three worlds".

89-90. On hearing these words of Brahmā, O splendid-faced lady, I concurred and said "So be it". Then I began to drink the poison that resembled death. As I drank the terrible poison frightening even the gods, O lady of excellent complexion, my throat immediately turned black.

91-92. On seeing the poison that had the lustre of the petal of blue lotus and that had appeared like the king of Serpents, Takṣaka, clinging to my throat and putting out its tongues, Brahmā, the grandfather of the worlds, possessor of excessive splendour, spoke: "O Mahādeva, of good rites, really you shine due to this throat".

93-94. O daughter of the excellent mountain, on hearing his words, even as the Devas and Daityas were watching along with Yakṣas, Gandharvas, Bhūtas, Piśācas, Nāgas and Rākṣasas, O sweet-faced lady, the terrible poison was contained in the throat. Hence I became famous as Nīlakaṇṭha (Blue-throated).

95. O daughter of the king of mountains, on seeing the Kālakūṭa, that poison of fierce potency, being retained by me in the throat, Devas and Daityas were wonder-struck.

96. Then, O fair lady with the gait of inebriated elephant,

all the Devas and Daityas, Nāgas and Rākṣasas spoke thus with palms joined in reverence:

97. "Wonderful is your strength, prowess and valour. Oh, wonderful is the strength of your Yoga. O lord of Devas, wonderful is your lordship, O lord, whose dishevelled hair is flooded with Gaṅgā water.

98. You alone are Viṣṇu, the four-faced Brahmā and Yama, the god of death; you alone are the bestower of boons; you alone are the sun, the moon, the earth and the water.

99. You alone are sacrifice, the rites and observances; you alone are the past and future. You alone are the origin and end; you alone are both gross and subtle Puruṣa.

100. You alone are the subtlest of the subtle; you alone are the fire and the wind; you alone are the creator, protector and annihilator of the world, both mobile and immobile."

101. After saying these words and bowing their heads, the leading Devas, the noble souls, went to Meru in their aerial chariots.

102. Thus the greatest of secrets, the holiest of holy things, the story of what is famous as Nīlakaṇṭha has been narrated to you.

103. This story has been narrated by the self-born deity. It is the sacred story that quells sins. I shall now mention the fruit accruing to that person who retains this story recounted by Brahmā.

104. O fair lady of good loins, on reaching his body; poison from mobile and immobile things becomes ineffective immediately.

105. It quells inauspiciousness and removes (the effect of) bad dreams. The person attains the love of women and leadership in royal assembly.

106. In disputes he becomes victorious; in battle he attains valour; on expedition he attains welfare; he has perpetual riches in his house.

107-109. I shall tell his goal at the dissolution of his body, O excellent-faced lady. He becomes blue-throated, green-moustached and moon-crested; he attains three eyes; he holds the trident in his hand, and has bull as his vehicle; he holds the Pināka bow;[1] he becomes as strong as Nandin with deeds as glorious as the exploits of Nandin. At my behest he wanders over all the worlds; his movement is unimpeded like that of the wind. He gains my strength and lives as such till the final dissolution of the world.

110. O beautiful lady, I shall now mention the goal both here and hereafter of those persons who are my devotees and who hear this story.

111. A Brāhmaṇa secures (attains mastery over) Vedas; a Kṣattriya conquers the earth; a Vaiśya derives profit; and a Śudra attains happiness.

112. A sick man is freed from ailments; a man in bondage attains release; a pregnant woman gets a son; and a virgin gets a good husband. Everyone regains everything he loses in this world as in the other.

113. On hearing this divine story of the Lord, one obtains the same fruit as is obtained when one hundred thousand cows are duly gifted away.

114. He who commits to memory one verse or half of it, one quarter of a verse or even half of it, attains Rudra's Loka.

115. After recounting this story of pious fruits to the Goddess, the Lord with the moon embellishing his crest, the Lord beloved of Guha, went along with Umā to the cave of Kiṣkindha seated on his bull.

116. After recounting this story of great length quelling sins, Vāyu went away. After studying everything, the excellent Brāhmaṇas went to the auspicious path of Āditya.

1. This type of liberation is called *Sārūpya*, 'similarity of appearance'.

CHAPTER FIFTYFIVE

Hymn to the Liṅga of Śiva[1]

The Sages enquired :

1. O eloquent one, who is the greatest in regard to attributes, activities and power ? We wish to hear clearly the description of his good, wonderful qualities in detail.

Sūta said :

2. In this connection they cite this ancient anecdote about the greatness and omnipotence of the great Ātman, Mahādeva.

3. Formerly this was narrated by Viṣṇu when he had conquered the three worlds after binding Bali. The deity of great prowess became the lord of the three worlds formerly.

4-6. When the Daityas were destroyed, when the Lord of Śacī was delighted, all the Devas including Indra came to see the Lord. They came near the ocean of milk where Viṣṇu, the Ātman of cosmic form, stayed. After approaching the noble-souled, the Puruṣa, Viṣṇu, all the Siddhas, Brāhmaṇas, Yakṣas, Gandharvas, Apsaras-s, Nāgas, celestial sages, rivers and mountains eulogised him.

7. "O Lord, you are the creator and sustainer of the worlds. By your grace the three worlds attain imperishable welfare. The Asuras have been conquered and Bali has been bound by you".

8. On being thus addressed by Devas, Siddhas and the sages, Viṣṇu, the excellent of Puruṣas, replied to them.

9-10. "May this be heard, O excellent Devas, I shall mention the cause; the achievement has come at the very outset, thanks to the grace of that Lord alone who is the creator of all living beings, who is Time (*Kāla*), the creator of Time, and by whom the worlds have been created along with Brahmā by means of his Māyā power.

---

1. Rudra and Agni (Fire-god) have been identified in Vedic times. Liṅga worship is not Phallus-worship but the Purāṇic transformation of Vedic fire worship. The origin of or manifestation of the Liṅga of Śiva is told in different Purāṇas, e.g. Liṅga 17, KP II. 38, Bd. P. 2.26.

11. Formerly, when the three worlds were plunged in unmanifest darkness and when the living beings had been retained inside my belly, I lay myself down.

12. Assuming the form of the thousand-headed, thousand-eyed thousand-legged deity, holding the conch, discus and mace in the hands, I lay down in the pure limpid waters.

13-14. In the meantime, from a distance I espied a person of unmeasured splendour who blazed with his brilliance resembling a hundred suns.

The person, endowed with great Yogic power, had four faces and was of golden lustre (complexion). He wore a deer-skin and was embellished with a water-pot (*Kamaṇḍalu*). Within a moment that excellent person came near.

15-16. Then he who was Brahmā, who was bowed to by the worlds, spoke to me—"O lord, who are you ? Whence have you come ? Why do you stay here. Tell me. I am the maker of the worlds. I am self-born. I have faces all round". Thus addressed by Brahmā, I spoke to him.

17. "I am the creator and destroyer of the worlds again and again". While we were talking like this with a desire to overpower each other, a well established flame was seen on the northern side.

18. On seeing that flame we two were surprised. By that splendour all the waters sparkled.

19. When that excessively surprising and mysterious flame began to increase in size, Brahmā and I hastened towards that flame.

20-22. The massive column of flame stood touching heaven and earth. In the midst of it we saw the unmanifest Liṅga of excessive brilliance[1], highly illuminated and of the size of *Pradeśa* (the distance between the thumb and the little finger). The Liṅga shone in the middle. It was neither made of gold nor of silver nor of stone. It could not be specified. It was inconceivable. It was sometimes perceptible and sometimes imperceptible. It had great splendour and was very terrible. It

1. The identity of Rudra and Fire-god is stated in RV.II.1.7; Śatapatha Br. III. 3.1.10, VI.1.3.10; Tait. Br. I.1.5.8-9; Tāṇḍya Brāhmaṇa XII.4.24.

increased in size excessively at that time. It appeared extensive through the series of flames and appeared terrific (to all beings).

23. Who can reach the limits of this terrible looking Liṅga, the cause of Mantra (Vedas), which was piercing through the heaven and the earth?

24. Then Brahmā told me, "You go down cautiously. Let us know the limits of this Liṅga, the great Ātman.

25. I shall go up as far as the limit is reached". Thus we came to an agreement and went up and down.

26. I went downwards for a thousand years. But I did not see the limit. Undoubtedly I was frightened.

27. Similarly Brahmā too was exhausted. He could not see the limit. There itself in that great expanse of water, Brahmā met me again.

28. Both of us were surprised. We were deluded by the Māyā of that great Ātman. We stood there (as if) we had lost our consciousness.

29. We bowed to the Lord engaged in meditation—the Lord who is the source of origin and the cause of (destruction) of all the worlds.

30. With palms joined in reverence Brahmā (and I) paid obeisance to the trident-bearing Śarva (Śiva), the unmanifest, the mighty god of terrible roar and a frightening form having curved fangs.

31. "O lord of the worlds and Devas, obeisance be to you. O great lord of Bhūtas, obeisance be to you. Hail to you, O external one, the cause of origin of the Siddhas. O lord, the support of the universe, obeisance be to you.

32. You are the great Brahman, the Supreme Lord and the imperishable. You are the great region and the excellent Vāmadeva. You are Lord Rudra, Śiva and Skanda.

33. You are Yajña (Sacrifice), Vaṣaṭkāra, Oṁkāra, the great goal. You are Svāhākāra and Namaskāra. You are the purifier of all sacred rites.

34. You alone are Svadhākāra. You are the Mantra for repetition. You are the sacred rites, observances, the Vedas, the worlds and all the Devas.

35. You are the sound (the quality) of Ākāśa; you are the eternal source of living beings. You are the attribute of smell in

the earth, of taste in the waters and of colour in the fire, O Maheśvara.

36. You are the attribute of touch in vāyu. You are the lord Moon in the embodied form. You are the perfect knowledge in Budha. O lord of Devas, you are the seed in the Prakṛti.

37. O lord, you are the maker of living beings. You are Kāla, Mṛtyu, Yama, the destroyer. You support the three worlds. You alone create them.

38. By means of your eastern face, you manifest Indra-hood. O lord, by means of your southern face you annihilate the worlds (as Yama).

39. By means of the western face you exhibit your Varuṇa-hood. Your Moon-hood is established by means of your northern face.

40-42a. O Lord, you shine in various forms. You are the eternal source of all the worlds. O Lord of Devas, the Ādityas, the Vasus, Rudras, Maruts, the two sons of Aśvinī, Sādhyas, Vidyādharas, Nāgas, Cāraṇas, the noble-souled Vālakhilyas and all those persons accomplished and those others who perform rites regularly, are also born of you.

42b-43. Umā, Sītā, Sinīvālī, Kuhū, Gāyatrī, Lakṣmī, Kīrti, Dhṛti, Medhā, Lajjā, Kṣānti, Vapus, Svadhā, Puṣṭi, Kriyā, Sarasvatī, the goddess of speech, Sandhyā and Rātri too are born of you, O Lord of Devas.

44. O Lord having the lustre of ten thousand suns, obeisance be to you. Bow to you, O Lord having the lustre of thousand moons. Hail to you, O Lord assuming the form of a mountain. Obeisance to you, O reservoir of all good qualities.

45. Obeisance be to you, O Lord holding a spear with a sharp edge. Obeisance to you, O Lord applying ashes to the skin. O Rudra, bow to you having the Pināka in your hand and bearing a discus and an arrow.

46. Obeisance be to you, O Lord, whose body is embellished (besmeared) with ashes. Obeisance be to you, O Lord, who destroyed Kāma. O Lord, hail to you, wearing golden apparel. Obeisance be to you, O Lord, having golden arms.

47. Obeisance be to you, O gold-formed lord. Bow to you, O gold-naveled Lord. Bow to you of wonderful form with a thousand eyes. Obeisance be to you, O Lord of golden semen.

48. Obeisance be to you, O gold-complexioned Lord. Hail to you, O gold-wombed Lord. Obeisance be to you, O Lord with gold bark-garments. Obeisance be to you, O lord, the bestower of gold.

49. Obeisance be to you, O Lord with golden necklace. Obeisance be to you, O Lord roaring terrifically.

50. Obeisance be to you, O Lord of terrific speed. Bow to you, O Śaṅkara, O blue-throated one. Obeisance be to you, O Lord with a thousand arms. Hail to you, O Lord, fond of dance and playing on instruments."

51. On being eulogised thus, the lord, the great Yogin of great intellect, became manifest. He had the lustre equal to that of a crore suns.

52-55. Then the delighted Mahādeva, appeared worthy of being addressed. He seemed to be devouring the sky with his thousands and crores of mouths, though he had only a single neck and a single mass of hair. He was bedecked in different kinds of ornaments. His body looked wonderful and variegated. He wore different (kinds of) garlands and (besmeared himself) with unguents. He held Pināka bow in his hand. The Lord wielding a spear was seated on a bull. He wore the hide of a black antelope. He assumed a terrible form with a skull in his hand. Wearing a serpent for the sacred thread, he offered protection to Devas. He laughed boisterously producing sound like a kettle-drum and the rumbling cloud wherewith the sky was reverberated.

56. At that loud sound of the great Ātman, we became frightened. Then the great Yogin said : "O excellent Devas, I am greatly delighted.

57. Both of you, see this Māyā. Give up fear. Both of you are born of my body. You are ancient and former beings.

58. This Brahmā, grandfather of the worlds, is my right arm. Viṣṇu is my left arm. He always stands by me in times of war. I am delighted with you. I shall grant whatever you desire."

59. Then both of us were delighted in the mind. We fell at his feet again. Then we, the pious great souls, spoke again.

60. "If you are pleased and if boons are to be bestowed on us, O Lord of Devas, let there be devotion in us for you."

61. "O blessed ones, may it be thus. Both of you create different kinds of subjects". After saying thus the Lord vanished there itself.

62. Thus the great power of that Yogin has been narrated to you. All this has been created by him. We are only nominal causes.

63. This form termed 'Śiva' is unknown and unmanifest. It is incomprehensible and unperceivable. Persons with intellectual vision alone can perceive it.

64. Perform obeisance to that Lord of Devas by whose grace persons with intellectual vision can perceive subtle and incomprehensible things.

65. O Mahādeva, obeisance be to you. O Maheśvara, obeisance be to you. O most excellent one among Devas and Asuras, O swan of the mind, obeisance be to you."

Sūta said :

66. On hearing this, Devas paid homage to the great Ātman, Śiva and went to their abodes.

67. He who recites this hymn of Īśvara, the great Ātman, obtains all desires and becomes free from sins.

68. All this in respect to the ancient Brahman was mentioned by the mighty Viṣṇu only due to the grace of Mahādeva. Everything in respect of the power of Maheśvara has been thus recounted to you.

CHAPTER FIFTYSIX

Description of Pitṛs

Śāṁśapāyana enquired :

1. O Sūta, how the king Purūravas, son of Ilā, used to go to heaven during the new moon day in every month? How did he perform (libation) to Pitṛs?

Sūta replied :

2. O Śāṁśapāyana, I shall now recount to you the superhuman power of (Purūravas), the son of Ilā. I shall mention how he contacted with the Sun and the noble-souled Moon.

3-5. I shall mention all these things in order—the increase and decrease of the Moon consisting of the essence of the waters during the bright and the dark halves of the month, the fixation (decision) about the fortnight dedicated to Pitṛs, the acquisition of nectar from the Moon, the *Tarpaṇa* offerings to Pitṛs, the vision of the Pitṛs who had extracted the Soma juice from the Kavya fire, and how Purūravas, the son of Ilā, propitiated Pitṛs. I shall mention the *Parvans* also (all in due order).

6. When both the Moon and the Sun come into conjunction with the same constellation, on the same night, in the same orbit, it shall be known as *Amāvāsyā* (the New Moon).

7-8. He (Purūravas) used to go to see his maternal and paternal grand-fathers, the Moon and the Sun, on every *Amāvāsyā*. After making obeisance to them, he used to keep waiting. For the sake of the Pitṛs, he used to extract exudation from the delighted Moon. In every month Purūravas, son of Ilā, stayed in the heaven and worshipped the Moon with devotion along with Pitṛs.

9-10. Pitṛs and the Moon partake of the Kavya offerings for two lavas.[1] Worshipping Sinīvālī[1] during the time of its appearance, Purūravas understood the duration of the new moon called Kuhū and worshipped Kuhū too.[2] Biding his time he used to see the Moon in conjunction with the Sun (?)

11-13. Whence will the nectar ooze out from Soma for the satisfaction for a period of a month ? It is by (replenishment) for fifteen days (of the bright half) by the flow of nectar. After drinking it in the dark half, it is being milked by the rays with

---

1. *Lava*=the 60th part of twinkling of the eye.—MW 898.

2. Verses 9-10 etc. state, Amāvāsyā is of two kinds: (i) when Amāvāsyā merged with the 14th *tithi* of the dark half, it is Sinivāli and (ii) when it merged with the 1st *tithi* of the next day (of the bright half) it is Kuhū. Sinīvāli is a divinity in RV. She is the sister of gods and bestower of progeny (RV II. 32. 6-7). Kuhū is a divinity invoked for wealth and sons (AV. VII. 47.1).

that lunar honey (nectar) given to him for oblating them to Pitṛs. The King propitiated his Pitṛs namely Saumyas, Barhiṣads, Kāvyas and Agniṣvāttas[1] by offering the nectar in accordance with injunctions.

14. *Ṛtu* (Season) which is spoken of as Agni is considered as Saṁvatsara, since Ṛtus are born of it. *Ārtavas* (smaller division of time such as a fortnight) are born of *Ṛtus* (Seasons).

15. *Ārtavas* are called half-months. Pitṛs are the sons of the year. *Ṛtus* are grandfathers. The months and the *Ṛtus* are the sons of the year.

16. Devas are the great-grandfathers. The five years (forming a Yuga) are the sons of Brahmā. Saumyas are born of the Moon. Kāvyas are the sons of Kavi.

17. Devas born of Soma, and the imbibers of the Soma juice, are known as *Upahūtas*. The Kāvyas are known as *Ājyapās*. (All) the classes of Pitṛs become satisfied thus.

18-19. Pitṛs are classified into three (only): Kāvyas, Barhiṣads and Agniṣvāttas. *Ṛtus* who are householders and performers of sacrifices are definitely Barhiṣads. Agniṣvāttas are also householders and performers of sacrifices. They are *Ārtavas*. Understand that Kāvyas are *Aṣṭakāpatis* (Lords of Aṣṭakas). Now understand the five years.

20. Among them Agni is *Saṁvatsara* and the Sun is *Parivatsara*. The Moon is *Idvatsara* and Vāyu is *Anuvatsara*.

21. Rudra is the *Vatsara* among them. The five years of the nature of Yugas are known as *Lekhas*, *Uṣmapās* and *Divākīrtyas*.

22. These imbibe the nectar in heaven every month. As long as he lived, Purūravas gratified them with that.

23-25. Since the nectar oozes out of the Moon every month, understand that it is the nectar for Pitṛs, the drinkers of Soma

1. According to Śatapatha Br. II. 6.1-7, those who performed a Soma sacrifice are *Somavantaḥ Pitaraḥ* (prob. Saumyas hereof); those who offered cooked oblations like *Caru* were *Barhiṣadaḥ Pitaraḥ*; those who offered no sacrifices but were consumed by fire in cremation after death were *Agniṣvāttāḥ Pitaraḥ*. Later during Smṛti period classes of Pitṛs increased and their connotation was changed. Thus we find in vv. 16-19 here, *Saumyas* are the sons of Soma & the imbibers of Soma; *Kāvyas* are the sons of Kavi (Śukra?) imbibers of ghee. *Ṛtus* are householders and performers of sacrifices; they are Barhiṣads. The non-performers of sacrifices are *Ārtavas* and *Agniṣvāttas*.

juice. The nectar is called *Amṛta*, *Saumya*, *Sudhā* and *Madhu*. The thirty-three Devas known as *Chandajas* drink the fifteen watery Kalās of the Moon gradually in the dark half. After drinking the nectar for a month till caturdaśī (fourteenth day), they depart.

26. Being thus drunk by Devas, the Moon remains with only the fifteenth part left on the Amāvāsyā day.

27. Pitṛs then drink the nectar for two Kalās on the new moon day, when the Moon develops by the Suṣumna ray of the Sun.

28. When the Moon is completely exhausted after being drunk, the Sun develops it by his Suṣumna ray for Pitṛs, the drinkers of Soma.

29. When the digits of the Moon are exhausted completely, the Sun develops it gradually by one fraction everyday. When the digits dwindle it becomes dark and when they develop it becomes white.

30. Thus the body of the Moon is developed by the power of the Sun. On the full moon day the Moon is complete in disc and white in colour. Thus is the decrease and increase of the Moon in the dark and bright halves.

31. The Moon with Pitṛs is known as *Idvatsara*. He is surrounded by fifteen rays shedding the nectar Sudhā.

32-33. I shall now explain the *Parvans* and the junctions of *Parvans*. Just as the sugarcane-stem and the bamboo have knots in their joints, so also the bright and dark halves have *Parvans*. Their knots and joints differ in respect of the full moon day and the new moon day. *Tṛtiyā* (the 3rd *Tithi*) and other tithis (lunar days) are the *Parvans* of the fortnight.

34. Since the rites such as of kindling fire are performed during the *Parvans*,[1] they are auspicious. If there is the overlapping of Pratipad in the evening, that time belongs to the full moon.

---

1. According to VP III.11.118-119, the 14th Tithi, 8th Tithi, Amāvāsyā and Purṇimā, the Sun's passage from one *rāśi* to another are called Parvans.

35. When the Sun is stationed in *Vyatīpāta*[1] at a deviation of half meridian (?) line at a distance of a Yuga the meridian of the Moon is risen duly by the distance of a Yuga.

36. This is because (the Sun and the Moon) glance each other after the elapse of the full moon (period), and that time their minutes of declination are the same.

37. Calculation proceeds on the basis of the time and direction of the Sun. That is the time prescribed for the rite to be performed instantly.

38. When the Moon is full after a complete period of a *pakṣa* (half-month) but the *Pūrṇimā* is the joint of the night (i.e. when it rises one digit less than the full) it is looked after by Pitṛs along with Devas, and hence it is known as *Anumati Pūrṇimā.*

39. The Moon shines very brilliantly on the full moon night. Sages call it *Rākā* because the Moon delights then.

40. The night on which the Moon and the Sun stay together in the same constellation is called Amāvāsyā. It is the fifteenth night (after the full moon).

41. The Moon is clear on the full moon day. The moon and the Sun are full in the afternoon and see each other in the Vyatīpāta. That is the full moon day.

42. When (the period of Amāvāsyā) is over, the Sun and the Moon coming together see each other, it is called *Darśa.*

43-44. In the Amāvāsyā, at the joints of the *Parvans*, there is the short time of two *Lavas*—the time taken to utter the two syllables ku-hu. It is remembered to be the time (for the sacred rites). In the Amāvāsyā when the Moon is completely invisible, it comes into contact with the Sun from the midday to the midnight. It suddenly gets released from the Sun in the morning. The Sun comes out in the midday, after remaining in conjunction for two *Kalās.*

45-46. On the *Pratipad* day of the bright half, the Moon gets released from the Sun's disc. The time of getting released from the disc is the appropriate time for *Āhuti* of *Darśa* and *Vaṣaṭkriyā.* The

---

1. The text is rather obscure. *Sūrya-Siddhānta* XI.1.2 defines Vyatipāta as follows:

"When the Moon and the Sun are on apposite sides of either solstice and their minutes of declination are same, it is Vyatipāta. The sum of their longitudes is half a circle i.e. 180.° Normally there are 13 Vyatipātas in a year.

time of Amāvāsyā shall be known as *Ṛtumukha* (first day of the season).

47. During the day in the Amāvāsyā Parvan (in the dark half) the Moon remains emaciated. Therefore, on the Amāvāsyā day the Sun is swallowed by the evil planets in the firmament.

48. The names of the Tithis have been assigned by the honoured and sensible scholars in accordance with the digits of the Moon.

49-50. The Sun and the Moon see each other on that day. It comes out and separates itself from the disc of the Sun gradually. For the duration of two *Lavas*, the Moon touches the Sun in the course of the day and the night. That is the (auspicious) time for *Darśa* and *Vaṣaṭkriyā*.

51. The Amāvāsyā (which gets mixed with the *Pratipad*, the first day, of the next fortnight for) the duration of as much time as is required for the cuckoo to utter Ku-hū is called Ku-hū.

52. (Defective) When the Moon is emaciated (due to loss of digits) yet has the remnant of a (slight digit of the measure of) Sinīvālī and the Amāvāsyā enters the Sun (gets mixed up with the last part of the *caturdaśī* day), it is called *Sinīvālī*.

53. The duration of *Parvan* in both is equal. Vaṣaṭkriyā in the Vyatīpāta of the Sun and the Moon (is forbidden?). The two types of full moon (i.e. *Anumati* and *Rākā*) have already been explained.

54. The auspicious time on the Pratipad and Pūrṇimā is for the duration of two Mātrās. The auspicious time in Ku-hū and Sinīvālī is also the same (two mātrās).

55. The auspicious time when the Moon is in the spheres of the Sun and fire has the duration of one *Kalā*.

56. Thus, it is the bright half (in which) during the 'joints' of Parvans of night the glorious Moon with its full disc gets eclipsed.

As the Moon is replenished in the fifteenth (day) it is Pūrṇimā (the full moon day).

57. In fifteen nights the Moon develops fully by putting on fifteen Kalās, adding one everyday. There is no sixteenth Kalā in the Moon. On the fifteenth day after the full moon, it becomes emaciated completely.

58. Thus are these Pitṛs, Devas, the drinkers of Soma and the replenishers of Soma, *Ārtavas* and *Ṛtus* (seasons). Hence Devas worship them.

59. Henceforth I shall describe the Pitṛs who partake of the monthly *Śrāddha*. I shall mention their goal, their inherent strength and the procedure of the *Śrāddha*.

60. The departure of the deceased and their return cannot be comprehended even by well-accomplished penance. Then how can it be perceived through the physical eye ?

61. These *Pitṛs* who are *Śrāddhadevas*, are known as Laukika (Worldly) *Pitṛs*. Devas, Saumyas and Yajvans are all *Ayonijas* (not born of a womb).

62. All these *Pitṛs* are Devas, for the latter make them flourish. There are human *Pitṛs* while others are proclaimed as *Laukika* (worldly) *Pitṛs*.

63. (The human *Pitṛs* are) father, grand-father, great-grand-father. Those who perform *Yajñas* with Soma are known as Soma-sacrificers.

64. Those who are mentioned as Yajvans are *Barhiṣads*. Engaged in holy rites, they remain happy and content till they take another body.

65-67. Those who perform sacrifices and preside over them are known as *Agniṣvāttas*. Those who adhere to their duties in virtue of their stages in life, those who closely follow the traditions, those who do not blunder in the performance of their rites with faith, those who are engaged in the holy rites till death, after being endowed with celibacy, penance, *Yajña*, progeny, faith, learning and charitable gifts (are also called *Agniṣvāttas*.)

68. After reaching heaven they rejoice along with Devas, Pitṛs and the subtle-bodied Soma-drinkers and they worship *Pitṛmāns* (?)

69. Only those who performed holy rites and were blessed with progeny are praised. Oblations and food-offerings are given to them by their kinsmen and persons born of their families.

70. Partaking of the monthly *Śrāddha*, the *Somalaukikas* become satisfied. They are human *Pitṛs* and partake of monthly *Śrāddhas*.

71-73. Others get entangled in their actions and rebirths in wombs. Fallen from their *Āśrama* duties and devoid of Svadhā and Svāhā, these wicked persons with their bodies pierced become ghosts in the abode of Yama. They bewail their former acts in their abodes of torture. They live long, (are) dry, pale, naked, hungry and thirsty, wandering here and there.

74. Desirous of water, they roam hither and thither near rivers, lakes, tanks and wells. They covet foodstuffs left by others. They tremble and move about here and there.

75-76. They move from one place of torture to another. They are thrown in different hells like Śālmalī, Vaitaraṇī, Kumbhīpāka, Karambhavālukā, Asipatravana and Śilāsaṁpeṣaṇa by (as a result of) their own activities.

77-78. It is here that they have their miserable hellish abodes devoid of joys of heaven. Offering three Piṇḍas to those who passed to the other world by uttering their names and Gotras, they offer Piṇḍas anticlockwise on the ground strewn over with Kuśa grass. Thus they propitiate the Pitṛs abiding in their places after death (or in their abodes as *Pretas* or Ghosts).

79-80. Those who do not go to the abode of torture are born in any of the five types of living beings according to their (previous) activities. Whatever may be the birth taken by them, whether of animals or of immobile beings, they get their natural food in their respective births as a result of the offerings of food by the kinsmen in the course of Śrāddha.

81. The offering of food in *Śrāddha* shall be made at the auspicious time to deserving persons. Then alone it reaches the place where the departed kinsman stays.

82. Just as the calf is able to seek and find out its mother-cow even if it is lost among other cows, so also the *mantra* chanted in the course of *Śrāddha* carries the gifts to the *Pitṛs*.

83. So also the *Śrāddha* offered through the Mantras reaches the manes. So Sanatkumāra, who had discovered the movements of the departed souls by his divine vision, could explain how food in *Śrāddha* could reach the manes.

84. These *Pitṛs* are known as Bahvīkas, Uṣmapās and Divākīrtyas. The dark half is their day-time and the bright half is their night for sleep.

85. Thus these Pitṛs are Devas and Devas are Pitṛs. Ṛtus and Ārtavas are declared as Pitṛs mutually.

86. Thus these godly Pitṛs and the human ones are delighted by *Śrāddha* rites offered to them.

87. Thus *Pitṛs* have been explained. The greatness of Pitṛs, the imbibers of Soma, is decisively mentioned in the Purāṇas.

88-89. Thus all these have been briefly explained: the contact of Purūravas with the Sun, Pitṛs and the Moon, his acquisition of the nectar and the performance of the *Tarpaṇa* to *Pitṛs*, the duration of the full moon and the new moon and the abode of Pitṛs. This is the eternal *Śarga* (Creation).

90. The Universal form of all has been mentioned but partially. It is impossible to enumerate (describe) it in full. It should be trusted faithfully by one who wishes prosperity.

91. The creation of Svāyambhuva Manu has indeed been described by me in detail and in accordance with the sequence.

What more should I describe to you ?

CHAPTER FIFTYSEVEN

The Cycle of Yugas :[1] *Their Characteristics*

The Sages said:

1. We wish to know the nature and reality of the (sets of) four Yugas which occurred formerly in the Svāyaṁbhuva Manvantara.

---

1. Although this Purāṇa accepted the Vedic tradition and regarded a Yuga period as consisting of five years (*vide supra* ch. 50 p. 343, fn. 3), here it follows Manu I.61-74, 79-86. According to Manu, the 1st Yuga, Kṛta, has a duration of 4000 years of Devas with 400 divine years of the dawn (*Sandhyā*) of the Age and 400 divine years of transition from Kṛta to the next Age (*Sandhyāṁśa*). The other Yugas, viz. Tretā, Dvāpara ahd Kali consist respectively of a period of 3000,2000 and 1000 years of Devas, each yuga preceded by and followed by *Sandhyā* and *Sandhyāṁśa*, each extending over a period of 300, 200, 100 years of Devas. This theory superseded the Vedic one and has been adopted by Purāṇas e.g. KP. I chs. 51 and 53, NP. I ch. 41, VP. I.3., Bd. P. I.2.29 &30 and Mbh. Vana. chs 149 and 188.

Sūta said :

2. In the context of the description of the earth etc. I have already said about the four Yugas. Now I shall recount them in detail. (Listen and) understand them.

3-4. Calculating everything and mentioning in detail, I shall narrate in full the six aspects viz. : *Yuga*, *Yugabheda* (difference in Yugas), *Yugadharma* (the particular characteristics of each Yuga), *Yugasandhi* (the junction of Yugas), *Yugāṁśa* (the parts of Yugas) and *Yugasandhāna* (the joints of Yugas).

5. The human year can be understood (calculated) by means of valid working knowledge. Calculating on the basis of that year, I shall explain the four Yugas.

6. The time taken to utter a short syllable is equal to a Nimeṣa. Nimeṣa, Kāṣṭhā, Kalā and Muhūrta are the units of time.[1]

7. Fifteen Nimeṣas constitute a Kāṣṭhā, thirty Kāṣṭhās make one Kalā, thirty Kalās make one Muhūrta. Thirty Muhūrtas make one full day and night.

8. The sun demarcates the human as well as the divine days and nights. The day is intended for activity and the night is meant for sleep.

9. A (human) month constitutes the day and night of the Pitṛs. Its division is thus: The dark half is the day for them and the bright half is their night for sleep.

10. Thirty human months make one month of the Pitṛs. On

---

1. Verses 6-20 give the units of Time, the smallest unit being Nimeṣa, the time required to utter one *mātrā* (a short vowel). The following are the terms to denote the particular periods.

15 Nimeṣas (18 according to Manu) = 1 Kāṣṭhā; 30 Kāṣṭhās = 1 Kalā; 30 Kalās = 1 Muhūrta; 30 Muhūrtas = complete day (day and night); 30 days = 1 month = one day + night of Pitṛs.

30 Human months = 1 Month of Pitṛs
360 Human months = 1 year of Pitṛs
Human Uttarāyaṇa (6 months) = Day of Devas
Human Dakṣiṇāyana (6 months) = Night of Devas
360 Human Years = 1 Year of Devas.
3030 Human Years = 1 Saptarṣi Year.
9090 Human Years = 1 Krauñca (Dhruva in Bd. P. I.2.29.18) Year.
360000 Human Years = 1000 Years of Devas.

the basis of the human calculation, three hundred and sixty months constitute a year of the Pitṛs.

11. A hundred human years constitute three years and four months of Pitṛs.

12. A human year in accordance with the human calculation is one day and one night of the Devas. This is the conclusion in this scripture.

13. The divine day and night together make a human year. A further classification is that the Uttarāyaṇa period (northern transit of the sun) is the day and the Dakṣiṇāyana period (southern transit of the sun) is the night (of Devas).

14. Thirty of the days and nights of the gods or thirty human years make one divine month.

15. One hundred human years make three divine months and three divine days. Thus is the divine reckoning for division of time.

16. Three hundred and sixty years according to the human calculation constitute one divine year.

17. Three thousand and thirty years according to human calculation constitute one year of the Seven Sages (Saptarṣis) or the Great Bear.

18. Nine thousand and ninety human years make one Krauñcan year (Dhruva year in Bd. P.I. 2.29.18).

19. Thirty-six thousand human years should be known as one hundred divine years. Thus is the calculation of the divine unit of time.

20. Persons well versed in calculation say that three hundred and sixty thousand years reckoned on the basis of human time units constitute a thousand divine years.

21. It is thus that the sages sang about the divine calculation. They have formulated reckoning of the Yugas and their duration on the basis of the divine calculation.

22. Wise people know that there are four Yugas in Bhārata Varṣa.[1] The first one is Kṛta, then follow Tretā, Dvāpara and Kali. One should reckon these Yugas in this order.

23. They say that Kṛta Yuga consists of four thousand years. The *Sandhyā* (Transition period) consists of as many (i.e.

1. It is strange that the yuga-system should be restricted to India only.

four) hundred years. The *Sandhyāṁśa* (part of the junction with the next Yuga) is equal to the *Sandhyā* period.

24. In the other Yugas, their *Sandhyās* and *Sandhyāṁśas* there is gradual reduction of thousand and hundred years.

25. Tretā contains three hundred years. Its *Sandhyā* and *Sandhyāṁśa* consist of three hundred years.

26. The wise say that Dvāpara contains two thousand years. The *Sandhyā* consists of two hundred years and the *Sandhyāṁśa* is equal to *Sandhyā*.

27. The learned say that Kaliyuga consists of a thousand years. Its *Sandhyā* is of a hundred years and the *Sandhyaṁśa* is equal to *Sandhyā*.

28. This period of twelve thousand (divine) years is known as (Mahā) Yuga. The four Yugas are Kṛta, Tretā, Dvāpara and Kali.

29. In this world the calculation of years is based on human level. Now I shall mention the duration of Kṛta Yuga in accordance with that type of calculation.[1]

30. The duration is one million four hundred and forty thousand years. As for Kali Yuga, it is one-fourth of the adove.

31. Thus the specific duration of time of the four Yugas excluding the *Sandhyās* and *Sandhyāṁśas* is declared.

32. Including the *Sandhyās* and *Sandhyāṁśas* the duration of the four yugas is four million three hundred and twenty thousand human years.

33. Thus seventyone sets of Caturyugas consisting of Kṛta, Tretā etc., constitute a Manvantara.

34-36. Now understand the unmber of human years constituting a Manvantara. It will be thirty crores, six millions and seven hundred and twenty thousand human years (306720000 years). The number of years constituting a Manvantara has been calculated by Dvijas, the experts in calculating time. Thus the duration of a Manvantara and that of Yugas has been stated.

37. The first (Kṛta) Yuga has four thousand years. The remaining Yugas, viz. Tretā, Dvāpara and Kali, I shall explain.

---

1. Our text records the duration of Kṛtayuga and the total number of human years in *Caturyugas*. It means verses pertaining to the periods of other Yugas are deleted (For these vide Bd. P.I.2. 29-31-36).

38. Previously, while engrossed in describing the lineage of the sages, the two Yugas have been mentioned to you as they had come in due order. It is not possible to describe separately the two connected Topics coming in the same context simultaneously.

39 In the beginning of Tretā, Manu and the Seven Sages popularised the sacred rites of Vedic and Smṛti origin, directed by Brahmā.[1]

40. The Seven Sages expatiated on the Vedic sacred rites such as Marriage, *Agnihotra* and the like on the basis of Ṛk, Yajur and Sāman.

41. The Svāyaṁbhuva Manu expatiated on the conduct of life based on Smṛti injunctions, traditionally handed down and referring to the duties of the different castes and stages of life.

42-44. The Seven Sages and Manu were endowed with truthfulness, celibacy, learning and penance. They had performed penace in accordance with the order of sages. Hence in the beginning of Tretā Yuga, the Mantras manifested themselves to them without their undergoing physical or mental effort. In the first Kalpa those Mantras along with *Tāraka* (Oṁkāra) and others had already appeared before the Devas.

45. When the (original) Siddhis ceased to exist, these (others) began to function. Thousands of those Mantras which existed in the past Kalpas manifested themselves in their intellect once again.

46. The Seven Sages popularised the Ṛk, Yajus, Sāman and the Atharvan mantras and Manu propagated the rites in accordance with Smṛtis.

47. In the beginning of Tretā, the Vedas were one undivided and unified whole, because Dharma alone prevailed. But they are classified in Dvāpara age due to the shortage of life.

48. In the Kali and Dvāpara ages, divine sages and Devas without birth or death were created by penance by the Self-born Deity.

---

1. Verses 39-85 describe the happy life in Tretāyuga (cf. Mt. P. 142).

49. Following their righteous conduct, along with their lineage, they perform their respective duties in different Yugas. The Vedic texts, with ancillaries, function* with uniform meaning in every age.

50. *Ārambha* (expedition or enterprise) was a sacrifice for Kṣattriyas. *Havis* (offering of ghee etc.) was the *Yajña* to Vaiśyas. Śūdras had service as *Yajña* and excellent Brāhmaṇas had *Japa* (chanting of Mantras) as their *Yajña*.

51. All the castes rejoiced in Tretā age. They were protected righteously. They performed holy rites. They were happy and flourishing. They were blessed with progeny.

52. Kṣattriyas obeyed the (advice etc. of) Brāhmaṇas, Vaiśyas obeyed Kṣattriyas, Śūdras followed Vaiśyas. People cooperated and collaborated with one another.

53. Their activities were auspicious. Their holy rites and duties of castes and stages of life too were auspicious, in thought, mind, words and actions. Thus in Tretā age their activities remained unimpaired.

54. In Tretāyuga, people were equally endowed with the same span of life, good intellect, strength, beauty, health and righteousness.

55-57. Brahmā had stipulated the duties of the different castes and different stages of life. But out of delusion the subjects strayed away from sacred rites. They argued and quarrelled with one another. They approached Prajāpati Manu. Manu, the son of Brahmā, realized the state of affairs. He, the creator, the Man, begot of Śatarūpā two sons Priyavrata and Uttānapāda. These two were the first kings.

58. Thence arose a line of kings wielding the staff of power of punishment. Since they delighted the subjects, kings were called "*Rājānaḥ*".

59-60. In order to check and control those men who commit sins in secret and (hence) are difficult to be subdued, and in order to establish righteousness on the earth, the divisions of

*For *vikrīḍante* in our text here, Bd. P. I.2.29.54 reads *vikriyante* 'undergo changes' (in every *yuga*).

castes have been laid down in Tretā Yuga. The compilations of Vedic texts, both Mantras and Brāhmaṇas, have been made by the sages.

61. (The institution of) Yajña has been initiated by Devas, namely Yāmas, Śuklas and Japas all fully equipped with the requisites.

62. Formerly, in the Svāyaṁbhuva Manvantara, Yajñas were set in vogue by Devas under the leadership of Indra, the enjoyer of the universe.

63. Truthfulness, Japa, penance and charity are the main virtues in Tretā age. The practice of holy rites and rituals declines and the virtue of truthfulness prevails.

64. Renouncing their staff (of punishment due to its superfluity ?) those excessively fortunate kings became performers of sacrifice and expounders of the Vedas.

65. Their eyes were as large as lotus petals. Their chests were broad, and their bodies were well-built. They were vigorous and capable of slaying lions. They walked majestically like the elephants in rut.

66. They wielded great bows. They were endowed with all good characteristics. They were *Nyagrodha-parimaṇḍalas* (as explained in the next verse).

67. The word 'Nyagrodha' denotes two (both the) arms. Hence Nyagrodha means *Vyāma* (extended arms). He whose height extends as much as a *Vyāma*, he whose girth and height are equal, should be known as a *Nyagrodha-parimaṇḍala*.

68. The following seven[1], viz. a discus, a chariot, a jewel, a spouse, a treasure, a horse and an elephant, are regarded as super-gems (*ati-ratna*).

69. They say that the following seven are the inanimate jewels of the sovereigns of the worlds, viz. a discus, a chariot,

1. The idea that an emperor possesses excellent gems (*ati-ratnas*) is found in Pali, e.g. *Sudarsana Sutta, Dīgha Nikāya*. Here verses 68 and 69 give different lists of seven 'inanāmate jewels'. V. 70 enumerates 'living, animate, jewels'. Thus an emperor is (or should be) in possession of 13 jewels. The representation of a *cakravartin* at Jagayya Petta (2nd cent. B.C.) shows a combination of both animate & inanimate jewels and one more feature—at the touch of the emperor's hand the sky, showers gold coins.

a jewel, a sword, an excellent bow (the fifth *ratna*), a flag and a treasure.

70. The seven jewels (of an emperor) possessing life are mentioned as follows : queen, family-priest, commander-in-chief, chariot-maker, minister, horse and elephant (lit. elephant-cub).

71. These fourteen jewels are divine. They have been naturally acquired by the noble-souled ones. These fourteen jewels should be assigned to all emperors (i.e. all emperors should possess these).

72. In all the Manvantaras of the past and future, the emperors are born on the earth with a part of Viṣṇu.[1]

73-74. The precious gems are conducive to the welfare of all emperors of the past, present and future born in the Yugas Tretā etc. These four are very wonderful, viz. strength, piety, happiness and wealth (among the emperors).

75. Wealth, dharma, love, fame and victory attained by kings without any conflict are on a par with one another.

76. They excel even the sages by means of (spiritual powers such as) *Aṇimā* (minuteness) and others the power of Lordship, learning and penance. They overpower Devas, Dānavas and human beings by their strength and austere penance.

77. They are born with super-human marks visible on their bodies. They have a circle of hair on their forehead (between the eyebrows); their tongue sweeps their mouths. Their teeth and lips are copper-coloured; their hair stand facing up; and they have the Śrīvatsa scar (on the chest).

78. Their arms extend to their knees; their palms are marked with net and bull; they are very tall (*Nyagrodha-pariṇāhas*); they have shoulders like those of lions; their penises are well shaped. Their gait is as stately as that of a lordly elephant. Their chin bones are broad.

79. There are lines of wheel and fish on the soles of their

1. Verses 72-80 state the then idea about a model emperor.

feet and of conch and lotus on their palms. They live upto eightyfive thousand years as kings without signs of old age.

80. They have unimpeded movement in four places, viz. in the firmament, in the ocean, in the nether regions and on the mountains.

81. Sacrifice, charity, penance and truthfulness are the holy rites in Tretā Age. During this age, Dharma functions in accordance with the division of castes and stages of life.

82. *Daṇḍa-nīti* (administration of Justice), aims at the establishment of the bounds of decency. All the subjects are jolly, well built, free from ailments. Their minds are fully contented.

83. Only a single unified Veda with four sub-divisions prevails in Tretā Age. People live upto three thousand years.

84. Surrounded by sons and grandsons, people die in due order (of seniority in age). This is the characteristic feature of Tretā Age. (Now) understand the *Tretā-Sandhyā* (Transition from Tretā Yuga).

85. The traits of Tretā Age continue to one-fourth of the *Sandhyā* and the traits in the *Sandhyā* continue to one-fourth of the Yuga.

Śāṁśapāyana said :

86. How did Yajña function in the beginning of Tretā age formerly in the Svāyaṁbhuva Manvantara ? Please explain it precisely.

87-88. How did they again make the classification and arrangement of the castes and stages of life when the *Sandhyā* too had elapsed along with Kṛta Age and a fraction of it alone remained, and Tretā age set in ? How was *Yajña* made to function, after gathering all the requisites.

On hearing this, *Sūta said* :

O Śāṁśapāyana, now listen to this.

89-90. I shall mention how in the beginning of Tretā Age Yajña was set in vogue. When there was plenty of rain, the plants grew and agriculture became established. People set about building houses, hermitages and cities. Then Indra the, enjoyer of the universe, arranged the division of castes and stages of life and compiled the Mantras into *Saṁhitās*. He prescribed (specific) Mantras for rites leading to fruits here and hereafter.

91. Thus, Indra, the enjoyer of the universe, along with other Devas, initiated *Yajña* (the institution of sacrifice) together with all its requisites.

92. When the horse-sacrifice was instituted, the sages arrived there and began to perform sacrifices with the holy sacrificial beasts. On hearing about it, people assembled there to witness it.

93-97. When the Ṛtviks were busily engaged in sacrificial rites, when the Vedic mantras were recited, when the leading *Adhvaryus* moved about hurriedly and quickly, when the holy sacrificial beasts were being killed, when the offerings of ghee were poured into the fire by the divine *Hotṛs*, when the noble Devas were invoked and when they partook of their shares in the sacrifice, the sages began to worship Devas in the form of sense-organs (i.e. their presiding deities) who existed in the beginning of the Kalpas. The *Adhvaryus* who were great sages got ready at the time of *praiṣa* to slay the animals. On seeing the animals in their pitiable condition, the great sages collectively asked Indra[1]—"What is this sacrificial rite of yours ?

98. Desirous of a rite involving violence to life you have started an extremely sinful activity. O leading and excellent Deva, in this *Yajña* of yours the slaughter of animals is not a desirable act.

99. An evil activity has been started by you for destroying Dharma through animal-slaughter. This is not Dharma. This is an evil, sinful act. Violence can never be a Dharma.

100-101. If Your Honour wishes to perform the Yajña do it as per injunctions in the Vedas. You may worship by means of the Yajña that will not cause the violation (dissipation) of Dharma. O great god, perform the Yajña with the sacrifice-worthy seeds, which does not involve violence (*Hiṁsā*)—the

1. Verses 97-102 record the Brahmanical protest against animal-sacrifice. A germinable seed is also prohibited as it involves Hiṁsā. Only old seeds incapable of germinating into sprouts should be used.

seeds which are kept for the maximum period of three years and which do not germinate (into sprouts). O Indra ! This great Dharma (rite) has been laid down formerly by the self-born god (Brahmā)."

102. In this way Indra, the enjoyer of the universe, was asked by the sages, the seers of Reality: 'Say with what objects, mobile (living) or immobile (inanimate), Yajña shall be performed?'

103. The great sages eagerly seeking truth got tired of the dispute. Coming to a compromise with Indra they asked lord Vasu:

The Sages said:

104. "O excessively intelligent king, O son of Uttānapāda, how was the procedure of Yajña seen by you ? Please tell us. O lord, clear our doubts."

105. On hearing their words, the king remembered the Vedic texts and, without pondering over the strong or weak points, he explained the facts about Yajña. The king said : "The Yajña shall be performed as laid down in the sacred texts.

106. It shall be performed with sacrificial animals or seeds and fruits. Violence is the nature of Yajña. This is what appears to me.

107. Inasmuch as the Mantras in the Saṁhitās, as revealed to the sages endowed with penance and the visions of Tāraka and other mantras, are indicative of violence, what I have said now is based on that authority. Hence it behoves you to forgive me.

108. O Brāhmaṇas, if those statements in Mantras are authoritative, let the *Yajña* function on those lines, otherwise those statements will become false".

Thus those sages of Yogic communion were rendered unable to reply (silenced by him).

109-110. Glancing at the world below they said—"For that purpose be quiet. Though a king, you have uttered a lie. So enter the nether world". As soon as this was uttered, the king entered the nether world. Having been a resident of the upper regions, he now became a resident of the nether regions.[1]

111. Thanks to that statement of the sages, he became a resident of the nether regions. Attempting to clear doubts in Dharma matters, King Vasu (in the nether world) went below.

112. No person, even if he be very learned, should express a decisive opinion all by himself, in regard to the disputed points of Dharma. The way of Dharma is very subtle. It has many loopholes and is inscrutable.

113. Excepting Svāyambhuva Manu, none of Devas and sages can pronounce a judgment on Dharma.

114. So, violence was not approved as a means to Dharma by the great sages.[2] Thousands and crores of sages have attained heaven by means of their activities.

115. For the same reason, the sages do not unduly praise charity or Yajña. By making gifts of even insignificant articles such as bulbous root, fruit, vegetables or waterpot, in accordance with their means, the sages have become established in heaven.

116. *Adroha* (absence of ill-feeling), *Alobha* (absence of covetousness), *Dama* (self-control), Bhūtadayā (kindness to living beings), *Tapas* (penance), *Brahmacarya* (celibacy), *Satya* (truthfulness), *Anukrośa* (compassion and tenderness), *Kṣamā* (forgiveness) and *Dhṛti* (fortitude)—these are roots of Dharma but extremely difficult to achieve.

117. Yajña consists of piety and Mantras; Tapas is of the nature of observance of fast; one attains Devas through Yajña and Vairāgya (detachment) through penace.

118. Brāhmaṇhood is attained through *Karmasannyāsa* (renunciation of the fruits of Karman). Assimilation (in the supreme Ātman) is obtained through detachment. *Kaivalya* (complete identity with Brahman) is obtained through perfect knowledge. These are the five goals of life.

119. Thus, formerly, in the Svāyambhuva Manvantara, a

1. The fall of Vasu for supporting animal-sacrifice shows that violence to life even for religious purpose was condemned at the time of the Purāṇa. The legend is found in *Mbh. Śānti.* 337. 13-16.

2. Verses 114-118 establish the superiority of the path of knowledge (*jñāna-mārga*) over *karma-mārga* includinσ sacrifices.

dispute arose between Devas and sages in regard to the practice of Yajña.

120. Then, after witnessing that wonderful procedure (of Yajña) through violence and disregarding the suggestions of Vasu, the sages returned to the place whence they had come.

121-123. When the sages had gone away, Devas completed the Yajña and attained the fruits. It is heard that many Brāhmaṇa-Kṣatriya kings had attained *Siddhis* through penance. These include Priyavrata, Uttānapāda, Dhruva, Medhātithi, Vasu, Sumedhas, Virajas, Śaṅkhapāt, Rajas, Prācīnabarhis, Parjanya, Havirdhāna and other kings. These and many other kings attained Siddhis and went to heaven. They were saintly kings of great prowess whose fame was well-established.

124. Hence by all means, in regard to everything, penance surpasses *Yajña*. It was by penance that the universe was created by Brahmā.

125. So, Yajña can never excel penance. All this (visible universe) has its roots in penance. In this manner Yajña was set in vogue in the Svāyambhuva Manvantara. From that time onwards the performance of Yajñas continued as Yugas rolled on.

CHAPTER FIFTYEIGHT

Description of the Four Yugas

Sūta said :

1. Henceforth I shall explain the traits of Dvāpara[1] age. When Tretā Yuga ends, Dvāpara sets in.

2. In the beginning of Dvāpara, the attainment of *Siddhis* by the people is as it was in Tretā Yuga. But as the Yuga advances, the *Siddhis* disappear.

---

1. This chapter describes the state of society, religion, religious texts etc. in Dvāpara Age. The deterioration and confusion in social, religious and other conditions in Dvāpara show how a backround of chaotic conditions was developing for Kali Age.

3-4. Then the following vices begin to appear in the people at the time of Dvāpara. : covetousness, lack of fortitude, trading mentality, war-mindedness, indecision about principles, inter-mixture of castes, indecision about duties, destruction of sacrificial plants and animals, pride, arrogance, impatience and weakness. These vices provoked by Rajas and Tamas Guṇas prevail in Dvāpara Age.

5. In Kṛta Age Dharma is natural; in Tretā it is sought and attained. In Dvāpara it becomes agitated and intensly affected, and in Kali it perishes.

6. In Kali Age the order of the castes gets destroyed. The discipline of the different stages of life is disturbed and confused. Doubts (due to variance) in Śrutis and Smṛtis begin to rise.

7. Owing to the difference between Śrutis and Smṛtis, no decision is arrived at. Due to indecision, principles of Dharma cannot be declared. When the principles diverge, there is difference of opinion among men.

8. Owing to mutual difference in their views and delusion, no definite decision as to what is Dharma and what is not, can be arrived at.

9. In view of the defects in the causes and the indecisions therein, differences in opinion arise leading to these peculiarities of outlook (or philosophy).

10. Multiplicity of scriptures has been created by the people of different (philosophical) outlooks. A single unified Veda is divided into four in Tretā Age.

11. Due to the short span of life as found in Dvāpara Yuga, the Veda is classified into four by Vedavyāsas (in Dvāpara Yugas).

12. The Vedas are further sub-divided into Mantras and Brāhmaṇas by the descendants of sages by alterations on accents, syllables etc. in accordance with their different outlooks.

13. The Saṁhitās of the Ṛk, Sāman and Yajur Vedas were compiled by sages expert in Śrutis occasionally with general and special (known as Vedic *Vikṛtis*) changes according to different standpoints.

14. Consequently Brāhmaṇa (works), Kalpa Sūtras and Mantra-Pravacanas (different scriptural texts) came into existence.

Some were abandoned by authoritative teachers while others were retained.

15. In Dvāpara Age Brāhmaṇas began to disregard the rules of conduct and stages of life. Formerly there was one Yajurveda; later it was bifurcated (into Śukla and Kṛṣṇa Yajurveda).

16. This entire scriptural lore became confused by the general and perverted interpretations. By the discourses on (the interpretation of) the Yajurveda, it was greatly impaired.

17. So also, by means of innumerable alterations and variations, the Atharvan, Ṛk and Sāman have been confused in Dvāpara by the people of different views.

18. These diverse and different versions do not perish in spite of alterations in Dvāpara Age. They continue to function but in Kaliyuga they perish.

19. Effects of these contrarieties and errors take shape in Dvāpara itself as calamities such as draughts, premature deaths, epidemics.

20. Due to miseries born of verbal, mental and physical acts, despondency and indifference to worldly life sets in, as a result of which they begin to ponder over the ways of relief from misery.

21. The pondering leads to detachment; from detachment, defects (of the worldly life) are seen. As a result of seeing defects, there is the possibility of spiritual knowledge in Dvāpara Age.

22. In Dvāpara Age, rival (scriptures and sects) crop up against the scriptures which were honoured formerly in the first Svāyaṁbhuva Manvantara.

23. There are variations and alterations in the science of Āyurveda, Jyotiṣa and the ancillaries of the Vedas; there are doubts and variations in regard to the texts on political economy and logic.

24. There are diversities and variations in the Smṛti texts. Separate systems and schools (of theology and philosophy) are established. In Dvāpara Yuga difference of opinion starts among men.

25. The life of all living beings in Dvāpara Age becomes arduous involving bodily strain. Livelihood is possible only by mental, verbal and physical strain.

26-27. Covetousness, lack of fortitude, mercantile activities, wars, indecision in regard to philosophical principles, handling and editing of the Vedic texts, inter-mixture of holy rites, diseases, sickness, greed, slaughter, breakdown in the system and rules of castes and stages of life, and susceptibility to passion and hatred—all these are rampant in Dvāpara Age.

28-29. The traits of Dvāpara are evident in the *Sandhyā* period but a little. They become deficient in quality. In the quarter of the *Sandhyā* period, a part of it persists.

30. Now listen and understand the traits of Kaliyuga[1]. At the close of transitional period of Dvāpara, Kaliyuga begins.

31. These are the characteristics of Kaliyuga: violence, jealousy, falsehood, deception and slaughter of ascetics. These are the characteristics of Kali Age which people inherit.

32. Affected by the traits of the Age, entire Dharma deteriorates. It is doubtful whether the livelihood (of the people) can be achieved even by putting up mental strain, physical exertion or prayers.

33. In Kali Age, there are fatal diseases. There is perpetual fear of hunger. There is terrible danger of drought. Vision is blurred and rendered perverse.

34. In Kaliyuga, people do not accept the authority of Smṛtis. Some die in the womb, others die in youth. Some die in old age and some in childhood, in Kali Yuga.

35. In Kali age people are unrighteous, unmindful of the rules of conduct, fierce in anger but deficient in power and splendour. They always utter falsehood.

36. There is danger and fear to people owing to wrong performance of sacrifices, neglect of (Vedic) studies, evil conduct, misleading religious scriptures and faults in the performance of holy rites of Brāhmaṇas.

---

1. This gloomy picture of Kali Age is found in almost all Purāṇas e.g. *Mbh. Vana.* chs. 188, 190, Br. P. chs. 229-230, Mt. P. 144. . 32-47, VP. VI. 1.

The consensus of Purāṇas shows that this was probably the actual state of Indian society when the Purāṇas came to be written.

37. In Kali age creatures are affected by passion and greed. They become violent, deceptive, malicious, hot-tempered, impatient and untruthful.

38. There is much of agitation and turbulence at the advent of Kaliyuga. There is no regular study of the Vedas. The Brāhamaṇas do not perform Yajñas. All men inclusive of Kṣattriyas and Vaiśyas gradually decay.

39. Low-born and insignificant persons have contact with Brāhmaṇas in sharing beds, seats and food in Kali Age.

40. Kings are mainly Śūdras propagating heretic ideas. People never hesitate to kill a child in the womb. They behave in such a way.

41. Longevity, intellect, strength, beauty and familyprestige decline. Śūdras behave like Brāhmaṇas and Brāhmaṇas adopt the ways of Śūdras.

42. When the end of the Yuga approaches, thieves and robbers administer kingdoms like kings; kings adopt the methods of thieves and robbers. Servants are bereft of love, friendship and loyalty (to their masters).

43. Women become unchaste and disinterested in holy rites. They become fond of wine and meat. When Kali Age sets in, they resort to deceptive means.

44. In Kali Age beasts of prey become more numerous and owerful. Cattles die and dwindle. Saintly men withdraw and keep aloof.

45. At that time excessively fruitful but very subtle Dharma becomes difficult of access. Since the conduct of life of those who enjoy, in the various stages of life, is loose and unbridled, Dharma gets shaken.

46. Then, when the end of the age approaches, even the great goddess like the earth will yield but little fruit. Śūdras will begin to perform penance.

47. But piety practised for one day (in Kali Yuga) is equal to that practised for a month in Dvāpara and a year in Tretā Age.

48. The kings never protect the subjects. They appropriate their shares in oblations. Towards the end of the Yuga, they become eager solely to protect themselves.

49. The kings do not belong to the Kṣattriya clan. Vaiśyas maintain themselves with the help of Śūdras. The noble Brāhmaṇas perform obeisance to Śūdras at the end of Kali Age.

50. In Kali Age there will be (wicked) persons in the guise of sages. When the Yuga is about to come to a close, the god of rains will shower in a mysteriously haphazard manner.

51. In this base Yuga, people will have trading propensity, By false measures, the buyers will be deceived of their due share in the commodities.

52. The whole society abounds in heretics of foul conduct and activity with their false appearance. Men will be in a minority and women will be many, when the end of Kaliyuga is imminent.

53. People will be begging too much of one another. They will habitually eat meat. They will be using harsh words. They will not be straightforward or free from jealousy.

54. No one helps in return for the help received. People will get emaciated and weak. They will indulge unhesitatingly in the activities causing downfall. That is the characteristic of the Yuga coming to a close.

55. The earth will be devoid of good men. It will be desolate. In countries and cities, there will be groups and cliques.

56. The earth will be deficient in water and less fertile. Protectors (i.e. those who ought to protect) will not protect. They will not exercise control over the administration.

57. People will take away others' gems and jewels. They will molest other men's wives. They will be passionate with a wicked heart. They will revel in violent sinful activities.

58. The men have unlikeable consciousness (?) They keep their hair untied and dishevelled. Towards the close of the Yuga, men less than sixteen years will begin to procreate.

59. When the close of Yuga is imminent, Śūdras exhibiting their white teeth, with clean shaven heads and wearing ochre-coloured robes will perform sacred rites, proclaiming that they have conquered the sense-organs.[1]

1. Probably a reference to Buddhist monks, as Buddhism prevailed all over India at the time of these Purāṇas.

60. There will be thieves stealing foodcrops and garments. There will be looters robbing other robbers and abductors of murderers.

61. When perfect knowledge and holy rites disappear in the world, when people become inactive (in religious matters) even worms, mice and serpents will attack men.

62. Abundance, welfare, good health and ability will become rare. Owls will begin to infest the countries afflicted by the fear of hunger.

63. The maximum life expectation of the people afflicted by misery will be a hundred years. In Kali Yuga, the Vedas will be seen in some places and not seen in some places.

64-66. Yajñas are forsaken when Dharma receives a setback. There will be many types of heretics like wearers of ochre-coloured robes (Buddhists), Jainas and Kāpālikas (skull-bearing mendicants). There will be sellers of the Vedas and of the sacred places. Heretics antagonistic to the discipline and arrangement of different castes and stages oflife will be born. When Kali Yuga sets in, the Vedas will not be studied. Śūdras will be experts and authorities in the affairs of Dharma.

67. Kings born of Śūdra women will not perform Yajñas. The subjects will murder women and slaughter cows. Coming to mutual clash, they will kill one another. And in this way, people will try to accomplish (their object).

68. Due to the spread of misery, people will be short-lived. Realms will be exterminated. Sickness, delusion, dejection, unhappiness and all *Tāmasic* activities prevail in Kali Age.

69. People will kill and destroy children in wombs. With the advent of Kali, longevity, strength and beauty begin to decline. The highest life expectation of men afflicted by misery will be a hundred years.

70. The Vedas will be seen somewhere and not seen in some places. When Dharma is harassed Yajñas are forsaken.

71. At that time men will attain *Siddhi* in a short time. Blessed people, leading excellent Brāhmaṇas will perform holy rites at the end of the Yuga.

72. For those who perform the holy rites enjoined by the Śrutis and Smṛtis, without the least tinge of jealousy, the

performance of holy rites for a year in Tretā Yuga is equal to that for a month in Dvāpara Age. An intelligent man performing these in Kali Age according to his capacity, shall attain the same fruit in a day.

73-74. This is the condition in Kali Age. Now understand the condition in the part of the junction (*Sandhyāṁśa*) from me. In every Yuga the achievements (*Siddhis*) shrink and dwindle by three-fourths. In accordance with the nature of the Yuga, the *Sandhyās* stay by a quarter. In accordance with the nature of the *Sandhyās* they are established in their parts by a quarter.

75-76. Thus when the period of junction (*Sandhyāṁśa*) approaches at the close of the (Kali) Yuga, a king, the chastiser of the wicked people, will be born after the death (fall) of Bhṛgus. He (will be) Candramas by *Gotra* (of the Lunar race). He will be called Pramiti. He was born of a part of Viṣṇu formerly in the Svāyaṁbhuva Manvantara.

77. He wandered over the earth for full twenty years. He led an army consisting of cavalry, chariots and elephants.

78. He was surrounded by hundreds and thousands of Brāhmaṇas armed with weapons. He killed Mlecchas in thousands.

79. He went everywhere. After killing the kings born of Śūdra women, he exterminated the heretics.

80. He killed thousands of persons who were not religious and righteous. He killed those born of mixed castes as well as those who depended on them.

81-83. He killed the *Udīcyas* (northerners), *Madhya Deśyas* (people of the Middle Land), mountain-dwellers, easterners, westerners, dwellers in Vindhya and Aparānta. He killed the southerners, Draviḍas, Siṁhalas, Gāndhāras, Pāradas, Pahlavas, Yavanas, Tuṣāras, Barbaras, Cīnas, Śūlikas, Daradas, Khasas, Laṁpākas, Ketas, and the different tribes of Kirātas.

84. Setting his wheel (of religious victory) in motion, the powerful lord, the destroyer of Mlecchas, roamed over the earth. He could not be thwarted by any living being.

85. He was born of a part of Lord Viṣṇu. This valorous hero was known as Pramiti by people knowing what happened in the previous birth.

86-88. In the previous Kali Yuga, he was of Candramas Gotra (Lunar race). When he was thirtytwo (he started his victorious march). For twenty years, he continued to slay men and other living beings in thousands. By his firm action, he rendered the earth a relic (memento) of his valour. Due to his anger provoked by mutual causes (bilateral relations) or suddenness, he subdued Vṛṣalas who were generally unrighteous. Thereafter, he attained eternal rest along with his followers in the region (confluence ?) of Gaṅgā and Yamunā.

89-91. When he thus passed away along with his ministers and faithful soldiers, after exterminating all the kings and Mlecchas in thousands, when the period of the part of *Sandhyā* arrived at the end of the Yuga, and when only a few of the people remained scattered here and there, the unchecked people became active in the world in groups. They harassed one another and sought help of one another.

92. When anarchy prevailed as a result of the Yuga (coming to a close), and when there was doubt and suspense everywhere among the subjects, they became frightened of one another.

93. They were exhausted and agitated. Eager to preserve their own lives, they left their wives and homes. They became extremely miserable and died.

94. When Dharma based on the Vedas and Smṛtis became defunct, people killed one another devoid of the bounds of decency, affection, friendship or shame.

95. Their span of life dwindled to twentyfive years. They became short-sized. They abandoned their wives and sons. Their sense-organs became agitated and their minds dejected.

96. Oppressed by drought and scanty rain, they were forced to abandon cultivation. Being utterly miserable, they left their lands and countries and lived in the frontier.

97. They began to resort to rivers, oceans, wells and mountains. They maintained themselves on fruits and roots, wine and meat. They became very miserable.

98. They wear bark garments and deer skins. They have no wives or sons. They fall off from the system of castes and stages of life. They resort to a terrible promiscuous intermixture of castes.

99. They reach the limit of misery. Only a few of them survive. They are oppressed by old age, sickness and hunger. Due to misery they become indifferent to worldly existence.

100. Due to this despondency and indifference, they begin to ponder. By pondering over they attain the state of equanimity. In the state of equanimity they are enlightened. Due to enlightenment they become pious.

101. When those subjects surviving at the end of Kali Age are thus enlightened, in a single day and night the Yuga is transformed.

102. After making their minds enchanted Kṛtayuga sets in due to the power of the inevitable destiny.

103. When Kṛtayuga begins to function again, the few subjects surviving from Kaliyuga become the subjects of Kṛtayuga.

104. Those Siddhas who stay move about and are seen clearly. The Seven Sages are also ever present there.

105. Brāhmaṇas, Kṣattriyas, Vaiśyas and Śūdras who are to serve as seeds for future generation become non-differentiated from those who are born of Kali.

106. The Seven Sages instruct them and the others too in the two types of Dharma prescribed by Śrutis and Smṛtis as well as in the conduct pertaining to the castes and stages of life.

107. Then in Kṛta Yuga, people (subjects) perform the sacred rites. To the subjects of the Kṛta Age Dharma based on Śrutis and Smṛtis is laid down by the Seven Sages.

108. For establishment of Dharma among the subjects, the Sages remain in authority over the whole of Manvantara and stay on (live) to the end of the Yuga.

109-110. Just as new shoots grow from the roots of grasses that are burnt during the summer in the forest-fire, so also the new Yuga grows out of the old Yuga. Till the end of the Manvantara this series goes on without break.

111. Happiness, longevity, strength, beauty, virtue

(Dharma), wealth and love—all these become reduced by one fourth from one Yuga to another.

112. In the parts of junctions of Yugas (*Sandhyāṁśas*) the *Siddhis* of Dharma become almost extinct. Thus, O Brāhmaṇas, the *Pratisandhi* (the period of transition between Yugas) has been narrated to you.

113-114. By means of this alone should all the sets of four Yugas be known. When the set of four Yugas repeats a thousand times, it is the day of god Brahmā. His night is also of the same duration. In it, there is simplicity and inactiveness of the Bhūtas (elements).

115. This alone is the trait of all Yugas. Seventy-one cycles of the sets of four Yugas occurring successively constitute a Manvantara.

116. In a single set of four Yugas everything happens in the manner you have heard now. In the other sets of four Yugas also the same thing happens in the same order.

117. The differences that occur in the various creations are confined to twentyfive, neither more nor less.

118. So also the Kalpas and the Yugas are similar in characteristics. This alone is the characteristic sign of all the Manvantaras.

119. So also the transitions of the Yugas occur naturally. They are eternal as well. But the living beings that undergo modifications in the form of dissolution and re-creation cannot be permanent.

120. Thus the characteristics of Yugas have been briefly mentioned, the Yugas of the past and future in all Manvantaras.

121-122. In respect of the future Manvantaras the traits shall be inferred from the previous one. In the Manvantaras whether of the past or of the future, know that the Manvantaras shall be explained by the present one; one Kalpa is explained by explaining another.[1]

123-124. The eight classes of Devas, sages and Manus are also similar in all Manvantaras in names, forms and purposes.

---

1. cf. *Dhātā yathāpūrvam akalpayat*
—*Mahānārāyaṇīya Up*. 5.7.

The division of the four castes and stages of life is the same in every Yuga.

125. The Lord arranges for the creation and the division of castes and stages in the different Yugas in accordance with the nature of those Yugas for the purposes of fulfilling the functions, in the respective Yugas.

126. The topic has been narrated in brief. Now listen to and understand the creation of the world. I shall explain the situation in different Yugas in details and in proper order.

CHAPTER FIFTYNINE

Yugas and Classes of People : Lineage of Sages

Sūta said :

1. Listen to and understand the details of those subjects who are born in the different Yugas. I shall mention in which Yuga demons, serpents, cattles, birds, Piśācas, Yakṣas and Rākṣasas are born and how long they live.

2. Piśācas, Asuras, Gandharvas, Yakṣas, Rākṣasas and Pannagas (serpents) live for the whole period of the Yuga, unless they are killed by someone.

3. The span of life of human beings, animals, birds and immobile beings fluctuates everywhere in accordance with the traits of the Yuga.[1]

4. Instability in regard to the span of life of living beings is seen in Kali Yuga. The maximum life expectation of human beings in this Yuga is a hundred years.

5-7. The height of Devas and Asuras is one hundred and fiftyeight *Aṅgulas* in Kali age. In human beings (?) the height is gradually reduced by seven times seven *Aṅgulas*

1. The Purāṇic author believes (as will be seen later) that there has been a continuous deterioration in height or physical built and other faculties of *all* the subjects of creation.

from that of Devas and Asuras. It is remembered by persons born in Kali Age that their height from foot to head is eightyfour *Aṅgulas* as measured with their own fingers. This stature of human beings is further reduced towards the end of the Yuga.

8. In all the periods of Yugas of the past and future man has the height of eight spans (*Tālas* i.e. *Vitasti* or the distance between the tips of the little finger and the thumb when both are extended) measuring with his own fingers.

9. He who is nine *Tālas* high from foot to head with arms extending upto the knees when they are close together, is worshipped even by Devas.

10. In every Yuga the height of cows, horses, elephants, buffaloes and immobile beings varies as follows :

11. The hump of bulls is seventysix *Aṅgulas*. The height of elephants is full hundred and eight *Aṅgulas*.

12. The height of horses is fifty *Aṅgulas* and that of trees is a thousand *Aṅgulas* less by forty *Aṅgulas* (i.e. nine hundred sixty).

13. The constitution of the bodies of Devas is as a matter of fact similar to that of human beings.

14. It is said that the body of Devas is endowed with exceptional intellect. The human body is said to be equipped with less intelligence than that of Devas.

15. Thus the life of gods and human beings has been explained. Now listen to the description of animals, birds and immobile beings.

16. Cows, goats, buffaloes, horses, elephants, birds and trees are useful in sacrificial and all other rites.

17. They are born again in the same form in the abodes of Devas. They, of auspicious forms, are such as can be enjoyed by the Devas as they pleased.

18. With the forms befitting them, either mobile or immobile, and with charming sizes as are known to those conversant with reality, they become happy.

19. I shall now explain the remaining ones (*Śiṣṭas* or cultured people) constituting *Sat-s* and *Sādhus* (saints).[1] The

1. Verses 21-32 explain the concept of *Dharma* and what is *Śrauta Dharma* and *Smārta Dharma*. The characteristics of Dharma are given in vv. 40-55.

word *'sat'* indicates Brahman. Those who possess it, are called *santas* due to their similarity with Brahman.

20. Those who are neither infuriated nor elated in regard to the tenfold object of senses and eight types of causes of bondage, are called *Jitātmans* (who are self-controlled).

21. Inasmuch as Brāhmaṇas, Kṣattriyas and Vaiśyas are engaged in two types of Dharma, the general and the special, they are called *Dvijātis*.

22. The knowledge of Śrauta and Smārta rites utilised by the different castes in their different stages of life and leading to heaven or salvation is called Real Dharma.

23-25. A Brahmacārin acting in the interest of his preceptor is an ascetic because he amasses learning. A householder is an ascetic because he accomplishes holy rites. A Vaikhānasa is called an ascetic, because he performs penance in the forest. The aspiring ascetic is called *Sādhu*, because he practises Yogic exercises. Thus all these—the religious student, the householder, the forest-dwelling hermit and the recluse are called *Sādhus* because they perform the *Āśrama Dharmas* (duties of their stage of life).

26. Neither Devas, nor Pitṛs, nor sages nor human beings can be of different views if they correctly say "This is Dharma", "This is not".

27. The two words, "*Dharma*" and "*Adharma*" refer to rites. Auspicious rites are *Dharmas* and inauspicious rites are *Adharmas*.

28. The word *Dharma* is derived from √*dhṛ* 'to hold' or 'to support. If *Dharma* does not sustain or if it is not conducive to greatness it is *Adharma*.

29. The *Dharma* that leads a person to achieve his desire is taught by preceptors. They call these persons *Ācāryas*—preceptors : old persons devoid of greediness, self-possessed, non-arrogant, well disciplined and straightforward.

30. A preceptor practises those principles himself; he establishes a code of good conduct; he collects (and masters) meanings of scriptures and is endowed with (practices) restraints and observances.

31. After learning the Vedas from the ancients, the Seven

Sages expatiated on the Śrauta Dharma. The Vedas are Ṛk, Yajus and Sāman. They are the very limbs of the Veda.

32. After remembering the code of conduct of life current in the previous Manvantara, they explained it once again. Hence that Dharma is known as Smārta Dharma. It refers to different castes and stages of life.

33. Both the types of Dharma are called "*Śiṣṭācāra*" (the conduct of the cultured). The word *Śiṣṭa* has come from the word *Śeṣa* (survivor, remainder).[1] Hence *Śiṣṭācāra* is the conduct of life for those who remain (i.e. survived the Manvantara).

34-35. The righteous persons who survive after a Manvantara are Manu and the Seven Sages. They remain for the continuity of the people and for the purpose of establishing virtue (*Dharma*). Manu and other Śiṣṭas have been enumerated by me before. That which has been practised regularly in every Yuga by those *Śiṣṭas* (shall be known as *Śiṣṭācāra*).

36. Study of the three Vedas, agriculture, administration of justice and government, sacrifice, adherence to the (the duties of) castes and stages of life—all these are practised by the *Śiṣṭas* including Manu and his predecessors. That *Śiṣṭācāra* is eternal.

37. The following eight are characteristic *Śiṣṭācāras*: charity, truthfulness, penance, absence of greed, learning, sacrifice, procreation and sympathy.

38. Since the *Śiṣṭas* (survivors), Manu and the Seven Sages, practise this in all the Manvantaras, it is known as *Śiṣṭācāra*.

39. That which is heard (i.e. refers to Śrutis) shall be known as Śrauta (Dharma); that which is remembered (i.e. refers to *Smṛtis*) is called Smārta (Dharma). Performance of sacrifice, study of the Vedas etc. are Śrauta Dharmas and observance of the duties of castes and stages of life is called Smārta Dharma. I shall state the characteristics and the various parts of this Dharma.

40. After seeing and on being asked about it (if) a person does not conceal facts and states them in proper sequence

---

1. Verses 33-38 present a unique definition of *Śiṣṭa* and what is *Śiṣṭācāra*. Manu XII. 109 and Vasiṣṭha (Smṛti) VI. 143 differ. They insist on scholarship (Vedic), ability to draw correct inference and persuade people to follow Vedic teaching. Mt. P. 145.34-35 supports our text & derives it from √*śiṣ* 'to remain'

(as they occurred), it is the characteristic (sign of) *Satya* (truthfulness).

41. Celibacy, Japa, silence and fasting—these are the roots of penance. Penance is hard and very difficult of achievement.

42. The sacrificial animals, the requisite materials, the ghee offerings, the Ṛk, Sāman and Yajus Mantras, Ṛtviks and the sacrificial gifts—the collection of all these constitutes Yajña*.

43. Viewing all living beings as one's own self, looking impartially towards friends and foes is called *Dayā* (sympathy, mercy).

44. One shall not strike back or rebuke when struck or rebuked. Restraint in thought, speech and action and forgiveness is called endurance.

45. Refraining from taking other man's belongings left unprotected by the master, or thrown out on the ground, is called here as non-covetousness.

46. Abstinence from sexual acts, neither brooding nor imagining about it and complete sexual detachment is called celibacy (*Brahmacarya*).

47. If the sense-organs do not adopt a wrong path either for oneself or for others, it is the sign of quiescence or restraint.

48. He who does not get infuriated when thwarted in the ten-fold sensual object and in the eight causes of worldly bondage is considered a conqueror.

49. If a person feels that he must give unto a deserving person whatever is liked by him most or the money (or things) that has come to him duly and justly, that is the characteristic sign of *Dāna* (Charity).

50. Charity is of three types: the lowest, superiormost, and middling. That which leads to liberation (from *Saṁsāra*) is of the highest type; that which is given for the achievement of one's selfish ends is the lowest; that which is given to all beings out of pity or their proper sharing with the kins is the middling (type of *Dāna*).

51. That which is enjoined by Śrutis and Smṛtis, that which conforms to the observance of the duties of castes and stages of

***Yoga* in the text obviously a misprint.

life, that which is not contrary to the practice of the cultured (*Śiṣṭas*) and that which arises from contact with the saintly and the good, is *Dharma.*

52. Absence of hatred for what is not liked, abstention from undue praise of what is liked, refraining from overdelightedness, repentance and dejection is called detachment.

53. *Sannyāsa* means eschewing the fruits of actions performed or intended to be performed. Abandonment of what is good and what is not good is called *Tyāga.*

54. The knowledge of the transformation from the unmanifest and undifferentiated into the non-sentient and the difference and distinction between the sentient and non-sentient is called *Jñāna* (real knowledge).

55. These are the characteristic signs of the various ancillaries of Dharma as mentioned by the sages who knew the principles of Dharma in the previous Svāyambhuva Manvantara.

56. I shall now mention the procedure of the Manvantara and the mode of behaviour of the people of one caste with the members of the other castes and among themselves. In every Manvantara, the system of the Vedas differs.

57-58. (The Vedic Mantras of) Ṛk, Yajus and Sāman remain the same in respect of every deity as before. In spite of the dissolution of elements, *Śatarudriya,* the procedure of sacrificial offerings as well as *Stotra* (hymns or prayers) function as before.

The *Stotras* are of four types: *Dravya-stotra* (prayer for sacrificial material); *Guṇastotra* (prayer for qualities); *Karma-stotra* (eulogy of proper rites), and the fourth is the eulogy of *Abhijanas* (lineage).

59. In all the Manvantaras Brahmā initiates the four types of *stotras* in regard to Devas even as they come into being. Thus the origin of the collection of Mantras is of four types.

60-62a. As the sages perform severe and extremely difficult penance, the Mantras of different Vedas, Atharva, Ṛk, Yajur and Sāman, appear before them severally in the same manner as in the previous Manvantaras. They (the Mantras) appear from five sources: satisfaction, fear, misery, happiness and sorrow, born of the totality of their penance, vision or by chance.

62b. Now (here) I shall explain the *Ṛṣitva* (the state of being a Ṛṣi) of sages along with their characteristics.

63. Among the past and the future, the sages are said to be of five types. Hence I shall recount the origin of sages and of *Ārṣa* (whatever pertains to the Ṛṣis).

64-65. When the Guṇas were in (a state of) equilibrium, there was the annihilation of everything. There were no Devas anywhere. As if due to their assimilation (*atideśa*) it (*Pradhāna*) unintelligently functions for the sake of *Cetana* (the conscious one). Thereby it was presided over by *Cetana* (the conscious principle) without its awareness.

66. Both of them function like the fish and the water. The *Tattva* (Pradhāna) presided over by consciousness (the conscious Puruṣa) functions through Guṇas.

67. Since the cause is present the effect functions in the same way. The object functions due to the subject. The *Artha* (meaning) functions due to its meaningfulness (state of possessing meaning).

68. The differences which are materialised by *Kāla* (Time) are due to the intrinsic nature of the cause. They become explicitly manifest in due course as Mahat and other principles.

69. From *Mahat*, *Ahaṁkāra* (Cosmic Ego) is evolved; from Ego the (Subtle) elements. The different elements are evolved due to mutual interaction. The cause immediately transforms (itself) into action.

70. Just as a burning fire-brand spreads its sparks all round simultaneously while falling, so also the conscious Principle (*Kṣetrajña*) that transforms itself due to the action of Time manifests himself.

71. Just as a glow-worm is suddenly seen in blinding darkness, so also *Mahat* is evolved out of the unmanifest and shines like a glow-worm.

72. The Principle of Consciousness stays at the entrance to the great chamber where the embodied principle *Mahat* stays.

73. *Mahat* is seen beyond *Tamas* (the dark principle) on account of its distinct disparity. The Śruti says, "The con-

scious Principle, the knower, stays there itself at the end of darkness".

74. As it (*Mahat*) was transforming, *Buddhi* (Intellect) manifested itself in four ways viz. perfect knowledge, detachment, glory and Dharma.

75. All these are its evolutes and well-shaped too. It is called *Siddhi* (Evolute) as it is effected through the transformation of embodied *Mahat*.

76. He (*Puruṣa*) stays in the body (*Pur*) and possesses the knowledge of the body. He is called *Puruṣa* as he dwells in the *Pur* (body), and is called *Kṣetrajña* due to his knowledge of the body.

77. Since he has knowledge of the *Kṣetra* (body), he is called *Kṣetrajña*. Therefore the Lord is called Intellect (*Mati*). Since he abides with *Buddhi* (Intellect), he is of the nature of knowledge (Bodha). For the accomplishment (of task of the world?) this non-intelligent entity, both manifest and unmainfest, is pervaded (by the Intelligent Principle).

78. Thus it is the conscious principle that dissociates itself from the objects of sense-organs. It is this very principle that cognizes the objects as worthy of being enjoyed.

79. The root √*ṛṣ* means 'to go'. It refers to the Vedas, truthfulness and penance. He who is devoted to these three and attains Brahman is called '*Ṛṣi*'.[1]

80. The *Ṛṣi* who attains the knowledge of the great unmanifest principle and abstains from worldly attachment simultaneously is called *Paramarṣi*.

81. From the root √*ṛṣ* meaning "to go", the name *Ṛṣi* has been derived. Since the mental sons of Brahmā are self-born, they are Īśvaras (endowed with spiritual power).

82. He who is not restricted or delimited by measures is called great. Those who attain the Great Principle by means of attributes are called *Maharṣis*. They are the seers who can penetrate beyond intellect.

83. The hearts of those powerful (mental sons) are auspicious. Eschewing ego and ignorance (*Tamas*), they have attained sagehood.

1. Verses 79-107 clarify the concept 'Ṛṣi' and give the details of the different classes of Ṛṣis, e.g. composers of the Mantras and Brāhmaṇas etc. and explanations of 'Maharṣi' etc. These also give the families of sages.

84. Hence those who have a real insight and knowledge of the *Bhūtādi* (Cosmic Ego) are called *Ṛṣis* (Sages). The sons of *Ṛṣis* (Sages) who are born of womb through sexual intercourse are called *Ṛṣikas*.

85. Those (spiritually) powerful ones realize the *Tanmātras* (subtle elements) and *Satya* (the truth). The Seven Sages, therefore, are the supreme realizer of the Truth.

86. The sons of the sages are known as *Ṛṣiputras*. Since they have attained learning and the mastery of the principles, they are called *Śrutarṣis*. They are keen observers of the true wisdom.

87. They are of five classes. Their names are *Avyaktātmā, Mahātmā, Ahaṁkārātmā, Bhūtāmā* and *Indriyātmā*. They practise five kinds of knowledge. Listen to the five classes of sages by their names.

88. The following are powerful lords self-born as the mental sons of Brahmā: Bhṛgu, Marīci, Atri, Aṅgiras, Pulaha, Kratu, Manu, Dakṣa, Vasiṣṭha and Pulastya, ten in all.

89. As they are born of the sage and are hence (spiritually great), they are called *Maharṣis*. Know the names of the sages who were the sons of these great sages (*Maharṣis*).

90-91. Kāvya, Bṛhaspati, Kaśyapa, Uśanas, Utathya, Vāmadeva, Apojya, Aiśija, Kardama, Viśravas, Śakti, Vālakhilya and Dhara. These are called sages because they had attained that stage through their knowledge.

92-94. Understand that the *Ṛṣikas*, sons of sages, were born of wombs. Vatsara, Nagrahū, Bhāradvāja, Bṛhaduttha, Śaradvān, Agastya, Auśija, Dīrghatamas, Bṛhaduktha, Śaradvata, Vājaśravas, Suvitta, Suvāk, Veṣaparāyaṇa, Dadhīca, Śaṅkhamān and king Vaiśravaṇa—these are called *Ṛṣikas*. They attained *Ṛṣihood* (status of *Ṛṣis*) through truthfulness.

95. Īśvaras, Ṛṣikas and others are the seers (creators of Mantras). Now listen to their names.

96-97. Bhṛgu, Kāvya, Pracetas, Dadhīca, Ātmavān, Aurva, Jamadagni, Vida, Sārasvata, Adviṣeṇa, Arūpa, Vītahavya, Sumedhasa, Vainya, Pṛthu, Divodāsa, Praśvāra, Gṛtsamān and Nabha : these nineteen sages were the expounders of Mantras.

98-102, Aṅgiras, Vedhasa, Bhāradvāja, Bāṣkali, Amṛta, Gārgya, Śeni, Saṃhṛti, Purukutsa, Māndhātā, Ambarīṣa, Āhārya, Ajamīḍha, Ṛṣabha, Bali, Pṛsadaśva, Virūpa, Kaṇva, Mudgala, Yuvanāśva, Paurukutsa, Trasaddasyu, Sadasyumān, Utathya, Bharadvāja, Vājaśravas, Āyāpya, Suvitti, Vāmadeva, Augaja, Bṛhaduktha, Dīrghatapas and Kakṣīvān : these thirty-three are excellent descendants of Aṅgiras. These are *Mantrakṛts* (Composers i.e. seers of Mantras). Now understand the descendants of Kāśyapa.

103. Kāśyapa, Vatsara, Vibhrama, Raibhya, Asita and Devala these six belong to the family of Kāśyapa and they are the expounders of Brahman.

104. Atri, Arcisana, Śyāmāvān, Niṣṭhura, the intelligent sage Valgūtaka and Pūrvātithi—these are the descendants of Atri. They are great sages (*Maharṣis*) and seers of Mantras.

105-106. Vasiṣṭha, Śakti, Parāśara, (the fourth one) Indrapramati, (the fifth) Bharadvasu, (the sixth) Maitrāvaruṇa, (the seventh) Kuṇḍina, (the eighth) Sudyumna, the ninth Bṛhaspati and the tenth Bharadvāja—these ten are the composers of Mantras and Brāhmaṇas.

107. These are the creators (seers of Mantras) and destroyers of unrighteousness. This characteristic of the Vedas is prescribed for all the branches of the Veda.

108-110. The word *Hetu* (reason of inference) is derived from √*hi* 'to destroy'.[1] 'That which destroys what is argued by the opponent' is called *Hetu*. Or it may be from √*hi* 'to go'—'that which enables one to the acquisition of the meaning' is *Hetu*. It helps to arrive at a definite (decisive) meaning of a statement after refuting the opponent's standpoint. Preceptors say that it means *Nindā* (censure) when the statements (of the opponents) are censured due to their defects.

111. The word '*Praśaṁsā*' (Praise) is derived from the root √*śaṁs* with the prefix *Pra*—. A statement is praised by virtue of its merits. 'This is this', 'This is not this'—this sort of indecision is called *Saṁśaya* (Doubt).

112. The concept of *Purākalpa* is due to its having taken place in the past.

113. The events of ancient times cannot be decided by Mantras, Brāhmaṇas, Kalpas and Nigamas, howsoever genuine

1. Verses 108-117 explain some terms such as *Hetu, Praśaṁsā, Sūtra etc.*

and detailed. What is said indecisively is called a make-believe.

114. Just as this, so also is that; this is also so, this is the tenth instruction of the Brāhmaṇa.

115. This is the early definition of the Brāhmaṇa laid down by the learned. Later on its *Vṛtti* (commentary) (on every word) was composed by Brāhmaṇas.

116. The utility of the Mantras is in the prescribed rites through injunctions. The word '*Mantra*' is derived from √*mantṛ* —'to whisper'. And the word Brāhmaṇa signifies a person who maintains the injunctions of Brahmā.

117. The knowers of Sūtras called that (statement) as *Sūtra* which consists of very few syllables, is free from ambiguity, full of essence, which is comprehensive in application yet devoid of superfluous adjuncts and contains no objectionable word.

CHAPTER SIXTY

Description of Holy Places : The Death of Śākalya

1. On hearing his words the sages said to Sūta of wide knowledge—"O intelligent Sir, how were the Vedas classified before ? Please tell us that."

Sūta said :

2. O highly intelligent sage, in the Svāyaṁbhuva Manvantara, when Dvāpara had set in, Brahmā said this to Manu. I shall repeat it.

3. "O dear one, when a Yuga passes away, Brāhmaṇas become deficient in energy and vigour. All of them become enveloped by the defects of the new Yuga.

4. Only very little (of the previous glory) remains to be seen. Only a ten-thousandth part of what existed originally at the beginning of Kṛta Age remains.

5. Power, splendour, strength and eloquence—everything

perishes. Hence Vedas should be classified, lest there should be utter destruction (of that lore).

6. When the Vedas perish, Yajña perishes. When Yajña perishes, Devas perish. Then everything perishes.

7. The original Vedas consisted of four Pādas and a hundred thousand Mantras. It has increased ten times. The entire Yajña yields all desires".

8. On being addressed thus, Lord Manu, engaged in the welfare of the worlds said, "So be it". He divided the Vedas into four books (compendia).

9. It was at the instance of Brahmā and with a desire for the well-being of the world (that he divided the Veda). It is by the present classification of the Vedas that you have to imagine the (extent etc. of) the Vedas.

10. I shall narrate to you (the classification of the Vedas) in accordance with present Manvantara. It is by adopting the process of inference of what is beyond perception that you understand (the classification), O excellent ones.

11. In this Yuga, the son of Parāśara who is glorified as a part of Viṣṇu and who is well-known as Dvaipāyana, the scorcher (vanquisher) of enemies, was made Vyāsa[1] (the arranger of the Vedas).

12-13. Urged by god Brahmā, he undertook the work of classifying the Veda. He adopted four disciples for (preservation and continuity of) of the Vedas. (They were) Jaimini, Sumantu, Vaiśaṁpāyana, Paila (was the fourth of them) and the fifth Lomaharṣaṇa.

14. He formally made the Brāhmaṇa Paila the propounder of the Ṛgveda and Vaiśaṁpāyana the expounder of the Yajurveda.

15. He accepted Jaimini as the propounder of the Sāma Veda. Similarly he took the excellent sage Sumantu as the expounder of the Atharva Veda.

1. Verses 11-23 describe how Kṛṣṇa Dvaipāyana classified the Vedic lore and gave it to his students as follows :

N. of Student	*Veda assigned*
Jaimini	Sāma Veda
Sumantu	Atharva Veda
Vaiśaṁpāyana	Yajur Veda
Paila	Ṛg Veda
Lomaharṣaṇa	Itihāsa & Purāṇa

16. The saintly Lord accepted me as the narrator of Itihāsa and Purāṇas.

17. The Yajurveda was one single compilation. He divided it into four. There were four sacrificial priests. He organised sacrifice through them.

18. He ordained the work of the priest *Adhvaryu* by means of Yajur Mantras, that of *Hotṛ* by Ṛk mantras, that of *Udgātṛ* by the Sāman Mantras and that of *Brahmā* (the presiding priest) by Atharvan Mantras. He established Brahmā in the Yajña by means of the Ātharvaṇa (Veda).

19. Thereafter, he picked up (selected) Ṛk Mantras and compiled the Ṛg Veda. He ordained the duties of Hotṛ, the performer of a sacrifice and the benefactor of the world.

20. With the Sāmans, (he) arranged Sāmaveda and thereby evolved Udgātṛ. By means of Atharva Veda he established rites for kings.

21. He, an expert in the meanings of the Purāṇas, composed the compendiums of Purāṇas by compiling narratives, sub-narratives, poems and songs, and the traditional conduct of the ancient races.

22. Whatever remained he included in the Yajurveda and organised it with sacrifice. It is the definite decision of scriptures that Yajurveda is that which enables one to perform sacrifice.

23. He gathered the scattered Yajur Mantras duly, with the collaboration of Ṛtviks who were the masters of the Vedas. By means of it the horse-sacrifice is performed. It is utilised in it.

24-25. Taking up the Ṛk Mantras, Paila divided them into two groups.[1] He handed them over to his two disciples, one

---

1. Verses 24-31 describe the division of the Ṛgveda & the line of teachers.

Paila

Indrapramati — Markaṇḍeya — Satyasravas — Satyahita

Bāṣkala — 4 Branches each given to
(1) Bodha
(2) Agnimāṭhara
(3) Parāśara
(4) Yājñavalkya

section was given to Indrapramati and the other was given to Bāṣkala. The excellent Brāhmaṇa Bāṣkali composed four Saṁhitās (compendiums) and taught his disciples who were suitable and who served him attentively.

26. He taught the first branch (compilation) to Bodha, the second to Agnimāṭhara, the third to Parāśara and the last to Yājñavalkya.

27. The excellent Brāhmaṇa Indrapramati taught the blessed and renowned Mārkaṇḍeya one of the Saṁhitās.

28. Mārkaṇḍeya of great fame, taught his eldest son Satyaśravas. Satyaśravas taught to Satyahita.

29. That master (of Vedic Lore) taught his son Satyaśrī who was truthful, noble-souled and eagerly devoted to truthfulness and piety.

30. Satyaśrī had three very brilliant disciples. They were highly learned and very anxious to learn scriptures.

31. Śākalya was the first among them. Another was Rathantara. The third was Bharadvāja, son of Bāṣkala. The three were the expounders of the branches of that Veda.

32. In the horse-sacrifice of Janaka the Brāhmaṇa Śākalya (also known as) Devamitra, perished as he was too proud of his knowledge.[1]

Ancient Teachers of Ṛgveda

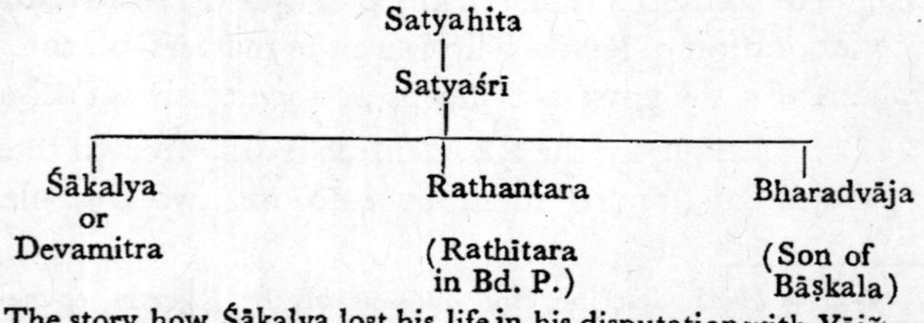

1. The story how Śākalya lost his life in his disputation with Yājñavalkya is told in vv. 33-63. The story is based on the legend recorded in *Bṛhadāraṇyaka Upa.* III. 8.12-26 Our Purāṇa does not mention that Gārgī Vacaknavī accepted defeat from Yājñavalkya before Śākalya accepted Yājñavalkya's challenge. It also does not state that it was Śākalya's inability to state about "Upaniṣadic Puruṣa" that cost him head and not about the superiority of Sāṅkhya or Yoga as given in this Purāṇa.

The episode throws light on the philosophic disputations in the royal courts of ancient India, though the Purāṇa gives a brief summary of the disputation.

Śāṁśapāyana said :

33. How did that sage, too proud of his knowledge, perish? How did the argument arise in the horse-sacrifice of Janaka?

34. Why did the argument arise at all and with whom? Narrate all this in the manner that happened, as far as you know.

On hearing the words of the sages Sūta replied:

Sūta said :

35. At the horse-sacrifice of Janaka there was a great congregation of sages. Thousands of sages, desirous of witnessing the sacrifice of the saintly king Janaka, came there from various places.

36. On seeing the Brāhmaṇas assembled there, a desire to know more about them arose in him. "Who is the most excellent Brāhmaṇa among these? How shall I decide it?". Thinking thus in his mind, he conceived of an intelligent method.

37. He collected a thousand cows, more than a thousand gold pieces and gems, slaves and villages. He then announced to the sages: "O excellent and blessed ones, I bow to you all with my head.

38. O excellent Brāhmaṇas, the wealth that is brought here is offered to the most excellent sage among you. It is offered as the price of your learning".

39. On hearing the words of Janaka, those sages, experts in the Vedas, saw and coveted the vast wealth. With full confidence in their knowledge, they began to challenge one another.

40. With their minds hovering round the wealth, one said, "This wealth (should be) mine". Another said, "Tell me. Is this not mine? Why are you in doubt?" Thus as a result of the allurement of wealth, they began to argue with one another.

41-43. There was a great scholar Yājñavalkya, son of Brahmavāha. He was highly brilliant, a great saint. He was born of the very body of Brahmā. The most excellent among the knowers of Brahman, he told his disciple clearly, "O, take away this wealth. O dear one, take this home. This is undoubtedly mine. I am the expounder of all the Vedas. None else is equal to me. If any Brāhmaṇa wishes to challenge me, let him do so without delay".

44. Thereupon that vast concourse of Brāhmaṇas became agitated like the ocean at the time of dissolution. The cool and calm Yājñavalkya smilingly told them :

45. "O learned ones, O speakers of truth, do not be angry. Trying to know one another, we shall argue in the proper manner".

46-47. Then their arguments took various turns. They discussed thousands of important topics on the subtle subject of philosophy. The secular, Vedic and spiritual topics were also discussed. All branches of leaning were touched. In the course of argument some cursed and some exhibited their excellent qualities. The kings were excluded from discussion. Thus the Brāhmaṇas continued discussion for the sake of wealth.

48. The sages ranged on one side. Yājñavalkya stood on the other side. Thereafter, all those sages were individually questioned by the intelligent Yājñavalkya. They however failed to reply.

49. After defeating the sages in argument, the sage Yājñavalkya of great splendour, a repository of Brahmanic knowledge, spoke to Śākalya who had initiated discussion:

50. "O Śākalya, speak out what you have to say. Why are you sitting meditating quietly? Full of sluggishness and false prestige, you are like a pair of bellows inflated by wind"

51. On being attacked thus Śākalya with his face and eyes red like copper due to anger, spoke to Yājñavalkya harshly in the presence of all sages:

52. "Ignoring (abandoning) us as well as these excellent Brāhmaṇas like blades of grass, you wish to seize all by yourself the vast wealth offered for learning."

Heairng this from Śākalya, Yājñavalkya spoke:

53. "Know that the strength of persons established in Brahman, is their learning and their insight into reality.

54. Desire is connected with wealth. Hence we desire wealth. Brāhmaṇas consider that asking question freely out of desire is the wealth of Brāhmaṇas. Hence we ask questions as we please.

55. This has been the condition laid down by the saintly king Janaka. Hence the wealth is being taken by me".

On hearing his words, the infuriated Śākalya spoke to Yājñavalkya asking questions as he pleased:

56. "Now tell me the answers to these questions precisely". Then a great debate ensued between the two experts in Brahman.

57. Śākalya asked him more than a thousand questions. Yājñavalkya answered those all even as the sages were listening.

58. When Śākalya ceased arguing, Yājñavalkya said, "O Śākalya, answer a single question of mine, which I willingly put to you. The stake for this argument is a curse. If you are unable to answer you will die".

59. Urged by him, a question was asked by Yājñavalkya. Unable to understand its answer, Śākalya died immediately.

60. Śākalya died being afflicted by inability to answer the question. Thus there was a great dispute between the sages covetous of wealth and Yājñavalkya.

61-62. Answering hundreds and thousands of questions put by all of them, Yājñavalkya, who had deep penetration into the essence of those questions took the entire wealth. He spread his fame everywhere. He, the sage of controlled senses, left for home along with his disciples and was quite happy.

63. Śākalya (otherwise known as) Devamitra, was a noble, excellent Brāhmaṇa. He was intelligent and excellent among those who know the implications of grammar. He had composed five Saṁhitās.

64. He had five disciples, viz. Mudgala, Golaka, Khālīya, Matsya and Śaiśireya (the fifth one).

65. Śākapūrṇa Rathītara expounded (compiled) three Saṁhitās. This excellent Brāhmaṇa composed Nirukta as his fourth work.

66. He had four disciples, viz. Ketava, Dālaki, Dharmaśarman and Devaśarman. They were Brāhmaṇas who observed holy rites.

67. When Śākalya died those present there incurred the sin of Brahmin-slaughter. Worried thus they approached Brahmā.

68. On knowing mentally their situation, Brahmā sent them to Pavana Pura. "All of you go there, your sin will be washed off immediately.

69. After bowing to the twelve suns, the deity Vāluka, the eleven Rudras and particularly the son of Vāyu (Hanumān) and after taking a dip in the four holy pools, you will surmount (expunge) the sin of Brāhmaṇa's slaughter".

70. On hearing this, they hastened to that city. They performed holy ablution in accordance with injunctions and visited the deities.

71. They bowed to Uttareśvara. By the grace of Vāḍavas they became free from sins and attained the solar region.

72. Ever since that time, that holy centre became a destroyer of sins. This holy city of Vāyu had been built by the Wind-god formerly.

73. When Hanumān, the son of the Wind-god, born of (the womb of) Añjanā, the great god of truthful exploits was born, this holy centre was created by Vāyu, the son of god Brahmā.

74-75. Here the Śūdras born in the world and dedicated to the Brāhmaṇas were taxed heavily for their livelihood and for the performance of Brahma Yajña. In this manner, the great administration of the Brāhmaṇas took root here. Even a slayer of cow, an ungrateful person, a wine addict or the defiler of one's preceptor's bed becomes free from all sins after bowing to Vāḍāditya.

CHAPTER SIXTYONE

Lineage of Prajāpati

The sages said :

1-2. Bhāradvāja, Yājñavalkya, Gālaki, Sālaki, the intelligent Śatabalāka, the excellent Brāhmaṇa Naigama and Bharadvāja, son of Bāṣkala[1]—all these expounded three Saṁhitās. Rathītara composed the fourth work called Nirukta.

3-4. He had three noble-souled disciples endowed with good qualities. They were the intelligent Nandāyanīya, the wise Pannagāri and the third one Āryava (Ārjava in Bd. P.). They were of praise-worthy, holy observances due to their penance. They were devoid of passions, endowed with very great splendour and masters of the knowledge of Saṁhitās. Hence they were called *Bahvṛcas* by whom Saṁhitās were propagated.

5-6. The sage of the spiritual lineage of Vaiśaṁpāyana composed Yajurveda. Eightysix auspicious Saṁhitās of Yajus (r) Mantras had been composed by him.[2] He passed them over to his disciples. They grasped them in accordance with the injunctions. The sage Yājñavalkya of great penance alone was left out. But he too composed eightysix alternative Saṁhitās.

7. Each of these three had three subdivisions. Thus there arose nine different schools.

8. The three main schools are Udīcyas (the northerners), Madhyadeśas (those of the middle countries) and Prācyas (the easterners). Śyāmāyani became the chief of the northern school.

9. These are the three regional heads.[3] Āruṇi was eulogised as the first and foremost of those who had been established in the Madhyadeśa. Ālambi was the first among the easterners.

---

1. The academic genealogy of Bahvṛcas :

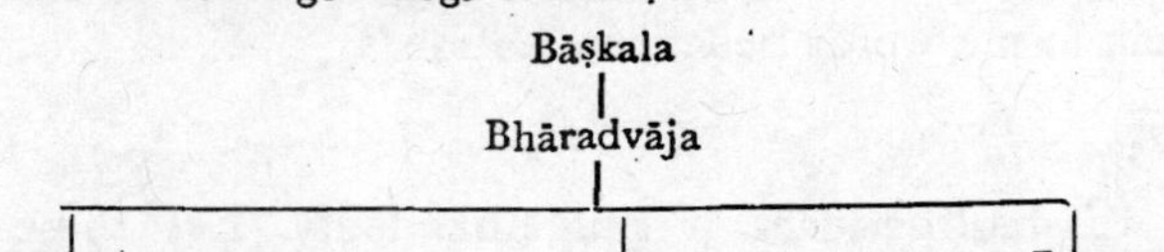

2. cf. *yajur-vedasya ṣaḍaśīti bhedā bhavanti* /
—CVS, p. 31

3. Our text reads : *trayodaśyādayaḥ* 'Trayodaśin and others'. The name 'Trayodaśin' does not occur in this chapter or elsewhere. The figure 'Thirteen' is inapplicable. Bd. P. in this context reads *trayodeśyādayaḥ* (I.2.35.13) which means '(There are thus) three regional heads'. '*Trayodaṣyādayaḥ*' hereof seems to have lost a *mātrā* of original '*deśya*'—a scribal error for °*deśya* in Bd.P. Hence I accepted the reading °*deśyādayaḥ*' from Bd. P.

10. All these Brāhmaṇas who expounded the Saṁhitās are also called '*Carakas*'.

On hearing his words, the sages who were desirous of hearing, asked Sūta:

11. "What was the reason whereby the Adhvaryus were called *Carakas* ? What was it that they performed ? For what reason they were termed thus ?"

Thus requested Sūta explained to them how they came to acquire the designation *Caraka*.

Sūta said :[1]

12. O excellent Brāhmaṇas, the sages had to perform a rite. They went to the top of Meru and conferred with one another as follows :

13. "O excellent Brāhmaṇas, he who does not come here within seven nights shall have to perform expiatory rite for Brāhmaṇa's slaughter. This is proclaimed as our stipulated condition."

14. Then all the sages, except Vaiśaṁpāyana, reached the place where they were required to as per condition, within seven nights. Their attendants too came along with them.

15. At the instance of the Brāhmaṇas he (Vaiśaṁpāyana) intended to perform the expiatory rite for Brāhmaṇa slaughter. Gathering together his disciples, Vaiśaṁpāyana said :

16. "O excellent Brāhmaṇas, all of you perform expiatory rite for Brāhmaṇa's slaughter on my behalf. All of you come and speak to me words beneficent to me."

Yājñavalkya said :

17. "I shall perform it single-handedly. Let these sages

---

1. While explaining the term '*Caraka*' Sūta tells the story why Vaiśaṁpāyana asked Yājñavalkya to recant Yajurveda taught to him. Yājñavalkya instantly obeyed and the blood smeared recanted Yagur Mantras went upto the Sun god who returned to him those very Mantras which went to him. The story of Yājñavalkya receiving Yajur-veda from the Sun-god is found in *Mbh-Śanti* 318.6-12. But there Yājñavalkya is not ordered by Vaiśampāyana to recant Yajurveda. It was the Sun-god and Yājñavalkya who assumed the form of a horse at the time of transmitting the Veda.

stand by. Purified by my own penance I shall raise up (develop) my (spiritual) strength."

18. On being thus addressed, the infuriated Vaiśaṁpāyana spoke to Yājñavalkya : "Return so me whatever you have learnt from me".

19. On being commanded thus, that sage Yājñavalkya, the most excellent among the knowers of Brahman, vomited the embodied forms of Yajur-Mantras smeared with blood and gave them back to his preceptor.

20. O Brāhmaṇas, then he meditated and worshipped the Sun-god. What was vomited rose up in the sky and stood near the Solar Brahman.

21. The delighted Sun handed over the Yajur-Mantras which had gone up to the solar disc. The Sun-god gave them to the intelligent Brahmarāti (in Bd. P.) Yājñavalkya who had assumed the form of a horse.

22. Thenceforth, the Brāhmaṇas who began the study of the Yajus handed over to Yājñavalkya in the form of a horse (*Vājin*) became known as Vājins.

23. Those by whom the expiatory rite for Brahma-hatyā (Brāhmaṇa-slaughter) was performed are remembered as *Carakas*[1] because of their performance of atonement (for Brāhmaṇa's slaughter). The disciples of Vaiśaṁpāyana are called *Carakas*.

24-26. These were called *Carakas*. Now understand the *Vājins*, the disciples of Yājñavalkya. They were[2] : Kaṇva, Vaidheya, Śālin, Madhyandina, Śāpeyī, Vidigadha, Āpya, Uddala, Tāmrāyaṇa, Vātsya, Gālava, Śaiśiri, Āṭavī, Parṇī, Vīraṇī and Saṁparāyaṇa. These fifteen are known as *Vājins*. Thus there are hundred and one alternative Saṁhitās.

---

1. A popular etymology of *Caraka* (SKD p. 435) derives it from √*car* 'to go,' 'to know' and hence *caraka* is a knower of Vedas and medical science' and quotes from *Bhāva Prakāśa* how Śeṣa espied diseases and sufferings on the earth and composed a medical treatise out of compassion. Here it means 'a follower of a branch of Black Yajurveda who follows special practices and rites different from those in Śatapatha Br. (vide MW. 389).

2. Cf. The list of disciples of Yājñavalkya in CVS, p. 32. It differs in some names from the list given here. Even the list in Bd. P.I.2.35.28-30 also differs from our text.

27. Jaimini taught his son Sumantu.[1] Sumantu taught his son Sutavan. Sutavan taught his son Sukarman.

28. After learning in a short while a thousand Saṁhitās, Sukarman, expounded them to his thousand disciples having the brilliance of the Sun.

---

1. Verses 27-48 give the genealogy of Sāma Veda teachers. It differs much from the list of Sāma Veda teachers in CVS pp. 43-46. The Bd. P. list (in I.2.35. 31-55) is also somewhat different from our Purāṇa. Our text gives following genealogy.

Jaimini
|
Sumantu
|
Sutvan
|
Sukarman (Studied 1000 Saṁhitas)

[1000 disciples, one per Saṁhitā. But as noted here and in CVS p. 43, Indra killed them all. After their death, two new dtsciples studied under him as shown here.]

Pauṣyañjin studied and taught 500 *Saṁhitās* to Northerners | king Hiraṇyanābha studied 500 *Saṁhitās* and taught them to Easterners

School of Pauṣyañjin—Northern Sāma-Singers [Northeın (udīcya) Sāmagas]

Lakokṣin | Kuthumi | Kuśitin | Lāṅgali

(i) *School of Lokākṣin*

Rāṇāyaniya | Taṇḍi-putra | Mūla-cārin | Kaiti-putra | Sātya-pūtra

(ii) *School of Kuthumi—His three sons*

as disciples viz. (1) Aurasa, (2) Rasapāsara (prob. Parāśara as in Bd. P), (3) Bhāgavitti.

(iii) *Disciples of Parāśara, Kuthumi's disciple*

(1) Āsurāyaṇa, (2) Vaiśakhya, (3) Vedavṛddha (4) Prācīṇa-yoga-putra (5) Patañjali.

(iv) *Disciples of Lāṅgali, disciple of Pauṣyañjin*

(1) Bhāluki, (2) Kāmahāni, (3) Jaimini (4) Lomagāyin, (5) Kaṇḍa, (6) Kolaha.

Eastern School of Sāma-singers

King Hiraṇyanābha (of Kausikagotra) composed 24 *Saṁhitās* and taught one each to the following students :

(1) Rāḍa, (2)Mahāvīrya, Rāḍavīya in Bd.P., (3) Pañcama, (4) Vāhana, (5) Tālaka (6) Pāṇḍaka, (7) Kālika, (8) Rājika (9) Gautama [Māṇḍuka in Bd. P,] (10) Ajabasta, (11) Somarāja, (12) Pṛṣṭhaghna (Puṣṭi in Bd. P.),

29. Indra killed all of them because they pursued their studies even on prohibited days. Then Sukarman performed a fast unto death, for the sake of his disciples.

30. On seeing him infuriated, Indra granted him a boon : "Two disciples of great prowess and brilliance of fire you will have.

31. They will be highly intelligent and will study all the thousand Saṁhitās. They will be blessed. O excellent Brāhmaṇa, do not be angry."

32. After saying this to the renowned Sukarman and seeing him mollified, the glorious Indra vanished there itself.

33. O excellent Brāhmaṇas, the intelligent Pauṣyañjin was his first disciple and king Hiraṇyanābha of Kuśika race was the second.

34. Pauṣyañjin taught five hundred Saṁhitās. The auspicious disciples of Pauṣyañjin were generally the northerners.

35. The powerful Kauśikya taught five hundred Saṁhitās. The disciples of Hiraṇyanābha are known as the easterners and the Sāmagas.

36. Lokākṣī, Kuthumi, Kuśītī and Lāṅgali were the four disciples of Pauṣyañjin. Now know their divisions (branches).

37. Rāṇāyanīya, son of Taṇḍi, the highly learned Mūlacārin, Kaitiputra and Sātyaputra—know these to be the disciples of different branches of Lokākṣin.

38. Kuthumi had three sons, viz. Aurasa, Rasapāsara and the brilliant Bhāgavitti. These three were famous as *Kauthumas*.

39. The two sages Śauridyu and Śṛṅgiputra performed holy rites. Rāṇāyanīya and Saumitri were experts in Sāmaveda.

40. Śṛṅgiputra of great penance expounded three Saṁhitās, O excellent Brāhmaṇas, to Caila, Prācīnayoga, Surāla.

---

(13) Parikṛṣṭa, (14) Ulūkhalaka, (15) Yavīyasa, (16) Vaiśāla (Śāli in Bd. P.), (17) Aṅgulīya, (18) Kauśika, (19) Sālimañjari-satya, (20) Kāpīya (Pāka in Bd. P.), (21) Kānika (Kānini in Bd. P.), (22) Parāśara.

Two names are either missing or we have to presume that the founder teachers—Hiraṇyanābha and Prince Kṛta (mentioned in Bd. P. and accepted as an alternative explanation of Kṛta-śiṣyaḥ in v. 44)—should be added to make up the number twentyfour in the above list.

41-42. Pārāśarya, disciple of Kuthumi, expounded six Saṁhitās. Āsurāyaṇa, Vaiśākhya, Vedavṛddha, Parāyaṇa, Prācīnayogaputra and intelligent Patañjali are known as the six disciples of Pārāśarya, the disciple of Kuthumi. Lāṅgali and Śālihotra expounded six Saṁhitās each.

43. Bhāluki, Kāmahāni, Jaimini, Lomagāyina, Kaṇḍa and Kolaha—these six are known as *Lāṅgalas*. These were the disciples of Lāṅgalī and they popularised these Saṁhitās.

44. Hiraṇyanābha, who was the son of a king who had disciples [or who had as his disciple Kṛta, the son of a king] and who was the most excellent among men, composed twenty-four Saṁhitās. Listen and understand the names of those disciples whom he taught.

45-47. Rāḍa, Mahavīrya, Pañcama, Vāhana, Tālaka, Pāṇḍaka, Kālika, Rājika, Gautama, Ajabasta, Somarāja, Pṛṣṭhaghna, Parikṛṣṭa, Ulūkhalaka, Yavīyasa, Vaiśāla, Aṅgulīya, Kauśika, Sālimañjarisatya, Kāpīya, Kānīka and the righteous Parāśara—all these were ancient singers of Sāman.

48. Two sages, the most excellent among the Sāman-singers, are said to be Pauṣyañji and Kṛti. They are the composers of Saṁhitās.

49. O Brāhmaṇas, Sumantu divided the Atharva Veda into two and handed the entire Veda to Kabandha.[1] Know its order.

1. Verses 49-55 give the genealogy of the teachers of the Atharva Veda and its branches. It is different from the list in CVS, pp. 46-49 and to some extent from the Bd. P.

The genealogy of teachers of the Atharva is as follows:

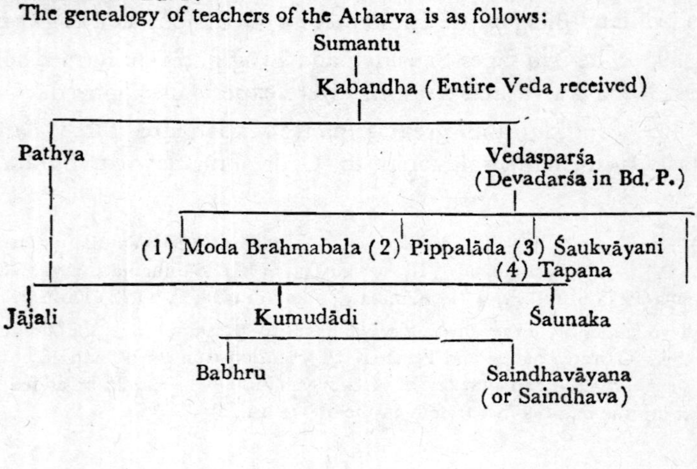

50. Kabandha divided it into two and taught one to Pathya and the second to Vedasparśa. Vedasparśa divided it again into four.

51. Moda Brahmabala, Pippalāda, Śaukvāyani the knower of Dharma, and Tapana—thase were the four disciples of Vedasparśa (who were) firm in holy rites.

52. Know the excellent threefold division (i.e. disciples and sons) of Pathya. They were Jājali, Kumudādi and the third Śaunaka.

53. After dividing it into two, Śaunaka gave one to Babhru. The intelligent one gave the second Saṁhitā to the disciple named Saindhavāyana.

54-55. Saindhava gave it to Muñjakeśa. The Saṁhitā was divided again into two. The alternative Saṁhitās of the Atharva Veda are five[1], viz. Nakṣatrakalpa, Vaitāna, (the third) Saṁhitāvidhi, the fourth Aṅgiras-kalpa and the fifth Śānti-kalpa. O excellent sages, the Purāṇa too was expounded by me after dividing it into six.

56-57. O Brāhmaṇa! In Purāṇic lore,[2] the following are my disciples, firm in religious austerities (or persevering in Purāṇic lore): Sumati, the intelligent scion of Atri's Gotra, Kāśyapa, Akṛtavraṇa, Bhāradvāja, Agnivarcas, Vasiṣṭha, Mitrayu, Sāvarṇi, Somadatti, Suśarman and Śāṁśapāyana. Three of them composed three Saṁhitās which were further divided into three.

58. The composers of the Saṁhitās were Kāśyapa, Sāvarṇi

Muñjakeśa
[According to Bd. P. Saindhava had another name Muñjakeśa]

1. The divisions of the Atharva Veda are five (1) Nakṣatra Kalpa, (2) Vaitāna (prob. Vidhāna Kalpa as in CVS.), (3) Saṁhita Vidhi (prob. Saṁhita Kalpa of CVS p. 46), (4) Aṅgiras Kalpa, (5) Śānti Kalpa.

2. Verses 56-61 state the position of the Purāṇic lore: Although Lomaharṣaṇa had eleven disciples, only three of them—Kāśyapa, Sāvarṇi and Śāṁśapāyana composed Purāṇa Saṁhitas in addition to their Guru's work. There Saṁhitās had four *pādas* (parts) and 4000 verses. Only Śāṁśapāyana's Saṁhitā contained 8600 verses.

and Śāṁśapāyana. There is a fourth Saṁhitā named Sāmikā. It is the original Saṁhitā.

59. All of them have four Pādas. All of them expound the same matter. They were distinguished by separate readings like the recensions of the Vedas. Excepting Śāṁśapāyana's Saṁhitā each contains four thousand verses.

60. The Saṁhitās of Lomaharṣaṇa are original, then come the Saṁhitās of Kāśyapa. The third are the Saṁhitās of Sāvarṇi. All these can be readily understood by the scholars of Yajur Veda.

61. The Saṁhitās of Śāṁśapāyana are embellished by the topics of exhortation. There are eight thousand six hundred verses.

62. There are additional fifteen and ten along with ten (Ṛks ?) known as Vālakhilyas, Samapraikhas along with Sāvarṇas.[1]

63. The Sāman Mantras are eight thousand fourteen (in the Sāma Veda) including Āraṇyaka along with Homa. Sāmagas (Sāma-singers) sing them.

64. The Ādhvaryava Veda consists of twelve thousand Mantras including the Yajur (Veda) and Brāhmaṇas as compiled (classified) by Vyāsa.

65. It includes the *Grāmya, Āraṇyaka* and the *Mantrakaraṇa*. Henceforth the narratives will be known as *Pūrva-kathās* (former or ancient narratives).

66. The Ṛk, Brāhmaṇa and Yajus are remembered to have Grāmya, Āraṇya and Mantra (Sections). There are additional compilations (*Khila*) and supplementary ones (*Upakhila*) of Hāridravīya as also the Parakṣudras of Taittirīyas.

---

1. Verses 62-73 give the number of Mantras in Vedic Text. But after comparing the figures stated in this Purāṇa and those in CVS (Śaunaka's *Caraṇa-Vyūha-Sūtra*) and the published editions of Vedic texts, I am constrained to repeat what I said about the author of Bd. P. (Bd. P. I.2.35, p. 348, Footnote 2):

"It appears that our Purāṇa writers give traditional (hearsay) round figures without verifying (and counting the mantras) in the original Saṁhitās".

67. The Ṛk verses in the Vājasaneyī Saṁhitā are a hundred less than two thousand. The Brāhmaṇa portion contains four times that number.

68. The total number of Yajur Mantras and Ṛks is eight thousand eight hundred eighty plus a quarter more along with *Śukriya* (Sāmans belonging to Pravargya) and Khila (additional) Mantras (according to) Yājñavalkya.

69. Similarly listen to the extent of the Saṁhitā of Caraṇa[1]-Vidyās (sections of Vedic School—of Atharva ?). They contain six thousand twenty-six Ṛks. Yajur Mantras, it is said, are somewhat more than this.

70-71. There are eleven thousand twenty Ṛks (in Yajus). In the Saṁhitā of Bhṛgu, there are ten thousand three hundred and eighty Ṛks and a thousand Mantras. The number of Ṛks in Atharva Veda is more.

72-73. These are mentioned as five thousand. Some sages add nine hundred and eighty Ṛks. This is mentioned by Aṅgiras who includes the Āraṇyaka portion. Thus the number of Ṛks and the different recensions have been enumerated.

74. The composers of Ṛks are the cause of the differences in recensions. In all the Manvantaras, the recensional differences are the same.

75. The Vedic text which is the creation of Prajāpati is eternal. These variations are due to the non-eternal nature of Devas. Creation of Mantras takes place again and again[2] (in every Manvantara).

76. The determination of the names of the Devas takes place in each Manvantara. The divisions of Śruti in the Dvāpara Yuga have been narrated.

77. Thus, after handing over the Vedas and other mantras to his disciples, the holy lord, the excellent sage Vyāsa went to the forest for performing penance. These different recensions have been made by his disciples and their disciples.

78. The fourteen lores are the (six) Aṅgas (ancillary subjects), the four Vedas, Mīmāṁsā, Nyāya-vistāra (logic), Dharmaśāstra and Purāṇas.

---

1. Bd. P. (I.2.35.78) reads *Cāraṇa*—a school of the Atharva Veda.
2. Purāṇic writer believed that Devas are not eternal but *Mantras* are so and they manifest themselves again and again in the new world order, after the new creation of the world.

79. (If four more lores viz.) Āyurveda (Science of Medicine), Dhanur Veda (Science of Archery), Gāndharva-Veda (i.e. Musicology) and the fourth Arthaśāstra (Science of Economics and Politics) (are added) the number (of lores) becomes eighteen.[1]

80. It should be known that Brahmarṣis are the earliest ones, thereafter come Devarṣis and then Rājarṣis.[2] Thus the sources of origin of Ṛṣis are three. It is through sages of well-disciplined observances, that Ṛṣis were born.

81. Expounders of Brahman are born in the five Gotras, viz. among the descendants of Kaśyapa, Vasiṣṭha, Bhṛgu, Aṅgiras and Atri. They are called Brahmarṣis because they can go to (approach) Brahmā.

82-83. Devarṣis (Celestial Sages) are the sons of Dharma, Pulastya, Kratu, Pulaha, Pratyūṣa, Prabhāsa and Kaśyapa. Listen to the enumeration of their names. The Celestial Sages, Nara and Nārāyaṇa are the two sons of Dharma.

84. Vālakhilyas are the sons of Kratu; Kardama is the son of Pulaha. Kubera is the son of Pulastya and Acala is known as the son of Pratyūṣa.

85. Parvata and Nārada are the sons of Kaśyapa. They are remembered as Devarṣis (Celestial Sages), because they approach Devas.

86. Kings born in the race of Manu and in the dynasty of Aila (Purūravas), viz. Ailas, Aikṣvākas (descendants of Ikṣvāku) and Nābhāgas should be known as *Rājarṣis* (Royal Sages).

---

1. Traditionally the number of Vidyās (lores or sciences) is fourteen, but it becomes eighteen by adding four 'Subsidary Vedas.' CVS P. 47 has given the following relation between Vedas and Upavedas.

Veda		Upaveda
Ṛg Veda	—	Āyurveda (Science of Medicine)
Yajur Veda	—	Dhanurveda (Military Science)
Sāma Veda	—	Gandharvaveda (Musicology)
Atharva Veda	—	Arthaśāstra (Politics, Economics, Administration)

2. Verses 80-93 define the terms 'Brahmarṣi,' Devarṣi', 'Rājarṣi', describe their powers and give names of some of them.

87. They are called *Rājarṣis* because they have attained (*Ṛṣanti*) the Prajās (subjects) through delighting them (*Rañjanāt*). Brahmarṣis are considered to be established in Brahmaloka.

88. The auspicious Devarṣis (Celestial Sages) should be known as established in Devaloka.

89. The Celestial Sages (Devarṣis) and Rājarṣis are proclaimed as Brahmarṣis on account of their nobility of birth, penance, ability to utter (compose and recite) *Mantras*.

90-93. I shall now mention the characteristics of Devarṣis and others. They have the knowledge of the past, present and future. They always speak the truth. They are enlightened and they are united to (their) self. They are well-known through their penance. Even while in the womb, the darkness of ignorance has been dispelled by them. They practise the repetition of Mantras. Due to their Supreme Power, they are omnipresent. Devas, Brāhmaṇas and Kings are in communion with the sages. Those who study and practise the above are considered to be Ṛṣis. Seven of them with the following seven traits are remembered as Saptarṣis (the Seven Sages).[1]

94. They are long-lived; they compose Mantras; they are possessed of noble qualities; they are endowed with divine visions; they are enlightened; they practise virtue directly and make their lineage function.

95-96. Everyday they observe the six rites; they are flourishing householders; they believe in *Adṛṣṭa* (the Unseen Principle), the cause of Karmans, and act accordingly. They maintain their lives without rustic vulgarities; they prepare their own tasty dishes; they maintain families; they are prosperous externally and internally.

97. The arrangement of castes and stages of life in the Kṛta and other Yugas is made at the outset by them in each and every Age.

98. When the Tretā Yuga begins again, these seven sages again establish the castes and stages of life entirely. In their family heroes are born again and again.

1. Verses 94-98 describe the special qualifications, duties etc. of the Saptarṣis (Seven Sages) who are credited with a very long life.

99. When a son is born to a father, and when the son turns into a father, the line of sages continues without a break. The sages thus live till the end of the Yuga. The number of sages who are householders is said to be eightyeight thousand.

100. Those who resort to the Pitṛyāna to the south of Aryaman (the Sun god), take wives unto themselves and perform *Agnihotra* (domestic sacrifices). They are known as the cause of progeny.

101. Householders are innumerable. They resort to cremation ground. Eightyeight thousand of them are in the northern path.

102. Those sages of sublimated sexuality who are reported to have attained heaven, are reborn at the end of the Yuga as the composers of Mantras and Brāhmaṇas.

103. Thus they are repeatedly reborn in Dvāpara Ages. They are the composers of *Kalpa*-Texts (Ritualistic Texts), propounders of commentatorial literature on different sciences at the end of the Yuga.

104. When this Dvāpara is over, in the further Dvāpara Aśvatthāman, the son of Droṇa, will be the Vedavyāsa of great penance.[1]

105. In the future times the different recensions of the Vedas will be composed by him. By virtue of his great penance, he will attain eternal Brahman.

106. *Karman* is attained by penance; through *Karman* fame is attained; through fame truth is attained; and through truth eternal Brahman is attained.

107. From the eternal immortality is attained and from immortality essence of every object is attained. This eternal one-syllabled (*Om*) Brahman, is established in the Self (*Ātman*). It is called Brahman due to its greatness or (inconceivable) vastness.

108. It remains in the form of Praṇava and is known as *Bhūḥ*, *Bhuvaḥ*, *Svaḥ*. Obeisance to the Brahman of the form of Ṛk Yajus, Sāman and Atharvan.

---

1. Here only one future Vyāsa, viz. the Mahābhārata hero Aśvatthāman is mentioned as the full list is given in *supra* 23.109 ff.

109. Obeisance to that excellent Brahman that is known as the cause of the annihilation and origination of the Universe and that is the esoteric secret beyond *Mahat.*

110. It is unfathomable, unlimited and inexhaustible or imperishable. It is the source of the delusion of the Universe. It is the cause of the realization of human aims through enlightenment and activity.

111. It is the culminating point of those who adhere to the tenets of the Sāṅkhya philosophy, the goal which gives its association (?) It is the unmanifest, immortal, eternal Brahman, the cause of Prakṛti.

112. It is called Pradhāna, self-born, the secret and Sattva. It is indivisible, the essence of everything (*Śukra*), imperishable and multiformed.

113-114. In the Kṛta Yuga (as) there are no religious rites, how can there be a rite not done? In this world whatever is once done or whatever is committed or omitted, whatever has been heard or should be heard, whether good or bad, what should be known, pondered over, touched or enjoyed, seen, heard or realized (is so by Brahman).

115. Whatever has been shown by Him is the (only) knowledge of Devarṣis. Who can scrutinize that which He (Brahman) has pointed out*. It is the Lord alone who has declared all things to all.

116. When anything is done by anyone, he gets identified with it. What is done by one, is previously conceived by another (i.e. by Brahman).

117. When (even) a verbal effort (*vāṅmayam*) by anyone is made anywhere that is done by Him (Brahman) only. The act (merely) appears to be done by the doer.

118. Absence of passion, over-attachment, knowledge, ignorance, pleasure, displeasure, *dharma* and *adharma* (good and evil), happiness, sorrow, death, immortality, the state of being above, below or at the sides—all these are due to the unseen (*Adṛṣṭa*, destiny).

*Bd. P. reads: *yan na darṣitavān eṣaḥ* 'which he (Brahman) has not shown? A better reading.

119-120. In every Tretā Age Svāyaṁbhuva (Manu), the eldest son of Brahmā, the Supreme God, is the only knower of all lores which he classifies in the Dvāpara Age. In the Vaivasvata Manvantara, it is Brahmā who teaches that lore at the outset.

121. Being born frequently in the revolving cycles of the Yugas, the sages compose and propagate Saṁhitās.

122. It is mentioned before that there are eighty-eight thousand Śrutarṣis. They propagate these (Vedic) Saṁhitās again and again.

123. Those branches (of the Vedic lore) are rearranged again and again in every Yuga by them who, following the Southern Path, resorted to cremation grounds (= died).

124. In all (every) Dvāpara Age, (Vedic) Saṁhitās have been composed by Śrutarṣis. In their lineage, these recensions (branches of Veda) appear again and again. Those recensions and their composers survive till the end of the Yuga.

125. It should be known that the composition of all the different branches (of the Vedas) in the past and future Manvantaras takes place in a similar way.

126. (The composition of the branches of Veda) of the past (Manvantaras) have elapsed, those of the present (Manvantara) exist, and those of the future (Manvantara) will be described in the future.

127. The later Manvantara shall be understood through the earlier Manvantara. Both of them shall be understood through the present (Manvantara). The decision of the Manvantara is on this basis.

128. Thus Devas, Pitṛs, Sages and Manus go up and return along with the Mantras.

129-130. From Janaloka all Devas are born at the appropriate time again and again for ten[1] Kalpas. Then they are linked with inevitable destiny. Thereafter, they perceive that birth to be full of defects and associated with diseases[2].

---

1. For *Paśu Kalpa* of the Text Bd. P. I.2.35.153 reads *daṣa kalpān* which makes some sense and hence accepted here.

2. *Rāgapūrvakam* 'through passionateness' is inappropriate here, hence '*roga-pūrvakam*' from Bd. P, is accepted.

131. But till they see through this defective nature of these successive rebirths, they continue. The rebirths continue for ten Celestial Yugas before they stop.

132. From Janaloka they go to Tapoloka from whence they do not return. Thus thousands of Celestial Yugas have elapsed. In Brahmaloka they meet death along with sages.

133-135. It is impossible to describe in detail and in the proper order, the Manvantaras of the previous Kalpas that have gone before, because time is beginningless and they are innumerable. Hundreds and thousands of Manvantaras and Kalpas have gone along with the Pitṛs, Sages, Devas and sets of Seven Sages that are the creatures of time.

136-137. Dissolution at the end of a Manvantara and creation at the end of dissolution, of Devas, Ṛṣis, Pitṛs and Manus cannot be described in detail and in proper order even in hundreds of years. The details of creation and annihilation cannot be stated. Now understand the duration of a Manvantara, according to the human calculation.

138-140. Experts in enumeration have calculated the duration of a Manvantara. It is thirty crores sixty-seven million twenty thousand years excluding the period of transition. This duration of a Manvantara has been enumerated according to human years. Now I shall enumerate the duration of a Manvantara in celestial years.

141. The duration of a Manvantara according to the celestial calculation is eight hundred fiftytwo thousand years.

142. Fourteen times this period constitute the *Ābhūtasaṁplava* (the period of final dissolution). A thousand sets of four Yugas constitute a day of Brahmā.

143. All the living beings will be scorched by the rays of the Sun. Keeping Brahmā at the head, and accompanied by Devas, Sages and Dānavas, they will enter lord Maheśvara, the most excellent among Devas.

144. It is He who creates all beings again and again at the beginning of Kalpas. Thus, this is considered to be the *Sthiti Kāla* (the period of sustenance) of Manu along with Devas and Sages.

145. (The period) what is called Yuga has been already

recounted to you by me before. Now listen to and understand the interim period (*Pratisandhi*) of all Manvantaras.[1]

146. That which includes Kṛta and Tretā, Dvāpara and Kali is known as *Caturyuga* (set of four Yugas). When it revolves into seventyone cycles, it is the period of a Manvantara. Thus the lord has ordained.

147. The characteristics of the Manvantaras of the past or of the future are explained through (those of) the present one.

148. Thus the mode of creation of Svāyambhuva Manu has been narrated. I shall now mention the interim period which links it with the following Manvantara.

149. The Manvantaras in the future will also pass as in the previous period along with Devas and sages through the inevitability of destiny.

150. Those who have been the lords of the three worlds in this Manvantara, the Seven Sages, Devas, Pitṛs and Manus are known as *Sādhakas* throughout the period of this Manvantara.

151. Realising the expiry of their tenure and the fall from authority, they eagerly turn to go to Maharloka.

152. The deities who decline in this Manvantara survive Kṛta Yuga in the course of their life time.

153. In the meanwhile the future lords of Manvantaras, Deities, Pitṛs, Sages and Manus are born similarly.

154. In every Manvantara it is the surviving subjects at the end of Kaliyugas who constitute the earlier subjects of the Kṛta Yugas.

155. Just as the continuity of Kṛta Yuga is remembered as preceded by Kali Yuga by learned men, so also the beginning of Manvantaras is preceded by the end of (the previous) Manvantara.

156-157. When the earlier Manvantara declines and the later one begins to function, those who survive in the beginning of the Kṛta Yuga, viz. the Seven Sages and Manu, remain biding their time (performing penance).

158-161. When the creation of rain begins, they function actively for the proper working of the Manvantara and for the

---

1. Verses 145-176 describe *Pratisandhi*—transition from one Yuga or Manvantara to another.

continuity of lineage everywhere. Men and Women are born and they function as before. The plants begin to grow. In different places, the subjects build abodes and begin to live. Agricultural and other occupations begin to function according to the good and the virtuous guidance of the sages. When the mobile and immobile beings die, people become cheerless. Villages and cities are ruined. The setup of castes and stages of life is disturbed. At that time, the Seven Sages, Manu and those virtuous persons who survive the previous Manvantara exert themselves for procreation.

162-163. Even as they perform penance extremely difficult to be performed for the Devas, Asuras, Pitṛs, Sages, Serpents, Ghosts and Goblins, Gandharvas, Yakṣas and Rākṣasas are born as before on the death of the earlier persons.

164. The good people who have survived, begin to teach and propagate the good conduct of life. In the beginning of the Manvantaras, Manu and the Seven Sages initiate the holy rites. Human beings along with the Devas also perform those rites.

165-166. At the beginning of a Manvantara as in the beginning of the Tretā Yuga, when Devas and men become stabilised in Dharma, they absolve themselves from the idebtedness to Ṛṣis (sages) by observing celibacy, to Pitṛs by procereation and to the Devas by performance of sacrifices.

167. After remaining in the practice of virtue pertaining to the castes and stages of life for a hundred thousand years, and after establishing the set of three Vedas, agricultural and other occupations for livelihood, maintenance of law and order and the virtuous practice of the discipline of castes and stages of life, they desire to attain heaven.

168. After they have set out for heaven, they at the outset maintain all the virtues wholeheartedly.

169. At the end of the Manvantara, they abandon their abodes and go to Maharloka which is free from ailments, along with the Mantras.

170. Free from aberrations, endowed with mental Siddhis, these people of self-control, stay till the final dissolution, observing passage of the Manvantara.

171-172. When all these have passed away ultimately, when all the abodes become vacant everywhere in the three worlds, other Devas who had been staying in the heaven endowed with penance, well equipped with truthfulness, celibacy and learning occupy those places.

173. Among the Seven Sages, Manu, Devas and Pitṛs those who had been before die along with the future ones (?)

174. Their final dissolution takes place at the close of (all) Manvantaras. They continue endlessly in the same order in all the Manvantaras, till the final dissolution of all beings.

175. Thus the characteristics of the inter-link of the past Manvantaras and future have been declared by Svāyaṁbhuva Manu.

176. The sequence of the Manvantaras of the past and future is snapped entirely through the final dissolution.

177. After the lapse of the Manvantaras, these attain Maharloka; from Maharloka they go to Jana, Tapaḥ and Satya Lokas.

178-179. As observed by those who have that sort of mystic experience and as proved by manifold testimony, they stay in Satya Loka, but when aberrations set in at the hour of dissolution of Manvantara, they leave off Satya Loka and with devotion they enter the body of lord Nārāyaṇa, of vast incomprehensible size.

180. In all the changes of Manvantaras that have been functioning for a long time, the world of living beings does not remain (the same) even for a moment. Due to the nature of destiny, it (the world) undergoes changes by way of decrease or increase.

181. Thus the narrative of the Manus, who are virtuous, who have been praised by the sages and who are endowed with divine vision has been recounted partly in detail and partly in brief. This narrative was originally composed by Vāyu. This can be understood by the people only by their divine power.

182. All the changes refer to saintly kings, Celestial Sages, Brahmarṣis, Devas, Serpents, the lord of Devas, the Seven Sages, the Pitṛs and Prajāpatis.

183. It is highly meritorious to eulogise the lords born of noble families, endowed with splendour, excellent intellect, fame and renown.

184. It is conducive to the attainment of heaven. It is very holy, highly esoteric, capable of granting progeny. It should be recited during great *parvan* days. It is conducive to the removal of the effects of bad dreams and is conducive to longevity.

185. Resort to the great principle Sumaheśa for attaining *Siddhis*. Resort to this Purāṇa which contains the narratives of Prajāpatis, Devas, Sages, the well-known yet sacred origination of the unborn Lord and for the fulfilment of my narration.

186. Thus I have described the Svāyaṁbhuva Manvantara in detail and in the proper order. What more shall I describe to you?